THE POETICAL WORKS
OF
ROBERT BROWNING

General Editor: IAN JACK

THE OXFORD ENGLISH TEXTS
EDITION OF THE POETICAL WORKS
OF ROBERT BROWNING

THE POETICAL WORKS
OF
ROBERT BROWNING

Volume V

MEN AND WOMEN

EDITED BY

IAN JACK
AND
ROBERT INGLESFIELD

CLARENDON PRESS · OXFORD

1995

Oxford University Press, Walton Street, Oxford OX2 6DP

Oxford New York
Athens Auckland Bangkok Bombay
Calcutta Cape Town Dar es Salaam Delhi
Florence Hong Kong Istanbul Karachi
Kuala Lumpur Madras Madrid Melbourne
Mexico City Nairobi Paris Singapore
Taipei Tokyo Toronto
and associated companies in
Berlin Ibadan

Oxford is a trade mark of Oxford University Press

Published in the United States
by Oxford University Press Inc., New York

British Library Cataloguing in Publication Data
Data available

Library of Congress Cataloging in Publication Data
(Revised for vol. 5)
Browning, Robert, 1812–1889.
The poetical works of Robert Browning.
Vol. 3 edited by Ian Jack and Rowena Fowler.
Vol. 4 edited by Ian Jack, Rowena Fowler, and Margaret Smith.
Vol. 5 edited by Ian Jack and Robert Inglesfield.
Includes bibliographical references and index.
Contents: v. 1. Pauline; Paracelsus—v. 2. Strafford; Sordello— v. 5. Men and women.
I. Jack, Ian Robert James. II. Smith, Margaret, 1931–   . III. Fowler, Rowena.
IV. Inglesfield, Robert. V. Title.
PR 4203.J3 1983   821'.8   82–12603
ISBN 0–19–812790–1

1 3 5 7 9 10 8 6 4 2

Typeset by Pure Tech India Ltd, Pondicherry
Printed in Great Britain
on acid-free paper by
Biddles Ltd,
Guildford and King's Lynn

PREFACE AND
ACKNOWLEDGEMENTS

THE order of the poems in this volume is that of the first edition of *Men and Women* (1855), but the text is based on that of *The Poetical Works of Robert Browning* as published in 1888/9. Robert Inglesfield is responsible for the preparation of the text and the textual part of the general Introduction, Ian Jack for the remainder of the general Introduction, the introductions to the individual poems, and the commentary.

The wealth of Browning material in America is a reminder of the early and generous appreciation of his work in that country. Two of the libraries to which we are indebted are now grouped in the Special Collections section of New York Public Library: the Berg Collection and the Carl H. Pforzheimer Collection. We also wish to thank the authorities of the Pierpont Morgan Library, the Huntington Library, and the Smithsonian Institution, as well as those of the libraries of the University of Texas, the University of Iowa, and the University of Syracuse. The Librarian of Wellesley College has been most helpful, as have Betty Coley and Rita S. Humphrey of the Armstrong Browning Library at the University of Waco.

In this country we are grateful to the authorities of the British Library, the Library of the Fitzwilliam Museum, the Library of Somerville College, and to the Curator of Castle Howard; and particularly to the staff of Cambridge University Library, where we have both spent many hours. Miss Myrtle Moulton-Barrett has again allowed us to quote briefly from unpublished letters in her collection.

No one has given us so much personal assistance as Dr Philip Kelley, whose indispensable edition of *The Brownings' Correspondence* reached volume xii in 1993. Without the privilege of access to letters which are to appear in his later volumes we should not have been able to write our general Introduction, in which we try to throw light on the composition of the poems with which we are concerned. Dr Kelley's co-editor, Mr Scott Lewis, has been equally helpful.

The initials 'P.K.' in our notes refer to the letters listed in *The Brownings' Correspondence: A Checklist*, by Philip Kelley and the late Ronald Hudson, an essential volume for those engaged in any detailed study. We wish to thank John Murray, London, for permission to quote from certain MS letters.

So many other friends and colleagues have assisted us in our five years' labour that we must beg forgiveness from any whom we may fail to mention. We wish to thank Professor Barrie Bullen, Mr J. A. B. Cuddon, Dr John Deathridge, Dr Eamon Duffy, Professor John Emerton, Dr Rowena Fowler, Professor Cecil Lang, Dr John Lindon, Dr Richard McCabe, Professor Barbara Melchiori, Mr Michael Meredith, Mr Peter Porter, and above all Mrs Margaret Smith, who did so much to set the textual policy of the edition on a sound basis. Dr Bill Grimstone and Professor Michael Reeve are not the only Fellows of Pembroke College to have responded patiently to particular questions. Dr Leofranc Holford-Strevens has read our work with the vigilance of a meticulous scholar, while Dr Bonnie Blackburn has assisted us in musical matters.

The General Editor has been indebted to the generosity of the Leverhulme Foundation for an Emeritus Fellowship which greatly encouraged him and went far to meeting the necessary expenses of this undertaking.

Volume IV contains a list of the titles and first lines of the poems in *Dramatic Lyrics* and *Dramatic Romances and Lyrics*. This volume provides similar guidance for *Men and Women*. The promised list of all the short poems published before *The Ring and the Book* will be in Volume VI, which will contain *Dramatis Personæ*.

I. J., R. I.

31 March 1994

CONTENTS

INTRODUCTION

The only complete poem in *Men and Women* known to have been written before 1853 is 'The Guardian-Angel: A Picture at Fano.'[1] 'As to poetry', EBB wrote to a friend from Florence on 11 April 1851, 'he has not done much in it since last spring',[2] a reference to the publication of *Christmas-Eve and Easter-Day* on 1 April 1850. The sale of that strange double-poem was disappointing, as had been that of the *Poems* of 1849. On 3 May 1851 the two poets left Casa Guidi for what proved to be an absence of almost eighteen months. It took them two months' leisurely travel to reach Paris, with more than a month in Venice *en route*. But for visits to London in 1851 and 1852,[3] Paris was to be their home until 23 October 1852. Throughout this period, which was the prologue to the writing of the poems in *Men and Women*, Browning was sustained by the encouragement not only of his wife but also of a number of friends in England. A letter from B. W. Procter ('Barry Cornwall') dated 23 May 1851 provides eloquent testimony of one friend's belief in him. He hopes that Browning will 'receive . . . kindly' an informal verse-epistle addressed to him which Procter had written at intervals between 1839 and 1850 and had just published in the enlarged edition of his *English Songs, and Other Small Poems*. More important than this appeal to him to enrol himself among 'The few great names which Memory / Has rescued from the oblivious deep Abyss!'[4] was probably the last paragraph of the prose letter itself, in which Procter commented on Tennyson's appointment as Poet Laureate and went on to pay Browning a compliment which must have meant a great deal to him. Tennyson, Procter wrote,

is very clever, & has written some exceedingly good things—& has very wisely (a word in your ear) taken the trouble of finishing & polishing off some of the poems till they are *sure* of being approved. Nevertheless, he is

---

[1] See p. 409. 'Part the First' of 'Saul' had also been written and published: see pp. 355 ff.

[2] 11 April [1851]. EBB to Clotilda Elizabeth Stisted: MS: Castle Howard.

[3] 23 July–25 September 1851; 6 July–12 October 1852.

[4] *English Songs*, pp. xxix–xxx (lines unnumbered).

a little lower than the angels; & I think that a friend of mine has more of the material of a great poet in him, & if he will condescend to do his best . . . the world will agree with me.[1]

In spite of the chill at heart which Elizabeth always felt when she thought of her unrelenting and inaccessible father, their visit to London in 1851 proved a most encouraging one. When they called on the Tennysons in July, as she told her sister Henrietta, the Laureate

had Robert's poems with him, and had been reading them aloud the previous evening . . . he pressed on us the use of his house and two servants at Twickenham as long as we stayed in England . . . We are both pleased and touched to the heart.[2]

Browning's old friend Joseph Arnould made a similar offer. Fanny Kemble left tickets for her Shakespeare reading. John Forster gave them a 'magnificent dinner at Thames Ditton in sight of the swans', and they breakfasted with the aged Samuel Rogers. They also 'passed an evening with *Carlyle* . . . a very warm friend of Robert's.'[3] Voluntary exiles as they were, they must have been reassured that they remained valued members of English literary life. Their reception owed a great deal to Elizabeth's celebrity as a poet, a great deal too to the sensation caused by their near-elopement; but *Paracelsus* and the two *Bells and Pomegranates* pamphlets containing short poems (reprinted in the *Poems* of 1849) had established Browning's reputation with the small body of well-informed people keenly interested in poetry. In France the gifted Joseph Milsand published a long and informative article on his work in the course of the year.[4]

On 17 October, when they were established in the Avenue des Champs-Élysées, EBB reported that Browning now had a room of his own 'to write in.'[5] We do not know of anything that he wrote

---

[1] PK 51: 18; see L. A. Brewer, *My Leigh Hunt Library: Autograph Letters* (Iowa City, 1938), 311–12. Cf. Donald Smalley, 'Joseph Arnould and Robert Browning: New Letters (1842–50) and a Verse Epistle': PMLA 80 (March 1965), 90 ff.

[2] Huxley, 136–7.

[3] PK 51: 35.

[4] *La Revue des deux mondes*, 11 (Nouvelle période), (1851), 661–89. On account of this article EBB told Milsand that she was 'bound to [him] as the critic who of all others, in or out of England, had approached my husband's poetry in the most philosophical spirit and with the most ardent comprehension': PK 52: 14.

[5] Ogilvy, 53.

at this time, but his friends continued to encourage him. On 5 November Procter was explicit:

Tell me . . . what you are doing. I should like to see a book of your lyrics—any book of yours indeed;—but lyrics (like your others) indicative of your different moods of thought & feeling—would draw less upon your time than any long elaborate poems—& might be quite as popular perhaps. They might be dotted down at once as the easy expression of your mood—one at a time. Twould amount to a book before you would be aware of it . . . How many things you will see where you are—how many things you *are* seeing now—how many dreams—everyone of which will suggest a poem to you. There is one crossing your brain at this moment—Is it about Waring? or whom?[1]

On 17 December, thanking Sir Thomas Noon Talfourd for a poem which he had addressed to him in *Household Words*, Browning wrote: 'For my poor poetry—it has been the best I could do—it should have been far better to deserve your sympathy and recognition: what it may be, hereafter—in whatever I may be able to effect yet—there is no saying.'[2] On 8 March 1852 Carlyle added his powerful voice to the chorus which was now urging Browning to write more:

We decidedly need a man or two like you, if we could get them! Seriously, dear Browning, you must at last gird up your loins again; and give us a right stroke of work:—I do not wish to hurry you . . . but I remind you what is expected; and say with what joy I, for one, will see it arrive.—Nor do I restrict you to Prose, in spite of all I have said and still say: Prose or Poetry, either of them you can master . . . in whatever form your own *Daimon* bids . . . go with your best speed.[3]

*

Since it has been disputed whether Browning began writing the poems which comprise *Men and Women* in 1852 or 1853,[4] it will be best to begin by setting out the evidence.

[1] MS: University of Iowa.

[2] *Letters*, 37.

[3] *Carlyle Letters*, 293. 'You are not permitted to be silent much longer', Carlyle had written a few weeks earlier: ibid. 290.

[4] Most editors and others have been content to follow DeVane's date, 1852. In his 2nd ed., however, he mentions in a footnote Johnstone Parr's important brief article, 'The Date of Composition of Browning's *Love among the Ruins*': PQ 32 (1953), 443–6, which briefly argues for 1853.

In a letter of 5 June 1854 Browning told John Forster that he had
ready a number of poems 'not written before last year.'[1] That
means that he had begun writing in Florence, in 1853. It is a
particularly important statement because it was made so soon after-
wards. In 1866, however, he told A. W. Hunt that he had written
'Childe Roland' in Paris.[2] Since the Brownings were not in Paris
in 1853 or 1854, that points to 1852. The same date is given by
Furnivall, who reported that he 'wrote *Love among the Ruins*,
Women and Roses, and *Childe Roland* in three successive days, 1, 2 &
3 January, 1852.'[3] The apparent precision of this statement has
appealed to biographers and others, yet it is certainly inaccurate.
'Love among the Ruins' was probably written in 1854, and in any
case we have a draft which suggests that it was not dashed off, in
anything like its final form, in a single day. In 1887 Browning told
a visitor who asked about 'Childe Roland' that 'one year in
Florence' he had been 'rather lazy', and therefore resolved to 'write
something every day': 'Well, the first day I wrote about some roses,
suggested by a magnificent basket that some one had sent my wife.
The next day "Childe Roland" came upon me as a kind of dream
. . . I finished it the same day, I believe.'[4] This points to 1853 or
1854, which he spent in Italy. His belief, at the end of his life, that
the poem was 'finished . . . the same day' is very hard to accept,
when we consider that it contains more than 200 lines and is in a
most unusual stanza.

In her *Life*, first published in 1891, Mrs Orr complicates matters.
She gives Paris as the place where the writing began, and tells us that
Browning 'repeatedly determined to write a poem every day, and
once succeeded for a fortnight in doing so.'[5] Like Furnivall, Mrs
Orr will have derived this information from Browning in his

---

[1] *New Letters*, 77.

[2] Ibid., 172–3. The Brownings were in Paris from 26 September 1851 to 5 July 1852,
from mid-July 1852 for about a month, and for a few days the same October.

[3] Furnivall's Additions to his *Browning Bibliography*, p. 159 in our copy. Unfortunately
different sets of *Browning Society Papers* often differ in their pagination: see W. S.
Peterson, *Interrogating the Oracle: A History of the London Browning Society* (Athens, Ohio,
1969), App. A.

[4] Whiting, 261.

[5] pp. 362, 361.

seventies, when his memory was untrustworthy,[1] and we may well doubt whether he ever wrote a poem a day for two weeks. Neither his letters nor those of EBB mention any such feat, which might surely have been recorded at the time. Such an exaggeration (as we must take it to be) is yet of interest, as a reminder that when the mood was on him Browning could compose, probably in draft form, 'at a great rate', as EBB told Val Prinsep.[2]

Such conflicting statements are not very surprising. Many of us find it difficult to remember in which year an event took place, when we look back many years later. What is more, a poem is not always written at one time—nor does the germ of a poem always lead to immediate composition. Browning told W. M. Rossetti that 'he seldom or never, unless in quite brief poems, [felt] the inspiring impulse and [set] the thing down into words at the same time': he often stored up a subject long before he used it.[3] It is possible that this explains the prominence of Paris in Browning's account of the origin of *Men and Women*. 'Robert likes Paris excessively', EBB wrote in the last week of 1851, 'and I dont much wonder, because people pay him great attention.'[4] If the city had suited her health they might well have settled there. She preferred Florence above all for its climate, although even she commented on the 'great silence, the stagnation in the air' which she found there: 'I want Robert to have more amusement than he can have here under [even] genial conditions', she added. On 14 November she told Sarianna how pleased she was to find herself back in her own house: 'Robert has been perfectly demoralised by Paris', she wrote, '& thinks [Florence] as dull as possible after the boulevards; "no life, no variety".' He had not been out 'a single evening' since they had arrived. Procter's letter of 5 November 1852 seems remarkably prescient: things noted down in Paris (on paper, or in Browning's memory), observations, and dreams, no doubt lay fallow until their day came. 'Respectability' need not have been written there—

---

[1] Cf. Vol. IV, pp. 95–6, and *Life*, 365.
[2] Val Prinsep met Browning in the winter of 1859/60, bearing an introduction from Rossetti: see Mrs Orr's *Life*, 224–5.
[3] W. M. Rossetti, *Rossetti Papers* (1903), 302.
[4] PK 51: 88; *Letters of EBB*, ii. 93; PK 52: 146.

there is no reason to suppose that it was—yet Paris clearly provided the germ of it.

There is a remarkable contrast between the letters of the Brownings written in 1852 and those of the following year. In the former we have not found any reference to his writing poetry: in the latter, on the other hand, there is a running commentary on the composition of many of the poems (unfortunately unspecified) which were to be collected in 1855. There is no hint of the burst of activity ascribed by Furnivall to the first three days of 1852, but a letter from EBB dated 15–17 January 1853 provides evidence of what was surely the inspiration of 'Women and Roses.' 'On new year's day', she wrote to Arabella, 'an anonymous bouquet came addressed to the "Olive-eyed prophet". The most splendid roses, not monthly roses indeed!'[1] This was surely the 'magnificent basket' to which Browning referred.

The same letter mentions that they were both 'doing a little writing, & passing a happy tranquil time'. On 24 February he wrote to Milsand, thanking him for his article in the *Revue des deux mondes*, and making the famous avowal: 'I am writing a sort of first step towards popularity (for me!) "Lyrics" with more music and painting than before, so as to get people to hear and see . . . something to follow, if I can compass it!'[2] That same day EBB told his sister that he was 'looking delightfully well', adding: 'he's the joy of my eyes just now, as well as of the rest of me—and he is writing good in all ways.'[3] She mentions, none the less, that he 'misses the blaze of life' in Paris.

While the inconsistencies in Browning's own remarks preclude all certainty, our tentative conclusion is that the writing of the poems with which we are concerned occurred almost entirely during the years 1853–5. Paris had greatly stimulated him: subjects for poems no doubt occurred to him while he was there: he may have drafted a few lines, or a stanza or two. That he wrote any complete poem during this visit we have no evidence.

*

[1] PK 53: 6. The roses were the gift of Jane Willis-Sandford.
[2] PK 53: 14. Cf. W. Thomas, 'Deux lettres inédites de Robert Browning à Joseph Milsand': *Revue germanique* (Paris), 12 (1921), 251.
[3] PK 53: 13.

On 2 March 1853 EBB told Arabella that he was engaged on 'a collection of Lyrics in which he will assert himself as an original writer I dare say—there will be in them a good deal of Italian art . . . pictures, music. Both he & I mean to make a success if we can.'[1] Three days later he himself wrote to Chapman to tell him that he would give him 'something saleable, one of these days—see if I don't.'[2] On the seventeenth he wrote to Kenyon:

I am trying if I can't take people's ears at last, by the lyrical tip; if they have one,—and make songs & such like at a great rate—*that* being your presidency in my "works"—at all events, I do my best & think I may have found out and set right some old cranks & hitches which used to stop my success so cruelly.[3]

While EBB was pleased that the recent production of *Colombe's Birthday* had been a *succès d'estime*, what she wanted Browning to do was to 'write dramatic poems for the world, and not dramas for the players,'[4] and it is clear that she knew that this was what he was now doing. Our gleaning from the letters of the early part of this extraordinary year may end fittingly with a quotation from one of her letters to Julia Martin:

We have had a most happy winter at Florence . . . very quiet, & very busy, . . . two good elements of enjoyment after all . . . Not one evening has even he been out, throughout this winter. We have stayed here, dreaming over the fire, reading heaps of books . . . We have been writing too.[5]

The intensity with which he was writing at this time is shown by EBB's remark, about 1 May, that he had 'nearly enough lyrics to print', as he had told her the other day.[6] Which of them, if any, she had seen we do not know; for the most part he seems not to have shown her anything until he was satisfied with it. Evidence of his writing is everywhere in her letters, however. On 14 May she told Henrietta that they were 'by no means idle. We write and we read.'[7] In June she assured Arabella that they would be in London in 1854 to see their books through the press.[8] In early July, commenting on the success of *Uncle Tom's Cabin*, 'the great bassoon' of

---

[1] PK 53:15. EBB was working on *Aurora Leigh*.   [2] *New Letters*, 59.
[3] PK 53:23.   [4] PK 53:26.   [5] PK 53:34.
[6] PK 53:38.   [7] Huxley, 186.   [8] PK 53:55.

the literary concert, she added that she and Robert 'must do what we can to keep a little tune alive.'[1] On the 15th they fled the heat of Florence and went up to Bagni di Lucca, where they had been so happy after the birth of their child. 'The mountains are wonderful in beauty', she exclaimed in a letter to Miss Mitford, '& we mean to buy our holiday by doing some work.'[2] They had a large house with 'a separate sittingroom for Robert to write in', she told her brother: '. . . & we are going to work hard, George—if Robert does not make good use of that cheerful little blue room with two windows, I shall give him up, I say.'[3] He was so delighted with his study that, as she told Sarianna, 'nobody is to enter even the room next to it': she expected 'a great deal of work from him under such brilliant circumstances'. About 1 August she reported that he was indeed being 'rather industrious for him', adding: 'He likes Lucca & so do I', and some nine days after that we have a glimpse of their method of composition:

Robert is working at a volume of lyrics, of which I have seen but a few, and those seemed to me as fine as anything he has done. We neither of us show our work to one another till it is finished. An artist must, I fancy, either find or *make* a solitude to work in, if it is to be good work at all.[4]

On 24 August she mentioned to Isabella Blagden that they were 'doing a little work between the holidays,'[5] and on 9 September, a month before their return to Florence, she similarly informed Mrs Ogilvy that they were 'doing work in a sort of lazy way—& mean to have finished in time for England next summer'. On 7 October she told her brother that they had been very happy at Lucca, '& not idle either. Robert especially has done a great deal of work, & will have his volume ready for the spring without failure, he says.'[6] We know that 'In A Balcony' was written at this time, since Browning uncharacteristically dated it ('Bagni di Lucca, 1853') in the 1868 edition of his *Poetical Works*.

---

[1] PK 53:60.   [2] Raymond and Sullivan, iii. 388.
[3] Landis, 187; PK 53:68.   [4] PK 53:78; *Letters of EBB*, ii. 131.
[5] Edward C. McAleer, 'New Letters from Browning to Isa Blagden', PMLA 66 (1951), 599; Ogilvy, 109.
[6] Landis, 200.

Back in Casa Guidi, where they remained for only five weeks, she told Mrs Henry Francis Cust that Browning had 'nearly prepared his bookfull of lyrics', and that they would visit London next year 'to see them through the press'.[1] In Rome, she insisted to Isabella Blagden, 'Robert must have a dressing room which he could sit and write in as well—dear Isa, see to *that*.'[2] 'I am in stress and strain', Browning told Forster on the eve of their setting out, 'with a great day's work before me'.

*

The six months which they spent in Rome, from 23 November to 28 May 1854, are characterized by the same eagerness on Browning's part to have his poems ready for the printer, while we notice that EBB's work on *Aurora Leigh* was beginning to fall behind. 'Robert is hard at work with his poems', she told her brother on 10 January, '& I too do a little work most days.'[3] On the 24th she assured Mrs Ogilvy that he 'at least' would be ready by the summer. His determination held even when friendship made legitimate demands, which they both met with characteristic generosity. When the Storys lost their six-year-old son and they took charge of their sick little girl, they were both halted in their tracks: 'We, both of us, wait for calms before we do anything with Art.'[4] Yet while in the same letter written on 19 February she reports that she herself has been 'thrown out of the habit of work', she tells Mrs Ogilvy that he still 'swears he shall have his book ready in spite of everything for printing in June when we shall be in London for the purpose.'

During the spring two minor concessions to friendship enable us to date the composition of one of the *Men and Women* poems, as well as that of another piece which Browning never collected. On 13 March Procter asked each of them to provide 'a scrap of verse' for *The Keepsake*, an Annual edited by an impoverished niece of Lady Blessington.[5] EBB sent him two short poems which appeared in the 1854 publication, but Browning's contribution, 'Ben

---

[1] PK 53: 113.   [2] McAleer, PMLA 66 (1951), 600; *New Letters*, 66.
[3] Landis, 214; Ogilvy, 112.   [4] Ogilvy, 115.
[5] PK 54: 38. 'The year before last I got something from Carlyle', Procter went on,'—& something from Tennyson. Now I come to the Brownings.'

Karshook's Wisdom', was held back until 1856. It is dated 'Rome, April 27, 1854.'[1] The same month Arabella asked each of them for a poem to help a favourite charity of hers. EBB wrote 'A Plea for the Ragged Schools of London', dated from Rome on 20 March; while Browning sent 'The Twins', which was to be the only piece in *Men and Women* to have been published before.[2]

His friends in England were still taking a keen interest in his poetic career. 'I hope that you are writing more lyrics', Procter wrote in the letter asking for a contribution'—& that you will publish them, together with those already printed, in a small pocket popular shape.'[3] Perhaps he was thinking of the format of the 1851 edition of his own *English Songs*. On 2 April Browning told Forster that his new book was to contain 'a set of poems, of various show and substance, not one poem.' On 5 June he wrote to him again, mentioning that he must soon be 'in London, or Paris at farthest, to print [his] poems' 'You enquire about these', he added, 'and, I think, are anticipating another guess matter than I shall have to show . . . what I have written [is] only a number of poems of all sorts and sizes and styles and subjects—not written before last year, but the beginning of an expressing the spirit of all the fruits of the years since I last turned the winch of the wine press. The manner will be newer than the matter. I hope to be listened to, this time, and I am glad I have been made to wait this not very long while.' Six days later he told Story that he was 'trying to make up for wasted time in Rome and setting [his] poetical house in order.'[4]

There was also the matter of setting their financial house in order. On 6 June EBB reported that they were thinking of 'offering the

---

[1] See below, p. 495.

[2] In a sixpenny pamphlet, *Two Poems by Elizabeth Barrett and Robert Browning* (Chapman and Hall, 1854).

[3] *New Letters*, PK 54:38; *New Letters*, 75, 77 (corrected).

[4] Hudson, 33. It is surprising that Browning should refer to time 'wasted' in Rome. His first biographer, William Sharp, names seven poems written, in whole or in part, at that time—poems which include 'Love among the Ruins', 'Fra Lippo Lippi', 'Holy Cross Day', part of 'Karshish', and the completion of 'Saul'—and while this may be an exaggeration, it seems likely that the months in Rome were productive. Sharp expresses his indebtedness for 'serviceable information' to Browning's son and to other 'relatives and intimate friends', and adds that 'in one or two instances' he had guidance from the poet himself. (See his *Life*, p. 9).

proofs of [their] new works to any publisher over the water who will pay us properly for the advantage of bringing out a volume in America simultaneously with the publication in England'.[1] Two days later she told Sarianna that Browning was talking about money, 'of waiting for *that*, among other hindrances to setting out directly' for London.[2] The same day she revealed to Mrs Ogilvy that, unlike her own, his book was ready 'to see through the press in London'.[3] 'Poetry makes a bad *metier*', she added. On 1 July Browning asked Chapman to be 'so good as to give us the half year's account, which will be more interesting than usual, just now', since they both had books in progress and were 'anxious to know the signs of the times'.[4] Within three weeks EBB had to tell Miss Mitford that they could not afford to visit England:

A ship was to have brought us in something, and brought us in nothing instead, with a discount—the consequence of which is that we are transfixed at Florence, & unable even to 'fly to the mountains' as a refuge from the summer heat. It has been a great disappointment to us all.[5]

On 23 August Browning wrote to James T. Fields, the American publisher whose firm had pirated his *Poems* of 1849, and whom he had met in England two years later, telling him that he expected to bring out in London, next season, 'a collection of new Poems, containing about 5000 lines', and asking what Fields would offer him for advance proofs.[6]

Fortunately Florence was not as hot as usual, that summer. An addition by EBB to a letter of Robert's to William Page, dated 9 September, makes it clear that they continued to write: 'we have been . . . very happy . . "with books & work and healthful play", as the old hymn says'.[7] On 19 October she was able to report that their

[1] *Letters of EBB*, ii. 170.
[2] Ibid., 168 (redated, as PK 54:77).
[3] Ogilvy, 122, 123.
[4] *New Letters*, 78.
[5] *Letters of EBB*, ii. 172. As Margaret Forster explains, 'She had an income from her shares in her Uncle Sam's ship, the *David Lyon* . . . which had not yet reached her': *Elizabeth Barrett Browning: A Biography*, (1988, Paladin ed. 1990), 208.
[6] Jack, 'Browning on *Sordello* and *Men and Women*', 186.
[7] PK 54:103.

'pecuniary affairs are promising better results for next year', so that they would probably be able to visit England.[1] Meanwhile they continued working. On 16 November she told Harriet Hosmer, the American sculptor, that they saw 'next to nobody, but make up a rare fire and get on a little with our work'.[2] 'We shall remain here till May', she wrote to Mrs Martin, 'and then, if God pleases, go north—to Paris and London. Robert and I are at work on our books.'[3]

When we consider that *Men and Women* as published contains 7,267 lines, as against 'about 5000 lines' of Browning's estimate the previous August, we can understand the growing excitement evident in the letters about the beginning of 1855. His creative urge had perhaps never been so powerful. On 10 January EBB told Arabella that he was 'fond of asking [her] to "wish him good-fortune" ' when he went out 'to walk or to his room to write'.[4] On 6 March she reported to Mrs Ogilvy that while she herself was 'not nearly at an end of the composition even' of her long poem, he had 'at least all his rough work done':[5] a valuable glance behind the scenes. About 20 March another of her letters makes it clear that he had been writing a great deal more. He declared that he would have 'at least seven thousand' lines, and had begun to wonder whether he would not have 'to split his great heap of poems into two volumes', as in fact he did.[6] Early in April she excuses him from writing to Isabella because 'after the necessary hard work every morning he wants his slippers'.[7] On 20 April, from a letter to Mrs Martin, we learn more: 'We have quantities of work to do, and small time to do it in. He is four hours a day engaged in dictating to a friend of ours who transcribes for him . . . We go to England or at least to Paris, next month, but it can't be early'.[8] The identity of the friend becomes apparent in a letter to Sarianna about the same time:

---

[1] *Letters of EBB*, ii. 178.

[2] *Harriet Hosmer*, ed. Cornelia Carr (1913), 47.

[3] *Letters of EBB*, ii. 182.   [4] PK 55:14.   [5] Ogilvy, 134.

[6] PK 55: 37. He probably did so about this time. Some rearrangement of the poems no doubt followed. Cf. Peterson, 33.

[7] PK 55: 42.   [8] *Letters of EBB*, ii. 192–3.

He is overwhelmed with business just now in getting his poems tran-
scribed—he wont let me do it, but submits to use Isa Blagden who is very
goodnatured & pleased to be useful to him . . . and now for four hours
together every morning he is at her house & at dictation—Then he comes
home to work more . . . The fact is we are crushed into a corner with our
work—So little time to do it in![1]

On the 27th she tells Henrietta that they are both 'swallowed up
[in]work', adds that his poems will be ready for the summer, and
states that they are 'magnificent, and will raise him higher than he
stands'.[2] 'We are up early working, working', she goes on, giving a
further valuable glimpse of these days. 'Penini's lessons I never
neglect—then I write.—Then dinner—then I criticise Robert's
MSS'. Of course we have none of her criticisms, but their value
may be guessed at from the tact and insight which she had displayed
in her remarks on *Dramatic Romances and Lyrics*.[3]

Meanwhile money had arrived, and on 13 May we hear that they
are definitely going to England 'in a week or two or three, and we
take between us some sixteen thousand lines, eight on one side,
eight on the other, which ought to be ready for publication. I have
not finished my seventh thousand yet; Robert is at his mark'.[4] Two
days later she tells Arabella that 'Robert has six thousand lines
written out clear, & the rest nearly ready. I haven't a line written out,
but between six & seven thousand are ready.' On the 19th she tells
Sarianna that they are both 'in a treadmill, each on a side', adding:
'Robert gets on excellently with his dictation—has about six thou-
sand lines copied. The poems are magnificent.' Her letter to Ruskin
dated 2 June suggests that she was worried about the possible
reception of Browning's poems, as well as of her own: 'Will you set
me down as arrogant, if I say that the longer I live in this writing and
reading world, the more convinced I am that the mass of readers
never receive a poet . . . without intermediation. The few under-
stand, appreciate, and distribute to the multitude below'.[5]

---

[1] PK 55:40. Isa was eager to help, and had even provided a specimen of her
handwriting, which EBB described as 'perfect': [c.April 1855]. EBB to Isabella Blagden.
MS Fitzwilliam Museum.
[2] Huxley, 215, 216.   [3] See our Vol. IV, pp. 3 ff.
[4] *Letters of EBB*, ii. 195; PK 55:54; PK 55:55.   [5] *Letters of EBB*, ii. 200

They reached Paris on 24 June, and left it for London on 11 July.

*

About 7 August EBB wrote an excited letter to Mrs Jameson:

The best news I can give you is that Robert has printed the first half volume of his poems, and that the work looks better than ever in print, as all true work does brought into the light. He has read these proofs to Mr. Fox . . . , who gives an opinion that the poems are at the top of art in their kind . . . The poems, for variety, vitality, and intensity, are quite worthy of the writer, it seems to me, and a clear advance in certain respects on his previous productions.[1]

About the same time she wrote to Mrs Martin, explaining that they could not leave London, being 'at the end of [their] purse', and 'bound to London by business engagements; a book in the press (Robert's two volumes), and *proofs* coming in at all hours'. Printing went ahead rapidly. On the 10th Browning wrote to Milsand:

I sent you yesterday what you are to receive today—the first volume of my poems . . . [They] go under the distinctive title of "Men and Women"—they being really dramatic attempts and not a collection of miscellanies. The second volume shall follow very soon—it is printed as far as page 176, and—as you conjectured—I waited for it before I sent the first, not wisely.[2]

On 6 September Browning wrote to Fields, whose response to his earlier letter had clearly been favourable:

I find that my poems are grown so considerably as to fill *two* books, *not* one. The first is before me, in the same type & form as 'Maud', but with 260 pages instead of 154: and two thirds of the second volume are printed—(it will extend to the same number of pages.) My publisher will bring them out at the end of October or beginning of November, I *believe*—You see, there are therefore two books to dispose of.[3]

---

[1] *Letters of EBB*, ii. 209, 207.

[2] W. Thomas, 'Lettres inédites de Robert Browning à Joseph Milsand', *Revue germanique* 12, 422–3 (corrected). Browning is referring to a proof of vol. I. Mrs Orr tells us that he 'invariably sent [Milsand] his proof-sheets for final revision, and was exceedingly pleased with such few corrections as his friend was able to suggest': *Life*, 176.

[3] Jack, 186–7.

He added in a note that the volumes would appear 'under a distinctive name, which I don't mention yet', and explained:

I wish to make the greater impression by a broad-side rather than a succession of poppings. These poems, too[,] are *all new entirely*—unpublished I mean. They are the best of me, hitherto and for some time to come probably—and I have given my whole mind to the correcting & facilitating. Only two critics have seen the first vol: yet—but they are our best, in my opinion. And all of their judgment that it becomes me to report is, that the work will *sell*. I propose therefore that you should give me two thirty pounds for two books: say so, and I will at once transmit the proofs to you with my best wishes for your success as well as their own.

A week later EBB explained to Henrietta that she could not 'choose to be away from Robert just when [she was] of most use to him every day in the proof-sheets.—No it would not be possible'.[1] It seems that the proofs may even have encroached on the sacred time set aside for Pen's lessons.[2] On 18 September she wrote optimistically to Mrs Jameson:

we are getting on prosperously with Robert's work which will be out in November at farthest, in two volumes, under the name of "Men & Women" . . . which I think it deserves, from its extraordinary variety of life, in situation & character. I am full of hope about it, & belief in the power displayed in it—and it seems to me that the improved clearness of expression will give it a better chance than any of his former poems, with the exoteric class of readers—Mr Fox of Oldham, & Mr Forster have read most of the proofs, & are very favorable in their verdict. Fox, especially, has been intensely pleased. Forster makes more drawbacks . . . considers that obscurities remain—but looks forward to a "success" in spite of them. How I shall long to hear your thought! There are many art-poems, as well as poems of passion & description. You will like some if not others, I am very certain. The first volume has been sent in proof to our friend Milsand, for the use of the "Revue des deux mondes," . . and he has used a word in answer which I must whisper to you . . "colossal".[3]

We hear of Milsand's reaction to the first volume in a letter which he wrote to W. H. Darley five days later:

---

[1] PK 55:119.   [2] PK 55:120.   [3] PK 55:121.

On the very eve of my departure from Paris I had received in proof the
first of Browning's two volumes. I have read it and as Buloz does not
see any other translators to replace me, I am trying (though without
too much success up to now) to translate passages from it. One cannot say
that this poetry possesses charm, but it is strangely striking. What a
powerful and extraordinary mind is that of Browning! Yet I cannot but
believe that he has not chosen his true terrain. The passages are a sort
of ~~poetic~~ dramatic monologues in which he brings on the stage imaginary
personages to represent what he sees in human nature. I imagine that he
is wrong not to bring on the scene his own personality which is certainly
his most striking side. Above all his own ideas would need to be expressed
more explicitly. It is no less true that such as they are, and even because
of their strange quality, these passages produce on me a sort of supernatural
effect.[1]

On 21 September EBB had told Isabella Blagden that Browning
was 'close at the end of his work',[2] adding that she would receive a
copy, as (we may reflect) she was surely entitled to expect. This was
an exciting time. On the 22nd Browning wrote out and dated his
fair copy of 'One Word More', while within a week there occurred
the most memorable of their meetings with the Tennysons. The
Laureate 'spent the whole day with us', Browning told John Ken-
yon on 1 October, 'dining, smoking and bidding us, as "brother-
poets" tell him,—as he would tell us—how we wrote, composed
&c'.[3] He returned the next day and stayed until two the following
morning, reading them

the whole of Maud—a business of one hour and a half—reciting in the
proper places two unfinished and unwritten portions, and *describing* two
other . . . he read strikingly and peculiarly—as he said, between a song and
a recitation . . . He stopped ever and anon to comment on his own work
with an adorable naïveté—calling attention to this and the other nicety,—

---

[1] Our translation of an extract from a letter in a private collection, whose owner does
not wish to be named. The letter is important because it includes the first occurrence
of the phrase 'dramatic monologue' known to us, 'dramatic' being an afterthought.
Milsand first wrote 'des espèces de monologues poétiques', then substituted 'dra-
matiques' for 'poétiques'. François Buloz was the editor of the *Revue des deux mondes*,
but the article appeared in the *Revue contemporaine*, 28 (1856), 511 ff., apparently because
Milsand was held up by indisposition: *New Letters*, 86.
[2] PK 55: 123.   [3] PK 55: 127.

telling us how this passage was originally penned, and how he fain would alter the other.

These cordial and confidential evenings—'worth many travels & pains to have gained'—must have seemed to Browning a most hopeful prologue to the publication of his own great collection; yet he noticed that Tennyson was 'a good deal annoyed by the little men of the little papers' who attacked him, an omen of the ordeal to which he himself was to be subjected within a matter of days.

In this same important letter Browning sent Kenyon the last part of his second volume; his tone makes it clear that his generous patron had disappointed him by his failure to appreciate his new work as he had hoped that he would:

With this, you will get the last of the second volume—, it seemed better to wait for the end of it all than to send and write at once—tho' your letter of about a fortnight since made the waiting a hard business. How kindly,—and too kindly,—you speak of "Saul"! Yet, I know, you write just as kindly,—and perhaps with some pain to yourself, when you cannot give me the praise you feel I should be glad to have. In your few criticisms on "Saul", I quite agree, thanking you heartily for the same: I restore "so docile" (altered to get an anapaest there) and alter in the other places. I should mention that I have gone over the preceding portion of the two volumes perhaps half a dozen times or more very carefully, making minute improvements which "tell" on the general effect. In your remarks on the little or no pleasure you derive from dramatic—in comparison with lyric—poetry (understanding the vulgar or more obvious form of drama,—scene & dialogue,—for lyrics may be dramatic also in the highest sense)—I partake your feeling to a great degree: lyric is the oldest, most natural, most *poetical* of poetry, and I would always get it if I could: but I find in these latter days that one has a great deal to say, and try and get attended to, which is out of the lyrical element and capability—and I am forced to take the nearest way to it: and then it is undeniable that the common reader is susceptible to plot, story, and the simplest form of putting a matter "Said I", "Said he" & so on. "The whole is with the Gods" as Cleon sums up in one of the things I send you. Well, dear Mr Kenyon, of this you are sure, I hope and believe,—that I have done my very best, with whatever effect and acceptance.[1]

[1] Peterson, 28–9: 'so docile', l. 37.

Two days later EBB told Henrietta that the book was printed and would be out by the end of October or the beginning of November, and that it was dedicated to 'me in a poem at the close'.[1] On the same day she told Arabella that they had 'just despatched Robert's last proof', adding that she was 'most sanguine about the work, believing in it, I for one'.[2]

Another letter from Browning to Fields, also of 3 October, repeated his request that he should receive £60 for the two volumes, but supplied him with the information he desired without waiting for a reply. Fields now learned the title for the first time, and the anticipated date of publication in England—'at the end of this, or the beginning of next month'.[3] As for the proofs from which the American edition was to be printed: 'I send as many sheets as are "worked"—the remainder, and the second Volume, shall be forwarded almost immediately, the whole being in type. Vol. I extends to pp. 260. Good luck to us both!' A postscript added the next morning informed Fields that Browning was sending 'the *whole of Vol. I*: the 2^{d} to follow as soon as possible'. Fields agreed to £60. On the 9th Browning wrote to him again:

With this you will receive the second volume . . . the Book was advertised to appear "in October"—but I undertake to postpone publishing till the 10th or as much later in next Month as Mr Chapman's arrangements allow: with a week's start of this second—for the first volume,—and with this second in your hands,—say by the 22—you will be indisputably ahead of anybody intending to print from the first published copy,—which cannot reach the U. S. before the 22 Nov. at earliest. I wish you success with all my heart.[4]

Browning's next letter to Fields (from Paris) confirms that publication was delayed to suit him. It is dated 26 October:

I hope that by this time you are in possession of the parcel . . . containing the Two volumes complete . . . [Chapman] deferred publication at my request till the 10th Nov.—tho' he had announced the book for the end of

[1] Huxley, 230.
[2] PK 55: 133.
[3] Jack, 188–9.
[4] Ibid., 189–90.

the current month,—begging you, of course, not to begin operations before him. I was very attentive to the proofs, and hoped to find the printing as faultless as one can expect: but on giving the thing a final supervision here I perceive so many little-or-nothings as amount to something I would remedy if it were possible—as it is *not*, in the English copies,—but may be, perhaps, in your American edition: I therefore subjoin a list of *errata*, and leave the matter to your discretion—if they don't come too late, your book will beat the first delivery of ours, you see. Should any other trifle occur to me, you shall hear of it in like manner.[1]

This happy and expectant letter includes a reference to their long meeting with Tennyson, and reminds Fields that Browning will be eager to hear 'how [his] poems "take" with my American readers,—whose sympathy I am very anxious to keep'.

On 30 October, writing from Paris, EBB told Mrs Kinney that they had seen the volumes through the press in England, though they were not yet published. 'I hold that they will set him high', she continued, '—in his own place—and several critical friends who glanced over the proofs confirmed this impression.'[2] The following day Browning wrote to Chapman, referring to 'that miraculous Mr. Fields', and asking 'how our affair goes on'. He was anxious to know how well 'the trade' was subscribing, and was glad to notice the 'advertisements in the weekly papers—all prominent and eye-catching'. He sent a list of people who were to receive complimentary copies.[3]

*

The two volumes came out on 10 November.[4] 'Though the book was only published on Saturday we hear good news of the promise of success', EBB wrote on the 15th:

"the trade" having "subscribed" (as they call it) largely—that is—having made large orders—so that the expenses were covered after three days. Robert will stand higher than ever through these poems—I am ready to die for them, at the stake, that they are his ablest works. They are making

---

[1] Ibid., 191. The *Athenæum* for 6 October had carried an advertisement for *Men and Women*, to be published 'In October': p. 1142.

[2] Bosco, 91.

[3] *New Letters*, 81–4.

[4] Not 17 November, as often stated. The date is clear from EBB's letter, and from Chapman and Hall's advertisement in the *Athenæum* for 10 November (p. 1315): '*This day*'.

translations of nearly half of them for the "Revue des deux Mondes", and Mr. Milsand told me quietly the other day, that he considered the poems "superhuman"—Mark that! Only superhuman!¹

Unfortunately the first review to appear, that in the *Athenæum*, proved deeply disappointing. The second sentence poses a rhetorical question which recalls the fierce attacks of the reviewers of the early part of the century: 'Who will not grieve over energy wasted and power misspent?' It is curious that the balance should come down so decidedly against a poet in whose love poems the critic discerns 'power and passion . . . and, together with power and passion, a tenderness such as few men now command'.² He admires 'Any Wife to any Husband', 'A Serenade at the Villa', the opening of 'In a Year' and 'the epilogue in which the Poet lays his work at the feet of his wife'. Although he recognizes the power of 'Holy-Cross Day' and 'The Heretic's Tragedy', he dislikes them, and cannot understand why 'one who can pour out his thoughts, fancies, stores of learning, and emotions, with an eloquent and direct sincerity' such as we find in 'The Patriot' should 'prefer to rhyme the pleadings of a casuist, or the arguments of a critic, or the ponderous discoursings of some obsolete schoolman' to 'themes in which every one can answer to his sympathies, and . . . modes of the lyre which find their echoes wherever hearts and ears know aught of music'. As for the versification, he finds in it 'an amount of extravagant licence, belonging to the superfluity of power for which only those who have studied versification as an art will be able to account or apologize'. It is as if the critic had caught a view, however imperfect, not only of Browning's power, but also of the nature of his genius, yet turned away in impatience and disapproval:

We had hoped that 'Men and Women' would enable us to register progress in the poet's mind (always rich to overflowing) and in the artist's hand (always able to draw whatever its owner pleased). The riches and the ability are there, but the employment and the expression of them seem to us, on the whole, more perverse, personal, and incomplete than they were formerly.

---

¹ Huxley, 233.   ² *Athenæum*, 17 November 1855, 1327–8.

It is not surprising that EBB should have complained to Isabella Blagden that Browning had been treated very shabbily. The second notice of consequence, that in the *Saturday Review*, is no better, beginning as it does with the judgement that 'It is really high time that this sort of thing should, if possible, be stopped'.[1] On 1 December John Forster, fortified by his reading of the proofs, found a great deal to praise in the pages of the *Examiner*, and provided readers with generous quotations. Browning described this review as the best so far: 'as for the worst, there's no saying *that*. The serious notices are to come, it is to be hoped'.[2] On the 17th he urged Chapman not to 'take to heart the zoological utterances' he himself had 'stopped [his] ears against at Galignani's of late. "Whoo-oo-oo-oo" mouths the big monkey—"Whee-ee-ee-ee" squeaks the little monkey.'[3]

A common theme was taken up once more by George Brimley in *Fraser's* for January 1856: that Browning was a greatly gifted poet who was not fulfilling his potential because he failed to respect himself and his public as Tennyson did. The review in the *Westminster* is anonymous, like the rest of these cited here, but is now known to be the work of George Eliot. She insists that to understand Browning the reader 'must exert himself'.[4] 'Turning from the ordinary literature of the day to such a writer', she remarks, ' . . . is like turning from Flotow's music, made up of well-pieced shreds and patches, to the distinct individuality of Chopin's Studies or Schubert's Songs. Here, at least, is a man who has something of his own to tell us, and who can tell it impressively, if not with faultless art.' She quotes from 'How It Strikes A Contemporary' as possibly describing the poet himself, and particularly praises 'Fra Lippo Lippi', 'Bishop Blougram's Apology', 'Karshish', and 'In a Balcony'. She gives generous extracts, particularly from the first of these. She has one serious reservation, however: 'He has *chosen*

---

[1] 24 November, 69.

[2] *New Letters*, 84.

[3] Ibid., 85. Galignani's bookshop and reading room, where English papers might be seen, was at no. 18 rue Vivienne. *Galignani's Messenger*, published daily, helped Englishmen abroad to keep abreast of home news.

[4] *Westminster Review*, 65 (January 1856), 290–1, 295–6.

verse as his medium; but of our greatest poets we feel that they had no choice.'

Writing in the *British Quarterly Review* for the same month, David Masson gives a balanced view:

As regards the objections popularly taken to the quality of his thought and to his strange choice of themes and materials, these, it seems to us, are not properly objections at all, but rather indications of his peculiar place and rank among British poets. That . . . much of Mr. Browning's poetry is and must always remain 'caviare to the general' must of course be admitted; but we have yet to learn that a man may not be a great poet, and yet be 'caviare to the general'. It may be that the greatest poets of all are those whose genius enables them to thrill the most universal human emotions, and so to command the largest constituencies; but surely, if the select and most cultured minds of a time can have a poet all to themselves, or nearly so, handling the questions which they handle, and leading them out in new tracks which have for them all the interest of blended curiosity and familiarity, that is also a great gain to the community.[1]

Two further reviewers who were among the 'most cultured minds' of the time were Milsand, whose long notice has already been referred to,[2] and William Morris, whose review in the *Oxford and Cambridge Magazine* is perceptive on 'Karshish', 'Cleon', and 'Bishop Blougram' (classed together because 'all three [have] to do with belief and doubt'), rightly stressing their dramatic quality. He highly praises the poems 'about art' and the two about music. He particularly admires 'Before' and 'After', but picks out the love poems, and 'Childe Roland', as the best pieces of all. Morris places Browning 'high among the poets of all time, and . . . first, or second, in our own', and remarks that it is 'a bitter thing' to see the way in which he has been generally received. 'I wonder what the critics would have said to *Hamlet, Prince of Denmark*', he comments, 'if it had been first published by Messrs. Chapman and Hall in the year 1855.'[3]

The book was reviewed surprisingly widely: Philip Kelley has traced more than forty reviews or brief notices, in this country and in America, though some of them are of negligible importance. The balance of judgement was decidedly unfavourable, bearing out

---

[1] xxiii. 151 ff.   [2] Above, p. xxiv n[1].   [3] (March 1856), 162–72.

EBB's remark on the need for 'intermediation'.[1] It is ironical that it should have been to Ruskin that she made that observation: well disposed as he was to her and her husband, his struggle with *Men and Women* can only be described as a mixture of comedy and farce. Most of the few favourable reviews were by friends of Browning's, and even they were aware of the obstacles standing in the way of any large sale. Rossetti, who was proud to 'boast of some intimacy with the glorious Robert', wrote to William Allingham: 'What a magnificent series is *Men and Women*. Of course you have it half by heart ere this.'[2] He deplored the 'comparative stagnation, *even among those I see*, and complete torpor elsewhere, which greet this my Elixir of Life': this seemed to him a terrible sign of the times, particularly when contrasted with the 'flurry and skurry' about *Maud*, published a few weeks earlier. An older friend, Carlyle, took some time to acknowledge his copy, until he could tell Browning that he had read 'many of the Pieces again and again': 'nor was it a difficulty of *conscience* that has kept me silent', he continued; 'my approval was hearty and spontaneous . . . and indeed I believe myself to stand among the first ranks of your readers in that particular'.[3] Since Browning 'seemed to have such a faith in the old Stager and fellow-climber', however, he sent him 'a few rough human words' of advice, 'such as the day gives':

It is certain there is an excellent opulence of intellect in these two rhymed volumes . . . I shall look far, I believe, to find such a pair of *eyes* as I see busy there inspecting human life . . . The keenest just insight into men and things;—and all that goes along with really good *insight*: a fresh valiant manful character, equipped with rugged humour, with just love, just contempt, well carried and bestowed;—in fine a most extraordinary power of expression; such I must call it, whether it be 'expressive' *enough*, or not. Rhythm there is too, endless poetic fancy, symbolical *help* to express; . . . if not melody always or often (for that would mean finish and

---

[1] Quoted on p. xxi, above.

[2] *Rossetti Letters*, i. 278.

[3] *Letters of Thomas Carlyle*, 297–300. Over Christmas, Carlyle told Browning else-where, on two evenings he had heard Lady Ashburton reading, 'superlatively', poems from *Men and Women*: 'we sat (being intelligent creatures, all), in rapt attention . . . and understood everything': MS letter quoted in *Rossetti Letters* i. 287 n. (It was not she, but the second Lady Ashburton who was later to propose marriage to Browning).

perfection) . . . Such a faculty of talent, "genius" if you like the name
better, seems to me *worth* cultivating, worth sacrificing onself to tame and
subdue into perfection;—none more so, that I know, of men now alive.
Nay, in a private way, I admit to myself that here apparently is *the finest*
poetic genius, finest possibility of such, we have got vouchsafed us in this
generation . . . Said genius, too, I perceive, has really *grown* . . . since I saw
it last . . .

Well! but what is the shadow side of the Picture, then? . . . My friend,
it is what they call 'unintelligibility!' That is a fact: you are dreadfully diffi-
cult to understand; and that is really a sin . . . God knows I too understand
very well what it is to be 'unintelligible' so-called. It is the effort of a man
with very much to say, endeavouring to get it said in a not sordid or
unworthy way, to men who are at home chiefly in the sordid, the prosaic,
inane and unworthy.

Browning must 'mend' this fault, Carlyle insists: 'A writing man is
there to be understood: let him lay that entirely to heart, and
conform to it patiently; the sooner the better!'

Ruskin was much less perceptive, yet his letter of 2 December
deserves to be quoted here, both because of its oddity and because
of the reply which it elicited from Browning, as striking a self-
justification as he ever wrote. Ruskin was so put out by the 'mass
of conundrums' he found in *Men and Women* that he compelled
Rossetti 'to sit down before him and lay siege for one whole
night'.[1] He must have made little indeed of the poems before this
session, since his letter shows him puzzled by simple matters even
after it. 'I cannot at all make up my mind about these poems of
yours', he wrote

and so far as my mind *is* made up, I am not sure whether it is in the least
right. Of their power there can of course be no question—nor do you
need to be told of it; for everyone who *has* power of this kind, knows
it—*must* know it. But as to the Presentation of the Power, I am in great
doubt. Being hard worked at present, & not being able to give the cream
of the day to poetry—when I take up these poems in the evening I find
them absolutely and literally a set of the most amazing Conundrums that
ever were proposed to me.[2]

---

[1] *Rossetti Letters*, i. 283.
[2] D. J. DeLaura, 'Ruskin and the Brownings', 324 ff.

He therefore proposes to 'read with [him], one poem—as I read it to myself, with all my comments and questions', a procedure which produces the strange results recorded in full in our notes to 'Popularity'. Ruskin then continues: 'Now, that is the way I read, as well as I can, poem after poem, picking up a little bit here & there & enjoying it, but wholly unable to put anything together'. He likes 'Cleon' immensely, and understands almost all of it; relishes 'Fra Lippo Lippi', though he is puzzled (oddly enough) by the grated orris root and by the phrase 'There's for you'. In 'By the Fire-Side' he is 'dead beat' only by stanzas 41–3. He goes on:

There is a stuff and fancy in your work which assuredly is in no other living writer's, and how far this purple of it *must* be within this terrible shell; and only to be fished for among threshing of foam & slippery rocks, I don't know. There are truths & depths in it, far beyond anything I have read except Shakespeare—and truly, if you had just written Hamlet, I believe I should have written to you, precisely this kind of letter—merely quoting your own Rosencrantz against you—'I understand you not, my Lord'.

He regrets that he cannot 'write in enthusiastic praise', but assures Browning that he can 'Still less . . . write in blame'. He urges him to make 'the real virtue' of his work 'acceptable & profitable to more people'.

He disputes a metrical point,[1] denies that a poet of such dramatic power should 'let *himself* come up, as you constantly do, through all manner of characters, so that every now and then poor Pippa herself shall speak a long piece of Robert Browning', and finds his ellipses (much as EBB had done) difficult and indeed 'Unconscionable':

before one can get through ten lines, one has to patch you up in twenty places, wrong or right, and if one hasn't much stuff of one's own to patch with! You are worse than the worst Alpine Glacier I ever crossed. Bright, & deep enough truly, but so full of Clefts that half the journey has to be done with ladder & hatchet.

---

[1] See 'Saul', 20 n. (below, p. 364).

He greatly admires 'The Bishop Orders his Tomb' from *Dramatic Romances and Lyrics*, which Rossetti had shown him, and ends what he realizes to have turned out a less friendly letter than he had intended by pleading that even if he is wrong, and his state of mind 'soon change[s] to a more acceptant one' about the poems, it will yet certainly represent 'the feelings of a good many more, besides myself, who ought to admire & learn from you, but can't because you are so difficult'.

Browning was wise enough to wait a week before replying to a letter which he must have found bitterly disappointing. He hoped that 'subsequent readings' might enable Ruskin to understand more.

For your bewilderment more especially noted—how shall I help *that*? We don't read poetry the same way, by the same law; it is too clear. I cannot begin writing poetry till my imaginary reader has conceded licences to me which you demur at altogether. I *know* that I don't make out my conception by my language; all poetry being a putting the infinite within the finite. You would have me paint it all plain out, which can't be; but by various artifices I try to make shift with touches and bits of outlines which *succeed* if they bear the conception from me to you. You ought, I think, to keep pace with the thought tripping from ledge to ledge of my 'glaciers', as you call them; not stand poking your alpen-stock into the holes, and demonstrating that no foot could have stood there;—suppose it sprang over there? In *prose* you may criticise so—because that is the absolute representation of portions of truth, what chronicling is to history—but in asking for more *ultimates* you must accept less *mediates*, nor expect that a Druid stone-circle will be traced for you with as few breaks to the eye as the North Crescent and South Crescent that go together so cleverly in many a suburb. Why, you look at my little song ['Popularity'] as if it were Hobbs' or Nobbs' lease of his house, or testament of his devisings . . . Do you think poetry was ever generally understood—or can be? Is the business of it to tell people what they know already, as they know it, & so precisely that they shall be able to cry out—"Here you should supply *this*—*that*, you evidently pass over, & I'll help you from my own stock'? It is all teaching, on the contrary, and the people hate to be taught. They say otherwise,—make foolish fables about Orpheus enchanting stocks & stones, poets standing up and being worshipped,—all nonsense & impossible dreaming. A poet's affair is with God, to whom he is accountable, and of whom is his reward: look elsewhere, and you find misery enough. Do you believe people understand *Hamlet*?[1]

The critical reception of *Men and Women* was no doubt the greatest disappointment of Browning's poetical career. No second edition was called for in England. His hope that these poems might prove less 'esoteric' than his earlier work was disappointed. If his reputation continued to grow—and it did—it did so slowly, and mainly among his friends, his friends' friends, and the sort of intelligent and pertinacious readers who were to form the nucleus of the Browning Society in 1881. In America, however, things went distinctly better.[2] Both *The Albion* and *Putnam's Magazine* printed serious and favourable reviews in December 1855. As EBB was to write on 7 April 1860, nobody in England

except a small knot of pre-Raffaelite men, pretends to do him justice . . . As a sort of lion, Robert has his range in society, and, for the rest, you should see Chapman's returns; while in America he's a power, a writer, a poet. He is read—he lives in the hearts of the people. "Browning readings" here in Boston; "Browning evenings" there.[3]

Eventually, in 1863, the 'Third Edition' of *The Poetical Works of Robert Browning* made its appearance, in three volumes,[4] to be followed by a new collection of poems, *Dramatis Personæ*, the following year. The appearance of a six-volume edition of his work, in 1868, the year in which *The Ring and the Book* began to appear, marked the growth of his reading public.

Three features of our brief introductions to the individual poems should perhaps be mentioned. In the last paragraph we usually make some comment on the metrical form which Browning has employed. We do this because metre commonly receives too little attention from modern readers. No poem can be read satisfactorily

---

[1] Collingwood, i. 199–202.

[2] See, in particular, Louise Greer, *Browning and America* (Chapel Hill, NC, 1952).

[3] *Letters of EBB*, ii. 370.

[4] Browning counted the two-volume *Poems* of 1849, described on its title-page as 'A New Edition', as his second edition: it is, of course, incomplete, omitting *Sordello*. The three-volume edition of 1865, although only very slightly revised from 1863, is described as 'Fourth Edition'. From 1868, unwillingly, Browning included *Pauline*.

without being read aloud, even if it is only to the reader's inner ear—and the remarkable variety of these poems is clearly a deliberate display of metrical virtuosity on Browning's part. Of course questions of metre often give rise to disagreement; but debate can only prove helpful to the fuller appreciation of his poetry. In general we have followed Browning and his contemporaries in using the classical metrical terminology.

At the end of each introduction we give what seems to us the most likely date of composition. Such datings are commonly tentative, and we must remember that a poem is not always written at one time, while all the poems in this collection were subject to revision in 1855. When we have no information we use the formula '1853/5'.

Below the date we give the classification of the poem as determined in 1863, when the first of the three volumes of *The Poetical Works* bears the subtitle 'Lyrics, Romances, Men, and Women'.[1] This classification, which Browning retained in subsequent collected editions, is explained in a note facing the first page of the text:

In this Volume are collected and redistributed the pieces first published in 1842, 1845, and 1855, respectively, under the titles of "Dramatic Lyrics," "Dramatic Romances,"[2] and "Men and Women."

THE TEXT

The set of proofs of the first edition of *Men and Women* originally belonging to Browning's painter friend Frederic Leighton, and now

---

[1] We have omitted the comma after 'Men,' which is unhelpful; Browning did so after 1865.

[2] In fact *Dramatic Romances and Lyrics* (1845). Browning had become aware that the word 'Lyrics', however widely defined, could not be used to describe narrative poems. The most important word, not only for the first two collections but for his short poems as a whole, is 'Dramatic'. With rare exceptions ('One Word More', for example), his poems are 'always Dramatic in principle, and so many utterances of so many imaginary persons, not mine', as he wrote in the Advertisement to *Dramatic Lyrics* (1842). See our Vol. III. While the word 'Dramatic' does not appear on the title-page, in *1863* or *1865*, or at the beginning of each category of poems, its omission has no significance. From *1868* onwards it is more prominent.

in the Huntington Library, provides remarkable evidence of the extensive and meticulous revision that the poet carried out, with Elizabeth's help and encouragement, at the proof stage—confirming his remark in the letter to Fields that 'I have given my whole mind to the correcting & facilitating', and his later remark in the letter to John Kenyon (1 October), 'I have gone over the preceding portion of the two volumes perhaps half a dozen times or more very carefully, making minute improvements which "tell" on the general effect.'[1] This set was presumably one of several sets of first proofs that Browning received or arranged to be sent to Milsand and others; we must suppose that he made the actual revisions in another set that has not survived. (The sheets of the two volumes that he sent to Fields on 3 and 9 October were revised proofs on which the American edition was based.) Textual collation of the Huntington proofs with the first edition reveals hundreds of textual variants, in both substantives and accidentals; in several places the type has been reset or repositioned. The proofs also contain a number of manuscript revisions in Browning's hand that were clearly made at a later stage. In the Huntington proofs the two volumes, corresponding to those of the first English edition, are bound in one; the pagination of the first volume is discontinuous, with pp. 129–92 in the pagination of the first edition, consisting of sheets K–N, numbered 145–208. 'Memorabilia', the last poem of the first volume in the published text, is omitted, though the title appears in the table of contents, which exactly corresponds to that of the first edition. Except for this omission the arrangement of the poems is the same as in the first edition: apart from obvious pairings ('Love in a Life', 'Life in a Love'; 'Before', 'After'; 'In Three Days', 'In a Year'; 'One Way of Love', 'Another Way of Love'), Browning seems in his arrangement of the poems to have tried to emphasize their variety, including that of verse-form. Textual collation of the proofs with the published text shows that the only poems not revised in proof were 'After', 'In a Year', 'Women and Roses', 'Two in the Campagna' and 'Another Way of Love'; several were

---

[1] On the Huntington proofs see William S. Peterson, 'The Proofs of Browning's *Men and Women*': SBC 3: 2 (1975), 23–39, and Allan C. Dooley, 'Further Notes on *Men and Women* Proofs': SBC 5: 1 (1977), 52–4.

revised very heavily, including the longest poem in the collection, 'Bishop Blougram's Apology'.

Several of the titles were revised at the proof stage, including those of 'An Epistle of Karshish', 'The Patriot', and 'Old Pictures in Florence', which appears in the proofs with the title 'Opus Magistri Jocti' (vol. ii, p. 31). Most of the revisions, both in substantives and accidentals, are obviously intended to remove some of the more difficult, loose, or awkward turns of expression, to improve the rhythm or metrical structure, or, in the case of the numerous alterations to the punctuation, to tighten up or clarify sentence structure. Browning and his wife clearly worked on the proofs with close attention to textual detail. Lines 226–37 of 'Fra Lippo Lippi' illustrate the kind of revisions that are made. Line 227 in the proofs, 'Having a friend, you see—the Corner-house—', where the phrasing and use of dashes are doubtless intended to suggest a discreet, indirect hint, becomes clearer in the published text, 'Having a friend, you see, in the Corner-house!', and two lines later, in ll. 229–30, 'Those great rings serve more purposes than one, | To plant a flag in,', 'one' is altered to 'just'—'just | To plant a flag in,'. Lines 231–3 in the proofs, 'the old grave eyes | Still peeping o'er my shoulder as I work, | The shaking heads—"It's Art's decline, my son!', become in the first edition '—the old grave eyes | Are peeping . . . The heads shake still—', and the slightly cumbersome l. 236, 'Brother Lorenzo, that's his single peer,', becomes 'Brother Lorenzo stands his single peer.', with the full stop replacing the unsatisfactory end-of-line comma.

'Old Pictures in Florence' was revised particularly heavily in proof. The last two stanzas of the poem, xxxv and xxxvi (ll. 273–88), seem to have presented special difficulties. Line 276 in the proofs, 'Turn the Bell-tower's alto to altissimo.', becomes in the first edition 'Turning the Bell-tower's altaltissimo.': the typographical error in the last word was included in the list of 'errata' that Browning sent to Fields on 26 October 1855. Lines 278–9, 'Shall the Campanile, . . . Soar up', are condensed to 'The Campanile, . . . Soars up'. In the proofs the concluding stanza opens with the abrupt 'So said, so done. That morning . . .' (l. 281), which is revised to 'Shall I be alive that morning . . .', reinforcing the sense of joyful anticipation and, through the introduction of the first person, preparing us for the expression of personal delight in the last line. 'When with' in l. 285 in the proofs is replaced by the more concise 'As,'. The oddly cluttered phrasing of the last two lines of the stanza in the proofs, 'Why, to hail him, the vindicated Giotto, | Thanking God for it all, the first am I!', is replaced in the first edition by 'Foreseeing the day that vindicates Giotto | And Florence together, the first am I!'

The revisions of punctuation frequently involve the replacement of dashes, especially at line-endings, by commas, colons, semi-colons, full stops, or exclamation marks. The heavy use of dashes in the proofs undoubtedly reflects Browning's practice at this time. In 'An Epistle of Karshish', for example, 'results—' at the end of l. 153, and 'eyes—' at the end of l. 156 become 'results;' and 'eyes.'; similarly in 'Bishop Blougram's Apology' the succession of dashes in 'fear—' (l. 325), 'crude—' (l. 328), 'upon—' (l. 329) and 'take—' (l. 331), all of them occurring at line-endings, become 'fear:', 'crude.', 'upon:' and 'take!'—the sentence structure becoming correspondingly tighter and more definite. In 'Fra Lippo Lippi' and 'Bishop Blougram's Apology', both in the first volume, the reset-ting that the revisions necessitated resulted in the repositioning of type, with lines being transferred from one page to the next. In 'Bishop Blougram's Apology' ll. 370–2 are repeated in the proofs, appearing first at the foot of p. 224 and, in slightly different, apparently revised form, at the head of the following page, which is the first page of sheet Q; curiously, this repetition of lines occurs at the end of a series of pages, beginning with 215–16, in which one, two, and finally three lines are transferred in the published text. Repositioning and resetting of type are also evident in 'A Toccata of Galuppi's', 'Transcendentalism', and 'Saul'.

The manuscript revisions in the Huntington proofs, as we have seen, were clearly made later than the far more extensive revision carried out at the proof stage for the first edition. The revisions include several corrections of typographical errors, together with a number of substantive revisions, the majority occurring in 'Old Pictures in Florence'; only one of these revisions coincides with the reading of the first edition ('Old Pictures in Florence', 261). The revisions to 'Old Pictures in Florence' in the proofs are close to another series of revisions, also in Browning's hand, made in a copy of the second volume of the first edition of *Men and Women* that belonged at one time to the poet's friend Thomas Woolner, and now in the George Arents Research Library, Syracuse University. The list of 'errata' to the first edition included in the letter that Browning wrote to Fields from Paris on 26 October 1855 contains twenty-eight items, most of them substantive alterations, but some corrections to spelling and punctuation. Browning specifically asks that the line-continuations in 'Up at a Villa—Down in the City' should be repositioned: '(Print the half-lines *nearer the end*, as is done in "Galuppi" or, still better, in "Saul":—they would be read more easily)'.[1] The list includes almost all the substantive revisions to 'Old Pictures in Florence' made in the Huntington proofs. None of the 'errata' that Browning lists was actually incorporated in the American edition.[2] A second, shorter list was included in a letter that he wrote to Dante Gabriel Rossetti, also from Paris, three days later— the letter accompanying a copy of the first edition. Browning remarks, 'I perceive some blunders in my poems, which I shall not, I think, draw attention to, but quietly correct hereafter. But it happens unluckily that the worst of them occur just in a thing I would have you like if it might be—so, please alter the following in your copy before you begin it, won't you?'[3]

In a letter of 31 October to his publisher Edward Chapman, Browning dithers about whether to include a list of errata. 'In looking over the book,' he remarks, 'I find a few errors, and a passage or two susceptible of improvement—but I avoid calling attention to them by making a list of *errata;* still, should there be a demand, by any strange chance, for more copies than are struck off, I will send the corrections to you.' A little later he admits, 'My wife is not of my opinion about the undesireableness of appending the

[1] Quoted in Jack, 'Browning on *Sordello* and *Men and Women*', 192.
[2] The 'errata' include two examples of dropped letters that do not actually occur in the first edition; a possible explanation is that in 'giving the thing a final supervision', as he puts it in the same letter (p. 191), Browning was using revises rather than a copy of the edition itself.
[3] *Letters*, 42. The reference is to 'Old Pictures in Florence'.

errata. Of course, I should prefer by a great deal that they were adopted. What do you say? I attach importance to the mere stops, but there are a few blunders that affect the sense, and not all of them my fault, neither. I subjoin the list; do what you think best.' Finally he decides to mention only two 'blunders' that 'affect the sense and are the printers'. Vol. II. Page 9. Line 8. you painting—*read*, I painting. Page 47, line 12 altallissimo—*read* alt to altissimo.'[1]

On 29 November, anticipating the publication of the American edition of *Men and Women*, Browning wrote from Paris to his publishers, Ticknor and Fields of Boston, assigning them publishing rights:

I take advantage of the opportunity of the publication in the United States of my "Men and Women,"—for printing which, you, through being more righteous than the Law, have liberally remunerated me,—to express my earnest desire that the power of publishing in America this and every subsequent work of mine may rest exclusively with you & your house.[2]

Two thousand copies of this edition (which is in one volume, as against the two volumes of the English edition) were published on 8 December; dated '1856', it is described on the reverse of the title-page as the 'author's edition'. The text follows that of the English original very closely. A second impression of 500 copies was published on 11 February of the following year.

The sexto-decimo volume of *Selections from the Poetical Works of Robert Browning*, edited by John Forster and Bryan W. Proctor and published by Chapman and Hall in December 1862[3] (dated '1863'), includes twenty poems from the collection of 1855, under the heading 'Men and Women'. In the Preface, dated '*November, 1862*', the editors explain that though the volume 'is published with Mr. Browning's sanction', he 'is in no respect responsible' for the choice of poems. In fact all twenty poems in the volume have been revised. In l. 3 of 'A Toccata of Galuppi's', for example, 'although I give you credit,' becomes 'although I take your meaning,'; in

---

[1] *New Letters*, 82–4. The actual reading is 'altaltissimo' ('Old Pictures in Florence', 276).

[2] This letter, now in the Armstrong Browning Library, was printed in the edition of 1863 and subsequent American editions.

[3] Listed under 'New Books' in *Athenæum*, 27 December (no. 1835, p. 845a).

'Bishop Blougram's Apology', l. 389, 'catch a thing within a thing,' becomes 'catch a wheel within a wheel,'; l. 864 of the same poem, 'Men are not gods, but, properly, are brutes.' becomes 'Men are not angels, neither are they brutes.'; and in the last line of ' "De Gustibus" ', l. 46, 'so it still shall be!' becomes 'so shall ever be.'—an important revision. In 'Andrea del Sarto', an entire line is added (l. 96), 'Speak as they please, what does the mountain care?'. There are a number of substantive revisions that do not appear in any later text: for example in 'Fra Lippo Lippi', l. 125, 'He learns the look of things, minds none the less'; 'Bishop Blougram's Apology', l. 878, 'In these the bounteous pastures of this life'; 'Saul', l. 327, 'In the shuddering forests' new dusk; in the sudden wind-thrills;'; and 'Two in the Campagna', l. 54, 'Onward, wherever light winds blow,'. Among the numerous changes to punctuation there is a noticeable tendency, as in the revisions in proof, to replace dashes.

The three-volume 1863 edition of the *Poetical Works*, described on the title-page as the 'third edition', was published by Chapman and Hall between May and August of that year, the three volumes appearing separately;[1] the revised three-volume 'fourth edition' appeared in March 1865;[2] and the following September *A Selection from the Works of Robert Browning*[3] was published in the Moxon's Miniature Poets series, the first volume of which, a selection of Tennyson, had appeared the previous January. In the 1863 *Poetical Works* all but one of the poems of *Men and Women* are included in three sections, 'Lyrics', 'Romances', and 'Men, and Women', in the first volume; 'In a Balcony' appears among the 'Tragedies and Other Plays' in the second volume.[4] The poems are extensively revised. In the last two stanzas of 'Old Pictures in Florence', for example, there are several important revisions, including the recasting of l. 274, 'Sober, expurgate, spare of an "*issimo*,")' (reading of

---

[1] Listed under 'New Books' in *Athenæum*, 9 May (no. 1854, p. 617a), 27 June (no. 1861, p. 843a) and 29 August (no. 1870, p. 271b). During printing of the 1863 edition one sheet (D of vol. i) was cancelled because of the omission of a line ('A Lovers' Quarrel', 122): see Nathaniel I. Hart, 'A Browning Letter on the *Poetical Works* of 1863': NQ 219 (1974), 213–15.

[2] Listed under 'New Books' in *Athenæum*, 25 March (no. 1952, p. 422a).

[3] Listed under 'New Books' in *Athenæum*, 30 September (no. 1972, p. 434c).

[4] See Lawrence Poston, 'Browning Rearranges Browning': SBC 2: 1 (1974), 39–54.

the first edition) as 'Expurgate and sober, with scarcely an "*issi-mo*,")'; the troublesome l. 276 becomes 'And turn the Bell-tower's *alt* to *altissimo:*'; and l. 287, 'Foreseeing the day that vindicates Giotto', becomes 'At least to foresee that glory of Giotto', perhaps slightly clarifying the meaning.

The 1865 *Poetical Works*[1] incorporates further revisions, many of them substantive: for example, line 179 of 'Childe Roland to the Dark Tower Came', 'Fool, to be dozing at the very nonce,' (reading of the 1863 *Poetical Works*), becomes more consciously archaic, 'Dotard, a-dozing at the very nonce,'. The *Selection* of 1865 includes twenty-one of the poems of *Men and Women*; in the prefatory note, dated '*March* 21, 1865', Browning refers to the volume as 'a little gathering from the lightest' of his poems. In preparing the *Selection* he made further revisions, concentrating particularly on punctuation. An incomplete printer's copy has survived, bound together with two incomplete sets of proofs, in a volume now in the Harry Ransom Humanities Research Center of the University of Texas at Austin. The printer's copy contains alterations and revisions in Browning's hand as well as printer's notes; in the first set of proofs there are a few manuscript corrections and queries, some of the corrections evidently by Browning himself, and in the second numerous revisions and instructions in the poet's hand. In the printer's copy 'One Way of Love', which appears without its companion-piece 'Another Way of Love', is given the title 'Song', which it retains in the published text (the poem does not appear in either set of proofs). The printer's copy also includes 'One Word More', with the title altered to 'Adapted from "One Word More" '; a total of forty lines of the poem are deleted, and ll. 140–1 are conflated to 'Pray you, take and keep my men and women,'. In a note at the beginning of the poem Browning has written, '*To go last in the volume*'. The abbreviated poem is included in the second set of proofs. The first, more incomplete set, which is actually bound in with the leaves of the printer's copy, includes 'Transcendentalism' and 'Childe Roland'. The second set is much fuller, though pp. 33–148 are missing. Browning's notes to the printer

---

[1] See Allan C. Dooley, 'The Textual Significance of Robert Browning's 1865 *Poetical Works*': *Papers of the Bibliographical Society of America*, 71 (1977), 212–8.

include general instructions at the beginnings of gatherings: obviously he received and worked on the proofs in separate gatherings. On the first page he wrote '*For Press*', an instruction repeated several pages later. 'Old Pictures in Florence' was quite heavily revised—much more heavily than any other poem—before being entirely deleted; and similarly 'Transcendentalism' received one revision before being entirely deleted (two other poems not in the collection of 1855 are also deleted). Several revisions, mostly corrections of typographical errors or alterations to punctuation, are made to 'Master Hugues of Saxe-Gotha', 'A Grammarian's Funeral', and 'Childe Roland'. It is worth noting that in both sets of proofs the word 'Pashing' in l. 72 of 'Childe Roland' is queried, presumably by the printer; in the second set Browning has written 'stet'. The revisions to 'Childe Roland' include the recasting of l. 152, 'patches where some leanness' as 'patches raw where leanness', a revision that appears in the published *Selection* but in no later text. At the end of the volume there are two leaves containing proofs of the prefatory note, the second heavily revised by Browning; on it he has written 'Send a revise of this.'

The six-volume *Poetical Works* of 1868 was published by Smith, Elder,[1] the volumes appearing at monthly intervals from March to August.[2] Writing to George Smith in December 1867 he expressed his eagerness to make a start on the business of revising his poems: 'I will begin whenever you like,—and give the edition so thorough a looking-to, if your printers will mind me, that it shall be the ultimate thing, and all revisions cease afterwards';[3] and in January, returning the proofs of the first volume, he makes clear his satisfaction with their appearance, adding, 'the printing is capital: the minute corrections, nine out of ten, mere oversights of my own.'[4]

[1] On the editions of 1868, 1870, and 1875 see Walter Barnes, 'Two Robert Brownings: the Edition of 1868', in *The Warden's Meeting: A Tribute to John Sparrow* (Oxford University Society of Bibliophiles; Oxford, 1977), 58–60; and Michael Meredith, 'Learning's Crabbed Text: a Reconsideration of the 1868 Edition of Browning's *Poetical Works*'; SBC 13 (1985), 97–107; on Browning's break with Edward Chapman see *New Letters*, 393–400.

[2] Vols. i and vi are listed under 'New Books' in *Athenæum*, 29 February (no. 2105, p. 323a) and 1 August (no. 2127, p. 145a).

[3] 10 December 1867; quoted in Meredith, 98.

[4] 4 January 1868; quoted in Meredith, 98.

In the 1868 edition the poems of *Men and Women* are divided
between three sections, 'Dramatic Lyrics', 'Dramatic Romances',
and 'Men and Women', corresponding to those of the *Poetical
Works* of 1863 and 1865, in vols. iii, iv, and v respectively, with 'In
a Balcony' appearing separately in vol. vi. As well as substantive
revisions the text incorporates numerous revisions of punctuation
and capitalization. Because of an oversight on the part of the
printers the six volumes had to be entirely reset two years later,
printing taking place between May 1870 and the following January.
Browning took the opportunity to make some revisions: a notable
feature of this edition of 1870–1 is the frequent substitution of the
contracted forms 'o' ' and 'i' ' for 'of' and 'in'. Further revisions
appear in the reprint of 1875, which was printed from stereotype
plates.[1] Writing to Smith on 14 January 1875, requesting the six
volumes of the edition of 1870–1, Browning stated that he would
'engage to go through them thoroughly for, I hope, the last time.'[2]
Three volumes of the copy in which Browning made the revisions
(iii, v, and vi) are now in the Gordon N. Ray Collection in the
Pierpont Morgan Library. In later reprints the deterioration of the
stereotype plates resulted in serious loss of type, notably in end-of-
line punctuation.

The volume of *Selections* published by Smith, Elder in December
1872[3] contains seventy-one poems, thirty-five of them from the
collection of 1855; in the prefatory note, dated 'May 14, 1872',
Browning declares that in selecting the poems '*by simply stringing
together certain pieces on the thread of an imaginary personality, I present
them in succession, rather as the natural development of a particular
experience than because I account them the most noteworthy portion of my
work*', adding that he does not '*apprehend any more charges of being
wilfully obscure, unconscientiously careless, or perversely harsh*'. Eight
years later, in May 1880,[4] Smith, Elder published a complementary
'Second Series' of *Selections*, containing fifty-six poems, twelve of

[1] Vols. i–iv and vi were printed in September and October; a corresponding reprint
of vol. v was printed in April 1877.
[2] Quoted in Meredith, 101.
[3] Advertised in *Athenæum*, 14 December (no. 2355, p. 782a).
[4] Listed under 'New Books' in *Athenæum*, 15 May (no. 2742, p. 631c).

them from *Men and Women*. Both volumes were subsequently reprinted. In May 1884 a 'new and cheaper edition' of both volumes of *Selections* appeared;[1] they were entirely reset. The 1886 reprint was available in a single volume, published by Suttaby & Co., with 'photographic illustrations by Payne Jennings'—clearly intended for a more popular readership. Browning revised his poems for both the 1872 and 1880 volumes and the 1884 *Selections*; most of the substantive revisions do not appear in later editions. Line 979 of 'Bishop Blougram's Apology', however, first introduced in the 1880 Second Series, 'Long rumpled, till creased consciousness lay smooth.', was to reappear in slightly revised form in the 1888–9 *Poetical Works*.

By November 1887 Browning and Smith were planning a new edition of the *Poetical Works*.[2] In the middle of January Browning completed the correction of the poems in the six-volume *Poetical Works*, using either the 1875 or a later reprint, and by the end of February the first proofs had arrived. The first of sixteen volumes of the 'New and Uniform Edition', printed from stereotype plates, was issued about 26 April 1888;[3] 3,000 trade copies (1,000 for America) and 250 large-paper copies were printed. The remaining volumes followed at monthly intervals, the last about 27 July 1889[4] (vols. i–viii of this impression are dated '1888', vols. ix–xvi '1889'). Browning was pleased with the accuracy of the new edition, and when he returned the last proofs on 5 June he enclosed a note acknowledging the 'display of knowledge, as well as intelligence' of the proof-reader at Spottiswoode & Co., the printers.[5] Nevertheless, from April he sent Smith lists of corrections to the earlier volumes, intended to be used in the preparation of a second impression; at the same time he seems to have made corrections and

---

[1] Advertised in *Athenæum*, 3 May (no. 2949, p. 579); in 'Our Library Table' on 31 May (no. 2953, p. 693c) the writer welcomes the *Selections*, 'which appear in a cheaper form, to meet what, we are glad to say, is an increasing taste for Mr. Browning's poetry.'

[2] See Michael Hancher, 'Browning and the *Poetical Works* of 1888–1889': BN 6 (1971), 25–7; Philip Kelley and William S. Peterson, 'Browning's Final Revisions': BIS 1 (1973), 87–118; and Allan C. Dooley, 'Browning's *Poetical Works* of 1888–1889': SBC 7 (1979), 43–69.

[3] Advertised in *Athenæum*, 21 April (no. 3156, p. 488b).

[4] Advertised in *Athenæum*, 27 July (no. 3222, p. 117a).

[5] Quoted in Kelley and Peterson, p. 95.

revisions in his own copy. By 29 August, when he left for Italy, he had completed the correction of vols. i–x; the remaining volumes were never corrected. Shortly before his departure Browning transcribed his corrections and revisions, apparently from his own copy, into a large-paper copy of the 1888–9 edition belonging to his friend James Dykes Campbell: this copy is now in the British Library. A separate list in Browning's hand, probably made for his own use, was in his possession at the time of his death, and is now in Brown University Library, Providence, Rhode Island. The Dykes Campbell copy and the Brown University list each contain corrections that do not appear in the other; a considerable number of the corrections, moreover, were not included in the second impression, or were included in inaccurate form. Most of the corrections and revisions in the Dykes Campbell copy and the Brown University list are concerned with punctuation, many involving the correction of defective end-of-line punctuation; there are, however, several substantive revisions, including a few in the poems of *Men and Women*. It is not clear when printing of the second impression, from corrected stereotype plates, took place, though an advertisement for Smith, Elder in the *Athenæum* of 5 October, specifying that volumes were available 'bound separately',[1] suggests that several of the volumes had been issued by this date; from the beginning of January, however, the edition was once more regularly advertised. Browning's death on 12 December may have provided an incentive to make the sixteen-volume set available as soon as possible. All the volumes of the second impression are dated '1889'.

For the present edition the text of the 1888–9 first impression of the *Poetical Works* has been used as copy-text. For several reasons the second impression cannot be regarded as reliable. As we have seen, a number of Browning's corrections were not incorporated, and the poet did not see the proofs; moreover, even in the early states the end-of-line punctuation is frequently defective. The 1888–9 text has been collated with extant manuscripts, with all the authoritative earlier editions, and with the text of the 1889 second

---

[1] No. 3232, p. 468. In the second impression the contents of each volume appear on the spine.

impression. The corrections and revisions in the Dykes Campbell copy and the Brown University list have, except where clearly inaccurate, been adopted as emendations. Obvious typographical errors in the copy-text have been emended; other emendations are based, where possible, on readings of earlier editions. The order of the poems is that of the first edition of 1855.

Note on the recording of variants

Printed editions

We aim to record substantive variants, and variants in accidentals which significantly affect the meaning. Variants not recorded are, for example, apostrophes denoting omission of letters (shouldst/ should'st, adored/ador'd); capitalization and spelling variants of no special importance (East/east—unless personification is involved; Thy/thy when unambiguously referring to God; ancles/ankles; recognise/recognize etc.); with a few exceptions, alternation between colons and semicolons, and between dashes and colons or semicolons; hyphenation unless it indicates a different meaning; and commas with a minimal influence on the meaning. A one-word lemma will normally be a punctuation variant. The words before and after substantive variants are given to aid identification, except when the variant begins or ends a line, when only one accompanying word or phrase is given. The editions or chronological series of editions in which the variants occur are specified in the textual note (see list of abbreviations and signs used in the textual notes, pp. lvii–lviii below).

Manuscripts

In recording variants in manuscripts, of which there are few for the poems of *Men and Women*, and in manuscript revisions in printed texts, as well as lists of corrections occurring in Browning's letters, the same criteria have been applied as with printed editions. For the signs used in the recording of manuscript variants, see the list of abbreviations and signs on pp. lv–lvi below.

REFERENCES AND ABBREVIATIONS

Note: the place of publication is given if it is not London or Oxford

Allen   F. C. Allen, *A Critical Edition of Robert Browning's 'Bishop Browning's Apology'* (Salzburg Studies in English Literature, 60; Salzburg 1976).

Altick   R. D. Altick, 'Memo to the Next Annotator of Browning': VP 1 (1963), 61–8.

Andrès   Glenn Andrès, John M. Hunisak and A. Richard Turner, *The Art of Florence*, 2 vols. (Abbeville Press, New York, 1988).

Barrett   see Landis.

Berdoe   *The Browning Cyclopaedia*, ed. Edward Berdoe, 2nd ed. (1892).

Biographie universelle   *Biographie universelle, ancienne et moderne*, 52 vols. (Paris, 1811–28).

BIS   *Browning Institute Studies*, annual volumes, 1973–90.

BN   *The Browning Newsletter* (Armstrong Browning Library, Waco, Tex.)

Boase   T. S. R. Boase, *Giorgio Vasari: The Man and the Book* (Princeton, 1979).

Bosco   R. A. Bosco, 'The Brownings and Mrs. Kinney: A Record of Their Friendship', BIS 4 (1976), 57–124.

Brewer   [E. C.] *Brewer's Dictionary of Phrase & Fable*, 6th ed. (1962).

Browning and Domett   *Robert Browning and Alfred Domett*, ed. Frederic G. Kenyon (1906).

BSN *Browning Society Notes* (Browning Society of London).

BST *Browning Society Papers*, 3 vols., 1881–91 (i.e. the Transactions of the original Browning Society. See Peterson, *Interrogating the Oracle*, Appendix A, for an account of this confusing publication).

Carlyle Letters   Letters of Thomas Carlyle to John Stuart Mill . . . and Robert Browning, ed. A. Carlyle (1923).

Carlyle: *New Letters of Thomas Carlyle*, ed. Alexander Carlyle, 2 vols., 1904.

Carlyle: *Works* (Centenary ed., 30 vols., 1896–9).

Centenary Selection   A Centenary Selection from Robert Browning's Poetry, ed. Michael Meredith (1989).

Checklist *The Brownings' Correspondence: A Checklist*, compiled by Philip Kelley and Ronald Hudson, The Browning Institute and Wedgestone Press (Winfield, Kan., 1978; supplements in later vols. of BIS)

Collections see Kelley and Coley.

Collingwood W. G. Collingwood, *The Life and Work of John Ruskin*, 2 vols. (1893).

Cook, *Browning's Lyrics: An Exploration*, by Eleanor Cook (Toronto, 1974).

Cook and Wedderburn see Ruskin.

Cooke George Willis Cooke, *A Guide-Book to the . . . Works of Robert Browning* (Cambridge, Mass., 1891).

Correspondence *The Brownings' Correspondence*, ed. Philip Kelley and Ronald Hudson (to vol. viii), ed. Philip Kelley and Scott Lewis (Wedgestone Press, Winfield, Kans., 1984–).

Cruden Alexander Cruden, *A Complete Concordance to the Old and New Testament* (Student's Edition, London and New York, 1894).

Dearest Isa: Robert Browning's Letters to Isabella Blagden, by Edward C. McAleer (Austin, Tex. and Edinburgh, 1951).

DeLaura, 'Ruskin and the Brownings': *Bulletin of the John Rylands Library*, 54 (1971–2), 314–56.

DeLaura, 'Browning's Painter Poems': PMLA 95 (May 1980), 367–88.

DeLaura, 'Some Notes on Browning's Pictures and Painters': SBHC (Fall 1980), 7–16.

DeVane, *Browning's Parleyings* William Clyde DeVane, *Browning's Parleyings: The Autobiography of a Mind* (New Haven, 1927).

DeVane *A Browning Handbook*, by William Clyde DeVane, 2nd ed. (New York, 1955; 1st ed., 1935).

DGR Letters Letters of Dante Gabriel Rossetti, ed. Oswald Doughty and John Robert Wahl, 4 vols. (1965–7).

Domett *The Diary of Alfred Domett 1872–1885*, ed. E. A. Horsman (1953).

Drew Philip Drew (ed.), *Robert Browning: A Collection of Critical Essays* (1966).

EBB Elizabeth Barrett Browning.

ELH *English Literary History*.

ELN *English Language Notes*.

Encyclopædia Britannica 11th ed., 29 vols. (1910–11).

Farquhar [Maria Farquhar], *Biographical catalogue of the principal Italian Painters, by a Lady*, ed. Ralph N. Wornum (1855).

Gosse *Robert Browning: Personalia*, by Edmund Gosse (Boston and New York, 1890). (Part of the impression was sold in London in 1891, under the imprint of T. Fisher Unwin).

Griffin and Minchin *The Life of Robert Browning*, by W. Hall Griffin, completed and edited by H. C. Minchin, 3rd ed., revised and enlarged (1938; 1st ed., 1910).

Hadow *Browning's Men and Women 1855*, ed. G. E. Hadow (1911).

Handbook A Handbook to the Works of Robert Browning, by Mrs Sutherland Orr, 7th ed. (1896, 1st ed. 1885). As William S. Peterson points out (*Trumpeter*, p. 124 n), Browning 'read both the first and second editions . . . in proof', and in a few instances provided prose statements of the meaning of passages.

Hatcher Harlan Henthorne Hatcher, *The Versification of Robert Browning* (Ohio State University, Columbus, 1928).

Hellstrom Ward Hellstrom, 'Time and Type in Browning's *Saul*', ELH 33 (1966), 370–89.

HLQ *Huntington Library Quarterly*

Hood T. L. Hood, 'Browning's Ancient Classical Sources'; *Harvard Studies in Classical Philology* 33 (1922), 79–180.

Hudson (ed.), *Browning to his American Friends*, ed. Gertrude Reese Hudson (1965).

Huxley *Elizabeth Barrett Browning: Letters to her Sister*, ed. Leonard Huxley (1929).

Jack Ian Jack, *Browning's Major Poetry* (1973).

Jack 'Browning on *Sordello* and *Men and Women*: Unpublished Letters to James T. Fields', HLQ XLV, no. 3 (Summer 1982), 185–98.

Jameson Mrs Jameson *Memoirs of Early Italian Painters*, 2 vols., 1845.

Jamieson *An Etymological Dictionary of the Scottish Language*, by John Jamieson, 2 vols. (Edinburgh, 1808).

JEGP *Journal of English and Germanic Philology*.

Johnson Samuel Johnson, *A Dictionary of the English Language*, 9th ed., 2 vols. (1806).

Kelley and Coley *The Browning Collections: A Reconstruction with Other Memorabilia*, compiled by Philip Kelley and Betty A. Coley, Armstrong Browning Library, Baylor University, Texas (1984).

Kelley and Hudson   *The Brownings' Correspondence: A Checklist*, compiled by Philip Kelley and Ronald Hudson, The Browning Institute and Wedgestone Press (Winfield, Kan., 1978).

Kintner   *The Letters of Robert Browning and Elizabeth Barrett Barrett 1845–1846*, ed. Elvan Kintner, 2 vols. (Cambridge, Mass., 1969).

Landis   *Letters of the Brownings to George Barrett*, ed. Paul Landis and R. E. Freeman (Urbana, Ill., 1958).

Lanzi   *The History of Painting in Italy*, by Abate Luigi Lanzi, trans. Thomas Roscoe, new ed. (1847).

Learned Lady   *Learned Lady: Letters from Robert Browning to Mrs Thomas FitzGerald*, ed. Edward C. McAleer (Cambridge, Mass., 1966).

Lemprière   *A Classical Dictionary*, by J. Lemprière, 5th ed. (1804).

Letters   *Letters of Robert Browning Collected by Thomas J. Wise*, ed. Thurman L. Hood (1933).

Letters of EBB   *The Letters of Elizabeth Barrett Browning*, ed. Frederic G. Kenyon, 2 vols. (1898).

Life   *Life and Letters of Robert Browning*, by Mrs Sutherland Orr, new ed. rev. by Frederic G. Kenyon, (1908; 1st ed. 1891).

Litzinger and Smalley   *Browning: The Critical Heritage* Boyd Litzinger and Donald Smalley (eds.), (1970).

Longman   *The Poems of Browning*, ed. John Woolford and Daniel Karlin, Vols. I–II (1826–46), 1991.

Lytton   *Letters from Owen Meredith (Robert, First Earl of Lytton) To Robert and Elizabeth Barrett Browning*, ed. Aurelia Brooks Harlan and J. Lee Harlan (Baylor University, Waco, Tex., n.d.).

Maynard   *Browning's Youth*, by John Maynard (Cambridge, Mass., 1977).

Melchiori   Barbara Melchiori, *Browning's Poetry of Reticence* (Edinburgh and London, 1968).

Meredith   *More than Friend: The Letters of Robert Browning to Katharine de Kay Bronson*, ed. Michael Meredith (Armstrong Browning Library and Wedgestone Press, 1985).

Miller *Robert Browning: A Portrait* (1952).

MLQ   *Modern Language Quarterly*.

MP   *Modern Philology*.

New Grove   *The New Grove Dictionary of Music and Musicians*, ed. Stanley Sadie, 20 vols. (1980).

New Letters *New Letters of Robert Browning*, ed. William Clyde DeVane and Kenneth Leslie Knickerbocker (1951).

New Letters of Thomas Carlyle, ed. A. Carlyle, 2 vols. (1904).

New Poems *New Poems by Robert Browning and Elizabeth Barrett Browning*, ed. Sir Frederic G. Kenyon (1914).

NQ *Notes and Queries*.

ODEP *Oxford Dictionary of English Proverbs*, 3rd ed., ed. F. P. Wilson (1970).

OED² *Oxford English Dictionary*, 2nd ed., ed. J. A. Simpson and E. S. C. Weiner, 20 vols. (1989).

Ogilvy *Elizabeth Barrett Browning's Letters to Mrs. David Ogilvy 1849–1861*, ed. Peter N. Heydon and Philip Kelley (1974).

Orr See *Handbook* and *Life*.

Parleyings *Browning's Parleyings: The Autobiography of a Mind*, by William Clyde DeVane (New Haven, 1927).

Parr Johnstone Parr, 'Browning's *Fra Lippo Lippi*, Vasari's Masaccio, and Mrs. Jameson': ELN, June 1968.

Personalia see Gosse.

Peterson William S. Peterson, 'The Proofs of Browning's *Men and Women*', SBC 3 (Fall 1975), 23–39.

Pettigrew and Collins *Robert Browning: The Poems*, Volume I, ed. John Pettigrew, supplemented and completed by Thomas J. Collins (Penguin English Poets, Harmondsworth, Yale University Press, New Haven, 1981).

Pittaluga Mary Pittaluga, *Filippo Lippi* (Florence, 1949).

PK References in the style 'PK 53:24' are to letters listed in *Checklist*.

PMLA *Publications of the Modern Language Association of America*.

Porter and Clarke *The Complete Works of Robert Browning*, ed. Charlotte Porter and Helen A. Clarke, 12 vols. (New York, 1898); published in different formats, at different times, and under various titles, e.g. as the Florentine Edition, the Camberwell Edition, etc.

PQ *Philological Quarterly*.

Raymond William O. Raymond, *The Infinite Moment and Other Essays in Robert Browning*, 2nd ed. (Toronto, 1965).

Raymond and Sullivan *The Letters of Elizabeth Barrett Browning to Mary Russell Mitford 1836–1854*, ed. Meredith B. Raymond and Mary Rose Sullivan, Armstrong Browning Library, etc., 3 vols. (1983).

RES   *The Review of English Studies.*

Rio   *The Poetry of Christian Art*, trans. from the French of A. F. Rio (1854).

Riverside   *Riverside Edition of The Poetic and Dramatic Works of Robert Browning*, 6 vols. (Cambridge, Mass., 1899).

Rossetti Letters   *Letters of Dante Gabriel Rossetti*, ed. Oswald Doughty and John Robert Wahl, 4 vols., (1965–7).

Ruskin   *The Works of John Ruskin*, ed. E. T. Cook and A. Wedderburn, 39 vols. (1903–12).

SBC   *Studies in Browning and his Circle* (Armstrong Browning Library, Waco, Tex.)

SEL   *Studies in English Literature*

Sharp   William Sharp *Life of Robert Browning* (1890).

SP   *Studies in Philology.*

Story   Henry James, *William Wetmore Story and his Friends*, 2 vols. (1903).

Symons, Arthur   *An Introduction to the Study of Browning*, rev. ed. (1906).

Tilley   M.P. Tilley, *A Dictionary of the Proverbs in England in the Sixteenth and Seventeenth Centuries* (Ann Arbor, Mich., 1950).

TLS   *Times Literary Supplement.*

Trésor   *Trésor de la langue française*, directed by Paul Imbs (1971–).

Trumpeter   *Browning's Trumpeter: The Correspondence of Robert Browning and Frederick J. Furnivall 1872–1889*, ed. William S. Peterson (Washington, DC, 1979).

Turner   *Browning: Men and Women*, ed. Paul Turner (1972).

UTQ   *University of Toronto Quarterly.*

Vasari   *Lives of the most eminent Painters, Sculptors, and Architects*, trans. from the Italian of Giorgio Vasari by Mrs Jonathan Foster, 5 vols. (1850–2).

VP   *Victorian Poetry* (Morgantown, W. Va.)

Wedgwood   *Robert Browning and Julia Wedgwood*, ed. Richard Curle (1937).

Whiting   Lilian Whiting, *The Brownings: Their Life and Art* (1911).

Worsfold   *Browning's Men and Women*, ed. Basil Worsfold, 2 vols., (1904).

Note: references to Shakespeare are to *William Shakespeare: The Complete Works* (Tudor Edition), ed. Peter Alexander (1951).

Abbreviations and signs used in the textual notes

*	Emendation.
†	So in text (e.g. four dots appear in text and do not indicate an omission by the editors).
. . . .	Omission by the editors.
{ }	Comment by the editors.
[ ]	Addition or substitution in MS.
⟨ ⟩	Deletion in MS.
|	Division between lines.
BrU	Brown University list of revisions in RB's hand to vols. iv–x of *Poetical Works*, 1888–9.
DC	Copy of *Poetical Works*, 1888–9, formerly belonging to James Dykes Campbell and containing revisions by RB, now in the British Library.
PM	Copies of vols. iii, v, and vi of *Poetical Works*, 1870–1, containing revisions by RB, now in the Gordon N.Ray Collection, Pierpont Morgan Library.
Fields	Corrections to *Men and Women* listed in RB's letter to James T. Fields, 26 October 1855
Rossetti	Corrections to *Men and Women* listed in RB's letter to D. G. Rossetti, 29 October 1855.
Taylor	Revisions to 'Memorabilia' in copy of vol. ii of *Poetical Works*, 1865, in Robert H. Taylor Collection, Princeton University.
Woolner	Revisions in copy of vol. ii of *Men and Women*, 1855, presented to Thomas Woolner, now in George Arents Research Library, Syracuse University.
1845	*Dramatic Romances and Lyrics*, 1845.
1849	*Poems by Robert Browning*, 1849.
1854	*Two Poems by Elizabeth Barrett and Robert Browning*, 1854.
1855P	Proofs of *Men and Women*, 1855, in Huntington Library.
1855P/MS	Manuscript revisions in Huntington proofs.
1855	*Men and Women*, 2 vols., 1855.
1856	*Men and Women*, Boston, 1856.

1865	*The Poetical Works of Robert Browning . . . Fourth Edition*, 3 vols., 1865.
1865SPC	Printer's copy for *A Selection from the Works of Robert Browning*, 1865.
1865SPC/MS	Manuscript revisions in printer's copy of *A Selection*, 1865.
1865SP	Proofs of *A Selection*, 1865.
1865SP/MS	Manuscript revisions in proofs of *A Selection*, 1865.
1865S	*A Selection from the Works of Robert Browning*, 1865.
1868	*The Poetical Works of Robert Browning*, 6 vols., 1868.
1870	*The Poetical Works of Robert Browning*, 6 vols., 1870–1.
1872S	*Selections from the Poetical Works of Robert Browning*, 1872.
1875	*The Poetical Works of Robert Browning*, 6 vols., 1875–7.
1880S	*Selections from the Poetical Works of Robert Browning*, Second Series, 1880.
1884S	*Selections from the Poetical Works of Robert Browning*, First and Second Series, 2 vols., 1884.
1888	*The Poetical Works of Robert Browning*, 16 vols., 1888–9.
1889	*The Poetical Works of Robert Browning*, second impression, 16 vols., 1889.

MEN AND WOMEN.

BY

ROBERT BROWNING.

IN TWO VOLUMES.

VOL. I.

LONDON:

CHAPMAN AND HALL, 193, PICCADILLY.

1855.

VOLUME I

LOVE AMONG THE RUINS

THE original title of this poem was 'Sicilian Pastoral', a useful indication of the genre to which it is related. It is 'Sicilian' not because Browning ever visited Sicily, but because he is writing, in his own manner, under the influence of Theocritus and his followers. Maynard describes the manuscript as 'an early or possibly a first draft',[1] yet the variants between it and the text of *1855* are (as he concedes) 'relatively few', and it could equally be late.

Scholars have discussed the setting, which is probably composite.[2] The Brownings loved to visit the Campagna outside Rome during their residence in that city from late November 1853 to late May 1854.[3] It was no doubt during the spring that they went there with Leighton, Ampère, Harriet Hosmer, and the Kemble sisters, Fanny being particularly delighted to have luncheon 'in the midst of all that was lovely in nature and picturesque in the ruined remains of Roman power'. As Johnstone Parr pointed out, the Brownings are likely to have consulted Murray's *Handbook for Travellers in Central Italy*, where they would have read that 'the present aspect of the Campagna should excite a contrast with the eventful drama once enacted on its surface'.[4] Murray mentions the 'magnificent aqueducts which span the Campagna with their colossal arches', and the 'ruins of Bovillæ . . . [with] portions of the circus, the theatre, and the ancient walls', as well as the distant view of Rome 'with its domes and towers and obelisks, rising in solitary grandeur amidst the ruins of the desolate Campagna, like an oasis in the desert'. As he wrote the poem Browning may also have been drawing on his memories of various travel books, and such works as Rollin's *Ancient History*. Parr quotes particularly tellingly from *The Cities and Cemeteries of Etruria*, by George Dennis, with its description of Veii, once 'preferred by the Romans to the Eternal City itself',

---

[1] John Maynard, 'Browning's "Sicilian Pastoral" ': *Harvard Library Bulletin*, 20 (1972), 436 ff.

[2] See Johnstone Parr, 'The Site and Ancient City of Browning's *Love among the Ruins*': PMLA 68 (1953), 128 ff.

[3] Griffin and Minchin, 194. Cf. our introduction to 'Two in the Campagna'.

[4] 2nd ed., 1850, p. 286, followed by a quotation from pp. 569–70.

now void and desolate, without one house or habitant, its temples and palaces level with the dust, and nothing beyond a few fragments of walls, and some empty sepulchres, remaining to tell the traveller that here Veii was. The plough passes over its bosom, and the shepherd pastures his flock on the waste within it.[1]

In the MS we find seven numbered sections, each consisting of twelve lines with a slight gap between the first six and the second. In *1855* there are fourteen sections of six lines, an arrangement which remains in *1863* and *1865*. From *1868* onwards Browning reverted to seven sections of twelve lines. As a rule six lines describe the scene in which the speaker (a shepherd) finds himself, while the following six lines deal with the past. In the fifth stanza (of the original and final text) only ll. 57, 58, and part of 59 deal with the past.

The most striking metrical feature of the piece is the alternation of long lines with short, each pair forming a couplet. The long lines have ten or eleven syllables, usually with three principal stresses. The fact that a few lines open with stressed syllables has led some critics to describe the poem as trochaic, a description belied by most of the lines. The predominant foot in many lines is the anapaest, and the final syllable is always stressed. The first line ends with two iambs. Line 79 is an iambic pentameter. The short lines are cretics. The music created by the contrast between the long lines and the arresting brevity of the short gives the piece its character.

DeVane's statement that the poem 'was written in an apartment in the Champs Elysées in Paris, on January 3, 1852' derives from Griffin and Minchin,[2] who appear to be relying on Furnivall's claim that it and 'Women and Roses' and 'Childe Roland' were written 'in three successive days, 1, 2 & 3, January 1852'. In the Introduction we have shown that this claim is untenable. Sharp's date, 1853–4 (p. 166), is preferable.

Date: 1854
1863: *Dramatic Lyrics*

---

[1] 2 vols., 1848, i. 15. A friend points out the parallel in Propertius, IV, x. 27–30.
[2] p. 189: cf. p. xii ff above.

LOVE AMONG THE RUINS.

I.

WHERE the quiet-coloured end of evening smiles,
    Miles and miles,
On the solitary pastures where our sheep
    Half-asleep
Tinkle homeward thro' the twilight, stray or stop   5
    As they crop—
Was the site once of a city great and gay,
    (So they say)
Of our country's very capital, its prince
    Ages since   10
Held his court in, gathered councils, wielding far
    Peace or war.

II.

Now,—the country does not even boast a tree,
    As you see,
To distinguish slopes of verdure, certain rills   15
    From the hills
Intersect and give a name to, (else they run
    Into one)

---

title *MS* Sicilian Pastoral   {in *MS* the poem is divided into twelve-line stanzas, numbered in arabic numerals, with a space between the sixth and seventh lines of each stanza; in *1855P–65* the poem is divided into six-line stanzas, numbered in arabic numerals in *1855P–56*, and roman in *1863S–65*}   1 *MS* of even smiles
*2 {reading of *MS, 1870–84S*} *1855P–68, 1888, 1889* miles   8 *MS* So . . . . say;
9 *MS* Was our   11 *MS* in, had his councils, sent afar   *13 {reading of *MS*, *1855P–84S*, DC, BrU} *1888, 1889* tree   17 *MS, 1855P* to, else   18 *MS, 1855P* one—

5 *Tinkle homeward*: cf. Thomas Gray, 'Elegy Written in a Country Churchyard', 8: 'And drowsy tinklings lull the distant folds'.

6 *crop*: graze.

7 *great and gay*: cf. Spenser, 'The Ruines of Time', 55–6.

11 *wielding*: commanding, determining.

Where the domed and daring palace shot its spires
        Up like fires   20
O'er the hundred-gated circuit of a wall
        Bounding all,
Made of marble, men might march on nor be pressed,
        Twelve abreast.

III.

And such plenty and perfection, see, of grass   25
        Never was!
Such a carpet as, this summer-time, o'erspreads
        And embeds
Every vestige of the city, guessed alone,
        Stock or stone—   30
Where a multitude of men breathed joy and woe
        Long ago;
Lust of glory pricked their hearts up, dread of shame
        Struck them tame;
And that glory and that shame alike, the gold   35
        Bought and sold.

IV.

Now,—the single little turret that remains
        On the plains,
By the caper overrooted, by the gourd
        Overscored,   40

---

*23 {reading of *1868–84S*, DC, BrU, *1889*} MS prest *1855P–65* prest, *1888* pressed
26 MS was,   34 MS, *1855P* tame,   39 MS Which the caper roots a-top
of, by   40 MS Oversoared,

---

19 *shot its spires*: cf. Spenser, 'Ruines of Rome: by Bellay', 16: 'And sharped
steeples high shot up in ayre' (Pettigrew); and Cowper, 'To the Immortal Memory of
the Halibut', 17–18: 'where Hibernia shoots/Her wondrous causeway far into the
main'.

21 *hundred-gated*: Gk. ἑκατόμπυλος, used of Egyptian Thebes in the *Iliad*, ix. 383.
Herodotus reports that there were a hundred gates in the circuit of the wall of Babylon:
Histories, i. 179.

29 *guessed alone*: only to be guessed at.

39 *caper*: a shrub (*Capparis spinosa*) which grows in S. Europe.
    overrooted: covered over with roots: cf. MS.

While the patching houseleek's head of blossom winks
     Through the chinks—
Marks the basement whence a tower in ancient time
     Sprang sublime,
And a burning ring, all round, the chariots traced   45
     As they raced,
And the monarch and his minions and his dames
     Viewed the games.

V.

And I know, while thus the quiet-coloured eve
     Smiles to leave   50
To their folding, all our many-tinkling fleece
     In such peace,
And the slopes and rills in undistinguished grey
     Melt away—
That a girl with eager eyes and yellow hair   55
     Waits me there
In the turret whence the charioteers caught soul
     For the goal,
When the king looked, where she looks now, breathless, dumb
     Till I come.   60

VI.

But he looked upon the city, every side,
     Far and wide,
All the mountains topped with temples, all the glades'
     Colonnades,

---

41 *MS* [Which] ⟨Where⟩ the   43 *MS* Was the   47 *MS* While the
61 *MS* But the city he looked out on, every   63 *1884S* glades,

41 *patching*: 'That patches or covers with patches': OED², with no other example.
43 *basement*: base.
44 *sublime*: lofty. L. *sublimis*.
49 *quiet-coloured*: repeated from l. 1.
51 *folding*: being enclosed in their pen.
   fleece: sheep (by synecdoche).
53 *undistinguished*: not clearly perceived.
57 *caught soul*: gained courage or inspiration.

All the causeys, bridges, aqueducts,—and then,   65
    All the men!
When I do come, she will speak not, she will stand,
    Either hand
On my shoulder, give her eyes the first embrace
    Of my face,   70
Ere we rush, ere we extinguish sight and speech
    Each on each.

VII.

In one year they sent a million fighters forth
    South and North,
And they built their gods a brazen pillar high   75
    As the sky,
Yet reserved a thousand chariots in full force—
    Gold, of course.
Oh heart! oh blood that freezes, blood that burns!
    Earth's returns   80
For whole centuries of folly, noise and sin!
    Shut them in,
With their triumphs and their glories and the rest!
    Love is best.

---

72 *MS* each!   77 *MS* And yet mustered five-score chariots in *1855P* And reserved   79 *MS* that [tingles] ⟨freezes⟩, blood   81 *MS* sin—   83 *MS* with their grandeurs and *MS, 1855P* rest—   *1855–65* rest.   84 *MS This* is best! *1855P* This is best!   *1855–65* best!

65 *causeys*: raised paths or roads. 'Applied esp. to the Roman roads': OED².
77 *a thousand chariots*: cf. MS.
80 *Earth's returns*: all that life vouchsafed.

A LOVERS' QUARREL

A COLLECTION of poems in which love is so prominent a theme would be incomplete without an account of a quarrel. As early as 9 November 1845 Browning humorously complained to EBB that he had 'not had *every* love-luxury, ... where is the proper, rationally to-be-expected—"lovers' quarrel?" '.[1] Karlin has concluded that the poem draws on 'the winter months of 1846–7 which the Brownings spent at Pisa',[2] an argument strengthened by a fact which he does not mention, that in December 1846 Pisa had 'actual snow, the first time for five years!'.[3] He rightly concedes that the 'setting, and the contemporary events to which it alludes, belong to a different place and later time'. We have no reason to believe that the quarrel which lies behind the poem corresponded to anything in the lives of the two poets.

There are twenty-two stanzas, each of seven lines. The rhyme scheme is *aabbaaa*. Lines 1, 2, 5, 6, and 7 have three stresses each, while lines 3 and 4 have two.[4] The initial syllable of the first line of every stanza is stressed, as (usually) is the initial syllable of the sixth line. The basic metrical pattern may be shown thus:

> Runnels, which rillets swéll,
> Must be dancing dówn the déll,
> With a foaming héad
> On the béryl béd
> Paven smooth as a hérmit's céll;
> Eách with a tále to téll,
> Could my Lóve but atténd as wéll.

The poem may well have been written in 1853. Stanza v refers to the marriage of Napoleon III and Eugénie at the end of January. On 4 March EBB told her sister Henrietta that there had been snow in Florence, and that 'all the mountains round [were] white'.[5]

Date: 1853
1863: Dramatic Lyrics

---

[1] Kintner, i. 262.
[2] 'Browning's Poetry of Intimacy': *Essays in Criticism*, 33 (January 1989), 47 ff., at p. 56.
[3] Huxley, 9.
[4] The indentation of the sixth line of each stanza is misleading, if it is taken to indicate that it rhymes with ll. 3 and 4.
[5] Huxley, 177.

A LOVERS' QUARREL.

I.

Oн, what a dawn of day!
How the March sun feels like May!
    All is blue again
    After last night's rain,
And the South dries the hawthorn-spray.   5
    Only, my Love's away!
I'd as lief that the blue were grey.

II.

Runnels, which rillets swell,
Must be dancing down the dell,
    With a foaming head   10
    On the beryl bed
Paven smooth as a hermit's cell;
    Each with a tale to tell,
Could my Love but attend as well.

III.

Dearest, three months ago!   15
When we lived blocked-up with snow,—
    When the wind would edge
    In and in his wedge,

---

10 *1855P–65S* a foamy head   11 *1855P* O'er each beryl   15 *1855P* ago
17 *1855P* the cold would

   1 *dawn of day*: as in Tennyson, 'The Death of the Old Year' (1832), 11.

   2 *feels like May!*: 'The spring has surprised us here', EBB wrote to Miss Mitford on 15 March 1853: '. . . The sun is powerful—we are rejoicing in our Italian climate': Raymond and Sullivan, iii. 381.

   5 *the South*: the South wind.

   7 *as lief*: I'd be as glad.

   8 *Runnels . . . rillets*: cf. Shelley, *Prometheus Unbound*, iv. 196: 'two runnels of a rivulet'.

    rillets: small rivulets, as in Keats, *Endymion*, ii. 945, and Tennyson, 'Recollections of the Arabian Nights' (1830), 48.

   12 *Paven*: paved, mainly a poetical form, as in *Comus*, 885, and Shelley, 'Spirit of Plato', 2.

In, as far as the point could go—
   Not to our ingle, though,   20
Where we loved each the other so!

IV.

Laughs with so little cause!
We devised games out of straws.
   We would try and trace
   One another's face   25
In the ash, as an artist draws;
   Free on each other's flaws,
How· we chattered like two church daws!

V.

What's in the "Times"?—a scold
At the Emperor deep and cold;   30
   He has taken a bride
   To his gruesome side,
That's as fair as himself is bold:
   There they sit ermine-stoled,
And she powders her hair with gold.   35

---

20 *ingle*: hearth, fire (often Sc. and Northern).

29 *What's in the "Times"?*: Louis Napoleon became Emperor of the French, as Napoleon III, on 2 December 1852, marrying Eugénie de Montijo in a civil ceremony on 29 January 1853, and in Notre-Dame the following day. *The Times* carried full reports, stressing the extravagance of the wedding. On 31 January, as Turner mentions, it stated that Eugénie's dresses cost £40,000 and that the bride and bridegroom sat on thrones on a carpet of ermine. Eugénie was indeed 'fair', and Napoleon was passionately in love with her: 'cold' and 'gruesome' refer to his political character. In *Le Gouvernement du Deux Décembre* (London, 1853, p. 437 n.) Victor Schoelcher described him as 'the hideous author of 2 December', with reference to the *coup d'état* of that date (see Jasper Ridley, *Napoleon III and Eugénie*, 1979). Whereas Browning was strongly opposed to Napoleon, EBB regarded him as 'an extraordinary man . . . & a man, too, with better stuff in him than is supposed by the Times Newspaper & the English nation generally. But I have no enthusiasm for him on the other side, after all', she added '. . . he does not allow of enough liberty for me' (Raymond and Sullivan, iii. 380).

VI.

Fancy the Pampas' sheen!
Miles and miles of gold and green
     Where the sunflowers blow
     In a solid glow,
And—to break now and then the screen—   40
     Black neck and eyeballs keen,
Up a wild horse leaps between!

VII.

Try, will our table turn?
Lay your hands there light, and yearn
     Till the yearning slips   45
     Thro' the finger-tips
In a fire which a few discern,
     And a very few feel burn,
And the rest, they may live and learn!

VIII.

Then we would up and pace,   50
For a change, about the place,
     Each with arm o'er neck:
     'T is our quarter-deck,
We are seamen in woeful case.
     Help in the ocean-space!   55
Or, if no help, we'll embrace.

---

36 *1855P* sheen,   40 *1855P* break once a while the   49 *1884S* learn.
52 *1855P–56* neck.   54 *1855P* case: 56 *1855P* embrace!

---

36 *Fancy the Pampas' sheen!*: another of the amusements of the lovers is to think of
the great shining plains of S. America.

43 *will our table turn?*: on 16 May 1853 EBB told John Kenyon that they had 'tried
the table experiment in this room a few days since . . . and failed; but we were
impatient, and Robert was playing Mephistopheles, . . . and there was little chance of
success under the circumstances': *Letters of EBB*, ii. 116–17.

47 *in a fire*: spiritualists believed that a mysterious force manifested itself on occasion
through people of sensitive temperaments (streaming from their finger-tips), and that
this explained mesmerism. Cf. 'Mesmerism', 63–5.

49 *live and learn!*: proverbial (ODEP 473ab).

IX.

See, how she looks now, dressed
In a sledging-cap and vest!
　　'T is a huge fur cloak—
　　Like a reindeer's yoke   60
Falls the lappet along the breast:
　　Sleeves for her arms to rest,
Or to hang, as my Love likes best.

X.

Teach me to flirt a fan
As the Spanish ladies can,   65
　　Or I tint your lip
　　With a burnt stick's tip
And you turn into such a man!
　　Just the two spots that span
Half the bill of the young male swan.   70

XI.

Dearest, three months ago
When the mesmerizer Snow
　　With his hand's first sweep
　　Put the earth to sleep:
'T was a time when the heart could show   75
　　All—how was earth to know,
'Neath the mute hand's to-and-fro?

58 *1855P* vest; *1855, 1856* vest.   74 *1855P–56, 1884S* sleep, *1863–68* sleep! *1870–75*
sleep   77 *1855P–56* to-and-fro!

61 *lappet*: flap, lapel, or overlapping part. The lovers are now in the far North.

64 *flirt*: open and close swiftly, in the manner of a coquette with a fan.

69 *the two spots*: 'probably the nostrils, which, in the Mute Swan, might appear to a
casual observer as two black spots taking up about half the width of the orange-coloured
bill': Turner.

72 *the mesmerizer Snow*: an appropriate image, given EBB's deep interest in
mesmerism.

XII.

Dearest, three months ago
When we loved each other so,
    Lived and loved the same   80
    Till an evening came
When a shaft from the devil's bow
    Pierced to our ingle-glow,
And the friends were friend and foe!

XIII.

Not from the heart beneath—   85
'T was a bubble born of breath,
    Neither sneer nor vaunt,
    Nor reproach nor taunt.
See a word, how it severeth!
    Oh, power of life and death   90
In the tongue, as the Preacher saith!

XIV.

Woman, and will you cast
For a word, quite off at last
    Me, your own, your You,—
    Since, as truth is true,   95
I was You all the happy past—
    Me do you leave aghast
With the memories We amassed?

XV.

Love, if you knew the light
That your soul casts in my sight,   100
    How I look to you
    For the pure and true

---

78 *1872S* ago!   98 *1855P* memories you amassed?   *102 {reading of DC, BrU, *1889*} *1855P–88* true,

---

89 *severeth*: cf. *Paradise Lost*, ix. 958: 'Our state cannot be severed, we are one' (Adam to Eve).

91 *as the Preacher saith*: 'Death and life are in the power of the tongue': Prov. 18: 21.

And the beauteous and the right,—
　　Bear with a moment's spite
When a mere mote threats the white!   105

XVI.

What of a hasty word?
Is the fleshly heart not stirred
　　By a worm's pin-prick
　　Where its roots are quick?
See the eye, by a fly's foot blurred—   110
　　Ear, when a straw is heard
Scratch the brain's coat of curd!

XVII.

Foul be the world or fair
More or less, how can I care?
　　'T is the world the same   115
　　For my praise or blame,
And endurance is easy there.
　　Wrong in the one thing rare—
Oh, it is hard to bear!

XVIII.

Here's the spring back or close,   120
When the almond-blossom blows:
　　We shall have the word
　　In a minor third
There is none but the cuckoo knows:
　　Heaps of the guelder-rose!   125
I must bear with it, I suppose.

---

122 _1863_ {line omitted in some copies}   123 _1855P–65S_ In that minor

105 _threats_: 'threat [vb.] is seldom used but in poetry': Johnson.
　　the white: of the eyeball. Cf. Matt. 7: 3, etc.
112 _curd_: the whitish covering of the brain.
123 _in a minor third_: 'The interval in the cuckoo's notes increases as spring progresses.
The time of the minor third is towards the middle of spring': Pettigrew and Collins.
Cf. 'A Toccato of Galuppi's', 19 n.
125 _the guelder-rose_: the flower of the snowball tree.

XIX.

Could but November come,
Were the noisy birds struck dumb
    At the warning slash
    Of his driver's-lash—   130
I would laugh like the valiant Thumb
    Facing the castle glum
And the giant's fee-faw-fum!

XX.

Then, were the world well stripped
Of the gear wherein equipped   135
    We can stand apart,
    Heart dispense with heart
In the sun, with the flowers unnipped,—
    Oh, the world's hangings ripped,
We were both in a bare-walled crypt!   140

XXI.

Each in the crypt would cry
"But one freezes here! and why?
    "When a heart, as chill,
    "At my own would thrill
"Back to life, and its fires out-fly?   145
    "Heart, shall we live or die?
"The rest, . . . settle by-and-by!"

---

147 *1855P–65, 1868* settle it by and by!" *1865S* settle it by-and-by!"

    131 *the valiant Thumb*: in some versions of his story Tom Thumb is a hero. See *The Famous History of Tom Thumb*, in John Ashton, *Chap-Books of the Eighteenth Century* (1882), 213: 'Yet none compar'd to brave Tom Thumb / In acts of Cavalry'. Cf. below, p. 131.

    135 *gear*: things, superfluities.

    138 *unnipped*: by frost or cold.

    140 *crypt*: hiding-place, as in 'The Italian in England', 41.

    148 *efface the score*: cancel my debt.

XXII.

So, she'd efface the score,
And forgive me as before.
   It is twelve o'clock: 150
   I shall hear her knock
In the worst of a storm's uproar,
   I shall pull her through the door,
   I shall have her for evermore!

148 *1855P* So she'll efface   150 *1855P–56* Just at twelve o'clock   152 *1872S,*
1884S uproar:

154 *I shall have her for evermore*: cf. 'Porphyria's Lover' and perhaps 'Mesmerism'.

EVELYN HOPE

THIS is part of the suite of pieces about love which includes 'Love among the Ruins', 'A Lovers' Quarrel', 'A Woman's Last Word', 'By the Fire-Side', 'Any Wife to any Husband', 'In Three Days', and 'In a Year'. It is not known to be associated with any particular young woman.

There are seven stanzas of eight lines each. The rhyme-scheme is *aba bcdcd*. The number of syllables in each line varies from seven to eleven. Each line has four stresses, the dominant foot being the iamb, variegated by the anapaest. The three opening lines, however, open with a stressed syllable, as do a number of other lines.

Date: 1853/5
1863: Dramatic Lyrics

EVELYN HOPE.

I.

BEAUTIFUL Evelyn Hope is dead!
 Sit and watch by her side an hour.
That is her book-shelf, this her bed;
 She plucked that piece of geranium-flower,
Beginning to die too, in the glass;   5
 Little has yet been changed, I think:
The shutters are shut, no light may pass
 Save two long rays thro' the hinge's chink.

II.

Sixteen years old when she died!
 Perhaps she had scarcely heard my name;   10
It was not her time to love; beside,
 Her life had many a hope and aim,

---

1 *1855* dead *Fields* dead.   5 *1855P–63S* glass.   7 *1855P* shut, nor light
11 *1855P* love, beside:

Duties enough and little cares,
   And now was quiet, now astir,
Till God's hand beckoned unawares,—   15
   And the sweet white brow is all of her.

III.

Is it too late then, Evelyn Hope?
   What, your soul was pure and true,
The good stars met in your horoscope,
   Made you of spirit, fire and dew—   20
And, just because I was thrice as old
   And our paths in the world diverged so wide,
Each was nought to each, must I be told?
   We were fellow mortals, nought beside?

IV.

No, indeed! for God above   25
   Is great to grant, as mighty to make,
And creates the love to reward the love:
   I claim you still, for my own love's sake!
Delayed it may be for more lives yet,
   Through worlds I shall traverse, not a few: 30
Much is to learn, much to forget
   Ere the time be come for taking you.

V.

But the time will come,—at last it will,
   When, Evelyn Hope, what meant (I shall say)
In the lower earth, in the years long still,   35
   That body and soul so pure and gay?

---

27 *1855P–63S* love,—   31 *1855P–68* learn and much   34 *1855P–63S*
meant, I . . . . say,

  20 *spirit, fire and dew*: the fourth element, earth, is omitted.

  21 *thrice as old*: Browning became forty in 1852.

  30 *not a few*: Browning was interested in the notion that each of us lives many
times.

Why your hair was amber, I shall divine,
   And your mouth of your own geranium's red—
And what you would do with me, in fine,
   In the new life come in the old one's stead.   40

VI.

I have lived (I shall say) so much since then,
   Given up myself so many times,
Gained me the gains of various men,
   Ransacked the ages, spoiled the climes;
Yet one thing, one, in my soul's full scope,   45
   Either I missed or itself missed me:
And I want and find you, Evelyn Hope!
   What is the issue? let us see!

VII.

I loved you, Evelyn, all the while.
   My heart seemed full as it could hold?   50
There was place and to spare for the frank young smile,
   And the red young mouth, and the hair's young gold.
So, hush,—I will give you this leaf to keep:
   See, I shut it inside the sweet cold hand!
There, that is our secret: go to sleep!   55
   You will wake, and remember, and understand.

---

41 *1855P–63* lived, I . . . . say, so   *49 {reading of DC, BrU, *1889*} *1855P, 1888*
while *1855–63S* while; *1863–84S* while!   50 *1855P–68* hold—*1872S, 1884S* hold;
54 *1855P* hand— *1855–65* hand.   55 *1855P–65* secret! . . . . sleep;

---

   44 *spoiled*: despoiled, plundered.

UP AT A VILLA—DOWN IN THE CITY

(AS DISTIṅGUISHED BY AN ITALIAN PERSON OF QUALITY)

IT is possible that this poem was written in 1853. The suggestion for it probably came from the contrast between life in Florence and life in Bagni di Lucca. On 3 July 1853 Browning told William Allingham that they had been very happy in Florence for eight months, but that they now wished to escape from the heat of 'this great summertime': 'the best will be when we go . . . to a Villa up in the hill-country next week . . . in Giotto's country, the Mugello'.[1] This was their second escape to Bagni di Lucca, which they had first visited for three months in 1849, when they lived 'at the heart of a hundred mountains sung to continually by a rushing mountain stream'.[2] Climate aside, the village among the hills was a complete contrast to Florence, where, from their small balcony in the Piazza Pitti, the Brownings had occasionally the excitement of watching a procession making its way past. On 13 September 1847 EBB had written excitedly to her sisters:

Forty thousand strangers were in Florence—I mean, inhabitants of the different Tuscan states, deputations and companies of various kinds; and for above three hours the infinite procession filed under our windows—with all their various flags and symbols, into the Piazza Pitti . . . The magistracy came first . . . and then the priesthood—and then and then—class after class—troops of peasants and nobles . . . [3]

The Person of Quality differs greatly in intelligence and in his views from EBB, however. To him the news that 'only this morning, three liberal thieves were shot' is simply grist to his mill, as are the rebuke of the Archbishop and 'some little new law of the Duke's'. In this wholly dramatic poem we sense that we are hearing of a city much smaller than Florence.

'Up at a Villa' is not only the work of a keen observer of Italian life, but also a riposte to the ancient tradition of poems praising the serenity of living in the country, the tradition of Horace's Second Epode ('Beatus

---

[1] *Letters to William Allingham*, ed. H. Allingham and E. Baumer Williams (1911), 95–6.
[2] *Letters of EBB*, i. 412.
[3] Huxley, 43.

ille') and Martial's 'Epigram to Himself' (x. 47), described by Røstvig as perhaps 'the most important key poem of English neo-classicism'.[1] Browning's speaker is very different, of course, and his lack of discrimination reminds us that the poem owes a good deal to a different tradition of English poetry, that exemplified above all in certain pieces by Swift, such as 'Mrs Harris's Petition' and 'Mary the Cook-Maid's Letter to Dr Sheridan'. Here is a short passage from another of Swift's poems:

> Next day, to be sure, the Captain will come,
> At the head of his troop, with trumpet and drum:
> Now, madam, observe, how he marches in state:
> The man with the kettle-drum enters the gate;
> *Dub, dub, adub, dub.* The trumpeters follow,
> *Tantara, tantara,* while all the boys holler.
> See, now comes the Captain all daubed in gold lace:
> O' lor'! the sweet gentleman! look in his face;
> And see how he rides like a lord of the land,
> With the fine flaming sword that he holds in his hand.[2]

The strange metrical form of the piece surely expresses the high spirits in which it must have been written. The ten stanzas, of varying length, rhyme as follows: *aaa bbb ccc dddddd eeff gghhh iiiii jjkklll mmmnnooppqqrrsstt uuvvwwwwxx.* It will be noticed that there are no cross-rhymes: all rhymes occur in couplets, triplets, or larger sets, up to six in st. iv. Each line has six main stresses, with a marked caesura in the middle. There is a mixture of trisyllabic and dissyllabic feet which gives the effect of a gossip's chatter. Whether the trisyllabic lines contain dactyls or anapaests depends on the opening syllable, so that these terms are here of little use:

> Houses in four straight lines, | not a single front awry:
> You watch who crosses and gossips, | Who saunters, who hurries by.

Date: 1853/4
1863: *Dramatic Lyrics*

---

[1] *The Happy Man*, by Maren-Sofie Røstvig (Oslo and Oxford, 1954), 82.
[2] 'The Grand Question Debated whether Hamilton's Bawn should be turned into a Barracks or a Malthouse', 87 ff.

UP AT A VILLA—DOWN IN THE CITY.

(AS DISTINGUISHED BY AN ITALIAN PERSON OF QUALITY.)

I.

HAD I but plenty of money, money enough and to spare,
The house for me, no doubt, were a house in the city-square;
Ah, such a life, such a life, as one leads at the window there!

II.

Something to see, by Bacchus, something to hear, at least!
There, the whole day long, one's life is a perfect feast;   5
While up at a villa one lives, I maintain it, no more than a beast.

III.

Well now, look at our villa! stuck like the horn of a bull
Just on a mountain-edge as bare as the creature's skull,
Save a mere shag of a bush with hardly a leaf to pull!
—I scratch my own, sometimes, to see if the hair's turned
wool.   10

IV.

But the city, oh the city—the square with the houses! Why?
They are stone-faced, white as a curd, there's something to
take the eye!
Houses in four straight lines, not a single front awry;
You watch who crosses and gossips, who saunters, who
hurries by;
Green blinds, as a matter of course, to draw when the sun
gets high;   15
And the shops with fanciful signs which are painted properly.

---

2 *1855P–56* city-square.   8 *1855P–68* a mountain's edge as   13 *1855P–65* awry!

4 *by Bacchus*: a common Italian oath.
9 *shag of a bush*: a shaggy bush.
12 *a curd*: the substance formed when acid mixes with milk.

V.

What of a villa? Though winter be over in March by rights,
'T is May perhaps ere the snow shall have withered well off
   the heights:
You've the brown ploughed land before, where the oxen
   steam and wheeze,
And the hills over-smoked behind by the faint grey
   olive-trees.   20

VI.

Is it better in May, I ask you? You've summer all at once;
In a day he leaps complete with a few strong April suns.
'Mid the sharp short emerald wheat, scarce risen three
   fingers well,
The wild tulip, at end of its tube, blows out its great red bell
Like a thin clear bubble of blood, for the children to pick
   and sell.   25

VII.

Is it ever hot in the square? There's a fountain to spout and
   splash!
In the shade it sings and springs; in the shine such foam-bows
   flash
On the horses with curling fish-tails, that prance and paddle
   and pash

---

21 *1855P–65* you've   22 *1855P–65* suns!   *27 {reading of *1855P–84S*, DC,
BrU, *1889*} *1888* foam bows

   20 *over-smoked*: covered by smoke: the only example of the verb in this sense in
OED².
   23 *fingers*: the breadth of a finger is commonly taken as three-quarters of an inch.
   27 *foam-bows*: bows 'similar to a rainbow, formed by sunlight upon foam or spray':
OED². Browning may have found the word in Tennyson's 'Œnone', 60.
   28 *the horses*: sea-horses, as traditionally portrayed, drawing the chariots of Neptune
and Proteus: cf. Virgil, *Georgics*, iv. 389.
      pash: 'the action of striking or beating water as by the feet of a horse', described
by OED² as 'rare', with the comment: 'Browning's use is prob. due to the exigency of
rime': 'Pash', vb. 5. It also occurs in 'Childe Roland', 72.

Round the lady atop in her conch—fifty gazers do not abash,
Though all that she wears is some weeds round her waist in
     a sort of sash.   30

VIII.

All the year long at the villa, nothing to see though you linger,
Except yon cypress that points like death's lean lifted forefinger.
Some think fireflies pretty, when they mix i' the corn and
     mingle,
Or thrid the stinking hemp till the stalks of it seem a-tingle.
Late August or early September, the stunning cicala is shrill,   35
And the bees keep their tiresome whine round the resinous
     firs on the hill.
Enough of the seasons,—I spare you the months of the fever
     and chill.

IX.

Ere you open your eyes in the city, the blessed church-bells
     begin:
No sooner the bells leave off than the diligence rattles in:
You get the pick of the news, and it costs you never a pin.   40
By-and-by there's the travelling doctor gives pills, lets blood,
     draws teeth;
Or the Pulcinello-trumpet breaks up the market beneath.
At the post-office such a scene-picture—the new play,
     piping hot!

---

29 *1855P–68* in the conch—   30 *1855P–65* sash!   31 *1855P–68* villa, nothing's
to   33 *1855P–68* mix in the   35 *1855P* cicala blows shrill,   38 *1855P–*
68 Ere opening your   42 *1855P* the Pulcinello's trumpet breaks beneath!
43 *1855P* a huge picture—the

---

29 *conch*: a large shell, traditionally associated with Venus.
32 *cypress*: a tree associated with death and graveyards.
34 *thrid*: thread their way through.
35 *the stunning cicala*: whereas a single cicala emits a small sound, the noise of a swarm
can be 'stunning'. Unlike the speaker here, EBB was delighted when she heard 'the
cicale sing all day': Ogilvy, 101.
39 *diligence*: a public stage-coach.
42 *Pulcinello-trumpet*: the trumpet proclaiming a sort of Punch-and-Judy show.
43 *a scene-picture*: apparently a poster advertising the play: not in OED².

And a notice how, only this morning, three liberal thieves
    were shot.
Above it, behold the Archbishop's most fatherly of rebukes,   45
And beneath, with his crown and his lion, some little new
    law of the Duke's!
Or a sonnet with flowery marge, to the Reverend Don
    So-and-so
Who is Dante, Boccaccio, Petrarca, Saint Jerome and
    Cicero,
"And moreover," (the sonnet goes rhyming,) "the skirts of
    Saint Paul has reached,
"Having preached us those six Lent-lectures more unctuous
    than ever he preached."   50
Noon strikes,—here sweeps the procession! our Lady borne
    smiling and smart
With a pink gauze gown all spangles, and seven swords stuck
    in her heart!
Bang-whang-whang goes the drum, *tootle-te-tootle* the fife;
No keeping one's haunches still: it's the greatest pleasure in
    life.

---

44 *1855P* shot!   50 *1855P* us six Lenten lectures more   54 *1855P* life!

46 *the Duke's*: a reference to Leopold II, grand-duke of Tuscany (1797–1870).
During his first twenty years he granted his people a constitution, and a National Guard,
despite the mandates of Austria; but by the early 1850s he had abandoned his liberal
stance. Cf. the use of 'liberal' above.

47 *Don*: a title of respect, normal for priests at the time.

48 *Who is Dante*: i.e. he is absurdly praised as the equal of great writers and godly
men of the most various kinds. St Jerome is mentioned as a great writer because he
produced the Latin translation of the Bible, completed *c*.404. He was by far the most
learned of the Fathers.

50 *Lent-lectures*: Lent is the period from Ash Wednesday to Easter-eve, commemora-
ting the fasting of Christ in the wilderness.

    unctuous: Johnson's last definition of 'unction' is 'Any thing that excites piety and
devotion', though he does not give a corresponding meaning for the adjective.

51 *our Lady*: the Virgin Mary.

52 *seven swords*: for the Seven Sorrows of Mary: Simeon's Prophecy, the Flight into
Egypt, Christ Missed, the Betrayal, the Crucifixion, the Deposition from the Cross, and
the Entombment.

X.

But bless you, it's dear—it's dear! fowls, wine, at double the rate.   55
They have clapped a new tax upon salt, and what oil pays
    passing the gate
It's a horror to think of. And so, the villa for me, not the city!
Beggars can scarcely be choosers: but still—ah, the pity, the
    pity!
Look, two and two go the priests, then the monks with
    cowls and sandals,
And the penitents dressed in white shirts, a-holding the
    yellow candles;   60
One, he carries a flag up straight, and another a cross with
    handles,
And the Duke's guard brings up the rear, for the better
    prevention of scandals:
Bang-whang-whang goes the drum, *tootle-te-tootle* the fife.
Oh, a day in the city-square, there is no such pleasure in life!

55   *1855P* rate!   56 *1855P* new impost on salt,   57 *1855P* of! and
60 *1855P–56* candles.   *61 {reading of *1855P–84S*, DC, BrU} *1888* handles.
1889 handles   62 *1855P–56* scandals.   63 *1855P* fife,—

56 *salt . . . oil*: both were highly taxed when they were brought into the towns.
58 *Beggars can scarcely be choosers*: proverbial (ODEP 42a).
60 *yellow candles*: in sign of mourning and contrition.
62 *scandals*: i.e. interruptions of any kind.

A WOMAN'S LAST WORD

THE title of this poem perhaps echoes ironically the saying that a woman will always have the last word.

The first and third lines of each stanza have six syllables, the second and fourth, three. The longer lines are trochaic trimeters, while each of the short lines is a cretic. The rhyme scheme of each stanza is *abab*, the rhymes of the longer lines being double: in sts. i, ii, iv, vi, vii, and x, however, the second syllable of the 'rhyme' in the third line is simply a repetition of the last syllable in the first: *more, Love, / before, Love, / words are? / birds are*, etc. This makes the first syllable of such rhymes particularly emphatic. 'Love' is the last word of the first and third lines in the first and last stanzas, as of st. vii.

Date: 1853/5
1863: *Dramatic Lyrics*

A WOMAN'S LAST WORD.

I.

LET'S contend no more, Love,
   Strive nor weep:
All be as before, Love,
   —Only sleep!

II.

What so wild as words are?   5
   I and thou
In debate, as birds are,
   Hawk on bough!

8 *Hawk on bough*: while a hawk (danger) is close to us.

III.

See the creature stalking
    While we speak!   10
Hush and hide the talking,
    Cheek on cheek!

IV.

What so false as truth is,
    False to thee?
Where the serpent's tooth is   15
    Shun the tree—

V.

Where the apple reddens
    Never pry—
Lest we lose our Edens,
    Eve and I.   20

VI.

Be a god and hold me
    With a charm!
Be a man and fold me
    With thine arm!

VII.

Teach me, only teach, Love!   25
    As I ought
I will speak thy speech, Love,
    Think thy thought—

---

10 *1855P–56* speak—   12 *1884S* cheek.   20 *1855P–63* I!   22 *1855P–56* charm—   *24 {reading of *1855P–84S*, DC, BrU, *1889*} *1888* arm

15 *the serpent's tooth*: cf. Ps. 140:3: 'They have sharpened their tongues like a serpent', echoed in *King Lear*, I. iv. 288.

16 *the tree*: Gen. 3.

VIII.

Meet, if thou require it,
    Both demands,   30
Laying flesh and spirit
    In thy hands.

IX.

That shall be to-morrow
    Not to-night:
I must bury sorrow   35
    Out of sight:

X.

—Must a little weep, Love,
    (Foolish me!)
And so fall asleep, Love,
    Loved by thee.   40

32 *1855P–56* hands!   36 *1855P–56* sight.   38 *1855P–56* —Foolish me!
40 *1855P* thee!

FRA LIPPO LIPPI

WHETHER or not his father owned an edition of Vasari's famous book, *Le Vite de' più eccellenti Pittori, Scultori, et Architettori*,[1] Browning is likely to have heard of Fra Filippo Lippi (*c.*1406–69) in his boyhood, from the account (for example) in vol. xxiv of the *Biographie universelle*.[2] As we have noticed earlier,[3] on 24 March 1846 Elizabeth Barrett was struck by his easy familiarity with Vasari, and reminded him that the *Vite* 'is not the handbook of the whole world'.[4] When they married and went to Italy circumstances immediately reminded them of the great historian of painting, since for the first six months they lived in Pisa, occupying rooms 'close to the Duomo & Leaning Tower, in the great Collegio built by Vasari!'[5] The injunction 'see Vasari', in 'Old Pictures in Florence', was one which Browning himself was to follow throughout his years in Italy.

The *Vite* was first published in 1550, to be succeeded by a much revised edition in 1568. While *1568* has been the basis of most later editions, as it was of the translation by Mrs Jonathan Foster in *1850–2*, Browning knew *1550* too;[6] he also knew the most recent edition of the Italian text, that published in Florence from 1846, which he owned and which he refers to when defending his mistaken belief that Masaccio was a pupil of Lippi's.[7] In the same letter he insists that he had 'looked into the matter' of the priority between these two painters 'long ago, and long before I thought of my own poem, from my interest in the Brancacci frescos, indeed in all early Florentine art'. He probably began to study the Capella Brancacci soon after their arrival in Florence in 1847. The present poem was no doubt one of those 'with more music and painting than before' which he

---

[1] The familiar title, that of the second edition.

[2] xxiv (1819), 545–9.   [3] See Vol. III, p. 4.   [4] Kintner, i. 553.

[5] Raymond and Sullivan, iii. 194.

[6] *1550* has *Architetti* (so spelt) first in the title. Landor's copy, presumably a gift to Browning, was inscribed by him to his son in 1863 (Kelley and Coley, A 2378). The 2nd ed., with '*Pittori*' mentioned first in the title, was published in Florence in 1568 (3 parts in 2 vols.) Browning also owned (Kelley and Coley, A 2379) the 13–vol. ed., Florence 1846–57 ed. V. Marchese, G. Pini, and C. and G. Milanesi. We quote from the translation of the 2nd ed., by Mrs Jonathan Foster (5 vols., 1850–2), which contains in footnotes important passages from the 1st ed. For an excellent account of the *Lives* one may turn to T. S. R. Boase, *Giorgio Vasari: The Man and the Book* (Princeton, N. J., 1979).

[7] *Letters*, 104. See Kelley and Coley, A 2379.

told Milsand that he was writing, early in 1853.[1] On 13 April EBB described him as 'fond of digging at Vasari . . . making him a betwixt and between to other writers'.[2]

Invaluable as Vasari is, his *Lives* are not wholly reliable in biographical detail. As T. S. R. Boase pointed out, each of them is 'a short tale, illustrating some facet of human nature', following 'the method of the Italian *novella*, of which Boccaccio was the great exemplar'.[3] Vasari's 'account of the friar escaping from a window by making a rope of his bedclothes corresponds verbally with a passage from Bandello's *novella* LVIII'. Whether or not this points to a common source for Vasari and Bandello, we notice that Browning carries forward the process of fashioning a tale by omitting and changing Vasari's narrative in accordance with his own purposes. He omits, for example, one episode given prominence in Landor's *Imaginary Conversation* between 'Fra Filippo Lippi and Pope Eugenius the Fourth', a dialogue which may even have prompted the writing of his poem:[4] that in which Lippi is said to have been captured by pirates and to have remained their prisoner in 'Barbary' for eighteen months, until he was released as a tribute to his skill in painting. He follows Mrs Foster, who omits the words 'furore amoroso, anzi bestiale',[5] in softening his description of Lippi's amorous nature. He cuts the episode in which Lippi tricked the nuns to whose care Lucrezia Buti had been entrusted and 'bore her from their keeping', as a result of which they 'were deeply disgraced, and the father of Lucrezia was so grievously afflicted . . . that he never more recovered his cheerfulness'.[6]

Browning assigns Lippi a different position in the history of Italian painting from that given him by Vasari. Believing as he did that Masaccio

[1] See above, p. xiv. Cf. note to l. 156, below.

[2] *Robert Browning: A Portrait*, by Betty Miller (1952), 175.

[3] Boase, 51. Bandello's *novelle* were not published until 1554, but they may well have circulated in manuscript. Apart from a common source, the correspondences between him and Vasari may, as Boase acknowledges, be due to his taking the story from the *Vite*. Borghini recommended the *novelle* of Franco Sacchetti to Vasari for his second edition, 'because of the stories about artists that they contained' (ibid.)

[4] See Landor, *Works* (2 vols., 1846), ii. 282. Landor makes Lippi tell the Pope how he and a friend (a *canonico*) went on the river one evening, to sing to a guitar certain 'gay Florentine songs, some of which were of such a turn and tendency' that they might 'sound better on water, and rather far from shore'. They took with them two boys and 'the good canonico's pretty niece', dressed as a boy.

[5] For the Italian we have used the two-text edition of Rosanna Bettarini and Paola Barocchi (Florence, 1966–). The quotation (from the later text) is from vol. III (*Testo*), p. 616.

[6] *Lives*, ii. 79–80.

was Lippi's pupil, not his master, Browning gives Lippi the role which
Vasari assigns to Masaccio.[1] Vasari tells us that Masaccio 'first attained the
clear perception that painting is no other than the clear imitation . . . of all
the forms presented by nature'.[2] In his portrayal of the consecration of the
church of the Carmine he 'painted the portraits of a great number of
the citizens who make part of the procession, clothed in hoods and
mantles',[3] in such a manner that they were readily identifiable. The
contrast between such a painter and artists 'to whom the cultivation of art
was a sacred vocation'—what she terms 'the great schism in modern
art'—is emphatically stated by the Brownings' friend Anna Jameson at the
beginning of her section on Fra Lippo Lippi in her *Memoirs of Early Italian
Painters*. On the one side, she writes:

We now find . . . a race of painters . . . profoundly versed in the knowledge of the
human form, and intent on studying and imitating the various effects of nature in
colour and in light and shade, without any other aspiration than the representation
of beauty for its own sake. . . . On the other hand, we find a race of painters to
whom . . . the representation of beauty [was] a means, not an end; by whom
Nature in her various aspects was studied and deeply studied, but only for the
purpose of embodying whatever we can conceive or reverence as highest, holiest,
purest in heaven and earth.[4]

Here we have the contrast between Lippi's own view, at ll. 283 ff., and
that of 'The Prior and the learned' at ll. 175–98 and 233–7.

Browning did not sympathize with the censorious attitude to Lippi
which was gaining ground in his time. In 1836 a conservative Roman
Catholic critic, A. F. Rio, published *De la poésie chrétienne*, in which he
wrote that Lippi's soul was 'devoid of refinement and dignity', as might be
seen by 'the round and curly heads of his angels, and their fanciful
costume' in 'The Coronation of the Virgin'; he added that 'no ray of
beatitude illumines their countenances . . . they always suggest the idea
that they are placed there to perform some *espiègleries*'.[5] The following

---

[1] See below, l. 273 n. Modern historians of art agree about the importance of
Masaccio, who died young, yet 'brought about a complete revolution in painting':
E. H. Gombrich, *The Story of Art* (1956), 165.
[2] *Lives*, i. 401.
[3] Ibid. 408.
[4] *Memoirs*, i. 114; 110–11.
[5] English translation, *The Poetry of Christian Art* (1854), 90. Browning knew Rio's
work: cf. l. 228 n., below. In Vol. IV, p. 355 we failed to recognize the satirical reference
to Rio in *Christmas-Eve*, ll. 671–2: 'To frame those portents which impart / Such
unction to true Christian Art'.—On Rio's influence, see DeLaura, 'Browning's Painter
Poems'.

year Franz Kugler similarly deplored the fact that in this painting 'the sacred event is entirely transposed to this world'.[1] In the same tone the Brownings' friend Anna Jameson observed that 'he was the first who desecrated [religious] subjects by introducing the portraits of women who happened to be the objects of his preference at the moment'.[2] Browning is so far from sharing such severe views that he brings his poem to its triumphant conclusion by making Lippi play with the notion that one of the same young girls, 'a sweet angelic slip of a thing', will address the Almighty on his behalf, so that he may escape censure. We note that, to give his poem this climax, he changes the time at which the painting is executed: whereas Vasari tells us that this was the first of Lippi's works to bring him to the attention of Cosimo de' Medici, Browning's painter boasts of his connection with Cosimo when he is caught by the guards at the beginning of the poem, promising to paint the picture at the end of it, as a work of atonement.[3]

On a famous occasion already mentioned, on 27 September 1855, Tennyson dined with the Brownings and read *Maud* to them, emotionally, and with numerous comments to draw attention to its merits. 'Yes, and it *was* wonderful', EBB wrote, ' . . . and he read exquisitely in a voice like an organ, rather music than speech'.[4] W. M. Rossetti contrasts the manner of reading of the two poets. He tells us that Tennyson's

grand deep voice sways onward with a long-drawn chaunt, which some hearers might deem monotonous, but which gives noble value and emphasis to the metrical structure and pauses. Browning's voice, which was at once rich and peculiar, took much less account of the poem as a rhythmical whole; his delivery had more affinity to that of an actor, laying stress on all the light and shade of the composition—its touches of character, its conversational points, its dramatic give-and-take. In those qualities of elocution in which Tennyson was strong, and aimed to be strong, Browning was contentedly weak; and *vice versa*.[5]

Browning's choice was of course 'Fra Lippo Lippi', described by George Eliot as 'a poem at once original and perfect in its kind'.[6] We cannot be

---

[1] *Handbook of Painting . . . in Italy, Translated by a Lady*, ed. Sir Charles Eastlake, 2nd ed., 2 vols. (1851), i. 198.

[2] *Memoirs*, i. 114.

[3] This seems generally to have escaped notice. An obvious alternative explanation, that Browning confused the chronology, is implausible. It is conceivable, but also unlikely, that he simply makes Lippi pluck a name from the air, to impress the guards, although he does not yet know Cosimo.

[4] *Letters of EBB*, ii. 213.

[5] Quoted in R. B. Martin, *Tennyson: The Unquiet Heart* (1980), 394.

[6] *Westminster Review*, 65 (January 1856), 291.

certain when it was written, but if it was during the Brownings' stay in
Rome between the last week of November 1853 and the end of the
following May, as Sharp states,[1] then it is later than 'Andrea del Sarto' and
must surely have presented itself to the poet as a companion poem of the
sort that he liked to write. The two were printed one after the other in
1863 and subsequently, 'Fra Lippo Lippi' first and 'Andrea' after, perhaps
because Lippi was born in the first decade of the century and del Sarto
some eight years later.

Date: 1853/4
1863: *Men and Women*

FRA LIPPO LIPPI.

I AM poor brother Lippo, by your leave!
You need not clap your torches to my face.
Zooks, what's to blame? you think you see a monk!
What, 't is past midnight, and you go the rounds,
And here you catch me at an alley's end   5
Where sportive ladies leave their doors ajar?
The Carmine's my cloister: hunt it up,
Do,—harry out, if you must show your zeal,
Whatever rat, there, haps on his wrong hole,
And nip each softling of a wee white mouse,   10
Weke, weke, that's crept to keep him company!

4 *1855P–65* What, it's past   *1855P* rounds?   6 *1855P* ajar!   *1855, 1856* ajar.

Title: 'Fra'=*Frater*, Brother. Mrs Foster comments that while 'it was customary, on
entering the convent, to change the baptismal name for some other', this custom seems
not to have been observed with Lippi (Vasari, ii. 74 n.).

3 *Zooks*: an archaic oath, abbreviated from 'God's hooks', referring to 'the nails or
"hooks" used in the crucifixion of Jesus': *Centenary Selection*, 179.

7 *The Carmine*: the Carmelite church or monastery. Cf. 81 n. Vasari tells us that when
Lippi was placed there as a boy the chapel 'had then been newly painted by Masaccio,
and this being exceedingly beautiful, pleased Fra Filippo greatly, wherefore he fre-
quented it daily'. In class, 'in place of studying, he never did any thing but daub his own
books, and those of the other boys, with caricatures, whereupon the prior determined
to give him all means . . . for learning to draw': ii. 74.

10 *softling*: cf. Keats, *Endymion*, iv. 316.

[1] p. 166. Cf. below, l. 156 n.

Aha, you know your betters! Then, you'll take
Your hand away that's fiddling on my throat,
And please to know me likewise. Who am I?
Why, one, sir, who is lodging with a friend   15
Three streets off—he's a certain . . . how d' ye call?
Master—a . . . Cosimo of the Medici,
I' the house that caps the corner. Boh! you were best!
Remember and tell me, the day you're hanged,
How you affected such a gullet's-gripe!   20
But you, sir, it concerns you that your knaves
Pick up a manner nor discredit you:
Zooks, are we pilchards, that they sweep the streets
And count fair prize what comes into their net?
He's Judas to a tittle, that man is!   25
Just such a face! Why, sir, you make amends.
Lord, I'm not angry! Bid your hangdogs go
Drink out this quarter-florin to the health
Of the munificent House that harbours me
(And many more beside, lads! more beside!)   30
And all's come square again. I'd like his face—

12 *1855P–84S* betters?   18 *1855P–68* In the   22 *1855P* you!   *1855–65* you.
26 *1855P–56, 1863, 1865* why,   27 *1855P* angry! Have your

17 *Cosimo of the Medici*: Cosimo the Elder (1389–1464), the great Florentine mer-
chant, politician, and patron of the arts. According to Vasari his attention was drawn to
Lippi by the painting described at the end of this poem, and he 'was thereby rendered
his most assured friend': ii. 76.
18 *the house*: the Medici-Riccardi Palace, built c.1446–57, for Cosimo. Cf. 'The
Statue and the Bust'. Here and elsewhere we have consulted *The Art of Florence*, by
Glenn Andrès, John M. Hunisak, and A. Richard Turner, (2 vols., Abbeville Press, New
York, 1988).
20 *affected*: became fond of. Cf. 'an Epistle', 228.
   gullet's-gripe: probably Browning's compound: 'gripe', squeeze.
21 *knaves*: servants, but with a strong suggestion of the modern meaning.
22 *a manner*: decent manners.
25 *Judas to a tittle*: the very image of Judas Iscariot.
27 *hangdogs*: degraded fellows.
28 *quarter-florin*: the coin called in English the 'florin' was first issued in Florence in
1252, in gold. Later the word was used for an English gold coin, and later for other
coins. OED² comments that 'the "flower" from which the Florentine coin took its
name' may have alluded to the name of the city.
31 *come square*: settled.

His, elbowing on his comrade in the door
With the pike and lantern,—for the slave that holds
John Baptist's head a-dangle by the hair
With one hand ("Look you, now," as who should say)   35
And his weapon in the other, yet unwiped!
It's not your chance to have a bit of chalk,
A wood-coal or the like? or you should see!
Yes, I'm the painter, since you style me so.
What, brother Lippo's doings, up and down,   40
You know them and they take you? like enough!
I saw the proper twinkle in your eye—
'Tell you, I liked your looks at very first.
Let's sit and set things straight now, hip to haunch.
Here's spring come, and the nights one makes up bands   45
To roam the town and sing out carnival,
And I've been three weeks shut within my mew,
A-painting for the great man, saints and saints
And saints again. I could not paint all night—
Ouf! I leaned out of window for fresh air.   50
There came a hurry of feet and little feet,
A sweep of lute-strings, laughs, and whiffs of song,—
Flower o' the broom,

35 *1855P* hand, "look   *1855–65* ("look   *1855P* say,   38 *1855P* like! and you
40 *1855P* What, works about the city, up   46 *1855P* sing at carnival,
50 *1855P* air;

33 *the slave*: Lippi painted the Feast of Herod for the Duomo at Prato, but in that
only the forearm and hand of the slave are to be seen, at the far left: Pittaluga, pls. 122–3.
Since Lippi refers more than once to cruel expressions, it is interesting to note that
Vasari comments on the 'brutal rage' of the men who stoned St Stephen to death, a
scene portrayed on the other side of the same chapel; one of them in particular is a
terrifying study in cruelty of expression.

34 *a-dangle*: cf. *The Ring and the Book*, i. 1313, and viii. 781. OED² cites no other author.

41 *they take you?*: they appeal to you?

46 *sing out carnival*: It. *far carnevale*, to make merry. The duration of the period of
carnival before Lent has varied at different times and in different places. Cf. Byron,
Beppo, sts. vi ff.

47 *three weeks*: two days in Vasari (ii. 77).
    mew: cage, prison.

52 *whiffs*: snatches of song. OED² has no other example of this meaning.

53 *Flower o' the broom*: here and at ll. 68–9, 110–11, 238–9 and 248–9 Browning is
imitating the *stornello* (also called *ritornello* or *fiore*), a snatch of song of two or three

Take away love, and our earth is a tomb!
Flower o' the quince,   55
I let Lisa go, and what good in life since?
Flower o' the thyme—and so on. Round they went.
Scarce had they turned the corner when a titter
Like the skipping of rabbits by moonlight,—three slim shapes,
And a face that looked up . . . zooks, sir, flesh and blood,   60
That's all I'm made of! Into shreds it went,
Curtain and counterpane and coverlet,
All the bed-furniture—a dozen knots,
There was a ladder! Down I let myself,
Hands and feet, scrambling somehow, and so dropped,   65
And after them. I came up with the fun
Hard by Saint Laurence, hail fellow, well met,—
Flower o' the rose,
If I've been merry, what matter who knows?
And so as I was stealing back again   70
To get to bed and have a bit of sleep
Ere I rise up to-morrow and go work
On Jerome knocking at his poor old breast

---

56 *1855P–65* what good's in   *60 {reading of *1855P–70, 1875*} *1872S, 1884S, 1888,*
1889 up . .   64 *1855P–65* down

verses, usually starting with the name of a flower. In Italian the first line has commonly
five syllables, while the second (and third, if there are three lines) has eleven. Browning
has four syllables in his first line, from ten to twelve in his second. Porter and Clarke
give translations of the Tuscan versions of two of the songs he uses: 'Flower of the pine!
/ Call me not ever happy heart again, / But call me heavy heart, O comrades mine' and
'Flower of the broom! / Unwed thy mother keeps thee not to lose / That flower from
the window of the room.'

   61 *into shreds it went*: Vasari (ii. 77) tells of an occasion when Cosimo de' Medici had
confined Lippi 'that he might not waste his time in running about'. After two days,
however, Lippi made his escape in this manner, 'and for several days gave himself up to
his amusements'. Cosimo never again had him shut up. For a marked similarity between
this passage in Vasari and Bandello's *Novella LVIII*, see Introduction, above.
   67 *Saint Laurence*: the church of S. Lorenzo, first built in the fourth century, rebuilt
in the eleventh, and transformed, on the orders of the Medici, by Brunelleschi, from
*c.*1421. It became the Medici family church and burial place. Lippi painted an Annun-
ciation for it: Vasari, ii. 78.
   hail fellow, well met: a traditional phrase. Tilley, H 15.
   73 *Jerome*: St Jerome (*c.*342–420) was a passionate advocate of the monastic life. Vasari
tells us that there was 'a figure of St. Jerome doing penance . . . in the *guardaroba* of

With his great round stone to subdue the flesh,
You snap me of the sudden. Ah, I see!   75
Though your eye twinkles still, you shake your head—
Mine's shaved—a monk, you say—the sting's in that!
If Master Cosimo announced himself,
Mum's the word naturally; but a monk!
Come, what am I a beast for? tell us, now!   80
I was a baby when my mother died
And father died and left me in the street.
I starved there, God knows how, a year or two
On fig-skins, melon-parings, rinds and shucks,
Refuse and rubbish. One fine frosty day,   85
My stomach being empty as your hat,
The wind doubled me up and down I went.
Old Aunt Lapaccia trussed me with one hand,
(Its fellow was a stinger as I knew)
And so along the wall, over the bridge,   90
By the straight cut to the convent. Six words there,
While I stood munching my first bread that month:
"So, boy, you're minded," quoth the good fat father
Wiping his own mouth, 't was refection-time,—
"To quit this very miserable world?   95
"Will you renounce" . . . "the mouthful of bread?" thought I;
By no means! Brief, they made a monk of me;

80 *1855P* Tell   89 *1855P* Its . . . . knew,   96 *1855P* . . . the   *1855, 1856,*
1863, 1865 . . . The   *1863S* . . The   *1855P–65* bread? thought

Duke Cosimo' by Lippi. He is often portrayed striking his breast with a stone. It is
possible that Browning is referring to a St Jerome in his own possession (of uncertain
attribution): see DeLaura, 'Some Notes', 7–8.

80 *What am I a beast for?*: Vasari writes frankly of the 'furore amoroso, anzi bestiale'
(amorous and indeed animal frenzy) which led Lippi to escape from Cosimo's palace.
See p. 32 above.

81 *I was a baby*: as Vasari tells us, 'By the death of his father he was left a friendless
orphan at the age of two years, his mother having also died shortly after his birth. The
child was for some time under the care of a certain Mona [Madonna] Lapaccia, his
aunt, . . . who brought him up with very great difficulty till he had attained his eighth
year, when . . . she placed him in the . . . convent of the Carmelites': ii. 74.

84 *shucks*: husks, shells.

86 *as empty as your hat*: a proverbial phrase.

97 *Brief*: in brief.

I did renounce the world, its pride and greed,
Palace, farm, villa, shop and banking-house,
Trash, such as these poor devils of Medici   100
Have given their hearts to—all at eight years old.
Well, sir, I found in time, you may be sure,
'T was not for nothing—the good bellyful,
The warm serge and the rope that goes all round,
And day-long blessed idleness beside!   105
"Let's see what the urchin's fit for"—that came next.
Not overmuch their way, I must confess.
Such a to-do! They tried me with their books:
Lord, they'd have taught me Latin in pure waste!
Flower o' the clove,   110
All the Latin I construe is, "amo" I love!
But, mind you, when a boy starves in the streets
Eight years together, as my fortune was,
Watching folk's faces to know who will fling
The bit of half-stripped grape-bunch he desires,   115
And who will curse or kick him for his pains,—
Which gentleman processional and fine,
Holding a candle to the Sacrament,
Will wink and let him lift a plate and catch
The droppings of the wax to sell again,   120
Or holla for the Eight and have him whipped,—
How say I?—nay, which dog bites, which lets drop
His bone from the heap of offal in the street,—
Why, soul and sense of him grow sharp alike,

100–1 *1855P* such poor devils as these Medici | Give their . . . . to—and all
106 *1863S* next: 107 *1855P* over much   108 *1855P–65* they . . . . books.
109 *1855P* Lord, Latin they'd . . . . me in . . . . waste.   111 *1872S, 1884S* "Amo"
115 *1855P* grape-bunch that he eyes,   117 *1855P* What gentleman processioning
and   121 *1855P* whipped;—   123 *1855, 1856* street!   124 *1855P–*
56 —The soul

---

117 *processional*: OED[2] knows no earlier example of the word in this sense. With the
proof reading cf. Carlyle, *French Revolution*, II. iii. 7: 'Jean Jacques too . . . processioned.'
118 *the Sacrament*: 'the eucharist; the holy communion': Johnson.
120 *the droppings of the wax*: cf. l. 148 n.
121 *the Eight*: the magistrates of Florence, 'the Council of Eight'.

He learns the look of things, and none the less   125
For admonition from the hunger-pinch.
I had a store of such remarks, be sure,
Which, after I found leisure, turned to use:
I drew men's faces on my copy-books,
Scrawled them within the antiphonary's marge,   130
Joined legs and arms to the long music-notes,
Found eyes and nose and chin for A's and B's,
And made a string of pictures of the world
Betwixt the ins and outs of verb and noun,
On the wall, the bench, the door. The monks looked black.   135
"Nay," quoth the Prior, "turn him out, d' ye say?
"In no wise. Lose a crow and catch a lark.
"What if at last we get our man of parts,
"We Carmelites, like those Camaldolese
"And Preaching Friars, to do our church up fine   140
"And put the front on it that ought to be!"
And hereupon he bade me daub away.

---

125 *1863S* things, minds none   126 *1855P–63* For admonitions from   128 *1855P*
Which, now that I   *{reading of *1855P–84S*} *1888, 1889* use.   130 *1855P* them
on the   131 *1863S* the square music-notes,   132 *1855P–65* Found nose and
eyes and   135 *1855P* monks were mazed.   140 *1855P* Friars, shall do
141 *1855P* be!   142 *1855P–65* hereupon they bade   *1855P* away,

---

127 *remarks*: observations.

130 *antiphonary's marge*: an antiphonary or antiphone is a collection of chants for the
Office Hours.

131 *music-notes*: the reading of *1863S* is interesting: the single notes would be square,
in chant notation, but the ligatures would be longer. Since chant notation is black, not
hollow, the 'A's and B's' of l. 132 are not musical notes, but letters of the alphabet.

137 *Lose a crow and catch a lark*: proverbial.

139 *those Camaldolese*: originally the Camaldolese or Camaldulians were a religious
order leading the life of hermits, but later many of its members were closer to the
Benedictine manner of living. There were also Camaldolese nuns: for one of their
houses Andrea del Sarto painted a remarkable picture of 'the Dead Christ mourned over
by Our Lady': Vasari, iii. 213–14. Cf. l. 236 n.

140 *Preaching Friars*: the Dominicans, who had among their number Fra Angelico:
see l. 235 n. (Although friars are not in the strict sense monks, it is usual to use the words
monk and monasticism in a wide sense). The great church of the Dominicans, founded
in 1246 and built in stages during the next century, is S. Maria Novella, which contains
Masaccio's 'The Holy Trinity'.

141 *And put the front on it*: begun in 1268, the Carmine church was later enlarged and
altered.

Thank you! my head being crammed, the walls a blank,
Never was such prompt disemburdening.
First, every sort of monk, the black and white,   145
I drew them, fat and lean: then, folk at church,
From good old gossips waiting to confess
Their cribs of barrel-droppings, candle-ends,—
To the breathless fellow at the altar-foot,
Fresh from his murder, safe and sitting there   150
With the little children round him in a row
Of admiration, half for his beard and half
For that white anger of his victim's son
Shaking a fist at him with one fierce arm,
Signing himself with the other because of Christ   155
(Whose sad face on the cross sees only this
After the passion of a thousand years)
Till some poor girl, her apron o'er her head,
(Which the intense eyes looked through) came at eve
On tiptoe, said a word, dropped in a loaf,   160
Her pair of earrings and a bunch of flowers
(The brute took growling), prayed, and so was gone.

143 *1855P* head was crammed, their walls   *1855–65* crammed, their walls
144 *1855P* disemburdening!   146 *1855P* them, good and bad: *1855P–84S*
then, folks at   151 *1855P* a ring   156 *1855P* only that   159 *1855P–65*
Which . . . . through, came   160 *1855P* word, threw in   162 *1855P* The
. . . . growling, prayed   *1855–65* The . . . . growling, prayed,   *1855P–63* and then was

144 *disemburdening*: no other example in OED[2].

145 *the black and white*: the Dominicans are known as the Black Friars, the Carmelites
as the White Friars.

148 *cribs*: petty thefts.
        barrel-droppings: cf. Donne, 'Satire II', 82–3 (pointed out to us by Michael
Meredith).

150 *safe*: by the law of the medieval Church a fugitive from justice could take refuge
in a church.

156 *Whose sad face*: DeLaura, 'Some Notes', p. 10, suggests that the line may have
been prompted by a passage in *The Stones of Venice*, vol. iii. (published in late July 1853).
After describing the splendid façade of St Mark's, Ruskin writes of the commonplace
people who do not pause to glance at it, whose lives are unaffected by its beauty:
'unregarded children', even, ' . . . their throats hoarse with cursing,—gamble, and fight,
and snarl, . . . clashing their bruised centesimi upon the . . . church porch. And the
images of Christ and His angels look down upon it continually': *Works*, x (1904), 84–5.

157 *passion*: suffering, in prolongation of the Passion on the Cross.
162 *The brute*: i.e. the priest taking Confession.

I painted all, then cried " 'T is ask and have;
"Choose, for more's ready!"—laid the ladder flat,
And showed my covered bit of cloister-wall.   165
The monks closed in a circle and praised loud
Till checked, taught what to see and not to see,
Being simple bodies,—"That's the very man!
"Look at the boy who stoops to pat the dog!
"That woman's like the Prior's niece who comes   170
"To care about his asthma: it's the life!"
But there my triumph's straw-fire flared and funked;
Their betters took their turn to see and say:
The Prior and the learned pulled a face
And stopped all that in no time. "How? what's here?   175
"Quite from the mark of painting, bless us all!
"Faces, arms, legs and bodies like the true
"As much as pea and pea! it's devil's-game!
"Your business is not to catch men with show,
"With homage to the perishable clay,   180
"But lift them over it, ignore it all,
"Make them forget there's such a thing as flesh.
"Your business is to paint the souls of men—
"Man's soul, and it's a fire, smoke . . . no, it's not . . .
"It's vapour done up like a new-born babe—   185
"(In that shape when you die it leaves your mouth)

---

163 *1855P* I got all ready, cried   *1855P–63S, 1865* " 'tis *1863* 't is   164 *1855P*
for my head's full!"—laid   *165 {reading of *1855P–84S*, DC, BrU, *1889}* *1888*
cloister-wall   167 *1855, 1856* (taught   168 *1855P* bodies: "that's   *1855, 1856*
bodies) "that's   *1863S–65* "that's   172 *1855P* funked,   173 *1855P* betters
had to see . . . . say instead: 175 *1884S* "How!   179 *1855P* to maze men
180 *1855P* Mere homage   184 *1855P* a vapour . . no   186 *1855P* In . . . .
when they die . . . . leaves their mouth,

---

170 *the Prior's niece*: cf. ll. 196, 209, 387. As 'nephews' in 'The Bishop orders his
Tomb' are illegitimate sons, so the 'niece' is the Prior's mistress. Cf. 'the good
canonico's pretty niece' in Landor's *Imaginary Conversation* between Fra Lippo Lippi and
Pope Eugenius the Fourth.

172 *funked*: smoked, with an unpleasant smell. 'A low word': Johnson.

176 *the mark*: the true goal.

178 *pea and pea*: cf. the common phrase 'as like as two peas': Tilley, p. 136.

185 *a new-born babe*: cf. *Macbeth* I. vii. 21.

"It's . . . well, what matters talking, it's the soul!
"Give us no more of body than shows soul!
"Here's Giotto, with his Saint a-praising God,
"That sets us praising,—why not stop with him? 190
"Why put all thoughts of praise out of our head
"With wonder at lines, colours, and what not?
"Paint the soul, never mind the legs and arms!
"Rub all out, try at it a second time.
"Oh, that white smallish female with the breasts, 195
"She's just my niece . . . Herodias, I would say,—
"Who went and danced and got men's heads cut off!
"Have it all out!" Now, is this sense, I ask?
A fine way to paint soul, by painting body
So ill, the eye can't stop there, must go further 200
And can't fare worse! Thus, yellow does for white
When what you put for yellow's simply black,
And any sort of meaning looks intense
When all beside itself means and looks nought.
Why can't a painter lift each foot in turn, 205
Left foot and right foot, go a double step,
Make his flesh liker and his soul more like,
Both in their order? Take the prettiest face,
The Prior's niece . . . patron-saint—is it so pretty

---

188 *1855P* shows that.   *1855, 1856* soul.   189 *1855P* a-praising there,
1855, 1856 God!   190 *1855P–63* sets you praising,—   191 *1855P–63* our
heads   193 *1855P* arms,   194 *1872S, 1884S* time!   197 *1855P–65*
off—   198 *1855P* is that sense,

---

189 *Giotto*: Giotto di Bondone (d. 1337) is regarded as the founder of modern
painting.

196 *Herodias*: 'the daughter of Herodias', according to Matt, 14: 6, Mark 6: 22 (in AV
and Vulgate); but in Mark there is authority in the Greek MSS for 'his daughter
Herodias', and that is how the Eastern church has sometimes understood the matter.
The name Salome comes not from the Bible, but from Josephus, *Jewish Antiquities* xviii.
136–7 (not in connection with John).

200–1 *go further/ . . . fare worse*: proverbial (ODEP 306b).

203 *intense*: cf. Keats to his brothers, 21 December 1817: 'I . . . went . . . to see *Death
on the Pale Horse*. It is a wonderful picture, when [Benjamin] West's age is considered;
But there is nothing to be intense upon; no women one feels mad to kiss; no face
swelling into reality': *Letters*, ed. H. E. Rollins (2 vols., Cambridge, Mass., and
Cambridge, 1958).

You can't discover if it means hope, fear,   210
Sorrow or joy? won't beauty go with these?
Suppose I've made her eyes all right and blue,
Can't I take breath and try to add life's flash,
And then add soul and heighten them threefold?
Or say there's beauty with no soul at all—   215
(I never saw it—put the case the same—)
If you get simple beauty and nought else,
You get about the best thing God invents:
That's somewhat: and you'll find the soul you have missed,
Within yourself, when you return him thanks.   220
"Rub all out!" Well, well, there's my life, in short,
And so the thing has gone on ever since.
I'm grown a man no doubt, I've broken bounds:
You should not take a fellow eight years old
And make him swear to never kiss the girls.   225
I'm my own master, paint now as I please—
Having a friend, you see, in the Corner-house!
Lord, it's fast holding by the rings in front—
Those great rings serve more purposes than just
To plant a flag in, or tie up a horse!   230
And yet the old schooling sticks, the old grave eyes
Are peeping o'er my shoulder as I work,
The heads shake still—"It's art's decline, my son!
"You're not of the true painters, great and old;
"Brother Angelico's the man, you'll find;   235

211 *1855P* Won't   216 *1855P* I . . . . saw that—put . . . . same—   218 *1855P–*
65 invents,—   219 *1855P* Is not that somewhat? And the soul   *1855, 1856,*
1863, 1865 somewhat. And   220 *1855P* Find in yourself   *1855P–63S* thanks!
1863 thanks,   221 *1855P–56* well, well,   *1855P* short: *1863* short.
222 *1855P* That way the   225 *1855P–56* girls—   227 *1855P* see—the
Corner-house—   229 *1855P* than one,   232 *1855P* Still peeping
233 *1855P* The shaking heads—"It's

227 *the Corner-house*: cf. l. 18 n.
228 *it's fast holding*: i.e. the rings provide a secure hold. Rio describes Lippi as the
'famous monk, . . . who by his naturalism contributed more than any other artist to
corrupt the Florentine school': *The Poetry of Christian Art*, 347–8.
235 *Brother Angelico*: in *Memoirs of Early Italian Painters* Mrs Jameson divides a chapter
between Lippi and Guido di Pietro (c.1400–55), 'both of a religious order, . . . in all

"Brother Lorenzo stands his single peer:
"Fag on at flesh, you'll never make the third!"
Flower o' the pine,
You keep your mistr . . . manners, and I'll stick to mine!
I'm not the third, then: bless us, they must know!   240
Don't you think they're the likeliest to know,
They with their Latin? So, I swallow my rage,
Clench my teeth, suck my lips in tight, and paint
To please them—sometimes do and sometimes don't;
For, doing most, there's pretty sure to come   245
A turn, some warm eve finds me at my saints—
A laugh, a cry, the business of the world—
(*Flower o' the peach,*
Death for us all, and his own life for each!)
And my whole soul revolves, the cup runs over,   250
The world and life's too big to pass for a dream,
And I do these wild things in sheer despite,
And play the fooleries you catch me at,
In pure rage! The old mill-horse, out at grass
After hard years, throws up his stiff heels so,   255
Although the miller does not preach to him
The only good of grass is to make chaff.
What would men have? Do they like grass or no—

236 *1855P* Lorenzo, that's his . . . . peer,   *1855, 1856* peer.   242 *1855P–63S* so
1863, 1865 so,   244 *1855P–65* don't,   248 *1855P* Flower   249 *1855P*
each!   250 *1855–63S* runs o'er,   254 *1855P* rage: the   *1855–65* the

other respects the very antipodes of each other', adding that 'From this period we date
the great schism in modern art': i. 110. Guido was called 'Fra Angelico' on account of
the 'divine' skill notably displayed in his Coronation of the Virgin in the church of
S. Domenico di Fiesole, and in his work in the cloisters of San Marco in Florence. Vasari
tells us that he 'is said never to have painted a Crucifix without tears streaming from his
eyes': *Lives,* ii. 35. He is the only painter in the Western tradition to have been beatified.

236 *Brother Lorenzo*: Lorenzo Monaco (Piero di Giovanni, born *c.*1370, died after
1422) was a monk of the order of Camoldoli (cf. 139–40 n), who was brought up in the
tradition of the great Sienese masters, but was later influenced by Orcagna and other
Florentines. He has a good deal in common with Fra Angelico. See 'Old Pictures in
Florence', 208.

237 *Fag*: labour.

247 *business*: bustle.

250 *the cup runs over*: cf. Ps. 23: 5.

May they or mayn't they? all I want's the thing
Settled for ever one way. As it is,   260
You tell too many lies and hurt yourself:
You don't like what you only like too much,
You do like what, if given you at your word,
You find abundantly detestable.
For me, I think I speak as I was taught;   265
I always see the garden and God there
A-making man's wife: and, my lesson learned,
The value and significance of flesh,
I can't unlearn ten minutes afterwards.

You understand me: I'm a beast, I know.   270
But see, now—why, I see as certainly
As that the morning-star's about to shine,
What will hap some day. We've a youngster here
Comes to our convent, studies what I do,

260 *1855P–65* way: as   261 *1855P* tell so many   *1855P–65* yourself.
264 *1855P* Is found abundantly   267 *1855P* A-making man his wife—my
*269 {reading of *1863–84S*} *1855P–63S* minutes afterward. *1888, 1889* afterwards,
271 *1855P* I know as   273 *1855P* day. There's a

266 *the garden*: Gen. 2:18 ff.
267, 269 *learned . . . unlearn*: cf. *King Victor and King Charles*, 'King Victor', II, 13.
270 *I'm a beast*: cf. 80 n.
273 *a youngster*. Masaccio (Tommaso di Giovanni, 1401–c.1428) was Lippi's master, not his pupil. In 1866, taxed by Edward Dowden with error, Browning defended himself vigorously: 'I looked into the matter carefully long ago, and long before I thought of my own poem, from my interest in the Brancacci frescos, indeed in all early Florentine art. I believe the strange confusions and mistakes of Vasari are set tolerably right now: you may know, he took Lippino the son for Lippo the father': *Letters*, 104. Whereas Browning believed it 'certain that Masaccio did not begin the paintings . . . before 1440', we now know that by that date he had been dead for some twelve years. Since Browning mentioned Filippo Baldinucci (the author of *Delle Notizie de' Professori del Disegno*, 6 vols., 1681–1728) in this letter, DeVane assumed that it was Baldinucci who misled Browning into believing that Masaccio was Lippi's pupil. In an important article in ELN for March 1966, however, Johnstone Parr pointed out that Baldinucci, so far from making any such assertion, states that Lippi 'learned the art' from Masaccio (p. 198). Parr shows that Browning was misled by Vasari's erroneous statement that Lippi painted frescoes in the Brancacci chapel (in S. Maria del Carmine) while 'still very young' (ii. 74), and particularly by the notes in *Vite*, ed. by Gaetano Milanesi *et al.*, 13 vols. (Florence, 1846–57). Browning owned this edition, sometimes known as the 'Le Monnier edition': Kelley and Coley, A 2379. As Parr mentions, vols. iii and iv, which deal with Masaccio and Fra Lippo Lippi, appeared in 1848.

Slouches and stares and lets no atom drop: 275
His name is Guidi—he'll not mind the monks—
They call him Hulking Tom, he lets them talk—
He picks my practice up—he'll paint apace,
I hope so—though I never live so long,
I know what's sure to follow. You be judge!   280
You speak no Latin more than I, belike;
However, you're my man, you've seen the world
—The beauty and the wonder and the power,
The shapes of things, their colours, lights and shades,
Changes, surprises,—and God made it all!   285
—For what? Do you feel thankful, ay or no,
For this fair town's face, yonder river's line,
The mountain round it and the sky above,
Much more the figures of man, woman, child,
These are the frame to? What's it all about?   290
To be passed over, despised? or dwelt upon,
Wondered at? oh, this last of course!—you say.
But why not do as well as say,—paint these
Just as they are, careless what comes of it?
God's works—paint anyone, and count it crime   295
To let a truth slip. Don't object, "His works
"Are here already; nature is complete:
"Suppose you reproduce her—(which you can't)
"There's no advantage! you must beat her, then."

---

279 *1855P* live to see,   282 *1855P* You've . . . . world however, you're . . . . man.
284 *1868* colours, light and   286 *1855P–65* do   291 *1855–63S* passed o'er,
despised?   292 *1855P–63S* course, you   293 *1855P* say? Paint
294 *1855P* it,   298 *1855P* you reproduced her—

276 *Guidi*: his father was Ser Giovanni di Simone Guidi.

277 *Hulking Tom*: Vasari tells us that 'He was remarkably absent and careless of externals', and for this reason was called 'Masaccio', 'awkward' or 'clumsy': i. 402–3. The name served to distinguish 'Big Tom' Masaccio from 'Little Tom' Masolino, who also worked on the Brancacci murals.

283 *The beauty and the wonder*: cf. Shelley, *Epipsychidion*, 29.

290 *These are the frame to*: according to Mrs Jameson (loc. cit.), Lippi 'was one of the earliest painters who introduced landscape backgrounds, painted with some feeling for the truth of nature'.

For, don't you mark? we're made so that we love   300
First when we see them painted, things we have passed
Perhaps a hundred times nor cared to see;
And so they are better, painted—better to us,
Which is the same thing. Art was given for that;
God uses us to help each other so,   305
Lending our minds out. Have you noticed, now,
Your cullion's hanging face? A bit of chalk,
And trust me but you should, though! How much more,
If I drew higher things with the same truth!
That were to take the Prior's pulpit-place,   310
Interpret God to all of you! Oh, oh,
It makes me mad to see what men shall do
And we in our graves! This world's no blot for us,
Nor blank; it means intensely, and means good:
To find its meaning is my meat and drink.   315
"Ay, but you don't so instigate to prayer!"
Strikes in the Prior: "when your meaning's plain
"It does not say to folk—remember matins,
"Or, mind you fast next Friday!" Why, for this
What need of art at all? A skull and bones,   320
Two bits of stick nailed crosswise, or, what's best,
A bell to chime the hour with, does as well.
I painted a Saint Laurence six months since

---

300 *1855P–68* mark,   302 *1855P* see,   311 *1855P–65* oh, oh,   312 *1855P*
men will do   313 *1855P* no trap for   316 *1855P–56* prayer"   *1863S*
prayer,"   317 *1855–63S* Prior!   *1855P* when a meaning's   318 *1855P–84S*
to folks—remember   319 *1855P–63* Friday."

---

300 *we're made so*: a commonplace of aesthetics, from the time of Aristotle.
307 *cullion*: 'A scoundrel; a mean wretch': Johnson.
    hanging: gloomy-looking, often with a play on 'hang', as OED² notes.
Cf. *Measure for Measure*, IV. ii. 29.
313 *This world's no blot for us*: 'The words which Browning put into the mouth of . . .
Filippo Lippi, as George Eliot realized when she reviewed *Men and Women*, are not so
much the sentiments of a Renaissance painter as those of a mid-Victorian, and they
derive as much from *Modern Painters* as from any fourteenth-century theory of art':
J. B. Bullen, *The Expressive Eye: Fiction and Perception in the Work of Thomas Hardy*,
(1986), 253. For George Eliot's review, see p. xxix. above.

At Prato, splashed the fresco in fine style:
"How looks my painting, now the scaffold's down?"   325
I ask a brother: "Hugely," he returns—
"Already not one phiz of your three slaves
"Who turn the Deacon off his toasted side,
"But's scratched and prodded to our heart's content,
"The pious people have so eased their own   330
"With coming to say prayers there in a rage:
"We get on fast to see the bricks beneath.
"Expect another job this time next year,
"For pity and religion grow i' the crowd—
"Your painting serves its purpose!" Hang the fools!   335

—That is—you'll not mistake an idle word
Spoke in a huff by a poor monk, Got wot,
Tasting the air this spicy night which turns
The unaccustomed head like Chianti wine!
Oh, the church knows! don't misreport me, now!   340
It's natural a poor monk out of bounds
Should have his apt word to excuse himself:
And hearken how I plot to make amends.
I have bethought me: I shall paint a piece
. . . There's for you! Give me six months, then go, see   345

---

324 *1855P–56* style.   328 *1855P* That turned the   *1855–63* That turn
331 *1855P–63* When coming   *1855P* rage,   *1855, 1856* rage.   332 *1855P*
beneath: 333 *1855P* year!   334 *1855P* So pity   340 *1855P* Don't
343 *1855P* But hearken

323–4 *a Saint Laurence . . . at Prato*: St Lawrence was martyred at Rome, probably in
258. There is a tradition that he was roasted on a grid. No St Lawrence by Lippi is
known at Prato.

333 *Expect another job*: Vasari records that the Flagellation, painted for the Basilica
of S. Croce by Andrea dal Castagno, was 'scratched and injured by children and
simple folks, who have maltreated the head, arms, and almost the entire persons
of the Jews, as though they would thereby avenge the injuries inflicted on the Sa-
viour': ii. 97. Castagno, who studied the work of Masaccio, probably worked with
Lippi.

345 *There's for you*: 'I don't know *What's* for you', Ruskin complained': see DeLaura,
'Ruskin and the Brownings', 326.

Something in Sant' Ambrogio's! Bless the nuns!
They want a cast o' my office. I shall paint
God in the midst, Madonna and her babe,
Ringed by a bowery flowery angel-brood,
Lilies and vestments and white faces, sweet   350
As puff on puff of grated orris-root
When ladies crowd to Church at midsummer.
And then i' the front, of course a saint or two—
Saint John, because he saves the Florentines,
Saint Ambrose, who puts down in black and white   355
The convent's friends and gives them a long day,
And Job, I must have him there past mistake,
The man of Uz (and Us without the z,
Painters who need his patience). Well, all these
Secured at their devotion, up shall come   360
Out of a corner when you least expect,
As one by a dark stair into a great light,

---

346 *1855P* Ambrogio's: bless   *1855, 1856* Ambrogio's . . . (bless   *1863S* Ambrogio's
. . . bless   347 *1855P–68* cast of my   *1855, 1856* office) I   353 *1855P–68*
then in the   354 *1855P* Florentines.   355 *1855P* Sant' Ambrose,
357 *1855P* I mean to set there   358 *1855P* Uz and   359 *1855P* Who . . . .
patience—I at least. Well, these   360 *1855P* their devotions, up there comes
1855–63 their devotions, up

346 *Something in Sant' Ambrogio's*: the painting is now in the Galleria dell'Accademia
in Florence. It has often been reproduced, e.g. in the first ed. of Griffin and Minchin
(1910), in Pittaluga, and in Andrès (in colour).

347 *a cast o' my office*: a specimen of my skill, probably with a sexual *double entendre*.

349 *a bowery flowery angel-brood*: cf. introd. p. 33.

351 *orris-root*: Ruskin complained that he had looked for this 'in the Encyclopaedia'
without success: he would have done better to look in Johnson. Browning replied that
it is 'a corruption of *iris*-root—the Florentine lily, the *giaggolo*, of world-wide fame as a
good savor': Collingwood, i. 202.

354 *Saint John*: John the Baptist, the patron saint of Florence, whose tall figure
appears standing at the extreme right of the picture. His garment (like a paint-brush) is
of camel-hair; cf. Matt. 3:4, Mark 1:6.

355 *Saint Ambrose*: Ambrose (d. Milan 397), after whom the church is named. He is
the mitred figure standing at the extreme left.

356 *day*: life.

357 *Job*: in the left foreground, he is identified by a sash over his shoulder with his
name on it.

358 *The man of Uz*: 'There was a man in the land of Uz, whose name was Job':
Job 1: 1.

Music and talking, who but Lippo! I!—
Mazed, motionless and moonstruck—I'm the man!
Back I shrink—what is this I see and hear?   365
I, caught up with my monk's-things by mistake,
My old serge gown and rope that goes all round,
I, in this presence, this pure company!
Where's a hole, where's a corner for escape?
Then steps a sweet angelic slip of a thing   370
Forward, puts out a soft palm—"Not so fast!"
—Addresses the celestial presence, "nay—
"He made you and devised you, after all,
"Though he's none of you! Could Saint John there draw—
"His camel-hair make up a painting-brush?   375
"We come to brother Lippo for all that,
"*Iste perfecit opus!*" So, all smile—
I shuffle sideways with my blushing face
Under the cover of a hundred wings
Thrown like a spread of kirtles when you're gay   380

---

364 *1855P* moon struck. I'm   368 *1855P* company?   374 *1855P* draw?
377 *1855P* so,   379 *1855P* And under cover

363 *I!*: in the *Biographie universelle* (xxiv. 546a) Browning will have read that in this
figure 'the painter has portrayed himself . . . in the character of a worshipper'. Such was
the tradition. It should be noted, however, that Vasari does not say this. While it is true
that it is implied by the portrait in *1568* (ii. 194 ff.), Boase has pointed out (p. 68) that
fewer than a hundred of the 144 alleged portraits in that edition have any claim 'to be
considered true likenesses'. As Montgomery Campbell argued in the *Burlington
Magazine* for 1912 (xxi. 194 ff.), the kneeling figure to the right of the picture must be
the Canon of S. Lorenzo who ordered the work, the Very Revd Francesco Maringhi,
who was Prior of the church and who endowed a chaplaincy. The painting was moved
from above the high altar by one of his successors. The words '*Is perfecit opus*' do not
mean 'he painted the work' but 'he completed the work'. Line 377 suggests that
Browning supposed that the last two letters, making 'Is' into 'Iste', are concealed by the
scroll. They would not change the meaning.
    Carmichael does not see Lippi himself anywhere in the painting; but Pittaluga
(p. 175) argues that it is likely that he portrayed himself as the monk near the left of the
picture, behind Job (who seems to be contemplating him). He supports his head with
one hand, and looks sideways at us as we admire the painting. Vasari tells us that in
another of his works, 'The Feast of Herod', there is 'A portrait of Fra Filippo himself,
taken with his own hand by help of a mirror': ii. 82.
    364 *Mazed*; bewildered, dazed.
    380 *kirtles*: gowns, petticoats.

And play hot cockles, all the doors being shut,
Till, wholly unexpected, in there pops
The hothead husband! Thus I scuttle off
To some safe bench behind, not letting go
The palm of her, the little lily thing 385
That spoke the good word for me in the nick,
Like the Prior's niece . . . Saint Lucy, I would say.
And so all's saved for me, and for the church
A pretty picture gained. Go, six months hence!
Your hand, sir, and good-bye: no lights, no lights! 390
The street's hushed, and I know my own way back,
Don't fear me! There's the grey beginning. Zooks!

383 *1855P* husband—So I   386 *1855P* That said the . . . . me i' the
*387 {reading of *1855P–84S*} *1888, 1889* niece . .

---

381 *hot cockles*: 'A rustic game in which one player lay face downwards, or knelt
down with his eyes covered, and being struck on the back by the others in turn, guessed
who struck him': OED². A game of romps.
386 *in the nick*: in the nick of time.
387 *the Prior's niece . . . Saint Lucy*: cf. 170 n. Saint Lucy was martyred at Syracuse,
probably in Diocletian's persecution. She died a virgin, there being a story that she was
miraculously saved from exposure in a brothel.
389 *six months hence*: cf. introduction, above, p. 34.

A TOCCATA OF GALUPPI'S

THIS poem may well have been written in 1853, as one of the 'lyrics with more music and painting than before'.[1] Baldassare Galuppi (1706–85) was a composer, conductor, and instrumentalist of great fame in his day. In 1748 he was chosen to be *vicemaestro* of the *cappella ducale* of St Mark's, and in 1762 he became its *maestro*, the highest musical appointment in Venice. Charles Burney considered him one of the four best opera composers of his age.[2]

A toccata is a piece in a free style, 'usually for keyboard . . . incorporating virtuoso elements designed to show off a player's "touch" '.[3] In 1887 Browning told an enquirer that he had 'had once in [his] possession two huge manuscript volumes almost exclusively made up of [Galuppi's] "Toccata-pieces"—apparently a slighter form of the Sonata to be "touched" lightly off'.[4] These volumes have not been identified. In *New Grove*, vii. 138 James L. Jackman lists under Galuppi's instrumental compositions '125 or more sonatas, toccatas' etc., in manuscripts now scattered among numerous libraries. When asked about the piece in question in 1880 Browning answered that he 'had only a general fancy of the character of Galuppi's music floating in [his] head,—no particular piece', when he wrote the poem.[5]

His first visit to Venice, in the spring of 1838, had proved a memorable one. He remained there for more than half of the time that he was able to stay in Italy. The impression it made on him is recorded in *Sordello*, the poem on which he was labouring, and for which he was seeking inspiration. In iii. 723–6 he records the significance that the extraordinary city had for him:

> Venice seems a type
> Of Life—'twixt blue and blue extends, a stripe,
> As Life, the somewhat, hangs 'twixt nought and nought:
> 'T is Venice, and 'tis Life.

His second visit, in 1851, when he and EBB occupied an apartment on the Grand Canal for a month, was much less memorable. After sharing his

---

[1] See above, p. xiv.
[2] For an article on Burney's possible influence on the poem, see n. to l. 18.
[3] *The New Oxford Companion to Music*, ed. Denis Arnold (2 vols., 1983).
[4] Letter to Henry G. Spaulding, first published in Herbert E. Greene, 'Browning's Knowledge of Music': PMLA 62 (1947), 1099.
[5] PK 80: 34.

wife's 'ecstasy' at first, he grew 'uncomfortable, & nervous, & unable to eat or sleep', finding that the 'moist, soft, relaxing' air did not suit him.[1] To EBB it was all very different:

The Heaven of it is ineffable—Never had I touched the skirts of so celestial a place. The beauty of the architecture, the silver trails of water up between all that gorgeous colour & carving, the enchanting silence, the moonlight, the music, the gondolas . . . I mix it all up together & maintain that nothing is like it, nothing equal to it, not a second Venice in the world.

They led 'a truly Venetian life', going in a gondola to the Lido, to a feast at Chioggia, to a play, to an opera.

While the brilliance with which Browning recreates the effect of music on his speaker has been generally acknowledged, too much attention has perhaps been devoted to the musical terms in st. vii—as if to punish the poet for his tendency to boast of his knowledge of music. He had a profound love of music, he knew more about music than most people, but at times music was in danger of becoming his 'violon d'Ingres'. A recent critic has justly remarked that he 'makes his meaning apparent with words which are manifestly untechnical, words which are confusing, to different degrees, from a strictly musical point of view. To complain that Browning is musically inaccurate is to fail to appreciate the offhand, oblique way in which he lets his speaker come to the point.'[2] We must also remember that Browning is a dramatic poet. His speaker in this poem has never been 'out of England', knows little of the layout of Venice, and is remarkably complacent: a rather limited autodidact, one might say. It is not self-evident that Browning would have chosen to endow with mastery of the technical language of a musician a man who is so ill informed on other matters. As we have commented elsewhere, 'It is sometimes difficult to be sure when Browning blundered, when . . . he "was not careful to be correct", and when (as he once explained) a blunder was part of his characterization of a speaker, as in his use of 'High Priest' for 'Chief Rabbi' in 'Filippo Baldinucci on the Privilege of Burial', st. xxvi.'[3] Replying to a correspondent who must have objected to a misquotation from Pope in The Inn Album, he remarked that 'the careless fellow was

[1] Raymond and Sullivan, iii. 322–3.
[2] Stefan Hawlin, 'Browning's "A Toccata of Galuppi's": How Venice once was dear': RES 41 (1990), 496–509 at 503.
[3] Our Vol. III, p. 202 n. (referring to the 'great text in Galatians' and the 'High Priest'). 'I really believe that when I try to put myself in the place of any ignorant person who figures in a poem', Browning wrote to an enquirer, 'I adopt his very ignorance': David George, 'Four New Browning Letters', SIB (Spring 1974), 62.

made purposely unsure in his quotations'.[1] No one (we take it) has ever supposed that Browning believed that the Sermon on the Mount was delivered by St Praxed, as the dying Bishop seems to imagine.[2]

The piece consists of fifteen stanzas, each a triplet, so that the rhymes go from *aaa* to *ooo*. Each line has fifteen syllables, with a marked caesura, commonly after the fourth foot. Good modern critics have described the metre as dipodic,[3] but it is simpler to follow Browning's own description of it as 'purely Trochaic',[4] so that we count eight feet, the last lacking the unstressed syllable. Tennyson had used a similar metre in 'Locksley Hall',[5] and Browning in 'Home-Thoughts, from the Sea'. The subtlety with which the metre is handled becomes apparent if we compare the first stanza, which reads like the work of a versifier attempting trochees for the first time, with a notably awkward and prosaic result, with the subtle rhythms of the remainder of the poem. We realize that the first stanza is not the result of clumsiness, but is designed to make clear to the reader the sort of man the speaker is.

Date: 1853/4
1863: *Dramatic Lyrics*

A TOCCATA OF GALUPPI'S.

I.

OH Galuppi, Baldassaro, this is very sad to find!
I can hardly misconceive you; it would prove me deaf and blind;
But although I take your meaning, 't is with such a heavy mind!

1 *1855P* OH!   2 *1855P, 1863S* you; that would   3 *1855P* But if I must give
you credit, 'tis   *1855, 1856* I give you credit, 'tis

1 *Oh, Galuppi, Baldassaro*: the characterization of the speaker begins with the inversion of Galuppi's name; he gives it as he might have found it in a reference book, and mis-spells the Christian name.

[1] See 'Letters from Robert Browning to the Rev. J. D. Williams, 1874–1889', ed. Thomas J. Collins and Walter J. Pickering, BIS 4 (1976), 46.
[2] Cf. Vol. IV, p. 74, n. to l. 95. On the general question of inaccuracies see Ian Jack, ' "Commented it must be": Browning annotating Browning': BIS 9 (1981), 59–77.
[3] e.g. John E. Schwiebert, 'Meter, Form and Sound Patterning in Robert Browning's "A Toccata . . ." ', SBHC 14 (1986), 17–18; and Hawlin, loc. cit.
[4] *Letters*, 196.
[5] 'Mr Hallam said to me that the English people liked verse in trochaics, so I wrote the poem in this metre': Tennyson's note, Eversley ed., ii (1908), 341.

II.

Here you come with your old music, and here's all the good
  it brings.
What, they lived once thus at Venice where the merchants
  were the kings,   5
Where Saint Mark's is, where the Doges used to wed the sea
  with rings?

III.

Ay, because the sea's the street there; and 't is arched by . . .
  what you call
. . . Shylock's bridge with houses on it, where they kept the
  carnival:
I was never out of England—it's as if I saw it all.

IV.

Did young people take their pleasure when the sea was warm
  in May?   10

8 *1855–63S* carnival!   9 *1855P–65* all!

6 *Saint Mark's*: one of the great buildings of the world, the present St Mark's
is the third church on its site. About 1063 the Doge Domenico Contarini
(*c.*1041–*c.*1071) began to remodel the building. Byzantine workmen and Lombards
worked together on an edifice which combines two architectural styles. His succes-
sor Domenico Selvo (*c.*1071–84) decreed that every Venetian merchantman return-
ing from the East must bring back marbles or fine carvings for the adornment of St
Mark's.

   the Doges: from 697 to 1797 Venice was a republic, with the Doge at the apex of
its government, 'the embodiment of the Venetian state in all its majesty but hemmed
in always by his six Councillors, the . . . Signoria': John Julius Norwich, *A History of
Venice* (2 vols., 1977, 1981: Penguin Books, 1 vol., 1983), p. 283. The Doge held office
for life. Every year, on Ascension Day, there occurred the *Sposalizio del Mar*, in
which he celebrated the symbolic marriage of Venice with the sea by casting a precious
ring from the state ship, the 'Bucintoro', into the Adriatic. Cf. Byron, *Childe Harold*, iv.
91 ff.

8 *Shylock's bridge*: the Ponte del Rialto. The Rialto is the quarter where the Exchange
was situated: see *The Merchant of Venice*, I. iii. 101 and III. i. 37 ff. The speaker is vague
about the layout of the city.

   the carnival: the period of feasting and merry-making preceding Lent. Cf. the
opening of Byron's *Beppo*. Throughout Lent the devout should abstain from meat in
memory of Christ's fast in the wilderness.

Balls and masks begun at midnight, burning ever to mid-day,
When they made up fresh adventures for the morrow, do
    you say?

V.

Was a lady such a lady, cheeks so round and lips so red,—
On her neck the small face buoyant, like a bell-flower on its bed,
O'er the breast's superb abundance where a man might base
    his head?   15

VI.

Well, and it was graceful of them—they'd break talk off and
    afford
—She, to bite her mask's black velvet—he, to finger on his
    sword,
While you sat and played Toccatas, stately at the clavichord?

VII.

What? Those lesser thirds so plaintive, sixths diminished, sigh
    on sigh,

11 *1855P, 1863S* masks began at   *1855P* mid-day;   12 *1855P* Then they
13 *1855P* red;   16 *1855–65* (and . . . . them)   18 *1855P* clavichord.

11 *masks*: parties of pleasure during which the company is masked.
    burning: blazing.
14 *a bell-flower.* Campanula, a genus of plants with bell-shaped blossoms.
16 *afford*: spare the time.
18 *the clavichord*: this instrument looks 'like a small rectangular piano—usually a sort
of box that can be placed upon a table for playing'. Its tone 'is soft and ethereal . . .
unlike the harpsichord, [it] offers virtually unlimited opportunity of modifying the tone
by means of the touch': *The Oxford Companion to Music*, by Percy Scholes, 10th ed., rev.
by J. O. Ward (1970). Arguing that Charles Burney's *The Present State of Music in France
and Italy* and *The Present State of Music in Germany* are relevant to this poem, David
Lindley mentions that the only instrument Galuppi had in his work-room when Burney
visited him was 'a little clavichord'; and that when he visited C. P. E. Bach that
composer sat down 'to his *Silbermann clavichord*', his 'favourite instrument', and played
with 'delicacy, precision, and spirit': 'In the pathetic and slow movements, whenever
he had a long note to express, he absolutely contrived to produce, from his instrument,
a cry of sorrow and complaint, such as can only be effected upon the clavichord': see
'A Possible Source for Browning's "A Toccata of Galuppi's" ', *BSN*, December 1979,
1–2. Browning is likely to have known Burney's books.
19 *lesser.* we should now say 'minor'. Cf. *Parleyings*, 'Charles Avison', 337–8: 'Into
the minor key first modulate—/Gently with A, now—in the Lesser Third!)'. The
interval A–C is a minor third.

Told them something? Those suspensions, those solutions—
   "Must we die?"   20
Those commiserating sevenths—"Life might last! we can
   but try!"

VIII.

"Were you happy?"—"Yes."—"And are you still as
   happy?"—"Yes. And you?"
—"Then, more kisses!"—"Did *I* stop them, when a million
   seemed so few?"
Hark, the dominant's persistence till it must be answered to!

IX.

So, an octave struck the answer. Oh, they praised you, I
   dare say!   25
"Brave Galuppi! that was music! good alike at grave and
   gay!
"I can always leave off talking when I hear a master play!"

---

20 *1863S* "must   21 *1855P* last we   22 *1855P* are you happy?"—"Yes—
And *1855–63S* "Yes—And you?"   23 *1855P–56* kisses"—*1855P* I   24 *1863,*
1865 Hark!   26 *1855P* music,   27 *1855P–68* play."

---

   sixths diminished: the speaker is showing off, and becoming confused in his attempt
to sound technical. If this meant anything (a friend advises us) it would mean 'not a
perfect fifth (e.g. C–G) but its enharmonic equivalent (e.g. C–A♭♭), which has virtually
no place in practical music, and surely none in Galuppi's'.

   20 *Those suspensions, those solutions*: 'A suspension is the holding on of a note in one
chord into the following chord. It produces a discord, which is only resolved (a
solution) when the note falls a degree to a note appropriate to the second chord. The
terms aptly symbolize reluctance to die, combined with the realization that in the
harmony of things one cannot stay, after the time has come for one to go': Turner.

   21 *commiserating sevenths*: probably 'minor sevenths', Hawlin comments, 'which
would be "commiserating" because they are mild dissonances and quite unlike the
acutely dissonant minor sixths'. A minor seventh (e.g. C–B♭) has 'a gentle mourn-
ful feeling, which is made the more woeful by its undermining of the normal joy-
ful feeling of the major triad supporting it': Deryck Cooke, *The Language of Music*
(1959) 74.

   23 *more kisses!*: counting kisses is an ancient theme in love poetry. See Catullus v. 7
and such later poets as Johannes Secundus (*Basia*), and Thomas Stanley ('Kisses by
Secundus').

   24 *the dominant's persistence*: of all the degrees of the scale the dominant is most
intimately related to the keynote.

X.

Then they left you for their pleasure: till in due time, one by
    one,
Some with lives that came to nothing, some with deeds as
    well undone,
Death stepped tacitly and took them where they never see
    the sun.   30

XI.

But when I sit down to reason, think to take my stand nor
    swerve,
While I triumph o'er a secret wrung from nature's close reserve,
In you come with your cold music till I creep thro' every nerve.

XII.

Yes, you, like a ghostly cricket, creaking where a house was
    burned:
"Dust and ashes, dead and done with, Venice spent what
    Venice earned.   35
"The soul, doubtless, is immortal—where a soul can be
    discerned.

XIII.

"Yours for instance: you know physics, something of geology,

---

28 *1855P* Thus they *1868, 1870* for your pleasure: 30 *1855P–63* Death came
tacitly   31 *1855P* reason,—say I'll take   32 *1855P* When I   *1855, 1856*
Till I   35 *1855P* earned,   *1855–65* earned!   36 *1855P* immortal—if a
37 *1855P–56, 1863–70, 1875* instance,

    30 *Death stepped tacitly*: cf. Ovid, *Tristia*, IV. x. 27: 'tacito passu labentibus annis': as
the years passed with silent pace.

    32 *reserve*: 'Store kept untouched, or undiscovered': Johnson.

    33 *creep*: shiver.

    34 *creaking*: with reference to the harsh persistent sound made by crickets, which are
fond of warmth.

    35 *Dust and ashes*: cf. Horace, *Odes*, IV. vii. 16: 'pulvis et umbra sumus'; *Book of Common
Prayer*, Order for the Burial of the Dead: 'earth to earth, ashes to ashes, dust to dust'.

    dead and done with: as in 'Master Hugues', 8.

    Venice spent: perhaps cf. the proverbial 'Spend as you get': ODEP.

"Mathematics are your pastime; souls shall rise in their degree;
"Butterflies may dread extinction,—you'll not die, it cannot be!

XIV.

"As for Venice and her people, merely born to bloom and
    drop,   40
"Here on earth they bore their fruitage, mirth and folly were
    the crop:
"What of soul was left, I wonder, when the kissing had to
    stop?

XV.

"Dust and ashes!" So you creak it, and I want the heart to
    scold.
Dear dead women, with such hair, too—what's become of all
    the gold
Used to hang and brush their bosoms? I feel chilly and grown
    old.   45

---

40 *1855P–63* and its people,   *1855P* to blow and   41 *1855P* crop,   *1855, 1856*
crop.

---

38 *souls shall rise in their degree*: in the next life.

39 *Butterflies*: since Gk. ψυχή means both 'soul' and 'butterfly', the contrast between the brief life of the one and the supposed immortality of the other is a common topic in poetry.

41 *bore their fruitage*: cf. 'Chapman's Masque of the Middle Temple and Lincoln's Inn, 1612–13', in J. Nichols, *The Progresses of King James the First* (4 vols., 1828), ii. 583: 'Freely Earth her frutage bearing'.

BY THE FIRE-SIDE

WHEN he was asked about this poem, Browning replied that 'all but the personality is fictitious—that is, the portraiture only is intended to be like—the circumstances are a mere imaginary framework'.[1] This confirms the conclusion of the unsophisticated reader that the speaker is the poet himself, and his 'perfect wife' Elizabeth.

In her *Life* Mrs Orr tells us that 'the scene of the declaration in *By the Fireside* was laid in a little adjacent mountain-gorge to which he walked or rode':[2] 'adjacent', that is, to Bagni di Lucca. Before 1855 they had spent two holidays there, and both are relevant. In 1849 they went there when Browning was still looking back over his own life as he strove to recover from the shock of his mother's death in March of that year. During this period of reflection and heightened awareness Elizabeth showed him the poems which she had written about her love for him, 'Sonnets from the Portuguese'.[3] They found exceptional happiness among the mountains. 'We have taken a sort of eagle's nest in this place', she wrote to Miss Mitford in July,

. . the highest house of the highest of the three villages which are called the Bagni di Lucca, & which lie at the heart of a hundred mountains, sung to continually by a rushing mountain-stream. The sound of the river & of the cicala is all the noise we hear . . . I think my husband's spirits are better already . . . it seems like a dream when I find myself able to climb the hills with Robert & help him to lose himself in the forests . . . The air of this place seems to penetrate the heart, & not the lungs only: it draws you, raises you, excites you . . . And the beauty, & the solitude . . . all is delightful to me. What is peculiarly beautiful & wonderful, is the variety of the shapes of the mountains. They are a multitude—and yet there is no likeness. None, except where the golden mist comes & transfigures them into one glory . . . the mountain there wrapt in the chestnut forest, is not like that bare peak which tilts against the sky . . nor like that serpent-twine of another which seems to move & coil, in the moving, coiling shadow.[4]

Four years later they were in the same vicinity. It was on this occasion that she told Miss Mitford that they intended to 'buy' their holiday 'by

---

[1] David George, 'Four New Browning Letters . . . to the Rev. James Graham': SBC, 2: 1 (1974), 62.

[2] p. 188.

[3] See Gardner B. Taplin, *The Life of Elizabeth Barrett Browning* (New Haven, 1957), 234 and 444 n. 19

[4] Raymond and Sullivan, iii, 272–3.

doing some work'.[1] Conditions were favourable for writing. 'It's a large house with a second sittingroom . . . a house withdrawn from the village & curtained in by a row of seven plane trees in which the cicale sing all day'.[2] Among the congenial company which added to their happiness was the American sculptor William Wetmore Story, one of whose letters describes an expedition to Prato Fiorito:

The day was glorious, and after climbing an hour we arrived at a little old church, near by which the view was magnificent. The grand limestone mountains spring sharply up, with deep patches of purple shade and little grey towns perched here and there on the lower spines. Under the trees here we spent nearly an hour, and then took our donkeys and horses again, and, after an hour and a half, passing over wild and grand scenery, with mountain-streams dripping and tumbling, and now and then over beds of red-veined jasper, we rounded a height bold and rugged as the Alps and saw before us the soft green velvety dome of Prato Fiorito.[3]

The comparison with Alpine scenery is a clue to Browning's 'imaginary framework'. Stanza ix, in which 'Alp meets heaven in snow!', contains a more precise description of the setting: we are told that a 'speck of white' at the edge of the little lake which can be seen below is Pella, a village near Lake Maggiore. In fact the Brownings never reached that part of Italy, but J. E. Lindsay pointed out that early in 1847 they were eagerly planning such a trip.[4] Since we know that they owned a copy of Murray's *Hand-Book for Travellers in Switzerland, . . . Savoy and Piedmont,*[5] we can make an intelligent guess at what attracted them about this vicinity, which was very shortly to become popular with travellers. The description of 'the Colma, the slope with which Browning's setting corresponds', includes this passage:

the ride is one of great interest, from the beautiful sites and views which it offers. A steep path leads up the mountain side to Arola, amidst the richest vegetation; vines, figs, gourds, and fruit-trees, make the course a vast garden. Magnificent forest-trees offer their shade, and the road in some places passes amidst precipices of granite in a state of decomposition, which offers an interesting study to the geologist . . . Above these granitic masses, the path continues through scenes resembling the most beautiful park scenery of England, and then opens upon the Col de Colma, a common, where a boundless scene is presented of the lakes

---

[1] Cf. p. xvi, above.   [2] Ogilvy, 101.   [3] Story, i. 273–4.

[4] See Jean Stirling Lindsay, 'The Central Episode of Browning's *By the Fire-Side*': SP 39 (1942), 571–9, and David Robertson, 'Browning on the Colle di Colma': BSN July 1975. Writing before Taplin cleared the matter up, Lindsay naturally believed that EBB had given Browning the 'Sonnets from the Portuguese' in 1847.

[5] Kelley and Coley, A 1692. It was the 3rd ed. (1846).

of Orta, Varese, and the plains of Lombardy, and towards the Alps, of Monte Rosa.[1]

The descent on the other side 'is not less beautiful':

The Val Sesia is seen in the deep distance, richly wooded and studded with churches and villages; the path leads down through pastoral scenes, which sometimes recall the most agreeable recollections of home to an English traveller; then changes almost suddenly to the deep gloom of a ravine, where there are quarries . . . buried in a forest of enormous walnut and chestnut trees.[2]

A place imagined, read about, longed for, can be as vivid in the mind as a place visited. The 'vale in Ida' in 'Œnone' was suggested to Tennyson by the Pyrenees. The setting of 'By the Fire-Side' owes its origin to something as commonplace as a guide-book. The poem may well have been written in Bagni di Lucca, during the holiday on which (as Story mentions) the Brownings were 'busily engaged in writing, he on a new volume of lyrical poems and she on a tale or novel in verse'.[3]

The poem is written in five-line stanzas, a form often used by Browning, in numerous variations. The rhyme-scheme, *ababa*, is the same as that of 'Two in the Campagna'; but the lines are a mixture of iambs and anapaests, and the last line of each stanza is a trimeter, not a tetrameter.

Date: 1853
1863: Dramatic Lyrics

BY THE FIRE-SIDE.

I.

How well I know what I mean to do
    When the long dark autumn-evenings come;
And where, my soul, is thy pleasant hue?
    With the music of all thy voices, dumb
    In life's November too!   5

---

2 *1855P–63* come,   4 *1855P* of thy

  3 *hue*: mood. OED[2] cites 'Our mental hue'.
  4 *thy voices*: those of his dramatic characters.

          [1] p. 271.   [2] Ibid.   [3] Story, i. 267.

II.

I shall be found by the fire, suppose,
   O'er a great wise book as beseemeth age,
While the shutters flap as the cross-wind blows
   And I turn the page, and I turn the page,
Not verse now, only prose!   10

III.

Till the young ones whisper, finger on lip,
   "There he is at it, deep in Greek:
"Now then, or never, out we slip
   "To cut from the hazels by the creek
"A mainmast for our ship!"   15

IV.

I shall be at it indeed, my friends:
   Greek puts already on either side
Such a branch-work forth as soon extends
   To a vista opening far and wide,
And I pass out where it ends.   20

---

7 *1855P, 1872S, 1884S* age;   8 *1855P* How the   12 *1855P* There
13 *1855, 1856* Now or never, then, out   15 *1855P* ship.   *1855, 1856* ship."
*16 {reading of DC, BrU, *1889*} *1855P* friends; *1855–84S* friends! *1888* friends

12 *deep in Greek*: for Browning's lifelong passion for Greek see any biography, his letters, or our notes to *Pauline* and 'Artemis Prologizes'.

18 *Such a branch-work*: 'The outside paths, which he will explore first, will show him the common English growths (hazel trees), namely the knowledge acquired in and from England. Each inner path will have rarer kinds of trees; the innermost of all, the rarest. When he shall have explored all the other paths, he will come at last to the innermost sanctuary of the wood's vista, and pursue that inner path alone, knowing the rest by heart. This innermost path is his own inner life; and pursuing it in retrospect, he will come to Italy, where his youth was spent, and at last reach the first beginning of his life, the moment when his own and his wife's spirits became first blended into one . . . He will find himself once more on that very mountain path where his troth was plighted': John T. Nettleship, *Robert Browning: Essays and Thoughts* (1890), 26.

V.

The outside-frame, like your hazel-trees:
    But the inside-archway widens fast,
And a rarer sort succeeds to these,
    And we slope to Italy at last
And youth, by green degrees.   25

VI.

I follow wherever I am led,
    Knowing so well the leader's hand:
Oh woman-country, wooed not wed,
    Loved all the more by earth's male-lands,
Laid to their hearts instead!   30

VII.

Look at the ruined chapel again
    Half-way up in the Alpine gorge!
Is that a tower, I point you plain,
    Or is it a mill, or an iron-forge
Breaks solitude in vain?   35

22 *1855P–63* inside-archway narrows fast,   32 *1855P, 1865S* gorge: *1855–65*
gorge.   33 *1855P* tower which I

    22 *widens*: note revision. 'Browning . . . changed "narrows" to "widens", deciding that it was better to suggest what the vista looked like to one walking down it': G. Tillotson, 'A Word for Browning': *Sewanee Review*, 72 (1964), 395.

    24 *slope*: move backwards in time.

    25 *by green degrees*: cf. Marvell, 'The Garden', 48.

    28 *Oh woman-country*: 'I may love Italy as a mistress, while my native country claims from me the proper and just regard due to a wedded wife': Lord Charlemont's letter of thanks to Baretti, for the dedication of his *Account of the Manners and Customs of Italy* (2 vols., 1768–9). The MS of the letter is in *H. M. C. Twelfth Report, Appendix, Part X, The Manuscripts and Correspondence of the First Earl of Charlemont, Vol. I, 1745–1783* (1891), 293. We are indebted to Mr John Lindon of University College, London for this information. We do not know where Browning found the quotation.

    31 *the ruined chapel*: cf. ll. 68 ff, and 167. While there is an old church near Bagni di Lucca, it is likely that Browning is describing a chapel more like that of which he had read, also in northern Italy. Robertson tells us of a 'wayside chapel of the Madonna di Loretto' which had a lunette above the door, in the porch. Understandably, however, the details do not fit, nor are the numbers 'Five, six, nine' to be found on it (l. 95).

    32 *the Alpine gorge*: see Introduction.

    33 *point*: point out. Cf. Pope, *Odyssey*, xxiv. 106, and 'Bishop Blougram', 448.

VIII.

A turn, and we stand in the heart of things;
  The woods are round us, heaped and dim;
From slab to slab how it slips and springs,
  The thread of water single and slim,
Through the ravage some torrent brings!   40

IX.

Does it feed the little lake below?
  That speck of white just on its marge
Is Pella; see, in the evening-glow,
  How sharp the silver spear-heads charge
When Alp meets heaven in snow!   45

X.

On our other side is the straight-up rock;
  And a path is kept 'twixt the gorge and it
By boulder-stones where lichens mock
  The marks on a moth, and small ferns fit
Their teeth to the polished block.   50

XI.

Oh the sense of the yellow mountain-flowers,
  And thorny balls, each three in one,
The chestnuts throw on our path in showers!
  For the drop of the woodland fruit's begun,
These early November hours,   55

---

42 *1855P* And the speck   45 *1855P–65* snow.   49 *1855P* moth, while small
52 *1855P–63* And the thorny   53 *1855P* throw in this path of ours,   *1855, 1856*
showers,

---

37 *heaped*: lofty, rising. Cf. Shelley, 'A Vision of the Sea', 128: 'The heaped waves'.

43 *Pella*: see introduction, above: 'Surely they are on the Orta side of the Colle di Colma': Robertson, 11.

44 *the silver spear-heads*: the pattern formed by the snow which adheres to the sides of a mountain.

48 *mock*: imitate.

50 *teeth*: roots.

51 *the sense*: our awareness.

54 *the drop*: cf. 'the fall of the leaf'. No other example of 'drop' in this sense in OED[2].

XII.

That crimson the creeper's leaf across
   Like a splash of blood, intense, abrupt,
O'er a shield else gold from rim to boss,
   And lay it for show on the fairy-cupped
Elf-needled mat of moss,   60

XIII.

By the rose-flesh mushrooms, undivulged
   Last evening—nay, in to-day's first dew
Yon sudden coral nipple bulged,
   Where a freaked fawn-coloured flaky crew
Of toadstools peep indulged.   65

XIV.

And yonder, at foot of the fronting ridge
   That takes the turn to a range beyond,
Is the chapel reached by the one-arched bridge
   Where the water is stopped in a stagnant pond
Danced over by the midge.   70

XV.

The chapel and bridge are of stone alike,
   Blackish-grey and mostly wet;
Cut hemp-stalks steep in the narrow dyke.
   See here again, how the lichens fret
And the roots of the ivy strike!   75

---

59 *1855P* it to show

56 *crimson*: vb.
58 *boss*: the protuberant centre of a shield.
60 *Elf-needled*: i.e. the mat looks as if it had been sewn by elves.
61 *rose-flesh mushrooms*: Henry James quotes a letter of Story's relating to this time:
'The whole day in the same woods with the Brownings . . . In the afternoon we . . .
found wondrous *fungi*, some red as coral': Story, i. 274–5.
    undivulged: unrevealed.
64 *freaked*: flecked or irregularly streaked, as in Milton, 'Lycidas', 144.
73 *the narrow dyke*: a hemp-dyke is a small pond in which green hemp is steeped.
74 *fret*: gnaw at the rock.

XVI.

Poor little place, where its one priest comes
   On a festa-day, if he comes at all,
To the dozen folk from their scattered homes,
   Gathered within that precinct small
By the dozen ways one roams—   80

XVII.

To drop from the charcoal-burners' huts,
   Or climb from the hemp-dressers' low shed,
Leave the grange where the woodman stores his nuts,
   Or the wattled cote where the fowlers spread
Their gear on the rock's bare juts.   85

XVIII.

It has some pretension too, this front,
   With its bit of fresco half-moon-wise
Set over the porch, Art's early wont:
   'T is John in the Desert, I surmise,
But has borne the weather's brunt—   90

XIX.

Not from the fault of the builder, though,
   For a pent-house properly projects
Where three carved beams make a certain show,
   Dating—good thought of our architect's—
'Five, six, nine, he lets you know.   95

81 *1855P* Who drops from   82 *1855P* Or climbs from   *1872S, 1884S* the hemp-dresser's low   83 *1855P* Or the   86 *1855P* front;   88 *1855P* Set o'er the

81 *charcoal-burners*: men who make charcoal, by partly burning wood.

83 *grange*: 'A farm; generally a farm with a house at a distance from neighbours': Johnson.

84 *wattled cote*: as in *Comus*, 344. Browning may have come on the phrase again in Arnold's 'The Scholar Gipsy', in his *Poems. A New Edition* (1853).

85 *juts*: cf. Tennyson, 'Morte d'Arthur', 50: 'juts of pointed rock'.

87 *half-moon-wise*: a nonce-formation. Cf. 31 n.

89 *John in the Desert*: Matt. 3. A common subject for painters.

95 *'Five, six, nine'*: for 1569: see l. 178.

XX.

And all day long a bird sings there,
    And a stray sheep drinks at the pond at times;
The place is silent and aware;
    It has had its scenes, its joys and crimes,
But that is its own affair.   100

XXI.

My perfect wife, my Leonor,
    Oh heart, my own, oh eyes, mine too,
Whom else could I dare look backward for,
    With whom beside should I dare pursue
The path grey heads abhor?   105

XXII.

For it leads to a crag's sheer edge with them;
    Youth, flowery all the way, there stops—
Not they; age threatens and they contemn,
    Till they reach the gulf wherein youth drops,
One inch from life's safe hem!   110

XXIII.

With me, youth led . . . I will speak now,
    No longer watch you as you sit

---

99 *1855P* scenes, and joys   103 *1855P* I look   110 *1855P–84S* from our
life's

98 *The place is silent and aware*: a good example of Ruskin's 'pathetic fallacy', though
his definitive account of it occurs in 1856, in vol. iii of *Modern Painters*.

101 *My Leonor*: in Beethoven's opera, *Fidelio, or Married Love* (first produced in 1805)
Florestan's devoted wife Leonora rescues him from prison, removing his chains.
Browning attended *Fidelio* 'in the first season of German opera here', in May 1832:
Kintner, i. 156, 158 n.

107 *Youth, flowery*: for the traditional image of youth in flower see e.g. Catullus
lxviii. 16. Browning may be remembering the name Prato Fiorito.

108 *contemn*: despise, ignore (it). Sometimes confused with 'condemn'. In 'Bad
Dreams. IV', 21–3, in *Asolando*, Browning rhymes the two words.

110 *life's safe hem*: edge. Cf. 'Bishop Blougram's Apology', 395: 'the dangerous edge
of things'.

Reading by fire-light, that great brow
  And the spirit-small hand propping it,
Mutely, my heart knows how—   115

XXIV.

When, if I think but deep enough,
  You are wont to answer, prompt as rhyme;
And you, too, find without rebuff
  Response your soul seeks many a time,
Piercing its fine flesh-stuff.   120

XXV.

My own, confirm me! If I tread
  This path back, is it not in pride
To think how little I dreamed it led
  To an age so blest that, by its side,
Youth seems the waste instead?   125

XXVI.

My own, see where the years conduct!
  At first, 't was something our two souls
Should mix as mists do; each is sucked
  In each now: on, the new stream rolls,
Whatever rocks obstruct.   130

XXVII.

Think, when our one soul understands
  The great Word which makes all things new,

118 *1855P–63* without a rebuff   119 *1855P–65S* The response   *{reading of *1872S, 1884S*} *1855P–70, 1875, 1888, 1889* time   120 *1855P* flesh stuff—   *1855, 1856* flesh-stuff—   123 *1855P* how blind I was, it   125 *1855P–56* instead! 129 *1855P* Into each now,   *1855–63* Into each

113 *that great brow*: a description of EBB.
127–8 *our two souls / Should mix*: cf. Donne, 'The Ecstasy', 35–6: 'Love, these mixed souls doth mix again, / And makes both one, each this and that'. Cf. 'Any Wife to any Husband', 50: 'our inmost beings met and mixed'.
132 *the great Word*: Rev. 21: 5. Cf. 2 Cor. 5: 17.

When earth breaks up and heaven expands,
　　How will the change strike me and you
In the house not made with hands?   135

XXVIII.

Oh I must feel your brain prompt mine,
　　Your heart anticipate my heart,
You must be just before, in fine,
　　See and make me see, for your part,
New depths of the divine!   140

XXIX.

But who could have expected this
　　When we two drew together first
Just for the obvious human bliss,
　　To satisfy life's daily thirst
With a thing men seldom miss?   145

XXX.

Come back with me to the first of all,
　　Let us lean and love it over again,
Let us now forget and now recall,
　　Break the rosary in a pearly rain,
And gather what we let fall!   150

XXXI.

What did I say?—that a small bird sings
　　All day long, save when a brown pair

---

141 *1855P* And who   148 *1855P–56* and then recall,   150 *1855P* And pick
up what

135 *the house not made with hands*: 2 Cor. 5:1: 'For we know that . . . we have a
building of God, an house not made with hands, eternal in the heavens'.
138 *in fine*: in a word.
149 *break the rosary*: cf. Browning to Julia Wedgwood, 'I have expressed it all in-
sufficiently, and will break the chain up, one day, and leave so many separate little
round rings to roll each its way, if it can': Wedgwood, 123, referring to 'James Lee's
Wife'.

Of hawks from the wood float with wide wings
   Strained to a bell: 'gainst noon-day glare
You count the streaks and rings.   155

XXXII.

But at afternoon or almost eve
   'T is better; then the silence grows
To that degree, you half believe
   It must get rid of what it knows,
Its bosom does so heave.   160

XXXIII.

Hither we walked then, side by side,
   Arm in arm and cheek to cheek,
And still I questioned or replied,
   While my heart, convulsed to really speak,
Lay choking in its pride.   165

XXXIV.

Silent the crumbling bridge we cross,
   And pity and praise the chapel sweet,
And care about the fresco's loss,
   And wish for our souls a like retreat,
And wonder at the moss.   170

XXXV.

Stoop and kneel on the settle under,
   Look through the window's grated square:
Nothing to see! For fear of plunder,
   The cross is down and the altar bare,
As if thieves don't fear thunder.   175

154 *1855P, 1855, 1863–65S* 'gainst the noon-day   *1856* 'gainst the noonday
173 *1855P–65S* for

154 *to a bell*: to the shape of a bell, as hawks close their wings.
164 *convulsed*: too deeply moved.
171 *settle*: bench.
175 *As if thieves*: thieves would be superstitiously afraid of stealing from a church.

XXXVI.

We stoop and look in through the grate,
  See the little porch and rustic door,
Read duly the dead builder's date;
  Then cross the bridge that we crossed before,
Take the path again—but wait!   180

XXXVII.

Oh moment, one and infinite!
  The water slips o'er stock and stone;
The West is tender, hardly bright:
  How grey at once is the evening grown—
One star, its chrysolite!   185

XXXVIII.

We two stood there with never a third,
  But each by each, as each knew well:
The sights we saw and the sounds we heard,
  The lights and the shades made up a spell
Till the trouble grew and stirred.   190

XXXIX.

Oh, the little more, and how much it is!
And the little less, and what worlds away!

---

178 *1855–63* date,   179 *1855P–68* bridge we   183 *1855, 1856* bright.
185 *1855P–68* star, the chrysolite!   187 *1855, 1856* well.

181 *Oh moment, one and infinite!*: cf. 'The Last Ride Together', 108, and Browning's description of poetry as 'a putting of the infinite within the finite'.

185 *its chrysolite!*: a name given to several different gems, including topaz. Some of its associations are indicated in George F. Kunz, *The Curious Lore of Precious Stones* (Philadelphia, 1913, repr. New York 1971). It was said that it could only be seen in the dark. There was a belief that it could dissolve enchantments and put evil spirits to flight: see his p. 67.

190 *the trouble*: probably Browning's premature declaration of love, in May 1845, which deeply disconcerted EBB. He asked her for his letter back, and destroyed it: see Kintner, i. 72. If this is the reference, it emphasizes that the poem is an imaginative work, though inspired by reality, since the declaration of course occurred before Browning and EBB went to Italy.

191 *Oh, the little more*: It. 'il poco più' and 'il poco meno', the little more and the little less: terms used in music, and in art-criticism: 'Just heaven! how does the *poco più*

How a sound shall quicken content to bliss,
  Or a breath suspend the blood's best play,
And life be a proof of this!   195

XL.

Had she willed it, still had stood the screen
  So slight, so sure, 'twixt my love and her:
I could fix her face with a guard between,
  And find her soul as when friends confer,
Friends—lovers that might have been.   200

XLI.

For my heart had a touch of the woodland-time,
  Wanting to sleep now over its best.
Shake the whole tree in the summer-prime,
  But bring to the last leaf no such test!
"Hold the last fast!" runs the rhyme.   205

XLII.

For a chance to make your little much,
  To gain a lover and lose a friend,
Venture the tree and a myriad such,
  When nothing you mar but the year can mend:
But a last leaf—fear to touch!   210

196 *1855P* willed so, still   197 *1855, 1856* her.   200 *1855P* been—
202 *1855P* best: 204 *1855P* bring the . . . . leaf to no . . . . test,   *1855, 1856* test.
1863–65S test: 205 *1855P–56* fast!" says the   208 *1855P* Tug though you
venture a . . . . such;   209 *1855P* Nothing   *1855–63* mend!   210 *1855,*
1856 touch.

and the *Poco meno* of the Italian artists; the insensible, more or less, determine the precise
line of beauty . . . in the statue!': Laurence Sterne, *Tristram Shandy*, II. vi.

  195 *life*: one's whole life.
  200 *lovers that might have been*: a favourite theme of Browning's, as in 'The Statue and
the Bust', 'Youth and Art', and 'Dîs aliter Visum'.
  201 *a touch of the woodland time*: cf. 54–5. The speaker was in autumnal mood. He felt
that this was no time to shake the tree, to get its fruit: one should not risk touching the
last leaf. What would be best of all would be if the leaf came eddying down to him. (It is
a common superstition that it is lucky if one catches a falling leaf, or if it settles on one.)
  205 *'Hold the last first'*: we have not found the rhyme.
  209 *When nothing you mar*: when you do no damage which the year will not be able
to put right, as it progresses.

XLIII.

Yet should it unfasten itself and fall
   Eddying down till it find your face
At some slight wind—best chance of all!
   Be your heart henceforth its dwelling-place
You trembled to forestall!   215

XLIV.

Worth how well, those dark grey eyes,
   That hair so dark and dear, how worth
That a man should strive and agonize,
   And taste a veriest hell on earth
For the hope of such a prize!   220

XLV.

You might have turned and tried a man,
   Set him a space to weary and wear,
And prove which suited more your plan,
   His best of hope or his worst despair,
Yet end as he began.   225

XLVI.

But you spared me this, like the heart you are,
   And filled my empty heart at a word.

---

212 *1855P* Eddying it down   213 *1855, 1856* (best . . . . all!)   *1863* (best . . . . all)
217 *1855P* so brown and   219 *1855P–68* a very hell   221 *1855P–65S* Oh,
you   222 *1855P* him such a   225 *1855P* And end   *1865S* began!
227 *1855P* filled up my . . . . word:

---

213 *chance*: luck, since many believe that it is lucky to catch a falling leaf.
216–17 *Worth how well . . . how worth*: valuable, deserving. An unusual construction.
222 *to weary and wear*: as in 'James Lee's Wife', 114. OED² cites James VI and I, *A Counterblast to Tobacco*, 'weaken, wearie and weare nature' (ed. Arber, 108).
223 *prove*: discover.
226 *heart*: a term of endearment, as in *Othello*, I. iii. 301.
227 *filled my empty heart*: cf. 'The Statue and the Bust', 15 and 25 ff.

If two lives join, there is oft a scar,
　　They are one and one, with a shadowy third;
One near one is too far.　　　　　　　　　　230

XLVII.

A moment after, and hands unseen
　　Were hanging the night around us fast;
But we knew that a bar was broken between
　　Life and life: we were mixed at last
In spite of the mortal screen.　　　　　　235

XLVIII.

The forests had done it; there they stood;
　　We caught for a moment the powers at play:
They had mingled us so, for once and good,
　　Their work was done—we might go or stay,
They relapsed to their ancient mood.　　　240

XLIX.

How the world is made for each of us!
　　How all we perceive and know in it
Tends to some moment's product thus,
　　When a soul declares itself—to wit,
By its fruit, the thing it does!　　　　　245

228 *1855P–63* If you join two lives, there　　230 *1855P* One beside one
232 *1855, 1856* fast.　　　237 *1855P–63* a second the　　238 *1855P* us here for
1855P–65S and for good,　　242 *1855P* we see and

230 *one near one is too far*: one other ('a shadowy third') near either of the lovers
prevents their lives joining perfectly.
231 *hands unseen*: Cook, 134, points out how 'the world is seen as a stage' here.
234 *we were mixed at last*: cf. 127–8 and n.; and RB to EBB, 25 December 1845: 'that
I may forever,—certainly during our mortal "forever"—mix my love for you, and . . .
your love for me': Kintner i. 343.
235 *the mortal screen*: cf. 196.
236 *The forests*: 'the very sound of a "forest" is something peculiarly delightful and
untried to me. I know hills well . . . but now I want forests, or quite, quite mountains,
such as you have not in England': *Letters of EBB*, i. 370 (1848).
237 *the powers*: supernatural agencies.
238 *They had mingled us*: cf. Donne, 'To Sir Henry Wotton', l: 'Sir, more than kisses,
letters mingle souls', and Browning, 'Cristina', 40.
245 *By its fruit*: cf. Matt. 7: 16 etc.

L.

Be hate that fruit or love that fruit,
  It forwards the general deed of man,
And each of the Many helps to recruit
  The life of the race by a general plan;
Each living his own, to boot.   250

LI.

I am named and known by that moment's feat;
  There took my station and degree;
So grew my own small life complete,
  As nature obtained her best of me—
One born to love you, sweet!   255

LII.

And to watch you sink by the fire-side now
  Back again, as you mutely sit
Musing by fire-light, that great brow
  And the spirit-small hand propping it,
Yonder, my heart knows how!   260

LIII.

So, earth has gained by one man the more,
  And the gain of earth must be heaven's gain too;
And the whole is well worth thinking o'er
  When autumn comes: which I mean to do
One day, as I said before.   265

---

247 *1855P* It goes to the   *1884S* man: 248 *1855P* the millions helps recruit
249 *1855P–56* plan,   250 *1855P* Each man with his   251 *1855P–56* that
hour's feat,   *1863* that hour's feat;   252 *1855P* So took   *1855, 1856* degree.
253 *1855P* There grew   261 *1855P–56* So the earth   *1863–68* So, the earth
1855P–68 man more,   262 *1855P–65* too,   264 *1855P–63* When the
autumn

---

256 *by the fire-side*: cf. RB to EBB (1846): 'there is a chair . . . which occupies the
precise place, stands just in the same relation to *this* chair I sit on now, that yours stands
in and occupies—to the left of the fire: and, how often, how *always* I turn in the dusk
and *see* the dearest real Ba with me': Kintner, i. 555. See 112 ff, above.

ANY WIFE TO ANY HUSBAND

WITH 'A Lovers' Quarrel', 'A Woman's Last Word', 'In A Year' and 'Another Way of Love', this is one of five poems in *Men and Women* in which the speaker is a woman. It may be read in relation to EBB's *Sonnets from the Portuguese*, written by her during the courtship. Whereas the sonnets are subjective, however, this poem is dramatic. Unlike the speaker here, EBB wished her husband to marry again after her death, brushing aside his passionate denial of any such possibility: see our note to the last line of the poem.

The style is much more emphatic and conversational than that of the *Sonnets*. Each stanza consists of six iambic pentameters, rhyming *aabccb*. The pentameter base is handled with remarkable freedom.

Date: 1853/4
1863: Dramatic Lyrics

ANY WIFE TO ANY HUSBAND.

I.

My love, this is the bitterest, that thou—
Who art all truth, and who dost love me now
  As thine eyes say, as thy voice breaks to say—
Shouldst love so truly, and couldst love me still
A whole long life through, had but love its will,   5
  Would death that leads me from thee brook delay.

II.

I have but to be by thee, and thy hand
Will never let mine go, nor heart withstand
  The beating of my heart to reach its place.

---

6 *1855P* And death . . . . thee brooked delay!   *1855–65S* delay!   8 *1855P–63*
Would never   *1855P–56* go, thy heart   9 *1855P* place:

When shall I look for thee and feel thee gone?   10
When cry for the old comfort and find none?
      Never, I know! Thy soul is in thy face.

III.

Oh, I should fade—'t is willed so! Might I save,
Gladly I would, whatever beauty gave
      Joy to thy sense, for that was precious too.   15
It is not to be granted. But the soul
Whence the love comes, all ravage leaves that whole;
      Vainly the flesh fades; soul makes all things new.

IV.

It would not be because my eye grew dim
Thou couldst not find the love there, thanks to Him   20
      Who never is dishonoured in the spark
He gave us from his fire of fires, and bade
Remember whence it sprang, nor be afraid
      While that burns on, though all the rest grow dark.

V.

So, how thou wouldst be perfect, white and clean   25
      Outside as inside, soul and soul's demesne

10 *1855P–63* When should I   *1855P* gone,   13 *1855P* should change—'tis . . . .
so! could I   *1855–65S* might   19 *1855–63* And 'twould not   *1865, 1865S* And
't would not   21 *1855P* Who will not be dishonoured   23 *1855P* it sprung,
nor   24 *1855P* rest grew dark.

12 *Thy soul is in thy face*: cf. Cicero, *Orator* 60: 'nam ut imago est animi vultus, sic
indices oculi': proverbial.
17 *all ravage leaves that whole*: cf. RB to EBB, Kintner, i. 531: 'what I build my future
on . . . is that one belief that you *will not alter*, will just remain as you are—meaning by
"*you*," the love in you, the qualities I have *known* . . . Keeping these, if it be God's will
that the body passes,—what is that?'
18 *soul makes all things new*: cf. Rev. 21: 5.
21 *the spark*: cf. Pope, 'The Dying Christian to his Soul', 1–2: 'Vital spark of heav'nly
flame! / Quit, oh quit this mortal frame.'
22 *his fire of fires*: 'Fire is a symbol of the holiness and justice of God': Cruden,
referring to Deut. 4: 24 etc.
26 *outside as inside*: cf. Luke 11: 39.
    demesne: realm.

Alike, this body given to show it by!
Oh, three-parts through the worst of life's abyss,
What plaudits from the next world after this,
    Couldst thou repeat a stroke and gain the sky!   30

VI.

And is it not the bitterer to think
That, disengage our hands and thou wilt sink
    Although thy love was love in very deed?
I know that nature! Pass a festive day,
Thou dost not throw its relic-flower away   35
    Nor bid its music's loitering echo speed.

VII.

Thou let'st the stranger's glove lie where it fell;
If old things remain old things all is well,
    For thou art grateful as becomes man best:
And hadst thou only heard me play one tune,   40
Or viewed me from a window, not so soon
    With thee would such things fade as with the rest.

VIII.

I seem to see! We meet and part; 't is brief;
The book I opened keeps a folded leaf,
    The very chair I sat on, breaks the rank;   45
That is a portrait of me on the wall—
Three lines, my face comes at so slight a call:
    And for all this, one little hour to thank!

---

33 *1855P* Because thy   *34 {reading of *1865–84S*, DC, BrU, *1889*} *1855P–63*,
1888 day   36 *1855P* Or bid   37 *1855P* fell,   38 *1855P* things keep but
old   43 *1855–65S* we   48 *1855P* little hour's to thank: *1855–63* little
hour's to thank.

---

30 *repeat a stroke*: one of Johnson's definitions of 'stroke' is 'a masterly or eminent
effort'.
    gain the sky: reach the heights.
35 *relic-flower*: probably Browning's coinage.
37 *the stranger's glove*: thrown in his path in coquetry.
45 *breaks the rank*: has not been put back in its place.

IX.

But now, because the hour through years was fixed,
Because our inmost beings met and mixed,   50
   Because thou once hast loved me—wilt thou dare
Say to thy soul and Who may list beside,
"Therefore she is immortally my bride;
   "Chance cannot change my love, nor time impair.

X.

"So, what if in the dusk of life that's left,   55
"I, a tired traveller of my sun bereft,
   "Look from my path when, mimicking the same,
"The fire-fly glimpses past me, come and gone?
"—Where was it till the sunset? where anon
   "It will be at the sunrise! What's to blame?"   60

XI.

Is it so helpful to thee? Canst thou take
The mimic up, nor, for the true thing's sake,
   Put gently by such efforts at a beam?
Is the remainder of the way so long,
Thou need'st the little solace, thou the strong?   65
   Watch out thy watch, let weak ones doze and dream!

---

53 *1855P–63* bride,   54 *1855P* change that love . . . . impair—   *1855, 1856*
change that love,   56 *1855P* A foot-sore traveller of his sun   57 *1855P* from
his path   58 *1855P* past him, come . . . . gone—   60 *1855P* sunrise: what's
1855–65S what's   61 *1855P–65S* canst   63 *1865S* such effort at
65 *1855P* need'st their little

---

50 *our inmost beings met and mixed*: cf. Donne, 'The Ecstasy', 35–6: 'Love, these mixed
souls doth mix again, / And makes both one, each this and that'. Cf. 'By the Fire-Side',
127–8.

54 *Chance cannot change my love*: cf. Shakespeare, *Sonnets*, CXVI. 2–4: 'Love is not
love / Which alters when it alteration finds, / Or bends with the remover to remove'.
   nor time impair: cf. Young, *Night Thoughts*, vii. 985–6: 'But Truth / No Years
impair'. EBB owned the poem: Kelley and Coley, A 2510.

55 *the dusk of life*: cf. Young, *The Centaur not Fabulous*, v: 'To grope out our weary
way, through the dusk of life, to our final home'.

66 *thy watch*: in the military sense, spell of duty.

XII.

—Ah, but the fresher faces! "Is it true,"
Thou'lt ask, "some eyes are beautiful and new?
    "Some hair,—how can one choose but grasp such wealth?
"And if a man would press his lips to lips   70
"Fresh as the wilding hedge-rose-cup there slips
    "The dew-drop out of, must it be by stealth?

XIII.

"It cannot change the love still kept for Her,
"More than if such a picture I prefer
    "Passing a day with, to a room's bare side: 75
The painted form takes nothing she possessed,
Yet, while the Titian's Venus lies at rest,
    A man looks. Once more, what is there to chide?"

XIV.

So must I see, from where I sit and watch,
My own self sell myself, my hand attach   80
    Its warrant to the very thefts from me—
Thy singleness of soul that made me proud,
Thy purity of heart I loved aloud,
    Thy man's-truth I was bold to bid God see!

XV.

Love so, then, if thou wilt! Give all thou canst   85

67 *1855P–65S* "—Ah, ... faces! Is   *1855P* true,   68 *1855P* Or not, some
71 *1855P* wilding hedge-cup-rose there   73 *1855P* "As if it changed the love kept
still for   *1855, 1856* love kept still for   74 *1855P* Much more than such
1855–63 Much more than, such   *1855P–63* picture to prefer   75 *1855, 1856* side.
78 *1855P* I gaze—and, once   *82 {reading of *1855P–84S*} *1888, 1889* proud.
85 *1855P* Love them, then,

  67 *the fresher faces!*: cf. Kintner, ii. 650: 'Dearest beloved, when I used to tell you to
give me up, & imagined to myself how I should feel if you did it . . . the chief *pang* was
the idea of another woman!'
  71 *the wilding hedge-rose-cup*: cf. Scott, *The Lady of the Lake*, IV. i. 5.
  77 *the Titian's Venus*: Tiziano Vecellio or Vecelli (*c.*1485–1576). Titian painted Venus
on many occasions. The painting most likely to be in Browning's mind is the 'Venus of
Urbino', in the Uffizi in Florence.

Away to the new faces—disentranced,
  (Say it and think it) obdurate no more:
Re-issue looks and words from the old mint,
Pass them afresh, no matter whose the print
  Image and superscription once they bore!   90

XVI.

Re-coin thyself and give it them to spend,—
It all comes to the same thing at the end,
  Since mine thou wast, mine art and mine shalt be,
Faithful or faithless, sealing up the sum
Or lavish of my treasure, thou must come   95
  Back to the heart's place here I keep for thee!

XVII.

Only, why should it be with stain at all?
Why must I, 'twixt the leaves of coronal,
  Put any kiss of pardon on thy brow?
Why need the other women know so much,   100
And talk together, "Such the look and such
  "The smile he used to love with, then as now!"

XVIII.

Might I die last and show thee! Should I find

87 *1855P* (Say so and think so) obdurate   *1855P–75* more,   93 *1865S* be;
94 *1872S, 1884S* faithless: 95 *1855P* my hoard,—at last shalt come   101 *1855P*
"such   103 *1855P* should

  86 *disentranced*: freed from my spell over him. Cf. *Sordello*, vi. 351.

  87 *obdurate*: unyielding.

  88 *Re-issue*: imagery from coining is particularly common in seventeenth-century poetry. Cf., e.g., *Julius Caesar*, IV. iii. 72, and Donne, 'A Valediction :of Weeping', 3–4.

  92 *the same thing at the end*: proverbial.

  90 *Image and superscription*: Matt. 22: 20, Luke 20: 24.

  94 *sealing up the sum*: making up your book. Cf. Ezeki. 28: 12: 'Thou sealest up the sum'.

  98 *coronal*: garland.

  103 *Might I die last*: Cf. *Sonnets from the Portuguese*, XLIII. 13–4: 'and, if God choose, / I shall but love thee better after death'.

Such hardship in the few years left behind,
    If free to take and light my lamp, and go   105
Into thy tomb, and shut the door and sit,
Seeing thy face on those four sides of it
    The better that they are so blank, I know!

XIX.

Why, time was what I wanted, to turn o'er
Within my mind each look, get more and more   110
    By heart each word, too much to learn at first;
And join thee all the fitter for the pause
'Neath the low doorway's lintel. That were cause
    For lingering, though thou calledst, if I durst!

XX.

And yet thou art the nobler of us two: 115
What dare I dream of, that thou canst not do,
    Outstripping my ten small steps with one stride?
I'll say then, here's a trial and a task—
Is it to bear?—if easy, I'll not ask:
    Though love fail, I can trust on in thy pride.   120

XXI.

Pride?—when those eyes forestall the life behind
The death I have to go through!—when I find,

104 *1870–84S* Such hardships in   111 *1855, 1856* first,   112 *1855P* To join
113 *1855P* lintel—that   *1865S* lintel: that   114 *1855P* thou call me, if
115 *1855, 1856* two.   120 *1855P* can hold on by thy   122 *1855P* through—

106 *Into thy tomb*: if this was suggested by Eumolpus' tale of the widow of Ephesus in the *Satyricon* of Petronius Arbiter (sect. 111), the speaker is telling us that she would have behaved very differently. Browning owned the book: Kelley and Coley, A 1841.

108 *so blank*: cf. l. 75.

113 *the low doorway's lintel*: that of the tomb. Cf. Dunbar, 'In Wintir'; 38–9: 'Albeid that thow wer never sa stout, / Undir this Lyntall sall thou lowt'.

115 *thou art the nobler*: the traditional belief. Cf. EBB, *Sonnets from the Portuguese*, XVI, 2: 'thou art more noble and like a king'.

Now that I want thy help most, all of thee!
What did I fear? Thy love shall hold me fast
Until the little minute's sleep is past   125
And I wake saved.—And yet it will not be!

123 *1855P* Now, when I   126 *1855P* saved!—

125 *the little minute's sleep*: a traditional image.

126 *it will not be!*: i.e. unlike the speaker here, EBB was determined that Browning should not feel bound to refrain from another marriage, after her (anticipated) death. 'I've stopped him twenty times in such vows as never to take another wife, & the like', she wrote to Arabella in 1854. '. . I've held his lips together with both hands . . I wouldn't have it!': PK 54: 55.

AN EPISTLE

CONTAINING THE STRANGE MEDICAL EXPERIENCE OF
KARSHISH, THE ARAB PHYSICIAN.

As Maureen Wright pointed out in the TLS for 1 May 1853,[1] 'Karshish' represents Arabic *qāsiš*, 'one who gathers', commonly with reference to gathering sticks or straw. She added that the parallel verb in Hebrew, *qāšaš*, has the same meaning, citing Exod. 5: 7 and 1 Kgs. 17: 12. Browning could read Hebrew, though his knowledge of the language has been described as 'limited'.[2]

The source of the poem is John 11, where we read how Lazarus of Bethany[3] was sick, and died, and how, four days after his death, Christ came to his grave, and cried 'Lazarus, come forth':

And he that was dead came forth, bound hand and foot with graveclothes: and his face was bound about with a napkin. Jesus said unto them, Loose him, and let him go.

Then many of the Jews which . . . had seen the things which Jesus did, believed on him.

This is the famous chapter in which Christ proclaims: 'I am the resurrection, and the life: he that believeth in me, though he were dead, yet shall he live'. Browning will have known it from his earliest days.

We note that the poem is an 'Epistle', and that its opening follows the standard formula for ancient letters, exemplified in Rom. 1: 1–7 and at the beginning of 1 and 2 Corinthians, and Galatians.

EBB was deeply disconcerted to find that her sister Henrietta failed to understand the poem. Telling her that she had been '*right* and *kind* to be frank and tell us your secret mind about Lazarus', she continued:

And you must do *us* justice, and understand that no want of reverence, much less blasphemy, was intended by that poem, the object of which is in the highest degree reverential and Christian. It is one of my great favorites—(and we have this

---

[1] p. 285. 'The word qāshish is the active participle of the Arabic verb qāshash, to gather . . . The "r" in Browning's spelling of the word is there in order to ensure the correct pronunciation with the long letter "a" '.

[2] Arnold Cheskin, ' 'Tis only the Coat of a Page to borrow': BSN 1990, 31.

[3] Not to be confused with Lazarus in Luke 16: 20, in the parable of the beggar and the rich man.

morning a letter from Mr. Ruskin, author of the Stones of Venice, a most Christian man, calling it his favorite,)[1] and among all the criticisms we have heard, private and public, such an idea as yours seems to have occurred to no one.

The Arabian physician considers the case of Lazarus as "a case"—represents it as such a man would, who had never heard of Christ before, or conceived of the miracle. It is a view *from without* of the raising from the dead, &c—and shows how this must have impressed the thinkers of the day, who came upon it with wondering, unbelieving eyes, for the first time. The way in which Lazarus is described as living his life after his acquaintance with the life beyond death, strikes me as entirely sublime, I confess.[2]

To her other sister Arabella she expressed her astonishment at such misunderstanding: 'Can any one say rationally that the poem is not for the honour of the Lord? It seems to me wonderful that a dramatic intention should be so mistaken'.

Sharp tells us that this poem was written 'in part' in Rome during the Brownings' visit there (from late November 1853 to late May 1854).[3] It invites comparison with other of Browning's poems, such as *Paracelsus*, 'Saul', 'Imperante Augusto Natus Est', 'A Death in the Desert', and particularly 'Cleon'.

Date: 1854
1863: *Men and Women*

---

[1] 'I can't say I have really made out any one yet', Ruskin wrote in the depressing letter we have quoted above (pp. xxxii ff), 'except the epistle from the Arabian physician, which I like immensely.'
[2] Huxley, 235–6. Cf. PK 55: 161.
[3] p. 166.

AN EPISTLE

CONTAINING THE STRANGE MEDICAL EXPERIENCE OF
KARSHISH, THE ARAB PHYSICIAN.

KARSHISH, the picker-up of learning's crumbs,
The not-incurious in God's handiwork
(This man's-flesh he hath admirably made,
Blown like a bubble, kneaded like a paste,
To coop up and keep down on earth a space   5
That puff of vapour from his mouth, man's soul)
—To Abib, all-sagacious in our art,
Breeder in me of what poor skill I boast,
Like me inquisitive how pricks and cracks
Befall the flesh through too much stress and strain,   10
Whereby the wily vapour fain would slip
Back and rejoin its source before the term,—
And aptest in contrivance (under God)
To baffle it by deftly stopping such:—
The vagrant Scholar to his Sage at home   15

Title:*1855P* THE MEDICAL . . . . OF BEN KARSHISH,   *1884S* EPISTLE.
3 *1855P* This   6 *1855P* soul—   13 *1855P–65* contrivance, under God,

---

1 *Karshish*: see introduction. 'Cf. Matthew 15: 27, where a non-Israelite woman claims help from Jesus, saying: "yet the dogs eat of the crumbs which fall from their masters' table". Thus the non-Christian Karshish is picking up crumbs of Christianity': Turner.

2 *God's handiwork*: cf. Ps. 19: 1. See too Quarles, *Emblems*, iii. 10. 26: 'I am thy handy-work, thy creature, LORD', For Browning and Quarles see Vol. I, p. 157 n.

3 *admirably made*: cf. *Hamlet*, II. ii. 303.

4 *Blown like a bubble*: cf. Edward Young, *Love of Fame*, ii, last para.: 'What are men . . . But *bubbles* on the rapid stream of Time?'

   paste: 'The material of which a person is figuratively said to be made': OED², 'Paste', sb. 4.

5 *a space*: for a while.

6 *That puff of vapour*. 'For what is your life? It is even a vapour, that appeareth for a little time, and then vanisheth away': Jas. 4: 14. Cf. 'Fra Lippo Lippi', 184–6.

7 *Abib*: like Karshish, an imaginary person. Cf. the Arabic name Habīb, literally 'friend'.
12 *the term*: the due time.

15 *vagrant*: wandering. We are reminded of *Paracelsus*, and of 'The Scholar-Gipsy', published in Arnold's *Poems. A New Edition* in November 1853.

Sends greeting (health and knowledge, fame with peace)
Three samples of true snakestone—rarer still,
One of the other sort, the melon-shaped,
(But fitter, pounded fine, for charms than drugs)
And writeth now the twenty-second time.   20

My journeyings were brought to Jericho:
Thus I resume. Who studious in our art
Shall count a little labour unrepaid?
I have shed sweat enough, left flesh and bone
On many a flinty furlong of this land.   25
Also, the country-side is all on fire
With rumours of a marching hitherward:
Some say Vespasian cometh, some, his son.
A black lynx snarled and pricked a tufted ear;
Lust of my blood inflamed his yellow balls: 30
I cried and threw my staff and he was gone.
Twice have the robbers stripped and beaten me,
And once a town declared me for a spy;
But at the end, I reach Jerusalem,
Since this poor covert where I pass the night,   35
This Bethany, lies scarce the distance thence

---

16 *1855P*   greeting,   health . . . . peace,   19 *1855P* But . . . . drugs,—
21 *1855P–56* Jericho,   28 *1855P* son—   29 *1855P* ear,   30 *1855P*
balls.   33 *1855P* spy.   *1855–63* spy,

17 *snakestone*: 'A porous or absorbent substance regarded as efficacious in curing snake-bite or as a remedy against poison': OED².

21 *Jericho*: an important town some five miles north of the Dead Sea.

26 *all on fire*: cf. *Henry V*, Act II, Chorus: 'Now all the youth of England are on fire'.

27 *marching hitherward*: as in *King Lear*, IV. iv. 21.

28 *Vespasian cometh*: this would date the epistle to AD 69/70. Titus Flavius Vespasianus was emperor 69–79. In 66 Nero had appointed him to quell the Jewish rebellion; proclaiming himself emperor he deputed his eldest son to carry on the war in Palestine. In 71 father and son celebrated a magnificent triumph for the capture of Jerusalem.

29 *A black lynx*: 'the Syrian lynx is distinguished by black ears': Porter and Clarke.

30 *balls*: eyeballs.

36 *Bethany*: 'Now Bethany was nigh unto Jerusalem, about fifteen furlongs off': John 11: 18. On the eastern slope of the Mount of Olives, it was a favourite retreat of Jesus, and the home of Lazarus.

A man with plague-sores at the third degree
Runs till he drops down dead. Thou laughest here!
'Sooth, it elates me, thus reposed and safe,
To void the stuffing of my travel-scrip   40
And share with thee whatever Jewry yields.
A viscid choler is observable
In tertians, I was nearly bold to say;
And falling-sickness hath a happier cure
Than our school wots of: there's a spider here   45
Weaves no web, watches on the ledge of tombs,
Sprinkled with mottles on an ash-grey back;
Take five and drop them . . . but who knows his mind,
The Syrian runagate I trust this to?
His service payeth me a sublimate   50
Blown up his nose to help the ailing eye.
Best wait: I reach Jerusalem at morn,
There set in order my experiences,
Gather what most deserves, and give thee all—

---

43 *1855P–63* say,   *48 {reading of *1855P–84S*} *1888, 1889* them . .   51
1855P eye:

   37 *plague-sores*: cf. *King Lear*, II. iv. 223.
     degree: stage of development.
   40 *void the stuffing*: empty out the contents.
     scrip: a small bag or satchel, especially one carried by a pilgrim.
   41 *Jewry*: Judaea (sometimes the whole of Palestine).
   42 *A viscid choler*: sticky bile.
   43 *tertians*: fevers or agues characterized 'by the occurrence of a paroxysm every third
(i.e. every alternate) day': OED.
   44 *falling-sickness*: epilepsy, as in *Julius Caesar*, I. ii. 250 ff.
   45 *school*: of medical men.
     wots of: knows (arch.)
     a spider: spiders were long believed to possess an occult power of healing, whether
administered internally or applied externally. Pliny cites a number of such remedies.
The reference is to one of the species of 'jumping spiders', which do not weave webs
and are variously coloured.
   47 *mottles*: spots or blotches.
   49 *runagate*: deserter, fugitive, or vagabond.
   50 *payeth*: pays for.
     sublimate: a powder derived from a solid which has been heated to a vapour, often
(as here) for inhalation.

Or I might add, Judæa's gum-tragacanth   55
Scales off in purer flakes, shines clearer-grained,
Cracks 'twixt the pestle and the porphyry,
In fine exceeds our produce. Scalp-disease
Confounds me, crossing so with leprosy—
Thou hadst admired one sort I gained at Zoar—   60
But zeal outruns discretion. Here I end.

    Yet stay: my Syrian blinketh gratefully,
Protesteth his devotion is my price—
Suppose I write what harms not, though he steal?
I half resolve to tell thee, yet I blush,   65
What set me off a-writing first of all.
An itch I had, a sting to write, a tang!
For, be it this town's barrenness—or else
The Man had something in the look of him—
His case has struck me far more than 't is worth.   70
So, pardon if—(lest presently I lose
In the great press of novelty at hand
The care and pains this somehow stole from me)
I bid thee take the thing while fresh in mind,
Almost in sight—for, wilt thou have the truth?   75
The very man is gone from me but now,
Whose ailment is the subject of discourse.
Thus then, and let thy better wit help all!

62 *1872S, 1884S* stay!   *1855P* gratefully;   65 *1855P* thee, though I
70 *1855P* than it's worth.   78 *1855P–65* all.

    55 *gum tragacanth*: a substance obtained from certain spiny shrubs of the genus
Astragalus and used as a vehicle for drugs.
    57 *porphyry*: slabs or blocks of porphyry were used for grinding drugs on.
    58 *Scalp-disease*: such as psoriasis, perhaps.
    59 *crossing so*: seeming so similar.
    admired: wondered at.
    Zoar: the one of the five cities of the plain which was spared: Gen. 19: 20–3, cf.
Deut. 29: 23.
    63 *price*: payment.
    67 *tang*: desire.
    71 *presently*: soon.
    72 *press of novelty*: crowd of new things.
    78 *wit*: understanding.

'T is but a case of mania—subinduced
By epilepsy, at the turning-point   80
Of trance prolonged unduly some three days:
When, by the exhibition of some drug
Or spell, exorcization, stroke of art
Unknown to me and which 't were well to know,
The evil thing out-breaking all at once   85
Left the man whole and sound of body indeed,—
But, flinging (so to speak) life's gates too wide,
Making a clear house of it too suddenly,
The first conceit that entered might inscribe
Whatever it was minded on the wall   90
So plainly at that vantage, as it were,
(First come, first served) that nothing subsequent
Attaineth to erase those fancy-scrawls
The just-returned and new-established soul
Hath gotten now so thoroughly by heart   95
That henceforth she will read or these or none.
And first—the man's own firm conviction rests
That he was dead (in fact they buried him)
—That he was dead and then restored to life
By a Nazarene physician of his tribe: 100
—'Sayeth, the same bade "Rise," and he did rise.

---

81 *1855P–63* days,   84 *1855P* which were fit to   *{reading of *1855P–84S*, DC,
BrU, *1889*} *1888* know   87 *1855P–65* flinging, so . . . . speak, life's
*{reading of *1855P–84S*, DC, BrU, *1889*} *1888* wide   89 *1855P–56* entered pleased
to write   *91 {reading of *1855P–84S*, DC, BrU, *1889*} *1888* were   93 *1855P*
erase her fancy-scrawls;   *1855, 1856* erase the fancy-scrawls   94 *1855P* And the
returned and   *1855, 1856* Which the returned and   95 *1855P* Hath got them
now   96 *1863S* or those or   100 *1855P* a Nazarite physician

79 *subinduced*: brought about as a consequence of.
81 *some three days*: four days, according to John 11: 17.
82 *exhibition*: in a medical sense, the administration of a remedy: OED² II. 4.
89 *conceit*: notion.
90 *was minded*: wished.
92 *First come, first served*: proverbial: ODEP.
100 *Nazarene*: 'Nazarite' (*1855P*) is an error, since a Nazarite is quite different from
a Nazarene: cf. 'Holy Cross Day', 10 n.
101 *'Sayeth*: Browning uses this form thrice in this poem, but nowhere else.
   the same bade "Rise": John 11: 43 ff.

"Such cases are diurnal," thou wilt cry.
Not so this figment!—not, that such a fume,
Instead of giving way to time and health,
Should eat itself into the life of life,   105
As saffron tingeth flesh, blood, bones and all!
For see, how he takes up the after-life.
The man—it is one Lazarus a Jew,
Sanguine, proportioned, fifty years of age,
The body's habit wholly laudable,   110
As much, indeed, beyond the common health
As he were made and put aside to show.
Think, could we penetrate by any drug
And bathe the wearied soul and worried flesh,
And bring it clear and fair, by three days' sleep!   115
Whence has the man the balm that brightens all?
This grown man eyes the world now like a child.
Some elders of his tribe, I should premise,
Led in their friend, obedient as a sheep,
To bear my inquisition. While they spoke,   120
Now sharply, now with sorrow,—told the case,—
He listened not except I spoke to him,
But folded his two hands and let them talk,

---

102 *1855P* cry—   120 *1855P* inquisition—while

102 *diurnal*: of daily occurrence.

103 *fume*: 'Idle conceit; vain imagination': Johnson.

107 *the after-life*: possibly playing on the usual sense, 'the life after death', but meaning primarily 'the later part of his life': cf. Scott, *Harold the Dauntless*, VI. xix. 12.

109 *Sanguine*: 'Abounding with blood more than any other humour; cheerful': Johnson.

fifty years of age: the implication of St John's narrative is that the miracle took place in the last months of Jesus' life: since the Crucifixion occurred in the early 30s AD, it would seem that he was nearer 70 than 60 when Karshish was writing.

110 *habit*: state (Johnson).

laudable: 'Healthy; salubrious': Johnson's second sense, which he illustrates from a medical work.

112 *As he were*: as if he were.

114 *And bathe the wearied soul*: cf. Milton, *Comus*, 810–12.

worried: torn, tormented.

116 *balm*: 'Any thing that sooths or mitigates pain': Johnson.

118 *premise*: first explain.

Watching the flies that buzzed: and yet no fool.
And that's a sample how his years must go.   125
Look, if a beggar, in fixed middle-life,
Should find a treasure,—can he use the same
With straitened habits and with tastes starved small,
And take at once to his impoverished brain
The sudden element that changes things,   130
That sets the undreamed-of rapture at his hand
And puts the cheap old joy in the scorned dust?
Is he not such an one as moves to mirth—
Warily parsimonious, when no need,
Wasteful as drunkenness at undue times?   135
All prudent counsel as to what befits
The golden mean, is lost on such an one:
The man's fantastic will is the man's law.
So here—we call the treasure knowledge, say,
Increased beyond the fleshly faculty—   140
Heaven opened to a soul while yet on earth,
Earth forced on a soul's use while seeing heaven:
The man is witless of the size, the sum,
The value in proportion of all things,
Or whether it be little or be much.   145
Discourse to him of prodigious armaments
Assembled to besiege his city now,
And of the passing of a mule with gourds—
'T is one! Then take it on the other side,
Speak of some trifling fact,—he will gaze rapt   150

---

124 *1863S* fool: 128 *1855P–63S* With straightened habits   *1872S, 1884S*
straitened habitude and tastes   130 *1855P* things?   131 *1863S* the
undreamed rapture   133 *1863S* such a one   134 *1855P–56* parsimonious,
when's no   *1855P* need;   137 *1863S* such a one: *1855P* one,   *1855, 1856* one.
138 *1855P* law,   139 *1855P–63* here—we'll call   142 *1855–63* Heaven.

135 *undue*: inappropriate.

137 *The golden mean*: 'Auream quisquis mediocritatem / Diligit': Horace, *Odes*, II.
x. 5–6: 'Whoever loves the golden mean'.

141 *Heaven opened*: Ezek. I: I: 'the heavens were opened, and I saw visions of God':
Cf. Matt. 3: 16 etc.

143 *witless*: without knowledge, unaware, as in the Epilogue to *Dramatis Personæ*, 66.

With stupor at its very littleness,
(Far as I see) as if in that indeed
He caught prodigious import, whole results;
And so will turn to us the bystanders
In ever the same stupor (note this point)   155
That we too see not with his opened eyes.
Wonder and doubt come wrongly into play,
Preposterously, at cross purposes.
Should his child sicken unto death,—why, look
For scarce abatement of his cheerfulness,   160
Or pretermission of the daily craft!
While a word, gesture, glance from that same child
At play or in the school or laid asleep,
Will startle him to an agony of fear,
Exasperation, just as like. Demand   165
The reason why—" 't is but a word," object—
"A gesture"—he regards thee as our lord
Who lived there in the pyramid alone,
Looked at us (dost thou mind?) when, being young,
We both would unadvisedly recite   170
Some charm's beginning, from that book of his,
Able to bid the sun throb wide and burst
All into stars, as suns grown old are wont.
Thou and the child have each a veil alike
Thrown o'er your heads, from under which ye both   175

151 *1855P* stupor from its   156 *1855P* eyes—   *1855–63S* eyes!   157 *1855P*
doubt brought wrongly   161 *1855P* Nor pretermission   *1855–63* of his daily
craft—   *1855P, 1865* craft—   164 *1855P–56* Will start him   165 *1855P* like:
demand   *1855–65* like! demand   166 *1855P* why—'tis but "a   169 *1855P–*
65 us, dost   *1855P–63S* mind, when   *1863, 1865* mind?—when   170 *1863S*
Either would   171 *1855P* beginning in that   173 *1855P* wont—
174 *1855P* and this man's child have a

155 *stupor*: astonishment.
156 *opened*: in the spiritual sense.
158 *Preposterously*: 'In an inverted or reversed order': OED²; or perhaps just 'perversely'.
161 *pretermission*: passing over, neglect.
167 *our lord*: cf. ll. 254–5, below.
169 *mind*: remember (Scots, and North.).

Stretch your blind hands and trifle with a match
Over a mine of Greek fire, did ye know!
He holds on firmly to some thread of life—
(It is the life to lead perforcedly)
Which runs across some vast distracting orb   180
Of glory on either side that meagre thread,
Which, conscious of, he must not enter yet—
The spiritual life around the earthly life:
The law of that is known to him as this,
His heart and brain move there, his feet stay here.   185
So is the man perplext with impulses
Sudden to start off crosswise, not straight on,
Proclaiming what is right and wrong across,
And not along, this black thread through the blaze—
"It should be" baulked by "here it cannot be."   190
And oft the man's soul springs into his face
As if he saw again and heard again
His sage that bade him "Rise" and he did rise.
Something, a word, a tick o' the blood within
Admonishes: then back he sinks at once   195
To ashes, who was very fire before,
In sedulous recurrence to his trade
Whereby he earneth him the daily bread;
And studiously the humbler for that pride,

---

179 *1855P* (Perforcedly it . . . . lead)   183 *1855P* The universal life, the . . . . life,
1855–63 earthly   life!   185 *1855P* here: 186 *1855* impulses.
190 *1855P* be:"   193 *1855P* rise—   *1863S* rise: 194 *1855P–68* tick of the
196 *1855P–63* ashes, that was   199 *1855P* Most studiously

176 *a match*: 'Any thing that catches fire; generally a card, rope, or small chip of wood
dipped in melted sulphur': Johnson.

177 *Greek fire*: 'a combustible composition for setting fire to an enemy's ships, works,
etc.; so called from being first used by the Greeks of Constantinople': OED². An
anachronism, but some form of liquid fire was known earlier.

178 *some thread of life*: 'men direct themselves by a clew of thread in a labyrinth':
Johnson, 'Clew', 2. Cf. 'Mr Sludge', 1457.

179 *perforcedly*: no other example in OED².

184 *as this*: as well as that of this.

190 *"It should be"*: cf. *Macbeth*, I. vii. 44: 'Letting "I dare not" wait upon "I would" '.

194 *a tick*: a twitch, an irregular pulse-beat. Cf. 'Mr. Sludge', 478.

Professedly the faultier that he knows   200
God's secret, while he holds the thread of life.
Indeed the especial marking of the man
Is prone submission to the heavenly will—
Seeing it, what it is, and why it is.
'Sayeth, he will wait patient to the last   205
For that same death which must restore his being
To equilibrium, body loosening soul
Divorced even now by premature full growth:
He will live, nay, it pleaseth him to live
So long as God please, and just how God please.   210
He even seeketh not to please God more
(Which meaneth, otherwise) than as God please.
Hence, I perceive not he affects to preach
The doctrine of his sect whate'er it be,
Make proselytes as madmen thirst to do: 215
How can he give his neighbour the real ground,
His own conviction? Ardent as he is—
Call his great truth a lie, why, still the old
"Be it as God please" reassureth him.
I probed the sore as thy disciple should: 220
"How, beast," said I, "this stolid carelessness
"Sufficeth thee, when Rome is on her march
"To stamp out like a little spark thy town,

206 *1855P–63S* which will restore   210 *1863S* please: 212 *1855P* Which
. . . . otherwise, than   215 *1855, 1856* do.   217 *1855P–65* ardent

────────────

200 *Professedly*: avowedly.
202 *marking*: characteristic.
203 *prone*: i.e. complete.
210 *So long as God please*: subjunctive.
212 *(Which meaneth, otherwise)*: see the XIVth Article of the Church of England, 'Of
Works of Supererogation'.
213 *I perceive not he affects to preach*: in 'Blake and Browning' (MLN 41, November
1926, 464–6) R. D. Havens compares the account of Blake given by Crabb Robinson
with that of Lazarus in this poem. He mentions that Crabb Robinson met Blake in
1852, and the Brownings the same year, and comments that it is possible that he and
Browning discussed Blake 'and that *An Epistle* was influenced by this discussion'. As he
grants, this is a hypothesis, but the fact that John Kenyon was a close friend of the two
poets makes it tempting.
222 *when Rome is on her march*: cf. l. 28 and n.

"Thy tribe, thy crazy tale and thee at once?"
He merely looked with his large eyes on me.   225
The man is apathetic, you deduce?
Contrariwise, he loves both old and young,
Able and weak, affects the very brutes
And birds—how say I? flowers of the field—
As a wise workman recognizes tools   230
In a master's workshop, loving what they make.
Thus is the man as harmless as a lamb:
Only impatient, let him do his best,
At ignorance and carelessness and sin—
An indignation which is promptly curbed: 235
As when in certain travel I have feigned
To be an ignoramus in our art
According to some preconceived design,
And happed to hear the land's practitioners
Steeped in conceit sublimed by ignorance,   240
Prattle fantastically on disease,
Its cause and cure—and I must hold my peace!

      Thou wilt object—Why have I not ere this
Sought out the sage himself, the Nazarene
Who wrought this cure, inquiring at the source,   245
Conferring with the frankness that befits?
Alas! it grieveth me, the learned leech
Perished in a tumult many years ago,
Accused,—our learning's fate,—of wizardry,

228 *1855P* very beasts   231 *1855P* make—   235 *1855P* is curbed by fear;
1855, 1856 curbed.   236 *1855P–63* certain travels I   237 *1863S* Myself an
239 *1872S, 1884S* And happened to   243 *1855P–65* why   *1855P* ere thus

   228 *able*: strong.
   229 *flowers of the field*: cf. Ps. 103. 15, Isai. 40. 6.
   233 *let him do his best*: however hard he tries not to be impatient.
   236 *in certain travel*: like Paracelsus, Karshish is a 'vagrant Scholar' in search of
knowledge wherever he can find it.
   240 *sublimed*: rendered supremely ridiculous.
   246 *befits*: is befitting.
   247 *leech*: 'physician': Johnson.

Rebellion, to the setting up a rule   250
And creed prodigious as described to me.
His death, which happened when the earthquake fell
(Prefiguring, as soon appeared, the loss
To occult learning in our lord the sage
Who lived there in the pyramid alone)   255
Was wrought by the mad people—that's their wont!
On vain recourse, as I conjecture it,
To his tried virtue, for miraculous help—
How could he stop the earthquake? That's their way!
The other imputations must be lies: 260
But take one, though I loathe to give it thee,
In mere respect for any good man's fame.
(And after all, our patient Lazarus
Is stark mad; should we count on what he says?
Perhaps not: though in writing to a leech   265
'T is well to keep back nothing of a case.)
This man so cured regards the curer, then,
As—God forgive me! who but God himself,
Creator and sustainer of the world,
That came and dwelt in flesh on it awhile!   270
—'Sayeth that such an one was born and lived,
Taught, healed the sick, broke bread at his own house,
Then died, with Lazarus by, for aught I know,
And yet was . . . what I said nor choose repeat,
And must have so avouched himself, in fact,   275
In hearing of this very Lazarus
Who saith—but why all this of what he saith?

---

250 *1855P* a crown,   255 *1855P–56* That lived   256 *1855P–63* wont—
261 *1855P* Take but this one—   262 *1855P–63* respect to any   *1855P* fame,
1855–63 fame!   263 *1855P* And   265 *1855P* not—yet in   266 *1855P*
case.   268 *1855P–65* me—   270 *1884S* awhile.   271 *1863S* such a
One   276 *1855P* Lazarus.   277 *1855P* He saith—

251 *prodigious*: amazing.
252 *the earthquake*: Matt. 27: 51.
254 *our lord the sage*: cf. l. 168.
270 *dwelt in flesh*: John 1: 14 etc.

Why write of trivial matters, things of price
Calling at every moment for remark?
I noticed on the margin of a pool   280
Blue-flowering borage, the Aleppo sort,
Aboundeth, very nitrous. It is strange!

   Thy pardon for this long and tedious case,
Which, now that I review it, needs must seem
Unduly dwelt on, prolixly set forth!   285
Nor I myself discern in what is writ
Good cause for the peculiar interest
And awe indeed this man has touched me with.
Perhaps the journey's end, the weariness
Had wrought upon me first. I met him thus: 290
I crossed a ridge of short sharp broken hills
Like an old lion's cheek teeth. Out there came
A moon made like a face with certain spots
Multiform, manifold and menacing:
Then a wind rose behind me. So we met   295
In this old sleepy town at unaware,
The man and I. I send thee what is writ.
Regard it as a chance, a matter risked
To this ambiguous Syrian—he may lose,
Or steal, or give it thee with equal good.   300

---

279 *1855P* for record!   280 *1855P* a lake   285 *1855P–56* forth.
286 *1855P* I discern myself in   292 *1855P* cheek-teeth: out   296 *1884S* at
unawares,

---

278 *of price*: valuable.

281 *Blue-flowering borage*: *Borago officinalis*, which the ancients considered 'one of the
four "cordial flowers", for cheering the spirits; the others being the rose, violet, and
alkanet'. According to Pliny it 'produces very exhilarating effects' (Porter and Clarke).

291–2 *short sharp broken hills / Like an old lion's cheek teeth*: cf. a letter by EBB, 21
August 1853: 'Oh those jagged mountains, rolled together like pre-Adamite beasts &
setting their teeth against the sky!': Raymond and Sullivan, iii. 394. But Browning had
probably already used the same notion in 'Childe Roland', 176–7, 'those two hills on
the right, / Crouched like two bulls'; which may have suggested the image in EBB's
letter.

298 *a chance*: a gamble.

300 *with equal good*: it's all one.

Jerusalem's repose shall make amends
For time this letter wastes, thy time and mine;
Till when, once more thy pardon and farewell!

The very God! think, Abib; dost thou think?
So, the All-Great, were the All-Loving too—   305
So, through the thunder comes a human voice
Saying, "O heart I made, a heart beats here!
"Face, my hands fashioned, see it in myself!
"Thou hast no power nor mayst conceive of mine,
"But love I gave thee, with myself to love,   310
"And thou must love me who have died for thee!"
The madman saith He said so: it is strange.

---

302 *1855–63S* mine,   303 *1855P* Till then, once   306 *1855P* thunder came
a   307 *1855P* "Oh, ... here—   308 *1855P–56* myself.   *1863S–65*
Myself.   *1868* myself,   309 *1884S* mine: *310 {reading of *1855P–84S*,
DC, BrU, *1889*} *1888* love

---

301 *Jerusalem's repose*: cf. l. 34. The quiet time he looks forward to there.

304 *The very God!*: as Symons noted (p. 97), 'As in *Cleon* the very pith of the letter
is contained in the postscript'.

312 *The madman*: Lazarus. Cf. 215, 263–4.

MESMERISM

Franz Anton Mesmer (1733–1815), an Austrian who dabbled in various branches of scientific thought, observed some of the features of what we know as hypnotic suggestion, and devised a system of his own to account for them. In his conception of the underlying unity of everything in nature, and in his tendency to mysticism, he can be regarded as having something in common with Paracelsus. He believed that the planets affect human health, and, fascinated by experiments with electricity, formulated his theory of 'animal magnetism', a phenomenon to which he ascribed hypnotic effects. Discarding the magnets, however, he came to believe that some power of influencing others resided in himself. From the 1780s Paris was excited by his claims; he held exhibitions which had some of the characteristics of the séances of 'mediums'.

In England it was during the 1840s and 1850s that magnetism was most widely discussed. ' "*What are we to believe*" ', wrote a contributor to the *Quarterly Review* in September 1853,

> as to Mesmerism, Electro-Biology, Odylism, Table-Talking, and (we are almost ashamed to be obliged to add) Spirit-Rapping and Table-Turning, is a question which most persons have asked themselves or others during the last few years, and to which the answers have varied with the amount of information possessed by the respondent, with his previous habits of thought, with his love of the marvellous, or his desire to bring everything to the test of sober sense.[1]

In an early letter EBB asked Browning whether he was 'not aware that these are the days of Mesmerism & clairvoyance?', demanding to know whether he was an 'infidel'.[2] She defended mesmerism against the charge that it was associated with religious unbelief. Her friend Harriet Martineau had an enthusiastic interest in the subject, on which she had written seven letters in the *Athenæum* for 1845: she believed that mesmerism had cured her of cancer. Browning, on the other hand, was strongly disposed to be sceptical, describing a French friend of his whose 'poor brains are whirling with mesmerism in which he believes, as in all other unbelief'. Early the next year, however, he was more diplomatic, stressing that he was not wholly opposed: 'Understand that I do *not* disbelieve in Mesmerism—I only object to insufficient evidence being put forward as

---

[1] Vol. xciii, pp. 501–2. [2] Kintner, i. 31, followed by i. 110 and 424.

quite irrefragable—I keep an open sense on the subject—ready to be instructed . . . So, I shall read what you bid me, and learn all I can.' EBB thought it a terrible thing to put oneself in the power of another, but while she was revolted by the idea she was also attracted in spite of herself.

In this she was not alone. Most members of the intellectual class of the age were fascinated by the claims of mesmerism, not least the writers. 'With regard to my opinion on . . . Mesmerism', Dickens wrote in January 1842, 'I have no hesitation in saying that I have closely watched Dr. Elliotson's experiments from the first . . . and that after what I have seen with my own eyes and observed with my own senses, I should be untrue both to him and myself, if I should shrink for a moment from saying that I am a believer, and that I became so against all my precon- ceived opinions.'[1] Charlotte Brontë, Thackeray, and George Eliot were also keenly interested, as were such Continental and American writers as Balzac, E. T. A. Hoffmann and Edgar Allan Poe. Nathaniel Hawthorne, whom Browning described to his American publisher James T. Fields as 'the finest genius that had appeared in English literature for many years',[2] may well have provided the germ of this poem.[3] In *The House of the Seven Gables*, published in 1851, a young man tells the story of an ancestor of his own who had been a mesmerist, one Matthew Maule. By means of his power he had dominated a beautiful young woman, Alice Pyncheon. Whereas the mesmeriser and his subject are usually together at the time of the experiment, we notice that Maule is said to have possessed the power of summoning Alice from a distance:

Seated by his humble fireside, Maule had but to wave his hand; and, wherever the proud lady chanced to be—whether in her chamber, or entertaining her father's stately guests, or worshipping at church—whatever her place or occupation, her spirit passed from beneath her own control, and bowed itself to Maule.[4]

On one occasion he summoned her to 'wait upon his bride'. Inevitably she came, but the night was cold and wet, so that she caught a cold and died. In the narrator's words, 'he had taken a woman's delicate soul into his rude gripe, to play with;—and she was dead!'[5]

---

[1] *The Letters of Charles Dickens* (Pilgrim ed.), iii. 23.

[2] E. P. Gould, *The Brownings and America* (Boston, Mass., 1904), 65.

[3] See J. C. Austin, 'The Hawthorne and Browning Acquaintance': *Victorian News- letter*, 20 (1961), 14–15.

[4] Centenary ed., ed. Fredson Bowers *et al.* (Columbus, Ohio, 1965), 208–9 (repr. Oxford, 1991, ed. Michael Davitt Bell).

[5] Ibid. 210.

The piece is in five-line stanzas rhyming *abbaa*. Lines 2 and 3 of each stanza are dimeters, almost always consisting of an anapaest and an iamb, while the longer lines are trimeters, usually made up of one iamb and two anapaests, or two iambs and one anapaest. The movement of the verse tells us that we are listening to a man in a state of high excitement. In the words of Arthur Symons, 'The intense absorption, the breathless eagerness of the mesmerist, are rendered, in a manner truly marvellous, by the breathless and yet measured race of the verses—fifteen of them succeed one another without a single full-stop, or a real pause in sense or sound.'[1] The speaker may well be deranged, and his story an illusion. With great tact, however, Browning leaves 'the *actuality* of such phenomena an open question'.[2] 'Mesmerism' is a brief Gothic tale, told by a man who believes himself to possess paranormal powers.

Date: 1853/4
1863: *Dramatic Romances*

MESMERISM.

I.

ALL I believed is true!
    I am able yet
    All I want, to get
By a method as strange as new:
Dare I trust the same to you?   5

II.

If at night, when doors are shut,
    And the wood-worm picks,
    And the death-watch ticks,

---

1 *1855P* true;   *4 {reading of *1855P–84S*, DC, BrU, *1889*} *1888* new

8 *the death-watch*: superstitious people used to believe (some still do) that the sound made by the death-watch beetle is an omen of an approaching death.

[1] Arthur Symons, *An Introduction to the Study of Browning* (1894), 113. The number of stanzas without a full stop depends on the text one reads. In *1855* sts. 2–18 all end in dashes.
[2] James Fotheringham, *Studies of the Mind and Art of Robert Browning*, 4th ed. (1900), 463. Browning praised the first ed. of this 'very noticeable book': *Letters*, 279.

And the bar has a flag of smut,
And a cat's in the water-butt—   10

III.

And the socket floats and flares,
    And the house-beams groan,
    And a foot unknown
Is surmised on the garret-stairs,
And the locks slip unawares—   15

IV.

And the spider, to serve his ends,
    By a sudden thread,
    Arms and legs outspread,
On the table's midst descends,
Comes to find, God knows what friends!—   20

V.

If since eve drew in, I say,
    I have sat and brought
    (So to speak) my thought
To bear on the woman away,
Till I felt my hair turn grey—   25

VI.

Till I seemed to have and hold,
    In the vacancy
    'Twixt the wall and me,
From the hair-plait's chestnut gold
To the foot in its muslin fold—   30

---

23 *1855P* (Thus to   24 *1855P* So to   25 *1855P* That I

9 *a flag of smut*: a rag-like little piece of smut hanging from the bar of the grate.
11 *the socket*: the socket of the candle-stick is afloat with grease, which flares up.
15 *unawares*: unnoticed.
26 *to have and hold*: 'I take thee . . . to my wedded wife, to have and to hold': *Book of Common Prayer*, 'The Form of the Solemnization of Matrimony'. Cf. 'In a Balcony', 17 n.

VII.

Have and hold, then and there,
   Her, from head to foot,
   Breathing and mute,
Passive and yet aware,
In the grasp of my steady stare—   35

VIII.

Hold and have, there and then,
   All her body and soul
   That completes my whole,
All that women add to men,
In the clutch of my steady ken—   40

IX.

Having and holding, till
   I imprint her fast
   On the void at last
As the sun does whom he will
By the calotypist's skill—   45

X.

Then,—if my heart's strength serve,
   And through all and each
   Of the veils I reach
To her soul and never swerve,
Knitting an iron nerve—   50

---

38 *that completes my whole*: cf. the humorous claim of Aristophanes, in Plato's *Symposium*, that man is an incomplete creature who goes about seeking his other half.

40 *ken*: gaze.

45 *the calotypist's skill*: this is the first occurrence of 'calotypist' known to OED². The first example of 'calotype' occurs in 1841, in Fox Talbot's *Specification for Patent* No. 8842.3, in the phrase 'calotype paper'. The picture was produced 'by the action of light upon silver iodide, the latent image being subsequently developed and fixed by hyposulphite of soda'. While Fox Talbot was the English inventor of photography, L. J. M. Daguerre, his exact contemporary in France, produced similar results by a different process.

XI.

Command her soul to advance
And inform the shape
Which has made escape
And before my countenance
Answers me glance for glance—   55

XII.

I, still with a gesture fit   ·
Of my hands that best
Do my soul's behest,
Pointing the power from it,
While myself do steadfast sit—   60

XIII.

Steadfast and still the same
On my object bent,
While the hands give vent
To my ardour and my aim
And break into very flame—   65

XIV.

Then I reach, I must believe,
Not her soul in vain,
For to me again
It reaches, and past retrieve
Is wound in the toils I weave;   70

---

51 *1855P–63* Commanding that to

52 *inform the shape*: as if it had been a phantasm before.
65 *And break into very flame*: in 1845 Karl von Reichenbach (1788–1869) announced the discovery of 'odyl', a mesmeric influence which he believed to be present in certain crystals and magnets, and in people with a particular gift. Some people saw it as a flame. EBB refers to him in 1846 (Kintner, ii. 640), and in *Aurora Leigh*, vii. 566 (1856) a speaker refers to 'that od-force of German Reichenbach'.

XV.

And must follow as I require,
    As befits a thrall,
    Bringing flesh and all,
Essence and earth-attire,
To the source of the tractile fire: 75

XVI.

Till the house called hers, not mine,
    With a growing weight
    Seems to suffocate
If she break not its leaden line
And escape from its close confine.   80

XVII.

Out of doors into the night!
    On to the maze
    Of the wild wood-ways,
Not turning to left nor right
From the pathway, blind with sight—   85

XVIII.

Making thro' rain and wind
    O'er the broken shrubs,
    'Twixt the stems and stubs,
With a still, composed, strong mind,
Nor a care for the world behind—   90

---

80 *1855P–65* confine—   81 *1855P* night   84 *1855P–56* left or right
85 *1855P* the path, too blind   90 *1855P–63, 1872S, 1884S* Not a

---

74 *earth-attire*: body.

75 *tractile*: possessing the power of attraction (more properly 'tractive').

76 *called hers, not mine*: in *The House of the Seven Gables* the Pyncheon-house is, according to Maule, rightly his, and its oppressiveness is a constant theme in the book, right up to the departure of Phoebe with Holgrave.

79 *line*: tether.

85 *blind with sight*: unseeing, though with open eyes. Cf. l. 94.

86 *Making*: making her way. Cf. *Comedy of Errors*, I. i. 93.

XIX.

Swifter and still more swift,
　　As the crowding peace
　　Doth to joy increase
In the wide blind eyes uplift
Thro' the darkness and the drift!   95

XX.

While I—to the shape, I too
　　Feel my soul dilate
　　Nor a whit abate,
And relax not a gesture due,
As I see my belief come true.   100

XXI.

For, there! have I drawn or no
　　Life to that lip?
　　Do my fingers dip
In a flame which again they throw
On the cheek that breaks a-glow?   105

XXII.

Ha! was the hair so first?
　　What, unfilleted,
　　Made alive, and spread
Through the void with a rich outburst,
Chestnut gold-interspersed?   110

---

94 *1855P* wide level eyes　　　95 *1855P* drift,—　　　97 *1872S*, *1884S* dilate:
98 *1863* Not a　　　100 *1855P–56* true—　　　102 *1855P* lip!　　　110 *1855P–56*
gold-interspersed!

---

94 *uplift*: uplifted, as in *Paradise Lost*, i. 193, and Shelley, 'Fragments of an Unfinished Drama', 239.
95 *drift*: 'A storm; a shower': Johnson.
96 *the shape*: cf. ll. 122 and 125.
104 *in a flame*: cf. l. 65.
105 *breaks a-glow*: breaks into a glow.
106 *first?*: at first?
107 *unfilleted*: without a headband.

XXIII.

Like the doors of a casket-shrine,
          See, on either side,
          Her two arms divide
Till the heart betwixt makes sign,
"Take me, for I am thine!"   115

XXIV.

"Now—now"—the door is heard!
          Hark, the stairs! and near—
          Nearer—and here—
"Now!" and at call the third
She enters without a word.   120

XXV.

On doth she march and on
          To the fancied shape;
          It is, past escape,
Herself, now: the dream is done
And the shadow and she are one.   125

XXVI.

First I will pray. Do Thou
          That ownest the soul,
          Yet wilt grant control
To another, nor disallow
For a time, restrain me now!   130

---

*115 {reading of *1872S*} *1855P* Take . . . . thine—*1855–70, 1875, 1888, 1889* Take . . . .
thine! *1884S* "Take . . . . thine?"   116 *1855P–56* Now—now— . . . . heard
117 *1855P–56* Hark! . . . . stairs and   119 *1855P–56* Now! and   *120 {read-
ing of *1855–84S*, DC, BrU, *1889*} *1855P* word—*1888* word   126 *1855P* pray: do

---

111 *casket-shrine*: not in OED². The reference is to the sort of household shrine one
finds in old Italian houses. Having doors which are closed when they are not in use,
they resemble cupboards.
119 *at call the third*: as one would expect, with a spell.
129 *disallow*: forbid.

XXVII.

I admonish me while I may,
   Not to squander guilt,
   Since require Thou wilt
At my hand its price one day!
What the price is, who can say?   135

---

134 *1855P* day—

  133 *require Thou wilt*: cf. Luke: 12: 20.

A SERENADE AT THE VILLA

WHILE this poem was no doubt written between 1853 and 1855, nothing in it suggests a more precise date, far less any autobiographical significance. Browning no doubt decided that a poem of this genre would be appropriate in a collection of poems of which so many deal with love. We are reminded of his early ambition to write an opera,[1] and perhaps of the episode between Ottima and Sebald in *Pippa Passes*. Browning takes a traditional topos and gives it a characteristic twist. The unfortunate lover may remind us of the speakers of 'The Last Ride Together' and 'One Way of Love'. Stanza iv is strongly reminiscent of Wyatt.

Each stanza consists of five lines, rhyming *ababa*. The lines are catalectic trochaic tetrameters. Many are monosyllabic, as are four of the first five.

Date: 1853/5
1863: *Dramatic Lyrics*

A SERENADE AT THE VILLA.

I.

THAT was I, you heard last night,
 When there rose no moon at all,
Nor, to pierce the strained and tight
 Tent of heaven, a planet small:
Life was dead and so was light.   5

---

4 *Tent of heaven*: a traditional image, as befits a serenade. Cf. Sir John Davies, *Orchestra*, 54: 'Jove's blue tent'; Collins, 'Ode on the Poetical Character', 26: 'tented sky'; Shelley, 'The Cloud', 51, 55.

[1] In his youth he hoped to write 'this poem, the other novel, such an opera, such a speech &c &c' under different pen-names: see Vol. I, p. 4. Cf. p. 465n, below.

II.

Not a twinkle from the fly,
    Not a glimmer from the worm;
When the crickets stopped their cry,
    When the owls forbore a term,
You heard music; that was I.   10

III.

Earth turned in her sleep with pain,
    Sultrily suspired for proof:
In at heaven and out again,
    Lightning!—where it broke the roof,
Bloodlike, some few drops of rain.   15

IV.

What they could my words expressed,
    O my love, my all, my one!
Singing helped the verses best,
    And when singing's best was done,
To my lute I left the rest.   20

V.

So wore night; the East was gray,
    White the broad-faced hemlock-flowers:
There would be another day;
    Ere its first of heavy hours
Found me, I had passed away.   25

7 *1855–84S* worm.   22 *1855P* hemlock flowers,   23 *1855P–56* Soon would
come another

6 *the fly*: the firefly, see 46.
7 *the worm*: the glow-worm.
9 *a term*: for a while.
12 *suspired*: breathed deeply or heavily.
15 *some few drops*: (fell).
20 *To my lute I left the rest*: reminiscent of Sir Thomas Wyatt.
21 *wore*: gradually passed.

VI.

What became of all the hopes,
    Words and song and lute as well?
Say, this struck you—"When life gropes
    "Feebly for the path where fell
"Light last on the evening slopes,   30

VII.

"One friend in that path shall be,
    "To secure my step from wrong;
"One to count night day for me,
    "Patient through the watches long,
"Serving most with none to see."   35

VIII.

Never say—as something bodes—
    "So, the worst has yet a worse!
"When life halts 'neath double loads,
    "Better the taskmaster's curse
"Than such music on the roads!   40

IX.

"When no moon succeeds the sun,
    "Nor can pierce the midnight's tent
"Any star, the smallest one,
    "While some drops, where lightning rent,
"Show the final storm begun—   45

26 *1855P* hopes?   28 *1855P* "when   *32 {reading of *1868–84S*} *1888, 1889*
To {in *1855P–65S* double quotation marks appear only at the beginning and end of the
stanza}   *1855P* my steps from wrong,   *1855–65* my steps from   *34 {reading
of *1868–84S*} *1888, 1889* 'Patient   37 *1855P* worse   44 *1855P–63* lightning
went,

28 *Say, this struck you*: the poet's hope.
34 *the watches long*: cf. Ps. 63: 6.
40 *such music*: as that of the serenader.
      on the roads: of her journey through life.

X.

"When the fire-fly hides its spot,
    "When the garden-voices fail
"In the darkness thick and hot,—
    "Shall another voice avail,
"That shape be where these are not?   50

XI.

"Has some plague a longer lease,
    "Proffering its help uncouth?
"Can't one even die in peace?
    "As one shuts one's eyes on youth,
"Is that face the last one sees?"   55

XII.

Oh how dark your villa was,
    Windows fast and obdurate!
How the garden grudged me grass
    Where I stood—the iron gate
Ground its teeth to let me pass!   60

---

50 *1855* where those are   *51 {reading of *1855P–84S*} *1888, 1889* 'Has
52 *1855P* Proffering this help   57 *1855P* obdurate—

---

51 *a longer lease*: cf. Shakespeare, *Sonnets*, xviii. 4.
60 *Ground its teeth*: creaked on its hinges.

MY STAR

In her *Handbook* Mrs Orr remarks, sensibly, that this poem 'may be taken as a tribute to the personal element in love: the bright peculiar light in which the sympathetic soul reveals itself to the object of its sympathy'. Its importance to Browning himself, which has surprised some, is shown by his placing it at the start of his 1865 *Selection*. The attempt to identify the star in terms of astronomy is destined to failure. More to the point is a passage in a letter to EBB cited by Pettigrew and Collins: 'I believed in your glorious genius and knew it for a true star from the moment I saw it,—long before I had the blessing of knowing it was MY star, with my fortune and futurity in it.'[1]

In his later years Browning would often write a few lines from this poem in a lady's album, when a request was made to him. On one occasion he said that this was the only poem he could remember, and found that even in it he had made 'a few errors'. See Meredith, 164. Cf. Kelley and Coley, E 267–77.

Each of the short lines has two stresses. Line 1 is a choriambus, line 3 an iambic dimeter, while each of the other lines consists of an anapaest followed by an iamb. The longer lines, which are mainly anapaestic, have each four stresses.

Date: 1853/5
1863: *Dramatic Lyrics*

MY STAR.

ALL that I know
　　Of a certain star
Is, it can throw
　　(Like the angled spar)

{in *1872S*, *1884S* lines 1–8 are not indented}　　　4 *1855P* Like . . . . spar

---

4 *the angled spar*: a spar is a crystalline mineral which breaks into regular surfaces, and reflects light.

---

[1] Kintner, i, 261.

Now a dart of red,   5
　　Now a dart of blue;
Till my friends have said
　　They would fain see, too,
My star that dartles the red and the blue!
Then it stops like a bird; like a flower, hangs furled: 10
　　They must solace themselves with the Saturn above it.
What matter to me if their star is a world?
　　Mine has opened its soul to me; therefore I love it.

---

6 *1855P–63* blue,　　　9 *1855P* blue:　　　10 *1855P–56* bird,—

9 *dartles*: a frequentive form, conceivably of Browning's invention. OED² has no
earlier example, and only one later.

11 *Saturn*: the most remote of the planets known to ancient astronomy.

INSTANS TYRANNUS

THE title means 'the (or an) importunate tyrant'. The inspiration of the poem is the opening of the third Ode in Horace's Third Book, thus translated in an edition which Browning owned (probably from his boyhood):

The Rage of the Citizens commanding unjust Things, the threatning Visage of the pressing Tyrant; the South-Wind, the boisterous Commander of the restless *Adriatick* Sea, and the mighty Hand of thundering *Jupiter*, can never shake the just Man who is firm to his Purpose, from his steady Resolution. Nay, should the World tumble in Ruins about his Head, he would be fearless amidst the universal Wreck.[1]

Browning's speaker gives the poem a Christian ending different from anything in Horace's Ode.

We do not know when this poem was written, but in its suggestion of Æsop it reminds us of his boyhood, when his mother 'used to read Croxall's Fables to his little sister and him'.[2] In the 'Application' of 'The Fowler and the Ring-Dove' in that translation we read: 'This is another lesson against injustice; a topic in which our just Author abounds'. The fable of 'The Lion and the Mouse', which lies behind *Strafford*, IV. i. 56 ff., 'gives us to understand, that there is no person in the world so little, but even the greatest may, at some time or other, stand in need of his assistance; and consequently that it is good to use clemency'. One or two other Fables have somewhat similar morals.

The seven stanzas, of varying length, all consist of rhyming couplets; the first line of each couplet is a trimeter, the other a dimeter. The dominant foot is the anapaest.

Date: 1853/5
1863: Dramatic Romances

---

[1] *The Odes, Epodes, and Carmen Seculare*, trans. David Watson (1741): see *Correspondence*, iv. 269.
[2] *Life*, 26. In the 1813 ed. of Croxall's *Æsop's Fables* see pp. 29 and 56 ff.

INSTANS TYRANNUS.

I.

OF the million or two, more or less,
I rule and possess,
One man, for some cause undefined,
Was least to my mind.

II.

I struck him, he grovelled of course—   5
For, what was his force?
I pinned him to earth with my weight
And persistence of hate:
And he lay, would not moan, would not curse,
As his lot might be worse.   10

III.

"Were the object less mean, would he stand
"At the swing of my hand!
"For obscurity helps him and blots
"The hole where he squats."
So, I set my five wits on the stretch   15
To inveigle the wretch.
All in vain! Gold and jewels I threw,
Still he couched there perdue;
I tempted his blood and his flesh,
Hid in roses my mesh,   20

---

10 *1855P–56* As if lots might   17 *1855P–65* gold   18 *1855–63* perdue.

6 *force*: strength.
11 *"Were the object less mean*: so the speaker (the Tyrant) had reflected to himself.
13 *blots*: obscures, conceals. Cf. Shakespeare, *Venus and Adonis*, 184, and Cowper, *Table Talk*, 270.
16 *inveigle*: 'To persuade to something bad or hurtful': Johnson.
18 *Couched there perdue*: lay there in hiding.
20 *mesh*: net.

Choicest cates and the flagon's best spilth:
Still he kept to his filth.

IV.

Had he kith now or kin, were access
To his heart, did I press:
Just a son or a mother to seize!   25
No such booty as these.
Were it simply a friend to pursue
'Mid my million or two,
Who could pay me in person or pelf
What he owes me himself!   30
No: I could not but smile through my chafe:
For the fellow lay safe
As his mates do, the midge and the nit,
—Through minuteness, to wit.

V.

Then a humour more great took its place   35
At the thought of his face,
The droop, the low cares of the mouth,
The trouble uncouth
Twixt the brows, all that air one is fain
To put out of its pain.   40
And, "no!" I admonished myself,
"Is one mocked by an elf,

---

22 *1855P–65* filth!   23 *1855P* kin, some access   24 *1855P–56* heart, if I
25 *1855P* But a   *1855P–56* seize—   26 *1855P–65* these!   27 *1863S* Were
there simply   30 *1855P–56, 1863, 1865* himself.   31 *1855P–65* No! *1863S*
chafe,   36 *1872S, 1884S* face: 40 *1855P–63* pain—   41 *1855P–56*
And, no, I   *1863S* And, no! I

---

21 *cates*: dainties.
  spilth: spilling of wine, as in *Timon*, II. ii. 161.
23 *were*: there would be.
31 *chafe*: rage, as in *Antony and Cleopatra*, I. iii. 85.
33 *nit*: the egg or larva of a louse.
35 *a humour more great*: a more passionate mood (of anger).
42 *elf*: insignificant little creature.

"Is one baffled by toad or by rat?
"The gravamen's in that!
"How the lion, who crouches to suit   45
"His back to my foot,
"Would admire that I stand in debate!
"But the small turns the great
"If it vexes you,—that is the thing!
"Toad or rat vex the king?   50
"Though I waste half my realm to unearth
"Toad or rat, 't is well worth!"

VI.

So, I soberly laid my last plan
To extinguish the man.
Round his creep-hole, with never a break   55
Ran my fires for his sake;
Over-head, did my thunder combine
With my underground mine:
Till I looked from my labour content
To enjoy the event.   60

VII.

When sudden . . . how think ye, the end?
Did I say "without friend"?
Say rather, from marge to blue marge
The whole sky grew his targe
With the sun's self for visible boss,   65
While an Arm ran across
Which the earth heaved beneath like a breast

43 *1855P* rat,—   48 *1855P–56* Small is the   52 *1855P* worth!
57 *1855P–56* my thunders combine   58 *1855P* mine

44 *gravamen*: the most serious part of the offence.
47 *admire*: be astonished.
55 *creep-hole*: 'A hole into which any animal may creep to escape danger': Johnson.
Cf. *King Victor*, 1. 95.
57 *my thunder*: cf. Horace's 'thundering Jupiter'.
58 *mine*: explosive charge.

Where the wretch was safe prest!
Do you see? Just my vengeance complete,
The man sprang to his feet,   70
Stood erect, caught at God's skirts, and prayed!
—So, *I* was afraid!

---

69 *1884S* see!   *1855P*–65 just   72 *1863S* afraid.

71 *God's skirts*: cf. *Christmas-Eve*, 638.

A PRETTY WOMAN

DeVane suggested that 'the model' for this light-hearted piece was Mrs Jameson's niece Gerardine, whom the Brownings had seen a good deal of in 1846, when she was seventeen. The following year EBB described her as 'a gentle, caressing little creature',[1] observing that she was as yet scarcely adult, with 'no experience of men and women'. Browning was exasperated by Mrs Jameson's indulgence of a girl who, as he put it, 'couldn't be trusted to walk down a street by herself lest she should run away with the first man at the corner'. When he told Mrs Jameson what he 'should do if he had the misfortune of having a wife like Gerardine' she observed that '*three men out of every five would be in love with her forthwith*', adding sarcastically that of course she was speaking only of 'ordinary men'. EBB's amused conclusion was that the girl was 'just pretty and no more at most'.

While it is possible that she inspired this piece, DeVane's conclusion that, if so, the poem 'was probably written in 1847', carries little weight. Gerardine was not unique. It is unlikely that Browning would have written a short poem of this kind in 1847: even if she was in his mind as he wrote it, there is no reason to suppose that he would have written it immediately.

A light-hearted poem of hate, 'A Pretty Woman' makes a suitable if minor addition to a collection of poems in which the relations between men and women are considered in a great many lights. It is also a reminder, if such be needed, of the remarkable technical variety to be found in *Men and Women*.

Each of the stanzas rhymes *abba*, the first and last line of each having eight or nine syllables, the second and third having four. The short lines are usually trochaic, while the long lines are sometimes iambic and sometimes trochaic, with variations. The most remarkable feature of the piece is the rhyme-scheme. The short lines have double rhymes, with the peculiarity that the second rhyming syllable is often the same monosyllable, not merely the same sound: so we have 'you' at the end of ll. 6 and 7, and 'sake' at the end of ll. 10 and 11, where (as in some other cases) a triple rhyme includes two of the same words: *a word's sake/a sword's sake*. The longer lines all have triple rhymes; in some of them there is an even

[1] Huxley, 62, 63, 61, 62, 63.

more marked element of repetition. Lines 21 and 24, 49 and 52, and
perhaps 65 and 68 may be considered as having quadruple rhymes. This
excessive rhyming and chiming is an appropriate feature of a poem to a
young woman who is apostrophized six times as 'Sweet', to whom and of
whom nothing else can really be said.

Date: 1853/5
1863: *Dramatic Lyrics*

A PRETTY WOMAN.

I.

THAT fawn-skin-dappled hair of hers,
    And the blue eye
    Dear and dewy,
And that infantine fresh air of hers!

II.

To think men cannot take you, Sweet,   5
    And enfold you,
    Ay, and hold you,
And so keep you what they make you, Sweet!

III.

You like us for a glance, you know—
    For a word's sake   10
    Or a sword's sake,
All's the same, whate'er the chance, you know.

IV.

And in turn we make you ours, we say—
    You and youth too,

11 *1855P* sword's ache,   *1872S*, *1884S* sake:

Eyes and mouth too, 15
All the face composed of flowers, we say.

V.

All's our own, to make the most of, Sweet—
Sing and say for,
Watch and pray for,
Keep a secret or go boast of, Sweet! 20

VI.

But for loving, why, you would not, Sweet,
Though we prayed you,
Paid you, brayed you
In a mortar—for you could not, Sweet!

VII.

So, we leave the sweet face fondly there: 25
Be its beauty
Its sole duty!
Let all hope of grace beyond, lie there!

VIII.

And while the face lies quiet there,
Who shall wonder 30
That I ponder
A conclusion? I will try it there.

IX.

As,—why must one, for the love foregone,
Scout mere liking?

---

20 *1855, 1856* Sweet.   24 *1855, 1856* Sweet.   25 *1884S* there.
27 *1855P* All its duty,   30 *1855P* Do you wonder   34 *1855P* Despise liking?

---

23 *brayed you*: Cf. Prov. 27: 22: 'Though thou shouldest bray a fool in a mortar . . .
yet will not his foolishness depart from him'.

Thunder-striking   35
Earth,—the heaven, we looked above for, gone!

X.

Why, with beauty, needs there money be,
    Love with liking?
    Crush the fly-king
In his gauze, because no honey-bee?   40

XI.

May not liking be so simple-sweet,
    If love grew there
    'T would undo there
All that breaks the cheek to dimples sweet?

XII.

Is the creature too imperfect, say?   45
    Would you mend it
    And so end it?
Since not all addition perfects aye!

XIII.

Or is it of its kind, perhaps,
    Just perfection—   50
    Whence, rejection
Of a grace not to its mind, perhaps?

XIV.

Shall we burn up, tread that face at once
    Into tinder,

---

36 *1855P* Earth,—heaven,   47 *1855P* it,

33 *for the love foregone*: why must one reject the possibility of simply liking her,
because one has denied oneself love? Why should one blast the earth, just because the
heaven one hoped to see above it has disappeared?
39 *fly-king*: 'presumably the Purple Emperor butterfly': Turner.
51 *Whence, rejection*: so that (being perfect) it rejects a grace which is not to its mind?

And so hinder   55
Sparks from kindling all the place at once?

XV.

Or else kiss away one's soul on her?
    Your love-fancies!
    —A sick man sees
Truer, when his hot eyes roll on her!   60

XVI.

Thus the craftsman thinks to grace the rose,—
    Plucks a mould-flower
    For his gold flower,
Uses fine things that efface the rose:

XVII.

Rosy rubies make its cup more rose,   65
    Precious metals
    Ape the petals,—
Last, some old king locks it up, morose!

XVIII.

Then how grace a rose? I know a way!
    Leave it, rather.   70
    Must you gather?
Smell, kiss, wear it—at last, throw away!

58 *1855P* love-fancies—   61 *1855P* There's the   64 *1855, 1856* rose.
65 *1855P* Red rubies   69 *1855P* How   70 *1855P* rather!

59–60 *sees / Truer.* being in no state for passion.
61 *Thus the craftsman*: so a carver picks a real rose to enhance the effect of his carving, and spoils it in the process. Cf. 'to paint the lily' (*King John*, IV. ii. 11), now proverbial.

"CHILDE ROLAND TO THE DARK TOWER CAME"

IN the Introduction to this volume we have given our reasons for believing that this was one of the first of the poems in the collection to be written, perhaps at the beginning of 1853.[1] In 1889 Browning told an enquirer that he had been 'conscious of no allegorical intention in writing it'; he stated that 'one year in Florence [he] had been rather lazy', and therefore resolved to write 'something every day:'

Well, the first day I wrote about some roses . . . The next day 'Childe Roland' came upon me as a kind of dream. I had to write it, then and there, and I finished it the same day, I believe. But it was simply that I had to do it. I did not know then what I meant beyond that, and I'm sure I don't know now. But I am very fond of it.[2]

We are reminded of the stated origin of 'Kubla Khan', and of that of a poem by Yeats. Coleridge introduces his fragment by telling his readers that he had been in ill health, in the summer of 1797, and had been advised to take an anodyne:

from the effects of which he fell asleep in his chair at the moment that he was reading the following sentence, or words of the same substance, in 'Purchas's Pilgrimage': 'Here the Khan Kubla commanded a palace to be built, and a stately garden thereunto. And thus ten miles of fertile ground were inclosed with a wall.' The Author continued for about three hours in a profound sleep, at least of the external senses, during which time he has the most vivid confidence, that he could not have composed less than from two to three hundred lines; if that indeed can be called composition in which all the images rose up before him as *things*, with a parallel production of the correspondent expressions, without any sensation or consciousness of effort. On awaking he appeared to himself to have a distinct recollection of the whole, and taking his pen, ink, and paper, instantly and eagerly wrote down the lines that are here preserved.[3]

[1] See p. xii ff.

[2] Whiting, 261. The enquirer had been 'greatly impressed by Mr. Nettleship's analysis and interpretation' of the poem, 'and asked the author if he accepted it. "Oh, no," replied Mr. Browning; "not at all. Understand, I don't repudiate it, either; I only mean that I was conscious of no allegorical intention it writing it"'. See J. T. Nettleship, *Essays on Browning's Poetry* (1868), reprinted in his *Robert Browning: Essays and Thoughts* (1890).

[3] *The Complete Poetical Works of Samuel Taylor Coleridge*, ed. E. H. Coleridge (2 vols., 1912), i. 296.

At this moment the infamous 'person on business from Porlock' appeared, and after 'above an hour', when he left, Coleridge found that hardly anything remained in his mind of what had followed the lines which he published. Of his poem 'The Cap and Bells' Yeats wrote:

I dreamed this story exactly as I have written it, and dreamed another long dream after it, trying to make out its meaning, and whether I was to write it in prose or verse. The first dream was more a vision than a dream, for it was beautiful and coherent, and gave me the sense of illumination and exaltation that one gets from visions, while the second dream was confused and meaningless. The poem has always meant a great deal to me, though, as is the way with symbolic poems, it has not always meant quite the same thing. Blake would have said 'the authors are in eternity,' and I am quite sure they can only be questioned in dreams.[1]

It seems that 'Childe Roland', like 'Kubla Khan', may have come to Browning as a dream or vision accompanied by 'the correspondent expressions'.

He mentions dreams in several of his letters. In 1846, for example, he told EBB that he 'never *used* to dream unless indisposed, and rarely then . . . and *those* nightmare dreams have invariably been of *one* sort—I stand by (powerless to interpose by a word even) and see the infliction of tyranny on the unresisting—man or beast (generally the last)—and I wake just in time not to die'.[2] In the present case the role of illness may have been taken by his worry at having neglected his duty of writing poetry.

The epigraph points to literary associations, and it is evident that in his anxious condition Browning's subconscious took him back to early memories of stories told him when he was a small boy. As Harold Golder pointed out long ago,[3] the second and third lines of Edgar's song provide valuable evidence:

> Child Rowland to the dark tower came,
> His word was still 'Fie, foh, and fum,
> I smell the blood of a British man'.

The first of these lines (*King Lear*, III. iv. 178–80), which gave Browning his title and no doubt something of his inspiration, suggests a romance background, while the other two seem to take us back almost to his

---

[1] Note first published, with the poem, in *The Wind among the Reeds* (1899).
[2] Kintner, i. 399.
[3] 'Browning's *Childe Roland*', PMLA 39 (1924), 963–78. Golder is one of the friends specifically thanked by John Livingston Lowes in the preface to *The Road to Xanadu: A Study in the Ways of the Imagination* (1930).

infancy. Similar echoes of juvenile rhymes and tales may be found in a number of his other poems. In *Pauline* the poet describes dying as being like 'going in the dark / To fight a giant'. In *Paracelsus* the protagonist tells Festus that he would like to behave 'Like some knight traversing a wilderness'. In *Strafford* the statesman refers to himself as 'soon to rush / Alone upon a giant in the dark', and compares himself ironically to a youthful knight setting out on an adventure in which he will (the privilege of youth) be triumphant: 'You need not turn a page of the romance / To learn the Dreadful Giant's fate'. In *Easter-Day* the speaker reflects on the way in which we wake from dreams reproaching ourselves with having let 'the chance slip . . . When such adventure offered! Just / A bridge to cross, a dwarf to thrust / Aside, a wicked mage to stab— / And, lo ye, I have kissed Queen Mab!'[1] Further echoes of children's stories are to be found elsewhere. In *The Ring and the Book*, for example, we find the lines

> Yet heaven my fancy lifts to, ladder-like,—
> As Jack reached, holpen of his beanstalk-rungs! (i. 1346–7)

—while at the end of section 27 of *Pacchiarotto* 'Jack-in-the-Green' and 'Quilp-Hop-o'-my-thumb' are mentioned.

There is a particularly interesting reference in one of the poems in this volume, 'A Lovers' Quarrel', where the speaker reflects that if only November would come, he would 'laugh like the valiant Thumb / Facing the castle glum / And the giant's fee-faw-fum!'[2] Golder wrongly states that Tom Thumb is never a hero.[3] In *The Famous History of Tom Thumb*, an eighteenth-century chapbook, we are told that at a certain tourney at which Sir Lancelot du Lake, Sir Tristram, and Sir Guy all appeared, 'none compar'd to brave Tom Thumb / In acts of cavalry'.[4] Golder is probably right, however, in arguing that as a rule it is 'Not the Thumbs, but the Jacks of children's lore [who] seek out giants and laugh . . . at their "fee-faw-fums".'

Two other nursery stories which will have been known to Browning from his earliest years relate closely to the last line-and-a-half of the song in *King Lear*: *Jack the Giant-Killer* and *Jack and the Beanstalk*. The hero of each attacks a castle and conquers its tyrant. In Golder's words:

[1] *Pauline*, 1026–7; *Paracelsus*, i. 474; *Strafford* II. ii. 40–1 and 174–5; *Easter-Day*, 484–8. cf.
[2] Lines 131–3.
[3] Op. cit., 965.
[4] *Chap-Books of the Eighteenth Century*, ed. John Ashton (1882), 213 ('cavalry' = chivalry).

The connection of the valiant Jack with the valiant Thumb and of the castle glum with the Dark Tower gains significance in view of a similarity between the incidents of both these tales and those of *Childe Roland*. The hero of *Jack and the Beanstalk* travels, as does Roland, through a desolate country on his way to the giant's castle. In most chap-book versions this plain is described as "a desert, quite barren; not a tree, shrub, house, or living creature to be seen"; but in some forms of the tale this description is expanded to include "scattered fragments of stone; and at unequal distances, small heaps of earth . . . loosely thrown together". Even more interesting . . . is the last episode in *Jack the Giant-killer*. The hero comes at evening to the foot of a mountain, where he encounters a man 'with a head as white as snow'. This man guides him to a castle . . . where a host of lost adventurers, who had previously essayed the conquest of the tower, lie imprisoned. On arriving before the gates, Jack finds a golden trumpet hanging suspended by a silver chain, under which is written:

> 'Whoso can this trumpet blow,
> Shall soon the giant overthrow,
> And break the black enchantment straight,
> So all shall be in happy state'.[1]

Needless to say, Jack blows the trumpet. While we find faint suggestions of the plot of 'Childe Roland' in such tales, however, Roland's quest is very different, being notably an account of 'the failure of many and the triumph of one'.[2]

It is when we turn to those great repositories of story-telling, the prose romances, that we find examples of the type of quest which is the heart of Browning's poem. In them such features as the narrator's asking the way, the desolate landscape, the temptation to despair, the audience which watches the brave traveller, and the blowing of his horn, take on a deeper significance. As Golder points out, the 'fell cirque' beyond the river recalls 'the frightful battlefield of Roncevaux, with which the name of Roland has a direct connection'.[3] In the Second Part of *Don Bellianis*, for instance, a damsel speaks thus to the traveller:

as for the place where now we are, we know no other of it but that it is called the Desert of Death, and indeed it may properly enough be termed so, for I never was in any place so dolesome and melancholly as this is, there being no other light coming into this place but what a candle produceth, and the fields, which are but few, look as if no grass nor any other herb had ever grown there, and there are no trees but Yew grow here.[4]

---

[1] Op. cit. 966.   [2] Ibid. 967.   [3] Ibid. 969.

[4] *The Honour of Chivalry: Or, The Famous and Delectable History of Don Bellianis of Greece, Now newly Written in English*, by F[rancis] K[irkman] (1671), 36, 38. In the 1673 ed. of the First Part, title and sub-title are transposed.

As they walk in the Desert of Death they find a tablet on a tree 'whereon was inscribed: "If thou art so valiant as to undertake the ent[r]ance into this Castle, blow this Horn, and prepare thy self to be received".'

While emphasizing that other romances may be equally relevant, Golder singles out two because of their similarities to the poem. *The Renowned History of the Seven Champions of Christendom*, incidents from which Coleridge loved to act out as a little boy, is full of strange landscapes, magic horns, and lost adventurers. When St George comes to the country of the Amazons and finds it desolate, the Queen blames a necromancer who

'wrought the destruction of this my realm and kingdom; for by his magic art and damned charms, he raised from the earth a mighty tower . . ., wherein are such enchantments wrought, that the light of the sun and the brightness of the skies is quenched, and the earth blasted with a terrible vapour and black mist . . . whereby a general darkness overspread our land . . . so this country is clean wasted and destroyed, and my people fled out thereof'.[1]

When St George declares that he will overcome this enchantment, she warns him of the extreme peril: 'Most dangerous is the adventure . . . from whence as yet did never knight return; but if you be so resolute and noble-minded as to attempt the enterprise, . . . know brave knight, . . . that this tower lieth westward from hence about thirteen miles'. Undaunted, St George set out:

At last he found a mighty river, with streams as black as pitch, and the banks were so high, that the water could scarce be seen running underneath, and it was so full of serpents, that none could enter among them that ever returned back with life: about his head flew monstrous birds and divers griffins, who were able to bear away an armed knight, horse and all, and were in as great multitudes as though they had been starlings . . . In this dangerous manner rode he on, till he came to the gates of the enchanted tower.

In another episode he reaches a castle, outside which there hangs a trumpet, with this inscription:

> If any dare attempt this place to see,
> By sounding this, the gate shall open'd be;
> A trumpet here enchain'd by magic art,
> To daunt with fear the proudest champion's heart:
> Look thou for blows that enterest in this gate,
> Return in time, repentance comes too late.

---

[1] *The Seven Champions of Christendom* (1824), 148–50, 244.

When St George saw this, 'and had understood the meaning of those mystical letters, without any more tarrying, he set the silver trumpet to his mouth, and sounded such a vehement blast, that . . . the principal gate presently opened, and the draw-bridge was let down'.

The First Part of *Palmerin of England* deals, in a highly episodic way, with 'the adventure of Great Britain', the quest to free the son of the King, who has been imprisoned in a tower by a giant and his aunt, an evil enchantress. Almost all the best knights in Christendom were engaged in the under-taking, heroes from Greece, Spain, France and other countries; but when they 'happened unto the unfortunate forest of Great Britain . . . there were very few escaped, but for the most part were all lost in this unfortunate search', being 'unhappily . . . taken prisoners in this cruel enchanted castle'.[1] A letter from the Lady of the Lake to the Emperor of Greece had made it clear that this achievement was reserved for one man: many had 'and shall attempt [it], but he alone is ordained to finish this exploit'. Boldly, therefore, Palmerin, the 'Knight of Fortune', made his way 'strait on towards the place where it was said all adventurers were lost . . . not fearing the peril which he sought, for he was adventuring worthily.' Much later (the chronology is obscure) he asks 'which way the fortress lies where all adventurers find their end?', and receives the reply: 'I know not, and believe nobody knows; but as it should seem, it cannot be far hence, by what the man told me.' Accordingly Palmerin sets out along a valley, but 'because it was night, and he knew not well which way to take, he alighted, sitting down at the root of a tree'. He cannot sleep, desiring only 'to be at the castle, where he might have that to do which perforce would put [his 'troublous thoughts'] out of mind, and where he would prove his fortune, and make an end of the adventure or of himself, as so many others had done'. He makes his way into 'the Valley of Perdition', so called because so many knights had never returned from it; 'his forebodings told him that this was the fortress of the giant'. He knew that 'if he failed to end the adventure' the captivity of all the imprisoned knights 'must be perpetual'. Accordingly he engaged in a long and terrible battle with the giant, who 'did that day even more than was expected from him', yet 'seeing the battlements and windows of the fortress full of his friends, and remembering that they were in captivity, and the confidence which they placed in him, [Palmerin] fought with such heartiness and

---

[1] *Palmerin of England, by Francisco de Moraes* (4 vols., 1807), i. 175, 127, 79, 255, 348, 352–3, 355, 357, 359. Southey corrected the original text of the translation for this edition.

hardihood, that by dint of blows he laid the giant at his feet, and . . . smote off his head'.

A great poem and (more particularly) a great allegory in prose, which were both influenced by the romances, certainly helped to inspire Browning. The knights in *The Faerie Queene* often have to ask their way. In the third stanza of Book I, Canto VIII, for example, the Red Cross Knight blows 'an horne of bugle small' before the castle of Orgoglio, and so summons him to combat. It is a horn with extraordinary properties:

> No false enchauntment, nor deceiptfull traine
> Might once abide the terror of that blast,
> But presently was voide and wholly vaine:
> No gate so strong, no locke so firme and fast,
> But with that percing noise flew open quite, or brast.

Later in the same Canto (sts. xxx–xxxi) he encounters 'An old old man, with beard as white as snow', who was a 'very vncouth sight',

> For as he forward moou'd his footing old,
> So backward still was turnd his wrincled face,

a description which may perhaps have suggested the sinister look of the 'hoary cripple, with malicious eye / Askance' at the beginning of 'Childe Roland'. In Book II, Canto I, sts. xxi ff. we find that the ancient man is Archimago, and that it is his occupation to 'deceive good knights, / And draw them from pursuit of praise and fame'.

Browning knew *The Pilgrim's Progress* from his boyhood, and throughout his life Bunyan remained 'the object of [his] utmost admiration and reverence'.[1] At some point, unfortunately we do not know when, his father drew a 'beautiful illustrated map leading through town and country to the celestial city', as well as sketches relating to the story.[2] When William Hale White gave Browning a picture of Bunyan he was told that it would hang in his study 'by the side of Spenser and Milton'.[3] In Bunyan's masterpiece, as in 'Childe Roland', a pilgrim (on foot, unlike the knights of romance) makes his way through many difficulties towards a goal which represents salvation, or a kind of victory: a desolate landscape, the need to ask the way, and constant dangers which call for the utmost determination and courage, are present in both. Near the beginning, for example, when Christian asks why the way is so hard, he is told that

---

[1] *New Letters*, 251. [2] Maynard, 315. [3] *New Letters*, 252.

this *Miry slow*, is such a place as cannot be mended: It is the descent whither the scum and filth that attends conviction for sin doth continually run, and therefore it is called the *Slough of Dispond*: for still as the sinner is awakened about his lost condition, there ariseth in his soul many fears, and doubts, and discouraging apprehensions, which all of them get together, and settle in this place: And this is the reason of the badness of the ground.[1]

The second part of the description of 'the Valley of the Shadow of Death' may also have been in Browning's mind as he wrote his poem:

tho the first part of the Valley of the shadow of Death was dangerous, yet this second part which he was yet to go, was, if possible, far more dangerous: for from the place where he now stood, even to the end of the Valley, the way was all along set . . . full of Snares, Traps, Gins, and Nets here, and . . . full of Pits, Pitfalls, deep holes, and shelvings down there.

While Browning's poem was certainly influenced by *The Pilgrim's Progress*, the differences between the two are very striking. The professedly allegorical work is full of details and is much closer to everyday life than the poem which Browning wrote without any conscious 'allegorical intention'. While Bunyan's book has a great deal of the mundane about it, for all the theological significance of its people and places, Browning's poem presents a landscape of the imagination which has nothing in common with our waking lives.

The Childe is much lonelier than Christian, who constantly meets and talks with other people as he makes his pilgrimage. After the first stanza, with its sinister cripple with his eye 'Askance', the Childe is the only human being in the poem—though in the end he is watched by a spectral audience of 'the lost adventurers, my peers'. The animals which appear in Browning's phantasmagoria are sinister creatures suited to a nightmare: a howlet or a bat, a water-rat, a great black bird, 'Toads in a poisoned tank, or wild cats in a red-hot iron cage'. If it were not that Mrs Orr tells us (clearly on Browning's own authority) that 'the figure of a horse in the tapestry in his own drawing-room' inspired the 'stiff blind' creature, 'his every bone astare', in stanzas xiii–xiv, we should rather have associated it with some picture that Browning had seen in connection with his passionate opposition to vivisection.[2] The plants, which are surprisingly numerous, are as remote as possible from the roses so prominent in the poem said to have been written the previous day. 'For flowers',

---

[1] *The Pilgrim's Progress*, ed. J. B. Wharey, rev. R. Sharrock (1960), 15, 65.

[2] For Browning's views on vivisection, see Edward Berdoe, *Browning's Message to his Time* (1890).

we are told, we might 'as well expect a cedar grove!' Nothing flourishes in this terrible country but such as cockle, spurge, burr, thistles, dock's leaves, low scrubby alders, moss, and palsied oak. These seem natural products of marsh, 'Bog, clay, and rubble, sand and stark black earth'.

In the creation of this poem Browning's subconscious clearly played a dominant part. It is of interest that while he did not write it with any allegorical intention, he did not altogether repudiate Nettleship's interpretation, over-simplified and misleading as it now seems to us. The truth is surely that it is a symbolic poem, and we may be guided by Robert Penn Warren on 'The Ancient Mariner':

If we take the poem as a symbolic poem, we are not permitted to read it in the way which Coleridge called allegorical. We cannot, for instance, say that the Pilot equals the Church, or that the Hermit equals the 'idea of an enlightened religion which is acquainted with the life of the spirit' . . . This allegorical kind of reading makes the poem into a system of equivalents in a discursive sequence. But, as a matter of fact, we must read it as . . . operating on more than one thematic level, as embodying a complex of feelings and ideas not to be differentiated except in so far as we discursively explore the poem itself.[1]

It is said that when J. W. Chadwick asked Browning whether the meaning of the poem could be expressed in the phrase 'He that endureth to the end shall be saved', he replied 'Yes, just about that.'[2] While a symbolical poem is susceptible to more than one meaning, and cannot be limited to any supposedly authoritative interpretation, it is difficult to believe that the Childe fails. What happens to him after he has blown his horn we do not know: that is no doubt the point at which the sleeper awakes. But whatever is about to happen, there is surely a sense in which, by the very act of blowing the horn, 'Dauntless', the dreamer triumphs. Whether we are to suppose that he defeats the enemy who is to be found within the tower, or that he is killed by him, it is hard to believe that he i unsuccessful, even if death is the condition of his success, or failure 'b

---

[1] 'A Poem of Pure Imagination', in Warren's *Selected Essays* (ed. of 1958), 221. In th introduction to *The Dark Tower: And Other Radio Scripts* (1947), Louis Macneic acknowledges his debt to Browning's poem, which he similarly describes as 'a wor which does not admit of a completely rational analysis and [one which] still less adds u to any clear moral or message. This poem has the solidity of a dream; the writer of suc a poem, though he may be aware of the "meanings" implicit in his dream, must n take the dream to pieces, . . . must allow the story to persist as a story and not dwind into a diagram.'
[2] 'An Eagle Feather', in *The Christian Register*, 19 January 1888, 37–8. Quoted l DeVane. Chadwick was quoting Matt. 10: 22.

success also'.[1] It is tempting to suppose that it was written at the moment when Browning decided to make a supreme effort to justify his own faith in his destiny as a poet.[2]

The very unusual stanza, six pentameter lines rhyming *abbaab*, is a perfect vehicle for Browning's account of his nightmare journey. While the rhymes are arranged like those at the beginning of a Petrarchan sonnet, there is nothing reminiscent of a sonnet-sequence here. Syntactically most of the stanzas are self-contained, yet the onward movement of the narrative is never obstructed as it would be if the stanzas ended in couplets. The run-on lines contribute to the urgency of the verse-movement, as does the exceptionally free handling of the stresses.

Date: 1853
1863: Dramatic Romances

---

[1] Part of the running headline to *Sordello*, vi. 586: see Vol. II of this edition, p. 483.

'Prospice', written after EBB's death in 1861, is an account of a journey which may be compared with 'Childe Roland'. Browning told a schoolgirl who wrote for guidance in her interpretation of it that ll. 4–6 ('I am nearing the place, / The power of the night, the press of the storm, / The post of the foe') are 'figurative descriptions of what may be the circumstances of death: the hitherto unreached "place" (or "time") when the "Foe" is revealed in his terrors'. It 'behoves' the speaker to make proof of his 'manliness', so that His journey will end in 'victory'. See *Crusaders: The Reminiscences of Constance Smedley* (1929), pp. 12–14.

[2] It is not surprising that a number of further possible sources for this poem have been suggested, with varying degrees of plausibility. The influence of Dante's *Inferno*, which Browning certainly knew well, has been suggested by various writers, notably R. E. Sullivan (VP 5, 1967, 296–303); that of Malory's story of Sir Gareth of Orkney (Lionel Stevenson, 'The Pertinacious Victorian Poets'. UTQ 21 (1952), 232–45); and that of Poe's story, 'Metzengerstein', by Barbara Melchiori (*Browning's Poetry of Reticence*, 1968, 208–13). While these and other books no doubt contributed to 'Childe Roland', however, it is as well to remember a letter Browning wrote in his last days: 'I have to say that I never in the course of my life saw even the outside of Scott's "Bridal of Triermain" . . . nor have any notion of what the poem may be about: any such coincidence . . . must be altogether accidental': PK 89: 48.

"CHILDE ROLAND TO THE DARK TOWER CAME."

(See Edgar's song in "LEAR.")

I.

MY first thought was, he lied in every word,
  That hoary cripple, with malicious eye
  Askance to watch the working of his lie
On mine, and mouth scarce able to afford
Suppression of the glee, that pursed and scored   5
  Its edge, at one more victim gained thereby.

II.

What else should he be set for, with his staff?
  What, save to waylay with his lies, ensnare
  All travellers who might find him posted there,
And ask the road? I guessed what skull-like laugh   10
Would break, what crutch 'gin write my epitaph
  For pastime in the dusty thoroughfare,

III.

If at his counsel I should turn aside
  Into that ominous tract which, all agree,
  Hides the Dark Tower. Yet acquiescingly   15

---

note to title *1855P* (See the Fool's Song   3 *1855P* the lurking of   7 *1855P*
for, on his   9 *1855P–63* travellers that might   11 *1855P* break, whose crutch
13 *1855P* council   15 *1855P* Tower; yet

Title: CHILDE: a youth of gentle birth, particularly one aspiring to knighthood. The word is common in ballads, and in *The Faerie Queene*. It was given fresh currency in Scott's poems, and in *Childe Harold's Pilgrimage*.

3 *Askance*: looking sideways, slily.

7 *set*: posted.

14 *which, all agree*: Golder explains: 'These are, of course, not Roland's words, but the cripple's, which Roland quotes indirectly and ironically': p. 968 n. 19. This is a possible interpretation, but hardly probable. If we wish to press the point, in a poem that originated in 'a kind of dream', it may be that the traveller merely wishes to confirm

I did turn as he pointed: neither pride
Nor hope rekindling at the end descried,
   So much as gladness that some end might be.

IV.

For, what with my whole world-wide wandering,
   What with my search drawn out thro' years, my hope   20
   Dwindled into a ghost not fit to cope
With that obstreperous joy success would bring,—
I hardly tried now to rebuke the spring
   My heart made, finding failure in its scope.

V.

As when a sick man very near to death   25
   Seems dead indeed, and feels begin and end
   The tears and takes the farewell of each friend,
And hears one bid the other go, draw breath
Freelier outside, ("since all is o'er," he saith,
   "And the blow fallen no grieving can amend;")   30

VI.

While some discuss if near the other graves
   Be room enough for this, and when a day
   Suits best for carrying the corpse away,
With care about the banners, scarves and staves:
And still the man hears all, and only craves   35
   He may not shame such tender love and stay.

---

18 *1855P–56* end should be.   *{reading of *1863–84S*, DC, BrU, *1889*} *1888* be
26 *1855P* indeed;   29 *1855P* outside, "since   30 *1855P* amend"—
1855, 1856 amend")   33 *1855P* away;   34 *1855–65S* staves,—

---

the direction he has been told he should follow, but is so unfavourably impressed by the sinister cripple that he half believes that he must be lying.

   19 *world-wide wandering*: cf. Shelley, *Prometheus Unbound*, i. 325.

   25 *As when a sick man*: Livingston Lowes pointed out the striking parallel with Donne, 'A Valediction: forbidding Mourning': NQ 1953, 491–2. Christopher Ricks adds Tennyson, *The Princess*, vii. 136–9: NQ 1967, 374.

   34 *staves*: short rods carried in funeral processions.

VII.

Thus, I had so long suffered in this quest,
   ˙ Heard failure prophesied so oft, been writ
   So many times among "The Band"—to wit,
The knights who to the Dark Tower's search addressed   40
Their steps—that just to fail as they, seemed best,
   And all the doubt was now—should I be fit?

VIII.

So, quiet as despair, I turned from him,
   That hateful cripple, out of his highway
   Into the path he pointed. All the day   45
Had been a dreary one at best, and dim
Was settling to its close, yet shot one grim
   Red leer to see the plain catch its estray.

IX.

For mark! no sooner was I fairly found
   Pledged to the plain, after a pace or two,   50
   Than, pausing to throw backward a last view
O'er the safe road, 't was gone; grey plain all round:
Nothing but plain to the horizon's bound.
   I might go on; nought else remained to do.

X.

So, on I went. I think I never saw   55
   Such starved ignoble nature; nothing throve:
   For flowers—as well expect a cedar grove!

40 *1855P* Of those who   42 *1855P–63* fit.   45 *1855P* pointed: all
52 *1855P–63* To the   *1855P–56* gone!   *1855, 1856* round!   54 *1855P* on,

37 *quest*: 'In mediaeval romance: An expedition or adventure undertaken by a knight
to procure some thing or achieve some exploit': OED², 'Quest', sb. 6.
48 *estray*: a lost animal or person.
51 *view*: survey. Cf. *Paradise Lost*, ii. 190.
56 *Such starved ignoble nature*: a marked influence on this landscape was that of *The Art
of Painting in All its Branches*, by Gérard de Lairesse, translated by J. F. Fritsch. Browning
wrote on the fly-leaf of his copy of the 1778 edition: 'I read this book more often and
with greater delight, when I was a child, than any other.' On pp. 258–60 we read: 'I

But cockle, spurge, according to their law
Might propagate their kind, with none to awe,
    You'd think; a burr had been a treasure-trove.   60

XI.

No! penury, inertness and grimace,
    In some strange sort, were the land's portion. "See
"Or shut your eyes," said Nature peevishly,
"It nothing skills: I cannot help my case:
" 'T is the Last Judgment's fire must cure this place,   65
"Calcine its clods and set my prisoners free."

XII.

If there pushed any ragged thistle-stalk
    Above its mates, the head was chopped; the bents
    Were jealous else. What made those holes and rents

---

62 *1855P* portion. See   63 *1855P* eyes—said   65 *1855P–56* The Judgment's
fire alone can cure   66 *1855P* free.   69 *1855P* else! what

---

found myself as in a strange country, so very rugged, desolate and rocky, without paths
or roads, that I knew not where to walk; the ground was no where so even as to rest
on.' Among the objects which meet his eye are 'a morass abounding with vermin . . . a
small rivulet full of big and little clods of earth and pebbles . . . muddy water, decayed
and broken stones . . . barren shrubs and bushes, rough grounds, toads, snakes &c. . . .
I came to a large and hideous rock, split through . . . over-run . . . with moss and
barren shrubs. . . . on the left appeared an inaccessible ruined building, like an heap of
stone, swarming with adders, snakes and other venemous creatures. Behind me the
ground was so uneven, full of ups and downs, and pathless, that I thought it impossible
to get from the place . . . a frightful thunder-clap . . . shook the whole rock . . . [as well
as] a tomb crushed to pieces, and almost sunk into the ground [and] a frightful pool.'
See W. C. DeVane, 'The Landscape of Browning's *Childe Roland*': PMLA 40 (1925),
426–32.

58 *cockle*: a weed which grows among crops. Cf. Job 31: 40: 'Let thistles grow instead
of wheat, and cockle instead of barley'.
    spurge: a plant or weed 'noxious to man': OED², quoting Benjamin Stillingfleet.
59 *Might propagate their kind*: cf. Dryden, *Absalom and Achitophel*, 424.
60 *burr*: 'A rough head of a plant, . . . which sticks to the hair or clothes': Johnson
(with one 'r').
64 *It nothing skills*: it makes no odds, does not matter. This verb, almost always
negative in suggestion, is described by Johnson as 'Not in use'.
65 *the Last Judgment's fire*: 2 Pet. 3: 7.
66 *Calcine*: 'To burn in the fire to a calx or friable substance': Johnson.
68 *bents*: coarse grass, particularly grass with reedy stems.

In the dock's harsh swarth leaves, bruised as to baulk   70
All hope of greenness? 't is a brute must walk
   Pashing their life out, with a brute's intents.

XIII.

As for the grass, it grew as scant as hair
   In leprosy; thin dry blades pricked the mud
   Which underneath looked kneaded up with blood.   75
One stiff blind horse, his every bone a-stare,
Stood stupefied, however he came there:
   Thrust out past service from the devil's stud!

XIV.

Alive? he might be dead for aught I know,
   With that red gaunt and colloped neck a-strain,   80
   And shut eyes underneath the rusty mane;
Seldom went such grotesqueness with such woe;
I never saw a brute I hated so;
   He must be wicked to deserve such pain.

XV.

I shut my eyes and turned them on my heart.   85
   As a man calls for wine before he fights,
   I asked one draught of earlier, happier sights,

70 *1855P* leaves?—   71 *1855P* greenness—   79 *1855P–56* for all I
81 *1855, 1856* mane.   85 *1855P* heart;

70 *dock's . . . leaves*: dock is 'The common name of various species of . . . coarse weedy herbs': OED².

   swarth: black.

72 *Pashing*: to pash a thing is to 'break or dash [it] in pieces. According to OED² the verb was common 'from c1575 for some 60 years'.

76 *One stiff blind horse*: the tapestry is reproduced in *Collections*, plate 27. We know that the infant Pen Browning found it fascinating, and had a noise to indicate it, before he could talk: Ogilvy, 33. Cf. a remark made by Browning, when unwillingly acknowledging that he had Wordsworth in mind when he wrote 'The Lost Leader': 'just as in the tapestry on my wall I can recognise figures which have *struck out* a fancy, on occasion, that though truly enough thus derived, yet would be preposterous as a copy, so . . . I dare not deny the original of my little poem': *Letters*, pp. 166–7. Cf. our Vol. IV, p. 55.

80 *colloped*: a collop means a slice of meat: 'colloped' here may mean 'raw'. The tapestry hardly helps, but Browning was remembering it as seen in a dream.

   a-strain: first recorded in OED² in EBB's *Aurora Leigh* (1856), vi. 328.

Ere fitly I could hope to play my part.
Think first, fight afterwards—the soldier's art:
   One taste of the old time sets all to rights.   90

XVI.

Not it! I fancied Cuthbert's reddening face
   Beneath its garniture of curly gold,
   Dear fellow, till I almost felt him fold
An arm in mine to fix me to the place,
That way he used. Alas, one night's disgrace!   95
   Out went my heart's new fire and left it cold.

XVII.

Giles then, the soul of honour—there he stands
   Frank as ten years ago when knighted first.
   What honest man should dare (he said) he durst.
Good—but the scene shifts—faugh! what hangman-hands   100
Pin to his breast a parchment? His own bands
   Read it. Poor traitor, spit upon and curst!

XVIII.

Better this present than a past like that;
   Back therefore to my darkening path again!
   No sound, no sight as far as eye could strain.   105
Will the night send a howlet or a bat?
I asked: when something on the dismal flat
   Came to arrest my thoughts and change their train.

88 *1855P* part—   90 *1855P–56* old times sets   *1855P–63* rights!   95 *1855P–*
56 Alas!   98 *1855P* first: 99 *1855P–68* honest men should   100 *1855P–*
65S what hangman's hands   101 *1855P–65S* his   102 *1855P* it: poor
104 *1855P–65S* again.

---

91 *Cuthbert's . . . face*: it is clear that Cuthbert and Giles are not to be identified.
They are peers of Roland's who betrayed their trust.

92 *garniture*: adornment.

99 *What honest man should dare*: cf. *Macbeth*, I. vii. 46.

100 *hangman-hands*: cf. Thomas Campbell, 'To the Memory of the Spanish Patriots',
41: 'Your hangmen fingers'.

102 *Poor traitor*: cf. 'The Lost Leader'.

106 *howlet*: owl, as in *Pippa Passes*, iv. 277.

XIX.

A sudden little river crossed my path
  As unexpected as a serpent comes.   110
  No sluggish tide congenial to the glooms;
This, as it frothed by, might have been a bath
For the fiend's glowing hoof—to see the wrath
  Of its black eddy bespate with flakes and spumes.

XX.

So petty yet so spiteful! All along,   115
  Low scrubby alders kneeled down over it;
  Drenched willows flung them headlong in a fit
Of mute despair, a suicidal throng:
The river which had done them all the wrong,
  Whate'er that was, rolled by, deterred no whit.   120

XXI.

Which, while I forded,—good saints, how I feared
  To set my foot upon a dead man's cheek,
  Each step, or feel the spear I thrust to seek
For hollows, tangled in his hair or beard!
—It may have been a water-rat I speared,   125
  But, ugh! it sounded like a baby's shriek.

XXII.

Glad was I when I reached the other bank.
  Now for a better country. Vain presage!

115 *1855P–65S* all   116 *1855P* it,   120 *1855P* whit—   124 *1855P*
beard.   127 *1855P* bank—   128 *1855P* country! vain

111 *glooms*: the plural occurs in Collins, 'The Passions', 64, Tennyson, 'The Palace
of Art', xiv, and in several other places in Browning.

114 *bespate*: an unrecorded and odd formation from *arch.* 'bespit', spit on, sometimes
used of Christ's persecutors, as in the Wycliff version of Mark 14: 65.

    spumes: very rare in the plural.

117 *them*: themselves.

124 *tangled in his hair or beard!*: cf. Shelley, *The Revolt of Islam*, 2466–8: 'my old
preserver's hoary hair / With the flesh clinging to its roots, was strewed / Under my feet!'
See, too, Wordsworth, 'Peter Bell', 573 ff., and the opening of Book IV of *Sordello*.

128 *country*: tract of land, territory.

Who were the strugglers, what war did they wage,
Whose savage trample thus could pad the dank   130
    Soil to a plash? Toads in a poisoned tank,
    Or wild cats in a red-hot iron cage—

XXIII.

The fight must so have seemed in that fell cirque.
    What penned them there, with all the plain to choose?
    No foot-print leading to that horrid mews,   135
None out of it. Mad brewage set to work
Their brains, no doubt, like galley-slaves the Turk
    Pits for his pastime, Christians against Jews.

XXIV.

And more than that—a furlong on—why, there!
    What bad use was that engine for, that wheel,   140
    Or brake, not wheel—that harrow fit to reel
Men's bodies out like silk? with all the air
Of Tophet's tool, on earth left unaware,
    Or brought to sharpen its rusty teeth of steel.

131 *1855P–65S* toads   134 *1855P–56* What kept them   136 *1855P–56* it: mad

130 *pad*: beat down (dial.) Cf. l. 72 n.

131 *plash*: a marshy pool, a puddle; used in *Colombe's Birthday* III.258 for a pool of blood, like 'plesh' in *The Faerie Queene*, II. VIII. xxxvi. 9.

133 *fell cirque*: cruel circle. Cf. Keats, *Endymion*, iv. 769, and 'Hyperion', ii. 34: 'A dismal cirque'.

135 *mews*: prison (obs.) The plural form may be due to a misreading of *The Faerie Queene*, II. V. XXVII. 8–9: 'Captiv'd eternally in yron mewes, / And darksom dens'.

136 *brewage*: brewing.

141 *brake*: rack.

harrow: a device similar to an agricultural harrow, used as an instrument of torture. Cf. 1 Chr. 20: 3.

143 *Tophet's tool*: Tophet was a place near Gehenna where the Jews made human sacrifices to strange gods: 2 Kgs 23: 10. Later it became a site where refuse was kept burning, and so was taken as a symbol of Hell. Cf. Isa. 30: 33. In *The Pilgrim's Progress* Christian tells Evangelist that he is afraid he will 'fall into *Tophet*'. For the comments of EBB and Browning on sinister words, see Kintner ii. 590–1, 593–4, 620, quoted in our Vol. IV, pp. 295–6 n.

unaware: inadvertently.

XXV.

Then came a bit of stubbed ground, once a wood,   145
        Next a marsh, it would seem, and now mere earth
        Desperate and done with; (so a fool finds mirth,
Makes a thing and then mars it, till his mood
Changes and off he goes!) within a rood—
        Bog, clay and rubble, sand and stark black dearth.   150

XXVI.

Now blotches rankling, coloured gay and grim,
        Now patches where some leanness of the soil's
        Broke into moss or substances like boils;
Then came some palsied oak, a cleft in him
Like a distorted mouth that splits its rim   155
        Gaping at death, and dies while it recoils.

XXVII.

And just as far as ever from the end!
        Nought in the distance but the evening, nought
        To point my footstep further! At the thought,
A great black bird, Apollyon's bosom-friend,   160

147 *1855P* with; so   149 *1855P* goes: within   150 *1855P* rubble stones and
152 *1865SP/MS, 1865S* patches raw where leanness   157 *1855P, 1884S* end,
1872S end.   159 *1865SP, 1865S* further?   *1855P* at

145 *stubbed*: 'Having the stubs removed; grubbed up': OED².
146 *a marsh*: 'My . . . "marsh" was only made out of my head,—with some recollec-
tion of a strange solitary little tower I have come upon more than once in Massa-
Carrara, in the midst of low hills': *New Letters*, 172–3.
148 *Makes a thing*: proverbial. Cf. *Othello*, v. i. 4: 'It makes us or it mars us'. See
'Caliban upon Setebos', 97.
149 *a rood*: a measurement of length varying from six to eight yards.
150 *dearth*: famine, sterility.
151 *blotches rankling*: discoloured patches which seem to fester or breed corruption.
152 *leanness*: barrenness.
154 *palsied oak*: almost personified, hence 'him'.
160 *Apollyon's bosom-friend*: 'And they [the damned] had a king over them, which is
the angel of the bottomless pit, whose name in the Hebrew tongue is Abaddon, but in
the Greek tongue hath his name Apollyon': Rev. 9: 11. Apollyon is prominent in *The
Pilgrim's Progress*. He is 'hidious to behold' and 'cloathed with scales like a Fish' and has
'Wings like a Dragon': ed. J. B. Wharey, rev. R. Sharrock (1960), 56. In combat he
comes close to destroying Christian.

Sailed past, nor beat his wide wing dragon-penned
    That brushed my cap—perchance the guide I sought.

XXVIII.

For, looking up, aware I somehow grew,
    'Spite of the dusk, the plain had given place
    All round to mountains—with such name to grace   165
Mere ugly heights and heaps now stolen in view.
How thus they had surprised me,—solve it, you!
    How to get from them was no clearer case.

.

XXIX.

Yet half I seemed to recognize some trick
    Of mischief happened to me, God knows when—   170
    In a bad dream perhaps. Here ended, then,
Progress this way. When, in the very nick
Of giving up, one time more, came a click
    As when a trap shuts—you're inside the den!

XXX

Burningly it came on me all at once,   175
    This was the place! those two hills on the right,
    Crouched like two bulls locked horn in horn in fight;
While to the left, a tall scalped mountain . . . Dunce,
Dotard, a-dozing at the very nonce,
    After a life spent training for the sight!   180

---

166 *1855P* view: 167 *1855P* me, tell who knew,   168 *1855P* get through
them   *1855P–56* no plainer case.   174 *1884S* den.   177 *1884S* fight,
179 *1855P* Fool, to be caught blind at   *1855–63* Fool, to be dozing at   180 *1855P*
With my life spent in training

---

161 *dragon-penned*: with wings, or wing-feathers, like a dragon's.

165 *mountains*: cf. 'Karshish', 291–2.

174 *a trap shuts*: 'The nearer Roland comes to perceiving the Tower, the more
frequently and vividly he uses the trap image': S. H. Aiken, 'Structural Imagery in
"Childe Roland" ': BIS 5 (1977) 25.

178 *scalped*: with a naked summit.

179 *a-dozing*: the only use of this compound before 1868, in OED[2], is 'a-dose', in
Blackwood's Magazine, 66. 23 (1849).

XXXI.

What in the midst lay but the Tower itself?
　　The round squat turret, blind as the fool's heart,
　　Built of brown stone, without a counterpart
In the whole world. The tempest's mocking elf
Points to the shipman thus the unseen shelf　　　　185
　　He strikes on, only when the timbers start.

XXXII.

Not see? because of night perhaps?—why, day
　　Came back again for that! before it left,
　　The dying sunset kindled through a cleft:
The hills, like giants at a hunting, lay,　　　　190
Chin upon hand, to see the game at bay,—
　　"Now stab and end the creature—to the heft!"

XXXIII.

Not hear? when noise was everywhere! it tolled
　　Increasing like a bell. Names in my ears
　　Of all the lost adventurers my peers,—　　　　195
How such a one was strong, and such was bold,
And such was fortunate, yet each of old
　　Lost, lost! one moment knelled the woe of years.

---

187 *1855P* perhaps—why,　*1855–63* Why,　188 *1855P* that,　*192 {reading of *1855P–84S*} *1888, 1889* heft!　193 *1855P, 1865SP/MS, 1865S* everywhere:
1855, 1856 everywhere?　194 *1865SP/MS, 1865S* bell!　196 *1855P, 1856*
such an one

---

181 *the Tower*: cf. 146 n.

182 *blind as the fool's heart*: cf. Ps. 14: 1, 53: 1.

184 *The tempest's mocking elf*: possibly suggested by one of the small figures blowing
the winds in the blank spaces of old maps.

186 *start*: spring out of place. Cf. a book probably known to Browning, (George)
Anson, *A Voyage round the World* (1748), III. ii. 317: 'a but-end or a plank might start,
and we might go down immediately'. Cf. Kelley and Coley, A 67.

190 *a hunting*: a hunt, as in 'Chevy Chase', 10.

191 *the game*: the prey, that is the speaker.

192 *the heft*: i.e. thrust the weapon right in.

195 *my peers*: cf. *Paracelsus*, v. 160 ff. Here the reference is probably to earlier poets. In
Palmerin of England (see p. 134 above), the hero is encouraged when he sees 'the battlements
and windows of the fortress full of his friends' just before he slays the giant: Vol. I, p. 359.

XXXIV.

There they stood, ranged along the hill-sides, met
   To view the last of me, a living frame   200
   For one more picture! in a sheet of flame
I saw them and I knew them all. And yet
Dauntless the slug-horn to my lips I set,
   And blew. *"Childe Roland to the Dark Tower came."*

---

201 *1855P, 1865SP/MS, 1865S* picture: 204 *1865, 1865SP, 1868–84S* blew
"Childe   1865SP/MS, 1865S blew:

203 *the slug-horn*: the word occurs frequently in the poems Thomas Chatterton attributed to 'Thomas Rowley', meaning a clarion or war-trumpet. In 'Battle of Hastynges II', we find 'Some caught a slughorne, and an onsett wounde' (l. 99), in 'Ælla' 'Nowe to the warre lette all the slughornes sounde' (l. 808), and in 'The Tournament' 'lette the Slughorne sounde' (l. 90). Chatterton was misled about the word, an early spelling of 'slogan' (battle-cry), by Thomas Ruddiman's edition of *Virgil's Æneis*, trans. Gawin Douglas (Edinburgh, 1710).

204 *And blew*: blowing a trumpet is a common feature of romance: cf. *The Faerie Queene*, I. VIII. iii. 5 ff., notably iv. 8–9: 'No gate so strong, no locke so firme and fast, / But with that percing noise flew open quite, or brast'. Turner and others have cited Malory's *Le Morte Darthur*, VII. xv: 'fast by a sycamore tree . . . there hung an horn, the greatest that ever they saw . . .; and this Knight of the Red Launds had hanged it up there, that if there came any errant-knight, he must blow that horn, and then will he make him ready and come to do him battle . . . And therewith he spurred his horse straight to the sycamore tree, and blew so the horn eagerly that all the siege and the castle rang thereof. And then . . . they within the castle looked over the walls and out at windows.'

RESPECTABILITY

On 4 February 1852 Browning wrote to his brother-in-law, George Barrett:

people are waiting curiously for the sort of reception Montalembert will have to-morrow at the Institute, where he "reads himself in"—those who, as liberals, hate him most (for his ultra-montane bigotry, "legitimate" opinions & so forth) will see it their duty to applaud him to the echo, on the ground of his having broken with the government on its promulgation of the spoliation measures—just as if he had not done his utmost to help that government when it most needed help—and now that, in consequence, it can act as it pleases, Montalembert cries out on it & expects sympathy! None of mine shall he have when I hear him tomorrow, as I hope to do.[1]

The Institut de France comprises the original Académie Française and several other bodies. Charles-Forbes-René, comte de Montalembert (1810–70), publicist, historian and orator, fought for liberal Catholicism, particularly in regard to education and the power of the Church in secular affairs. Browning was present at his 'réception', an occasion which gave the new Academician much pleasure. Never since 1827, he recorded in his *Journal*,[2] had such a multitude of people been present; it was a crowd 'which was more elegant, if not above all more sympathetic' than any since that date. After he had delivered the customary eulogy on his predecessor, it fell to François Guizot, a man whom Browning thoroughly disliked,[3] to respond. He was the leader of the *doctrinaires*, the party which favoured a constitutional monarchy. He became Foreign Minister and Prime Minister, falling in 1848 and devoting the rest of his life to writing history. While Guizot's praise of Montalembert, a man whose opinions were so different from his own, provides an important line in the poem—an alternative title for which might be 'Hypocrisy'—it is also relevant that such receptions often figured prominently in the social calendar of Paris. In the spring of the same year EBB 'positively went to the Institute with Mrs. Jameson & Madame Mohl & the Countess de Colegno in order to see the reception of the poet Alfred de Musset—yes, & sate four hours, in a heat & crowd . . . I had set my mind on seeing this

[1] Landis, 170.
[2] R. P. Lecanuet, *Montalembert*, iii (Paris, 1912), 132.
[3] *Learned Lady*, 92.

reception. It is very difficult to get tickets, & we had the best-place tickets . . and it's a great sight . . . Lord Brougham came from England on purpose. There were all the great men of France there, almost—poor Guizot, Cousin . . . Montalembert, De Tocqueville . . . I am very glad I went—very.'[1]

Each stanza has eight lines, rhyming *abbacddc*. The first seven lines of each are iambic tetrameters, the eighth being a trimeter. Lines 6 and 14 have each an internal rhyme.

Date: 1853/4
1863: Dramatic Lyrics

RESPECTABILITY.

I.

DEAR, had the world in its caprice
   Deigned to proclaim "I know you both,
   "Have recognized your plighted troth,
"Am sponsor for you: live in peace!"—
How many precious months and years   5
   Of youth had passed, that speed so fast,
   Before we found it out at last,
The world, and what it fears?

II.

How much of priceless life were spent
   With men that every virtue decks,   10
   And women models of their sex,
Society's true ornament,—

---

10 *1855P* virtue deck

   9 *were*: would have been.
   10 *every virtue decks*: like the two following phrases, this is a cliché which might well be in inverted commas.

---

[1] PK 52: 54.

Ere we dared wander, nights like this,
   Thro' wind and rain, and watch the Seine,
   And feel the Boulevart break again   15
To warmth and light and bliss?

III.

I know! the world proscribes not love;
   Allows my finger to caress
   Your lips' contour and downiness,
Provided it supply a glove.   20
The world's good word!—the Institute!
   Guizot receives Montalembert!
   Eh? Down the court three lampions flare:
Put forward your best foot!

---

15 *1855P* And bid the   17 *1855P* love,   19 *1855P* Your lip's contour,
1855–65 Your lip's contour   21 *1855P* And then, rewards—the   23 *1855P*–
65 down

---

15 *Boulevart*: Browning has this spelling, for 'Boulevard', elsewhere. *Trésor* gives one
example, from 1803.
    break: burst.
23 *lampions*: Fr. Lights associated with celebrations.
24 *Put forward your best foot!*: i.e. let's hurry past!

A LIGHT WOMAN

NOWHERE does Browning pose a problem of conscience with more economy. The plot which is supposed to be offered to him for a play in fact constitutes a perfect short-story.

Each stanza has four lines rhyming *abab*. The first three lines of each are tetrameters, the fourth being a trimeter. Iambs and anapaests are the feet.

Date: 1853/5
1863: *Dramatic Romances*

A LIGHT WOMAN.

I.

So far as our story approaches the end,
    Which do you pity the most of us three?—
My friend, or the mistress of my friend
    With her wanton eyes, or me?

II.

My friend was already too good to lose,   5
    And seemed in the way of improvement yet,
When she crossed his path with her hunting-noose
    And over him drew her net.

III.

When I saw him tangled in her toils,
    A shame, said I, if she adds just him   10
To her nine-and-ninety other spoils,
    The hundredth for a whim!

---

10 *1865S* "A .... shame," .... "if   11 *1855P* To the nine-and-ninety
12 *1855P* Her hundredth,

---

9 *toils*: Johnson defines 'toil' as 'Any net or snare woven or meshed'. Cf. *Antony and Cleopatra*, v. ii. 343–5.

IV.

And before my friend be wholly hers,
　　How easy to prove to him, I said,
An eagle's the game her pride prefers,   15
　　Though she snaps at a wren instead!

V.

So, I gave her eyes my own eyes to take,
　　My hand sought hers as in earnest need,
And round she turned for my noble sake,
　　And gave me herself indeed.   20

VI.

The eagle am I, with my fame in the world,
　　The wren is he, with his maiden face.
—You look away and your lip is curled?
　　Patience, a moment's space!

VII.

For see, my friend goes shaking and white;   25
　　He eyes me as the basilisk:
I have turned, it appears, his day to night,
　　Eclipsing his sun's disk.

VIII.

And I did it, he thinks, as a very thief:
　　"Though I love her—that, he comprehends—   30
"One should master one's passions, (love, in chief)
　　"And be loyal to one's friends!"

---

13 *1865S* "And   14 *1855P* to show the fool (I said)   *1865S* him,"   15 *1865S*
"An   16 *1855P–63* at the wren   *1865S* instead!"   22 *1855P* face:
24 *1855P* But, patience,   25 *1855P, 1884S* white,   30 *1855P* her—and that
31 *1855P* passions, love, ... chief,

16 *a wren*: the eagle and the wren are conventionally contrasted. Cf. *Richard III*, I. iii.
71, and Cowper, *Table Talk*, 552–3: 'As if an eagle flew aloft, and then— / Stoop'd from
his highest pitch to pounce a wren'.

26 *basilisk*: 'A kind of serpent, called also a cockatrice, which is said to drive away all
others by his hissing, and to kill by looking': Johnson.

IX.

And she,—she lies in my hand as tame
 As a pear late basking over a wall;
Just a touch to try and off it came;   35
 'T is mine,—can I let it fall?

X.

With no mind to eat it, that's the worst!
 Were it thrown in the road, would the case assist?
'T was quenching a dozen blue-flies' thirst
 When I gave its stalk a twist.   40

XI.

And I,—what I seem to my friend, you see:
 What I soon shall seem to his love, you guess:
What I seem to myself, do you ask of me?
 No hero, I confess.

XII.

'T is an awkward thing to play with souls,   45
 And matter enough to save one's own:
Yet think of my friend, and the burning coals
 He played with for bits of stone!

XIII.

One likes to show the truth for the truth;
 That the woman was light is very true: 50
But suppose she says,—Never mind that youth!
 What wrong have I done to you?

34 *1855P* pear that hung basking *1855, 1856* pear hung basking 42 *1855–63*
guess. 46 *1855–63* own. 49 *1855P* Then one 51 *1855P–56* never
1865S "Never *1855P–63* youth— 52 *1865S* you?"

XIV.

Well, any how, here the story stays,
    So far at least as I understand;
And, Robert Browning, you writer of plays,   55
    Here's a subject made to your hand!

55 *1855P* So, Robert

55 *you writer of plays*: Browning never abandoned the ambition of writing for the theatre.

THE STATUE AND THE BUST

BROWNING told an enquirer that 'the fiction in the poem . . . comprises everything but the (legendary) fact that the lady was shut up there by a jealous husband, and that the Duke commemorated his riding past her window by the statue's erection, as you see it; so my old friend Kirkup, pre-eminently learned in such legends, told me'.[1] It seems that Browning invented everything else, including the bust: 'There are niches in the palace wall where such a bust might have been placed', he continued, ' "and if not, why not?" ' Giovanni Bologna's remarkable statue still dominates the centre of the Piazza della SS. Annunziata.[2] As for the bust, Thomas Hardy, meeting Browning at Mrs Procter's one day in 1887, remarked that

> looking at the 'empty shrine' opposite the figure of Ferdinand . . . he had wondered where the bust had gone to, and had been informed by an officious waiter . . . that he remembered seeing it in its place; after which he gave further interesting details about it, for which information he was gratefully rewarded. Browning smiled and said, "I invented it."[3]

For almost a third of the poem Browning follows the conventions of romance. Riding by, the great Duke sees a beautiful lady at her window, as so many heroes see their heroines for the first time, loves her instantly, and grows 'straightway brave and wise'. The lady has already asked her attendants who he is. In an instant they are deeply in love:

> He looked at her, as a lover can;
> She looked at him, as one who awakes:
> The past was a sleep, and her life began.

When they meet at a feast that very night the Duke is privileged to confer a kiss on the lady, 'As the courtly custom was of yore'. Some say they exchanged a word, which was heard only by the man who had that very day become the lady's husband. By the next morning she has decided to leave him:

---

[1] Browning to E. H. Yates. 22 August 1888 (PK 88:82). Text from *The New York Times*, 6 January 1890, p. 3. Seymour Kirkup was an artist, and the leader of a literary circle in Florence. Cf. p. 291n, below.

[2] It is illustrated in the first ed. of Griffin and Minchin.

[3] *The Life of Thomas Hardy*, 'by Florence Emily Hardy' (in fact his autobiography), ed. of 1970, p. 199.

> I fly to the Duke who loves me well,
> Sit by his side and laugh at sorrow.

She is going to behave much as the heroine of 'The Flight of the Duchess' has done:

> 'Tis only the coat of a page to borrow,
> And tie my hair in a horse-boy's trim,
> And I save my soul.

Abruptly, however, in the middle of l. 75, she remembers that her father 'tarries to bless [her] state', and this proves the first of many obstacles which lead to the lovers' delaying from week to week, from month to month, from year to year, until 'They found not love as it seemed before'. We notice that the moral question which has troubled so many readers is no problem in this world of romance.

In the remainder of the poem, in which the real world supersedes romance, we hear how the lovers tried to make the best of what remained to them, until they realized how little that was, 'And both perceived they had dreamed a dream'. And so the lady has a bust made, to fix her 'beauty never to fade', while the Duke commissions a statue to make posterity believe him a more resolute man than he had ever been; he will 'laugh in [his] tomb / At idleness which aspires to strive'.

In her *Handbook* Mrs Orr makes this one of four 'Didactic Poems' in Browning's work. It was no doubt influenced by 'the importance he attaches to a climactic moment in the lives of individuals',[1] and by his conviction that it would have been wrong if he and EBB had not married, for all the difficulties in their way. They of course had previously been unmarried. So are the Duke and the Lady when they fall in love, but it is only after the first night of her married life that they are at liberty to plan to run away together, and while such a project had caused little or no objection from critics of 'The Flight of the Duchess', in this poem it occasioned an outcry. As Berdoe put it, more bluntly than most,

If every woman flew to the arms of the man whom she liked better than her own husband, and if every governor of a city felt himself at liberty to steal another man's wife merely to complete and perfect the circle of his own delights, society would soon be thrown back into barbarism. The sacrifice to conventionality and the self-restraint these persons practised may have atoned for much that was defective in their lives. "Pecca fortiter" (sin bravely) said Luther; but it would be difficult to defend the doctrine on any principle of ethics.

---

[1] William O. Raymond, in his excellent essay on this poem, in *The Infinite Moment and Other Essays*, 2nd ed., rev. (Toronto, 1965), 218.

The moral presented in the final lines is proposed (it is clear) as something superior to everyday morality.[1] As they await 'the trump of doom' the frustrated lovers 'see not God . . . Nor all that chivalry of his, / The soldier-saints': unlike them they have failed to burn their way through the world to their point of bliss. To the objection that their love was a crime, the poet answers, 'a crime will do / As well . . . to serve as a test, / As a virtue golden through and through'. The sin which he imputes to 'each frustrate ghost'

> Is—the unlit lamp and the ungirt loin,
> Though the end in sight was a vice, I say.

It seems surprising that Browning did not argue that the total poem was dramatic: there is no reason why the 'I' of the final lines must be taken to apply to the poet himself; yet he accepted the identification. When he told this story he chose to draw from it what Edmund Gosse termed a 'non-obvious or inverted moral', as he planned to do in a poem which he had it in mind to write in his old age.[2] In 'The Statue and the Bust', as in that unwritten piece, what another poet might have applauded as self-restraint is 'shown to be, really, an act of tame renunciation, the poverty of the [lovers'] spirit being proved' by their willingness to be content with 'a benefit simply material'.

The rhythm of the poem is unusual. It is appropriate that it should remind us, but only faintly, of 'How they brought the good News', 'Though the Metidja' and indeed 'The Flight of the Duchess', poems in which riding is of central importance. Here the riding is hardly more important when performed by the Great-Duke than when represented by his statue: 'For I ride—what should I do but ride?' he asks weakly.[3] Each line has four stresses. The predominant feet are iambs and anapaests, the latter prominent in the first stanza, which establishes the reader's expectations. The stanza-form is an abbreviated form of *terza rima*, which creates a rapid movement that contrasts with the failure of the lovers to take action. There is a striking change of rhythm in the first stanza of the conclusion, which contains only one anapaest and opens with two iambs which we are tempted to call spondees. Alliteration is prominent, as often

---

[1] As Berdoe recognizes, to do him justice.

[2] Gosse, 85–7. Cf. *Browning's Major Poetry*, 177–8.

[3] 'It is curious to contrast Browning's attitude to sculptured forms in this poem with that of Keats in the 'Ode on a Grecian Urn'. Whereas Keats reflects that the lover on the Urn will love "for ever", as his beloved will be "for ever . . . fair", Browning sees the sculptured forms of his lovers as cold and dead, reflecting the futility of a man and woman who have lacked the courage to act': ibid., 175.

in *terza rima*. The inevitable suggestion of Dante is appropriate, since the reader is more than once reminded of him, most notably of *Inferno* iii. 34 ff.

We are told by Sharp (p. 166) that when the Brownings returned to Florence from the hills in the autumn of 1853 EBB found that the 'chill breath of the *tramontana* was affecting her lungs', so that they moved to Rome for the winter. If ll. 100–5 were suggested by this, as seems likely, then it is possible that the poem was written (or at least begun) there at that time. It is conceivable that the conclusion, which may be compared with that of 'Bishop Blougram's Apology', was added later, to obviate misunderstanding. In any event, it brings into the open the 'Application' of the story.[1]

Date: 1853/4
1863: Dramatic Romances

THE STATUE AND THE BUST.

THERE'S a palace in Florence, the world knows well,
And a statue watches it from the square,
And this story of both do our townsmen tell.

Ages ago, a lady there,
At the farthest window facing the East   5
Asked, "Who rides by with the royal air?"

1 *1855P* well;   2 *1855P* Square;   3 *1855P–56* do the townsmen   5 *1856* the furthest window

1 *a palace*: commentators have been confused about this, as Browning himself was when, in 1887, he told Wise that 'it was not from the Duke's Palace, but a window in that of the Riccardi, that the lady gazed at her lover' (*Letters*, 260). In fact Ferdinand is staring at the Palazzo Grifoni (now Budini Gattai), as Pettigrew and Collins point out. See *The Palazzi of Florence*, by L. G. Lisci, trans. J. Grillo (Firenze, 1985), i. 451 ff., with the illustration on p. 455. For the Riccardi Palace see ll. 33 ff. of the poem. Browning's misidentification may be found in all editions of Mrs Orr's *Handbook*. DeVane follows Mrs Orr.

1 'Application' is the term used at the end of each of Croxall's versions of Æsop's *Fables*, which were read to Browning and his sister when they were children. The present poem is a fable exemplifying the saying 'He who hesitates is lost'. Cf. Vol. II, 113–4 n, and p. 296n below.

The bridesmaids' prattle around her ceased;
She leaned forth, one on either hand;
They saw how the blush of the bride increased—

They felt by its beats her heart expand—   10
As one at each ear and both in a breath
Whispered, "The Great-Duke Ferdinand."

That self-same instant, underneath,
The Duke rode past in his idle way,
Empty and fine like a swordless sheath.   15

Gay he rode, with a friend as gay,
Till he threw his head back—"Who is she?"
—"A bride the Riccardi brings home to-day."

Hair in heaps lay heavily
Over a pale brow spirit-pure—   20
Carved like the heart of the coal-black tree,

Crisped like a war-steed's encolure—
And vainly sought to dissemble her eyes
Of the blackest black our eyes endure.

And lo, a blade for a knight's emprise   25
Filled the fine empty sheath of a man,—
The Duke grew straightway brave and wise.

---

19 *1855P–56* heaps laid heavily   23 *1855P* It vainly   *1855, 1856* Which vainly

15 *like a swordless sheath*: In *1 Henry IV*, II. iv. 240 Falstaff impertinently addresses the Prince as 'you tailor's yard, you sheath, you bow-case'.

18 *the Riccardi*: this powerful and wealthy family bought the Medici Palace in the seventeenth century and made considerable additions to it. At the time of Browning's story 'the Riccardi', or head of the family, is a follower of the Grand-Duke Ferdinand de' Medici (Ferdinando I de' Medici, 1587–1609), who intends to use him as a tool in his negotations with France.

20 *spirit-pure*: no other example in OED[2].

21 *the coal-black tree*: ebony. Cf. Byron, *Childe Harold's Pilgrimage*, 1. 569.

22 *crisped*: closely and stiffly curled; cf. *The Merchant of Venice*, III. ii. 92.
    encolure: mane.

23 *dissemble*: conceal.

25 *a blade*: cf. l. 15 n.
    emprise: knightly adventuring. Cf. *The Faerie Queene*, I. IX. iv, and *Childe Harold's Pilgrimage*, ii. 337: 'his deeds of chivalrous emprize'.

He looked at her, as a lover can;
She looked at him, as one who awakes:
The past was a sleep, and her life began.   30

Now, love so ordered for both their sakes,
A feast was held that selfsame night
In the pile which the mighty shadow makes.

(For Via Larga is three-parts light,
But the palace overshadows one,   35
Because of a crime which may God requite!

To Florence and God the wrong was done,
Through the first republic's murder there
By Cosimo and his cursed son.)

The Duke (with the statue's face in the square)   40
Turned in the midst of his multitude
At the bright approach of the bridal pair.

Face to face the lovers stood
A single minute and no more,
While the bridegroom bent as a man subdued—   45

Bowed till his bonnet brushed the floor—
For the Duke on the lady a kiss conferred,
As the courtly custom was of yore.

In a minute can lovers exchange a word?
If a word did pass, which I do not think,   50
Only one out of the thousand heard.

---

28 *1855P* can,   29 *1855P* awakes,   31 *1855P–56* As love   33 *1855P* pile
that the   40 *1855P* Duke, with . . . . Square   51 *1855P* the thousands heard.

33 *pile*: 'An edifice; a building' (Johnson).
     the mighty shadow: 'The partial darkening of the Via Larga [later Via Cavour] by
the overhanging mass of the Riccardi (formerly Medici) Palace is figuratively connected
in the poem with the "crime" of two of its inmates: the "murder," by Cosimo de'
Medici and his (grand)son Lorenzo, of the liberties of the Florentine Republic':
Handbook. In her second and later editions Mrs Orr apologizes for having wrongly
identified the 'crime' in her first. It was probably Browning who pointed out the error.

That was the bridegroom. At day's brink
He and his bride were alone at last
In a bedchamber by a taper's blink.

Calmly he said that her lot was cast,   55
That the door she had passed was shut on her
Till the final catafalk repassed.

The world meanwhile, its noise and stir,
Through a certain window facing the East,
She could watch like a convent's chronicler.   60

Since passing the door might lead to a feast,
And a feast might lead to so much beside,
He, of many evils, chose the least.

"Freely I choose too," said the bride—
"Your window and its world suffice,"   65
Replied the tongue, while the heart replied—

"If I spend the night with that devil twice,
"May his window serve as my loop of hell
"Whence a damned soul looks on paradise!

"I fly to the Duke who loves me well,   70
"Sit by his side and laugh at sorrow
"Ere I count another ave-bell.

" 'T is only the coat of a page to borrow,
"And tie my hair in a horse-boy's trim,
"And I save my soul—but not to-morrow"—   75

56 *1855P* And the . . . . passed through, shut   *59 {reading of *1863S*, *1872S*,
1884S, DC, BrU, *1889*} *1855P*, *1863–70*,   *1875*, *1888* East   *1855*, *1856* east
60 *1855P–56* She might watch   65 *1855*, *1856* suffice."   66 *1855P* So spoke
the tongue;   *1855*, *1856* So replied

57 *catafalk*: a stage or platform which supports a coffin in a church, or (as here) an
open hearse or funeral car.

68 *loop*: loophole.

72 *ave-bell*: the bell rung for prayers, at dawn and (as no doubt here) half an hour after
sunset.

(She checked herself and her eye grew dim)
"My father tarries to bless my state:
"I must keep it one day more for him.

"Is one day more so long to wait?
"Moreover the Duke rides past, I know;   80
"We shall see each other, sure as fate."

She turned on her side and slept. Just so!
So we resolve on a thing and sleep:
So did the lady, ages ago.

That night the Duke said, "Dear or cheap   85
"As the cost of this cup of bliss may prove
"To body or soul, I will drain it deep."

And on the morrow, bold with love,
He beckoned the bridegroom (close on call,
As his duty bade, by the Duke's alcove)   90

And smiled " 'T was a very funeral,
"Your lady will think, this feast of ours,—
"A shame to efface, whate'er befall!

"What if we break from the Arno bowers,
"And try if Petraja, cool and green,   95
"Cure last night's fault with this morning's flowers?"

The bridegroom, not a thought to be seen
On his steady brow and quiet mouth,
Said, "Too much favour for me so mean!

---

83 *1855, 1856* sleep.   87 *1855P* I drain   95 *1855P–56* And let Petraja,

81 *sure as fate*: proverbial.
86 *this cup of bliss*: cf. Ps. 23: 5.
94 *the Arno bowers*: Florence is on the River Arno.
95 *Petraja*: a country resort on the slopes of Mt. Morello.

"But, alas! my lady leaves the South;   100
"Each wind that comes from the Apennine
"Is a menace to her tender youth:

"Nor a way exists, the wise opine,
"If she quits her palace twice this year,
"To avert the flower of life's decline."   105

Quoth the Duke, "A sage and a kindly fear.
"Moreover Petraja is cold this spring:
"Be our feast to-night as usual here!"

And then to himself—"Which night shall bring
"Thy bride to her lover's embraces, fool—   110
"Or I am the fool, and thou art the king!

"Yet my passion must wait a night, nor cool—
"For to-night the Envoy arrives from France,
"Whose heart I unlock with thyself, my tool.

"I need thee still and might miss perchance.   115
"To-day is not wholly lost, beside,
"With its hope of my lady's countenance:

---

*100 {reading of *1863S–84S*} *1888, 1889* 'But, *1855P–56* "Alas! *1863S* alas,   *1855, 1856*
south.   *1863S* south!   102 *1855P* a canker to her rose of youth.   *1855, 1856*
youth.   103 *1855P–56* "No way   111 *1855P–56* art   his king!
*113 {reading of *1855P–68*} *1870–89* France

100 *leaves the South*: probably 'comes from the South', not merely 'hails from' but
'comes from' in the literal sense, with the present used vividly for the perfect. She may
(for example) come from some great Roman or Neapolitan family.

101 *"Each wind*: see p. 161. *the Apennine*: the range of mountains which stretches
down Italy like a backbone.

105 *the flower of life*: cf. 'In a Balcony', 265.

111 *Or I am the fool*: a verbal memory of an antithesis in *King Lear*, particularly in Act
I, Scene iv.

113 *the Envoy*: as Turner points out, Ferdinand was seeking good relations with
France, to counteract Spanish influence in Italy.

115 *miss*: lose my opportunity.

"For I ride—what should I do but ride?
"And passing her palace, if I list,
"May glance at its window—well betide!"   120

So said, so done: nor the lady missed
One ray that broke from the ardent brow,
Nor a curl of the lips where the spirit kissed.

Be sure that each renewed the vow,
No morrow's sun should arise and set   125
And leave them then as it left them now.

But next day passed, and next day yet,
With still fresh cause to wait one day more
Ere each leaped over the parapet.

And still, as love's brief morning wore,   130
With a gentle start, half smile, half sigh,
They found love not as it seemed before.

They thought it would work infallibly,
But not in despite of heaven and earth:
The rose would blow when the storm passed by.   135

Meantime they could profit in winter's dearth
By store of fruits that supplant the rose:
The world and its ways have a certain worth:

---

118 *1855P* ride!   128 *1855P–63S* one more   130 *1855P* They found, as
132 *1855P* Their love not all it had been before.   135 *1855P* by—   136 *1855P*
could gather in   137 *1855P* Winter's fruits   *1855–63* By winter's fruits
1855P rose,   138 *1855, 1863S, 1863* worth!

---

120 *well betide!*: much less common than 'ill betide!'

130 *wore*: wore on, passed.

134 *But not in despite*: but it would not work against the course of nature: the rose was sure to be past its best after the storm. Cf. *Antony and Cleopatra*, III. xiii. 39–40.

135 *blow*: shed its petals. Cf. Tennyson, 'The Lotos-Eaters', 47: 'petals from blown roses on the grass'.

137 *store of fruits*: the many fruits.

And to press a point while these oppose
Were simple policy; better wait: 140
We lose no friends and we gain no foes.

Meantime, worse fates than a lover's fate,
Who daily may ride and pass and look
Where his lady watches behind the grate!

And she—she watched the square like a book   145
Holding one picture and only one,
Which daily to find she undertook:

When the picture was reached the book was done,
And she turned from the picture at night to scheme
Of tearing it out for herself next sun.   150

So weeks grew months, years; gleam by gleam
The glory dropped from their youth and love,
And both perceived they had dreamed a dream;

Which hovered as dreams do, still above:
But who can take a dream for a truth?   155
Oh, hide our eyes from the next remove!

One day as the lady saw her youth
Depart, and the silver thread that streaked
Her hair, and, worn by the serpent's tooth,

140 *1855P* Were a simple policy—best wait   *1855, 1856* Were a simple policy—best
wait, *1863S* Were a simple policy: best wait,   *1863* Were a simple   *1884S* Were
simply policy;   141 *1855P–56* And lose   *1863S* And we   *1855P–63S* and gain
142 *1855P–63S* Meanwhile, worse   143 *1855P–63S* and lean and   144 *1855P*
grate.   146 *1855P* That holds one   147 *1855P–56* undertook.   148 *1855P*
picture came the   149 *1855P–56* from it all night   *1863S* picture all night
151 *1855P* But weeks . . . . months, and gleam   *1855, 1856* Weeks grew
152 *1855P–63S* from youth   153 *1855P, 1856* dream.   *1855* dream,
154 *1855P* It hovered . . . . above,   155 *1855P–63S* for truth?   159 *1855P*
and, traced by

140 *simple*: foolish.
151 *months, years*: note revision from *1855P*.
156 *remove*: step, stage.
159 *the serpent's tooth*: cf. Ps. 140: 3, and *King Lear*, I. iv. 287–9. See too 'A
Forgiveness'.

The brow so puckered, the chin so peaked,—   160
And wondered who the woman was,
Hollow-eyed and haggard-cheeked,

Fronting her silent in the glass—
"Summon here," she suddenly said,
"Before the rest of my old self pass,   165

"Him, the Carver, a hand to aid,
"Who fashions the clay no love will change,
"And fixes a beauty never to fade.

"Let Robbia's craft so apt and strange
"Arrest the remains of young and fair,   170
"And rivet them while the seasons range.

"Make me a face on the window there,
"Waiting as ever, mute the while,
"My love to pass below in the square!

"And let me think that it may beguile   175
"Dreary days which the dead must spend
"Down in their darkness under the aisle,

---

162 *1855P* The hollow-eyed and the haggard-cheeked,   *1855–63S* So hollow-
eyed   164 *1855P* "Call him here,"   165 *1855P* pass!   166 *1855P*
Carver, I call in aid,   167 *1855P* Who moulds the clay our touch would change,
1855–63S Who moulds the   169 *1855P* so true and   174 *1855P* square;
175 *1855P* "Let

162 *haggard-cheeked*: no other example in OED².
163 *glass*: mirror.
169 *Robbia's craft*: Luca della Robbia (1399/1400–1482) was a skilful sculptor, but is
particularly remembered as the inventor of glazed terracotta, usually with white figures
on a blue or polychromatic background. His factory was carried on by younger
members of his family, of whom the last died in 1566. This anachronism may be
compared, as evidence of fiction, with the absence from the poem of Christine of
Lorraine, whom Ferdinand married with great spectacle and ceremony in 1589.
171 *rivet*: fix.
      range: move (onwards).
172 *on the window*: i.e. on the window-sill.

"To say, 'What matters it at the end?
" 'I did no more while my heart was warm
" 'Than does that image, my pale-faced friend.'   180

"Where is the use of the lip's red charm,
"The heaven of hair, the pride of the brow,
"And the blood that blues the inside arm—

"Unless we turn, as the soul knows how,
"The earthly gift to an end divine?   185
"A lady of clay is as good, I trow."

But long ere Robbia's cornice, fine,
With flowers and fruits which leaves enlace,
Was set where now is the empty shrine—

(And, leaning out of a bright blue space,   190
As a ghost might lean from a chink of sky,
The passionate pale lady's face—

Eyeing ever, with earnest eye
And quick-turned neck at its breathless stretch,
Some one who ever is passing by—)   195

The Duke had sighed like the simplest wretch
In Florence, "Youth—my dream escapes!
"Will its record stay?" And he bade them fetch

Some subtle moulder of brazen shapes—
"Can the soul, the will, die out of a man   200
"Ere his body find the grave that gapes?

178 *1855P* say, what matters at   *1855–63S* matters at   180 *1855P* friend.
*184 {reading of *1863S–84S*} *1855P–56, 1888, 1889* Unless   *185 {reading of
1868–84S} *1888, 1889* The   190 *1855P* And,   *1855, 1856* (With, leaning
191 *1855P–63S* might from   195 *1855P* ever passes by—   *1855–63S* ever passes
by—)   196 *1855P–56* Duke sighed   197 *1855P* Florence "And so my
1855–63S Florence, "So, my   198 *1855P* and   199 *1855P* subte fashioner
of shapes— {revised in *1855P/MS*}   *1855–63S* subtle fashioner of shapes—
201 *1872S, 1884S* body finds the

   200 *the soul, the will*: cf. ll. 25–7.

"John of Douay shall effect my plan,
"Set me on horseback here aloft,
"Alive, as the crafty sculptor can,

"In the very square I have crossed so oft: 205
"That men may admire, when future suns
"Shall touch the eyes to a purpose soft,

"While the mouth and the brow stay brave in bronze—
"Admire and say, 'When he was alive
" 'How he would take his pleasure once!'   210

"And it shall go hard but I contrive
"To listen the while, and laugh in my tomb
"At idleness which aspires to strive."

So! While these wait the trump of doom,
How do their spirits pass, I wonder,   215
Nights and days in the narrow room?

Still, I suppose, they sit and ponder
What a gift life was, ages ago,
Six steps out of the chapel yonder.

202 *1855P–56* shall work my   203 *1855P, 1863S* Make me   *1855, 1856* Mould me
204 *1855P* Alive—the subtle artisan!   *1855–63S* Alive—(the subtle artisan!)
205 *1855P* I crossed   *1855, 1856* I cross so   *1855P* oft   *1855–65* oft!   206 *1855P*
when other suns   208 *1855P–56* brow are brave   212 *1855P–63S* listen
meanwhile and   213 *1855P* At the idleness   *1855, 1856* At indolence which
{in *1855P* there is no rule after l. 213}   214 *1855P–63* while

202 *John of Douay*: Jean Boulogne, known as Giovanni Bologna or Giambologna
(b. Douai 1529, d. Florence 1608). He worked on this statue 1601–8. He was celebrated
for his skill in indicating movement.

213 *idleness which aspires to strive*: those who expiate the sin of Sloth (*accidia*) in Dante's
Purgatorio are punished by having to run continually round and round, urging each
other to greater exertion with the cry 'Ratto, ratto, che il tempo non si perda / Per
poco amor' ('Haste! Haste! let no time be lost through little love'): xviii. 103.

214 *the trump of doom*: as in Milton, 'On the Morning of Christ's Nativity', 156; cf. 1
Cor. 15: 52.

216 *the narrow room*: the grave.

Only they see not God, I know,   220
Nor all that chivalry of his,
The soldier-saints who, row on row,

Burn upward each to his point of bliss—
Since, the end of life being manifest,
He had burned his way thro' the world to this.   225

I hear you reproach, "But delay was best,
"For their end was a crime."—Oh, a crime will do
As well, I reply, to serve for a test,

As a virtue golden through and through,
Sufficient to vindicate itself   230
And prove its worth at a moment's view!

Must a game be played for the sake of pelf?
Where a button goes, 't were an epigram
To offer the stamp of the very Guelph.

The true has no value beyond the sham: 235

---

220 *1855P–56* Surely they   *1855P* I trow   221 *1855P* And all   223 *1855P*
to a point   224 *1855P* For the . . . . life made manifest,   225 *1855P* They
had cut their way   *1855, 1856* had cut his   226 *1855P* hear your reproach—"but
1855, 1856 hear your reproach—   227 *1855P* Since their . . . . crime!"—And a
1855, 1856   crime!"   231 *1855P–56*   view.   234 *1855P*   Guelph—
235 *1855P* The real has . . . . sham,   *1855, 1856* sham.

221–2 *that chivalry of his,* / *The soldier-saints*: OED² has two fifteenth-century
examples of 'the chivalry of heaven'.

223 *Burn upward*: as in certain paintings.

225 *to this*: to no more than this.

227 *a crime*: cf. ll. 246 ('sin') and 248 ('vice').

   a crime will do: see 248 n. and 'Before', 13 n.

233 *Where a button goes*: where a button serves as counter (in a game), it would be a
jest to offer a real coin (a 'guelfo' was an old Florentine coin). Worsfold explains
'epigram' by saying: 'that is, a pithy comment upon the uses to which the names of
princes may be put. The engraving upon the coin ceases to be merely a "stamp" of the
Prince, out of whose mint it is issued, and therefore a guarantee of its value; it is an
epigram, in the literal sense of a pointed sentence, inscribed upon an object. It bears
witness to the vanity of human greatness'.

As well the counter as coin, I submit,
When your table's a hat, and your prize a dram.

Stake your counter as boldly every whit,
Venture as warily, use the same skill,
Do your best, whether winning or losing it,   240

If you choose to play!—is my principle.
Let a man contend to the uttermost
For his life's set prize, be it what it will!

The counter our lovers staked was lost
As surely as if it were lawful coin: 245
And the sin I impute to each frustrate ghost

Is—the unlit lamp and the ungirt loin,
Though the end in sight was a vice, I say.
You of the virtue (we issue join)
How strive you? *De te, fabula.*   250

236 *1855P* The coin than the counter, I submit.   237 *1855P* dram,
239 *1855P–63* as truly, use   241 *1855P–56* play—   *1855P* principle,   *1855,*
1856 principle!   246 *1855P* sin we impute   247 *1855P–56* Was, the
248 *1855P* a crime, we say.   *1855, 1856* a crime, I   249 *1855P* You with the
*250 {reading of DC, BrU} *1855P–84S fabula! 1888, 1889 fabula*

237 *When your table's a hat*: as in a game played in a bar (for example), for the next
drink.
246 *frustrate*: as in *Antony and Cleopatra*, v. i. 2.
247 *the unlit lamp and the ungirt loin*: cf. Luke 12: 35: 'Let your loins be girded about,
and your lights burning.' See too the parable of the foolish virgins, in Matt. 25: 1–13.
248 *a vice*: perhaps revised because the Grand-Duke, as ruler, could not have been
guilty of a crime. Otherwise the revision from 'crime' is hardly an improvement, 'since
it might be argued that a "crime" is a legal concept, whereas a "Vice" is a moral one,
so that it might be wrong (from the standpoint of an enlightened morality) to refrain
from committing what is technically a crime': Jack, 178.
250 *How strive you?*: cf. l. 213.
     De te, fabula: 'the story is about *you*': Horace, *Satires*, i. i. 69–70.

LOVE IN A LIFE

THIS poem forms a pair with 'Life in a Love', and in a limited sense reminds us of earlier paired poems such as 'Rudel to the Lady of Tripoli' and 'Cristina', bracketed as 'Queen-Worship' on their first appearance in *Dramatic Lyrics*. In each of the present pieces the lover is pursuing his mistress. There are two relevant passages in Browning's letters.[1] 'In this House of Life', he wrote to EBB on 5 April 1846, '—where I go, you go—where I ascend you run before,—where I descend, it is after you.' He is longing for the domesticity of marriage. In an earlier letter he had fancied himself meeting her 'on "the stairs"—stairs and passages generally, and galleries (ah, those indeed!—) all, with their picturesque *accidents*, of landing-places, and spiral height & depths, and sudden turns and visions of half open doors into what Quarles calls "mollitious chambers"—and above all, *landing-places*—they are my heart's delight—I would come upon you unaware on a landing-place in my next dream!'

While it is natural to take the house and its rooms literally, we notice that it might be interpreted allegorically as the house of thought which the lover and his mistress share, on which reading the 'suites', 'closets' and 'alcoves' would represent areas of her thought. There is a good account of this poem and the next in Cook, 143 ff.

The piece consists of two stanzas rhyming *abcddabc, efghhefg*, the first three lines of each having two stresses and the other lines having four. Analysis in terms of the conventional feet is perhaps unnecessarily complicated. A critic has complained that it is 'hard to tell' if certain feet in it 'are best scanned as upbeat anapaests or downbeat dactyls'[2]: on reading, however, most of the difficulty disappears. In both stanzas we note that ll. 1 and 4–6 are in falling rhythms, ll. 2–3 and 7–8 in rising. The fact that the first line of each stanza is a choriambus (/ x x /) suggests that Browning may have had Greek lyric forms in mind.

Date: 1853/5
1863: Dramatic Lyrics

---

1 Kintner, ii. 591; i. 404.
2 Stefan Hawlin, 'Browning's Voice': SBHC 20 (1990–1), 13–14.

LOVE IN A LIFE.

I.

ROOM after room,
I hunt the house through
We inhabit together.
Heart, fear nothing, for, heart, thou shalt find her—
Next time, herself!—not the trouble behind her   5
Left in the curtain, the couch's perfume!
As she brushed it, the cornice-wreath blossomed anew:
Yon looking-glass gleamed at the wave of her feather.

II.

Yet the day wears,
And door succeeds door;   10
I try the fresh fortune—
Range the wide house from the wing to the centre.
Still the same chance! she goes out as I enter.
Spend my whole day in the quest,—who cares?
But 't is twilight, you see,—with such suites to explore,   15
Such closets to search, such alcoves to importune!

---

1 *1855P* room;   4 *1855P* her!—   5 *1855P* herself—   6 *1855P* perfume:
7 *1855P* anew,   12 *1855P* centre:

5 *the trouble*: the stir, or trembling.
6 *perfume*: stressed on the second syllable, as in Johnson.
9 *wears*: passes. Cf. 'The Statue and the Bust', 130.
16 *alcoves*: like 'importune' this word has its stress on the second syllable in Johnson.

LIFE IN A LOVE

WHEREAS it is natural to read the preceding poem as the expression of a lover who is destined to succeed, the second lover is clearly destined to fail. His mood may be compared with that of the speaker in 'The Last Ride Together'. Since Browning 'of course' gave Mrs Orr 'whatever explanations she chose to consider necessary',[1] however, particular interest attaches to her remark that the second piece 'might be the utterance of the same person' as the first, 'when he has grasped the fact that the loved one is determined to elude him'. 'She may baffle his pursuit', she continues, 'but he will never desist from it, though it absorb his whole life.'

This is another metrical experiment. The rhyme-scheme is *abc deed fggf hihi jkjkabc*. After the amphibrach+trochee+iamb of the first three lines (repeated at the end) we find rising metre throughout (the first foot of l. 6 is inverted), a mixture of iambs and anapaests.

Date: 1853–5.
1863: *Dramatic Lyrics*

LIFE IN A LOVE.

ESCAPE me?
Never—
Beloved!
While I am I, and you are you,
   So long as the world contains us both,   5
   Me the loving and you the loth,
While the one eludes, must the other pursue.
My life is a fault at last, I fear:

---

8 *a fault*: one sense is no doubt that of a failure in hunting, when the pursuing hounds fail to follow the scent of their prey.

[1] Thomas J. Collins and Walter J. Pickering, 'Letters from Robert Browning to the Rev. J. D. Williams, 1874–1889', BIS 4. 38.

It seems too much like a fate, indeed!
   Though I do my best I shall scarce succeed.   10
But what if I fail of my purpose here?
It is but to keep the nerves at strain,
   To dry one's eyes and laugh at a fall,
And, baffled, get up and begin again,—
   So the chace takes up one's life, that's all.   15
While, look but once from your farthest bound
   At me so deep in the dust and dark,
No sooner the old hope goes to ground
   Than a new one, straight to the self-same mark,
I shape me—   20
Ever
Removed!

9 *1855P* indeed,   10 *1855P–56* succeed—   14 *1855P–56* up to begin
16 *1856* your furthest bound,   *1855P* bound,   18 *1855P–63* hope drops to

HOW IT STRIKES A
CONTEMPORARY

A notable anticipation of ll. 72–7 occurs in an early letter from Browning to EBB written on 9 July 1845:

tho' on other grounds I should be all so proud of being known for your friend by everybody, yet there's no denying the deep delight of playing the Eastern Jew's part here in this London—they go about, you know by travel-books, with the tokens of extreme destitution & misery, and steal by blind ways & by-paths to some blank dreary house, one obscure door in it—which being well shut behind them, they grope on thro' a dark corridor or so, and then, a blaze follows the lifting a curtain or the like, for they are in a palace-hall with fountains and light, and marble and gold, of which the envious are never to dream!¹

The title of this poem may have been suggested by early reading. In a note to 'Rephan', published in *Asolando*, Browning mentions its source as 'a very early recollection' of his, a prose story by Jane Taylor, who published a number of tales in *Youth's Magazine*, 1816–22. One of them (they were collected in 1824), 'How It Strikes a Stranger', describes 'a stranger of extraordinary appearance [who] was observed pacing the streets of one of the magnificent cities of the east, remarking with an eye of intelligent curiosity every surrounding object'.²

Another possible influence may have been 'an Elementary French book, on a new plan, which [Browning] "*did*" for [his] old French Master, and he published': *Le Gil Blas de la Jeunesse* (1835), in which there occur a housekeeper called Jacinte and a 'corregidor de Valladolid'.³

While the poem is dramatic, and set in Spain rather than Italy or France,⁴ it presents a version of Browning's belief that 'A poet's affair is with God, to whom he is accountable, and of whom is his reward'.⁵ It is

---

¹ Kintner, i. 118.

² *The Contributions of Q. Q. to a Periodical Work*, by Jane Taylor, 2 vols., (1824, 3rd ed. 1828), i. 204. Browning's sister Sarianna was given a copy by her mother: Kelley and Coley, A 2258.

³ Auguste Loradoux and Charles LeRoy, *Le Gil Blas de la Jeunesse*, 1835. See Lionel Stevenson, 'A French Text-Book by Browning': MLN 42 (May 1927), 299–305. How much Browning '*did*' is not clear: see Maynard, 254–5 and 441 n. 58.

⁴ Like 'Soliloquy of the Spanish Cloister' and 'The Confessional'.

⁵ Letter to Ruskin: above, p. xxxiv.

natural to connect it with the description of the 'objective poet' in the Essay on Shelley.[1]

'That old "corregidor" is a diamond', Carlyle wrote, '—*unequalled* since something else of yours I saw'.[2]

Date: 1853/5
1863: Men and Women

HOW IT STRIKES A CONTEMPORARY.

I ONLY knew one poet in my life:
And this, or something like it, was his way.

    You saw go up and down Valladolid,
A man of mark, to know next time you saw.
His very serviceable suit of black   5
Was courtly once and conscientious still,
And many might have worn it, though none did:
The cloak, that somewhat shone and showed the threads,
Had purpose, and the ruff, significance.
He walked and tapped the pavement with his cane,   10
Scenting the world, looking it full in face,
An old dog, bald and blindish, at his heels.
They turned up, now, the alley by the church,
That leads nowhither; now, they breathed themselves
On the main promenade just at the wrong time: 15
You'd come upon his scrutinizing hat,
Making a peaked shade blacker than itself
Against the single window spared some house

11 *1872S, 1884S* face: 15 *1855P–63S, 1872S, 1884S* time.

3 *Valladolid*: Valladolid was a royal city until 1561, when Philip III declared Madrid the *única corte* of Spain: it became the capital for a few years under Philip III.
14 *breathed themselves*: passed their time, enjoyed a break.
15 *wrong*: i.e. unfashionable.

[1] Our Vol. IV, pp. 424 ff.
[2] Cf. p. xxxi, above.

Intact yet with its mouldered Moorish work,—
Or else surprise the ferrel of his stick   20
Trying the mortar's temper 'tween the chinks
Of some new shop a-building, French and fine.
He stood and watched the cobbler at his trade,
The man who slices lemons into drink,
The coffee-roaster's brazier, and the boys   25
That volunteer to help him turn its winch.
He glanced o'er books on stalls with half an eye,
And fly-leaf ballads on the vendor's string,
And broad-edge bold-print posters by the wall.
He took such cognizance of men and things,   30
If any beat a horse, you felt he saw;
If any cursed a woman, he took note;
Yet stared at nobody,—you stared at him,
And found, less to your pleasure than surprise,
He seemed to know you and expect as much.   35
So, next time that a neighbour's tongue was loosed,
It marked the shameful and notorious fact,
We had among us, not so much a spy,
As a recording chief-inquisitor,
The town's true master if the town but knew!   40
We merely kept a governor for form,
While this man walked about and took account
Of all thought, said and acted, then went home,
And wrote it fully to our Lord the King
Who has an itch to know things, he knows why,   45

19 *1855P* work: 20 *1863* ferule   26 *1855P* turn his winch.   27 *1855P*
He took in books   28 *1855P* The fly-leaf   29 *1855P* wall,   33 *1855P*
He looked at nobody, they looked at   *1855–65* nobody,—they stared   34 *1855P*–
65 to their pleasure   35 *1855P–65* know them and   *1855P* much: 40 *1855P*
knew,   41 *1855P* Which merely   45 *1855P–63* He

19 *Moorish work*: the name of the city is Moorish. Valladolid was recovered from the
Moors in the tenth century.
20 *ferrel*: ferule.
28 *fly-leaf*: printed on a single sheet of paper.
31 *If any beat a horse*: Browning hated cruelty to animals. Cf. p. 136n[2] above.
39 *chief-inquisitor*: in relation to Spain 'inquisitor' inevitably suggests the Inquisition.
44 *our Lord the King*: the initial capitals appear in all editions.

And reads them in his bedroom of a night.
Oh, you might smile! there wanted not a touch,
A tang of . . . well, it was not wholly ease,
As back into your mind the man's look came.
Stricken in years a little,—such a brow   50
His eyes had to live under!—clear as flint
On either side the formidable nose
Curved, cut and coloured like an eagle's claw.
Had he to do with A.'s surprising fate?
When altogether old B. disappeared   55
And young C. got his mistress,—was 't our friend,
His letter to the King, that did it all?
What paid the bloodless man for so much pains?
Our Lord the King has favourites manifold,
And shifts his ministry some once a month;   60
Our city gets new governors at whiles,—
But never word or sign, that I could hear,
Notified to this man about the streets
The King's approval of those letters conned
The last thing duly at the dead of night.   65
Did the man love his office? Frowned our Lord,
Exhorting when none heard—"Beseech me not!
"Too far above my people,—beneath me!
"I set the watch,—how should the people know?
"Forget them, keep me all the more in mind!"   70
Was some such understanding 'twixt the two?

        I found no truth in one report at least—
    That if you tracked him to his home, down lanes

46 *1855–63* His   48 *1855P* well, 'twas not of easiness   *{reading of *1872S*,
1884S} *1855–70, 1875, 1888, 1889* ease   49 *1855P–70, 1875* came—   52 *1872S*,
1884S side o' the   58 *1855P* for all his pains?   60 *1863* His   *1855P* month,
63 *1855P* to the man   66 *1855P* Did this man   *1855P–65* frowned   67 *1855P*
Reproving when   *1863* Me   68 *1863* My   *1855P* Me,—   *1855–63* Me!
70 *1855P–63* Me   *{reading of *1855P–84S*} 1888, 1889* mind!'   71 *1855P–63* Two?

48 *tang*: suggestion.
58 *bloodless*: passionless.
63 *man about the streets*: as distinct from a 'man about town'.
64 *conned*: studied.

Beyond the Jewry, and as clean to pace,
You found he ate his supper in a room   75
Blazing with lights, four Titians on the wall,
And twenty naked girls to change his plate!
Poor man, he lived another kind of life
In that new stuccoed third house by the bridge,
Fresh-painted, rather smart than otherwise!   80
The whole street might o'erlook him as he sat,
Leg crossing leg, one foot on the dog's back,
Playing a decent cribbage with his maid
(Jacynth, you're sure her name was) o'er the cheese
And fruit, three red halves of starved winter-pears,   85
Or treat of radishes in April. Nine,
Ten, struck the church clock, straight to bed went he.

My father, like the man of sense he was,
Would point him out to me a dozen times;
" 'St—'St," he'd whisper, "the Corregidor!"   90
I had been used to think that personage
Was one with lacquered breeches, lustrous belt,
And feathers like a forest in his hat,
Who blew a trumpet and proclaimed the news,
Announced the bull-fights, gave each church its turn,   95

---

74 *1855P* the Ghetto and   77 *1855P* plate.   79 *1855P* that third stuccoed,
new house,   80 *1855P* Fresh-painted, more genteel than otherwise;
85 *1855P* And wine, three   86 *1855P* April; nine—   *1855, 1856* April! nine—
1863S–65 April! nine,   87 *1855P* clock, and to

74 *Jewry*: ghetto.

    as clean to pace: in *Six Months in Italy*, by Browning's friend George S. Hillard, (2
vols. 1853), we are told that the ghetto in Rome, squalid as it seems, 'is in some respects
the healthiest part of the city': ii. 41.

76 *four Titians*: cf. 'Any Wife to Any Husband', 77 n.

83 *cribbage*; a card game.

84 *Jacynth*: also the name of the waiting woman who becomes the wife of the
narrator, in 'The Flight of the Duchess'. Pettigrew and Collins point out that a
housekeeper called Jacinte appears in *Le Gil Blas de la Jeunesse* (see Introduction).

90 *Corregidor*: chief magistrate (Sp.)

92 *lacquered breeches*: varnished articles of attire were fashionable at this time. In *Vanity
Fair* (1847–8) Lord Tapeworm has 'high-heeled lacquered boots' (ch. 63).

And memorized the miracle in vogue!
He had a great observance from us boys;
We were in error; that was not the man.

I'd like now, yet had haply been afraid,
To have just looked, when this man came to die,   100
And seen who lined the clean gay garret-sides
And stood about the neat low truckle-bed,
With the heavenly manner of relieving guard.
Here had been, mark, the general-in-chief,
Thro' a whole campaign of the world's life and death,   105
Doing the King's work all the dim day long,
In his old coat and up to knees in mud,
Smoked like a herring, dining on a crust,—
And, now the day was won, relieved at once!
No further show or need for that old coat,   110
You are sure, for one thing! Bless us, all the while
How sprucely we are dressed out, you and I!
A second, and the angels alter that.
Well, I could never write a verse,—could you?
Let's to the Prado and make the most of time.   115

---

98 *1855P–56* I was in   100 *1855P* when that man   101 *1855P–65* gay
garret's   sides   105 *1855P* A whole   107 *1855P–65* to his knees
109 *1855P* the day's won, he's relieved . . . . once.   110 *1872S, 1884S* need of that
115 *1855P* time!

---

96 *memorized*: related, recorded.

97 *observance*: respectful attention.

101 *lined*: i.e. with flowers.

102 *truckle-bed*: 'A low bed running on truckles or castors, usually pushed beneath a
high or "standing" bed when not in use': OED[2].

103 *relieving guard*: as by the bier of an important personage, before a funeral.

108 *smoked*: weather-beaten.

109 *relieved*: in the military sense.

113 *alter that*: when we die.

115 *the Prado*: the fashionable place to promenade.

THE LAST RIDE TOGETHER

In this poem Browning again takes up one of the traditional topoi of love
poetry. It is a Valediction, like Drayton's 'Since there's no help, come let
us kiss and part' and the four Valedictions by John Donne: in fact it is a
Valediction forbidding Mourning. For all the self-abnegation in certain of
his love letters to Elizabeth, nothing could remind us less of Browning
than this speaker's acceptance of failure. By endowing the lover with his
own skill in casuistry, indeed, Browning enables him to regard failure as a
kind of transcendental success, the Last Ride becoming a sort of image of
eternity. One is reminded of a much greater poem, the 'Ode on a Grecian
Urn'. Where we expect a complaint, we find a celebration. It is not
surprising that the piece has been parodied, if never with any great degree
of success.[1]

Each of the ten stanzas consists of eleven iambic tetrameters, rhyming
aabbccddeeec. The strict regularity of the beat is varied in the fifth, tenth, and
eleventh line of each stanza, where an anapaest occurs as the second or
third foot.

Date: 1853/5
1863: *Dramatic Romances*

THE LAST RIDE TOGETHER.

I.

I said—Then, dearest, since 't is so,
Since now at length my fate I know,
Since nothing all my love avails,
Since all, my life seemed meant for, fails,
    Since this was written and needs must be—   5

---

1 *1855P* then,   4 *1855P* And all,

5 *written*: in the book of fate.

[1] The best known attempt is 'The Last Ride Together (from her Point of View)', by
J. K. Stephen, *Lapsus Calami* (1891).

My whole heart rises up to bless
Your name in pride and thankfulness!
Take back the hope you gave,—I claim
Only a memory of the same,
—And this beside, if you will not blame,   10
　　Your leave for one more last ride with me.

II.

My mistress bent that brow of hers;
Those deep dark eyes where pride demurs
When pity would be softening through,
Fixed me a breathing-while or two   15
　　With life or death in the balance: right!
The blood replenished me again;
My last thought was at least not vain:
I and my mistress, side by side
Shall be together, breathe and ride,   20
So, one day more am I deified.
　　Who knows but the world may end to-night?

III.

Hush! if you saw some western cloud
All billowy-bosomed, over-bowed
By many benedictions—sun's   25
And moon's and evening-star's at once—
　　And so, you, looking and loving best,

---

10 *1855P*—Or this   12 *1855P–56* hers,   16 *1855P–56* Right!   18
1855P vain, *1855, 1856* vain.   21 *1855P* deified   *1863* deified—   22 18
63 to-night.

12 *bent that brow*: a sign of passion, often of anger.

15 *breathing-while*: as in Shakespeare, *Venus and Adonis*, 1142.

21 *deified*: a common trope in poetry, since Sappho wrote lines translated by Ambrose Philips: 'Blest as th' Immortal Gods is he / The Youth who fondly sits by thee'.

22 *Who knows*: cf. Donne, 'Holy Sonnets', 13: 'What if this present were the worlds last night?'

24 *billowy-bosomed, over-bowed*: no other example of either compound in OED².

25 *many benedictions*: cf. Wordsworth, 'Ode: Immortality', sect. ix.

Conscious grew, your passion drew
Cloud, sunset, moonrise, star-shine too,
Down on you, near and yet more near,   30
Till flesh must fade for heaven was here!—
Thus leant she and lingered—joy and fear!
    Thus lay she a moment on my breast.

IV.

Then we began to ride. My soul
Smoothed itself out, a long-cramped scroll   35
Freshening and fluttering in the wind.
Past hopes already lay behind.
    What need to strive with a life awry?
Had I said that, had I done this,
So might I gain, so might I miss.   40
Might she have loved me? just as well
She might have hated, who can tell!
Where had I been now if the worst befell?
    And here we are riding, she and I.

V.

Fail I alone, in words and deeds?   45
Why, all men strive and who succeeds?
We rode; it seemed my spirit flew,
Saw other regions, cities new,
    As the world rushed by on either side.
I thought,—All labour, yet no less   50
Bear up beneath their unsuccess.
Look at the end of work, contrast
The petty done, the undone vast,

---

28 *1855P* Conscious you grew,   32 *1855P* fear—   *33 {reading of *1855–84S*}
1855P breast! *1888, 1889* breast {in DC there is a pencil revision (with a question mark),
evidently not by RB}   40 *1855P* miss: 42 *1865S* hated;   *1855P–65* tell?
43 *1855P* Where were I now   46 *1865S* strive;   49 *1855P* side:
51 *1855P* unsuccess: 53 *1855P* Done and Undone

---

29 *star-shine*: as in Tennyson, 'The Ballad of Oriana' (1830), 24.
47 *it seemed my spirit flew*: as if on a magic carpet. Cf. *Christmas-Eve*, 523 ff.

This present of theirs with the hopeful past!
I hoped she would love me; here we ride.   55

VI.

What hand and brain went ever paired?
What heart alike conceived and dared?
What act proved all its thought had been?
What will but felt the fleshly screen?
    We ride and I see her bosom heave.   60
There's many a crown for who can reach.
Ten lines, a statesman's life in each!
The flag stuck on a heap of bones,
A soldier's doing! what atones?
They scratch his name on the Abbey-stones.   65
    My riding is better, by their leave.

VII.

What does it all mean, poet? Well,
Your brains beat into rhythm, you tell
What we felt only; you expressed
You hold things beautiful the best,   70
    And pace them in rhyme so, side by side.
'T is something, nay 't is much: but then,
Have you yourself what's best for men?
Are you—poor, sick, old ere your time—
Nearer one whit your own sublime   75
Than we who never have turned a rhyme?
    Sing, riding's a joy! For me, I ride.

---

55 *1855P–56* me. Here   *59 {reading of *1855P–68, 1884S*, DC, BrU, *1889*}
1870–75, 1888 the fleshy screen?   60 *1855P* heave—   61–2 *1855P.* There is
the Poet's crown of years, | That page, the statesman life appears;   63 *1855P* A
flag   64 *1855P* The soldier's   66 *1855P* The riding   67 *1855P–65S*
well,   68 *1855P* The brain's beat   *1855, 1856* Your brain's beat   71 *1855P*
side by side—   76 *1872S, 1884S* who have never turned   77 *1855P* for

---

59 *the fleshly screen*: the limitations imposed by the human condition.
  61 *a crown*: a symbol of achievement, e.g. a brief obituary, a soldier's crude monument, a memorial inscription in Westminster Abbey.
  71 *pace them*: the image is from riding. OED² gives a quotation from 1727–41: 'Pace is
. . . that easy low motion wherein the horse raises the two feet of the same side at a time'.

VIII.

And you, great sculptor—so, you gave
A score of years to Art, her slave,
And that's your Venus, whence we turn   80
To yonder girl that fords the burn!
    You acquiesce, and shall I repine?
What, man of music, you grown grey
With notes and nothing else to say,
Is this your sole praise from a friend,   85
"Greatly his opera's strains intend,
"But in music we know how fashions end!"
    I gave my youth; but we ride, in fine.

IX.

Who knows what's fit for us? Had fate
Proposed bliss here should sublimate   90
My being—had I signed the bond—
Still one must lead some life beyond,
    Have a bliss to die with, dim-descried.
This foot once planted on the goal,
This glory-garland round my soul,   95
Could I descry such? Try and test!
I sink back shuddering from the quest.
Earth being so good, would heaven seem best?
    Now, heaven and she are beyond this ride.

81 *1855P* burn: 85 *1855P* this the sole praise of your friend,   86 *1855P*
"Greatly this Opera's   *88 {reading of *1855P–84S*, DC, BrU, *1889*} *1888* fine
91 *1855P* being; if I   92 *1855P* Why, one   93 *1855P* dim-descried:
97 *1855P–63* quest—

78 *great sculptor*: after the poet, a sculptor (or painter), and a composer, as often in Browning.

80–1 *we turn / To yonder girl*: cf. 'In a Balcony', 409–12.

88 *in fine*: in a word.

93 *dim-descried*: not in OED^2, but cf. Wordsworth, *An Evening Walk*, 164: 'dim between the lofty cliffs descried'.

95 *glory-garland*: cf. *In Memoriam*, xcvii. 3.

X.

And yet—she has not spoke so long!   100
What if heaven be that, fair and strong
At life's best, with our eyes upturned
Whither life's flower is first discerned,
    We, fixed so, ever should so abide?
What if we still ride on, we two,   105
With life for ever old yet new,
Changed not in kind but in degree,
The instant made eternity,—
And heaven just prove that I and she
    Ride, ride together, for ever ride?   110

---

*100 {reading of *1855P–84S*, DC, BrU, *1889*} *1888* long   101 *1855P* If . . . . that,
most fair, most strong,   103 *1855P* Where life's full flower   105 *1855P* If
we keep riding on,   *{reading of *1855P–84S*} *1888, 1889* two   ˈ   109 *1855P*
heaven prove just that   110 *1855P* together, and ever

104 *fixed so*: as in sculpture.
108 *The instant made eternity*: a close parallel to 'Der Augenblick ist Ewigkeit', in
Goethe's late poem, 'Vermächtnis': see M. Kowal, 'An Allusion to Goethe in Brown-
ing': NQ 235 (1990), 32–4.
109 *just prove*: just proves to be.

THE PATRIOT

AN OLD STORY

'An Old Story' because the ingratitude of mankind to its former heroes is no new thing. Whereas in 'The Lost Leader' the great man has abandoned the cause of progress, here the leader remains true but has been deserted by his people. The naming of Brescia in st. vi of the proof and *1855* makes it clear that Browning was thinking of the events of 1848–9, when, in the words of a contemporary, 'after Messina, Brescia and Catania had been put to fire and sword, despotism raised its loathed flag of victory and again bound the whole of Italy in brutal fetters'[1]. DeVane conjectures that the poem was written 'late in the spring of 1849', but provides no convincing evidence.

The five-line stanzas rhyme *ababa* and consist mainly of iambic tetrameters. Most lines include an anapaest, while several include two.

Date: 1853/5
1863: Dramatic Romances

THE PATRIOT.

AN OLD STORY.

I.

It was roses, roses, all the way,
   With myrtle mixed in my path like mad:
The house-roofs seemed to heave and sway,
   The church-spires flamed, such flags they had,
A year ago on this very day.   5

title {in *1855P* the full title is 'THE OLD STORY.'; the running title on p. 193 is, however, 'THE PATRIOT.'}   2 *1855P* mad,   *1855, 1856* mad.   5 *1855P–65S* day!

---

2 *myrtle*: myrtle is sacred to Venus, an emblem of love.

[1] Carlo Pisacane, *Guerra combattuta in Italia negli anni 1848–49*, ed. L. Maino (Rome, 1906), 313.

II.

· The air broke into a mist with bells,
    The old walls rocked with the crowd and cries.
Had I said, "Good folk, mere noise repels—
    "But give me your sun from yonder skies!"
They had answered, "And afterward, what else?"   10

III.

Alack, it was I who leaped at the sun
    To give it my loving friends to keep!
Nought man could do, have I left undone:
    And you see my harvest, what I reap
This very day, now a year is run.   15

IV.

There's nobody on the house-tops now—
    Just a palsied few at the windows set;
For the best of the sight is, all allow,
    At the Shambles' Gate—or, better yet,
By the very scaffold's foot, I trow.   20

V.

I go in the rain, and, more than needs,
    A rope cuts both my wrists behind;
And I think, by the feel, my forehead bleeds,
    For they fling, whoever has a mind,
Stones at me for my year's misdeeds.   25

---

7 *1855P–56* the crowds and   *1855P* cries: 8 *1855P* "Good folks mere   *1855,*
1856 "Good folks, mere   12 *1855P* keep: *1855, 1856* keep.   13 *1855P* do,
surely, I *1855P, 1856* undone,   *1855* undone   17 *1855P* Save the palsied
22 *1855P–56* behind,

6 *broke into a mist*: as it seemed to him, as he rode in triumph.

19 *at the Shambles' Gate*: Johnson defines shambles as 'the place where butchers kill
or sell their meat'.

VI.

Thus I entered, and thus I go!

In triumphs, people have dropped down dead.

"Paid by the world, what dost thou owe

"Me?"—God might question; now instead,

'T is God shall repay: I am safer so.   30

---

26 *1855P* So I entered this Brescia and quit it so!   *1855, 1856* entered Brescia, and
27 *1855P* In such triumphs some people . . . . dead: *1855, 1856* In such triumphs,
28 *1855P–56* "Thou, paid   29 *1855P* Me!"— . . . . might have questioned—but
now,   *1855, 1856* might have questioned: but now   30 *1855P* It is God who
requites: I   *1855, 1856* shall requite! I   *1863–65S* repay!

---

27 *triumphs*: triumphal processions.
30 *God shall repay*: Rom. 12: 19; cf. Luke 10: 35.

MASTER HUGUES OF SAXE-GOTHA

JOHN CHURTON COLLINS twice asked Browning about this piece. On the earlier occasion the poet told him that

The poem was little more than an actual description of what I saw with my own eyes. I happened one evening to stroll into a church—(I think he said it was at Antwerp)—and I made my way, I remember, to the organ-loft, where, though the service was over and the lights were being put out, the organ was still playing, and I looked down into the fast-emptying and fast-darkening church. I was struck with the picturesqueness of the scene and thought I would describe it in a poem. There began and ended the inspiration of the little trifle into which you have read so much.[1]

If Churton Collins was right in remembering Antwerp, it follows that the inspiration of the poem dates from 1838, when Browning visited the city before he returned to England after his first journey to Italy. It is conceivable that he found time to visit the church of St James, with its three paintings by Rubens, a baroque edifice much more ornate than the cathedral, though the latter contains the great painter's tomb. In another passage, more frequently cited, Browning

repeated what he had told me before that he had no allegorical intent in his head when he wrote the poem; that it was composed in an organ loft and was merely the expression of a fugue—the construction of which he understood, he said, because he had composed fugues himself: it was an involved labyrinth of entanglement *leading to nothing*—the only allegory in it was its possible reflection of the labyrinth of human life.[2]

It is impossible to believe that a poem of 149 lines was 'composed in an organ loft', though we must accept the repeated statement that it was in an organ-loft that 'Master Hugues' was conceived.

---

[1] 'Poetry and Symbolism: A Study of "The Tempest"': *Contemporary Review*, 1908, 65–7. Mrs Orr remarks: 'the dramatic situation has . . . a strong basis of personal truth'.

[2] L. C. Collins, *Life of John Churton Collins* (1912), 79. Churton Collins had told Browning his interpretation of the poem, namely that 'the fugue is life, Hugues what Sir Thomas Browne calls the first great composer, the student of the fugue the man who believes in the harmony and wisdom implicit in the scheme of things', and so on. (*Contemporary Review*, 1908, 66). He also asked Browning if he accepted the passage in Plato's *Apology* [22], which argues that 'anyone you please could give a better explanation of what poets in their inspiration mean than the poets themselves'. 'With some reservation, and making of course much allowance for the exaggerated way in which it was stated, this he said was undoubtedly and profoundly true.'

The two passages illustrate vividly the value of Browning's own replies to enquiries about the origins of his poems, but also the frailty of some of the evidence. If Antwerp was indeed the place in question (and here it is Churton Collins who was not sure) then the germ of the poem preceded its writing by about fifteen years, since Browning would surely have published it in *Dramatic Lyrics* or *Dramatic Romances and Lyrics* if it had been written by 1845, and it is unlikely to have been written between that year and 1853 or so.[1] We know that he played the organ whenever he could; if we are to believe 'an American author' who visited Casa Guidi in 1847, he had access to an organ in a 'monastery chapel'.[2] The association of the poem with an organ loft is no doubt authentic: whether the organ loft was in Antwerp is another matter.

We have abundant evidence of Browning's lifelong passion for music, from *Pauline* to *Asolando*. He chose Charles Avison, whose Grand March was one of the earliest musical memories of his life, for one of the finest of his *Parleyings*, and in it he refers to 'Great John Relfe, Master of mine, learned, redoubtable.'[3] 'I was studying the grammar of music', he once said in his old age, 'when most children are learning the multiplication table, and I know what I am talking about when I speak of music'.[4] Music and musicians were potent in his imagination, and it is not surprising that he, a composer himself, should have been inspired by music to the composition of several of his most memorable pieces.

Master Hugues is an imaginary composer, so named as to provide a rhyme for 'fugues':

had he been meant for the glorious Bach it were a shame to me indeed; I had in my mind one of the dry-as-dust imitators who would elaborate some such subject as

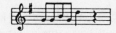

for a dozen pages together.[5] The "mode Palestrina" has no reference to organ-playing; it was the name given by old Italian writers on Composition to a certain

---

[1] See above, pp. xiv ff.   [2] Griffin and Minchin, 161.

[3] *Parleyings with Certain People of Importance*, VII. 81–2.

[4] Griffin and Minchin, 16.

[5] 'Since this motif exhibits the major triad on G', a friend comments, 'and the fugue is in F minor, Browning can have had in mind only a compositional procedure, not the specific work. His statement, however, is interesting for other reasons. He does not and cannot pretend that the readers who mistook Master Hugues for Bach had overlooked any clue in the text; the ordinary concert-goer in the nineteenth century, as opposed to the serious musician, was much less likely to know or appreciate Bach than his modern counterpart. On the other hand, in our own day, when "programme music" is out of favour, and serious criticism scorns to speak of "meaning", let alone "intent", we may

simple and severe style like that of the Master; just as, according to Byron, "the word Miltonic means sublime".[1]

The clue to the central part of the poem is the style of musical composition called a 'fugue' (L. *fuga*, flight). A quotation from the *New Oxford Companion to Music* will be helpful: a fugue is

a composition in which three or more voices enter imitatively one after the other, each giving chase to the previous voice which 'flies' before it. . . . Fugue is a style of composition rather than a principle of form, but nevertheless there is an accepted terminology to describe the various roles of each voice in the fugue. The first voice to enter carries the principal theme . . . which is known as the 'subject'. After this theme has been presented the second voice enters, transposing this subject to the dominant . . . these dominant entries are called 'answers'. The third voice then enters after the answer with the subject, and so it continues: an alternation of subject and answer until all the voices in the fugue have entered. This section of the composition is known as the 'exposition', which is concluded when the last voice to enter has presented the subject or answer.[2]

The poem is a narrative, told in the first person, with a marked element of comedy in it. The speaker is not a poet passing through a town, but the 'poor organist' of an ornate old church. In st. iii he is quickly setting to rights a pedal which is not as it should be. He thinks of the 'church saints' who, as he likes to fancy, keep an eye on the place at night. As he reflects on a purely imaginary fugue he seems to see the face of Master Hugues looking like the score of the music and supposes that he is complaining that while he plays the piece correctly he does not understand its 'intent'. He then thinks through the piece (sts. xii–xxi) and wonders whether the fugue is somehow Hugues's 'moral of life'. Do we weave a complicated web which we prefer to 'truth and nature'? In xxvi he begins to play the piece again, but as he does so he has the sense that 'Truth's golden o'er us although we refuse it', partly (at least) because we pay too much attention to the commentators of the past (xxv). In reaction he blares out a piece of music in 'the *mode Palestrina*'. The poem ends, as it began, in comedy, as he asks the sacristan whether he wants him to be found dead in the morning at the foot of the 'rotten-runged rat-riddled stairs' because he has no light to enable him to get down in safety.

well side with Master Hugues and his complex craftsmanship and look down our noses at the organist; is this wholly false to Browning's poem? After all, in "A Toccata" it is the shallow coxcomb who finds meaning in the music, rather as the monks sought pious effects in Fra Lippo Lippi's paintings'.

[1] Herbert E. Greene, 'Browning's Knowledge of Music': PMLA 62 (1947), 1098, Browning to H. G. Spaulding.

[2] *The New Oxford Companion to Music*, ed. Denis Arnold (2 vols., Oxford, 1983), i. 731.

Each stanza except the last rhymes *ababa*. The metre is predominantly dactylic: as a rule the first, second and fifth line of each stanza scan / x x /x x /, while lines 3 and 4 scan / x x / x x / x x /. From st. vii variations occur at the end of the line, which may become a trochee or a dactyl: in that stanza, for instance, 'runningly' and 'cunningly' in ll. 32 and 34 make these two lines completely dactylic just as they serve to convey the quality of the narrator's playing. The last stanza has nine lines, rhyming *ababcccb*: the last three lines being anapaestic (though the first of them opens with an iamb).

Date: 1853/4
1863: *Dramatic Lyrics*

MASTER HUGUES OF SAXE-GOTHA.

I.

HIST, but a word, fair and soft!
   Forth and be judged, Master Hugues!
Answer the question I've put you so oft:
   What do you mean by your mountainous fugues?
See, we're alone in the loft,—   5

II.

I, the poor organist here,
   Hugues, the composer of note,
Dead though, and done with, this many a year:
   Let's have a colloquy, something to quote,
Make the world prick up its ear!   10

---

1 *1855P* soft—

Title: *Saxe-Gotha*: since Hugues is 'one of the dry-as-dust imitators' of J. S. Bach, this locality is appropriate. Bach was born in Eisenach in 1685; four years before his death in 1750 it was united with Sachsen-Weimar (not in fact Sachsen-Gotha).
  1 *fair and soft*: cf. *Much Ado*, v. iv. 72.
  4 *fugues*: see introduction.
  9 *colloquy*: discussion, L. *colloquium*.

III.

See, the church empties apace:
 Fast they extinguish the lights.
Hallo there, sacristan! Five minutes' grace!
 Here's a crank pedal wants setting to rights,
Baulks one of holding the base.   15

IV.

See, our huge house of the sounds,
 Hushing its hundreds at once,
Bids the last loiterer back to his bounds!
 —O you may challenge them, not a response
Get the church-saints on their rounds!   20

V.

(Saints go their rounds, who shall doubt?
 —March, with the moon to admire,
Up nave, down chancel, turn transept about,
 Supervise all betwixt pavement and spire,
Put rats and mice to the rout—   25

VI.

Aloys and Jurien and Just—
 Order things back to their place,

---

11 *1855P* a-pace, *1855, 1856* a-pace. 12 *1855P–63* lights— 13 *1855P–*
65S five 15 *1855P* base! 18 *1855P–56* bounds

 11 *apace*: quickly.
 13 *sacristan*: the man who has charge of the contents of a church.
 14 *crank*: unsatisfactory, needing attention. The first example of this use in OED² is
from Carlyle, *Sartor Resartus*, 1. iii: 'the machinery . . . seemed crank and slack'.
 15 *Baulks one of*: prevents one from.
  holding: to prolong the note.
 18 *back to his bounds*: cf. 'Fra Lippo Lippi', 223, 341.
 19 *them*: the sounds.
 20 *the church-saints*: those after whom the church is called. Cf. 26.
 23 *nave*: the nave is the central part of a church, the chancel the part behind the altar,
and the transept the cross-part of a cruciform church.
 26 *Aloys*: Aloysius Gonzaga (1568–91), who died as a Jesuit novice, working in a
hospital for victims of the plague. 'Jurien' is not to be found in the *Bibliotheca Sanctorum*,

Have a sharp eye lest the candlesticks rust,
   Rub the church-plate, darn the sacrament-lace,
Clear the desk-velvet of dust.)   30

VII.

Here's your book, younger folks shelve!
   Played I not off-hand and runningly,
Just now, your masterpiece, hard number twelve?
   Here's what should strike, could one handle it cunningly:
Help the axe, give it a helve!   35

VIII.

Page after page as I played,
   Every bar's rest, where one wipes
Sweat from one's brow, I looked up and surveyed,
   O'er my three claviers, yon forest of pipes
Whence you still peeped in the shade.   40

IX.

Sure you were wishful to speak?
   You, with brow ruled like a score,
Yes, and eyes buried in pits on each cheek,
   Like two great breves, as they wrote them of yore,
Each side that bar, your straight beak!   45

---

31 *1855P* shelve: 33 *1855P* twelve,   34 *1855P* cunningly,   *1855, 1856*
cunningly.   41 *1855P* speak!   *1855–84S* speak,   45 *1855P* beak.

12 vols. (Istituto Giovanni XXIII, Rome, 1960–70), which aims at completeness. 'Just'
is presumably Justus, the fabulous boy-martyr of Beauvais.

   29 *the sacrament-lace*: the lace of the altar-cloth.
   32 *off-hand*: without preparation, at sight.
      runningly: It. *correntemente*.
   35 *helve*: handle of an axe.
   39 *claviers*: keyboards, banks of manuals.
   44 *Like two great breves*: in the musical notation of the later Middle Ages and
Renaissance the breve was written square; in this Baroque composer, however, we
should rather think of the oblong used in later printing ('of yore' is a reminder that in
the organist's day breves were hardly used at all). He seems to see Master Hugues
peeping from the score, with the bar-line as his beaklike nose and the breves as his eyes.

X.

Sure you said—"Good, the mere notes!
    "Still, couldst thou take my intent,
"Know what procured me our Company's votes—
    "A master were lauded and sciolists shent,
"Parted the sheep from the goats!"   50

XI.

Well then, speak up, never flinch!
    Quick, ere my candle's a snuff
—Burnt, do you see? to its uttermost inch—
    I believe in you, but that's not enough:
Give my conviction a clinch!   55

XII.

First you deliver your phrase
    —Nothing propound, that I see,
Fit in itself for much blame or much praise—
    Answered no less, where no answer needs be:
Off start the Two on their ways.   60

XIII.

Straight must a Third interpose,
    Volunteer needlessly help;

---

48 *1855P* votes!   49 *1855P* Masters were   *1855–63* Masters being lauded
50 *1855P* Parting the   54 *1855P* enough,   *1855, 1856* enough.   55 *1855P*
clinch.   60 *1855P–63* ways!

---

48 *our Company's votes*: Hugues is here supposed to have been elected organist by the
municipal governing body. So in 1707 Bach became organist of the church of St Blasius
in Mühlhausen, on the vote of the councillors.
49 *sciolists*: Johnson defines a sciolist as 'One who knows many things superficially'.
    shent: disgraced, ruined. Cf. Shakespeare, *Merry Wives*, I. iv. 33.
50 *the sheep from the goats*: Matt. 25: 32.
52 *a snuff*: 'A candle almost burnt out': Johnson, citing *Cymbeline*, I. vi. 86.
55 *a clinch*: 'the clinching of an argument, opinion, etc.': OED²,
56 *phrase*: 'The chief motive; technically the *proposta*, or main proposition, to which
the *risposta*, or reply, forms the complementary motive': Worsfold.

In strikes a Fourth, a Fifth thrusts in his nose,
   So the cry's open, the kennel's a-yelp,
Argument's hot to the close.   65

XIV.

One dissertates, he is candid;
   Two must discept,—has distinguished;
Three helps the couple, if ever yet man did;
   Four protests; Five makes a dart at the thing wished:
Back to One, goes the case bandied.   70

XV.

One says his say with a difference;
   More of expounding, explaining!
All now is wrangle, abuse, and vociferance;
   Now there's a truce, all's subdued, self-restraining:
Five, though, stands out all the stiffer hence.   75

XVI.

One is incisive, corrosive;
   Two retorts, nettled, curt, crepitant;
Three makes rejoinder, expansive, explosive;
   Four overbears them all, strident and strepitant:
Five . . . O Danaides, O Sieve!   80

---

65 *1855P–63* close!   67 *1855P–56* distinguished!   68 *1855P* did,
69 *1855P–56* protests,   70 *1855P–56* bandied!   75 *1855P* hence!

64 *the cry's open*: the hounds are yelping at the beginning of the pursuit. Cf. *Merry Wives*, IV. ii. 174–5: 'If I cry out thus upon no trail, never trust me when I open again'.
   a-yelp: no other example in OED[2].

67 *discept*: differ (from the previous speaker).

79 *crepitant*: making a crackling noise: no earlier example in OED[2].

79 *strepitant*: noisy: no earlier example.

80 *O Danaides, O Sieve!*: the Danaides, the fifty daughters of Danaus, king of Argus, promised their father that they would kill their husbands on the first night of their married lives, because of an old feud. All but one did, and 'were condemned to severe punishment in hell, and were compelled to fill with water a vessel full of holes, so that the water ran out as soon as poured into it and therefore their labour was infinite, and their punishment eternal'. Lemprière. The fugue seems similarly endless.

XVII.

Now, they ply axes and crowbars;
   Now, they prick pins at a tissue
Fine as a skein of the casuist Escobar's
   Worked on the bone of a lie. To what issue?
Where is our gain at the Two-bars?   85

XVIII.

Est fuga, volvitur rota.
   On we drift: where looms the dim port?
One, Two, Three, Four, Five, contribute their quota;
   Something is gained, if one caught but the import—
Show it us, Hugues of Saxe-Gotha!   90

XIX.

What with affirming, denying,
   Holding, risposting, subjoining,

84 *1855P* lie: 86 *1855P–63 rota!*   87 *1855P* On I drift,   *1855–63* drift.
Where   89 *1865SP/MS, 1865S* if we caught   90 *1855P* Saxe-Gotha.
92 *1855P* risposting,

82 *prick pins at a tissue*: in this old process the pins were not pricked into the cloth,
but on to some kind of tracing paper. The paper with the pin-pricked pattern was
then laid on the material, and a fine powder was rubbed over the paper to leave the
pattern on the material. This would be very quiet. Dr Jean Macqueen, our informant,
adds that 'There would be a parallel with the figure in the delicacy of the process,
and in the creation of a complex pattern from many tiny dots (cf. musical notes).' The
next line shows Browning moving from one sense of 'tissue' to another, namely fine
material.
   83 *a skein*: 'A knot of thread or silk wound and doubled': Johnson.
   Escobar. Antonio Escobar y Mendoza (1589–1669), a voluminous Spanish relig-
ious writer, best known as a casuist. The Fr. verb *escobarder*, to equivocate, derives from
his name.
   84 *the bone*: 'A sort of *bobbins*, made of trotter bones, for weaving bonelace': Johnson.
'Worked on the bone of a lie' means that the basis of the structure is false.
   85 *the Two-bars*: the double bar which marks the end of the work.
   86 *Est fuga, volvitur rota*: we have been unable to find a source for these words, which
are supposed to be a guide written in the music MS: 'fuga' no doubt means 'fugue',
'volvitur' means 'is being turned', and 'rota', 'wheel'.
   92 *risposting*: old spelling, from 'riposte', in fencing: 'A quick thrust given after
parrying a lunge'. Cf. 56 n.

All's like . . . it's like . . . for an instance I'm trying . . .
   There! See our roof, its gilt moulding and groining
Under those spider-webs lying!   95

XX.

So your fugue broadens and thickens,
   Greatens and deepens and lengthens,
Till we exclaim—"But where's music, the dickens?"
   "Blot ye the gold, while your spider-web strengthens
"—Blacked to the stoutest of tickens?"   100

XXI.

I for man's effort am zealous:
   Prove me such censure unfounded!
Seems it surprising a lover grows jealous—
   Hopes 't was for something, his organ-pipes sounded,
Tiring three boys at the bellows?   105

XXII.

Is it your moral of Life?
   Such a web, simple and subtle,
Weave we on earth here in impotent strife,
   Backward and forward each throwing his shuttle,
Death ending all with a knife?   110

XXIII.

Over our heads truth and nature—
   Still our life's zigzags and dodges,

---

94 *1855P* its gold moulding   98 *1855P–63* Till one exclaims—"But   101 *1855,*
1856 zealous.   102 *1855P–63* such censures unfounded!   110 *1855P* with his knife?

94 *groining*: 'The edge formed by the intersection of two vaults', or 'the rib or fillet of stone of wood with which this is usually covered': OED[2].
98 *the dickens*: this exclamation is first recorded in *The Merry Wives of Windsor*, III. ii. 17.
99 *blot*: conceal, obscure.
   the gold: the gold of truth.
100 *tickens*: a dialectal form of 'tickings', stout cotton or linen, here used for thread.
109 *shuttle*: cf. *Merry Wives*, V. i. 20: 'I know . . . life is a shuttle.'
110 *a knife*: perhaps suggested by Atropos, one of the Parcae, who bore a pair of scissors in her hand. Cf. 'Lycidas', 75–6.

Ins and outs, weaving a new legislature—
　　God's gold just shining its last where that lodges,
Palled beneath man's usurpature.   115

XXIV.

So we o'ershroud stars and roses,
　　Cherub and trophy and garland;
Nothings grow something which quietly closes
　　Heaven's earnest eye: not a glimpse of the far land
Gets through our comments and glozes.   120

XXV.

Ah but traditions, inventions,
　　(Say we and make up a visage)
So many men with such various intentions,
　　Down the past ages, must know more than this age!
Leave we the web its dimensions!   125

XXVI.

Who thinks Hugues wrote for the deaf,
　　Proved a mere mountain in labour?

---

115 *1855P* beneath Art's usurpature!　*1855–65S* usurpature!　116 *1855P* So men
o'erweave stars　117 *1855P* garland,　*1855–63* garland.　119 *1855P–63*
eye,—　125 *1855P–63* Leave the web all its　126 *1855P* Think you Hugues
1855P–56 deaf?　127 *1855P* Proves a

113 *legislature*: strictly the body that makes laws.

114 *that*: the 'legislature' which conceals the gold of the roof.

115 *Palled*: covered with a pall. Cf. *In Memoriam*, lxx. 7.

　　usurpature: the first occurrence of the word in OED² is in 'The Flight of the
Duchess', 473.

116 *stars and roses*: on the roof of the ornate church.

120 *glozes*: comments, often (as here) implying that they are useless.

122 *make up a visage*: adopt a suitably solemn expression.

127 *a mere mountain in labour*: from Horace, *De Arte Poetica*, 139: 'Parturiunt montes:
nascetur ridiculus mus', the mountains are in labour, [but only] a ridiculous mouse will
be born'.

Better submit; try again; what's the clef?
 'Faith, 't is no trifle for pipe and for tabor—
Four flats, the minor in F.   130

XXVII.

Friend, your fugue taxes the finger:
 Learning it once, who would lose it?
Yet all the while a misgiving will linger,
 Truth's golden o'er us although we refuse it—
Nature, thro' cobwebs we string her.   135

XXVIII.

Hugues! I advise *meâ pœnâ*
 (Counterpoint glares like a Gorgon)
Bid One, Two, Three, Four, Five, clear the arena!
 Say the word, straight I unstop the full-organ,
Blare out the *mode Palestrina*.   140

---

129 *1855P–63* 'Faith, it's no   130 *1855P* the minor's in   131 *1855, 1856*
finger.   135 *1855P* Art's crowned—for Nature—unking her! *1855–65S* thro'
dust-clouds we fling her!

 128 *clef*: before the mid-eighteenth century, the position of the clefs was not fixed;
the C clef, in particular, could stand on any line of the stave. The organist, looking to
see where the clefs are placed, observes the four flats of the key signature, and tells from
the music itself that it denotes F minor and not A flat major.

 129 *for pipe and for tabor*: the two are often yoked to indicate peaceful rejoicing (as in
Much Ado, II. iii. 15). A pipe was 'the small flageolet-like instrument held to the mouth
. . . with the left hand . . . whilst the right played the tabor, or small drum, hanging from
the body': *The Oxford Companion to Music*, 10th ed. (1970).

 135 *Nature*: as in 111.

  we string her. *1855* is somewhat clearer: 'we string her' may perhaps be compared
with 'fine-drawn' arguments. Cf. too *In Memoriam*, cxxiv. 8.

 136 *meâ pœnâ*: at my risk.

 137 *Counterpoint*: the rules governing the combination of simultaneous musical lines.

  a Gorgon: 'a monster with snaky hair, of which the sight turned beholders to
stone': Johnson. A friend points out that the image may have been suggested by the
appearance of the fugue on the page, each voice being similar to that above or below
it but at a short horizontal as well as vertical distance from it, looking like wavy lines
that suggest a Gorgon's snaky hair—'especially to a man who has had a vision of Master
Hugues's face in the form of a musical score'.

 138 *Bid One, Two, Three*: cf. sts. xii–xiv.

 139 *unstop*: 'To pull or draw out': OED².

XXIX.

While in the roof, if I'm right there,
   . . . Lo you, the wick in the socket!
Hallo, you sacristan, show us a light there!
   Down it dips, gone like a rocket.
What, you want, do you, to come unawares,   145
Sweeping the church up for first morning-prayers,
And find a poor devil has ended his cares
At the foot of your rotten-runged rat-riddled stairs?
   Do I carry the moon in my pocket?

---

141 *1855P* See in   144 *1855P–65S* rocket!   147 *1855P–56* devil at end of
his   148 *1855P–56* your rotten-planked rat-riddled

---

149 *Do I carry the moon*: cf. *Cymbeline*, III. i. 42–4: 'If Cæsar can hide the sun from us
with a blanket, or put the moon in his pocket, we will pay him tribute for light'.
Pointing this out, R. D. Altick writes: 'Note that "hide the sun . . . with a blanket" may
have suggested "Blot ye the gold, while your spider-web strengthens, / Blacked to the
stoutest of tickens" (ll. 99–100). For some reason *Cymbeline* was in the back of
Browning's mind as he wrote this poem; like the roof of the baroque church, "the roof
of [Imogen's] chamber," according to Iachimo (II. iv. 87–8), "With golden cherubins
is fretted." ' 'The Symbolism of Browning's "Master Hugues . . ." ', VP 3 (1965), 5 n.

BISHOP BLOUGRAM'S APOLOGY

DeVane's description of this poem as 'a by-product of Browning's work upon *Christmas-Eve and Easter-Day*'[1] is misleading. Whereas that strange double-poem has a marked subjective element, embodying as it does Browning's own reflections on religion at a crisis in his emotional life,[2] the Bishop is one of his triumphs of dramatization. The inspiration of the poem was clearly the restoration of the Catholic hierarchy in England in October 1850, commonly referred to at the time as the Papal Aggression.[3]

It does not follow that the 'Apology' was written immediately after that event. The clearest indication of time in the poem occurs in l. 938, where 'this war' is obviously the Crimean War, which began in 1854. Two further references seem to point to 1854/5: 'Up with the Immaculate Conception' (l. 704) must refer to the Bull *Ineffabilis Deus* of 8 December 1854, while the mention of 'The new edition, fifty volumes long' of the works of Balzac may refer to a preliminary announcement of an edition of his works which eventually began to appear in 1856.[4] Indeed 1854/5 seems to be the most likely date of composition, in which case the poem, which in some ways points forward to *Dramatis Personæ*, may have been one of the last-written of the pieces in *Men and Women*. It remains conceivable, of course, that it had been begun earlier.

The Roman Catholic community in England and Wales had been growing rapidly since 1770, when it numbered about 80,000. From 1815 the flow of Irish immigrants increased greatly. Estimates are inevitably inexact, but for our purpose it is enough to cite John Bossy's estimate that there were 'something like three quarters of a million' Catholics in England and Wales by 1851.[5] Whereas there had been only eight or nine Catholic chapels in London in 1800, by then there were thirty-five. Catholic emancipation, so long debated, had become a reality in 1829.

Nicholas Patrick Stephen Wiseman, whom Browning acknowledged as the original of his Bishop,[6] was born in Seville in 1802, the son of an Irish

---

[1] 'as the reference to Strauss (l. 577) shows', he oddly remarks.

[2] See our Vol. IV, p. 326.

[3] This has already been pointed out, e.g. by C. R. Tracy, 'Bishop Blougram': MLR 34 (1939), 422 ff. Useful background material may be found in J. L. Altholz, *The Liberal Catholic Movement in England* (1962).

[4] See below, note to l. 109.

[5] John Bossy, *The English Catholic Community 1570–1850* (1975), 298.

[6] See below, p. 209.

Catholic who spent much of his life in Spain.[1] In 1818 he began studying at the English College in Rome, of which he was later to become Rector. During Advent 1835 and Lent 1836 he gave courses of lectures in England which were designed to attract non-Catholics: their tone was 'apologetic' rather than polemical and they attracted large audiences which included such notabilities as Lord Brougham. In the latter year Wiseman and Daniel O'Connell, the great Irish nationalist, became the first proprietors of the *Dublin Review*, one of the most important of the sixty-seven Catholic newspapers, journals and other periodicals launched in England in the first half of the century.[2] It spoke for the better-educated part of the Catholic community, and played an important part in leading Anglo-Catholics towards Rome. When the Pope increased the number of vicars-apostolic in England in 1839, Wiseman was one of them. On 8 June 1840 he was consecrated Bishop of Melipotamus *in partibus* [*infidelium*] in the chapel of the English College in Rome, a strange title best described in a footnote.[3] In September 1850 he was elevated to the dignity of Archbishop of Westminster and created cardinal of the title-church of St Pudentiana. He thereupon issued a pastoral letter in which he announced that 'The great work . . . is complete . . . Your beloved country has received a place among the fair Churches which . . . form the splendid aggregate of Catholic Communion; Catholic England has been restored to its orbit in the ecclesiastical firmament, from which its light had long vanished, and begins now anew its course of regularly adjusted action round the centre of unity, the source of jurisdiction, of light and of vigour'.[4]

One result of such triumphalism was an outburst of popular indignation. Riots occurred outside many Catholic churches, and sometimes outside Anglican churches where the parson was a ritualist. On 5 November 'it was not Guy Fawkes, but Pius IX and Wiseman whom the London urchins burned in effigy'.[5] Two days later Lord John Russell proclaimed, in his *Letter to the Bishop of Durham*, that 'no foreign prince or potentate will be set at liberty to fasten his fetters upon a nation which has so long and so nobly vindicated its right to freedom of opinion, civil, political,

---

[1] Purely by chance, the Brownings had met Wiseman's mother, 'who has lived in Fano seven years', in 1848: *Life*, 151. Cf. p. 409, below.

[2] *The Wellesley Index to Victorian Periodicals*, ii, ed. Walter E. Houghton (Toronto, 1972), 11. The introductions to the sections on *The Dublin Review* and *The Rambler* provide valuable background for this poem.

[3] See l. 972 n., below.

[4] Wilfrid Ward, *The Life and Times of Cardinal Wiseman*, 2 vols. (1897), i. 542.

[5] Élie Halévy, *A History of the English People in the Nineteenth Century*, iv: *Victorian Years*, trans. E. I. Watkin (1951), 369.

and religious'.[1] *The Times* led the outcry, while churchmen and others published a great many pamphlets, such as *Romish Usurpation. The Supremacy of the Crown and Liberties of the British People Vindicated . . . in a Letter to the Rev. Dr. Wiseman, being a Reply to his Address to the People of England*, by the Rev. J. W. Worthington, D.D., and *A Letter on the Intrusion of a Roman Episcopate in England*, by the Rev. John Oates. The following year there appeared such further polemics as *Has Dr. Wiseman Violated the Law?* by Edward James, *Position and Prospects of the Protestant Churches . . . with reference to the proposed Establishment of a Catholic Hierarchy in this Country*, by T. Greenwood, M.A., Barrister at Law, and *The Probable Effect of the Late Papal Aggression considered in a Paper read before the Malton Clerical and Theological Society*, by William Pound, M.A. Between 1850 and 1852 Browning's friend Landor contributed to the *Examiner* eight ironical letters 'Addressed to His Eminence the Cardinal Wiseman, by a True Believer'[1].

Nothing in his upbringing disposed Browning to sympathy with Roman Catholicism. His father had been brought up in the Church of England, though on his marriage he followed his wife, who was a deeply religious woman, by becoming a member of the Independent Church at York Street. In his second letter to EBB Browning wrote: 'I don't think I shall let *you* hear, after all, the savage things about Popes and imaginative religions that I must say'.[2] Soon, however, he was expressing his delight that she, like himself, was 'a schismatic and frequenter of Independent Dissenting Chapels'.[3] In our introduction to *Christmas-Eve and Easter-Day* we have given a brief account of the baptism of their son 'at the French Evangelical Protestant Church' in Florence.[4] While Browning's views on religious matters remained undogmatic and somewhat vague, nothing that he saw of the Roman Catholic Church in Italy led him to admire it. For all his last-minute refusal to assent to the murder of Pippa, the Monsignor in Part IV of *Pippa Passes* has clearly led a worldly and evil life, while 'Soliloquy of the Spanish Cloister', 'The Bishop Orders his Tomb', and 'Confessional' (the last described by Alfred Domett as 'a sugar plum for the Puseyites'[5]) all give a highly unfavourable impression of the Catholic Church. We notice that the speaker in *Christmas-Eve* is not bidden by

---

[1] *The Complete Works*, ed. T. Earle Welby, 12 vols. (1927–31), xii (1931), 103–34. In the words of Disraeli, writing to Lady Londonderry on 20 April 1850, the Church question 'pervades all classes': *The Life of Benjamin Disraeli*, by W. F. Monypenny and G. E. Buckle, revised ed., 2 vols. (1929), i. 1063.

[2] Kintner, i. 7.   [3] Ibid. 143.   [4] Vol. IV, pp. 324–5

[5] Maynard, 105.

Christ to enter St Peter's (633), and the narrator's judgement of 'Rome's gross yoke' and all its 'errors and perversities' is explicit and uncompromising.[1] For all their splendour, and the masterpieces of art by which they are adorned, the churches of Florence and Rome must have seemed to Browning remote from true religious feeling.

Yet his dramatic genius predisposed him to take a deep interest in the men and women who give this collection of poems its title. We remember his surprising remark to EBB that in *Luria* he sympathized 'just as much' with the Florentines as with the Moor whom they treat so badly.[2] The Pope in *The Ring and the Book* is evidence that he was capable of creating an almost saintly Catholic. Such was not his aim, however, in the present poem.

'Apology' means 'Defence', as it had meant in Plato's *Apology of Socrates* and was to mean again in Newman's *Apologia pro Vita Sua*. When Sir Charles Gavan Duffy told Browning that he found Roman Catholicism 'habitually disparaged' in his poems,

Browning replied that the allusions to the Catholic Church, which I complained of, were mainly attributable to local circumstances. He had lived in Italy, and he took his illustrations of life from the facts which fell under his notice there; had he lived in England he would probably have taken them from the Church of which Forster was so enamoured. I said I had always assumed that one of his illustrations from the Catholic Church which was English and certainly unfriendly, Bishop Blogram [*sic*] was intended to suggest Cardinal Wiseman. Yes, he said, Bishop Blogram was certainly intended for the English Cardinal, but he was not treated ungenerously. I replied that I had lent that poem to a remarkably gifted young priest, who considered it more offensive than the naked scorn of Voltaire and Diderot.[3]

Here surely Browning was driven to the special pleading of a habitually polite man, but if indeed he used the words 'not treated ungenerously', it seems that he was not seriously concealing a marked degree of contempt for Wiseman. We find in this one often-quoted remark none of the embarrassment that he displayed when asked if he had used Wordsworth as a model in 'The Lost Leader'.[4] Whether he was fair to Wiseman is another question. His biographer, Wilfrid Ward, described the portrayal as 'quite unlike all that Wiseman's letters and the recollections of his friends

---

[1] See e.g. *Christmas-Eve*, 693 ff., 1242, and 1322 ff.
[2] Kintner, i. 26.
[3] Sir Charles Gavan Duffy, *My Life in Two Hemispheres* (Shannon, 2 vols., 1898), ii. 261.
[4] See our Vol. IV, p. 55.

show him to have been'.[1] We must also acknowledge that certain beliefs of Newman's are introduced, particularly with reference to modern 'miracles'.[2] Blougram is to a limited extent a composite figure.

The reviewer of *Men and Women* in the *Rambler*, a recently–founded and able Catholic review, had no doubt of the type of man whom Browning had in mind: 'of course the most unpleasant specimen of such a man would be the half-sceptical prelate, who sucks means of luxury out of a system the truth of which he does not—cannot believe', adding that 'The Catholic would, perhaps, pick out an Anglican bishop for an example of this class of persons; he must not, then, be too hard upon the Protestant poet for choosing a Catholic to exemplify his position.'[3] The reviewer severely censures Browning for making the original of his Bishop so readily identifiable:

it is scandalous in Mr. Browning *first* to show so plainly *whom* he means, when he describes an English Catholic bishop, once bishop *in partibus*, now a member of 'our novel hierarchy,' . . . one too, who, though an Englishman, was born in a foreign land; and *then* to go on sketching a fancy portrait which is abominably untrue, and to draw this person not only as an arch-hypocrite, but also as the frankest of fools. It is bad enough to assign a heap of disgusting qualities to a Catholic bishop in the abstract . . .; but it is far worse to attribute the hypocrisy and scepticism that he has forged in his own brain to any person whom he designates so plainly.

Browning described this as the 'most curious' review he had ever received, because it was 'from Cardinal Wiseman on *Blougram*, i.e. himself . . . certified to be his by Father Prout, who said nobody else would have dared put it in'.[4] Browning's amusement was understandable, but his informant, Francis Sylvester Mahony, a former Jesuit who wrote a great deal in periodicals under this pen-name and was a frequent visitor at Casa Guidi, was relying on gossip. We now know that the reviewer was Richard Simpson, a prolific contributor to the *Rambler* and a critic whose merits have recently been acknowledged.[5]

This is not the place to enumerate the many discussions and interpretations of the poem.[6] In her *Handbook* Mrs Orr describes it as

---

[1] *The Life and Times of Cardinal Wiseman* (2 vols, 1897), ii. 157.

[2] See C. R. Tracy, (p. 206, n3 above).

[3] *The Rambler*, OS 17 (= NS 5) January 1856, 71, 66.

[4] *Letters*, 195.

[5] See e.g. *Richard Simpson as Critic*, ed. David Carroll (1977).

[6] 'Browning's Apologetics', by F. E. L. Priestley (UTQ 1946, repr. in Litzinger and Knickerbocker) led DeVane to revise his account of the poem and to see the Bishop in

a defence of religious conformity in those cases in which the doctrines to which we conform exceed our powers of belief, but are not throughout opposed to them; its point of view being that of a Roman Catholic churchman, who has secured his preferment by this kind of compromise. It is addressed to a semi-freethinker, who is supposed to have declared that a man who could thus identify himself with Romish superstitions must be despised as either knave or fool; and Bishop Blougram has undertaken to prove that he is not to be thus despised; and least of all by the person before him.

The argument is thus special-pleading in the full sense of the word; and it is clear from a kind of editor's note with which the poem concludes, that we are meant to take it as such.

The note at the end (ll. 971–1014) is of particular interest because such a thing is rare in Browning's work: in the present volume that which concludes 'The Statue and the Bust' is the one clear analogue. There the poet is clearly anxious to point the moral of his story: here, in a slightly different way, he wants to guide the reader to the right interpretation of the monologue. It is curious to reflect on the different reading which the poem might have encouraged without the concluding lines, and tempting to speculate whether they were added to a piece already complete, to obviate misreading; but for such a hypothesis we have no evidence. It is particularly valuable to have the authoritative statement that the Bishop 'believed, say, half he spoke'. While Gigadibs[1] is not allowed to open his mouth, that is the common fate of the auditor of a monologue, and there is no reason to suppose that the Bishop seriously misrepresents the views of his 'friend', as he condescendingly calls him. Unlike Blougram the narrator obviously approves of the 'healthy vehemence' which leads the younger man to take ship for Australia, as Alfred Domett had done for New Zealand in 1842, so eliciting an interesting comment from Browning:

---

a much more favourable light. Other stimulating readings include W. O. Raymond, 'Browning's Casuists': SP 37 (1940), repr. in *The Infinite Moment* (Toronto, 1950); C. E. Tanzy, 'Browning, Emerson, and Bishop Blougram': *Victorian Studies* (1958), 255–66; R. E. Palmer, 'The Uses of Character in "Bishop Blougram's Apology" ': MP 58 (1960), 108–18; and S. Gilead, ' "Read the Text Right": Textual Strategies in Bishop Blougram's Apology': VP 24 (1986), 47–67.

[1] The name, much discussed, probably means something like 'whirligig', signifying a fickle and inconstant person. The word 'gig' can mean a top, a flighty girl, a fool, and a whim. 'Dib' is or was a game played by children. It has been suggested that Gigadibs owes something to Father Prout. Robert G. Laird, in ' "He did not sit five minutes": the Conversion of Gigadibs': UTQ 45, 1975–6, 295 ff. makes a good case for R. H. Horne as a more likely model. There is no need, however, to suppose that Browning had one particular individual in mind.

the little I, or anybody, can do as it is, comes of them *going to New Zealand*—partial
retirement and stopping the ears against the noise outside—but all is next to
useless—for there is a creeping magnetic assimilating influence nothing can block
out . . . What I meant to say was—that only in your present condition of life, so
far as I see, is there any chance of your being able to find out . . what is wanted,
and how to supply the want when you precisely find it.[1]

Date 1854/5
1863: Men and Women

BISHOP BLOUGRAM'S APOLOGY.

No more wine? then we'll push back chairs and talk.
A final glass for me, though: cool, i' faith!
We ought to have our Abbey back, you see.
It's different, preaching in basilicas,
And doing duty in some masterpiece   5
Like this of brother Pugin's, bless his heart!
I doubt if they're half baked, those chalk rosettes,
Ciphers and stucco-twiddlings everywhere;
It's just like breathing in a lime-kiln: eh?
These hot long ceremonies of our church   10

---

1 *1855P* Then   3 *1855P* see;

3 *our Abbey*: Westminster Abbey ceased to be an Abbey in the strict sense at the
Reformation, the monastery being dissolved in 1539. After four years as a bishopric, it
had an Abbot again under Mary; but Elizabeth reinstated the dean, with twelve
prebendaries. Some feared that Wiseman might lay claim to the Abbey.
4 *basilicas*: properly, a basilica is a church without transepts; but the term became a
papally awarded title for great churches such as St Peter's and St John Lateran.
6 *brother Pugin's*: A. Welby Pugin (1812–52) was an influential architect fascinated by
the Gothic. His conversion to Roman Catholicism in 1834 gave the Gothic Revival an
ethical and social foundation. His most celebrated book is *Contrasts: or a Parallel Between
the Noble Edifices of the Fourteenth and Fifteenth Centuries, and Similar Buildings of the Present
Day: Showing the Present Decay of Taste* (1836).
8 *Ciphers*: meaningless decorations.

---

[1] *Correspondence*, v. 355–6.

Cost us a little—oh, they pay the price,
You take me—amply pay it! Now, we'll talk.

So, you despise me, Mr. Gigadibs.
No deprecation,—nay, I beg you, sir!
Beside 't is our engagement: don't you know,   15
I promised, if you'd watch a dinner out,
We'd see truth dawn together?—truth that peeps
Over the glasses' edge when dinner's done,
And body gets its sop and holds its noise
And leaves soul free a little. Now's the time: 20
Truth's break of day! You do despise me then.
And if I say, "despise me,"—never fear!
I know you do not in a certain sense—
Not in my arm-chair, for example: here,
I well imagine you respect my place   25
(*Status*, *entourage*, worldly circumstance)
Quite to its value—very much indeed:
—Are up to the protesting eyes of you
In pride at being seated here for once—
You'll turn it to such capital account!   30
When somebody, through years and years to come,
Hints of the bishop,—names me—that's enough:
"Blougram? I knew him"—(into it you slide)

13 *1855P* Gigadibs!   18 *1855P–84S* the glass's edge   20 *1855P* little; now's
*21 {reading of DC, BrU, *1889*} *1855P, 1855, 1863S* 'Tis break *1856, 1863–88* 'T is break
22 *1855P* But if   *1855P–65* fear—   25 *1855P* I will imagine   27 *1855P–63*
indeed
___

12 *You take me*: you understand me.
13 *Gigadibs*: see above, p. 211 n.
17 *We'd see truth dawn*: see l. 21 n.
     truth that peeps: cf. the L. proverb, *in vino veritas*, 'in wine there is truth'.
19 *sop*: 'Any thing given to pacify: from the *sop* given to Cerberus': Johnson.
     and holds its noise: a deliberately vulgar idiom.
21 *Truth's break of day*: revised in *1889*, no doubt to obviate a misinterpretation:
cf. l. 17. Pettigrew and Collin state that the revision was for 'the second impression of
1888', but there was no such impression.
26 *entourage*: surroundings, circumstances, and particularly attendants.

"Dined with him once, a Corpus Christi Day,
"All alone, we two; he's a clever man: 35
"And after dinner,—why, the wine you know,—
"Oh, there was wine, and good!—what with the wine . . .
" 'Faith, we began upon all sorts of talk!
"He's no bad fellow, Blougram; he had seen
"Something of mine he relished, some review: 40
"He's quite above their humbug in his heart,
"Half-said as much, indeed—the thing's his trade.
"I warrant, Blougram's sceptical at times:
"How otherwise? I liked him, I confess!"
Che che, my dear sir, as we say at Rome,   45
Don't you protest now! It's fair give and take;
You have had your turn and spoken your home-truths:
The hand's mine now, and here you follow suit.

    Thus much conceded, still the first fact stays—
You do despise me; your ideal of life   50
Is not the bishop's: you would not be I.
You would like better to be Goethe, now,
Or Buonaparte, or, bless me, lower still,
Count D'Orsay,—so you did what you preferred,
Spoke as you thought, and, as you cannot help,   55
Believed or disbelieved, no matter what,

---

37 *1855P* was wine!   *{reading of *1855P–84S*} *1888, 1889* wine . .   40 *1884S*
review.   42 *1855P–63* trade—   44 *1880S* I like him   45 *1855P–56*
Che ch' é, my   46 *1855P* take,—   51 *1855P–63* I—   56 *1855P* what;

34 *Corpus Christi Day*: the Feast of the Blessed Sacrament, or Body of Christ,
observed by the Roman Catholic Church on the Thursday after Trinity Sunday: 'God's
great day' (*Sordello,* iii. 766). The suggestion (see Turner) that an ironic contrast is
intended between the bread and wine of the Last Supper and the good food and wine
of the present dinner seems unlikely, since the day is celebrated as a feast.
    45 *Che che*: come now!
    48 *you follow suit*: note the frequent imagery from games. Here they are playing cards:
the Bishop is to deal.
    54 *Count D'Orsay*: 1801–52, came to London from France as a young man, and was
taken up by the Earl and Countess of Blessington, becoming the lover of the Countess.
A wit, a dandy, and an artist, he is ubiquitous in the memoirs and letters of the time.
Browning despised him: Kintner, ii. 685.

So long as on that point, whate'er it was,
You loosed your mind, were whole and sole yourself.
—That, my ideal never can include,
Upon that element of truth and worth   60
Never be based! for say they make me Pope—
(They can't—suppose it for our argument!)
Why, there I'm at my tether's end, I've reached
My height, and not a height which pleases you:
An unbelieving Pope won't do, you say.   65
It's like those eerie stories nurses tell,
Of how some actor on a stage played Death,
With pasteboard crown, sham orb and tinselled dart,
And called himself the monarch of the world;
Then, going in the tire-room afterward,   70
Because the play was done, to shift himself,
Got touched upon the sleeve familiarly,
The moment he had shut the closet door,
By Death himself. Thus God might touch a Pope
At unawares, ask what his baubles mean,   75
And whose part he presumed to play just now.
Best be yourself, imperial, plain and true!

So, drawing comfortable breath again,
You weigh and find, whatever more or less

58 *1855P* yourself!   *1870, 1875* yourself,   62 *1855P–56, 1863–84S* argument)
1863S argument),   64 *1855P* you,   *1855, 1856, 1863* you.   65 *1855P* say—
67 *1855P–63* actor played Death on a stage   *1865, 1868–84S* actor played Death on a
stage,   69 *1855P* world,—   *1855–63* world,   70 *1855P* Who going
74 *1855P* himself: so God   *76 {reading of DC, BrU, *1889*} *1855P–88* now?

58 *loosed your mind*: were free in thought and expression.
62 *They can't*: an English pope would have been inconceivable. There has only been
one, in the twelfth century.
70 *tire-room*: dressing-room.
71 *shift himself*: change his clothes.
75 *At unawares*: unexpectedly (arch.) Browning uses the phrase a number of times,
notably in *Christmas-Eve*, 152.
76 *whose part*: that of Vicar of Christ on earth.
77 *imperial*: subject to no one.
78 *comfortable*: cheerful.

I boast of my ideal realized   80
Is nothing in the balance when opposed
To your ideal, your grand simple life,
Of which you will not realize one jot.
I am much, you are nothing; you would be all,
I would be merely much: you beat me there.   85

No, friend, you do not beat me: hearken why!
The common problem, yours, mine, every one's,
Is—not to fancy what were fair in life
Provided it could be,—but, finding first
What may be, then find how to make it fair   90
Up to our means: a very different thing!
No abstract intellectual plan of life
Quite irrespective of life's plainest laws,
But one, a man, who is man and nothing more,
May lead within a world which (by your leave)   95
Is Rome or London, not Fool's-paradise.
Embellish Rome, idealize away,
Make paradise of London if you can,
You're welcome, nay, you're wise.

                                        A simile!
We mortals cross the ocean of this world   100
Each in his average cabin of a life;
The best's not big, the worst yields elbow-room.
Now for our six months' voyage—how prepare?
You come on shipboard with a landsman's list
Of things he calls convenient: so they are!   105
An India screen is pretty furniture,
A piano-forte is a fine resource,

---

*80 {reading of DC, BrU, *1889*} *1855P, 1855* realised *1856–88* realized,   83 *1855P*
jot,—   86 *1855P* me,—listen why: *1855–68* why.   *1875* why!   96 *1855P*
Fool's-paradise;   102 *1855P* elbow room;   107 *1855P* a great resource;

97 *Embellish Rome*: imagine Rome as more beautiful than it is.
103 *our six months' voyage*: no particular voyage is referred to.

All Balzac's novels occupy one shelf,
The new edition fifty volumes long;
And little Greek books, with the funny type   110
They get up well at Leipsic, fill the next:
Go on! slabbed marble, what a bath it makes!
And Parma's pride, the Jerome, let us add!
'T were pleasant could Correggio's fleeting glow
Hang full in face of one where'er one roams,   115
Since he more than the others brings with him
Italy's self,—the marvellous Modenese!—
Yet was not on your list before, perhaps.
—Alas, friend, here's the agent . . . is 't the name?
The captain, or whoever's master here—   120
You see him screw his face up; what's his cry
Ere you set foot on shipboard? "Six feet square!"
If you won't understand what six feet mean,
Compute and purchase stores accordingly—
And if, in pique because he overhauls   125
Your Jerome, piano, bath, you come on board
Bare—why, you cut a figure at the first
While sympathetic landsmen see you off;

113 *1855P* add,   118 *1855P–63S* Yet 'twas not   *1863* Yet 't was not
119 *1855P–56*—Alas!   *1863S, 1863* Alas!   125 *1855P* because they overhaul
126 *1855P–84S* piano and bath,   127 *1855P* first!

109 *The new edition*: as C. R. Tracy pointed out (TLS, 24 January 1935, p. 8), it is likely that Browning saw a preliminary advertisement for an edition of the *Œuvres Complètes* in 55 volumes, which began to appear in 1856. The Brownings were great admirers of Balzac: 'When Robert and I are ambitious', EBB wrote to Miss Mitford in 1848, 'we talk of buying Balzac in full some day': *Letters of EBB*, i. 375.

110 *little Greek books*: probably the Tauchnitz series of Greek texts, published in Leipzig, a famous publishing centre. Browning owned several of their Greek texts, which have a typeface which looks like small italic.

113 *the Jerome*: the Madonna with St Jerome ('Day') in the Pinacoteca at Parma by Antonio Allegri (1489/94–1534), known as Correggio after his birthplace, a small city near Modena. 'His tints are delicate, his colouring rich and glowing; he creates the most powerful effects from . . . chiaroscuro'; Farquhar. The Bishop would have been delighted by what she terms the 'sensuous display of limb' in certain of his works.

125 *overhauls*: examines in detail, but here with the clear implication that such bulky luxuries are rejected. Cf. l. 156.

Not afterward, when long ere half seas over,
You peep up from your utterly naked boards   130
Into some snug and well-appointed berth,
Like mine for instance (try the cooler jug—
Put back the other, but don't jog the ice!)
And mortified you mutter "Well and good;
"He sits enjoying his sea-furniture;   135
" 'T is stout and proper, and there's store of it:
"Though I've the better notion, all agree,
"Of fitting rooms up. Hang the carpenter,
"Neat ship-shape fixings and contrivances—
"I would have brought my Jerome, frame and all!"   140
And meantime you bring nothing: never mind—
You've proved your artist-nature: what you don't
You might bring, so despise me, as I say.

Now come, let's backward to the starting-place.
See my way: we're two college friends, suppose.   145
Prepare together for our voyage, then;
Each note and check the other in his work,—
Here's mine, a bishop's outfit; criticize!
What's wrong? why won't you be a bishop too?

Why first, you don't believe, you don't and can't,   150
(Not statedly, that is, and fixedly
And absolutely and exclusively)
In any revelation called divine.
No dogmas nail your faith; and what remains
But say so, like the honest man you are?   155

129 *1855P* Not afterwards when,   *1855–63* Not afterwards, when,   *1855P–63S* seas
o'er,   133 *1855P–63* ice)   *1863S* ice),   134 *1855P* Then mortified
136 *1855P–63* it,   137 *1855P* Still, I've   138 *1855P* up: hang   *1855–63* up!
hang   140 *1855P* all!   144 *1855P* place   145 *1855P–63* suppose—
146 *1855P–63* then,   153 *1855P* divine—   155 *1855P* are!

129 *half seas over*: halfway on your voyage. The meaning 'half-drunk' had developed
by the beginning of the eighteenth century, and has now superseded the literal sense.
136 *store*: plenty.
139 *fixings*: fittings. Originally American slang.

First, therefore, overhaul theology!
Nay, I too, not a fool, you please to think,
Must find believing every whit as hard:
And if I do not frankly say as much,
The ugly consequence is clear enough.   160

Now wait, my friend: well, I do not believe—
If you'll accept no faith that is not fixed,
Absolute and exclusive, as you say.
You're wrong—I mean to prove it in due time.
Meanwhile, I know where difficulties lie   165
I could not, cannot solve, nor ever shall,
So give up hope accordingly to solve—
(To you, and over the wine). Our dogmas then
With both of us, though in unlike degree,
Missing full credence—overboard with them!   170
I mean to meet you on your own premise:
Good, there go mine in company with yours!

And now what are we? unbelievers both,
Calm and complete, determinately fixed
To-day, to-morrow and for ever, pray?   175
You'll guarantee me that? Not so, I think!
In no wise! all we've gained is, that belief,
As unbelief before, shakes us by fits,
Confounds us like its predecessor. Where's
The gain? how can we guard our unbelief,   180
Make it bear fruit to us?—the problem here.

156 *1855P* theology—   158 *1855P–63* hard,   159 *1855P* So if
160 *1855P* enough!   163 *1855P* say   164 *1855–65* (You're   *1855P* to show
you in   *1855, 1856* time)   *1863S–65* time.)   167 *1855P* solve;   169 *1855P*
In both   176 *1855, 1856* think.   179 *1855P* predecessor—where's
180 *1855P* unbelief?   181 *1855P* us,— . . . . here—

158 *Must find believing*: cf. the opening of *Easter-Day*.
177–8 *belief, / As unbelief before*: cf. Mark 9: 24.
178 *shakes us by fits*: cf. Donne, 'Holy Sonnets', xix. 12–13: 'So my devout fits come
and go away / Like a fantastic ague.'

Just when we are safest, there's a sunset-touch,
A fancy from a flower-bell, some one's death,
A chorus-ending from Euripides,—
And that's enough for fifty hopes and fears   185
As old and new at once as nature's self,
To rap and knock and enter in our soul,
Take hands and dance there, a fantastic ring,
Round the ancient idol, on his base again,—
The grand Perhaps! We look on helplessly.   190
There the old misgivings, crooked questions are—
This good God,—what he could do, if he would,
Would, if he could—then must have done long since:
If so, when, where and how? some way must be,—
Once feel about, and soon or late you hit   195
Some sense, in which it might be, after all.
Why not, "The Way, the Truth, the Life?"

---

187 *1855P* in one's soul,   190 *1855P* Perhaps: we   *1855–65* we   *1855P–56,*
1863, 1865 helplessly,—   195 *1855P* feel for it, and soon you hit upon
196 *1855P* all,   *1863S* all—

182 *Just when we are safest*: cf. a passage (cited by Pettigrew and Collins) from *The Gospel Narrative of Our Lord's Passion* (1841), by Isaac Williams, p. 436: 'God hath so constituted [Man] that every sense is an avenue to the heart . . . the sound of distant music or a plaintive note, a passing word, or the momentary scent of a flower, or the sound of a bell, or the retiring of the day . . . all these will touch a chord.' Williams, who had been Newman's curate and was now a Fellow of Trinity College, Oxford, argues that all such perceptions take us 'from the business of the world, from the buying and the selling', and remind us of 'the awful silence of that state which is beyond the grave, . . . the sepulchre of Christ'. The fact that Williams quotes ll. 74–6 of the *Antigone* of Sophocles in a footnote to the previous page may possibly have drawn Browning's attention to this passage. Cf. too *Childe Harold's Pilgrimage*, IV. xxiii–iv.

184 *A chorus-ending from Euripides*: Browning was passionately interested in Greek literature, particularly in the dramatists, and most of all in Euripides (480–406 BC). Porter and Clarke, followed by later annotators, suggest for this 'chorus-ending' the final lines which are to be found (with slight variations) in his *Helen, Bacchae, Andromache, Medea*, and *Alcestis*. In his own *Balaustion's Adventure: including a Transcript from Euripides* (1871) Browning gives this rendering: 'Many a hopeless matter Gods arrange. / What we expected, never came to pass: / What we did not expect, Gods brought to bear; / So have things gone, this whole experience through!' (ll. 2393–6).

190 *The grand Perhaps*: Altick points out the deathbed remark attributed to Rabelais: 'I am going to seek a big Perhaps': VP I (1963), 64–5.

191 *crooked*: not straightforward.

197 *The Way*: John 14: 6.

                                        —That way
Over the mountain, which who stands upon
Is apt to doubt if it be meant for a road;
While, if he views it from the waste itself,   200
Up goes the line there, plain from base to brow,
Not vague, mistakeable! what's a break or two
Seen from the unbroken desert either side?
And then (to bring in fresh philosophy)
What if the breaks themselves should prove at last   205
The most consummate of contrivances
To train a man's eye, teach him what is faith?
And so we stumble at truth's very test!
All we have gained then by our unbelief
Is a life of doubt diversified by faith,   210
For one of faith diversified by doubt:
We called the chess-board white,—we call it black.

       "Well," you rejoin, "the end's no worse, at least;
"We've reason for both colours on the board:
"Why not confess then, where I drop the faith   215
"And you the doubt, that I'm as right as you?"

       Because, friend, in the next place, this being so,
And both things even,—faith and unbelief
Left to a man's choice,—we'll proceed a step,
Returning to our image, which I like.   220

       A man's choice, yes—but a cabin-passenger's—
The man made for the special life o' the world—

199 *1855P* if it's a road at all,   *1855–63S* if it's indeed a   *1863–84S* be indeed a
200 *1865,* *1868–75* he view it   204 *1855P* then—to .... philosophy—
207 *1855P–56* faith,—   *1863S* faith—   208 *1855P–63S* test?   209 *1855P*
What have we gained,   *1855, 1856* What have we gained   210 *1855P–56* But a
211 {does not appear in *1855P*}   *1855, 1856* doubt.   212 *1855P* black!
213 *1855P–56* least,   *1863* least   214 *1855, 1856* board.   215 *1855P* then,
when I   216 *1855P* Which you retain, that   222 *1855P–68* life of the

199 *it be*: note revisions.
200 *the waste*: desert.
212 *the chess-board*: cf. 48 n.
221 *a cabin-passenger's*: a cabin-passenger travels comfortably, 'First Class'.

Do you forget him? I remember though!
Consult our ship's conditions and you find
One and but one choice suitable to all;   225
The choice, that you unluckily prefer,
Turning things topsy-turvy—they or it
Going to the ground. Belief or unbelief
Bears upon life, determines its whole course,
Begins at its beginning. See the world   230
Such as it is,—you made it not, nor I;
I mean to take it as it is,—and you,
Not so you'll take it,—though you get nought else.
I know the special kind of life I like,
What suits the most my idiosyncrasy,   235
Brings out the best of me and bears me fruit
In power, peace, pleasantness and length of days.
I find that positive belief does this
For me, and unbelief, no whit of this.
—For you, it does, however?—that, we'll try!   240
'T is clear, I cannot lead my life, at least,
Induce the world to let me peaceably,
Without declaring at the outset, "Friends,
"I absolutely and peremptorily
"Believe!"—I say, faith is my waking life: 245
One sleeps, indeed, and dreams at intervals,
We know, but waking's the main point with us,
And my provision's for life's waking part.
Accordingly, I use heart, head and hand
All day, I build, scheme, study, and make friends;   250
And when night overtakes me, down I lie,
Sleep, dream a little, and get done with it,
The sooner the better, to begin afresh.

---

224 *1855P* Consult the ship's   225 *1855P–65* all,   237 *1855P* days;
240 *1855P–56* however—   245 *1855, 1856, 1863, 1865* life.   *247 {reading
of *1855P–68*} *1870–89* us   248 *1855P* So my . . . . part—   249 *1855P* and
hands,   *1855–63* and hands   250 *1855P* friends,   253 *1855P* afresh—

237 *length of days*: a biblical phrase: e.g. Prov. 3: 16.

What's midnight doubt before the dayspring's faith?
You, the philosopher, that disbelieve,   255
That recognize the night, give dreams their weight—
To be consistent you should keep your bed,
Abstain from healthy acts that prove you man,
For fear you drowse perhaps at unawares!
And certainly at night you'll sleep and dream,   260
Live through the day and bustle as you please.
And so you live to sleep as I to wake,
To unbelieve as I to still believe?
Well, and the common sense o' the world calls you
Bed-ridden,—and its good things come to me.   265
Its estimation, which is half the fight,
That's the first cabin-comfort I secure:
The next . . . but you perceive with half an eye!
Come, come, it's best believing, if we may;
You can't but own that!

                    Next, concede again,   270
If once we choose belief, on all accounts
We can't be too decisive in our faith,
Conclusive and exclusive in its terms,
To suit the world which gives us the good things.
In every man's career are certain points   275
Whereon he dares not be indifferent;
The world detects him clearly, if he dare,
As baffled at the game, and losing life.
He may care little or he may care much
For riches, honour, pleasure, work, repose,   280

---

254 *1855P–65, 1884S* What's midnight's doubt   258 *1855P–65* you a man,
259 *1855P* unawares   261 *1855P* please,   263 *1855P* believe.
264 *1855P–68* sense of the   *267 {reading of *1855P–63*} *1865–89* first-cabin comfort
269 *1855P–56* we can—   270 *1855P–56* that.   277 *1855P–56* he is,
1863S, 1863 he dares,

---

254 *dayspring's faith*: cf. Luke 1: 78 (Allen).
259 *at unawares*: as in l. 75.

Since various theories of life and life's
Success are extant which might easily
Comport with either estimate of these;
And whoso chooses wealth or poverty,
Labour or quiet, is not judged a fool   285
Because his fellow would choose otherwise:
We let him choose upon his own account
So long as he's consistent with his choice.
But certain points, left wholly to himself,
When once a man has arbitrated on,   290
We say he must succeed there or go hang.
Thus, he should wed the woman he loves most
Or needs most, whatsoe'er the love or need—
For he can't wed twice. Then, he must avouch,
Or follow, at the least, sufficiently,   295
The form of faith his conscience holds the best,
Whate'er the process of conviction was:
For nothing can compensate his mistake
On such a point, the man himself being judge:
He cannot wed twice, nor twice lose his soul.   300

    Well now, there's one great form of Christian faith
I happened to be born in—which to teach
Was given me as I grew up, on all hands,
As best and readiest means of living by;
The same on examination being proved   305
The most pronounced moreover, fixed, precise
And absolute form of faith in the whole world—
Accordingly, most potent of all forms

---

283 *1855P–63S* these,   286 *1855P–63* his fellows would   *1855, 1856* otherwise.
291 *1855P* or be lost.   297 *1855P* was,   *1855, 1856* was.

291 *go hang*: cf. proof reading.
294 *he can't wed twice*: until the Act of 1857 came into force at the beginning of 1858 divorce was impossible in England except by a private Act, which was out of the question except for the very wealthy and influential.
298 *compensate*: stressed on the second syllable, as in Johnson and elsewhere in Browning.

For working on the world. Observe, my friend!
Such as you know me, I am free to say,   310
In these hard latter days which hamper one,
Myself—by no immoderate exercise
Of intellect and learning, but the tact
To let external forces work for me,
—Bid the street's stones be bread and they are bread;   315
Bid Peter's creed, or rather, Hildebrand's,
Exalt me o'er my fellows in the world
And make my life an ease and joy and pride;
It does so,—which for me's a great point gained,
Who have a soul and body that exact   320
A comfortable care in many ways.
There's power in me and will to dominate
Which I must exercise, they hurt me else:
In many ways I need mankind's respect,
Obedience, and the love that's born of fear: 325
While at the same time, there's a taste I have,
A toy of soul, a titillating thing,
Refuses to digest these dainties crude.
The naked life is gross till clothed upon:
I must take what men offer, with a grace   330
As though I would not, could I help it, take!
An uniform I wear though over-rich—

---

309 *1855P–65* friend,   313 *1855P–68* learning, and the   315 *1855P* are bread.
1855, 1856, 1863 are bread,   318 *1855P* And let them make . . . . joy,   *1855–65*
pride,   321 *1855P* ways—   323 *1855P* exercise, it hurts me   328 *1855P*
crude—   331 *1855P* take—   332 *1855P, 1856* uniform to wear   *1855* A
uniform to wear

311 *latter days*: a biblical phrase: e.g. Deut. 31: 29.

315 *and they are bread*: in Matt. 4: 3 and Luke 4: 3 Christ refuses the devil's temptation
to perform this miracle.

316 *Peter's creed*: while Peter is regarded as the foundation-stone of the Christian
Church, Hildebrand (*c*.1021–85), who became pope as Gregory VII in 1073, fought for
the independence of the Church from the secular power. In 1077 the Emperor
submitted to him, and did penance. There are important references to Hildebrand in
Sordello, notably at iii. 271–3, and v. 161 ff. and 216–17.

327 *a toy of soul*: a wild fancy.
    titillating: tempting, teasing.

328 *crude*: uncooked, unadorned.

Something imposed on me, no choice of mine;
No fancy-dress worn for pure fancy's sake
And despicable therefore! now folk kneel   335
And kiss my hand—of course the Church's hand.
Thus I am made, thus life is best for me,
And thus that it should be I have procured;
And thus it could not be another way,
I venture to imagine.

                    You'll reply,   340
So far my choice, no doubt, is a success;
But were I made of better elements,
With nobler instincts, purer tastes, like you,
I hardly would account the thing success
Though it did all for me I say.

                    But, friend,   345
We speak of what is; not of what might be,
And how 't were better if 't were otherwise.
I am the man you see here plain enough:
Grant I'm a beast, why, beasts must lead beasts' lives!
Suppose I own at once to tail and claws;   350
The tailless man exceeds me: but being tailed
I'll lash out lion fashion, and leave apes
To dock their stump and dress their haunches up.
My business is not to remake myself,
But make the absolute best of what God made.   355
Or—our first simile—though you prove me doomed

---

333 *1855P* mine,   334 *1855P–56* pure fashion's sake   335 *1855P* therefore—
now men kneel   *1855–68* now men kneel   *1870–84S* now folks kneel   337 *1855P*
thus is life best   338 *1855P* procured,   344 *1855P* You hardly
345 *1855P–56* it do all   *1855P* me you say.   347 *1855P* otherwise:
349 *1855P* lives—   *1863S* lives.   351 *1855P* me,   352 *1855P* lash mine
lion's-fashion and   353 *1855P* their buttocks up—   356 *1855P–68* you
proved me

---

338 *I have procured*: I have contrived that it should be so.
349 *a beast*: cf. 'Fra Lippo Lippi', 270.
353 *haunches*: note revision from proof.

To a viler berth still, to the steerage-hole,
The sheep-pen or the pig-stye, I should strive
To make what use of each were possible;
And as this cabin gets upholstery,   360
That hutch should rustle with sufficient straw.

    But, friend, I don't acknowledge quite so fast
I fail of all your manhood's lofty tastes
Enumerated so complacently,
On the mere ground that you forsooth can find   365
In this particular life I choose to lead
No fit provision for them. Can you not?
Say you, my fault is I address myself
To grosser estimators than should judge?
And that's no way of holding up the soul,   370
Which, nobler, needs men's praise perhaps, yet knows
One wise man's verdict outweighs all the fools'—
Would like the two, but, forced to choose, takes that.
I pine among my million imbeciles
(You think) aware some dozen men of sense   375
Eye me and know me, whether I believe
In the last winking Virgin, as I vow,
And am a fool, or disbelieve in her
And am a knave,—approve in neither case,
Withold their voices though I look their way: 380

365 *1855P* can see   369 *1855P* than I need—   *1855, 1856* than I need,   *1863S–*
65 than I need?   370–2 {in *1855P* lines 370–2 are repeated in altered form; the two
forms are here indicated by A and B}   370 *1855P* {A} soul;   371 *1855P* {A,
B} perhaps, but knows   372 *1855P* {B} fools'?   373 *1855P–68* that?
375 *1855P* You think,   376 *1855P* me: 380 *1855P* way

    357 *the steerage-hole*: the worst place in the ship. No other example of this compound
in OED[2].

    372 *One wise man's verdict*: cf. Plato, *Gorgias*, 490 A: 'One wise man is worth more
than ten thousand fools'.

    377 *the last winking Virgin*: in his *Lectures on the Present Position of Catholics in England*
(1851) Newman wrote: 'I think it impossible to withstand the evidence which is
brought for the liquefaction of the blood of St. Januarius at Naples, and for the motion
of the eyes of the pictures of the Madonna in the Roman States . . . I firmly believe that
the relics of the saints are doing innumerable miracles and graces daily, and that it needs

Like Verdi when, at his worst opera's end
(The thing they gave at Florence,—what's its name?)
While the mad houseful's plaudits near out-bang
His orchestra of salt-box, tongs and bones,
He looks through all the roaring and the wreaths   385
Where sits Rossini patient in his stall.

Nay, friend, I meet you with an answer here—
That even your prime men who appraise their kind
Are men still, catch a wheel within a wheel,
See more in a truth than the truth's simple self,   390

---

387 *1855P* answer there—   388 *1855P–56* For even   389 *1855P–56* a thing
within a thing,

---

only for a Catholic to show devotion to any saint in order to receive special benefits
from his intercession. I firmly believe that saints in their lifetime have before now raised
the dead to life': p. 298. See C. R. Tracy, MLR 34 (1939), 423. On p. 1 of the first
number of *Bentley's Miscellany* (1837) we find an anonymous poem, by Father Prout,
'The Bottle of St. Januarius': 'In the land of the citron and myrtle, we're told / That
the blood of a MARTYR is kept in a phial', this being the 'favourite FACT' of the
'profound LAZZARONI'. The Brownings had no doubt heard Prout on the subject, as
he visited them only too frequently. As Robert C. Schweik points out ('Bishop
Browning's Miracles': MLN 71, 1956, 416–18), Wiseman would not have credited such
claims. Apart from the composite nature of Blougram, Schweik suggests, Browning
may have been misled by a passage in a review of *Lavengro* in *Blackwood's Magazine*,
March 1851, 322–37: 'It is not safe now to deny miracles, to sneer at stories of winking
images, or to speak lightly of the liquefaction of the blood of St. Januarius. Cardinal
Wiseman, in his future attempts to familiarise us with the doctrines of saintly inter-
ference, will find a good deal of work already cut and dry for his hand . . . The chain
in the church of St. Peter ad Vincula has already been suspended around more than one
English neck, in token of the entire submission of the proselytes to the spiritual yoke of
Rome.'

382 *what's its name?*: *Macbeth*, first performed in Florence in 1847, in a version inferior
to the revised form of the opera prepared for Paris in the 1860s. Dr John Deathridge
tells us that the strange instruments mentioned are 'most likely metaphorical references
to the original orchestration, with its ghoulish effects for the witches', and other crude
effects.

384 *salt-box*: one authority describes this as 'a somewhat mysterious instrument, . . .
beaten with a rolling pin'. For the tongs and bones see *A Midsummer Night's Dream*,
IV. i. 27.

386 *Where sits Rossini*: Verdi sees that Rossini is not applauding. (As a matter of fact,
it is not known whether Rossini was present at the first performance).

388 *your prime men*: i.e. the best journalists.

389 *a wheel within a wheel*: see Ezek. 1: 16.

Confuse themselves. You see lads walk the street
Sixty the minute; what's to note in that?
You see one lad o'erstride a chimney-stack;
Him you must watch—he's sure to fall, yet stands!
Our interest's on the dangerous edge of things.   395
The honest thief, the tender murderer,
The superstitious atheist, demirep
That loves and saves her soul in new French books—
We watch while these in equilibrium keep
The giddy line midway: one step aside,   400
They're classed and done with. I, then, keep the line
Before your sages,—just the men to shrink
From the gross weights, cóarse scales and labels broad
You offer their refinement. Fool or knave?
Why needs a bishop be a fool or knave   405
When there's a thousand diamond weights between?
So, I enlist them. Your picked twelve, you'll find,
Profess themselves indignant, scandalized
At thus being held unable to explain
How a superior man who disbelieves   410
May not believe as well: that's Schelling's way!
It's through my coming in the tail of time,

392 *1855P* minute, ... in such?   393 *1855P* lad stand on a   394 *1855P*
stands.   395 *1855P* things—   397–8 *1855P–65* atheist, demireps | That love
and save their souls in   401 *1855P* with: 404 *1855P* refinement; fool
407 *1855P* them—your   412 *1855P* through one's coming

397 *demirep*: a woman with a bad reputation; cf. 'demi monde'.

398 *new French books*: EBB (in particular) was a great reader of French novels, notably
those of George Sand: *Lélia*, however, she 'could not read through for its vileness', she
told Miss Mitford: Raymond and Sullivan, ii. 127.

406 *diamond weights*: the weight of a diamond is assessed with extreme accuracy;
cf. *A Blot in the 'Scutcheon*, I. iii. 187.

407 *Your picked twelve*: an imaginary jury.

411 *Schelling's way*: F. W. J. von Schelling (1775–1854) was early influenced by Fichte
and Kant. As he grew older his philosophy transformed itself: latterly he tried to
reconcile it with Christianity. 'I take the opportunity of saying, once for all, that I never
read a line, original or translated, by Kant, Schelling, or Hegel in my whole life',
Browning wrote to Furnivall in 1882: *Trumpeter*, 51. These men were constantly
mentioned in the Reviews, however, and Browning will also have heard about them
from Carlyle and other friends.

412 *the tail of time*: at the last possible moment.

Nicking the minute with a happy tact.
Had I been born three hundred years ago
They'd say, "What's strange? Blougram of course believes;"   415
And, seventy years since, "disbelieves of course."
But now, "He may believe; and yet, and yet
"How can he?" All eyes turn with interest.
Whereas, step off the line on either side—
You, for example, clever to a fault,   420
The rough and ready man who write apace,
Read somewhat seldomer, think perhaps even less—
You disbelieve! Who wonders and who cares?
Lord So-and-so—his coat bedropped with wax,
All Peter's chains about his waist, his back   425
Brave with the needlework of Noodledom—
Believes! Again, who wonders and who cares?
But I, the man of sense and learning too,
The able to think yet act, the this, the that,
I, to believe at this late time of day!   430
Enough; you see, I need not fear contempt.

   —Except it's yours! Admire me as these may,
You don't. But whom at least do you admire?
Present your own perfection, your ideal,
Your pattern man for a minute—oh, make haste,   435

---

415 *1855P* strange? the man of   418 *1855P* interest—   421 *1855P–63* man
that write   422 *1855P* Think somewhat seldomer, read perhaps   423 *1855P*
disbelieve—who   425 *1855P* his throat, his   427 *1855P* Believes—again,
430 *1855P* day?   431 *1855P* contempt   432 {in *1868–80S* the line is in-
dented, but does not begin a new paragraph}   *1855P–65* admire   433 *1855P–56*
But what at   434 *1855P–63* own perfections, your   435 *1863S* a moment—oh,
*{reading of DC, BrU, *1889*} *1855P–84S* haste! *1888* haste

---

413 *Nicking*: catching.
   425 *Peter's chains*: 'An ironic juxtaposition of the "chains" that a conventional
believer would wear to hold a cross and rosary as opposed to the chains with which
Herod had St. Peter bound. See Acts 12. 3–11': Allen.
   426 *Brave*: showy, splendid.
   Noodledum: a word coined by Sydney Smith, writing anonymously in the
Edinburgh Review for January 1810 (xv. 305). It recurs in *The Two Poets of Croisic*, cvi. 2.

Is it Napoleon you would have us grow?
Concede the means; allow his head and hand,
(A large concession, clever as you are)
Good! In our common primal element
Of unbelief (we can't believe, you know—   440
We're still at that admission, recollect!)
Where do you find—apart from, towering o'er
The secondary temporary aims
Which satisfy the gross taste you despise—
Where do you find his star?—his crazy trust   445
God knows through what or in what? it's alive
And shines and leads him, and that's all we want.
Have we aught in our sober night shall point
Such ends as his were, and direct the means
Of working out our purpose straight as his,   450
Nor bring a moment's trouble on success
With after-care to justify the same?
—Be a Napoleon, and yet disbelieve—
Why, the man's mad, friend, take his light away!
What's the vague good o' the world, for which you dare   455
With comfort to yourself blow millions up?
We neither of us see it! we do see
The blown-up millions—spatter of their brains
And writhing of their bowels and so forth,
In that bewildering entanglement   460

---

439 *1855P* in   *1863S*—in   441 *1855P* that concession, recollect)   *1855–68*
recollect)   442 *1855P* (apart   444 *1855P–63* gross tastes you   *1855P*
despise)—   445 *1855P* star, his   446 *1855P* in what—   447 *1855P* It
shines   450 *1855P* as he,   453 *1855P* disbelieve?   *1855–65* disbelieve!
454 *1855–65* away.   455 *1855P–68* good of the   *1855P–65* which you'd dare
457 *1855P* it—

436 *Napoleon*: Napoleon was Emperor of France from 1804 to 1814, and again briefly
for 'the hundred days' in 1815, until he was defeated by Wellington at Waterloo. He
stands here for the epitome of a great man of action. Cf. l. 53, and 'Apparent Failure', 38.

448 *point*: point to, as in Pope's *Odyssey*, xxiv. 106, and in 'By the Fireside', 33.

452 *after-care*: a rare usage, to be distinguished from the modern sense of the
compound.

454 *take his light away!*: such was supposed to be a treatment for madness. Cf. *Twelfth
Night*, III. iv. 129 ff.

Of horrible eventualities
Past calculation to the end of time!
Can I mistake for some clear word of God
(Which were my ample warrant for it all)
His puff of hazy instinct, idle talk,   465
"The State, that's I," quack-nonsense about crowns,
And (when one beats the man to his last hold)
A vague idea of setting things to rights,
Policing people efficaciously,
More to their profit, most of all to his own;   470
The whole to end that dismallest of ends
By an Austrian marriage, cant to us the Church,
And resurrection of the old *régime*?
Would I, who hope to live a dozen years,
Fight Austerlitz for reasons such and such?   475
No: for, concede me but the merest chance
Doubt may be wrong—there's judgment, life to come!
With just that chance, I dare not. Doubt proves right?
This present life is all?—you offer me
Its dozen noisy years, without a chance   480
That wedding an archduchess, wearing lace,
And getting called by divers new-coined names,
Will drive off ugly thoughts and let me dine,

462 *1855P* time.   465 *1855P–63* hazy instincts, idle   466 *1855P* about Fate,
1855–63S about kings,   468 *1855P–56* The vague   470 *1855P* his,
473 *1855P–63 régime*.   1865 *régime*:   477 *1855P* come—   478 *1855P* not:
doubt   479 *1855P* all—   480 *1855P* dozen years with not a chance at all
1855, 1856 years with not a   482 *1855P* by half-a-dozen names

461 *eventualities*: consequences.
466 *"The State, that's I"*: Louis XIV is said to have remarked, 'l'État c'est moi'. The
Ohio editor quotes Napoleon, addressing a delegation of the *corps législatif* on 30
December 1813, as saying 'le trône c'est un homme et cet homme c'est moi'.
    quack-nonsense: a nonce-compound.
467 *hold*: stronghold, retreat.
472 *an Austrian marriage*: his first wife, Josephine, having failed to provide him with
an heir, Napoleon divorced her and married the Archduchess Marie Louise of Austria
in 1810. Since she was a member of the ruling Habsburg family, he thus allied himself
with 'the old *régime*'.
475 *Austerlitz*: on 2 December 1805 Napoleon had one of his most important
victories there, against the Austro-Russian armies.

Sleep, read and chat in quiet as I like!
Therefore I will not.

                    Take another case;   485
Fit up the cabin yet another way.
What say you to the poets? shall we write
Hamlet, Othello—make the world our own,
Without a risk to run of either sort?
I can't!—to put the strongest reason first.   490
"But try," you urge, "the trying shall suffice;
"The aim, if reached or not, makes great the life:
"Try to be Shakespeare, leave the rest to fate!"
Spare my self-knowledge—there's no fooling me!
If I prefer remaining my poor self,   495
I say so not in self-dispraise but praise.
If I'm a Shakespeare, let the well alone;
Why should I try to be what now I am?
If I'm no Shakespeare, as too probable,—
His power and consciousness and self-delight   500
And all we want in common, shall I find—
Trying for ever? while on points of taste
Wherewith, to speak it humbly, he and I
Are dowered alike—I'll ask you, I or he,
Which in our two lives realizes most?   505
Much, he imagined—somewhat, I possess.
He had the imagination; stick to that!
Let him say, "In the face of my soul's works
"Your world is worthless and I touch it not

---

484 *1855P* like—   485 *1855P* not. | Try another   *1880S, 1884S* case,
487 *1855P* the Poet's? shall   *1855–63, 1884S* the poet's? shall   488 *1855P–65*
Hamlets, Othellos—make   *492 1855P–56* life.   496 *1884S* praise,
497 *1884S* alone!   499 *1855P* I'm not Shakspeare,   501 *1855P* find
502 *1855P* of tastes   507 *1855P* that—   508 *1855P* "in

---

492 *The aim . . . makes great the life*: a characteristic sentiment in Browning: cf. 'Andrea
del Sarto', 97–8, 'A Grammarian's Funeral', 101 ff., and 'Rabbi Ben Ezra', 40–1.
497 *the well*: that which is well.
501 *want*: lack.

"Lest I should wrong them"—I'll withdraw my plea.   510
But does he say so? look upon his life!
Himself, who only can, gives judgment there.
He leaves his towers and gorgeous palaces
To build the trimmest house in Stratford town;
Saves money, spends it, owns the worth of things,   515
Giulio Romano's pictures, Dowland's lute;
Enjoys a show, respects the puppets, too,
And none more, had he seen its entry once,
Than "Pandulph, of fair Milan cardinal."
Why then should I who play that personage,   520
The very Pandulph Shakespeare's fancy made,
Be told that had the poet chanced to start
From where I stand now (some degree like mine
Being just the goal he ran his race to reach)
He would have run the whole race back, forsooth,   525
And left being Pandulph, to begin write plays?
Ah, the earth's best can be but the earth's best!

510 *1855P* them"—I should yield my cause: *1855, 1856* them"—I withdraw
512 *1855P* there!   514 *1855P* town,   517 *1855P* Would see a show, respect
the   518 *1855P* None more than, had   519 *1855P* "I, Pandulph, ...
cardinal:"   520 *1855P* should one who plays that   521 *1855P* Pandulph
Shakspeare made so fine,   523 *1855P* now—some   524 *1855P* reach—
527 *1855P* best—

513 *his towers and gorgeous palaces*: cf. *The Tempest*, IV. i. 152.
514 *the trimmest house*: Shakespeare bought New Place, the second largest dwelling in Stratford, in 1597. It had been built in the fifteenth century, and was known as The Great House.
516 *Giulio Romano's pictures, Dowland's lute*: a character in *The Winter's Tale*, at V. ii. 9 ff., refers to 'that rare Italian master, Julio Romano'. He lived from 1492 or 1499 to 1546, and was a sculptor as well as a painter and architect. Shakespeare's plays are full of references to the lute. The only specific reference to John Dowland (1562–1626) occurs in the eighth poem in *The Passionate Pilgrim*, a collection of twenty poems formerly attributed to Shakespeare, an attribution Browning may well have accepted.
517 *a show*: an exhibition, in a booth or elsewhere, of acrobats, dancers, etc.
    puppets: puppet-shows were common in Shakespeare's time: see, e.g., *Hamlet*, III. ii. 241.
519 *"Pandulph, of fair Milan cardinal"*: in *King John*, III. i. 135 Pandulph enters. King Philip of France says: 'Here comes the holy legate of the Pope', and the legate announces himself in these words. He exhibits Papal power by excommunicating King John and so obliging King Philip to break his alliance with England.
523 *degree*: status.

Did Shakespeare live, he could but sit at home
And get himself in dreams the Vatican,
Greek busts, Venetian paintings, Roman walls,   530
And English books, none equal to his own,
Which I read, bound in gold (he never did).
—Terni's fall, Naples' bay and Gothard's top—
Eh, friend? I could not fancy one of these;
But, as I pour this claret, there they are: 535
I've gained them—crossed St. Gothard last July
With ten mules to the carriage and a bed
Slung inside; is my hap the worse for that?
We want the same things, Shakespeare and myself,
And what I want, I have: he, gifted more,   540
Could fancy he too had them when he liked,
But not so thoroughly that, if fate allowed,
He would not have them also in my sense.
We play one game; I send the ball aloft
No less adroitly that of fifty strokes   545
Scarce five go o'er the wall so wide and high
Which sends them back to me: I wish and get.
He struck balls higher and with better skill,
But at a poor fence level with his head,
And hit—his Stratford house, a coat of arms,   550

---

530 *1855P* Venetian painting, Roman   532 *1855P* I have, bound . . . . never had)
533 *1855P*—Terni and Naples bay   *1855–65*—Terni and Naples'   536 *1855P*
I've seen them—   541 *1855P* Can fancy that he had it when   *1855–84S* had it
when   542 *1855P* that when fate allows   543 *1855P–84S* have it also
544 *1855P* game, *1855–65* game.   546 *1855P* Not five   547 *1855P* get—

---

533 *Terni's fall*: a famous waterfall north of Rome, often painted.
534 *fancy*: call up with the aid of my imagination.
538 *hap*: fate.
544 *I send the ball aloft*: 'I see no connection with real ('Royal') tennis', writes J. A. B.
Cuddon, the authority on sporting terms, 'or with any of the varieties of pelota. Nor can
I make any link with any of the forms of "fives" games. I don't understand the "poor
fence level", nor do I see what he's getting at with "scarce five go o'er the wall". Like
many preachers the Bishop is using an example from a realm of knowledge of which he
is ignorant.' How far Browning shared his ignorance is a matter for speculation.
550 *a coat of arms*: in 1596 the College of Heralds granted a coat of arms to
Shakespeare's father. From then on the poet appears in the records, 'gentleman'. See
S. Schoenbaum, *Shakespeare's Lives* (2nd ed., 1991), 16, 15.

Successful dealings in his grain and wool,—
While I receive heaven's incense in my nose
And style myself the cousin of Queen Bess.
Ask him, if this life's all, who wins the game?

Believe—and our whole argument breaks up.   555
Enthusiasm's the best thing, I repeat;
Only, we can't command it; fire and life
Are all, dead matter's nothing, we agree:
And be it a mad dream or God's very breath,
The fact's the same,—belief's fire, once in us,   560
Makes of all else mere stuff to show itself:
We penetrate our life with such a glow
As fire lends wood and iron—this turns steel,
That burns to ash—all's one, fire proves its power
For good or ill, since men call flare success.   565
But paint a fire, it will not therefore burn.
Light one in me, I'll find it food enough!
Why, to be Luther—that's a life to lead,
Incomparably better than my own.
He comes, reclaims God's earth for God, he says,   570
Sets up God's rule again by simple means,

---

551 *1884S* wool: 552 *1855P* receive the incense   553 *1855P* Bess—
561 *1855P–56* itself.   562 *1855P* You penetrate   *1863S* It penetrates our
564 *1855P* proves itself.   565 *1855P* success—   566 *1855P* burn!
567 *1855P* me, I'd find   569 *1855P* own—

---

551 *grain and wool*: in July 1605 Shakespeare made a large investment in the lease of tithes of these and other commodities in Stratford parish and villages nearby: Schoenbaum, 34.

553 *the cousin of Queen Bess*: a light-hearted allusion to the fact that sovereigns (such as Queen Elizabeth) and princes of the Church used the word 'cousin' in addressing or referring to each other.

562 *penetrate*: imbrue.

565 *Flare*: 'A sudden, quick, transitory blaze': Johnson.

568 *Luther*: the Bishop's tribute to Martin Luther (1483–1546), the great German religious reformer, is magnanimous, and perhaps a sign of a lack of Catholic fervour. We may contrast Gerard Manley Hopkins, (a convert) who, in 'The Wreck of the Deutschland' (written 1875–6), terms Luther the 'beast of the waste wood' (st. xx).

Re-opens a shut book, and all is done.
He flared out in the flaring of mankind;
Such Luther's luck was: how shall such be mine?
If he succeeded, nothing's left to do: 575
And if he did not altogether—well,
Strauss is the next advance. All Strauss should be
I might be also. But to what result?
He looks upon no future: Luther did.
What can I gain on the denying side?   580
Ice makes no conflagration. State the facts,
Read the text right, emancipate the world—
The emancipated world enjoys itself
With scarce a thank-you: Blougram told it first
It could not owe a farthing,—not to him   585
More than Saint Paul! 't would press its pay, you think?
Then add there's still that plaguy hundredth chance
Strauss may be wrong. And so a risk is run—
For what gain? not for Luther's, who secured
A real heaven in his heart throughout his life,   590
Supposing death a little altered things.

    "Ay, but since really you lack faith," you cry,
"You run the same risk really on all sides,
"In cool indifference as bold unbelief.
"As well be Strauss as swing 'twixt Paul and him.   595

572 _1855P_ done—   573 _1855P_ He could enjoy the   577 _1855P_ advance—
all   578 _1855P_ also—but   581 _1855P_ conflagration!   584 _1855P_ With
just a thank-you—since I told   585 _1855P_ to me   586 _1855P_ Paul: _1868_
Paul?   588 _1855P_ wrong—and   591 _1855P–63S_ things!   592 _1855P–_
56 really I lack   593 _1855P–56_ "I run   594 _1855P_ unbelief;

572 _Re-opens a shut book_: by translating the Bible. Luther translated the New
Testament from the Greek in 1522, and the Old Testament and Apocrypha in the
following years.
573 _Flared out_: probably a reference to the Renaissance in the northern countries of
Europe.
577 _Strauss_: David Friedrich Strauss published _Das Leben Jesu_ a critical analysis of the
gospel accounts of Christ's life, in 1835–6. In 1846 George Eliot translated the 4th ed.
into English. The Bishop regards Luther as halfway to this dangerous man.
585 _It could not owe a farthing_: cf. Rom. 13: 8: 'Owe no man any thing.'

"It's not worth having, such imperfect faith,
"No more available to do faith's work
"Than unbelief like mine. Whole faith, or none!"

 Softly, my friend! I must dispute that point.
Once own the use of faith, I'll find you faith.   600
We're back on Christian ground. You call for faith:
I show you doubt, to prove that faith exists.
The more of doubt, the stronger faith, I say,
If faith o'ercomes doubt. How I know it does?
By life and man's free will, God gave for that!   605
To mould life as we choose it, shows our choice:
That's our one act, the previous work's his own.
You criticize the soil? it reared this tree—
This broad life and whatever fruit it bears!
What matter though I doubt at every pore,   610
Head-doubts, heart-doubts, doubts at my fingers' ends,
Doubts in the trivial work of every day,
Doubts at the very bases of my soul
In the grand moments when she probes herself—
If finally I have a life to show,   615
The thing I did, brought out in evidence
Against the thing done to me underground
By hell and all its brood, for aught I know?
I say, whence sprang this? shows it faith or doubt?
All's doubt in me; where's break of faith in this?   620
It is the idea, the feeling and the love,
God means mankind should strive for and show forth
Whatever be the process to that end,—
And not historic knowledge, logic sound,
And metaphysical acumen, sure!   625

596 *1855P* Myself, for instance, have imperfect   597 *1855–63* Nor more
598 *1855P* like yours—whole *1855, 1856* like yours. Whole   *599 {reading of
1855P–84S*, DC, BrU, *1889}* *1888* point   601 *1855P* ground; you   604 *1855P*
doubt—how 606 *1855P* choice,   607 *1855P* own!   *608 {reading
of *1855P–84S}* *1888, 1889* soul?   609 *1855P* bears.   618 *1855P* know.
620 *1855P* me,   625 *1855P* sure.

"What think ye of Christ," friend? when all's done and said,
Like you this Christianity or not?
It may be false, but will you wish it true?
Has it your vote to be so if it can?
Trust you an instinct silenced long ago   630
That will break silence and enjoin you love
What mortified philosophy is hoarse,
And all in vain, with bidding you despise?
If you desire faith—then you've faith enough:
What else seeks God—nay, what else seek ourselves?   635
You form a notion of me, we'll suppose,
On hearsay; it's a favourable one:
"But still" (you add), "there was no such good man,
"Because of contradiction in the facts.
"One proves, for instance, he was born in Rome,   640
"This Blougram; yet throughout the tales of him
"I see he figures as an Englishman."
Well, the two things are reconcileable.
But would I rather you discovered that,
Subjoining—"Still, what matter though they be?   645
"Blougram concerns me nought, born here or there."

    Pure faith indeed—you know not what you ask!
Naked belief in God the Omnipotent,
Omniscient, Omnipresent, sears too much
The sense of conscious creatures to be borne.   650
It were the seeing him, no flesh shall dare.

626 *1855P* friend!   627 *1855P–56* You like this   634 *1855–63S* enough.
637 *1855P* one.   638 *1855P* man,"   639 *1855P–63* of contradictions in
1855P facts—   642 *1855P* Englishman.   643 *1855P* reconcilable—
646 *1855P* there?"   647 *1884S* indeed? you   650 *1855P* borne,   *651 {read-
ing of *1855–84S*, DC, BrU, *1889*} *1855P* dare—   *1888* dare

    626 *"What think ye of Christ"*: 'While the Pharisees were gathered together, Jesus
asked them, saying, What think ye of Christ?': Matt. 22: 41–2.
    632 *mortified*: 'In religious use . . . Dead to sin or the world; having the appetites and
passions in subjection; ascetic. Now *rare*': OED².
    640 *born in Rome*: see pp. 206–7, above.
    651 *no flesh shall dare*: in Exod. 33: 23 and *Christmas-Eve*, 434, however, the back of
the Lord is seen.

Some think, Creation's meant to show him forth:
I say it's meant to hide him all it can,
And that's what all the blessed evil's for.
Its use in Time is to environ us,   655
Our breath, our drop of dew, with shield enough
Against that sight till we can bear its stress.
Under a vertical sun, the exposed brain
And lidless eye and disemprisoned heart
Less certainly would wither up at once   660
Than mind, confronted with the truth of him.
But time and earth case-harden us to live;
The feeblest sense is trusted most; the child
Feels God a moment, ichors o'er the place,
Plays on and grows to be a man like us.   665
With me, faith means perpetual unbelief
Kept quiet like the snake 'neath Michael's foot
Who stands calm just because he feels it writhe.
Or, if that's too ambitious,—here's my box—
I need the excitation of a pinch   670
Threatening the torpor of the inside-nose
Nigh on the imminent sneeze that never comes.
"Leave it in peace" advise the simple folk:

654 *1855P* for,   657 *1855P* stress: 659 *1855P* The lidless eye, the
disemprisoned   661 *1855P* Than we, confronted   672 *1855P* comes
673 *1880S, 1884S* peace!"

652 *Creation's meant to show him forth*: cf. the title of John Ray's famous book, *The Wisdom of God Manifested in the Works of the Creation* (1691), often referred to by both Wesley and Paley.

658 *Under a vertical sun*: Livingston Lowes noted that 'Coleridge, like everybody else who read voyages at all, had met with the vertical sun at the Line a score of times': *The Road to Xanadu* (1930), 158. Browning had probably read a description of the vertical sun in *Eothen* (1844): he had met Kinglake in 1842: see our Vol. IV, p. 96.

662 *case-harden*: toughen.

664 *ichors o'er the place*: the verb is not in OED[2]. In Greek mythology 'ichor' is the fluid which flows in the veins of the gods. Here, as Porter and Clarke suggest, 'ichor' probably means serum, 'which exudes where the skin is broken, coats the hurt, and facilitates its healing'.

667 *the snake*: Rev. 12: 7–9 describes the conquest of Michael and his angels over 'the great dragon . . . that old serpent, called the Devil, and Satan'. Browning is probably remembering Raphael's 'St Michael and the Dragon' in the Louvre.

669 *box*: snuffbox.

Make it aware of peace by itching-fits,
Say I—let doubt occasion still more faith! 675

You'll say, once all believed, man, woman, child,
In that dear middle-age these noodles praise.
How you'd exult if I could put you back
Six hundred years, blot out cosmogony,
Geology, ethnology, what not, 680
(Greek endings, each the little passing-bell
That signifies some faith's about to die),
And set you square with Genesis again,—
When such a traveller told you his last news,
He saw the ark a-top of Ararat 685
But did not climb there since 't was getting dusk
And robber-bands infest the mountain's foot!
How should you feel, I ask, in such an age,
How act? As other people felt and did;
With soul more blank than this decanter's knob, 690
Believe—and yet lie, kill, rob, fornicate
Full in belief's face, like the beast you'd be!

No, when the fight begins within himself,
A man's worth something. God stoops o'er his head,
Satan looks up between his feet—both tug— 695

---

675 *1855P* I, give still occasion for more   676 *1855P* Why, once we all
677 *1855P* praise—   *680 {reading of *1855–84S*, DC, BrU, *1889*} *1855P* not—
1888 not   681 *1855P–63* endings with the   683 *1855P* again? *1880S*, *1884S*
again!   687 *1855P* foot—   688 *1855P* age?   689 *1855P* as
694 *1855P* something—

677 *that dear middle-age*: enthusiasm for the Middle Ages is a characteristic of the
Victorian period, when it had a marked influence on religion, as on literature and
painting. Here Browning endows Blougram with his own impatience with its excesses.
Cf. our Vol. IV, p. 98.

679 *cosmogony*: the study of the creation or development of the universe. The Bishop
is thinking of such influential works as *Vestiges of the Natural History of Creation* (1844),
by Robert Chambers.

681 *Greek endings*: branches of knowledge described by words ending in 'ology'.

685 *Ararat*: Noah's ark 'rested . . . upon the mountains of Ararat': Gen. 8: 4.

695 *both tug*: an image reminiscent of emblem books and religious pictures.

He's left, himself, i' the middle: the soul wakes
And grows. Prolong that battle through his life!
Never leave growing till the life to come!
Here, we've got callous to the Virgin's winks
That used to puzzle people wholesomely: 700
Men have outgrown the shame of being fools.
What are the laws of nature, not to bend
If the Church bid them?—brother Newman asks.
Up with the Immaculate Conception, then—
On to the rack with faith!—is my advice.   705
Will not that hurry us upon our knees,
Knocking our breasts, "It can't be—yet it shall!
"Who am I, the worm, to argue with my Pope?
"Low things confound the high things!" and so forth.
That's better than acquitting God with grace   710
As some folk do. He's tried—no case is proved,
Philosophy is lenient—he may go!

   You'll say, the old system's not so obsolete
But men believe still: ay, but who and where?
King Bomba's lazzaroni foster yet   715

---

696 *1855P–68* himself, in the   697 *1855P* grows: prolong . . . . life   702 *1855P*
bend?   703 *1855P–63S* them, brother   *1855P* asks;   704 *1855P* Out with
705 *1855P–63S* faith—   *1855P* advice—   *1855–63S* advice!   711 *1855P* As
folks do now—he's   *1855–84S* some folks do.   714 *1855P* But some men

699 *the Virgin's winks*: see 377 n.

703 *brother Newman asks*: in his *Lectures* (cf. above, 377 n.) Newman stated that
'Miracles to the Catholic are historical facts, and nothing short of this; and they are to
be regarded and dealt with as other facts': 294.

704 *the Immaculate Conception*: the Roman Catholic dogma that from the first
moment of her conception the Blessed Virgin Mary was kept free from all stain of
original sin, proclaimed by the Bull *Ineffabilis Deus* of Pope Pius IX, 8 December 1854.
It is a common error to confuse it with the Virgin Birth.

705 *On to the rack with faith!*: his ironical advice is that Faith should be tortured by
being stretched.

708 *the worm*: 'But I am a worm, and no man': Ps. 22: 6.

715 *King Bomba's lazzaroni*: i.e. the poorest of the poor in Naples. In his early years
Ferdinand II, king of the Two Sicilies, was popular with the poor, but later he became
more and more despotic. He was grossly superstitious, and was known as King Bomba
after the bombardment of Sicily in 1849. Cf. 'De Gustibus', 35–7.

The sacred flame, so Antonelli writes;
But even of these, what ragamuffin-saint
Believes God watches him continually,
As he believes in fire that it will burn,
Or rain that it will drench him? Break fire's law,   720
Sin against rain, although the penalty
Be just a singe or soaking? "No," he smiles;
"Those laws are laws that can enforce themselves."

 The sum of all is—yes, my doubt is great,
My faith's still greater, then my faith's enough.   725
I have read much, thought much, experienced much,
Yet would die rather than avow my fear
The Naples' liquefaction may be false,
When set to happen by the palace-clock
According to the clouds or dinner-time.   730
I hear you recommend, I might at least
Eliminate, decrassify my faith
Since I adopt it; keeping what I must
And leaving what I can—such points as this.
I won't—that is, I can't throw one away.   735
Supposing there's no truth in what I hold
About the need of trial to man's faith,
Still, when you bid me purify the same,
To such a process I discern no end.

---

722 *1855P–63* soaking? No, he 723 *1855P–63* Those *1855P* themselves! *1855–*
63 themselves. 725 *1855P–56* faith's the greater— 727 *1855P* than avouch
my 728 *1855P* The Naples liquefaction 731 *1855P* you interpose—"I
734 *1855P* this!" *1855–65* this! 735 *1855P* away! 736 *1855P* Suppose
there were no *1855P–65* I said 737 *1855P–63* of trials to 739 *1855P–65* end,

716 *Antonelli*: Cardinal Giacomo Antonelli (1806–76), an unscrupulous and grasping
man who was the papal Secretary of State from 1850; he was a master of reactionary
statecraft.

724–5 *my doubt is great, / My faith's still greater*: cf. Matt 21: 21.

728 *The Naples' liquefaction*: see 377 n, above.

732 *decrassify*: 'To divest of what is crass, gross, or material': OED[2], which gives no
earlier example.

739 *To such a process*: 'Browning has reproduced one of Newman's leading ideas.
About 1842, Newman wrote in the *Apologia*, he "came to the conclusion that there was

Clearing off one excrescence to see two,   740
There's ever a next in size, now grown as big,
That meets the knife: I cut and cut again!
First cut the Liquefaction, what comes last
But Fichte's clever cut at God himself?
Experimentalize on sacred things!   745
I trust nor hand nor eye nor heart nor brain
To stop betimes: they all get drunk alike.
The first step, I am master not to take.

You'd find the cutting-process to your taste
As much as leaving growths of lies unpruned,   750
Nor see more danger in it,—you retort.
Your taste's worth mine; but my taste proves more wise
When we consider that the steadfast hold
On the extreme end of the chain of faith
Gives all the advantage, makes the difference   755
With the rough purblind mass we seek to rule:
We are their lords, or they are free of us,
Just as we tighten or relax our hold.
So, other matters equal, we'll revert
To the first problem—which, if solved my way   760

---

740 *1863S* to find two;   *1855, 1856, 1863, 1865* two;   743 *1855P* First comes the
745 *1855P–63S* things?   747 *1855P* alike—   751 *1855P* retort—
754 *1855P* Of the   756 *1855–63* rule.   758 *1855P* relax that hold—
1855–63 relax that hold.   *759 {reading of *1855P–84S*} *1888, 1889* So, others matters

no medium, in true philosophy, between Atheism and Catholicity, and that a perfectly
consistent mind . . . must embrace either the one or the other" ': C. R. Tracy, 'Bishop
Blougram': MLR 34 (1939), 424 (referring to the edition of Wilfred Ward, 1913, 291).

744 *Fichte's clever cut*: J. G. Fichte (1762–1814) was an enthusiastic follower of Kant
who devised a scheme of his own, 'subjective idealism', according to which (in the
words of Bertrand Russell) 'the Ego is the only ultimate reality, and . . . exists because
it posits itself; the non-Ego . . . exists only because the Ego posits it': *History of Western
Philosophy* (1946), 744–5. This leaves God in an odd position. Allen mentions that Fichte
is reported as ending a lecture with the words, 'Tomorrow, gentlemen, I shall create
God': C. F. Harrold, *Carlyle and German Thought: 1819–1834* (New Haven, 1934), 36.

745 *Experimentalize*: first recorded in 1800: *The Life . . . of Robert Southey*, ed. C. C.
Southey, 6 vols. (1849–50), ii. 38.

748 *I am master not to take*: a Gallicism, *je suis maître de faire quelque chose*.

759 *other matters equal*: an absolute construction, L. *ceteris paribus*.

And thrown into the balance, turns the scale—
How we may lead a comfortable life,
How suit our luggage to the cabin's size.

Of course you are remarking all this time
How narrowly and grossly I view life,   765
Respect the creature-comforts, care to rule
The masses, and regard complacently
"The cabin," in our old phrase. Well, I do.
I act for, talk for, live for this world now,
As this world prizes action, life and talk: 770
No prejudice to what next world may prove,
Whose new laws and requirements, my best pledge
To observe then, is that I observe these now,
Shall do hereafter what I do meanwhile.
Let us concede (gratuitously though)   775
Next life relieves the soul of body, yields
Pure spiritual enjoyment: well, my friend,
Why lose this life i' the meantime, since its use
May be to make the next life more intense?

Do you know, I have often had a dream   780
(Work it up in your next month's article)
Of man's poor spirit in its progress, still
Losing true life for ever and a day
Through ever trying to be and ever being—
In the evolution of successive spheres—   785

761 *1855P* scale.   768 *1855P–63* phrase!   *1855P* do—   769 *1855P* talk of,
live in, this   770 *1855P–65* world calls for action,   774 *1855P–56* Doing
hereafter   777 *1855P–63* spiritual enjoyments: well,   778 *1855P–68* life in the
779 *1855P* the contrast more   783 *1855P* Losing its life

768 *"The cabin"*: see l. 101.

782 *progress*: see Georg Roppen, *Evolution and Poetic Belief* (Oslo and Oxford, 1956),
particularly 112 ff. Cf. 'Old Pictures in Florence', st. xxi.

785 *successive spheres*: cf. *Sordello*, vi. 551 ff. 'According to him', Henry Adams wrote
of Browning's conversation in 1863, 'the minds or souls that really did develope
themselves and educate themselves in life, could alone expect to enter a future career
for which this life was a preparatory course': *Selected Letters of Henry Adams*, ed. Newton
Arvin (New York, 1951), 43.

Before its actual sphere and place of life,
Halfway into the next, which having reached,
It shoots with corresponding foolery
Halfway into the next still, on and off!
As when a traveller, bound from North to South,   790
Scouts fur in Russia: what's its use in France?
In France spurns flannel: where's its need in Spain?
In Spain drops cloth, too cumbrous for Algiers!
Linen goes next, and last the skin itself,
A superfluity at Timbuctoo.   795
When, through his journey, was the fool at ease?
I'm at ease now, friend; worldly in this world,
I take and like its way of life; I think
My brothers, who administer the means,
Live better for my comfort—that's good too;   800
And God, if he pronounce upon such life,
Approves my service, which is better still.
If he keep silence,—why, for you or me
Or that brute beast pulled-up in to-day's "Times,"
What odds is 't, save to ourselves, what life we lead?   805

    You meet me at this issue: you declare,—
All special-pleading done with—truth is truth,
And justifies itself by undreamed ways.
You don't fear but it's better, if we doubt,
To say so, act up to our truth perceived   810
However feebly. Do then,—act away!
'T is there I'm on the watch for you. How one acts
Is, both of us agree, our chief concern:

---

793 *1855P* Algiers—   795 *1855P* Timbuctoo—   797 *1855P* world;
801 *1855P* upon it all   *1855–65* upon it all,   808 *1855P* ways—   810 *1855P*–
63 so, acting up   811 *1855P* However feeble; do that then,—   812 *1855P*
you—how   *1855–63* you!

---

791 *Scouts*: scorns.

795 *Timbuctoo*: a town in what is now Mali, the terminus of a caravan route across
the Sahara. The name is often used for any remote or outlandish place.

804 *pulled-up*: reprimanded, brought to book.

And how you'll act is what I fain would see
If, like the candid person you appear,   815
You dare to make the most of your life's scheme
As I of mine, live up to its full law
Since there's no higher law that counterchecks.
Put natural religion to the test
You've just demolished the revealed with—quick,   820
Down to the root of all that checks your will,
All prohibition to lie, kill and thieve,
Or even to be an atheistic priest!
Suppose a pricking to incontinence—
Philosophers deduce you chastity   825
Or shame, from just the fact that at the first
Whoso embraced a woman in the field,
Threw club down and forewent his brains beside,
So, stood a ready victim in the reach
Of any brother savage, club in hand;   830
Hence saw the use of going out of sight
In wood or cave to prosecute his loves:
I read this in a French book t' other day.
Does law so analysed coerce you much?
Oh, men spin clouds of fuzz where matters end,   835
But you who reach where the first thread begins,
You'll soon cut that!—which means you can, but won't,

---

815 *1855P* person that you are,   818 *1855P* counterchecks—   827 *1855P*–
63 the plain,   828 *1855P* Used both arms, and   830 *1855P* So lay . . . . the
sight   831 *1855P* the good of   832 *1855P* to set about the same—

---

819 *natural religion*: 'The Things knowable concerning God, and our Duty by the
Light of Nature, are called natural Religion': Isaac Watts, *Logick* (1725), II. v. Blougram
is caricaturing the concept.

833 *a French book*: probably Balzac's 'Physiologie du Mariage', where in 'Méditation
xvii, Théorie du lit', we find this: 'it is recognised that if originally man sought shady
caves, mossy ravines, and the roof of silicious caverns to provide a safe refuge for his
pleasures, it is because love delivers him defenceless to his enemies': see R. E. Neil
Dodge's letter in the TLS for 21 March 1935, p. 176, citing *Œuvres complètes* (Paris,
1927), xxxii. 202 ff. C. R. Tracy had suggested Stendhal's *De l'amour*, first published in
1822 (TLS 24 January 1935, p. 48); while Oscar Maurer later pointed to a passage in
Diderot's *Supplément au voyage de Bougainville*: VP vi (1968), 177–9.

834 *coerce*: restrain.

Through certain instincts, blind, unreasoned-out,
You dare not set aside, you can't tell why,
But there they are, and so you let them rule.   840
Then, friend, you seem as much a slave as I,
A liar, conscious coward and hypocrite,
Without the good the slave expects to get,
In case he has a master after all!
You own your instincts? why, what else do I,   845
Who want, am made for, and must have a God
Ere I can be aught, do aught?—no mere name
Want, but the true thing with what proves its truth,
To wit, a relation from that thing to me,
Touching from head to foot—which touch I feel,   850
And with it take the rest, this life of ours!
I live my life here; yours you dare not live.

      —Not as I state it, who (you please subjoin)
Disfigure such a life and call it names,
While, to your mind, remains another way   855
For simple men: knowledge and power have rights,
But ignorance and weakness have rights too.
There needs no crucial effort to find truth
If here or there or anywhere about:
We ought to turn each side, try hard and see,   860
And if we can't, be glad we've earned at least
The right, by one laborious proof the more,
To graze in peace earth's pleasant pasturage.
Men are not angels, neither are they brutes:

842 *1855P* hypocrite.   843 *1855P* get.   844 *1855P–63* Suppose he   *1855P*
all,   845 *1855P–63* instincts—   *1865* instincts: 847 *1855P* aught!—51 *1855P*
ours.   852 *1855P* you cannot live—   855 *1855P–63* While, in your
856 *1880S* rights.   859 *1855P* about   862 *1855P* more.   863–4 {lines
reversed in *1855P*}   863 *1855P* pasturage: 864 *1855P* not Gods, but, if you
like, are brutes   *1855, 1856* not gods, but, properly, are brutes.   *1863S, 1863* brutes.

    864 *Men are not angels*: 'The change from asserting to denying that men are brutes is
interesting', a friend comments on the revision here; 'what could freely be said in 1855
might by the end of Browning's life have made the Bishop an evolutionist.' *1855* echoes
Othello, III, iv. 149.

Something we may see, all we cannot see.   865
What need of lying? I say, I see all,
And swear to each detail the most minute
In what I think a Pan's face—you, mere cloud:
I swear I hear him speak and see him wink,
For fear, if once I drop the emphasis,   870
Mankind may doubt there's any cloud at all.
You take the simple life—ready to see,
Willing to see (for no cloud's worth a face)—
And leaving quiet what no strength can move,
And which, who bids you move? who has the right?   875
I bid you; but you are God's sheep, not mine:
"*Pastor est tui Dominus.*" You find
In this the pleasant pasture of our life
Much you may eat without the least offence,
Much you don't eat because your maw objects,   880
Much you would eat but that your fellow-flock
Open great eyes at you and even butt,
And thereupon you like your mates so well
You cannot please yourself, offending them;
Though when they seem exorbitantly sheep,   885
You weigh your pleasure with their butts and bleats
And strike the balance. Sometimes certain fears
Restrain you, real checks since you find them so;

865 *1855P–63* cannot see—   868 *1855P–56* a man's face—   *1855P* cloud,—
870 *1855P* if I once drop   871 *1855P–56* doubt if there's a cloud
872 *1855P–65* the simpler life—   873 *1855P–63* see—for   *1855P* race—
1855–63 face—   875 *1855P* who, with the   877 *1855P* Dominus"—you
878 *1855P* In these the pleasant pastures of this life,   *1855, 1856, 1863* In these the pleasant
pastures of this life *1863S* In these the bounteous pastures of this life   883 *1855P*
Well, in the main you *1855P–56* your friends so much {revised in *Fields*}   *1863S* so
much   885 *1855P* Though sometimes, when .... seem to exact too much,
886 *1855P* their kicks and butts,   *1855, 1856* and kicks   888 *1855P* Will stay
you—real fears, since

868 *a Pan's face*: note revision from *1855*. Cf. *Hamlet*, III. ii. 366 f.

877 *"Pastor est tui Dominus"*: '*Your* Lord is a shepherd', i.e. Blougram is not his Lord,
since Gigadibs is not a Roman Catholic. The Bishop is not quoting, but playing with
the opening words of Ps. 23.

880 *maw*: stomach.

885 *exorbitantly sheep*: sheeplike to excess.

Sometimes you please yourself and nothing checks:
And thus you graze through life with not one lie,   890
And like it best.

                        But do you, in truth's name?
If so, you beat—which means you are not I—
Who needs must make earth mine and feed my fill
Not simply unbutted at, unbickered with,
But motioned to the velvet of the sward   895
By those obsequious wethers' very selves.
Look at me, sir; my age is double yours:
At yours, I knew beforehand, so enjoyed,
What now I should be—as, permit the word,
I pretty well imagine your whole range   900
And stretch of tether twenty years to come.
We both have minds and bodies much alike:
In truth's name, don't you want my bishopric,
My daily bread, my influence and my state?
You're young. I'm old; you must be old one day;   905
Will you find then, as I do hour by hour,
Women their lovers kneel to, who cut curls
From your fat lap-dog's ear to grace a brooch—
Dukes, who petition just to kiss your ring—
With much beside you know or may conceive?   910
Suppose we die to-night: well, here am I,
Such were my gains, life bore this fruit to me,
While writing all the same my articles

889 *1863S* you sate yourself   *1855P* checks,   893 *1855P* Who cannot make . . . .
mine so, feed   896 *1855P* By the obsequious short horns' very   897 *1855,*
1856 yours.   899 *1855P* be—while, permit   902 *1868–84S* We have both
minds   *1855–63* alike.   905 *1855P–84S* young, ... old,   *1855P* day,
907 *1855P–63* to, that cut   908 *1855P* From yonder lap-dog's ears to   *1855–63*
lap-dog's ears to   909 *1855P* Dukes that petition   *1855–63* Dukes, that petition
1855P kiss my ring—   910 *1855P* conceive!

892 *you beat*: you win (intrans.)
895 *the velvet*: the softest part.
896 *wethers'*: a wether is a castrated male sheep.
904 *My daily bread*: Matt. 6: 11, Luke 11: 3.
913 *my articles*: while Wiseman was a prolific contributor to the *Dublin Review*,
almost all his pieces were on religious topics, although one or two were on Christian

On music, poetry, the fictile vase
Found at Albano, chess, Anacreon's Greek.   915
But you—the highest honour in your life,
The thing you'll crown yourself with, all your days,
Is—dining here and drinking this last glass
I pour you out in sign of amity
Before we part for ever. Of your power   920
And social influence, worldly worth in short,
Judge what's my estimation by the fact,
I do not condescend to enjoin, beseech,
Hint secrecy on one of all these words!
You're shrewd and know that should you publish one   925
The world would brand the lie—my enemies first,
Who'd sneer—"the bishop's an arch-hypocrite
"And knave perhaps, but not so frank a fool."
Whereas I should not dare for both my ears
Breathe one such syllable, smile one such smile,   930
Before the chaplain who reflects myself—
My shade's so much more potent than your flesh.
What's your reward, self-abnegating friend?
Stood you confessed of those exceptional
And privileged great natures that dwarf mine—   935

915 *1855P–56* Albano, or Anacreon's   *1863* chess, or Anacreon's   924 *1855P*
words—   925 *1855P–56* publish it   927 *1855P* Who'd laugh—the . . . .
arch-hypocrite: *1855, 1856, 1863* "Who'd sneer—the   928 *1855P* fool.
931 *1855P–63* Before my chaplain   934 *1855P* of these exceptional   935 *1855P*
natures dwarfing mine—

art and architecture. See *The Wellesley Index to Victorian Periodicals*, V, ed. J. H.
Slingerland, (Toronto, 1989), 849 ff. All articles were anonymous.

914 *fictile*: moulded by a potter.
915 *Albano*: an ancient Roman town, some 20 miles SE of Rome, famous for its
catacombs.
  Anacreon's Greek: Anacreon, the lyric poet, was born at Teos *c.*570 BC. He wrote
in an Ionic vernacular which differs from Attic Greek. Browning and EBB owned
several editions of his poems. The translations of some of the 'Anacreontea' (verses
wrongly attributed to him) in Pettigrew and Collins, ii. 943 ff. are by EBB. Most of the
poems he wrote and of those attributed to him deal with wine and love. Yet as a boy,
we are told, Browning 'was hushed to sleep by his father to the words of an ode of
Anacreon': Griffin and Minchin, 25.
934 *of*: i.e. one of.

A zealot with a mad ideal in reach,
A poet just about to print his ode,
A statesman with a scheme to stop this war,
An artist whose religion is his art—
I should have nothing to object: such men   940
Carry the fire, all things grow warm to them,
Their drugget's worth my purple, they beat me.
But you,—you're just as little those as I—
You, Gigadibs, who, thirty years of age,
Write statedly for Blackwood's Magazine,   945
Believe you see two points in Hamlet's soul
Unseized by the Germans yet—which view you'll print—
Meantime the best you have to show being still
That lively lightsome article we took
Almost for the true Dickens,—what's its name?   950
"The Slum and Cellar, or Whitechapel life

---

940 *1855P* object,   *1855–63* object!   942 *1855P* purple, these beat me—
943 *1855P* little these as   947 *1855P* which views you'll   950 *1855P–56*
what's the name?

938 *this war*: the Crimean War, 1854–6, in which England and France (and latterly
Turkey) opposed and defeated Russia.

939 *whose religion is his art*: Kant and Schiller defended the autonomy of art. René
Wellek points out that 'The phrase "art for art, and without purpose" ' can be found as
early as 1804, in Benjamin Constant's diary, while 'In a lecture course first given in 1818
(printed only in 1836)' Victor Cousin 'apparently spoke of the need of ". . . art-for-art's
sake" ': *A History of Modern Criticism: 1750–1950*, vol. III (New Haven, 1965, p. 30). The
phrase became more prominent in England as the century wore on.

941 *the fire*: that of genius.

942 *their drugget*: the coarse cloth of which their clothes are made.

945 *statedly*: regularly.

      Blackwood's Magazine: 'Maga' began to appear in 1817, and attained a large
circulation. EBB first published a number of her poems there, including 'The Cry of
the Children'. Browning encouraged her, but did not himself contribute.

947 *the Germans*: from the later eighteenth century Germany produced numerous
literary critics and aestheticians. *Hamlet* was of particular interest to them. See, above
all, Goethe, *Wilhelm Meisters Lehrjahre*.

949 *lightsome*: illuminating.

951 *Whitechapel*: 'a district of London, inhabited chiefly by persons of low character':
OED (in section first published in 1924). Dickens and others explored the area in their
fiction. In its early years the *Rambler* (see l. 960 n. below) serialized 'Scenes of Life in
London', some set in Whitechapel, to emphasize the Roman Catholic concern for the
poor.

"Limned after dark!" it made me laugh, I know,
And pleased a month, and brought you in ten pounds.
—Success I recognize and compliment,
And therefore give you, if you choose, three words   955
(The card and pencil-scratch is quite enough)
Which whether here, in Dublin or New York,
Will get you, prompt as at my eyebrow's wink,
Such terms as never you aspired to get
In all our own reviews and some not ours.   960
Go write your lively sketches! be the first
"Blougram, or The Eccentric Confidence"—
Or better simply say, "The Outward-bound."
Why, men as soon would throw it in my teeth
As copy and quote the infamy chalked broad   965
About me on the church-door opposite.
You will not wait for that experience though,
I fancy, howsoever you decide,
To discontinue—not detesting, not
Defaming, but at least—despising me!   970

Over his wine so smiled and talked his hour
Sylvester Blougram, styled *in partibus*
Episcopus, nec non—(the deuce knows what
It's changed to by our novel hierarchy)

---

952 *1855P* dark"   955 *1855P*–56 you please, three   956 *1855P* (The simple card and pencil scratch's enough)   961 *1855P*–63 sketches—   964 *1855P* soon will throw   970 *1855P* Degrading, but   974 *1855P* by the novel

960 *our own reviews*: such as the *Dublin Review* (p. 207 above), and the *Rambler* .

963 *"The Outward-bound"*: see Edward Young, *Night Thoughts*, l. 149–51: 'Thought outward-bound / . . . flies off / In fume and Dissipations'.

972 *in partibus*: bishoprics *in partibus* were a long-established institution, permitting episcopal rank to be bestowed on men required for other duties. The Latin phrase, with the word 'infidelium' added or understood, often applies to an area where there is no Catholic hierarchy. Since Wiseman was forbidden by law from having a territorial see in England, he chose to be titular bishop of Melipotamus, in commemoration of the martyrdom of a vicar apostolic of Tonquin who had held the same title. Melipotamus was in Crete. See Richard J. Schiefen, *Nicholas Wiseman and the Transformation of English Catholicism* (The Patmos Press, Shepherdstown, W. Va., 1984), 110–11. Cf. Allen, 237.

With Gigadibs the literary man,   975
Who played with spoons, explored his plate's design,
And ranged the olive-stones about its edge,
While the great bishop rolled him out a mind
Long crumpled, till creased consciousness lay smooth.

For Blougram, he believed, say, half he spoke.   980
The other portion, as he shaped it thus
For argumentatory purposes,
He felt his foe was foolish to dispute.
Some arbitrary accidental thoughts
That crossed his mind, amusing because new,   985
He chose to represent as fixtures there,
Invariable convictions (such they seemed
Beside his interlocutor's loose cards
Flung daily down, and not the same way twice)
While certain hell-deep instincts, man's weak tongue   990
Is never bold to utter in their truth
Because styled hell-deep ('t is an old mistake
To place hell at the bottom of the earth)
He ignored these,—not having in readiness
Their nomenclature and philosophy: 995
He said true things, but called them by wrong names.
"On the whole," he thought, "I justify myself
"On every point where cavillers like this
"Oppugn my life: he tries one kind of fence,
"I close, he's worsted, that's enough for him.   1000
"He's on the ground: if ground should break away

977 *1855P* Arranged its olive stones   978 *1855P–75* out his mind.   979 {does
not appear in *1855P–75*} *1880S, 1884S* Long rumpled, till   980 *1855P* half he said.
987 *1855P* convictions—such   989 *1855P* twice;   991 *1855P* Shall hardly
dare to   992 *1855P* Till one demonstrate it an   1856 hell-deep (it is an
993 *1855P* earth,—   997 *1855P* On . . . . whole, he thought, I   1000 *1855P*
him!   *1855, 1856, 1863, 1865* him;   1001 *1855–63* ground!   *1855P–68* if the ground

979 *Long crumpled*: this line was added in *1880S*.
982 *argumentatory*: not in OED² (which has 'argumentator').
990 *hell-deep instincts*: such as 'looking after Number One'?
999 *fence*: use of his sword (as in duelling).

"I take my stand on, there's a firmer yet
"Beneath it, both of us may sink and reach.
"His ground was over mine and broke the first:
"So, let him sit with me this many a year!"   1005

He did not sit five minutes. Just a week
Sufficed his sudden healthy vehemence.
Something had struck him in the "Outward-bound"
Another way than Blougram's purpose was:
And having bought, not cabin-furniture   1010
But settler's-implements (enough for three)
And started for Australia—there, I hope,
By this time he has tested his first plough,
And studied his last chapter of St. John.

1002 *1855P* I took my   1004 *1855P–63S* first.   1005 *1855P* year!
1006 *1855P* minutes; for a   1008 *1855P–63* (Something   1009 *1855P–63*
was)

1009 *Another way*: i.e. literally, not metaphorically (as in ll. 100 ff).

1011 *(enough for three)*: cf. ll. 104–5.

1012 *Australia*: the 1840s and 1850s were great periods of emigration to Australia.
Wool was the staple produce, while the discovery of gold in 1851 led to a rush of
prospectors. In 1842 Browning's close friend Alfred Domett (cf. Vol. III, pp. 224 ff.) had
emigrated to New Zealand. Turner points out that in Clough's poem *The Bothie of
Toper-na-Fuosich* (1848) the hero and his wife go there, 'Five hundred pounds in pocket,
with books, and two or three pictures, / Tool-box, plough, and the rest . . . There he
hewed, and dug; subdued the earth and his spirit': ix. 194–6.

1014 *his last chapter of St. John*: where he would have found the exhortations, 'Feed
my lambs . . . Feed my sheep . . . Feed my sheep'. Cf. l. 877 and n. The narrator hopes
that Gigadibs has abandoned fruitless religious disputation, and is now engaged in
agricultural life in Australia. Cf. a letter from EBB to her sister Sarianna: 'I have a distrust
of persons going to Australia, who are not prepared for manual labour': PK 53: 13
(24 February 1853).

MEMORABILIA

WHEN E. G. Kingsland asked Browning about the origin of this poem, he replied:

I was once in the shop of Hodgson, the bookseller, when a stranger, who was in conversation with Hodgson, spoke of something which Shelley had once told him. Suddenly the stranger turned towards me, bursting into a loud laugh as he saw my blanched face—for I was strangely moved.[1]

In a letter to Buxton Forman, Browning stated that the man who 'once [saw] Shelley plain' was in fact two men, one 'a bookseller I never saw before or since', who 'mentioned the poet carelessly', the other 'a friend who accompanied me to the shop' and who 'laughed at me for what he told my father was—"a look quite his own"—that is mine, I who was a boy at the time: so the twain became one flesh'.[2] The seed of this little poem was therefore planted when Browning was in the first flush of his enthusiasm for Shelley the poet and Shelley the man, almost thirty years before 'Memorabilia' was published.[3]

Browning told Buxton Forman that 'The "moor" had no name of its own except in the writer's head.' The eagle's feather which stands out against the blankness of the moor has literary origins. On 1 March 1842 Sarah Flower had written a poem for the birthday of Browning's friend W. J. Fox which includes the words 'His pen it hath come / From the wing of an eagle, / And tells of its home'. Since Browning knew Young's

---

[1] 'Robert Browning: Some Personal Reminiscences'. *Baylor University Browning Interests, Second Series* (Waco, Texas, July 1931), p. 32. Hodgson's Bookshop, which was near Wimpole Street, is mentioned several times in the letters in Kintner. It was the rendezvous from which the Brownings set out together for Italy.

[2] Browning to Buxton Forman, 30 March 1881 (PK 81: 84). We are indebted to the authorities of the Pforzheimer Library for a photocopy of the whole letter.

[3] In the *Christian Science Monitor* for 17 September 1956, p. 8, Horace Reynolds described what he took to be a manuscript of an early version of this poem, with a facsimile. It is not in Browning's hand. It is entitled 'Incident in a Life', and reads as follows: 'Did you once see Shelley—plain—/And he spoke to you, / And you spoke to him again? / It is strange and new. / You were living before that, / And you are living after, / And the memory I started at / Moves your laughter? / I travelled a moor with a name of its own / And a use in the world no doubt, / Yet for me a handsbreadth shines alone / Mid blank miles round about / Where I picked up on the heather / And put inside my breast / The moulted eagle-feather: / I forget all the rest.' While it is conceivable that this is an early draft, it reads more like someone's attempt to remember the poem.

Night Thoughts well, he may have remembered *Night the Second*, ll. 602–4: 'Had he dropt, / That Eagle Genius! O had he let fall / One feather as he flew'.

The piece is not in the proofs; it was probably added to avoid a blank page at the end of vol. i.

The verse form of st. i, three iambic tetrameters followed by an iambic trimeter, rhyming *abab*, is repeated with slight variations in the other stanzas: in st. iii, notably, there is an anapaest in every line (two in l. 10).

Date: 1853/5
1863: *Dramatic Lyrics*

MEMORABILIA.

I.

AH, did you once see Shelley plain,
  And did he stop and speak to you,
And did you speak to him again?
  How strange it seems and new!

II.

But you were living before that,   5
  And also you are living after;
And the memory I started at—
  My starting moves your laughter.

III.

I crossed a moor, with a name of its own
  And a certain use in the world no doubt,   10
Yet a hand's-breadth of it shines alone
  'Mid the blank miles round about:

---

*2 {reading of *1865–84S*} *1855–63* you? *1888, 1889* you   6 *1855–65* And you *1855–63* after,   *8 {reading of DC, BrU} *1855–84S* laughter! *1888, 1889* laughter 10 *1855–65* a use *Taylor, 1865S* doubt;

IV.

For there I picked up on the heather
And there I put inside my breast
A moulted feather, an eagle-feather!
Well, I forget the rest.

15

15 *1855–63* eagle-feather —

VOLUME II

ANDREA DEL SARTO

ON 16 November 1881 a member of the Browning Society wrote to F. J. Furnivall from Florence to point out that 'the *impulse*' to write this poem must have been the portrait of Andrea and his wife in the Pitti Palace.[1] He quoted the description from the catalogue of the gallery:

The painter, seen in three-quarter face, appears by the gesture of his left hand to appeal to his wife Lucrezia Fede. His right hand rests on her shoulder (his arm is around her, I may remark—an act of tenderness which has much to do with the pathos of the composition). Lucrezia is presented in full face, with a golden chain on her neck, and a letter in her hands.

Andrea has 'a pleading expression', while she looks straight ahead. It is now known that the painting is in fact a composite, that neither of the parts is by Andrea, and that neither he nor his wife is portrayed; but that is irrelevant for us. Furnivall was so excited by the letter that 'some fourteen hours' after receiving it he asked Browning whether it had in fact suggested his poem. 'He said, Yes, it had. Mr. Kenyon, . . . had askt him to buy for him, Mr. K., a copy . . . None was on sale, or to be got; and so Browning, as he couldn't send a copy of the painting, wrote what it told him in words, and sent his poem to Mr. Kenyon.'

Fortunately Browning's letter survives, as part of the collection at Wellesley.[2] 'I know the picture well', Browning replied to his friend's request on 17 March 1853, 'and esteem it just as you do'; but he went on to warn him that 'The business of copying is carried on with remarkable rascality here', and that a good copyist whom he had approached 'asks too much———for he considers two heads as two pictures, and wants 100 dollars for them.' Browning urged Kenyon rather to commission him to buy one of the fine original paintings by other masters still available in Florence.

---

[1] The letter, by Ernest Radford, is in BST, pp. 160–1.
[2] We print this passage by kind permission of the authorities of Wellesley College Library. The painting is illustrated in the first ed. of Griffin and Minchin.

Andrea del Sarto, the son of a Florentine tailor (*sarto*), is the subject of one of the longest of Vasari's *Lives*. He was born in 1486 (not 1488, as Vasari believed), and was a painter in whom 'art and nature combined to show all that may be done . . . , when design, colouring, and invention unite in one and the same person'; yet 'there was a certain timidity of mind, a sort of diffidence and want of force in his nature' which prevented him from attaining the 'elevation' which could 'have rendered him a truly divine painter.'[1] Vasari hints that the fact that his first master had been Gian Barile, 'a Florentine painter . . . of a coarse and plebeian taste',[2] may have been unfortunate, mentioning more than once that Andrea habitually asked low prices for his work, which his biographer clearly regards as a symptom of lack of a proper ambition and self-esteem.

The great mistake of his life, we are told, was his marriage to Lucrezia, a beautiful young widow whom he had known before the early death of her husband: as a result of this folly

he found that he had enough to do for the remainder of his days, and was . . . obliged to work much more laboriously than he had previously done; for in addition to the duties and liabilities which engagements of that kind are wont to bring with them, [he] found that he had brought on himself many others; he was now tormented by jealousy, now by one thing, now by another; but ever by some evil consequence of his new connection.[3]

This passage is from the second edition of the *Lives*. In the first Vasari makes much more of Andrea's unfortunate marriage, partly no doubt because he himself had been ill-treated by Lucrezia when he had worked in the studio in his youth. He tells us that her father had been 'poor and vicious', yet that she 'carried about her as much pride and haughtiness as beauty and fascination. She delighted in trapping the hearts of men, and among others ensnared the unlucky Andrea, whose immoderate love for her soon caused him to neglect the studies demanded by his art, and in great measure to discontinue the assistance which he had given to his parents.'[4] When the news of his marriage became known in Florence 'the respect and affection which his friends had previously borne to Andrea changed to contempt and disgust'. None of his pupils escaped ill-treatment at her hands: 'none could escape her blows'.

In Vasari's view all the misfortunes of Andrea's life were due to his foolish marriage, or to the weakness of character which led him to it. When the King of France became an admirer of his work he decided that he would like to visit that country, and was encouraged to go there by his

[1] *Lives*, iii. 180–1.   [2] Ibid. 181.   [3] Ibid. 194.   [4] Ibid. 194 n.

friends.[1] Eventually he set out to 'enter the service of His Majesty', and was royally received. If only he had reflected on the inferior circumstances of his life in Florence, Vasari comments,

and duly weighed the advantageous character of that position to which fate had conducted him, . . . he might have attained to great honours. But one day . . . there came to him certain letters from Florence . . . written to him by his wife, and from that time . . . he began to think of leaving France.

He left, promising to return with his wife, and adding 'that he would bring with him pictures and sculptures of great value', for which purpose the King provided him with money. But after several months 'he found himself at the end, not only of his own money, but what with building, indulging himself in various pleasures and doing no work, of that belonging to the French monarch also, the whole of which he had consumed. He was nevertheless determined to return to France, but the prayers and tears of his wife had more power than his own necessities, or the faith which he had pledged to the king: he remained therefore in Florence, and the French monarch was . . . greatly angered thereby'. As a result Andrea fell 'from a highly eminent position . . . to the very lowest, procuring a livelihood and passing his time as he best might'.

We know that Andrea also visited Rome 'to see the works of Raffaello and Michelagnolo, and to examine the statues and ruins of that city'.[2] If only he had remained there longer, in the opinion of Vasari,

he would without doubt have greatly enriched his manner as regarded style of composition, and would eventually have attained the power of imparting a more elevated character and increased force to his figures, which are qualities that have never been perfectly acquired by any but those who have been for some time in Rome . . . there were not wanting those who affirm that he would, in that case, have surpassed all the artists of his time.

Line 105 makes it clear that the monologue is set in 1525, when Raphael had been dead for five years. While Andrea's tone of voice, as conveyed by the handling of the blank verse (which has more in common with that of the Pope in *The Ring and the Book* than with that of 'Fra Lippo Lippi') would be appropriate to an elderly man, in fact he was at the height of his powers at this time; in 1525 he painted, and dated, the 'Madonna del Sacco'. Yet the poem is clearly designed as a 'twilight-piece' expressing the painter's mood as he contemplates his own 'work and self'. The line 'A common greyness silvers everything' describes the picture that he is

[1] Ibid. 199, 204–7.   [2] Ibid. 231–2.

thinking of painting. When he says that 'All is silvery grey, / Placid and perfect with my art', he is speaking in a mood of resigned depression. He is not in fact giving an accurate description of his own paintings, which Vasari and others have repeatedly praised for their skill in colouring. Maria Farquhar, writing in the very year in which *Men and Women* was published, goes so far as to tell us that his pictures 'are generally characterised by a simple cheerfulness, and indicate little of that resigned sentiment which constituted the chief element of the style of some of his immediate predecessors'.[1] This remarkable poem has sometimes led art lovers to misinterpret his work.

The writers of the principal modern monographs on del Sarto show that, financially at least, he was better off after his marriage than before.[2] They seek to base their account strictly on surviving documents. When due allowance has been made for Vasari's tendency to make each of his *Lives* a tale illustrating some facet of human nature however, there is surely something reductive about discarding the view of a man who had known him well, and known his wife. In any event Browning's Andrea is Vasari's Andrea.

It is to be noted that he had probably heard of Andrea at an early age. We know that he used to visit the Dulwich Gallery, which was within walking distance of his home, even as a child 'far under the age allowed by the regulations';[3] there he will have seen two paintings attributed to the master, both Holy Families with the Madonna. Hazlitt described one of them as 'only inferior to Raphael'.[4] In 1834 Browning wrote a trivial humorous piece, 'On Andrea del Sarto's "Jupiter & Leda" ', which we have printed in Vol. IV, pp. 444–5. No doubt his attention was drawn to Vasari by his father. In Florence, however, the *Lives* became his daily companion, and there he found most of Andrea's finest paintings within a short distance of his home.[5]

---

[1] Farquhar, p. 161a. It is to be noted that a long chapter is devoted to Andrea in H. Wölfflin's celebrated book, *Classic Art* (Eng. trans. 1952).

[2] S. J. Freedberg, *Andrea del Sarto*, 2 vols. (Cambridge, Mass. 1963), and John Shearman, *Andrea del Sarto*, 2 vols. (Oxford 1964).

[3] Kintner, i. 509.

[4] *Complete Works*, ed. P. P. Howe, (1932), x. 25. In vol. ii of Freedberg's study they are nos. 326–7. He describes both as copies (pp.186–7).

[5] It is possible, as Barbara Melchiori suggests (pp. 199 ff.), that Browning was influenced by Alfred de Musset's play, *André del Sarto* (1833); but we agree with her that there is no 'conclusive evidence'. A similar uncertainty hangs over the influence of a number of works on the history of Italian painting which Browning certainly knew. In his *Parleyings*, for example, DeVane argued strenuously that Baldinucci's *Delle Notizie de' professori del Disegno* influenced this poem, but any such influence would appear to have been minimal.

As we have mentioned above, Browning acknowledged to Furnivall
that the poem was suggested by Kenyon's request for a copy of the
supposed portrait of Andrea and his wife; it is probable that it was written
in 1853, and is earlier than 'Fra Lippo Lippi'.

Date: 1853
1863: *Men and Women*

ANDREA DEL SARTO.

(CALLED "THE FAULTLESS PAINTER.")

BUT do not let us quarrel any more,
No, my Lucrezia; bear with me for once:
Sit down and all shall happen as you wish.
You turn your face, but does it bring your heart?
I'll work then for your friend's friend, never fear,   5
Treat his own subject after his own way,
Fix his own time, accept too his own price,
And shut the money into this small hand
When next it takes mine. Will it? tenderly?
Oh, I'll content him,—but to-morrow, Love!   10
I often am much wearier than you think,
This evening more than usual, and it seems
As if—forgive now—should you let me sit
Here by the window with your hand in mine
And look a half-hour forth on Fiesole,   15
Both of one mind, as married people use,

title *1855P* (CALLED THE "FAULTLESS.")   2 *1872S*, *1884S* Lucrezia!   *1855P*
once,   12 *1872S*, *1884S* usual:

Title: the word 'Painter' was added in proof. Near the beginning of his *Life* Vasari
observes that Andrea's figures 'are entirely free from errors': the phrase 'Senza errori'
became a commonplace. Cf. the first proper guide-book to Florence, *Le Bellezze della
Città di Fiorenzà*, by Francesco Bocchi (Florence, 1591), first page of 'Tavola', and
p. 236.
  15 *Fiesole*: a small town NE of Florence, at no great distance from it. It stands on a
hill, and is distinguished by beautiful villas and a fine view of the city.

Quietly, quietly the evening through,
I might get up to-morrow to my work
Cheerful and fresh as ever. Let us try.
To-morrow, how you shall be glad for this!   20
Your soft hand is a woman of itself,
And mine the man's bared breast she curls inside.
Don't count the time lost, neither; you must serve
For each of the five pictures we require:
It saves a model. So! keep looking so—   25
My serpentining beauty, rounds on rounds!
—How could you ever prick those perfect ears,
Even to put the pearl there! oh, so sweet—
My face, my moon, my everybody's moon,
Which everybody looks on and calls his,   30
And, I suppose, is looked on by in turn,
While she looks—no one's: very dear, no less.
You smile? why, there's my picture ready made,
There's what we painters call our harmony!
A common greyness silvers everything,—   35
All in a twilight, you and I alike
—You, at the point of your first pride in me
(That's gone you know),—but I, at every point;

---

23 *1855P–63* lost, either; you   26 *1855P* on rounds!   32 *1855P–63* less!
33 *1855P–63* made.   38 *1855P* That's . . . . know,—but

25 *It saves a model*: 'he rarely painted the countenance of a woman in any place that
he did not avail himself of the features of his wife . . . he had her lineaments engraven
on his heart': Vasari, iii. 203.

26 *serpentining*: the only earlier use of the word in OED² occurs in a letter in *The Life
and Letters of Southey*, ed. C. C. Southey (6 vols.) ii (1850), 22, where Browning may
have found it. Here there is an obvious suggestion of the serpent in the Garden of Eden.

29 *my moon*: the moon is always changing. There is a possible echo of Dryden, *All
for Love*, IV. i. 297–8: 'Your Cleopatra; / Dolabella's Cleopatra; Everyman's Cleopatra':
see Richard D. Altick, ' "Andrea del Sarto": The Kingdom of Hell is within', in
Browning's Mind and Art, ed. Clarence Tracy (1968), p. 23.

34 *Our harmony*: Vasari praises 'a pleasing harmony in the colouring' of one of his
paintings, and states that 'He . . . taught the method of working in fresco with perfect
harmony' (*Lives*, iii. 192 and 236).

35 *A common greyness*: this is not from Vasari, who praises Andrea for his use of
colours, as does Maria Farquhar, who writes that. 'his colouring is powerful': p. 161a.

My youth, my hope, my art, being all toned down
To yonder sober pleasant Fiesole.   40
There's the bell clinking from the chapel-top;
That length of convent-wall across the way
Holds the trees safer, huddled more inside;
The last monk leaves the garden; days decrease,
And autumn grows, autumn in everything.   45
Eh? the whole seems to fall into a shape,
As if I saw alike my work and self
And all that I was born to be and do,
A twilight-piece. Love, we are in God's hand.
How strange now, looks the life he makes us lead;   50
So free we seem, so fettered fast we are!
I feel he laid the fetter: let it lie!
This chamber for example—turn your head—
All that's behind us! You don't understand
Nor care to understand about my art,   55
But you can hear at least when people speak:
And that cartoon, the second from the door
—It is the thing, Love! so such things should be—
Behold Madonna!—I am bold to say.
I can do with my pencil what I know,   60
What I see, what at bottom of my heart
I wish for, if I ever wish so deep—
Do easily, too—when I say, perfectly,
I do not boast, perhaps: yourself are judge,

---

39 *1855P* my hopes, my   *46 {reading of *1872S, 1884S*} *1855P–70, 1875, 1888, 1889*
shape   50 *1855P–65* lead!   51 *1855P–56* are: 54 *1855P–65* you
59 *1855P–63* Madonna, I   *63 {reading of *1855P–84S*, DC, BrU, *1889*} *1888*
too—what I

39–40 *all toned down / To . . . Fiesole*: Vasari believed that Andrea would have
benefited greatly if he had remained longer in Rome.

49 *A twilight piece*: cf. the more familiar term, Night Piece.

57 *cartoon*: a full-scale design for a painting or a work in a different material: from It.
cartone, a large sheet of paper.

59 *Madonna*: Our Lady. Vasari praises a number of Andrea's paintings of the Mother
of God, above all the 'Madonna del Sacco', in which Joseph leans on a sack, while Mary
has the infant Christ on her knee: iii. 221.

Who listened to the Legate's talk last week,   65
And just as much they used to say in France.
At any rate 't is easy, all of it!
No sketches first, no studies, that's long past:
I do what many dream of, all their lives,
—Dream? strive to do, and agonize to do,   70
And fail in doing. I could count twenty such
On twice your fingers, and not leave this town,
Who strive—you don't know how the others strive
To paint a little thing like that you smeared
Carelessly passing with your robes afloat,—   75
Yet do much less, so much less, Someone says,
(I know his name, no matter)—so much less!
Well, less is more, Lucrezia: I am judged.
There burns a truer light of God in them,
In their vexed beating stuffed and stopped-up brain,   80
Heart, or whate'er else, than goes on to prompt
This low-pulsed forthright craftsman's hand of mine.
Their works drop groundward, but themselves, I know,
Reach many a time a heaven that's shut to me,
Enter and take their place there sure enough,   85
Though they come back and cannot tell the world.
My works are nearer heaven, but I sit here.
The sudden blood of these men! at a word—
Praise them, it boils, or blame them, it boils too.
I, painting from myself and to myself,   90
Know what I do, am unmoved by men's blame
Or their praise either. Somebody remarks
Morello's outline there is wrongly traced,

65 *1872S, 1884S* week;   67 *1855P–63* it,   *1865, 1868* it;   77 *1855P —*I . . . .
matter—so   78 *1855P* Well, it is   *1855P–65* Lucrezia!   82 *1855P* mine!

65 *the Legate's talk*: a Legate is a Papal representative.
66 *in France*: see introduction, and l. 149 n.
76 *Someone*: Michelangelo.
78 *less is more*: because they are striving more, aiming higher.
80 *stopped-up brain*: cf. Chapman, *Iliad*, xv. 222: 'wheasing with a stopt-up spirit'.
88 *The sudden blood*: cf. *Paradise Lost*, ii. 738: 'my sudden hand'.
93 *Morello's outline*: Morello is the highest mountain in the Appenine range, and is
N. of Florence. 'His' (94) because It. *monte* is masculine.

His hue mistaken; what of that? or else,
Rightly traced and well ordered; what of that?   95
Speak as they please, what does the mountain care?
Ah, but a man's reach should exceed his grasp,
Or what's a heaven for? All is silver-grey,
Placid and perfect with my art: the worse!
I know both what I want and what might gain;   100
And yet how profitless to know, to sigh
"Had I been two, another and myself,
"Our head would have o'erlooked the world!" No doubt.
Yonder's a work now, of that famous youth
The Urbinate who died five years ago.   105
('T is copied, George Vasari sent it me.)
Well, I can fancy how he did it all,
Pouring his soul, with kings and popes to see,
Reaching, that heaven might so replenish him,
Above and through his art—for it gives way;   110
That arm is wrongly put—and there again—
A fault to pardon in the drawing's lines,
Its body, so to speak: its soul is right,
He means right—that, a child may understand.
Still, what an arm! and I could alter it: 115

96 {does not appear in *1855P–56*}   98 *1855P–65* all   *{reading of *1872S, 1884S*}
1855P–70, 1888, 1889 silver-grey   *100 {reading of *1868–84S*} *1855P–65* gain—
1888, 1889 gain,   110 *1855P* way,   113 *1855P–56* speak!   115 *1855P–63*
it.

96 *Speak as they please*: this line was added in *1863*.
97 *a man's reach*: cf. ll. 109–10.
106 *George Vasari*: Giorgio Vasari (1511–74), the author of the *Vite*, was himself an
outstanding painter and architect. Entering the service of Cosimo de' Medici perman-
ently in 1555, he redesigned and greatly improved the Palazzo della Signoria in
Florence. From 1560 he built the Uffizi. He remained on friendly terms with Andrea
from his early days in his studio.
111 *wrongly put*: as DeLaura points out, Rio remarks on the 'incorrect fore-
shortening' of the hand of the infant Christ in one of Raphael's early Madonnas: *The
Poetry of Christian Art*, 217. How closely Andrea studied Raphael is illustrated by a story
told by Vasari. When the Pope ordered that a painting of Raphael's much admired by
the Duke of Mantua should be sent to him, much against the will of the Florentines,
Andrea made a copy so exact that the owner could not 'distinguish the true and original
painting from the counterfeit': iii. 217. Later Vasari told the recipient of the subterfuge,
who continued highly to value the picture he had been given.

But all the play, the insight and the stretch—
Out of me, out of me! And wherefore out?
Had you enjoined them on me, given me soul,
We might have risen to Rafael, I and you!
Nay, Love, you did give all I asked, I think—   120
More than I merit, yes, by many times.
But had you—oh, with the same perfect brow,
And perfect eyes, and more than perfect mouth,
And the low voice my soul hears, as a bird
The fowler's pipe, and follows to the snare—   125
Had you, with these the same, but brought a mind!
Some women do so. Had the mouth there urged
"God and the glory! never care for gain.
"The present by the future, what is that?
"Live for fame, side by side with Agnolo!   130
"Rafael is waiting: up to God, all three!"
I might have done it for you. So it seems:
Perhaps not. All is as God over-rules.
Beside, incentives come from the soul's self;
The rest avail not. Why do I need you?   135
What wife had Rafael, or has Agnolo?

---

117 *1855P–65* me! out   119 *1855P–68, 1872S, 1884S* you.   *1870* you,
130 *1855P–63* with Angelo—   *1865* with Angelo: 131 *1855P–65* waiting. Up
136 *1855P–65* has Angelo?

116 *the play, the insight and the stretch*: of the mind and imagination of Raphael.

117 *Out of me*: beyond my reach.

119 *We might have risen to Rafael*: 'Had this master possessed a somewhat bolder and more elevated mind, . . . he would without doubt have been without an equal': Vasari, iii. 180–1.

125 *The fowler's pipe*: cf. 'The fowler's pipe sounds sweet till the bird is caught', ODEP, from T. Fuller, *Gnomologia* (1732), no. 4542.

129 *by*: compared with, beside.

130 *Agnolo*: Michelangelo Buonarroti (1475–1564), one of the great masters of the Italian Renaissance, sculptor, painter, architect, and military engineer. 'Agnolo' is the Florentine form of the name. The (Latinizing) standard form is 'Angelo', but he signed himself 'michelagniolo'.

133 *over-rules*: arch. in this sense.

136 *What wife had Rafael*: Raphael loved women, but not marriage. In the end he promised to marry, but he procrastinated and the lady died. In his will he left 'sufficient provision' for the mistress by whom 'he was enchained' in his last years: Vasari, iii. 59–60. Michelangelo was homosexual and did not marry.

In this world, who can do a thing, will not;
And who would do it, cannot, I perceive:
Yet the will's somewhat—somewhat, too, the power—
And thus we half-men struggle. At the end,   140
God, I conclude, compensates, punishes.
'T is safer for me, if the award be strict,
That I am something underrated here,
Poor this long while, despised, to speak the truth.
I dared not, do you know, leave home all day,   145
For fear of chancing on the Paris lords.
The best is when they pass and look aside;
But they speak sometimes; I must bear it all.
Well may they speak! That Francis, that first time,
And that long festal year at Fontainebleau!   150
I surely then could sometimes leave the ground,
Put on the glory, Rafael's daily wear,
In that humane great monarch's golden look,—
One finger in his beard or twisted curl
Over his mouth's good mark that made the smile,   155
One arm about my shoulder, round my neck,
The jingle of his gold chain in my ear,
I painting proudly with his breath on me,
All his court round him, seeing with his eyes,

---

142 *1884S* For me, 't is safer, if   154 *1856* finger on his   156 *1855P* about
your shoulder, round your neck,   157 *1855P* in your ear,   158 *1855P–56*
You painting {revised in *Woolner, Fields*}   *1855P* on you,

---

141 *compensates*: stressed on the second syllable, as in Johnson.

143 *something*: somewhat.

149 *That Francis*: François I (1494–1547), who became King of France in 1515, having admired two paintings by Andrea, sent for him in 1518. 'Having in due time arrived at the French court, [Andrea was] received by the monarch very amicably and with many favours, even the first day of his arrival was marked by proofs of that magnanimous sovereign's liberality and courtesy, since he at once received not only a present of money, but the added gift of very rich and honourable vestments. He soon afterwards commenced his labours, rendering himself so acceptable to the king as well as to the whole court, and receiving so many proofs of good-will from all, that his departure from his native country soon appeared . . . to have conducted him from the extreme of wretchedness to the summit of felicity': Vasari, iii. 204–5.

150 *Fontainebleau*: SE of Paris, where François had built himself a palace.

155 *his mouth's good mark*: the encouraging appearance of his mouth.

Such frank French eyes, and such a fire of souls   160
Profuse, my hand kept plying by those hearts,—
And, best of all, this, this, this face beyond,
This in the background, waiting on my work,
To crown the issue with a last reward!
A good time, was it not, my kingly days?   165
And had you not grown restless . . . but I know—
'T is done and past; 't was right, my instinct said;
Too live the life grew, golden and not grey,
And I'm the weak-eyed bat no sun should tempt
Out of the grange whose four walls make his world.   170
How could it end in any other way?
You called me, and I came home to your heart.
The triumph was—to reach and stay there; since
I reached it ere the triumph, what is lost?
Let my hands frame your face in your hair's gold,   175
You beautiful Lucrezia that are mine!
"Rafael did this, Andrea painted that;
"The Roman's is the better when you pray,
"But still the other's Virgin was his wife—"
Men will excuse me. I am glad to judge   180
Both pictures in your presence; clearer grows
My better fortune, I resolve to think.
For, do you know, Lucrezia, as God lives,

---

161 *1855P* Profuse, your hand   166 *1855P/MS* had I not   168 *1872S, 1884S*
grey: 172 *1863S* heart;   173 *1855P* to have ended there—if then   *1855,*
1856 to have ended there—then if   *1863S, 1863* to have ended there; then if
1865–84S to have ended there; then, if   180 *1855P* me!

160 *frank*: with an obvious play on words.
        such a fire of souls: such fervent souls.
161 *plying*: working.
166 *And had you not grown restless*: according to Vasari's first edition, Lucrezia 'wrote
with bitter complaints to Andrea, declaring that she never ceased to weep, and was in
perpetual affliction at his absence; dressing all this up with sweet words': iii. 206. In his
second edition he merely refers to 'certain letters'.
168 *live*: full of life.
169 *the weak-eyed bat*: as in William Collins, 'Ode to Evening', 9.
178 *The Roman's*: Raphael's. He spent his last twelve years in Rome.

Said one day Agnolo, his very self,
To Rafael . . . I have known it all these years . . .   185
(When the young man was flaming out his thoughts
Upon a palace-wall for Rome to see,
Too lifted up in heart because of it)
"Friend, there's a certain sorry little scrub
"Goes up and down our Florence, none cares how,   190
"Who, were he set to plan and execute
"As you are, pricked on by your popes and kings,
"Would bring the sweat into that brow of yours!"
To Rafael's!—And indeed the arm is wrong.
I hardly dare . . . yet, only you to see,   205
Give the chalk here—quick, thus the line should go!
Ay, but the soul! he's Rafael! rub it out!
Still, all I care for, if he spoke the truth,
(What he? why, who but Michel Agnolo?
Do you forget already words like those?)   200
If really there was such a chance, so lost,—
Is, whether you're—not grateful—but more pleased.
Well, let me think so. And you smile indeed!
This hour has been an hour! Another smile?
If you would sit thus by me every night   205
I should work better, do you comprehend?
I mean that I should earn more, give you more.
See, it is settled dusk now; there's a star;
Morello's gone, the watch-lights show the wall,

184 *1855P–65* day Angelo, his   186 *1855P* When   188 *1855P* it,
192 *1855P* you, pricked forward by   194 *1855P* and   199 *1855P–65* but
Michael Angelo?   203 *1855P* so!   207 *1855P* Lucrezia—I should

184 *Said one day Agnolo*: Bocchi tells us that Michelangelo remarked to Raphael one
day that 'there is in Florence a mannikin who, if he were employed on great matters,
as Raphael himself was, would have brought sweat to his brow': *Le Bellezze*, 232.

186 *the young man*: Raphael.

flaming out his thoughts: unusual, but cf. Ariel in *The Tempest*, I. ii. 197–8: 'in
every cabin, / I flam'd amazement'.

189 *scrub*: 'A mean fellow': Johnson.

192 *pricked on*: urged on.

209 *watch-lights*: lights carried by watchmen, according to OED[2], which has no other
example.

The cue-owls speak the name we call them by.   210
Come from the window, love,—come in, at last,
Inside the melancholy little house
We built to be so gay with. God is just.
King Francis may forgive me: oft at nights
When I look up from painting, eyes tired out,   215
The walls become illumined, brick from brick
Distinct, instead of mortar, fierce bright gold,
That gold of his I did cement them with!
Let us but love each other. Must you go?
That Cousin here again? he waits outside?   220
Must see you—you, and not with me? Those loans?
More gaming debts to pay? you smiled for that?
Well, let smiles buy me! have you more to spend?
While hand and eye and something of a heart
Are left me, work's my ware, and what's it worth?   225
I'll pay my fancy. Only let me sit
The grey remainder of the evening out,
Idle, you call it, and muse perfectly

214 *1855P–65* me. Oft   217 *1855P* mortar with bright   221 *1855P–56* loans!
225 *1863S* left to me,

210 *cue-owls*: 'A name applied to the Scops-owl . . ., common on the shores of the
Mediterranean': OED², which cites only this, and EBB's *Aurora Leigh* (1856), viii. 32.
'So called from their cry, which the Italians say is *chiù* or *ciù*': Riverside. Cf. *Aurora Leigh*,
viii. 32.

214 *King Francis may forgive me*: Vasari tells us that, on receiving letters from his wife,
Andrea asked the King's permission to go back to Florence, promising that he 'would
return without fail', bringing her with him, as well as 'pictures and sculptures of great
value. The king . . . gave him money for the purchase of those pictures and sculptures,
Andrea taking an oath on the gospels to return within the space of a few months': Vasari,
iii. 206. After a few months, however, Andrea had spent all the money, and was
persuaded by Lucrezia to remain in Florence. Francis 'was so greatly angered thereby,
that for a long time after he would not look at the paintings of Florentine masters, and
declared that if Andrea ever fell into his hands he would have no regard whatever to
the distinction of his endowments, but would do him more harm than he had before
done him good': iii. 207. Cf. above, pp. 260–1.

220 *Cousin*: lover, just as 'nephews' can mean illegitimate sons, and 'niece' mistress:
see 'The Bishop Orders', 3, and 'Fra Lippo Lippi', 170.

225 *ware*: 'something to be sold': Johnson.

226 *I'll pay my fancy*: I'll pay for what I like: 'fancy' perhaps in a slightly derogatory
sense: cf. 'fancy man'.

How I could paint, were I but back in France,
One picture, just one more—the Virgin's face,   230
Not yours this time! I want you at my side
To hear them—that is, Michel Agnolo—
Judge all I do and tell you of its worth.
Will you? To-morrow, satisfy your friend.
I take the subjects for his corridor,   235
Finish the portrait out of hand—there, there,
And throw him in another thing or two
If he demurs; the whole should prove enough
To pay for this same Cousin's freak. Beside,
What's better and what's all I care about,   240
Get you the thirteen scudi for the ruff!
Love, does that please you? Ah, but what does he,
The Cousin! what does he to please you more?

       I am grown peaceful as old age to-night.
I regret little, I would change still less.   245
Since there my past life lies, why alter it?
The very wrong to Francis!—it is true
I took his coin, was tempted and complied,
And built this house and sinned, and all is said.
My father and my mother died of want.   250
Well, had I riches of my own? you see
How one gets rich! Let each one bear his lot.
They were born poor, lived poor, and poor they died:
And I have laboured somewhat in my time
And not been paid profusely. Some good son   255

232 *1855P–65* is, Michael Angelo—   234 *1855P* friend—   241 *1855P–65*
ruff.

---

231 *Not yours*: cf. 25 n. Mrs Jameson, who describes Lucrezia as 'infamous', states that
'In general his Madonnas are not pleasing; they have, with great beauty, a certain
vulgarity of expression': *Memoirs*, ii. 80.

249 *And built this house*: building is one of the extravagances Vasari mentions. In his
first ed. he states that Andrea had 'even ordered a house to be built for them behind the
Nunziata': Vasari, iii. 207 and 206 n.

255 *And not been paid profusely*: a point to which Vasari keeps returning.

Paint my two hundred pictures—let him try!
Nò doubt, there's something strikes a balance. Yes,
You loved me quite enough, it seems to-night.
This must suffice me here. What would one have?
In heaven, perhaps, new chances, one more chance—   260
Four great walls in the New Jerusalem,
Meted on each side by the angel's reed,
For Leonard, Rafael, Agnolo and me
To cover—the three first without a wife,
While I have mine! So—still they overcome   265
Because there's still Lucrezia,—as I choose.

Again the Cousin's whistle! Go, my Love.

---

263 1855P–65 Rafael, Angelo and   267 1855P go my

256 *my two hundred pictures*: Freedberg lists 90 of which the whereabouts are known; but Andrea was a prolific painter, and a great many others have no doubt perished.

260 *In heaven, perhaps, new chances*: cf. l. 98.

261 *Four great walls in the New Jerusalem*: cf. Rev. 21: 15–16: 'And he [the angel] that talked with me had a golden reed to measure the city, and the gates thereof, and the wall thereof. / And the city lieth foursquare, and the length is as large as the breadth: and he measured the city with the reed, twelve thousand furlongs. The length and the breadth and the height of it are equal.'

262 *Meted*: measured.

263 *Leonard*: Leonardo.

BEFORE

THE *Athenæum* for 4 April 1846 contained a report of the trial of 'M. de Beauvallon for the murder of M. Dujarier . . . one of the most astonishing exhibitions that France, fertile in scenes of the kind, has presented'.[1] The writer was shocked by this duel between two men of letters, and by its public reception.

Till now, we were disposed to regard M. de Balzac's frightful delineation of the literary world of Paris as the fiction of an offended vanity . . . But the facts disclosed in the Court of Justice of Rouen exceed in moral degradation all that even he has imagined or copied. The scene of the quarrel—an *orgie* with all its accompaniments of loose women, gambling, &c. &c.; . . . the strange mixture of fine-sounding names (most of them have the aristocratic prefix) with the foulest and coarsest manners;—all this forms a combination which the corruptest imagination has not yet surpassed.

Dumas appeared as a witness. This was indeed an 'étude des mœurs', as the writer termed it, which was precisely of the kind calculated to appeal to Browning. When he referred to it in his letter to EBB the same day he did so in terms suggesting simple reprobation.[2] In her reply she was indignant that a man of such genius as Balzac should have been brought in 'so!' On 6 April Browning visited her for almost three hours, and it is clear that they disagreed about duelling. As she wrote the next day, she could not 'conceive of any *possible combination of circumstances*' which could excuse, far less justify, 'an honourable man's having recourse to the duellist's pistol'. She asked him to promise that he himself 'never will be provoked into such an act—never?', referring to O'Connell's vow, after killing his opponent in a duel, not to do such a thing again. This letter should be read as a whole, as should Browning's reply of 8 April for his defence of the practice for those (unlike himself, it seems) who are obliged to live in 'society':

I write all this to show the *not such irrationality* of the practice even on comparative-ly frivolous grounds . . and that those individuals to whom you once admit Society may be a legitimate enjoyment, must take such a course to retain the privileges they value . . . I excepted myself from the operation of this necessity.

---

[1] pp. 349–50.   [2] Kintner, ii. 588, 590, 595–7, 601–5, 607, 612.

Whereas he understood how a man might be obliged to fight a duel, in certain circumstances, EBB would have none of it. She distinguishes between 'the sacrifice of little or indifferent things, . . . in respect to mere manners & costume', and 'another class of sacrifice which should be refused by every righteous man'. By the tenth Browning realized that further argument was useless: 'YOU ARE RIGHT and I am wrong'.

While duelling was approaching its end at this time, at least in England, it had not become a mere matter of history, as it has now.[1] In 1821 John Scott, the editor of the *London Magazine*, was shot dead by J. H. Christie, on behalf of John Gibson Lockhart. Christie was tried for murder, but found not guilty. In 1829 the Duke of Wellington felt obliged to fight the Earl of Winchelsea, who had accused him of 'insidious designs, for the infringement of our liberties, and the introduction of Popery into every department of State'.[2] The Duke missed, and his opponent fired into the air and subsequently apologized. In 1840 Lord Cardigan wounded a Captain Tuckett with his second shot; feeling ran high, but he was acquitted. Three years later Lt.-Col. Fawcett was shot dead by his brother-in-law, who was obliged to flee the country. On 7 December EBB wrote to Miss Mitford:

Another atrocious example of the effects of the Duel-system! . . . some persons going as far as to regret the unhappy necessity of this commission of murder by grace of Society—and a very few, bold enough to protest against its wickedness. In the meantime the murdered man lies still in his red shroud . . . Is it not outrageous that men sh.^d act so, calling the crime "honour"?—"honorable men"![3]

The Prince Consort too was outraged by this case, in which (as often) 'a man, having first been insulted, must also expose himself to be shot, and branded in one event as a coward, or in another as a criminal'.[4] In April 1844 amended Articles of War were issued which went far to putting an end to 'so-called affairs of honour'.

---

[1] Never quite, perhaps. When the late Viscount Montgomery refused a duel with an Italian indignant at his suggestion that some of of his countrymen fought less than heroically during the Second World War, an unnamed Englishman fought on his behalf. The duel took place early in 1959, with swords. The Englishman wounded his antagonist in the arm, and honour was satisfied. See *The Times*, 20 February 1992, 12.

[2] A quotation from Winchelsea's letter, in the *Standard* for 16 March 1829, cited in *Correspondence*, viii. 80 n. EBB believed that men '*do* want moral courage' (p. 79), and therefore fear to refuse a challenge.

[3] Raymond and Sullivan, ii. 356.

[4] Sir Theodore Martin, *The Life of the Prince Consort*, 5 vols. (1875–80) i. 169–70. For a general account of the matter see V. G. Kiernan, *The Duel in European History* (1988).

'Before' and 'After' form a pair of dramatic monologues, the first being spoken by one of the seconds, a strong believer in duelling, the second by the survivor of the duel. On 14 March 1864 Browning replied to R. M. Ball, who had sought guidance:

The poem is the presumable defence of duelling, in behalf of a man who has been wronged, as the matter seems "before" the event [i.e. the duel]—How it seems afterwards being the subject of the succeeding piece. Verse [stanza] 4 is a method of saying "Whatever be the issue, the wrong doer will gain nothing: if he complete his offence by this additional sin, how will the rest of his life turn out, though God's justice do not visibly interpose in the course of it? (Verse 5) For let things go smoothly as they may, his conscience will soon become aware that there is a Retribution certainly waiting him, (Verse 6) and that all the toleration and indulgence of the present serve, like the luxuries conceded to a condemned felon, to enhance the final punishment: just so a wild beast plays with its victim.

Something like this I, at least, meant to say—and I hope I made it somewhat clearer.[1]

The speaker's confused manner of expression does his intelligence little credit: we notice that he wrongly supposes that the guilty man will win, and yet wishes the duel to proceed.

While each of the stanzas of the poem consists of two pairs of rhyming couplets, there are marked differences between the first and the second. The former pair have masculine rhymes and a marked caesura after the third foot. They scan (but for l. 22, which is irregular) / × / × / × | / × / × /. The latter have feminine rhymes and are (for the most part) in rising metre which contrasts with the falling metre of the former: in them the position of the caesura is sometimes uncertain. The contrast between the two halves of each stanza gives an effect of inconsistency which fits the character of the speaker.

It is unlikely that Browning would have written this piece at the time of his debate with EBB on the ethics of duelling,[2] although the notion of writing something of the kind may of course have come into his mind about that time. In our tentative dating we follow the reasoning of our Introduction.[3]

Date: 1853/4
1863: *Dramatic Lyrics*

---

[1] J. J. Campbell, 'Two Unpublished Browning Letters': NQ (March 1987), 41–2. In a subsequent letter, on 18 March 1864, Browning thanked Ball for pointing out a 'strange blunder' in l. 14 of 'Before' (see our textual note). 'As it reads now', he wrote of *1863*, 'the passage is nonsense'.
[2] Such is the view of the Longman editors.
[3] See above, p. xiv ff.

BEFORE.

I.

LET them fight it out, friend! things have gone too far.
God must judge the couple: leave them as they are
—Whichever one's the guiltless, to his glory,
And whichever one the guilt's with, to my story!

II.

Why, you would not bid men, sunk in such a slough,   5
Strike no arm out further, stick and stink as now,
Leaving right and wrong to settle the embroilment,
Heaven with snaky hell, in torture and entoilment?

III.

Who's the culprit of them? How must he conceive
God—the queen he caps to, laughing in his sleeve,   10
" 'T is but decent to profess oneself beneath her:
"Still, one must not be too much in earnest, either!"

IV.

Better sin the whole sin, sure that God observes;
Then go live his life out! Life will try his nerves,

2 *1855P–65* couple!   4 *1855P–65* story.   9 *1855P–56* Which of them's the
culprit, how   10 *1855P–56* God's the . . . . sleeve!   11 *1855P–56* 'Tis . . . .
her.   *12 {reading of *1863–84S*} *1855P–56* either. *1888, 1889* either!
13 *1855P–63* observes,   14 *1863* Than   *1855P–65* life will

2 *God must judge*: the traditional defence of duelling.

4 *to my story!*: I shall tell you his fate.

6 *Strike no arm out*: i.e. refrain from trying to escape from the foul and deadly swamp.

7 *embroilment*: quarrel.

8 *entoilment*: entanglement.

10 *God—the queen he caps to*: the guilty man must be as cynical in honouring God as
he is in honouring the queen.

13 *Better sin the whole sin*: it is better that he should sin the whole sin (we may be sure
that God observes), and then go on with his life, which will be a miserable one.

14 *Then go live*: on 18 March 1864 Browning thanked the same B. M. Ball 'for
pointing out the strange blunder' in *1863*, where 'Then' is misprinted 'Than', so making
the passage 'nonsense'.

When the sky, which noticed all, makes no disclosure,   15
And the earth keeps up her terrible composure.

V.

Let him pace at pleasure, past the walls of rose,
Pluck their fruits when grape-trees graze him as he goes!
For he 'gins to guess the purpose of the garden,
With the sly mute thing, beside there, for a warden.   20

VI.

What's the leopard-dog-thing, constant at his side,
A leer and lie in every eye of its obsequious hide?
When will come an end to all the mock obeisance,
And the price appear that pays for the misfeasance?

VII.

So much for the culprit. Who's the martyred man?   25
Let him bear one stroke more, for be sure he can!
He that strove thus evil's lump with good to leaven,
Let him give his blood at last and get his heaven!

---

18 *1855P–65* goes.   21 *1855P–56* constant to his   22 *1855P–56* eye on its
23 *1855P–56* end of all   26 *1855P–56* can.   28 *1855P–56* heaven.

15 *makes no disclosure*: gives no sign.

16 *her terrible composure*: cf. *The Ring and the Book*, xi. 1380: 'the terrible patience of God'.

18 *grape-trees*: vines. OED² cites the word in Dampier and elsewhere; and in two books on Jamaica, with which the families of both the Brownings had business connections.

20 *the sly mute thing*: there are suggestions of Eden about this garden.

21 *the leopard-dog-thing*: the nature of the creature which slinks beside him is left uncertain, though there is no doubt a reminiscence of the treacherous leopard in *Inferno*, i. 32. The speaker realizes that this is no Garden of Eden, but a prison, with a 'wild beast' in it. The medial rhyme in l. 22 adds to the sinister effect.

22 *eye*: spot.

23 *obeisance*: respect, as evidenced by bowing.

24 *misfeasance*: transgression.

25 *the martyr'd man*: the man who has to bear witness to the truth: Gk. $\mu\acute{\alpha}\rho\tau\nu\varsigma$, witness.

27 *evil's lump . . . to leaven*: 1 Cor. 5: 6–7.

28 *Let him give his blood*: the speaker assumes that the 'guiltless' man will lose his life.

VIII.

All or nothing, stake it! Trusts he God or no?
Thus far and no farther? farther? be it so!   30
Now, enough of your chicane of prudent pauses,
Sage provisos, sub-intents and saving-clauses!

IX.

Ah, "forgive" you bid him? While God's champion lives,
Wrong shall be resisted: dead, why, he forgives.
But you must not end my friend ere you begin him;   35
Evil stands not crowned on earth, while breath is in him.

X.

Once more—Will the wronger, at this last of all,
Dare to say, "I did wrong," rising in his fall?
No?—Let go, then! Both the fighters to their places!
While I count three, step you back as many paces!   40

---

29 *1855P–65* trusts   30 *1856* no further? further be   *1855P–56* so.   32 *1855P*
saving-clauses.   36 *1863, 1865* him!   37 *1855P* more, will   39 *1855P–*
56 then—both   *1863, 1865* both   *1855P–56* places—   40 *1855P–56* paces.

31 *chicane*: 'The art of protracting a contest by petty objection and artifice': Johnson.
Cf. *King Victor and King Charles*, 'King Victor', II. 68.

32 *sub-intents*: Fr. *sous-ententes*. No other example in OED[2].

33 *God's champion*: cf. *The Ring and the Book*, x. 1156–7: 'such championship / Of
God at first blush'.

35 *end my friend*: assume that the innocent man will fall.

37 *Once more*: the speaker turns to the antagonists.

38 *rising in his fall*: rising morally by confessing the wrong he has done.

40 *step back as many paces!*: a duel at six paces, with pistols, would be likely to prove
lethal. Cf. Kintner, ii. 596. Ridiculing duelling, in *Sartor Resartus*, II. viii, Carlyle
mentions twelve paces, the distance in Browning's 'Clive', 131.

AFTER

'Before' and 'After' form a diptych of the kind which appealed to Browning and which we first encounter in 'Johannes Agricola in Meditation' and 'Porphyria's Lover', two poems first published in the *Monthly Repository* in January 1836 and republished in *Dramatic Lyrics* in 1842 as 'Madhouse Cells', I and II. The present pair of poems may remind us of 'Meeting at Night' and 'Parting at Morning'.

'After' is divided into sections of 2, 8, 6, and 2 lines. It is written in alternate trimeters and dimeters, rhyming in pairs. Except in the last couplet the metre is predominantly anapaestic: in it there is an important variation of rhythm. Whereas one critic has suggested that the penultimate line has stresses only on 'here', 'lies' and 'place', one might counter (with only slight exaggeration) by claiming that every syllable in it, except 'in', calls for a stress, since 'I' and 'he' are contrasted, as are 'stand' and 'lie', and 'here' and 'his place'. The last line is a choriambus: *Cóver the fáce*.

Date: 1853/4
1863: Dramatic Lyrics

AFTER.

TAKE the cloak from his face, and at first
   Let the corpse do its worst!

How he lies in his rights of a man!
   Death has done all death can.
And, absorbed in the new life he leads,   5
   He recks not, he heeds
Nor his wrong nor my vengeance; both strike
   On his senses alike,
And are lost in the solemn and strange
   Surprise of the change.   10

2 *1855P–65* worst.

Ha, what avails death to erase
  His offence, my disgrace?
I would we were boys as of old
  In the field, by the fold:
His outrage, God's patience, man's scorn   15
  Were so easily borne!

I stand here now, he lies in his place:
  Cover the face!11

---

11 {no new paragraph in *1856*}   16 *1855P–65* borne.   18 *1855P–65* face.

IN THREE DAYS

MRS ORR describes this poem as 'doubtless a pure lyric, though classed as dramatic-lyrical'. That it has its origin in Browning's own experience seems likely. Betty Miller suggested that it was inspired by his separation from EBB in the summer of 1852, when he left her in London while he and Sarianna took his father to Paris.[1] Eleanor Cook connects it rather with the period of their courtship, when three days 'was an accustomed interval between Browning's later visits' to Wimpole Street:[2] 'remember there are three days before our Saturday', he wrote on 23 July 1846. In his next letter he explained that he had dated a letter 'Wednesday' instead of 'Thursday',

because all day long I was in that error—having been used to see you on *Mondays*, and to calculate my time by the number of days since I saw you—whence, knowing to my cost that two days had gone by since such an event, I thought what I wrote.

'I am very well considering there are three days to wait', he wrote in another letter, on 21 August. The poem has a rhetorical complexity which does not suggest that it was written on an immediate occasion.[3]

It consists of thirty-eight iambic tetrameters, divided into four stanzas, the first and second of seven lines each, the third of nine, and the last of fifteen. The rhyme-scheme is *abccddd / abeefff / gghhiijjj / akakaiaiiiccabc*. There is a triplet in each stanza, at the end of the first three and in ll. 31-3. Repetition is a marked feature of the poem, the opening lines being nearly repeated in the last three; ll. 9 and 29 look back to l. 2. The last stanza is built round the potent word 'fear'. Such patterning expresses admirably the impatience and anxiety of a lover. The poet's introspective tone reminds us of Wyatt and of the age subsequent to his.

Date: 1853/5
1863: Dramatic Lyrics

[1] *Robert Browning*, 170 n.
[2] *Browning's Lyrics*, 212.
[3] Kintner, ii. 898, 900, 983.

IN THREE DAYS.

I.

So, I shall see her in three days
And just one night, but nights are short,
Then two long hours, and that is morn.
See how I come, unchanged, unworn!
Feel, where my life broke off from thine,   5
How fresh the splinters keep and fine,—
Only a touch and we combine!

II.

Too long, this time of year, the days!
But nights, at least the nights are short.
As night shows where her one moon is,   10
A hand's-breadth of pure light and bliss,
So life's night gives my lady birth
And my eyes hold her! What is worth
The rest of heaven, the rest of earth?

III.

O loaded curls, release your store   15
Of warmth and scent, as once before
The tingling hair did, lights and darks
Outbreaking into fairy sparks,
When under curl and curl I pried
After the warmth and scent inside,   20
Thro' lights and darks how manifold—

---

4 *1855P–56* unworn—   13 *1855P–65* what

4 *unworn*: fresh.
12 *life's night*: the comparison of the beloved to the moon is found elsewhere in Browning, as in other poets: for example in 'Andrea del Sarto', 29, and 'One Word More', 188.
15 *store*: abundance, as in 'The Statue and the Bust', 137.
18 *outbreaking*: a favourite verb of Browning, who liked verbs with the prefix 'out'.
20 *After*: seeking.

The dark inspired, the light controlled!
As early Art embrowns the gold.

IV.

What great fear, should one say, "Three days
"That change the world might change as well   25
"Your fortune; and if joy delays,
"Be happy that no worse befell!"
What small fear, if another says,
"Three days and one short night beside
"May throw no shadow on your ways;   30
"But years must teem with change untried,
"With chance not easily defied,
"With an end somewhere undescried."
No fear!—or if a fear be born
This minute, it dies out in scorn.   35
Fear? I shall see her in three days
And one night, now the nights are short,
Then just two hours, and that is morn.

22 *1880S, 1884S* controlled,   23 *1855P* So early art embrowned the   *1855–63*
Art embrowned the   *1880S, 1884S* gold!   27 *1855P–65* befell."   35 *1880S,*
1884S minute, fear dies   38 *1880S, 1884S* morn!

23 *embrowns*: as the gold in early paintings turns brown with time.
33 *undescried*: as in *The Winter's Tale*, IV. iv. 669, and Tennyson, 'Isabel', 22.

IN A YEAR

BROWNING's placing of this immediately after 'In Three Days' exemplifies his fondness for pairing poems, whether or not they appear to belong together. Whereas in the previous poem a man is the speaker, eager for his next meeting with his beloved, in this poem a woman speaks, meditating on the decay of her lover's passion. It demonstrates Browning's understanding of a woman's experience of love, as do 'Another Way of Love', 'A Woman's Last Word', and 'Any Wife to any Husband'.[1]

While the lines with odd numbers scan / × / × /, it is the telling use of the short line called a cretic (/ × /) which does most to characterize the piece. While several of these short lines could be mistaken for anapaests, the majority could not: to read them so would fail to convey the profound sadness of the speaker. The rhyme scheme of each stanza is *abcadbcd*.

Date: 1853/5
1863 Dramatic Lyrics

IN A YEAR.

I.

NEVER any more,
    While I live,
Need I hope to see his face
    As before.

---

[1] In a letter to Edward Irenaeus Stevenson, who had asked whether the speaker in this poem was wife or mistress, and whether the person referred to was 'actually dead or only recreant', Browning replied: 'The little poem was meant to express the feeling of a woman towards a hopelessly alienated lover—husband, if you will. The summing-up of the account between much endeavour and as constant a resistance to it, leaves the result a mere "clay-cold clod" in the shape of a heart—to be "left" finally and altogether, when "what comes *next*?"—as something must.' The letter was printed in *The Independent* for 27 January 1887, and reprinted in another American publication, *The Critic*, on 29 January.

Once his love grown chill,   5
   Mine may strive:
Bitterly we re-embrace,
   Single still.

II.

Was it something said,
   Something done,   10
Vexed him? was it touch of hand,
   Turn of head?
Strange! that very way
   Love begun:
I as little understand   15
   Love's decay.

III.

When I sewed or drew,
   I recall
How he looked as if I sung,
   —Sweetly too.   20
If I spoke a word,
   First of all
Up his cheek the colour sprung,
   Then he heard.

IV.

Sitting by my side,   25
   At my feet,
So he breathed but air I breathed,
   Satisfied!
I, too, at love's brim
   Touched the sweet: 30
I would die if death bequeathed
   Sweet to him.

14 *1855P–56* begun.   19 *1855P–56* I sang,   23 *1855P–56* color sprang,
27 *1855P–63* breathed the air

V.

"Speak, I love thee best!"
    He exclaimed:
"Let thy love my own foretell!"   35
    I confessed:
"Clasp my heart on thine
    "Now unblamed,
"Since upon thy soul as well
    "Hangeth mine!"   40

VI.

Was it wrong to own,
    Being truth?
Why should all the giving prove
    His alone?
I had wealth and ease,   45
    Beauty, youth:
Since my lover gave me love,
    I gave these.

VII.

That was all I meant,
    —To be just,   50
And the passion I had raised,
    To content.
Since he chose to change
    Gold for dust,
If I gave him what he praised   55
    Was it strange?

VIII.

Would he loved me yet,
    On and on,
While I found some way undreamed

—Paid my debt! 60
Gave more life and more,
   Till, all gone,
He should smile "She never seemed
   "Mine before.

IX.

"What, she felt the while, 65
   "Must I think?
"Love's so different with us men!"
   He should smile:
"Dying for my sake—
   "White and pink! 70
"Can't we touch these bubbles then
   "But they break?"

X.

Dear, the pang is brief,
   Do thy part,
Have thy pleasure! How perplexed 75
   Grows belief!
Well, this cold clay clod
   Was man's heart:
Crumble it, and what comes next?
   Is it God? 80

67 *1855P–65* men,"   68 *1855P–63* smile.   73 *1855P–63S* brief.
75 *1855P–65* pleasure.   78 *1855P–63* heart.

OLD PICTURES IN FLORENCE

MRS ORR gives a good description of this poem as 'a fanciful monologue, spoken as by one who is looking down upon Florence, through her magical atmosphere, from a villa on the neighbouring heights':

The sight of her Campanile brings Giotto to his mind; and with Giotto comes a vision of all the dead Old Masters who mingle in spirit with her living men. He sees them each haunting the scene of his former labours in church or chapter-room, cloister or crypt; and he sees them grieving over the decay of their works, as these fade and moulder under the hand of time. He is also conscious that they do not grieve for themselves. Earthly praise or neglect cannot touch them more. But they have had a lesson to teach; and so long as the world has not learnt the lesson, their souls may not rest in heaven.[1]

This is clearly one of the poems 'with more music and painting than before' to which Browning referred in his letter to Milsand on 24 February 1853;[2] it may well have been begun, at least, by that time. It is to be seen in relation to 'Andrea del Sarto' and 'Fra Lippo Lippi'. Unlike these masterpieces, however, it is only in a limited sense 'dramatic', as the first stanza indicates. In the course of a stroll near Casa Guidi of the kind that Browning himself so often took, the narrator visits some of the famous churches in the area and muses on certain of the paintings which they contain, in particular those by the artists before Raphael who were receiving so much attention from Ruskin and the Pre-Raphaelites. In the final stanzas he associates the history of art and that of Italy, so reminding us of the affinity between this work and EBB's more ambitious *Casa Guidi Windows*.

Like his father, Browning was a born collector, and Florence was exciting territory for a man who knew so much about the history of the early Tuscan painters. It was of course merely foolish to suppose that first-rate paintings were lying about and might be picked up 'for trifling sums', as a writer in a short-lived periodical, the *Tuscan Athenæum*, was concerned to point out. 'The pictures which perhaps may be purchased here to advantage', he continued,

are those which have as yet escaped the endless coatings of varnish, or the *touchings-up* of a second rate restorer; they are to be found out by enquiring and

---

[1] *Handbook*, 208.   [2] Above, p. xiv.

hunting for, in remote palaces, streets, and corners, where an indefatigible picture-hunter (if he does not mind running up and down stair-cases, disturbing the proprietors at their meals, or even in bed, and wading through oceans of rubbish) may discover perhaps a gem, and certainly some second rate paintings of value, especially of the old Florentine school.[1]

'Robert has been picking up pictures at a few pauls each', EBB had written to Julia Martin on 4 May 1850:

'hole and corner' pictures which the 'dealers' had not found out; and the other day he covered himself with glory by discovering and seizing on (in a corn shop a mile from Florence) five pictures among heaps of trash; and one of the best judges in Florence (Mr. Kirkup) throws out such names for them as Cimabue, Ghirlandaio, Giottino, a crucifixion painted on a banner, Giottesque, if not Giotto, but *unique*, or nearly so, on account of the linen material, and a little Virgin by a Byzantine master. The curious thing is that two angel pictures, for which he had given a scudo last year, prove to have been each sawn off the sides of the Ghirlandaio, so called . . . It has been a grand altar-piece, cut to bits.[2]

In the course of the letter in which he warned Kenyon of the expense which he would incur if he ordered a copy of the painting attributed to Andrea del Sarto in which he was interested, and urged him rather to commission him to buy an original by some other artist of note, Browning told him that 'good things' by Ghirlandaio and Fra Lippo Lippi were still 'extant at Metzgers'—'who, by the way, I verily believe, has discovered the precious little picture by Giotto, of which Vasari says so much, and how he heard Michelagnolo admire it to hearts' content—"the death of the Virgin"—missing from S. Spirito in Vasari's time'.[3] We agree with Julia Markus that this takes us close to the genesis of 'Old Pictures in Florence',[4] and notice that the letter was written on 17 March, while the occasion described at the beginning of the poem was a 'warm March day'.

---

[1] *The Tuscan Athenæum*, 24 December 1847, p. 74 (see Julia Markus, ' "Old Pictures in Florence" Through *Casa Guidi Windows'*: BIS 6 (1978) 60). For this short-lived periodical, see G. Artom Treves, *The Golden Ring: The Anglo-Florentines 1847–1862*, trans. S. Sprigge (1956).

[2] *Letters of EBB*, i. 448 (to Julia Martin, not Mrs Jameson: see Kelley and Hudson, p. 64). Seymour Kirkup was a friend of the Brownings, often mentioned in their correspondence, and the leader of a literary circle in Florence. He had known Blake, and been present at the funeral of Keats, and that of Shelley. He told Browning the story on which 'The Statue and the Bust' is based: see p. 158, above. 'Giottino' was Tommaso di Stefano, of whom Vasari gives a brief Life.

[3] Cf. Vasari, i. 113. See n to l. 236, below.

[4] BIS 6, 44.

The earlier title of the poem was 'Opus Magistri Jocti', 'The Work of Master Giotto', and he, the greatest of the old painters with whom the piece is concerned, is of course its central figure. The description of Florence at the beginning immediately introduces 'the startling bell-tower Giotto raised' as its most remarkable feature, while the poem ends by looking forward to the eventual completion of this masterpiece, and invests the event with a momentous importance which corresponds (we notice) with the intention with which its construction had been set on foot by the Commune in 1334: the third element in the cathedral complex, it was to 'serve as a symbol not only of Florentine prowess but also of renewed civil unity', a great structure erected 'to the honor . . . of a powerfully united, greatly spirited, and freely sovereign people.'[1]

The fact that Browning mentions politics only at the end of 'Old Pictures' differentiates it sharply from EBB's *Casa Guidi Windows*. While it is a striking fact that so many of the painters named in his poem had already made their appearance in hers (Giotto, Michelangelo, Cimabue, Margheritone[2]), the passages about painters in her poem are directly related to contemporary Italian politics: in his, politics is confined to the last five stanzas, and it is questionable whether 'Art and politics are related as if the connection between the two had always been in his mind'.[3] He knew much more about 'the season / Of Art's spring-birth' than she did. He was constantly looking at paintings, and his knowledge of earlier Italian art had developed. It is clear that he had read Rio's book, *The Poetry of Christian Art*: as clear that he had disagreed with a good deal which he had found in it. He blamed Mary Shelley, for example, for clinging to 'Rio's skirts', and for the commonplace nature of her remarks once she let go of them: 'she had no eyes for the divine *bon-bourgeoisie* of his [Fra Angelico's] pictures; the dear common folk of his crowds, those who sit and listen (spectacle at nose and bent into a comfortable heap to hear better) at the sermon of the Saint'.[4] And he sees the difference between Greek art and these early Italian painters in relation to the whole sweep of the history of mankind.

It is not surprising that he had Rossetti in mind, when he published this poem, telling him that it was 'a thing I would have you like if it might be' in a letter in which he listed sixteen *corrigenda* in Vol. II of *Men and Women*, thirteen of them in the text of this poem.[5] We have already quoted

[1] Andrès, 98.

[2] *Casa Guidi Windows*, ed. J. Markus (New York, The Browning Institute, 1977), part i, ll. 68, 73, 354, 379, 390, 395.

[3] BIS 6, 50.   [4] Kintner, i. 190.   [5] *Letters*, 42.

Rossetti's praise of the 'magnificent' volumes.[1] 'I spent some most delight-
ful time with Browning at Paris', he wrote to William Allingham, 'both
in the evenings and at the Louvre, where (and throughout conversation)
I found his knowledge of early Italian art beyond that of anyone I ever
met,—*encyclopaedically* beyond that of Ruskin himself. What a jolly thing
is *Old Pictures at Florence*!'.[2] When Browning arrived in Italy with his wife
he already knew a great deal about Italian art, and particularly that of the
Renaissance. This poem is evidence of the growth of his knowledge of the
earlier painters, the painters who provided the English Pre-Raphaelites
with inspiration, and a name.

We do not know when 'Old Pictures in Florence' was written, though
it seems likely that it was one of the earlier pieces. The possibility that it
was not all written at one time is attractive. Lines 123–4 may have been
suggested by the chapter on 'The Nature of Gothic' in Vol. II of *The
Stones of Venice*, which was published on 28 July 1853. It is written in an
informal style, in eight-line stanzas rhyming *ababcdcd*, with four stresses to
the line. While the measure is basically iambic, every line has a trisyllabic
foot (an anapaest or occasionally a dactyl), and some have two. The
light-hearted tone of many passages comes out in such Hudibrastic rhymes
as *Theseus/knees' use* and *Giotto/not? O!* Revisions from proof are particu-
larly numerous.[3]

Date: 1853–4
1863: Dramatic Lyrics

---

[1] Above, p. xxxi.
[2] *DGR Letters*, i. 280. 'It seems all the pictures *desired* by the poet are in his possession
in fact', Rossetti continues. In her *Handbook* Mrs Orr remarks that Browning 'possesses
or possessed pictures by all the artists mentioned' (209 n). Some were rather unlikely
attributions. Cf. DeLaura, 'Some Notes on Browning's Pictures and Painters'.
[3] See above, p. xl.

OLD PICTURES IN FLORENCE.

I.

THE morn when first it thunders in March,
　　The eel in the pond gives a leap, they say:
As I leaned and looked over the aloed arch
　　Of the villa-gate this warm March day,
No flash snapped, no dumb thunder rolled　　　　5
　　In the valley beneath where, white and wide
And washed by the morning water-gold,
　　Florence lay out on the mountain-side.

II.

River and bridge and street and square
　　Lay mine, as much at my beck and call,　　　　10
Through the live translucent bath of air,
　　As the sights in a magic crystal ball.
And of all I saw and of all I praised,
　　The most to praise and the best to see
Was the startling bell-tower Giotto raised:　　　　15
　　But why did it more than startle me?

{in *1865SP* numerous revisions have been made; subsequently the entire poem has been deleted}　　title *1855P* OPUS MAGISTRI JOCTI.　　*{reading of *1855–84S*} *1888*, *1889* FLORENCE　　2 *1855P–56, 1880S, 1884S* say.　　7 *1855P–56* Washed *1855P–65* the morning's water-gold,　　*14 {reading of *1880S, 1884S*, DC, BrU, *1889*} *1855P–75, 1888* see,

---

Title in proof: 'The work of Master Giotto'. Cf. Vasari, 96 n, i. 101 n, 115 n.

3 *aloed*: no other example in OED², in this sense.

4 *this warm March day*: in 1853? See introduction.

5 *No flash snapped*: no flash of lightning stabbed downwards.

5 *dumb*: inarticulate.

6 *the valley beneath*: the poet is somewhere above the city. 'Perhaps the villa gate is that of Bellosguardo, pictured by Mrs. Browning in *Casa Guidi Windows*' (ll. 1178–84): Markus, BIS 6, 44.

7 *washed*: 'Of a water colour or monochrome drawing: Having the tints produced by colour laid on in "washes" ': OED².

15 *the startling bell-tower*: see introduction, above; cf. 'Casa Guidi Windows', i. 68–72. To say that Giotto 'raised' it is an over-simplification, since he died shortly after designing it. Andrea Pisano took over, with ideas of his own, and was succeeded in turn

III.

Giotto, how, with that soul of yours,
   Could you play me false who loved you so?
Some slights if a certain heart endures
   Yet it feels, I would have your fellows know!   20
I' faith, I perceive not why I should care
   To break a silence that suits them best,
But the thing grows somewhat hard to bear
   When I find a Giotto join the rest.

IV.

On the arch where olives overhead   25
   Print the blue sky with twig and leaf,
(That sharp-curled leaf which they never shed)
   'Twixt the aloes, I used to lean in chief,
And mark through the winter afternoons,
   By a gift God grants me now and then,   30
In the mild decline of those suns like moons,
   Who walked in Florence, besides her men.

V.

They might chirp and chaffer, come and go
   For pleasure or profit, her men alive—
My business was hardly with them, I trow,   35
   But with empty cells of the human hive;

---

19 *1855P* There be slights   20 *1855, 1856* It feels,   21 *1855P–56* 'Faith—I
27 *1855P–56* leaf they   *1865SP/MS* leaf, they   36 *1865SP/MS* But the empty

by Francesco Talenti. 'Each succeeding master adjusted his predecessor's design to accord with his own ideas': Andrès, i. 239.

18 *Could you play me false*: see introduction.
28 *in chief*: particularly.
32 *her men*: i.e. her living men.
33 *chaffer*: haggle.
36 *the human hive*: an image suggested by Bernard Mandeville, *The Fable of the Bees* (1714). For Browning's copy, see Kelley and Coley, A 1534. The first of the *Parleyings* (1887) is with Mandeville.

—With the chapter-room, the cloister-porch,
    The church's apsis, aisle or nave,
Its crypt, one fingers along with a torch,
    Its face set full for the sun to shave.   40

VI.

Wherever a fresco peels and drops,
    Wherever an outline weakens and wanes
Till the latest life in the painting stops,
    Stands One whom each fainter pulse-tick pains:
One, wishful each scrap should clutch the brick,   45
    Each tinge not wholly escape the plaster,
—A lion who dies of an ass's kick,
    The wronged great soul of an ancient Master.

VII.

For oh, this world and the wrong it does!
    They are safe in heaven with their backs to it,   50
The Michaels and Rafaels, you hum and buzz
    Round the works of, you of the little wit!
Do their eyes contract to the earth's old scope,
    Now that they see God face to face,

---

43 *1855P* in its system stops,   44 *1865SP/MS* One, each   *1855P–63* pains!
45 *1855P–56* clutch its brick,   52 *1856* wit;

    37 *chapter-room*: or chapter-house, a building attached to a cathedral or monastery where the members of a religious order meet to discuss their affairs.

    38 *apsis*: the apse is 'A semi-circular or polygonal recess . . . at the end of the choir, aisles, or nave of a church': OED².

    39 *fingers*: feels one's way.

    43 *latest*: last.

    44 *pulse-tick*: no other example in OED².

    47 *A lion*: 'His mother used to read Croxall's Fables to his little sister [Sarianna] and him. The story contained in them of a lion who was kicked to death by an ass affected him so painfully that he could no longer endure the sight of the book': *Life*, pp. 26–7. Croxall's edition, first published in 1722, was often reprinted. (Kelley and Coley, A 734 is inscribed by EBB's father.) See our Vol. II, p. 113 n. for another allusion to Æsop. Cf. p. 161n above.

    51 *Michaels*: Michelangelos.

    52 *wit*: understanding.

And have all attained to be poets, I hope? 55
    'T is their holiday now, in any case.

VIII.

Much they reck of your praise and you!
    But the wronged great souls—can they be quit
Of a world where their work is all to do,
    Where you style them, you of the little wit, 60
Old Master This and Early the Other,
    Not dreaming that Old and New are fellows:
A younger succeeds to an elder brother,
    Da Vincis derive in good time from Dellos.

IX.

And here where your praise might yield returns, 65
    And a handsome word or two give help,
Here, after your kind, the mastiff girns
    And the puppy pack of poodles yelp.

---

59 *1855P–56* where all their . . . . is to {revised in *1855P/MS, Woolner, Fields, Rossetti*}
62 *1865SP/MS* dreaming Old   *1855P–56* fellows,   63 *1855P–56* That a {revised
in *1855P/MS, Woolner, Fields, Rossetti*}   *1865SP/MS* succeeds an   65 *1855P–56*
praise would yield   67 *1855P* Why, after

54 *see God face to face*: 1 Cor. 13: 12.

55 *have all attained to be poets*: both Michelangelo and Raphael wrote poems, but the reference is probably rather to the title of Rio's *The Poetry of Christian Art*. In Vol. IV we missed the reference to his book in *Christmas-Eve*, 671–2: 'portents which impart / Such unction to true Christian Art'. Cf. p. 267n, above.

58 *But the wronged great souls*: but the great painters whom we know less of, and therefore value less highly—how can they cease to haunt the earth, until their work is acknowledged?

64 *Dellos*: Vasari (*Lives*, i. 327 ff.) tells us that Dello di Niccolo Delli was a Florentine painter, born late in the fourteenth century and still living in 1455. He specialized in painting mythological and other figures on cassoni (large chests in which the Florentines kept their valuables) and other pieces of furniture for wealthy householders. 'And as it is desirable to preserve some memorial of these old things', Vasari writes (i. 330), 'I have caused many of them to be retained in the palace of my lord the Duke Cosimo.' Browning may have seen in the Uffizi two small pictures attributed to him.

67 *girns*: (Sc.) snarls.

What, not a word for Stefano there,
    Of brow once prominent and starry,   70
Called Nature's Ape and the world's despair
    For his peerless painting? (See Vasari.)

X.

There stands the Master. Study, my friends,
    What a man's work comes to! So he plans it,
Performs it, perfects it, makes amends   75
    For the toiling and moiling, and then, *sic transit!*
Happier the thrifty blind-folk labour,
    With upturned eye while the hand is busy,
Not sidling a glance at the coin of their neighbour!
    'T is looking downward that makes one dizzy.   80

XI.

"If you knew their work you would deal your dole."
    May I take upon me to instruct you?
When Greek Art ran and reached the goal,
    Thus much had the world to boast *in fructu*—
The Truth of Man, as by God first spoken,   85
    Which the actual generations garble,

---

72 *1855P, 1855* painting (see Vasari)?   *1856* painting (see Vasari ?   *1863–84S* (see
73 *1855P–56* There he stands now. Study,   74 *1855P–65SP* so   76 *1855P–56*
and there's its transit! {revised in *1855P/MS, Woolner, Fields, Rossetti*}   80 *1855P*
'Tis the looking downward makes   *1855, 1856, 1880S, 1884S* downward makes
81 *1855P–56* If . . . . dole.   83 *1855P* When in Greece Art

  69 *Stefano*: This 'Florentine painter and disciple of Giotto', dated by Vasari 1301?–
1350?, 'was an artist of such excellence, that he not only surpassed all those who had
preceded him in the art, but left even his master, Giotto himself, far behind.' For his
work in the Campo Santo of Pisa and elsewhere he was considered 'the best of all the
painters who had appeared down to that time'. He 'was called by his brother artists, "the
ape of nature" ': *Lives*, i. 133 ff.
  76 *moiling*: labouring.
    sic transit: 'sic transit gloria mundi' (so passes the glory of the world), a sentence
used in the ceremony for the enthronement of popes.
  77 *the thrifty blind-folk labour*: schools for the blind had been founded from the late
eighteenth century.
  81 *your dole*: pay what you should pay (in praise). Inverted commas added from *1863*.
  84 *in fructu*: harvested.

Was re-uttered, and Soul (which Limbs betoken)
And Limbs (Soul informs) made new in marble.

XII.

So, you saw yourself as you wished you were,
    As you might have been, as you cannot be;   90
Earth here, rebuked by Olympus there:
    And grew content in your poor degree
With your little power, by those statues' godhead,
    And your little scope, by their eyes' full sway,
And your little grace, by their grace embodied,   95
    And your little date, by their forms that stay.

XIII.

You would fain be kinglier, say, than I am?
    Even so, you will not sit like Theseus.
You would prove a model? The Son of Priam
    Has yet the advantage in arms' and knees' use.   100
You're wroth—can you slay your snake like Apollo?
    You're grieved—still Niobe's the grander!

---

87 *1855P* Soul, which . . . . betoken,   88 *1855P* Limbs, Soul informs, were made
1855, 1856 informs) were made   91–2 *1855P–56* And bringing your own shortcom-
ings there, | You grew {revised in *1855P/MS, Woolner}* Fields, Rossetti (Earth . . . . there)
95 *1855P* by such grace   99 *1855P* would fain be a   *1855–65SP* You'd fain be a
1855P–65SP the   101 *1855P* You are wroth—   102 *1855P* You are grieved—

---

   87 *re-uttered*: no earlier example in OED[2].
   91 *Olympus*: the home of the gods.
   93 *by those statues' godhead*: compared with the divine nature of those statues.
   96 *date*: lifespan.
   98 *Theseus*: the reclining form of Theseus (or Dionysus) is one of the most
remarkable pieces of sculpture from the Parthenon Frieze (the Elgin Marbles).
   99 *The Son of Priam*: probably 'the Paris of the Ægina sculptures, kneeling and
drawing a bow, now in the Munich Glyptothek': Porter and Clarke.
   101 *Apollo*: on p. 210 of his *Selections* of 1880 Browning provided this comment:

   NOTE.—The space left here tempts to a word on the line about Apollo the
snake-slayer, which my friend Professor [Sidney] Colvin condemns, believing
that the God of the Belvedere grasps no bow, but the Ægis, as described in the
15th Iliad. Surely the text represents that portentous object (θοῦριν, δεινήν,
ἀμφιδάσειαν, ἀριπρεπέ'— μαρμαρέην) as "shaken violently" or "held im-
movably" by both hands, not a single one and that the left hand:

You live—there's the Racers' frieze to follow:
You die—there's the dying Alexander.

XIV.

So, testing your weakness by their strength,   105
    Your meagre charms by their rounded beauty,
Measured by Art in your breadth and length,
    You learned—to submit is a mortal's duty.
—When I say "you" 't is the common soul,
    The collective, I mean: the race of Man   110
That receives life in parts to live in a whole,
    And grow here according to God's clear plan.

---

108 *1855P–56* You learn—to . . . . is the worsted's duty.   111 *1865SP/MS* live a
112 *1855P–56* God's own plan.

ἀλλὰ σύ γ᾽ ἐν χείρεσσι λάβ᾽ αἰγίδα θυσανόεσσαν
τὴν μάλ᾽ ἐπισσείων φοβέειν ἥρωας Ἀχαιούς

and so on, τὴν ἄρ᾽ ὅ γ᾽ ἐν χείρεσσιν ἔχων—χερσὶν ἔχ᾽ ἀτρέμα, κ. τ. λ. Moreover, while he shook it he "shouted enormously," σεῖσ᾽, ἐπὶ δ᾽ αὐτός ἄυσε μάλα μέγα, which the statue does not. Presently when Teukros, on the other side, plies the bow, it is τόξον ἔχων ἐν χειρὶ παλίντονον. Besides, by the act of discharging an arrow, the right arm and hand are thrown back as we see: a quite gratuitous and theatrical display in the case supposed. The conjecture of Flaxman that the statue was suggested by the bronze Apollo Alexikakos of Kalamis, mentioned by Pausanias, remains probable,—though the "hardness" which Cicero considers to distinguish the artist's workmanship from that of Muron is not by any means apparent in our marble copy, if it be one.—Feb. 16, 1880.

Apollo was termed 'the snake-slayer' because, as soon as he was born, he destroyed with arrows the serpent Python. Zeus lent him the Ægis, his own shield. The epithets in brackets mean 'dreadful', 'terrible', 'fringed all round', 'very bright' and 'flashing' (*Iliad* xv. 308–9; xvii. 594). The two lines of verse (xv. 229–30) mean 'But take in your hands the tasselled aegis, and shake it fiercely over the Achaean warriors to terrify them.' The words following 'and so on' translate: 'this he carried in his hands' and 'moveless in his hands' (xv. 311, 318). The following words mean 'shouted enormously' (as Browning says), and 'holding in his hand his bent-back bow' (xv. 321, 443). In his *Lectures on Sculpture* (1829) p. 92, John Flaxman told his audience that 'The Apollo Belvedere is believed by the learned Visconti to be the work of Calamis'. ('Alexikakos' means 'warding off evil'). The reference to Pausanias is to his *Description of Greece*, I. iii. 4.

XV.

Growth came when, looking your last on them all,
　　You turned your eyes inwardly one fine day
And cried with a start—What if we so small 　　　　　　115
　　Be greater and grander the while than they?
Are they perfect of lineament, perfect of stature?
　　In both, of such lower types are we
Precisely because of our wider nature;
　　For time, theirs—ours, for eternity. 　　　　　　120

XVI.

To-day's brief passion limits their range;
　　It seethes with the morrow for us and more.
They are perfect—how else? they shall never change:
　　We are faulty—why not? we have time in store.
The Artificer's hand is not arrested 　　　　　　125
　　With us; we are rough-hewn, nowise polished:
They stand for our copy, and, once invested
　　With all they can teach, we shall see them abolished.

XVII.

'T is a life-long toil till our lump be leaven—
　　The better! What's come to perfection perishes. 　　　　　　130

---

114 *1865SP/MS* eyes inward one 　　　116 *1855P–56* Are greater, ay, greater the
1855–70 they! 　　117 *1855P* stature, 　　118 *1855P* And in 　　119 *1856* nature!
120 *1855P* eternity? 　　121 *1855P–56* range, 　　126 *1880S, 1884S* polished.
127 *1855P* They are set for 　　*129 {reading of 1865–84S} 1855P–63* 'Tis *1888* {some
copies} T is 　　*1888* {some copies}, *1889* 'T is 　　130 *1855P–65SP* what's

---

116 *the while*: all the time.
122 *seethes*: ferments.

124 *We are faulty—why not?*: the background here is Ruskin's chapter, 'The Nature
of Gothic', in vol. II of *The Stones of Venice* (published 28 July 1853). 'Accept this for a
universal law', Ruskin wrote, 'that neither architecture nor any other noble work of
man can be good unless it be imperfect . . . the first cause of the fall of the arts of Europe
was a relentless requirement of perfection': *Works*, ed. Cook and Wedderburn, X,
(1904), 204. This was part of his attack on the Renaissance.

129 *leaven*: for 'leavened': not in OED². Cf. Matt. 13: 33, etc.

Things learned on earth, we shall practise in heaven:
    Works done least rapidly, Art most cherishes.
Thyself shalt afford the example, Giotto!
    Thy one work, not to decrease or diminish,
Done at a stroke, was just (was it not?) "O!"   135
    Thy great Campanile is still to finish.

XVIII.

Is it true that we are now, and shall be hereafter,
    But what and where depend on life's minute?
Hails heavenly cheer or infernal laughter
    Our first step out of the gulf or in it?   140
Shall Man, such step within his endeavour,
    Man's face, have no more play and action
Than joy which is crystallized for ever,
    Or grief, an eternal petrifaction?

XIX.

On which I conclude, that the early painters,   145
    To cries of "Greek Art and what more wish you?"—

---

131 *1855P* Things half-learned on   *1855P–56* heaven.   *1863–65SP* Heaven.
133 *1855P–65SP* Thyself shall afford   135 *1855P* just—was . . . . not? "O!"
136 *1855P* While thy   137 *1855P–56, 1865SP/MS* true, we   138 *1855P–56*
And what—is depending on life's one minute?   139 *1855P* Waits celestial cheer
141 *1855P–56* And man, this step   142 *1855P* Has his face, do you think, no
1855P/MS Has Man's face,   *1855, 1856* His face, {revised in *Woolner, Fields, Rossetti*}
143 *1855P* Than a joy   144 *1855P* Or a grief,   *1855, 1856* petrifaction!
146 *1855P* To the cry of

---

131 *we shall practise in heaven*: cf. *Sordello*, iii. 925–7.

132 *Works done least rapidly*: *Ars longa, vita brevis* is the first aphorism of Hippocrates
(in its usual Latin form).

135 *'O!'*: when the Pope sent a messenger to Florence to enquire about Giotto,
wishing to have certain paintings executed for St Peter's, 'Giotto, who was very
courteous, took a sheet of paper, and a pencil dipped in a red colour; then, resting his
elbow on his side, to form a sort of compass, with one turn of the hand he drew a circle,
so perfect and exact that it was a marvel to behold.' This enabled the Pope to understand
'how far Giotto surpassed all the other painters of the time': Vasari, i. 102–3.

136 *is still to finish*: see introduction.

142 *play*: freedom of movement.

146 *Greek Art*: 'All that had been done in painting before Giotto, resolved itself into
the imitation of certain existing models . . . there was no new method; the Greekish

Replied, "To become now self-acquainters,
    "And paint man man, whatever the issue!
"Make new hopes shine through the flesh they fray,
    "New fears aggrandize the rags and tatters: 150
"To bring the invisible full into play!
    "Let the visible go to the dogs—what matters?"

XX.

Give these, I exhort you, their guerdon and glory
    For daring so much, before they well did it.
The first of the new, in our race's story,   155
    Beats the last of the old; 't is no idle quiddit.
The worthies began a revolution,
    Which if on earth you intend to acknowledge,
Why, honour them now! (ends my allocution)
    Nor confer your degree when the folk leave college.   160

XXI.

There's a fancy some lean to and others hate—
    That, when this life is ended, begins

---

147 *1855P, 1856* Replied, "Become   *1855P* self-acquainters!   148 *1855P* To
paint   149 *1855P* Make the new {revised in *1855P/MS*}   *1855, 1856* Make the
hopes {revised in *Woolner, Fields, Rossetti*}   150 *1855P–56* tatters   151 *1855P*
So we bring *1855, 1856* So bring   *1865SP/MS* We bring   *1855P–56, 1880S, 1884S*
play, 153 *1855P–56* I say, full honour and   *1855P/MS, Woolner, Fields* exhort, their
{revised in *Rossetti*}   156 *1855P–63* old,   158 *1855P* if we on the earth
intend {revised in *1855P/MS*}   *1855, 1856* on the earth we intend {revised in *Woolner,
Fields, Rossetti*}   159 *1855P* Let us honour   *1855, 1856* Honour them   *1855P–
65SP* now—   160 *1855P–56* confer our degree   *1855P–84S* the folks leave

---

types were everywhere seen, more or less modified . . . such seems to have been the
limit to which painting had advanced previous to 1280. [Then] Giotto appeared; and
almost from the beginning of his career he not only deviated from the practice of the
older painters, but stood opposed to them': Mrs Jameson, *Memoirs*, i. 48–9. See Rio's
third chapter.

147 *self-acquainters*: no doubt a nonce-compound, but 'self-acquaintance' is recorded
in OED². See DeLaura, 'Browning's Painter Poems', 382 ff., for a good discussion of
this passage.

149 *fray*: wear out. Cf. *Pippa Passes*, Introduction, 145.

156 *quiddit*: an archaic abbreviation of 'quiddity', excessive subtlety of argument.

160 *leave college*: here 'die'. Cf. l. 131.

New work for the soul in another state,
    Where it strives and gets weary, loses and wins:
Where the strong and the weak, this world's congeries,   165
    Repeat in large what they practised in small,
Through life after life in unlimited series;
    Only the scale's to be changed, that's all.

XXII.

Yet I hardly know. When a soul has seen
    By the means of Evil that Good is best,   170
And, through earth and its noise, what is heaven's serene,—
    When our faith in the same has stood the test—
Why, the child grown man, you burn the rod,
    The uses of labour are surely done;
There remaineth a rest for the people of God: 175
    And I have had troubles enough, for one.

XXIII.

But at any rate I have loved the season
    Of Art's spring-birth so dim and dewy;
My sculptor is Nicolo the Pisan,
    My painter—who but Cimabue?   180
Nor ever was man of them all indeed,
    From these to Ghiberti and Ghirlandajo,

---

172 *1855P–63* When its faith   174 *1855P–56* done.   175 *1855–63* God,
178 *1855P–65SP* dewy,   179 *1855P* And my   *1855, 1856* Pisan;   180 *1855P*
And my   *1863* And painter—

---

165 *congeries*: masses.

178 *spring-birth*: no other example in OED[2].

179 *Nicolo*: Nicola or Nicolo Pisano (1220/1225?–1284?). Vasari praises him and his brother Giovanni for having liberated sculpture and architecture 'from the rude and tasteless old Greek manner, and having displayed much greater power of invention in their compositions, as well as more grace of attitude in their figures': i. 60. Mrs Jameson states that he was 'the first to leave the stiff monotony of the traditional forms for the study of nature and the antique': *Memoirs*, i. 22.

180 *Cimabue*: Cenni di Pepi, called Cimabue (1240/50–1302?) is the subject of the first of Vasari's *Lives*. As Mrs Jameson remarks, 'To Cimabue for three centuries had been awarded the lofty title of "Father of Modern Painting" ', on the ground that he achieved 'the *miracle*, of having revived the art of painting': *Memoirs*, i. 5. To him is attributed the large *Maestà* from the church of S. Trinita in the Uffizi Gallery. He is seen

Could say that he missed my critic-meed.
So, now to my special grievance—heigh ho!

XXIV.

Their ghosts still stand, as I said before,   185
    Watching each fresco flaked and rasped,
Blocked up, knocked out, or whitewashed o'er:
    —No getting again what the church has grasped!
The works on the wall must take their chance;
    "Works never conceded to England's thick clime!"   190
(I hope they prefer their inheritance
    Of a bucketful of Italian quick-lime.)

XXV.

When they go at length, with such a shaking
    Of heads o'er the old delusion, sadly
Each master his way through the black streets taking,   195
    Where many a lost work breathes though badly—
Why don't they bethink them of who has merited?
    Why not reveal, while their pictures dree

185 *1855P* ghosts would stand,   *1855–63* ghosts now stand,   187 *1855–63* o'er
189 *1855P–56* chance,   194 *1855P–63* old delusions, sadly   198 *1855P* Why
won't they reveal,

as the essential forerunner of Giotto. In the *Purgatorio* Dante wrote: 'Credette Cimabue
nella pittura / tener lo campo, ed ora ha Giotto il grido, / sì che la fama di colui è
oscura': *Purgatorio*, xi. 94–6 ('Cimabue thought / To lord it over painting's field; and
now / The cry is Giotto's, and his name eclipsed': Cary).
  182 *Ghiberti*: Lorenzo Ghiberti (1378–1455), a Florentine sculptor celebrated for
the two great bronze doors of the Baptistery there, of which Michelangelo said:
'They are so beautiful, that they might fittingly stand at the gates of Paradise' (Vasari, i.
382).
    Ghirlandajo: (Domenico di Tommaso Bigordi, 1449–94), one of the painters
who decorated the Sistine Chapel in Rome.
  183 *critic-meed*: critical justice from me.
  186 *rasped*: scraped off.
  190 *"Works never conceded*: in 'Some Notes', 9, DeLaura suggests that this may be an
allusion to Mrs Jameson's comment on the possibility of fresco-painting in England, in
her *Visits and Sketches at Home and Abroad* (1834).
  198–9 *dree / Such doom*: undergo such a fate (Sc.)

Such doom, how a captive might be out-ferreted?
Why is it they never remember me?   200

XXVI.

Not that I expect the great Bigordi,
    Nor Sandro to hear me, chivalric, bellicose;
Nor the wronged Lippino; and not a word I
    Say of a scrap of Frà Angelico's:
But are you too fine, Taddeo Gaddi,   205
    To grant me a taste of your intonaco,
Some Jerome that seeks the heaven with a sad eye?
Not a churlish saint, Lorenzo Monaco?

---

199 *1855P–63* doom, that a captive's to be   200 *1855, 1856* Why do they
201 *1865SP/MS* I scarce expect   202 *1865SP/MS* Or Sandro   203 *1855P–*
56 Nor wronged   *1865SP/MS* Or the   204 *1855P–56* Angelico's.   206 *1855P*
To afford me   207 *1865SP/MS* A Jerome . . . . with sad   208 *1855, 1856* No
churlish

---

199 *out-ferreted*: no other example in OED².

201 *the great Bigordi*: Ghirlandaio; see 182 n.

202 *Sandro*: Alessandro di Mariano Filipepi, called Sandro Botticelli (1444/5–1510), now recognized as one of the greatest of the painters of the Italian Renaissance, seems to have been a pupil of Fra Lippo Lippi. Vasari praises him highly, but does not devote to him one of the longer of the Lives. In 'Botticelli and Nineteenth-Century England' (*Journal of the Warburg Institute*, 23 (1960), 292 ff) Michael Levey explains why the painter of 'The Birth of Venus' was so much less celebrated then than now.

203 *the wronged Lippino*: Filippino Lippi (*c.*1457–1504), the son of Fra Lippo Lippi. He was an admirable painter: see Vasari, ii. 274–84. There is hardly any other case of a son so nearly emulating his father in art. He was 'wronged' (in Browning's view) because he received too little credit for the large part he played in completing the paintings in the Brancacci Chapel in the Carmine Church in Florence, of which the principal painter was Masaccio.

204 *Frà Angelico*: see above, 'Fra Lippo Lippi', 235 n.

205 *Taddeo Gaddi*: died 1366: a godson and pupil of Giotto's who painted the frescoes of the Baroncelli Chapel in S. Croce, Florence, with their remarkable experiments with light. Vasari tells us that he had a particular devotion to St Jerome, 'having chosen him for the protector of his house', and mentions his painting of the saint in S. Maria Novella: *Lives*, i. 201. Mrs Jameson writes that 'His pictures are considered the most important works of the 14th century': *Memoirs*, i. 75.

206 *intonaco*: 'The final coating of plaster spread upon a wall or other surface, esp. for fresco painting': OED². For Giotto's use of intonaco, see Vasari, i. 101.

207 *Jerome*: now generally attributed to Masolino: DeLaura, 'Some Notes', 8.

208 *Lorenzo Monaco*: see 'Fra Lippo Lippi', 236.

XXVII.

Could not the ghost with the close red cap,
  My Pollajolo, the twice a craftsman,   210
Save me a sample, give me the hap
  Of a muscular Christ that shows the draughtsman?
No Virgin by him the somewhat petty,
  Of finical touch and tempera crumbly—
Could not Alesso Baldovinetti   215
  Contribute so much, I ask him humbly?

XXVIII.

Margheritone of Arezzo,
  With the grave-clothes garb and swaddling barret
(Why purse up mouth and beak in a pet so,
  You bald old saturnine poll-clawed parrot?)   220

---

213 *1855P* Not a Virgin   218 *1855P, 1865SP/MS* With grave-clothes
220 *1855P* Like a bald, saturnine,   *1855, 1856* bald, saturnine,

---

209 *cap*: see the illustration in the 2nd ed. of the *Vite*.

210 *Pollajolo*: Antonio Pollaiuolo (1431/2–1498) and his brother Piero (1443–96)
were both painters, sculptors, engravers, and goldsmiths. Vasari tells us that Antonio
'dissected many human bodies to study the anatomy, and was the first who investi-
gated the action of the muscles in this manner' (ii. 227). The Brownings owned
a painting of Christ tied to a column which was attributed to this painter: see Kelley
and Coley, Plate 16 (H 20). The attribution is no longer accepted: DeLaura, 'Some
Notes', 8–9.

211 *hap*: good luck.

214 *tempera*: distemper.

215 *Alesso Baldovinetti*: this painter (1425–1500) excelled in the precise details of his
paintings. Vasari tells us that in the Church of the Annunziata in Florence 'he
represented the Nativity . . . with such minuteness of care, that each separate straw, in
the roof of a cabin . . . may be counted' (ii. 66–7). His painting of an altar-piece in
tempera, Vasari tells us, 'has in several places peeled off' (65).

217 *Margheritone*: Vasari, who assigns him the dates 1236–1313, describes him as one
of the painters eclipsed by Cimabue and Giotto: i. 115 ff. The engraving of him in the
2nd ed. of the *Vite* shows a disgruntled and rather parrot-like face with angry eyes,
attired in something like a night-shirt surmounted by a turban: Mrs Orr describes this
as 'funeral garb', due to his annoyance at the success of Giotto and his followers
(*Handbook*, 210 n.). Cf. *Casa Guidi Windows*, i. 386–8: 'If wistfully / Margheritone
sickened at the smell / Of Cimabue's laurel, let him go!'

218 *barret*: 'A little flat cap; esp. the *Biretta*, worn by Roman Catholic clerics': OED².

220 *poll-clawed parrot*: cf. *2 Henry IV*, II. iv. 249.

Not a poor glimmering Crucifixion,
    Where in the foreground kneels the donor?
If such remain, as is my conviction,
    The hoarding it does you but little honour.

XXIX.

They pass; for them the panels may thrill,   225
    The tempera grow alive and tinglish;
Their pictures are left to the mercies still
    Of dealers and stealers, Jews and the English,
Who, seeing mere money's worth in their prize,
    Will sell it to somebody calm as Zeno   230
At naked High Art, and in ecstasies
    Before some clay-cold vile Carlino!

XXX.

No matter for these! But Giotto, you,
    Have you allowed, as the town-tongues babble it,—
Oh, never! it shall not be counted true—   235
    That a certain precious little tablet

---

221 *1855, 1856* No poor   222 *1855P* Where dim in   *Woolner* Whereby in
223 *1855P* such still remain,   224 *1855P–56* hoarding does   227 *1855P* Works
rot or are   *1855P/MS, Woolner, Fields* The pictures are   *1855, 1856* Rot or are
{revised in *Rossetti*}   *1865SP/MS* the mercy still   228 *1855P–56* English!
229 *1855P* Who see mere   *1855, 1856* Seeing mere   *1865SP/MS* in the prize,
230 *1855P* And sell   *1855, 1856* Who sell   *1855P–56* to some one calm   231 *1855P*
At the naked Art,   *1855, 1856* naked Art,   233 *1865SP/MS* for them! But
235 *1855, 1856* Never!

---

222 *kneels the donor*: painters often included a small portrait of the donor in pictures
of the period. Browning and his contemporaries mistook the portrait of the donor in
'The Coronation of the Virgin', by Fra Lippo Lippi, for the painter himself: see above,
p. 52n.

226 *tinglish*: a nonce-word. No other example in OED².

230 *Zeno*: Zeno (335–263BC) was the founder of the Stoic school of philosophers.

232 *Carlino*: Carlino Dolci (1616–86) was a slow and plodding painter. In the brief
entry in the *Encyclopaedia Britannica* (11th ed.) W. M. Rossetti tells us of the story that
'his brain was affected by seeing Luca Giordano . . . despatch more business in four or
five hours than he could have executed in as many months'. He was deeply pious, but
lacked invention.

234 *town-tongues*: not in OED².

236 *a certain precious little tablet*: Browning told an American scholar that this 'was a
famous "Last Supper", mentioned by Vasari, and gone astray long ago from the Church

Which Buonarroti eyed like a lover,—
　　Was buried so long in oblivion's womb
And, left for another than I to discover,
　　Turns up at last! and to whom?—to whom?　　240

XXXI.

I, that have haunted the dim San Spirito,
　　(Or was it rather the Ognissanti?)
Patient on altar-step planting a weary toe!
　　Nay, I shall have it yet! *Detur amanti!*
My Koh-i-noor—or (if that's a platitude)　　245
　　Jewel of Giamschid, the Persian Sofi's eye;
So, in anticipative gratitude,
　　What if I take up my hope and prophesy?

---

238 *1855P* Swallowed so　*1855, 1856* Buried　239 *1855P–56* Was left
240 *1855P–56* last,　242 *1855P* it not rather　243 *1855P–56* Stood on the
altar-steps, patient and weary too!　*1863* on altar-steps planting　244 *1855P–56*
yet, *detur 1863–65SP detur*　245 *1855P* or, if . . . . platitude,　246 *1855P–
65SP* eye!　247 *1855P* And so

---

of S. Spirito: it turned up, according to report, in some obscure corner, while I was in
Florence, and was at once acquired by a stranger. I saw it,—genuine or no, a work of
great beauty': letter dated 28 December 1886, illustrated as frontispiece to Hiram
Corson, *An Introduction to the Study of Robert Browning's Poetry* (Boston, 1899: 1st ed.
1886). Browning was confused, however. On 17 March 1853 he had written to John
Kenyon, telling him that he believed that the art-dealer Metzger 'has discovered the
precious little picture by Giotto of which Vasari says so much, and how he heard
Michelagnolo admire it to heart's content—"the death of the Virgin"—missing from S.
Spirito in Vasari's time': PK 53: 23. In 1886 he has confused the subject of the painting.
See Vasari, i. 113.

241 *San Spirito*: Brunelleschi designed this remarkable church for the Augustinians.
Work began in 1436, and continued long after his death in 1446.

242 *the Ognissanti*: the Church of all Saints, begun in 1251, was completely recon-
structed in 1627.

244 *Detur amanti!*: let it be given to the one who loves it!

245 *My Koh-i-noor*: this celebrated diamond ('Mountain of Light') had recently been
presented to Queen Victoria. It remains among the Crown Jewels.

246 *Jewel of Giamschid*: 'The celebrated fabulous ruby of Sultan Giamschid . . . from
its splendour, named Schebgerag, "the torch of night"; also the "cup of the sun", etc.':
Byron's note to *The Giaour*, 479.

XXXII.

When the hour grows ripe, and a certain dotard
   Is pitched, no parcel that needs invoicing,   250
To the worse side of the Mont Saint Gothard,
   We shall begin by way of rejoicing;
None of that shooting the sky (blank cartridge),
   Nor a civic guard, all plumes and lacquer,
Hunting Radetzky's soul like a partridge   255
   Over Morello with squib and cracker.

XXXIII.

This time we'll shoot better game and bag 'em hot—
   No mere display at the stone of Dante,
But a kind of sober Witanagemot
   (Ex: "Casa Guidi," *quod videas ante*)   260

---

249 *1855P–56* hour is ripe,   250 *1855P–56* Pitched,   251 *1855P* the worser
side   *1884S* the worst side   252 *1855P* We'll have, to begin   *1855, 1856* Have,
to begin   *1855P–56* rejoicing,   253 *1855P* of our shooting   254 *1855P* As
when civic guards, all   *1855, 1856* No civic guards, all   *{reading of *1855P–84S*, DC,
BrU, *1889*} *1888* lacquer   255 *1855P* We hunted Radetzky's   256 *1855P*
Over Mount Morello   257 *1855P–56* We'll shoot this time better   *1865SP/MS*
time shoot   258 *1855P* No stupid display   *1855,* *1856* No display
259 *1855P* a sober kind of Witan-agemot   *1855, 1856* of Witan-agemot {revised in
Woolner, Fields, Rossetti}   260 *1855P–56* ("Casa

249 *a certain dotard*: 'He concludes with an invocation to a future time when the
Grand Duke will have been pitched across the Alps, when art and the Republic will
revive together, and when Giotto's Campanile will be completed—which glorious
consummation, though he may not live to see, he considers himself the first to predict':
Handbook, 210. The reference is not to Leopold II, however, but to Count Radetzky,
the military governor of Lombardy-Venetia, born in 1766 but no dotard, as the
Piedmontese armies had learnt to their cost.

251 *Mont Saint Gothard*: a range of the Lepontine Alps: 'the worse side' is the Swiss side.

256 *Morello*: a mountain north of Florence.

258 *the stone of Dante*: cf. EBB, *Casa Guidi Windows*, 601–6: 'On the stone / Called
Dante's,—a plain flat stone, scarce discerned / From others in the pavement,—where-
upon / He used to bring his quiet chair out, turned / To Brunelleschi's church, and
pour along / The lava of his spirit when it burned.' As Julia Markus notes, ' "Il Sasso di
Dante" is on the right side of the Piazza del Duomo'.

259 *Witanagemot*: O.E. *witena gemōt*, 'meeting of wise men'.

260 *quod videas ante*: literally 'which see earlier', a reference to *Casa Guidi Windows*,
i. 617–9: 'thy favourite stone's elected right / As tryst-place for thy Tuscans to foresee /
Their earliest chartas from'.

Shall ponder, once Freedom restored to Florence,
How Art may return that departed with her.
Go, hated house, go each trace of the Loraine's,
And bring us the days of Orgagna hither!

XXXIV.

How we shall prologize, how we shall perorate,   265
Utter fit things upon art and history,
Feel truth at blood-heat and falsehood at zero rate,
Make of the want of the age no mystery;
Contrast the fructuous and sterile eras,
Show—monarchy ever its uncouth cub licks   270
Out of the bear's shape into Chimæra's,
While Pure Art's birth is still the republic's.

261 *1855P* To ponder, now Freedom's restored *1855P/MS* ponder, Freedom restored *1855, 1856* To ponder Freedom {revised in *Rossetti*} *1865SP/MS* ponder, freedom 263 *1855P* With the hated *1855P–56* Loraine's! 264 *1855P–56* hither. 266 *1855P* Say proper things *1855, 1856* Say fit *1865SP/MS* Utter choice things 267 *1855P* Set the true at *1855, 1856* Set truth *1855P–63* and the false at a zero 268 *1855P, 1863* And make *1855P–63* mystery! 269 *1863* Contrasting the 270 *1855P–56* monarchy its 271 *1855P–56* shape to the chimæra's— 272 *1855, 1856* Pure .... birth being still *1855P* birth was still *1855P–65SP, 1880S, 1884S* republic's!

263 *each trace of the Loraine's*: in 1737, on the death of the last of the Medici, the duchy passed to Francis, duke of Lorraine, and husband of Maria Theresa (daughter of the Emperor Charles VI); Francis became emperor, but the real power in the Habsburg lands remained with Maria Theresa; his descendants in the house of Habsburg-Lorraine are commonly counted Habsburgs, but Browning contemptuously uses the unimpressive name.

264 *Orgagna*: Andrea di Cione, active 1344–68, described as the finest and most versatile Tuscan artist of the mid-fourteenth century. He was the principal artist of the tabernacle for Or San Michele, in Florence, with the striking relief on the reverse which represents the Dormition and Assumption of the Virgin. He was influenced by Giotto and the painters of Siena, and was one of the most prolific of the masters of his time, as well as being a sculptor, architect and poet. Vasari attributes to him the frescoes of The Triumph of Death and the Last Judgement in the Campo Santo at Pisa.

265 *prologize*: cf. note on title of 'Artemis Prologizes', Vol. III, p. 218 n.

270 *its uncouth cub licks*: a reference to the old belief that bears lick their cubs into shape. The fabulous Chimaera was a lion in front, a snake at the rear, and a goat in the middle.

XXXV.

Then one shall propose in a speech (curt Tuscan,
    Expurgate and sober, with scarcely an *"issimo,"*)
To end now our half-told tale of Cambuscan,   275
    And turn the bell-tower's *alt* to *altissimo:*
And fine as the beak of a young beccaccia
    The Campanile, the Duomo's fit ally,
Shall soar up in gold full fifty braccia,
    Completing Florence, as Florence Italy.   280

XXXVI.

Shall I be alive that morning the scaffold
    Is broken away, and the long-pent fire,
. Like the golden hope of the world, unbaffled
    Springs from its sleep, and up goes the spire

---

273 *1855, 1856* (in   *1855P–56* speech, curt   274 *1855P* Sober, expurgate, spare of an *"issimo,"*   *1855P/MS* of alt*issimo,"*   *1855, 1856* Sober, expurgate, spare of an 275 *1855P* To finish our   *1855, 1856* Ending our   276 *1855P* Turn the Bell-tower's alto to altissimo.   *1855, 1856* Turning the Bell-tower's altaltissimo.   *Woolner, Fields* altissimo.   *Rossetti* altissimo.   278 *1855P* Shall the Campanile, 279 *1855P* Soar   *1855, 1856* Soars up   *1855P–56* gold its full   281 *1855P* So said, so done. That   *1865SP/MS* that morn the   284 *1865SP/MS* up burns the

274 *Expurgate*: for 'expurgated', a rare form.
    an 'issimo': a superlative, to be used sparingly in the Tuscan style here mentioned: 'altissimo' in 276 exemplifies the form.
   275 *our half-told tale*: the poet here compares himself to Chaucer, who, in *The Squire's Tale*, 'left half-told / The story of Cambuscan bold' (Milton, 'Il Penseroso', 109–10).
   276 *alt*: for *altissimo*. Architectural height is here expressed metaphorically as musical height: the octave 'in alt' is that from g'' (the note written on the top line of the treble stave) to f''' (about the top of a high soprano range), that above is 'in altissimo'.
   277 *fine*: slender.
    beccaccia: woodcock.
   279 *Shall soar up in gold*: Vasari, i. 114 gives a good account of work on the Campanile, begun 9 July 1334. He tells us that the height of the tower is 144 braccia (cubits), and that Giotto intended it 'to have been crowned by a spire or pyramid, of the height of fifty braccia', adding: 'but as this was in the old Gothic manner, the modern architects have always advised its omission'. Mrs Foster notes (p. 196 n.) that the braccio varies in length in different places, but that in Florence it is 23 inches. Cf. introduction, and 15 n. We have found no evidence that Giotto planned a golden campanile.
   282 *is broken away*: being made of wood.
   283 *unbaffled*: freed.

While "God and the People" plain for its motto,   285
  Thence the new tricolour flaps at the sky?
At least to foresee that glory of Giotto
  And Florence together, the first am I!

285 *1855P* When with "God   *1855, 1856* As, "God   286 *1855P* sky,
287 *1855P* Why, to hail him, the vindicated Giotto,   *1855, 1856* Foreseeing the day
that vindicates Giotto   288 *1855P* Thanking God for it all, the

285 *'God and the People'*: Mazzini's motto. Cf. *Casa Guidi Windows*, i. 499.
286 *the new tricolour*: the flag of Italian Nationalism, first raised in Romagna and the
Marches in 1831.

IN A BALCONY

IN *1868* the title is followed by 'Bagni di Lucca, 1853', so we can safely assign most of its composition to that happy and productive period. Sharp tells us that Browning returned to Florence 'with the MS. of the greater part of . . . "In a Balcony", composed mainly while walking alone through the forest glades':[1] the work was probably completed in Rome during the following winter.[2] There is no known source, but a likely stimulus was the production of *Colombe's Birthday*, in a shortened form, at the Haymarket Theatre in April 1853.[3]

In the original edition of *Men and Women* 'In a Balcony' is divided into three Parts, each beginning on a new page. At the end of the First Part we have the stage-direction. *He breaks from her: she remains. Dance-music from within.* The Second Part begins with the first entry of the Queen, to Constance, and ends with the stage-direction *She* [the Queen] *goes out. Dance-music from within.* Part I is a dialogue between Constance and Norbert, Part II a dialogue between the Queen and Constance. In Part III Norbert and Constance are together at the beginning and end, but the Queen is with them for much of the time, although she has only one speech. When the work was first reprinted, in *1863*, Browning placed it among the *Tragedies and other Plays* which constitute the second volume, after 'A Soul's Tragedy' and before 'Strafford', printed last. It was described as 'A Scene. 1855', the date being that of its first publication. From this time onwards there is no mention of Parts; a line occurs between what had been Parts I and II, but not between what had been Parts II and III. In *1868* 'In a Balcony' is separated from the dramas and printed at the beginning of Vol. VI, before *Dramatis Personæ*, with 'Bagni di Lucca, 1853' on the title-page. In *1888/9* it appears in Vol. VII; once again it bears the date '1853', but 'Bagni di Lucca' disappears, and there are no divisions.

Certain of these details are of interest in relation to Browning's attitude to the piece. In her *Handbook*, of which Browning himself read both the first and second editions in proof,[4] Mrs Orr describes it as 'a dramatic fragment, equivalent to the third or fourth act, of what might prove a tragedy or a drama, as the author designed'. It is difficult to judge how serious such an intention ever was, and unlikely that he could have

---

[1] *Life of Robert Browning*, 166.   [2] Ibid., 167.
[3] See Vol. III, pp. 433–4.   [4] *Trumpeter*, 124 n. 5.

planned to complete a play during his years in Italy. 'How odd the remembrance of play-going seems now', he had written to Forster on 12 April 1853, with reference to the imminent performance of *Colombe's Birthday*,'—seven years since I was away—and for three or four years previous I had become strange to the benches, or boards, should one say?'[1] For us it remains a Dramatic Scene, yet the strength of Browning's continuing interest in drama remains important. He was pleased when 'In a Balcony' was presented on 28 November 1884, under the auspices of the Browning Society, with Alma Murray (Mrs Forman) as Constance. As late as 1888, indeed, he told Furnivall that a letter from her had greatly interested him: 'It is a powerful incentive,—if I wanted one,—to try hard and do my very best, if the power to write a Tragedy be still in me,—or ever was . . . and this whether for the stage or no.'[2] Shortly before his death he told Mrs Bronson that he thought 'constantly' of his old ambition 'to write a tragedy better than anything [he had] done yet'.[3] The fact that he mentioned Norbert in 'One Word More' suggests that this work was to him one of the most important pieces in *Men and Women*.

'In a Balcony' was written during a period when Browning was speculating about love and looking back on the long months of his courtship. It is evident that Elizabeth left her influence on the work. There may be something of her early situation in that of the Queen, who is older (in her case much older) than the man she is persuaded to consider as her lover, and who has spent her life among books and pictures, away from the everyday bustle of life: there is certainly something of her in Constance, a highly intellectual woman who is determined not to stand in the way of what she sees as her lover's career.

Several reviewers singled out this piece for notice. Writing anonymously in the *Westminster Review* George Eliot observed that it 'is so fine, that we regret it is not a complete drama instead of being merely the suggestion of a drama', quoting ll. 509–19 and italicizing the last line.[4] An unidentified reviewer in *Bentley's Miscellany* regarded 'In a Balcony' as 'probably the most perfect specimen of even, sustained, and lofty eloquence afforded in this collection', ruling that

---

[1] *New Letters*, 61. 'Do you know', EBB wrote to Isa Blagden on 16 November 1855, 'I had thought of Miss Cushman as the "queen" "In the Balcony"—but the drama might not perhaps be strong enough in incident for the English stage. The French would accept it willingly': PK 55: 160.

[2] *Trumpeter*, 152.

[3] Meredith, 142.

[4] *Westminster Review*, lxv (January 1856), 295.

there are few better things in the best of its author's dramas; and that is saying more, by a great deal, than would be supposed by idle play-goers and railway-bookstall-keepers, whose gauge of excellence is the run of so many nights, and the run of so many copies. Let such as doubt Mr. Browning's possession of real dramatic talent, listen to his speakers "In a Balcony", and note the construction and quietly marked-out action of the piece; and they will surely abate their scepticism, or the avowal of it.'[1]

Date: 1853–4
1863: printed with the *Tragedies and other Plays* in Vol. II.

[1] *Bentley's Miscellany*, xxxix (January 1856), 69.

IN A BALCONY.

PERSONS.

NORBERT.
CONSTANCE.
THE QUEEN.

half-title {in *1868-75* the half-title includes the following date:} BAGNI DI LUCCA, 1853. list of 'persons' {appears in *1888, 1889*}

IN A BALCONY.

1853.

CONSTANCE *and* NORBERT.

Norbert. Now!
Constance.   Not now!
Norbert.   Give me them again, those hands:
Put them upon my forehead, how it throbs!
Press them before my eyes, the fire comes through!
You cruellest, you dearest in the world,
Let me! The Queen must grant whate'er I ask—   5
How can I gain you and not ask the Queen?
There she stays waiting for me, here stand you;
Some time or other this was to be asked;
Now is the one time—what I ask, I gain:
Let me ask now, Love!
      Constance.   Do, and ruin us.   10
      Norbert. Let it be now, Love! All my soul breaks forth.
How I do love you! Give my love its way!
A man can have but one life and one death,
One heaven, one hell. Let me fulfil my fate—
Grant me my heaven now! Let me know you mine,   15

title *1863, 1865* BALCONY. | A SCENE. | *1855*. {the date '1853.' appears in *1888, 1889*}
{in *1855P–63S* the poem is divided into three parts, the second and third beginning at
ll. 340 and 606 respectively; in these texts the title is followed by 'FIRST PART.'}
{in *1863, 1865* the following stage direction precedes the names of the two characters:}
In a Balcony.   1 *1855P–65* Now. .... now.   3 *1855P, 1855, 1863S–65*
through.   *1856* through,   5 *1855P–65* the   7 *1855P–65* you.
8 *1855P–56* asked,   10 *1868–84S* us!   12 *1855P–65* give   15 *1855P–65*
now.

---

2 *Put them upon my forehead*: Browning suffered from severe headaches, particularly
before his marriage. For a later occasion when EBB took his head 'in her two little
hands', see *Wedgwood*, 102.

12 *How I do love you!*: cf. EBB, *Sonnets from the Portuguese*, xliii: 'How do I love thee?
Let me count the ways.'

Prove you mine, write my name upon your brow,
Hold you and have you, and then die away,
If God please, with completion in my soul!

   Constance. I am not yours then? How content this man!
I am not his—who change into himself,   20
Have passed into his heart and beat its beats,
Who give my hands to him, my eyes, my hair,
Give all that was of me away to him—
So well, that now, my spirit turned his own,
Takes part with him against the woman here,   25
Bids him not stumble at so mere a straw
As caring that the world be cognizant
How he loves her and how she worships him.
You have this woman, not as yet that world.
Go on, I bid, nor stop to care for me   30
By saving what I cease to care about,
The courtly name and pride of circumstance—
The name you'll pick up and be cumbered with
Just for the poor parade's sake, nothing more;
Just that the world may slip from under you—   35
Just that the world may cry "So much for him—
"The man predestined to the heap of crowns:
"There goes his chance of winning one, at least!"

   Norbert. The world!

   Constance.   You love it. Love me quite as well,
And see if I shall pray for this in vain!   40
Why must you ponder what it knows or thinks?

   Norbert. You pray for—what, in vain?

   Constance.   Oh my heart's heart,

---

18 *1855P–65* soul.   19 *1855P–65* how . . . . man?   34 *1855P* more.
1863S more,   37 *1855P* crowns.   *1855–56* crowns!   38 *1855P–56* least"
39 *1868–84S* it!

   17 *Hold you and have you*: an echo of 'The Form of the Solemnization of Matrimony'
in the Book of Common Prayer. Cf. 'Mesmerism', 26.
   32 *pride of circumstance*: cf. *Othello*, III. iii. 358.
   34 *parade's sake*: Johnson defines 'parade' as 'Show; ostentation'.
   42 *my heart's heart*: cf. l. 752 below, and *Hamlet*, III. ii. 71.

How I do love you, Norbert! That is right:
But listen, or I take my hands away!
You say, "let it be now": you would go now   45
And tell the Queen, perhaps six steps from us,
You love me—so you do, thank God!
  Norbert.   Thank God!
  Constance. Yes, Norbert,—but you fain would tell your
   love,
And, what succeeds the telling, ask of her
My hand. Now take this rose and look at it,   50
Listening to me. You are the minister,
The Queen's first favourite, nor without a cause.
To-night completes your wonderful year's-work
(This palace-feast is held to celebrate)
Made memorable by her life's success,   55
The junction of two crowns, on her sole head,
Her house had only dreamed of anciently:
That this mere dream is grown a stable truth,
To-night's feast makes authentic. Whose the praise?
Whose genius, patience, energy, achieved   60
What turned the many heads and broke the hearts?
You are the fate, your minute's in the heaven.
Next comes the Queen's turn. "Name your own reward!"
With leave to clench the past, chain the to-come,
Put out an arm and touch and take the sun   65
And fix it ever full-faced on your earth,
Possess yourself supremely of her life,—
You choose the single thing she will not grant;
Nay, very declaration of which choice

---

43 *1855P–65* that . . . . right! 44 *1855P–65* away. 56 *1855P–56, 1863* That
junction 57 *1855P–65* anciently. 63 *1855P–63S* turn. Name . . . . reward!
69 *1855P–56* The very

---

49 *succeeds*: follows.
62 *the fate*: the destined one.
  your minute's in the heaven: astrological in suggestion.
64 *clench*: clinch.
  the to-come: as in Shelley, 'Letter to Maria Gisborne', 200, and *Hellas*, 148 and 854.
See too *Sordello*, v. 981 and vi. 206.

Will turn the scale and neutralize your work: 70
At best she will forgive you, if she can.
You think I'll let you choose—her cousin's hand?
   Norbert. Wait. First, do you retain your old belief
The Queen is generous,—nay, is just?
   Constance.   There, there!
So men make women love them, while they know   75
No more of women's hearts than . . . look you here,
You that are just and generous beside,
Make it your own case! For example now,
I'll say—I let you kiss me, hold my hands—
Why? do you know why? I'll instruct you, then—   80
The kiss, because you have a name at court;
This hand and this, that you may shut in each
A jewel, if you please to pick up such.
That's horrible? Apply it to the Queen—
Suppose I am the Queen to whom you speak: 85
"I was a nameless man; you needed me:
"Why did I proffer you my aid? there stood
"A certain pretty cousin at your side.
"Why did I make such common cause with you?
"Access to her had not been easy else.   90
"You give my labour here abundant praise?
" 'Faith, labour, which she overlooked, grew play.
"How shall your gratitude discharge itself?
"Give me her hand!"
   Norbert.   And still I urge the same.
Is the Queen just? just—generous or no!   95
   Constance. Yes, just. You love a rose; no harm in that:
But was it for the rose's sake or mine
You put it in your bosom? mine, you said—
Then, mine you still must say or else be false.

70 *1855P–65* work.　　78 *1855P–65* case.　　79 *1855P–65* me and hold
81 *1855P–84S* court,　　84 *1855P–56, 1863, 1865* horrible!　　85 *1855P–84S*
speak.　　87 *1855P* there crouched　　91 *1855P–84S* my labours here
1855P–56 praise:　　92 *1855P–56* labour, while she

You told the Queen you served her for herself;   100
If so, to serve her was to serve yourself,
She thinks, for all your unbelieving face!
I know her. In the hall, six steps from us,
One sees the twenty pictures; there's a life
Better than life, and yet no life at all.   105
Conceive her born in such a magic dome,
Pictures all round her! why, she sees the world,
Can recognize its given things and facts,
The fight of giants or the feast of gods,
Sages in senate, beauties at the bath,   110
Chases and battles, the whole earth's display,
Landscape and sea-piece, down to flowers and fruit—
And who shall question that she knows them all,
In better semblance than the things outside?
Yet bring into the silent gallery   115
Some live thing to contrast in breath and blood,
Some lion, with the painted lion there—
You think she'll understand composedly?
—Say, "that's his fellow in the hunting-piece
"Yonder, I've turned to praise a hundred times?"   120
Not so. Her knowledge of our actual earth,
Its hopes and fears, concerns and sympathies,
Must be too far, too mediate, too unreal.
The real exists for us outside, not her:
How should it, with that life in these four walls—   125

105 *1855P–56* all;   115 *1855P* But bring   *125 {reading of DC, BrU, *1889*}
1855P–84S walls,   *1888* walls

105 *Better than life*: more lifelike than life itself. Cf. 410–12, and 'The Last Ride Together', 80–1.
106 *dome*: building.
109 *The fight of giants*: the revolt of the Giants against the gods was a favourite theme for sculptors in antiquity, and was often used in the decoration of temple pediments. It was also a theme of the Italian painters of the Renaissance.
     the feast of gods: another common subject for painters, most splendidly treated by Bellini.
116 *Some live thing*: cf. 'The Last Ride Together', 78 ff.
123 *too far, too mediate*: too distant, too indirect.

That father and that mother, first to last
No father and no mother—friends, a heap,
Lovers, no lack—a husband in due time,
And every one of them alike a lie!
Things painted by a Rubens out of nought   130
Into what kindness, friendship, love should be;
All better, all more grandiose than the life,
Only no life; mere cloth and surface-paint,
You feel, while you admire. How should she feel?
Yet now that she has stood thus fifty years   135
The sole spectator in that gallery,
You think to bring this warm real struggling love
In to her of a sudden, and suppose
She'll keep her state untroubled? Here's the truth—
She'll apprehend truth's value at a glance,   140
Prefer it to the pictured loyalty?
You only have to say, "so men are made,
"For this they act; the thing has many names,
"But this the right one: and now, Queen, be just!"
Your life slips back; you lose her at the word: 145
You do not even for amends gain me.
He will not understand; oh, Norbert, Norbert,
Do you not understand?
    Norbert.   The Queen's the Queen:
I am myself—no picture, but alive
In every nerve and every muscle, here   150
At the palace-window o'er the people's street,
As she in the gallery where the pictures glow:
The good of life is precious to us both.
She cannot love; what do I want with rule?

132 *1855P–84S* than life,   135 *1855P–63S* And now   140 *1855P–65* appre-
hend   its   value   141 *1855P–63S* loyalty!   142 *1880S–84S* "So
143 *1855P–63S* act,   145 *1855P–65* And life   147 *1855P, 1855, 1863S–84S*
understand!   *148 {reading of DC, BrU, 1889}* *1855P–84S* Queen, *1888* Queen
151 *1855P–56* palace-window or in the   152 *1855P–56* glow.

130 *Rubens*: Peter Paul Rubens (1577–1640), the great Flemish painter.
139 *her state*: her stateliness. Cf. 397, and *King Victor and King Charles*, 'King Charles',
II. 210.

When first I saw your face a year ago   155
I knew my life's good, my soul heard one voice—
"The woman yonder, there's no use of life
"But just to obtain her! heap earth's woes in one
"And bear them—make a pile of all earth's joys
"And spurn them, as they help or help not this;   160
"Only, obtain her!" How was it to be?
I found you were the cousin of the Queen;
I must then serve the Queen to get to you.
No other way. Suppose there had been one,
And I, by saying prayers to some white star   165
With promise of my body and my soul,
Might gain you,—should I pray the star or no?
Instead, there was the Queen to serve! I served,
Helped, did what other servants failed to do.
Neither she sought nor I declared my end.   170
Her good is hers, my recompense be mine,—
I therefore name you as that recompense.
She dreamed that such a thing could never be?
Let her wake now. She thinks there was more cause
In love of power, high fame, pure loyalty?   175
Perhaps she fancies men wear out their lives
Chasing such shades. Then, I've a fancy too;
I worked because I want you with my soul:
I therefore ask your hand. Let it be now!

    Constance. Had I not loved you from the very first,   180
Were I not yours, could we not steal out thus
So wickedly, so wildly, and so well,
You might become impatient. What's conceived
Of us without here, by the folk within?

160 *1855P–56* not here;   161 *1868–84S* how   162 *1855P–63S* found she
was the   163 *1855P–56* to her—   *1863S* to her.   169 *1855P–56* And did
172 *1855P–56* And let me name   174 *1855P–56* was some cause—   175 *1855P–*
56 The love . . . . power, of fame,   177 *1855P–56* too.   179 *1855P–63S*
now.   183 *1855P–63S* might be thus impatient.   *184 {reading of DC,
BrU, *1889*}   *1855P–88* the folks within?

165 *white star*: propitious star.

Where are you now? immersed in cares of state—   185
Where am I now? intent on festal robes—
We two, embracing under death's spread hand!
What was this thought for, what that scruple of yours
Which broke the council up?—to bring about
One minute's meeting in the corridor!   190
And then the sudden sleights, strange secrecies,
Complots inscrutable, deep telegraphs,
Long-planned chance-meetings, hazards of a look,
"Does she know? does she not know? saved or lost?"
A year of this compression's ecstasy   195
All goes for nothing! you would give this up
For the old way, the open way, the world's,
His way who beats, and his who sells his wife!
What tempts you?—their notorious happiness
Makes you ashamed of ours? The best you'll gain   200
Will be—the Queen grants all that you require,
Concedes the cousin, rids herself of you
And me at once, and gives us ample leave
To live like our five hundred happy friends.
The world will show us with officious hand   205
Our chamber-entry, and stand sentinel
Where we so oft have stolen across its traps!
Get the world's warrant, ring the falcons' feet,

188 *1855P–56* what this scruple   189 *1855P–56* up, to   190 *1855P–56* corridor?
191 *1855P–56* sleights, long secresies,   192 *1855P–56* The plots inscrutable,
196 *1855P–56* nothing?   198 *1855P–56* wife?   200 *1855P–63* That you're
ashamed   *1865, 1868–84S* That you are ashamed   *1855P–56* you'll get
202 *1855P–56* cousin, and gets rid of   203 *1855P–56* And her at   204 *1855P–56*
live as our   207 *1855P–56* When we . . . . across her traps!   208 *1855P–56*
the falcon's foot,

192 *Complots*: as in *Pippa Passes*, iv. 128.
    telegraphs: telegrams. Cf. Tennyson, *The Princess* (1847), Prologue, 77, and
Clough, *Mari Magno* (written 1861), 'The Clergyman's Second Tale', 265.
193 *hazards of a look*: hazardous glances.
195 *this compression's ecstasy*: the ecstasy of being obliged to observe restraint.
Cf. 'Cristina and Monaldeschi' (in *Jocoseria*), l. 4. from end: 'Love burst compression'.
202 *Concedes*: grants (you).
208 *ring the falcons' feet*: oblige the falcons to hawk, i.e. oblige us to love.
Cf. 'Respectability'.

And make it duty to be bold and swift,
Which long ago was nature. Have it so!   210
We never hawked by rights till flung from fist?
Oh, the man's thought! no woman's such a fool.
   Norbert. Yes, the man's thought and my thought, which is
     more—
One made to love you, let the world take note!
Have I done worthy work? be love's the praise,   215
Though hampered by restrictions, barred against
By set forms, blinded by forced secrecies!
Set free my love, and see what love can do
Shown in my life—what work will spring from that!
The world is used to have its business done   220
On other grounds, find great effects produced
For power's sake, fame's sake, motives in men's mouth.
So, good: but let my low ground shame their high!
Truth is the strong thing. Let man's life be true!
And love's the truth of mine. Time prove the rest!   225
I choose to wear you stamped all over me,
Your name upon my forehead and my breast,
You, from the sword's blade to the ribbon's edge,
That men may see, all over, you in me—
That pale loves may die out of their pretence   230
In face of mine, shames thrown on love fall off.
Permit this, Constance! Love has been so long
Subdued in me, eating me through and through,
That now 't is all of me and must have way.
Think of my work, that chaos of intrigues,   235

---

209 *1863S* make that duty   210 *1855P–56* When long ago 'twas nature.   *1863S*
nature: have   211 *1855P–56* He never   *1884S* Hawk never   212 *1884S*
thought;   214 *1855P–63S* note.   217 *1855P–56* secresies.   *1863S* secresies.
218 *1855P* my life, and   *1855P–56* love will do {revised in *Fields*}   · *1863S* can dare
222 *1855P–56* motives you have named.   223 *1855P–63S* good. But   *1855P–56*
high.   226 *1855P–56* to have you   231 *1855P–56* off—   234 *1855P–*
65 now it's all

231 *shames*: imputations of shame.
233 *subdued*: suppressed.

Those hopes and fears, surprises and delays,
That long endeavour, earnest, patient, slow,
Trembling at last to its assured result:
Then think of this revulsion! I resume
Life after death, (it is no less than life,   240
After such long unlovely labouring days)
And liberate to beauty life's great need
O' the beautiful, which, while it prompted work,
Suppressed itself erewhile. This eve's the time,
This eve intense with yon first trembling star   245
We seem to pant and reach; scarce aught between
The earth that rises and the heaven that bends;
All nature self-abandoned, every tree
Flung as it will, pursuing its own thoughts
And fixed so, every flower and every weed,   250
No pride, no shame, no victory, no defeat;
All under God, each measured by itself.
These statues round us stand abrupt, distinct,
The strong in strength, the weak in weakness fixed,
The Muse for ever wedded to her lyre,   255
Nymph to her fawn, and Silence to her rose:
See God's approval on his universe!
Let us do so—aspire to live as these
In harmony with truth, ourselves being true!
Take the first way, and let the second come!   260
My first is to possess myself of you;
The music sets the march-step—forward, then!

239 1855P–63S revulsion.   243 1855P–68 Of the   248 1855P self-
abandoned—even each tree   250 1855P so, each small flower and weed the same,
252 1855P–56. itself!   1863S itself: 253 1855P–63S us, each abrupt,
256 1855P–84S The Nymph . . . . fawn, the Silence   1855P–63S rose   257 1855P–
63S And God's   259 1855P–63S true.   260 1855P–63S come.

245 trembling star: cf. Shelley, The Revolt of Islam, 3002.
248 self-abandoned: as in Cowper, Iliad, xii. 138.
256 Silence to her rose: The rose is a symbol of secrecy. Hence sub rosa, 'in confidence'.
262 the march-step: as a boy, Browning was delighted by a march by Charles Avison:
see Parleyings with Certain People of Importance, VII, and (for the music) DeVane,
Browning's Parleyings, 283.

And there's the Queen, I go to claim you of,
The world to witness, wonder and applaud.
Our flower of life breaks open. No delay!   265
   Constance. And so shall we be ruined, both of us.
Norbert, I know her to the skin and bone:
You do not know her, were not born to it,
To feel what she can see or cannot see.
Love, she is generous,—ay, despite your smile,   270
Generous as you are: for, in that thin frame
Pain-twisted, punctured through and through with cares,
There lived a lavish soul until it starved,
Debarred of healthy food. Look to the soul—
Pity that, stoop to that, ere you begin   275
(The true man's-way) on justice and your rights,
Exactions and acquittance of the past!
Begin so—see what justice she will deal!
We women hate a debt as men a gift.
Suppose her some poor keeper of a school   280
Whose business is to sit thro' summer months
And dole out children leave to go and play,
Herself superior to such lightness—she
In the arm-chair's state and pædagogic pomp—
To the life, the laughter, sun and youth outside: 285
We wonder such a face looks black on us?
I do not bid you wake her tenderness,
(That were vain truly—none is left to wake)

---

*267 {reading of DC, BrU, *1889*} *1855P–63* bone—   *1865–84S* bone: *1888* bone
270 *1855P* generous, despite   271 *1855P* are. Yes, in   *1855–63S* are. For,
273 *1855P* a generous soul   274 *1855P–84S* Debarred all healthy   277 *1855P–*
63S past.   279 *1855P* Men hate a gift as women hate a debt.   282 *1855P–*
63S out children's leave   286 *1855P–63S* such an one looks   288 *1855P–56*
—That . . . . wake—

265 *Our flower of life*: as in l. 458 below, and 'The Statue and the Bust', 105.
   breaks open: blooms.
267 *to the skin and bone*: one of several references to the Queen's poor physique.
272 *pain-twisted*: not in OED^2.
274 *Debarred*: deprived.
277 *acquittance*: settlement.
279 *as men a gift*: proverbial. Cf. ODEP 301b: 'Who receives a gift, sells his liberty.'

But let her think her justice is engaged
To take the shape of tenderness, and mark   290
If she'll not coldly pay its warmest debt!
Does she love me, I ask you? not a whit:
Yet, thinking that her justice was engaged
To help a kinswoman, she took me up—
Did more on that bare ground than other loves   295
Would do on greater argument. For me,
I have no equivalent of such cold kind
To pay her with, but love alone to give
If I give anything. I give her love:
I feel I ought to help her, and I will.   300
So, for her sake, as yours, I tell you twice
That women hate a debt as men a gift.
If I were you, I could obtain this grace—
Could lay the whole I did to love's account,
Nor yet be very false as courtiers go—   305
Declaring my success was recompense;
It would be so, in fact: what were it else?
And then, once loose her generosity,—
Oh, how I see it!—then, were I but you,
To turn it, let it seem to move itself,   310
And make it offer what I really take,
Accepting just, in the poor cousin's hand,
Her value as the next thing to the Queen's—
Since none love Queens directly, none dare that,

---

*289 {reading of DC, BrU, *1889*} *1855P–88* But,   291 *1855P–56* coldly do its
warmest deed!   *1863S–70* warmest need! {revised in PM}   292 *1855P–56* whit.
297 *1855P–63S* of that cold   298 *1855P–56* with; my love   299 *1855P–63S*
love.   303–4 *1855P* I could obtain this favour—I would lay | The whole of what I
304 *1855, 1856* Would lay   306 *1855P–63S* Declare that my   *1884S* Declaring
her success my recompense;   308 *1855P* then, when flows her   *1855–63S* once
loosed her   309 *1855P–56* As you will mark it—   *1863S* it—   *1884S* it! Oh,
were   310 *1863S* it, letting it   311 *1855P–56* it give the thing I
312 *1855P–56* Accepting so, in   313 *1855P–56* All value . . . . the queen—
314 *1855P–56* none loves her directly, none dares that!   *1863S–75* none loves Queens
1863S none dares that!   *1863–75* none dares that,

---

296 *on greater argument*: for a stronger reason.

And a thing's shadow or a name's mere echo   315
Suffices those who miss the name and thing!
You pick up just a ribbon she has worn,
To keep in proof how near her breath you came.
Say, I'm so near I seem a piece of her—
Ask for me that way—(oh, you understand)   320
You'd find the same gift yielded with a grace,
Which, if you make the least show to extort . . .
—You'll see! and when you have ruined both of us,
Dissertate on the Queen's ingratitude!
    Norbert. Then, if I turn it that way, you consent?   325
'T is not my way; I have more hope in truth:
Still, if you won't have truth—why, this indeed,
Were scarcely false, as I'd express the sense.
Will you remain here?
    Constance.   O best heart of mine,
How I have loved you! then, you take my way?   330
Are mine as you have been her minister,
Work out my thought, give it effect for me,
Paint plain my poor conceit and make it serve?
I owe that withered woman everything—
Life, fortune, you, remember! Take my part—   335
Help me to pay her! Stand upon your rights?
You, with my rose, my hands, my heart on you?
Your rights are mine—you have no rights but mine.
    Norbert. Remain here. How you know me!
    Constance.   Ah, but still—
    [*He breaks from her: she remains. Dance-music from*
                                     within.

315 *1855P–63S* A shadow of a thing, a   316 *1855P–63S* thing;   321 *1855P–*
56 And find   325 *1855P* So, if   *1863S* What, if   326 *1855P–63S* truth.
328 *1855P* Is scarcely false, I'll turn it such a way.   *1855, 1856* Is scarcely false, I'll so
express   *1863S* false, I'd so express   {before l. 339, 'SECOND PART.' appears in
1855P–63S}

333 *conceit*: idea.

Enter the QUEEN.

Queen. Constance? She is here as he said. Speak quick!   340
Is it so? Is it true or false? One word!
    Constance. True.
    Queen.   Mercifullest Mother, thanks to thee!
    Constance. Madam?
    Queen.   I love you, Constance, from my soul.
Now say once more, with any words you will,
'T is true, all true, as true as that I speak.   345
    Constance. Why should you doubt it?
    Queen.   Ah, why doubt? why doubt?
Dear, make me see it! Do you see it so?
None see themselves; another sees them best.
You say "why doubt it?"—you see him and me.
It is because the Mother has such grace   350
That if we had but faith—wherein we fail—
Whate'er we yearn for would be granted us;
Yet still we let our whims prescribe despair,
Our fancies thwart and cramp our will and power,
And while accepting life, abjure its use.   355
Constance, I had abjured the hope of love
And being loved, as truly as yon palm
The hope of seeing Egypt from that plot.
    Constance. Heaven!
    Queen.   But it was so, Constance, it was so!
Men say—or do men say it? fancies say—   360
"Stop here, your life is set, you are grown old.
"Too late—no love for you, too late for love—

---

340 *1855P–65* Constance!— . . . . Speak!   341 *1855P–56, 1863, 1865* is it true—
1863S is it true   *1868–84S* word?   343 *1855P–65* Madam!   347 *1855P–*
63S it.   353 *1855P* Howbeit we let such whims   *1855–84S* Howbeit we
354 *1855P* Such very fancies   *1855–84S* Our very fancies   *1855P–84S* will,|
*355 {editors' emendation}   *1855P–56* And so accepting   *1863S–84S* And so,
accepting   *1888, 1889* And while, accepting   *1855P–63S* abjure ourselves!
1863–84S abjure ourselves.   357 *1855P–65* And of being   358 *1855P–63S*
that turf.   359 *1855P–63S* so.

342 *Mother:* Mary.

"Leave love to girls. Be queen: let Constance love."
One takes the hint—half meets it like a child,
Ashamed at any feelings that oppose.   365
"Oh love, true, never think of love again!
"I am a queen: I rule, not love forsooth."
So it goes on; so a face grows like this,
Hair like this hair, poor arms as lean as these,
Till,—nay, it does not end so, I thank God!   370
   Constance. I cannot understand—
   Queen.   The happier you!
Constance, I know not how it is with men:
For women (I am a woman now like you)
There is no good of life but love—but love!
What else looks good, is some shade flung from love;   375
Love gilds it, gives it worth. Be warned by me,
Never you cheat yourself one instant! Love,
Give love, ask only love, and leave the rest!
O Constance, how I love you!
   Constance.   I love you.
   Queen. I do believe that all is come through you.   380
I took you to my heart to keep it warm
When the last chance of love seemed dead in me;
I thought your fresh youth warmed my withered heart.
Oh, I am very old now, am I not?
Not so! it is true and it shall be true!   385
   Constance. Tell it me: let me judge if true or false.
   Queen. Ah, but I fear you! you will look at me
And say, "she's old, she's grown unlovely quite
"Who ne'er was beauteous: men want beauty still."
Well, so I feared—the curse! so I felt sure!   390
   Constance. Be calm. And now you feel not sure, you say?

363 *1855P–70, 1880S, 1884S* love!" *1875* love!'   366 *1855P* Oh, ... of it again!
367 *1855P* love, indeed.   *1855–84S* love, indeed."   372 *1855P–56* men.
377 *1855P–63S* instant.   386 *1855P–63S* me!   387 *1855P–56* you—
389 *1855P–63S* beauteous!   390 *1855P–65, 1884S* sure.

389 *still*: always.

    Queen. Constance, he came,—the coming was not
        strange—
Do not I stand and see men come and go?
I turned a half-look from my pedestal
Where I grow marble—"one young man the more!   395
"He will love some one; that is nought to me:
"What would he with my marble stateliness?"
Yet this seemed somewhat worse than heretofore;
The man more gracious, youthful, like a god,
And I still older, with less flesh to change—   400
We two those dear extremes that long to touch.
It seemed still harder when he first began
To labour at those state-affairs, absorbed
The old way for the old end—interest.
Oh, to live with a thousand beating hearts   405
Around you, swift eyes, serviceable hands,
Professing they've no care but for your cause,
Thought but to help you, love but for yourself,—
And you the marble statue all the time
They praise and point at as preferred to life,   410
Yet leave for the first breathing woman's smile,
First dancer's, gipsy's or street baladine's!
Why, how I have ground my teeth to hear men's speech
Stifled for fear it should alarm my ear,
Their gait subdued lest step should startle me,   415
Their eyes declined, such queendom to respect,
Their hands alert, such treasure to preserve,

---

396 *1855P–63* one,—   403 *1855P–84S* Absorbed to . . . . at the state-affairs|
411 *1855P–84S* woman's cheek,

   393 *and see men come and go*: cf. 103–5, above.
   401 *extremes that long to touch*: 'extremes meet' is proverbial.
   410 *as preferred to life*: cf. 105, above.
   411 *Yet leave*: cf. 'The Last Ride Together', 80–1.
   412 *baladine's*: a *baladine* (Fr.) is a dancer, or street-performer. The word occurs in
Fifine at the Fair, 12, 101, 207.
   416 *declined*: cast down.
    queendom: the position or dignity of a queen, as in EBB, 'Dead Pan', xi.

While not a man of them broke rank and spoke,
Wrote me a vulgar letter all of love,
Or caught my hand and pressed it like a hand!   420
There have been moments, if the sentinel
Lowering his halbert to salute the queen,
Had flung it brutally and clasped my knees,
I would have stooped and kissed him with my soul.
    Constance. Who could have comprehended?
    Queen.   Ay, who—who?   425
Why, no one, Constance, but this one who did.
Not they, not you, not I. Even now perhaps
It comes too late—would you but tell the truth.
    Constance. I wait to tell it.
    Queen.   Well, you see, he came,
Outfaced the others, did a work this year   430
Exceeds in value all was ever done,
You know—it is not I who say it—all
Say it. And so (a second pang and worse)
I grew aware not only of what he did,
But why so wondrously. Oh, never work   435
Like his was done for work's ignoble sake—
Souls need a finer aim to light and lure!
I felt, I saw, he loved—loved somebody.
And Constance, my dear Constance, do you know,
I did believe this while 't was you he loved.   440
    Constance. Me, madam?
    Queen.   It did seem to me, your face
Met him where'er he looked: and whom but you
Was such a man to love? It seemed to me,
You saw he loved you, and approved his love,

---

418 *1855P–56* of these broke   419 *1855P–84S* Or wrote   420 *1855P–65*
hand.   425 *1855P–63S* comprehended!   437 *1855P–63S* It must have finer
aims to spur it on!   *1863–84S* It must have finer aims to lure it on'
443 *1855P–65* it   444 *1855P–84S* approved the love,

---

418 *broke rank*: left his station.
419 *vulgar*: ordinary.
422 *halbert*: a battle-axe mounted on a long handle.

And both of you were in intelligence.   445
You could not loiter in that garden, step
Into this balcony, but I straight was stung
And forced to understand. It seemed so true,
So right, so beautiful, so like you both,
That all this work should have been done by him   450
Not for the vulgar hope of recompense,
But that at last—suppose, some night like this—
Borne on to claim his due reward of me,
He might say "Give her hand and pay me so."
And I (O Constance, you shall love me now!)   455
I thought, surmounting all the bitterness,
—"And he shall have it. I will make her blest,
"My flower of youth, my woman's self that was,
"My happiest woman's self that might have been!
"These two shall have their joy and leave me here." 460
Yes—yes!
    Constance. Thanks!
    Queen.   And the word was on my lips
When he burst in upon me. I looked to hear
A mere calm statement of his just desire
For payment of his labour. When—O heaven,
How can I tell you? lightning on my eyes   465
And thunder in my ears proved that first word
Which told 't was love of me, of me, did all—
He loved me—from the first step to the last,
Loved me!
    Constance. You hardly saw, scarce heard him speak
Of love: what if you should mistake?
    Queen.   No, no—   470

---

445 *1855P–63S* And that you both were   *1863–84S* And so you both were
*{reading of *1855P–84S*, DC, BrU, *1889*}   *1888* intelligence   446 *1855P–84S* in
the garden,   455 *1855P–63S* now)   461 *1855P–65* yes—   463 *1855P*
Such a calm   464 *1855P–63S* In payment   465 *1855P–84S* you? cloud was
on   466 *1855P–84S* ears at that   469 *1855P–84S* You did not hear . . . you
thought he spoke   470 *1855P–84S* love?

---

445 *in intelligence*: in close touch, understanding each other.

No mistake! Ha, there shall be no mistake!
He had not dared to hint the love he felt—
You were my reflex—(how I understood!)
He said you were the ribbon I had worn,
He kissed my hand, he looked into my eyes,   475
And love, love came at end of every phrase.
Love is begun; this much is come to pass:
The rest is easy. Constance, I am yours!
I will learn, I will place my life on you,
Teach me but how to keep what I have won!   480
Am I so old? This hair was early grey;
But joy ere now has brought hair brown again,
And joy will bring the cheek's red back, I feel.
I could sing once too; that was in my youth.
Still, when men paint me, they declare me . . . yes,   485
Beautiful—for the last French painter did!
I know they flatter somewhat; you are frank—
I trust you. How I loved you from the first!
Some queens would hardly seek a cousin out
And set her by their side to take the eye: 490
I must have felt that good would come from you.
I am not generous—like him—like you!
But he is not your lover after all:
It was not you he looked at. Saw you him?
You have not been mistaking words or looks?   495
He said you were the reflex of myself.
And yet he is not such a paragon
To you, to younger women who may choose
Among a thousand Norberts. Speak the truth!
You know you never named his name to me: 500
You know, I cannot give him up—ah God,
Not up now, even to you!

473 *1855P–63S* reflex—how . . . . understood!   474 *1855P*   the   riband   I
476 *1855P–84S* love was the end   477 *1855P–63* pass,   478 *1855P–65*
yours—   480 *1855P–84S* But teach me how   *1855P–65* won.   481 *1855P–*
65 this   496 *1855P–63* myself—

473 *reflex*: reflection.

Constance.   Then calm yourself.

    Queen. See, I am old—look here, you happy girl!
I will not play the fool, deceive—ah, whom?
'T is all gone: put your cheek beside my cheek   505
And what a contrast does the moon behold!
But then I set my life upon one chance,
The last chance and the best—am *I* not left,
My soul, myself? All women love great men
If young or old; it is in all the tales: 510
Young beauties love old poets who can love—
Why should not he, the poems in my soul,
The passionate faith, the pride of sacrifice,
Life-long, death-long? I throw them at his feet.
Who cares to see the fountain's very shape,   515
Whether it be a Triton's or a Nymph's
That pours the foam, makes rainbows all around?
You could not praise indeed the empty conch;
But I'll pour floods of love and hide myself.

---

503 *1855P–75* girl, {revised in PM}   504 *1855P–84S* deceive myself;
506 *1855P–84S* Ah, what   513–14 *1855P–84S* The love, the . . . . faith, the sac-
rifice, | The constancy? I   516 *1855P–84S* And whether

---

507 *I set my life*: as a gambler.

508–9 *am I not left, / My soul, myself?*: asked about this passage by Furnivall, Browning
replied: 'The great obstacle, in the Queen's mind, to the possibility of her awakening
love, in the case of a young and handsome man, is her consciousness of being neither
young nor handsome,—and she seeks for an instance where, in default of these qualities,
the desired effect may be produced all the same. And this applies equally, or even more
forcibly, to the second instance she gives—when driven to an extremity,—that, though
all other attractions fail, men will find them in loving—not youth and beauty—but
soul—phantasy—even that poorest one of *rank*—which she *curses* in recognition of its
being the very poorest': *Trumpeter*, 102. Probably with reference to the simile about 'the
fountain's very shape' [515], he replied (immediately before the passage just quoted): 'all
I can reply is that the simile came in quite naturally and without stoppage of the Queen's
"passionate feeling"—as I conceived the character, at least: depend on it, I never
introduce a simile as an afterthought.'

512 *why should not he*: 'love' understood.

514 *death-long*: not in OED[2].

516 *a Triton's*: Triton, son of Neptune, is generally represented as blowing a
conch-shell.

517 *that pours the foam*: cf. 'Up at a Villa', 26 ff.

519 *But I'll pour*: quoting ll. 509–19, George Eliot italicized this line.

How I will love him! Cannot men love love?   520
Who was a queen and loved a poet once
Humpbacked, a dwarf? ah, women can do that!
Well, but men too; at least, they tell you so.
They love so many women in their youth,
And even in age they all love whom they please;   525
And yet the best of them confide to friends
That 't is not beauty makes the lasting love—
They spend a day with such and tire the next:
They like soul,—well then, they like phantasy,
Novelty even. Let us confess the truth,   530
Horrible though it be, that prejudice,
Prescription . . . curses! they will love a queen.
They will, they do: and will not, does not—he?
    Constance. How can he? You are wedded: 't is a name
We know, but still a bond. Your rank remains,   535
His rank remains. How can he, nobly souled
As you believe and I incline to think,
Aspire to be your favourite, shame and all?
    Queen. Hear her! There, there now—could she love
        like me?
What did I say of smooth-cheeked youth and grace?   540
See all it does or could do! so youth loves!
Oh, tell him, Constance, you could never do
What I will—you, it was not born in! I
Will drive these difficulties far and fast
As yonder mists curdling before the moon.   545
I'll use my light too, gloriously retrieve
My youth from its enforced calamity,

520 *1855P–65* `cannot   523 *1855P–56* too!   532 *1855P–63S* Curses!
533 *1855P–65* do. And   539 *1855P–65* there, there,

520 *How I will love him!*: see 12 n.
521 *loved a poet once*: probably, as Cooke suggested, Paul Scarron was the poet. The youthful Françoise d'Aubigné, the future Mme de Maintenon, married him when he was over forty and had been severely crippled by rheumatism for some ten years.
529 *phantasy*: imagination, imagining.
534 *You are wedded*: we hear nothing of her husband. Cf. 548.
545 *curdling*: coagulating. Cf. Shelley, *Prometheus Unbound*, II. iii. 22–7.

Dissolve that hateful marriage, and be his,
His own in the eyes alike of God and man.
    Constance. You will do—dare do . . . pause on what
        you say!   550
    Queen. Hear her! I thank you, sweet, for that surprise.
You have the fair face: for the soul, see mine!
I have the strong soul: let me teach you, here.
I think I have borne enough and long enough,
And patiently enough, the world remarks,   555
To have my own way now, unblamed by all.
It does so happen (I rejoice for it)
This most unhoped-for issue cuts the knot.
There's not a better way of settling claims
Than this; God sends the accident express: 560
And were it for my subjects' good, no more,
'T were best thus ordered. I am thankful now,
Mute, passive, acquiescent. I receive,
And bless God simply, or should almost fear
To walk so smoothly to my ends at last.   565
Why, how I baffle obstacles, spurn fate!
How strong I am! Could Norbert see me now!
    Constance. Let me consider. It is all too strange.
    Queen. You, Constance, learn of me; do you, like me!
You are young, beautiful: my own, best girl,   570
You will have many lovers, and love one—
Light hair, not hair like Norbert's, to suit yours:
Taller than he is, since yourself are tall.
Love him, like me! Give all away to him;
Think never of yourself; throw by your pride,   575
Hope, fear,—your own good as you saw it once,
And love him simply for his very self.
Remember, I (and what am I to you?)

550 *1855P–56* Pause   557 *1855P–63S* happen, I . . . . it,   567 *1855P–56,*
1863, 1865 could   568 *1880S–84S* consider!   569 *1855P–63S* like me.
572 *1855P–84S* yours,   573 *1855P–84S* And taller   *1855P–56* is, for you are
1863–84S is, for yourself   574 *1863S* me, give . . . . him!   *1855P–56, 1863, 1865* give

560 *express*: on purpose.
578 *to you*: in comparison to you.

Would give up all for one, leave throne, lose life,
Do all but just unlove him! He loves me.   580
   Constance. He shall.
   Queen.   You, step inside my inmost heart!
Give me your own heart: let us have one heart!
I'll come to you for counsel; "this he says,
"This he does; what should this amount to, pray?
"Beseech you, change it into current coin!   585
"Is that worth kisses? Shall I please him there?"
And then we'll speak in turn of you—what else?
Your love, according to your beauty's worth,
For you shall have some noble love, all gold:
Whom choose you? we will get him at your choice.   590
—Constance, I leave you. Just a minute since,
I felt as I must die or be alone
Breathing my soul into an ear like yours:
Now, I would face the world with my new life,
Wear my new crown. I'll walk around the rooms,   595
And then come back and tell you how it feels.
How soon a smile of God can change the world!
How we are made for happiness—how work
Grows play, adversity a winning fight!
True, I have lost so many years: what then?   600
Many remain: God has been very good.
You, stay here! 'T is as different from dreams,
From the mind's cold calm estimate of bliss,
As these stone statues from the flesh and blood.
The comfort thou hast caused mankind, God's moon!   605
   [*She goes out, leaving* CONSTANCE. *Dance-music from within.*

579 *1863S* for love, leave   580 *1855P–56* he   581 *1855P–56, 1863, 1865*
heart.   582 *1855P–56* one heart—   *1863S–65* one heart.   583 *1855P–63S*
"This   584 *1855P–56* does,   585 *1855P–65* coin.   586 *1855P–65* shall
588 *1855P–63S* (according . . . . worth)   593 *1855P–63S* yours.   595 *1855P–
56, 1863–84S* With my   598 *1855P–56* are all made   600 *1855P–65* years.
What   602 *1855P–65* here.   604 *1863S* from live flesh   stage direction
after l. 605 *1855P–56* out. *Dance-music*   {before l. 606 'PART THIRD.' appears
in *1855P–56*, and 'THIRD PART.' in *1863S* }

   605 *God's moon*: apparently Love, which reflects God, as the moon reflects the sun.

NORBERT *enters.*

Norbert. Well? we have but one minute and one word!
Constance. I am yours, Norbert!
Norbert.   Yes, mine.
Constance.   Not till now!
You were mine. Now I give myself to you.
  Norbert. Constance?
  Constance.   Your own! I know the thriftier way
Of giving—haply, 't is the wiser way.   610
Meaning to give a treasure, I might dole
Coin after coin out (each, as that were all,
With a new largess still at each despair)
And force you keep in sight the deed, preserve
Exhaustless till the end my part and yours,   615
My giving and your taking; both our joys
Dying together. Is it the wiser way?
I choose the simpler; I give all at once.
Know what you have to trust to, trade upon!
Use it, abuse it,—anything but think   620
Hereafter, "Had I known she loved me so,
"And what my means, I might have thriven with it."
This is your means. I give you all myself.
  Norbert. I take you and thank God.
  Constance.   Look on through years!
We cannot kiss, a second day like this;   625
Else were this earth no earth.
  Norbert.   With this day's heat
We shall go on through years of cold.
  Constance.   So, best!
—I try to see those years—I think I see.

---

606 *1855P–65* Well!   *1855P–56* word—   *1863S–65* word.   609 *1855P–65*
Constance!   614 *1855P–56* deed, reserve   615 *1880S, 1884S* Exhaustless to
the   616 *1855P–63S* taking,   619 *1855P–56* upon.   620 *1855P–63S*
but say   625 *1855P–63S* this,   627 *1855P–63S* best.

613 *largess*: bounty.
615 *Exhaustless*: unexhausted, inexhaustible.

You walk quick and new warmth comes; you look back
And lay all to the first glow—not sit down   630
For ever brooding on a day like this
While seeing embers whiten and love die.
Yes, love lives best in its effect; and mine,
Full in its own life, yearns to live in yours.
    Norbert. Just so. I take and know you all at once.   635
Your soul is disengaged so easily,
Your face is there, I know you; give me time,
Let me be proud and think you shall know me.
My soul is slower: in a life I roll
The minute out whereto you condense yours—   640
The whole slow circle round you I must move,
To be just you. I look to a long life
To decompose this minute, prove its worth.
'T is the sparks' long succession one by one
Shall show you, in the end, what fire was crammed   645
In that mere stone you struck: how could you know,
If it lay ever unproved in your sight,
As now my heart lies? your own warmth would hide
Its coldness, were it cold.
    Constance.   But how prove, how?
    Norbert. Prove in my life, you ask?
    Constance.   Quick, Norbert—how?   650
    Norbert. That's easy told. I count life just a stuff
To try the soul's strength on, educe the man.
Who keeps one end in view makes all things serve.
As with the body—he who hurls a lance

632 *1855P–84S* seeing the embers   640 *1855P–56* out in which you
646 *1855P–56* struck: you could not know,   648 *Fields* lies:

638 *shall*: note the stress on this word.

643 *decompose*: analyse, open out. Cf. Scott, *The Antiquary*, ch. iv, 4th para. from end: 'to decompose the motives of my worthy friend'.

645 *what fire was crammed*: cf. *Timon of Athens*, I. i. 24–5: 'The fire i' th' flint / Shows not till it be struck'. Cook points out that 'enclosed fire is an image that intrigued Browning': on pp. 264–5 she cites other examples.

651–2 *a stuff: / To try the soul's strength on*: cf. *Sordello*, i. 766–70.

652 *educe*: bring out.

Or heaps up stone on stone, shows strength alike: 655
So must I seize and task all means to prove
And show this soul of mine, you crown as yours,
And justify us both.
    Constance.   Could you write books,
Paint pictures! One sits down in poverty
And writes or paints, with pity for the rich.   660
    Norbert. And loves one's painting and one's writing, then,
And not one's mistress! All is best, believe,
And we best as no other than we are.
We live, and they experiment on life—
Those poets, painters, all who stand aloof   665
To overlook the farther. Let us be
The thing they look at! I might take your face
And write of it and paint it—to what end?
For whom? what pale dictatress in the air
Feeds, smiling sadly, her fine ghost-like form   670
With earth's real blood and breath, the beauteous life
She makes despised for ever? You are mine,
Made for me, not for others in the world,
Nor yet for that which I should call my art,
The cold calm power to see how fair you look.   675
I come to you; I leave you not, to write
Or paint. You are, I am: let Rubens there
Paint us!
    Constance. So, best!
    Norbert.   I understand your soul.
You live, and rightly sympathize with life,
With action, power, success. This way is straight;   680
And time were short beside, to let me change

655 *1855P–84S* alike,   656 *1855P–56, 1863–84S* So I will seize and use all
1863S So will I . . . . and use all   659 *1855P–65* one   661 *1855P–56* writing
too,   667 *1855P–56* take that face   675 *1855P–63S* That cold
677 *1855P–65* am. Let   678 *1855P–65* us.   680 *1855P–63S* success: this . . . .
straight.   681 *1855P–65* And days were

  657 *this soul of mine*: supply 'which'.
  666 *overlook*: see.
  677 *Rubens*: cf. 130. She no doubt points to a picture on the wall.

The craft my childhood learnt: my craft shall serve.
Men set me here to subjugate, enclose,
Manure their barren lives, and force thence fruit
First for themselves, and afterward for me   685
In the due tithe; the task of some one soul,
Through ways of work appointed by the world.
I am not bid create—men see no star
Transfiguring my brow to warrant that—
But find and bind and bring to bear their wills.   690
So I began: to-night sees how I end.
What if it see, too, power's first outbreak here
Amid the warmth, surprise and sympathy,
And instincts of the heart that teach the head?
What if the people have discerned at length   695
The dawn of the next nature, novel brain
Whose will they venture in the place of theirs,
Whose work, they trust, shall find them as novel ways
To untried heights which yet he only sees?
I felt it when you kissed me. See this Queen,   700
This people—in our phrase, this mass of men—
See how the mass lies passive to my hand

---

684 *1855P–84S* force the fruit   686 *1855P–84S* one man,   687 *1855P–56,*
1863 By ways   *1863S* With ways *1855P–84S* by themselves.   688 *1855P–63S*
create, they see   *1863–84S* create—they see   690 *1855P–84S* But bind in one
and carry out their   692 *1855P–84S* too, my first   694 *1855P–56* The
instincts   695 *1855P–56* discerned in me   696 *1855P–84S* nature, the new
man   698 *1855P–56* And whom they trust to find them out new ways   *1863S*
And whom they trust shall find them out new ways *1863–84S* And who, they . . . .
them out new ways   699 *1855P–63S* To the new heights   *1863–84S* To heights
as new which

---

686 *tithe*: share, originally 'The tenth part; the part assigned to the maintenance of
the ministry' (Johnson).

688 *no star*: of genius. Cf. 'Pictor Ignotus', 34–5.

692 *What if it see, too, power's first outbreak here*: in himself, he means: is he the 'the
new man' (l. 696, *1855*) who is to be the leader?

701 *this mass of men*: at the beginning of the first of his lectures *On Heroes,
Hero-Worship and the Heroic in History* Carlyle told his audience that history 'is at bottom
the History of . . . Great Men . . . the leaders of men . . . the modellers, patterns, and in
a wide sense creators, of whatsoever the general mass of men contrived to do or to
attain'. Browning was among his audience. Cf. *Sordello*, i. 468–9; *Luria*, v. 301; 'Bishop
Blougram's Apology', 756.

Now that my hand is plastic, with you by
To make the muscles iron! Oh, an end
Shall crown this issue as this crowns the first!   705
My will be on this people! then, the strain,
The grappling of the potter with his clay,
The long uncertain struggle,—the success
And consummation of the spirit-work,
Some vase shaped to the curl of the god's lip,   710
While rounded fair for human sense to see
The Graces in a dance men recognize
With turbulent applause and laughs of heart!
So triumph ever shall renew itself;
Ever shall end in efforts higher yet,   715
Ever begin . . .

> *Constance.*   I ever helping?
> *Norbert.*   Thus!
>   [*As he embraces her, the* QUEEN *enters.*
> *Constance.* Hist, madam! So have I performed my part.

You see your gratitude's true decency,
Norbert? A little slow in seeing it!
Begin, to end the sooner! What's a kiss?   720

> *Norbert.* Constance?
> *Constance.*   Why, must I teach it you again?

---

703 *1855P–84S* And how my . . . . plastic, and you   705 *1855P–56* first.
709 *1855P–56* In that uprising of   710 *1855P–56* The vase   711 *1855P–84S* for
lower men to   712 *1855P–56* dance they recognise   *1863S–75* dance all recognise
1880S, 1884S dance all recognize   715 *1855P–56* Ever to end   716 *1855P–*
56 Ever begun—   stage direction after l. 716 *1855P–56* her, enter the QUEEN.
717 *1855P–65* madam—so I have performed   *1868–84S* So I have performed
719 *1855P–65* a   720 *1855P–56* Begun to   *1855P–65* sooner.   721 *1855P–*
56, 1863–65 Constance!

---

703 *plastic*: capable of giving shape to.

706 *My will be on this people!*: optative or jussive: 'May my will . . .'

707 *the potter with his clay*: cf. 'Rabbi Ben Ezra', 151 ff.

709 *the spirit-work*: no other example of this compound in OED².

712 *The Graces in a dance*: the three Graces were goddesses of beauty, who spread the joy of Nature in the hearts of men and gods. They are commonly represented as scantily-clad or naked young women, as in Botticelli's 'Birth of Venus'.

718 *your gratitude's true decency*: the appropriate expression of your gratitude. She wishes the Queen to interpret their embrace as no more than this. Cf. l. 755.

You want a witness to your dulness, sir?
What was I saying these ten minutes long?
Then I repeat—when some young handsome man
Like you has acted out a part like yours,   725
Is pleased to fall in love with one beyond,
So very far beyond him, as he says—
So hopelessly in love that but to speak
Would prove him mad,—he thinks judiciously,
And makes some insignificant good soul,   730
Like me, his friend, adviser, confidant,
And very stalking-horse to cover him
In following after what he dares not face.
When his end's gained—(sir, do you understand?)
When she, he dares not face, has loved him first,   735
—May I not say so, madam?—tops his hope,
And overpasses so his wildest dream,
With glad consent of all, and most of her
The confidant who brought the same about—
Why, in the moment when such joy explodes,   740
I do hold that the merest gentleman
Will not start rudely from the stalking-horse,
Dismiss it with a "There, enough of you!"
Forget it, show his back unmannerly:
But like a liberal heart will rather turn   745
And say, "A tingling time of hope was ours;
"Betwixt the fears and falterings, we two lived
"A chanceful time in waiting for the prize:
"The confidant, the Constance, served not ill.
"And though I shall forget her in due time,   750
"Her use being answered now, as reason bids,
"Nay as herself bids from her heart of hearts,—

723 *1863S* minutes since?   733 *1855P–84S* face—   737 *1863S* overpasses
even his   741 *1855P–56* do say that   748 *1855P–56* prize.   749 *1855P*
confidant, I grant too, served   *1855P–56, 1865* ill;   *1863S, 1863* ill!

732 *stalking-horse*: an artificial horse behind which a fowler hid in pursuit of his game,
as in *As You Like It*, v. iv. 100.
736 *tops*: surpasses.
752 *heart of hearts*: cf. *Hamlet*, III. ii. 71.

"Still, she has rights, the first thanks go to her,
"The first good praise goes to the prosperous tool,
"And the first—which is the last—rewarding kiss."   755
  Norbert. Constance, it is a dream—ah, see, you smile!
  Constance. So, now his part being properly performed,
Madam, I turn to you and finish mine
As duly; I do justice in my turn.
Yes, madam, he has loved you—long and well;   760
He could not hope to tell you so—'t was I
Who served to prove your soul accessible,
I led his thoughts on, drew them to their place
When they had wandered else into despair,
And kept love constant toward its natural aim.   765
Enough, my part is played; you stoop half-way
And meet us royally and spare our fears:
'T is like yourself. He thanks you, so do I.
Take him—with my full heart! my work is praised
By what comes of it. Be you happy, both!   770
Yourself—the only one on earth who can—
Do all for him, much more than a mere heart
Which though warm is not useful in its warmth
As the silk vesture of a queen! fold that
Around him gently, tenderly. For him—   775
For him,—he knows his own part!
  Norbert   Have you done?
I take the jest at last. Should I speak now?
Was yours the wager, Constance, foolish child,
Or did you but accept it? Well—at least
You lose by it.
  Constance. Nay, madam, 't is your turn!   780
Restrain him still from speech a little more,
And make him happier as more confident!

755 *1855P–56* last—thankful kiss." 756 *1855P–65* Constance? 762 *1855P–*
63 accessible. 764 *1855P–56* When oft they *1863S–84S* When else they
1855P–84S wandered out into 765 *1863* constant towards its 768 *1855P–*
56 yourself—he 776 *1855P–65* part. 780 *1855P–56* Now madam,
1855P–63S turn. 782 *1855P–84S* happier and more 783 *1855P–63S* yet.

Pity him, madam, he is timid yet!
Mark, Norbert! Do not shrink now! Here I yield
My whole right in you to the Queen, observe!   785
With her go put in practice the great schemes
You teem with, follow the career else closed—
Be all you cannot be except by her!
Behold her!—Madam, say for pity's sake
Anything—frankly say you love him! Else   790
He'll not believe it: there's more earnest in
His fear than you conceive: I know the man!
    Norbert. I know the woman somewhat, and confess
I thought she had jested better: she begins
To overcharge her part. I gravely wait   795
Your pleasure, madam: where is my reward?
    Queen. Norbert, this wild girl (whom I recognize
Scarce more than you do, in her fancy-fit,
Eccentric speech and variable mirth,
Not very wise perhaps and somewhat bold,   800
Yet suitable, the whole night's work being strange)
—May still be right: I may do well to speak
And make authentic what appears a dream
To even myself. For, what she says, is true:
Yes, Norbert—what you spoke just now of love,   805
Devotion, stirred no novel sense in me,
But justified a warmth felt long before.
Yes, from the first—I loved you, I shall say:
Strange! but I do grow stronger, now 't is said.
Your courage helps mine: you did well to speak   810
To-night, the night that crowns your twelvemonths' toil:
But still I had not waited to discern
Your heart so long, believe me! From the first

784 *1855P–65* do   789 *1855P–63S* her.—   790 *1855P–63S* him.
792 *1855–65* man.   802 *1884S* —She may be   804 *1880S, 1884S* is truth.
805 *1855P–65* spoke but now   808 *1855P–63S* say,—   809 *1855P–56* said,
813 *1863, 1865* me.

798 *fancy-fit*: no earlier example in OED².
799 *variable*: fickle.

The source of so much zeal was almost plain,
In absence even of your own words just now   815
Which hazarded the truth. 'T is very strange,
But takes a happy ending—in your love
Which mine meets: be it so! as you chose me,
So I choose you.
     Norbert.   And worthily you choose.
I will not be unworthy your esteem,   820
No, madam. I do love you; I will meet
Your nature, now I know it. This was well.
I see,—you dare and you are justified:
But none had ventured such experiment,
Less versed than you in nobleness of heart,   825
Less confident of finding such in me.
I joy that thus you test me ere you grant
The dearest richest beauteousest and best
Of women to my arms: 't is like yourself.
So—back again into my part's set words—   830
Devotion to the uttermost is yours,
But no, you cannot, madam, even you,
Create in me the love our Constance does.
Or—something truer to the tragic phrase—
Not yon magnolia-bell superb with scent   835
Invites a certain insect—that's myself—
But the small eye-flower nearer to the ground.
I take this lady.
     Constance.   Stay—not hers, the trap—
Stay, Norbert—that mistake were worst of all!

---

816 *1855P–84S* Which opened out the   818 *1855P–56* so—   *1863S–65* so:
1855P–84S you choose me,   819 *1855P–65* choose!   821 *1855P* you,
822 *1855P–63S* it; this   *1855P–56* well,   826 *1855P–63S* finding it in
827 *1855P–56* I like that   829 *1855P–56* arms! . . . . yourself!   837 *1855P–*
56 ground: 838 *1855P–56* lady!   839 *1855P–65* all.

    816 *hazarded*: risked (telling).
    837 *eye-flower*: daisy, i.e. day's eye; cf. Chaucer, Prologue to the *Canterbury Tales*, 332.
Cf. too 'Transcendentalism', 26.

He is too cunning, madam! It was I,   840
I, Norbert, who . . .

 Norbert.   You, was it, Constance? Then,
But for the grace of this divinest hour
Which gives me you, I might not pardon here!
I am the Queen's; she only knows my brain:
She may experiment upon my heart   845
And I instruct her too by the result.
But you, sweet, you who know me, who so long
Have told my heart-beats over, held my life
In those white hands of yours,—it is not well!

 Constance. Tush! I have said it, did I not say it all?   850
The life, for her—the heart-beats, for her sake!

 Norbert. Enough! my cheek grows red, I think. Your test?
There's not the meanest woman in the world,
Not she I least could love in all the world,
Whom, did she love me, had love proved itself,   855
I dare insult as you insult me now.
Constance, I could say, if it must be said,
"Take back the soul you offer, I keep mine!"
But—"Take the soul still quivering on your hand,
"The soul so offered, which I cannot use,   860
"And, please you, give it to some playful friend,
"For—what's the trifle he requites me with?"
I, tempt a woman, to amuse a man,
That two may mock her heart if it succumb?
No: fearing God and standing 'neath his heaven,   865
I would not dare insult a woman so,
Were she the meanest woman in the world,

---

840 *1855P–56* (He . . . . madam!) it   *1863S* (He . . . . madam!)   843 *1855P–63S*
I should not   *1855P–65* here.   845 *1855P–84S* experiment therefore on my 846
1855P–63S result;   852 *1855P–63S* test!   855 *1855P–84S* me, did love prove
itself,   856 *1855P–75* I dared insult   858 *1855P–56, 1863, 1865* mine"
1863S mine:"   861 *1855P–56* some friend of mine,   865 *1855P–65* No!

---

848 *told*: counted.

858 *"Take back the soul*: I could imagine myself rejecting a woman's love, but never
telling her to offer it to 'some friend'.

865 *fearing*: reverencing, as in Ps. 103: 13, etc.

And he, I cared to please, ten emperors!
    Constance. Norbert!
    Norbert.   I love once as I live but once.
What case is this to think or talk about?   870
I love you. Would it mend the case at all
If such a step as this killed love in me?
Your part were done: account to God for it!
But mine—could murdered love get up again,
And kneel to whom you please to designate,   875
And make you mirth? It is too horrible.
You did not know this, Constance? now you know
That body and soul have each one life, but one:
And here's my love, here, living, at your feet.
    Constance. See the Queen! Norbert—this one more
           last word—   880
If thus you have taken jest for earnest—thus
Loved me in earnest . . .
    Norbert.   Ah, no jest holds here!
Where is the laughter in which jests break up,
And what this horror that grows palpable?
Madam—why grasp you thus the balcony?   885
Have I done ill? Have I not spoken truth?
How could I other? Was it not your test,
To try me, what my love for Constance meant?
Madam, your royal soul itself approves,
The first, that I should choose thus! so one takes   890
A beggar,—asks him, what would buy his child?
And then approves the expected laugh of scorn
Returned as something noble from the rags.
Speak, Constance, I'm the beggar! Ha, what's this?
You two glare each at each like panthers now.   895

---

872 *1855P–84S* Should such . . . . this kill love   873 *1855P–65* it.   875 *1855P–*
63 you pleased to   883 *1870–84S* which jest breaks up,   *1855P–56* up? {revised
in *Fields*}   886 *1855P–75* spoken the truth?   888 *1855P–75* me, and what
891 *1855P–65* child,

---

876 *And make you mirth*: to entertain you.
885 *Madam*: addressed to the Queen.

Constance, the world fades; only you stand there!
You did not, in to-night's wild whirl of things,
Sell me—your soul of souls, for any price?
No—no—'t is easy to believe in you!
Was it your love's mad trial to o'ertop   900
Mine by this vain self-sacrifice? well, still—
Though I might curse, I love you. I am love
And cannot change: love's self is at your feet!

                              [*The* QUEEN *goes out.*

   Constance. Feel my heart; let it die against your own!
   Norbert. Against my own. Explain not; let this be!   905
This is life's height.
   Constance.   Yours, yours, yours!
   Norbert.   You and I—
Why care by what meanders we are here
I' the centre of the labyrinth? Men have died
Trying to find this place, which we have found.
   Constance. Found, found!
   Norbert.   Sweet, never fear what she can do!   910
We are past harm now.
   Constance.   On the breast of God.
I thought of men—as if you were a man.
Tempting him with a crown!
   Norbert.   This must end here:
It is too perfect.
   Constance.   There's the music stopped.
What measured heavy tread? It is one blaze   915
About me and within me.
   Norbert.   Oh, some death
Will run its sudden finger round this spark

899 *1855P–65* you.   902 *1855P–84S* I should curse,   903 *1855P–63S*
change!   *1855P–65* feet.   stage direction after l. 903 · *1855P–56* [QUEEN
904 *1855P–56* own.   905 *1855P–65* own! explain . . . . be.   906 *1855P–65*
Yours! Yours! Yours!   908 *1855P–68* In the   *1855P–65* men   909 *1855P–
63S* place out, which   910 *1855P–63S* do—   914 *1855P–65* perfect!
915 *1855P–56, 1863, 1865* it

907 *meanders*: winding ways.

> And sever us from the rest!
> *Constance.*   And so do well.
> Now the doors open.
> *Norbert.*   'T is the guard comes.
> *Constance.*   Kiss!

918 *1855P–65* rest—   919 *1855P–65* open—*{reading of *1855P–84S*, BrU, *1889*}
1888 {some copies} Kiss

919 *Kiss!*: it is natural to suppose that the guard comes to lead the lovers away to the death of one or both of them. Such is the conclusion of most critics, including Elmer E. Stoll in *From Shakespeare to Joyce* (New York 1944, repr. in Drew). But when, in the last decade of his life, Browning read 'In a Balcony' aloud for a few friends, 'as full of dramatic interest . . . as if he had just written it', he demurred when one of those present 'said that it was a natural sequence that the step of the guard should be heard coming to take Norbert to his doom, as, with a nature like the queen's, who had known only one hour of joy in her sterile life, vengeance swift and terrible would follow on the sudden destruction of her happiness':

> 'Now, I don't quite think that', answered Browning, as if he were following out the play as a spectator. 'The queen had a large and passionate temperament, which had only once been touched and brought into intense life. She would have died, as by a knife in her heart. The guard would have come to carry away her dead body.'
> 'But I imagine that most people interpret it as I do', was the reply.
> 'Then', said Browning, with quick interest, 'don't you think it would be as well to put it in the stage directions, and have it seen that they were carrying her across the back of the stage?'
> Whether this was ever done I do not know; but it was wonderful to me, as showing the personal interest he took in his own creations.

See Meredith, 154–5. One may recall Browning's uncertainty (in retrospect) about the meaning of 'Then all smiles stopped together' in 'My Last Duchess': see Vol. III, pp. 187–8 n.

SAUL

ON 3 May 1845 Browning mentioned to Elizabeth Barrett 'a certain "Saul" I should like to show you one day', describing it as 'one of my Dramatic Romances'.[1] On the twenty-third she enquired about it; but it was not until three months later that he took her the manuscript of the uncompleted poem. He was obviously uncertain about it, but she replied at once:

your 'Saul' is unobjectionable as far as I can see . . . He was tormented by an evil spirit—but how, we are not told . . & the consolation is not obliged to be definite . . is it? A singer was sent for as a singer—& all that you are called upon to be true to, are the general characteristics of David the chosen, standing between his sheep & his dawning hereafter, between innocence & holiness, & with what you speak of as the 'gracious gold locks' besides the chrism of the prophet, on his own head—and surely you have been happy in the tone & spirit of these lyrics . . broken as you have left them. Where is the wrong in all this? For the right & beauty, they are more obvious—& I cannot tell you how the poem holds me & will not let me go until it blesses me . . & so, where are the 'sixty lines' thrown away?[2] I do beseech you . . you who forget nothing, . . to remember them directly, & to go on with the rest . . *as* directly (be it understood) as is not injurious to your health. The whole conception of the poem, I like . . & the execution is exquisite up to this point—& the sight of Saul in the tent, just struck out of the dark by that sunbeam, "a thing to see," . . not to say that afterwards when he is visibly 'caught in his pangs' like the king serpent, . . the sight is grander still. How could you doubt about this poem.

Browning commented that she had been 'lenient'.[3] A few days later, anxious about his health, she suggested that he might publish, in his next *Bell*, only the poems which were complete and required no retouching: he could put 'Saul' aside, meanwhile. From a letter which she wrote about 29 October, however, we learn that he had decided to publish it as it stood. She suggested that it might be wise 'to print it in the meanwhile as a fragment confessed . . sowing asterisks at the end. Because as a poem of yours it stands there & wants unity, and people can't be expected to

---

[1] Kintner, i. 55, followed by i. 173. The first part of this introduction is a revision of that to the original 'Saul', as published in 1845 and printed in Vol. IV in this edition.

[2] Since Browning now uses long verse, the 'sixty lines' become thirty or just over thirty, from l. 97 to the first seven words of l. 127.

[3] Ibid., 177, 185, 252, 315, 508.

understand the difference between incompleteness & defect, unless you make a sign'. 'Saul' is 'noble & must have his full royalty some day'.

On 9 December, a month after the publication of the pamphlet, she told him of the profound impression the poem had made on John Kenyon, insisting that 'the next parts must certainly follow & complete what will be a great lyrical work—now remember'. On 2 March 1846 she told him that Kenyon earnestly hoped that he would complete it, 'which you ought to do', she added, '. . must do—*only not now*', the final words a reminder of her continuing worry about his health. In fact he did not return to 'Saul' until the early 1850s.

The source is the First Book of Samuel. There we read that when the Israelites wanted a king, God told Samuel to anoint Saul.[1] When Saul proved disobedient by sparing Agag when he made war against his people, God was angry, and ordered Saul to anoint Jesse's youngest son, David, who was to be the chosen one. In 1 Samuel 16: 13 ff we hear how 'the Spirit of the Lord came upon David from that day forward', but 'departed from Saul':

And Saul's servants said unto him, Behold now, an evil spirit from God troubleth thee.

Let our lord now command thy servants which are before thee, to seek out a man, who is a cunning player on an harp: and it shall come to pass, when the evil spirit from God is upon thee, that he shall play with his hand, and thou shalt be well . . .

And David came to Saul, and stood before him: and he loved him greatly; and he became his armour-bearer . . .

And it came to pass, when the evil spirit from God was upon Saul, that David took an harp, and played with his hand: so Saul was refreshed, and was well, and the evil spirit departed from him.

This passage will have been familiar to Browning from a very early age, and must have assumed a particular importance for him because of the passion for music which once led him to say, 'when I was nine years old I should have been very indignant if you had told me that I was going to be anything else than a musician'.[2] It is not surprising that several of his most remarkable poems should deal with the power of music.

Apart from the passage in 1 Samuel, a number of other possible influences have been suggested; they are so numerous, indeed, that most of them remain no more than possibilities. As DeVane pointed out, it is likely

---

[1] 1 Sam. 9: 17; 16: 12.   [2] Maynard, 140.

that Smart's preface to his *Ode for Musick on St Cecilia's Day* had remained in Browning's memory:

It would not be right to conclude, without taking notice of a fine subject for an Ode on S. Cecilia's Day, which was suggested to the Author by his friend the learned and ingenious Mr. Comber . . . that is David's playing to King Saul when he was troubled with the evil Spirit. He was much pleased with the hint at first, but at length was deterred from improving it by the greatness of the subject, and he thinks not without reason. The chusing too high subjects has been the ruin of many a tolerable Genius.[1]

In the first part of 'Saul', as published in 1845, as in the completed poem, David (who has been sent for at Saul's bidding) describes the tunes which he played to him to relieve his depression: that which he was in the habit of playing to his sheep at the close of the day, those which attracted quails, crickets, and jerboas, 'the help-tune of our reapers', elegy, marriage-song, and battle-song; and finally the chorus which accompanied the Levites as they approached the altar. This brings him to the threshold of religion. He sings of the natural delights of living, and ends with praise of Saul himself, the mighty monarch.

We do not know why the poem was left at this point for several years. Like Christopher Smart, Browning may have been 'deterred . . . by the greatness of the subject'. He may simply have been tired, with so much other work in hand at a time when he was engaged in a slow and difficult courtship. The encouraging and perceptive comments of Elizabeth make it clear that he had originally been uncertain how to describe Saul's mental torment, and what consolation was to be provided by David. Some critics have suggested that he was held up by religious doubts. While that is conceivable, the poem is (after all) a dramatic one, the speaker being 'an imaginary person',[2] like the speakers in *Christmas-Eve and Easter-Day*, a fact too little regarded by critics who regarded it as a straightforward affirmation of the poet's own faith.

The thirty lines which succeed the original 'Part the First' no doubt derive from those which Browning told Elizabeth that he had 'thrown away'. In them we hear that Saul has been moved by David's songs, and is now 'released and aware'; yet he says nothing, and still appears despondent. So

---

[1] *The Poems of Christopher Smart*, 2 vols. (Reading, 1791), i. [40]. The third of Browning's *Colloquies with Certain People of Importance* is addressed to Smart.

[2] *Handbook*, 179, on *Christmas-Eve and Easter-Day*.

far David has offered him 'the wine of this life': what 'vintage more potent
and perfect' can he now provide?

Remembering vague thoughts that had come to him earlier in his life,
David begins to play again, moving from the natural life to spiritual
reflections. He bids Saul consider the value his existence will have for
Israel after his own death. Is he not the 'first of the mighty', as the first
King of Israel (and therefore, in a sense, the forerunner of Christ)? As he
sings in this higher strain, with supernatural prompting, Saul responds by
resuming 'His old motions and habitudes kingly'. When David tells him
of the praise which will be his in later history, Saul lays his hand on David's
brow. David feels a profound love for Saul, and wishes that he could give
him 'new life altogether'. As the truth dawns on him, that there is life after
death, he lays his harp aside, and simply speaks. After all the troubles of
this existence, he tells Saul, he will be received by

> A Face like my face . . . a Man like to me,
> Thou shalt love and be loved by, for ever: a Hand like this hand
> Shall throw open the gates of new life to thee! See the Christ Stand!

As he goes home, David reflects on the wonders of the night.

Whether he knew it by 1845, or came on it in the years between his
writing the first part of the poem and completing it, it is tempting to
conjecture that Browning had read *A Dissertation on . . . Poetry and Music,
To which is prefixed, The Cure of Saul. A Sacred Ode*, by Dr John Brown, a
work published in the same year as Smart's *Ode for Musick*.[1] Here is the
beginning of the Argument of Brown's Ode:

---

[1] See W. L. Phelps, 'Dr John Brown, The Cure for Saul': MLN 24 (1909), 162 ff.
DeVane is misleading in his description of the Ode. Other possible influences on
'Saul' have been adduced. In Vol. IV, p. 155, we have mentioned that it is tempting
to suppose that Browning knew the English translation of Herder's *Vom Geist der
ebräischen Poesie*, in which '*David in the presence of Saul*' is mentioned as a subject
which has attracted several poets, with a further statement (which amounts to a
recommendation to future writers) that so far none has 'yet stolen the harp of David,
and produced a poem, such even as Dryden's ode . . . where Timotheus plays before
Alexander': Vol. II, p. 197 of James Marsh's translation. Carlyle's enthusiasm for Herder
renders this the more likely. Another suggestion is that of A. S. Cook, mentioned
in Porter and Clarke, iv. 374–5: that the tunes played by David and described in ll. 36
ff. owe something to the Greek romance by Longus, *Daphnis and Chloe*, ii. 35 and 13.
iv. 15.

In 'The Shaping of Saul': JEGP 44 (1945), 360–6, J. A. S. McPeek argued for the
influence of Sir Thomas Wyatt's *Seven Penitential Psalms*, a case which seems to us to
stop short of the convincing. Griffin and Minchin state (p. 129) that Browning knew
Alfieri's drama, *Saulle*, but its influence has not been proved. Other possibilities are

SAUL, for his Disobedience to Heaven, is afflicted with the Fiend of MELAN-CHOLY. DAVID is sent for, to cure him by the Power of Music. He comes, attended with a Choir of Shepherds; and, as the means of dispelling SAUL's Despair, he sings the Creation of the World, and the happy Estate of our First Parents in Paradise. SAUL is moved by the Representation; but expostulates with DAVID, 'why, when others are happy, He should be miserable'.

At this point David, 'to convince him that Guilt is the Source of Misery, sings the Fall of Man, and his Expulsion from Paradise'. On Saul becoming angry David 'awakens his Conscience, and terrifies him, by singing the Fate and Punishment of Guilt':

SAUL, struck with Horror, attempts to kill himself. But being prevented by his Friends, DAVID sooths his Anguish, by invoking Repentance and divine Mercy to compose his Passions. SAUL relents into virtuous Sorrow. But his Despair return-ing, DAVID calls on his attendant Choir to raise a more sublime and affecting Strain. This hath its Effect; and SAUL melts into Tears of Penitence. DAVID now comforts him with the Return of the divine Favour. To banish the Remains of Pride, he then sings his own Happiness in the humble Station of a Shepherd. Still farther to compose the Monarch's Griefs, by a Strain of soft Music he throws him into a gentle Slumber; invoking celestial Visions to transport him to the Regions of the Blessed, and change his Anguish into Joy. The desired Effects appear in his Countenance: The Fiend departs: And SAUL awakes in perfect Tranquillity. DAVID then concludes with a Song of Triumph on the Powers of Harmony, and the seraphic Hymn that attended her, as the Minister of Heaven, on the Creation of the World.

Whether or not Browning knew Brown's *Sacred Ode*, a comparison of the two poems is illuminating. In Browning's poem David comes to Saul alone, not with 'a Choir of Shepherds'. Saul does not expostulate about his own misery, nor does David awaken his conscience. Although 'Saul' is indeed an illustration of 'the Powers of Harmony', its conclusion is much more than 'A Song of Triumph'. Instead of complaining, becoming angry, terrified, attempting suicide and the rest, Saul hardly stirs throughout, and utters only three words, 'It is good.' In the greater part of the poem, sections iv–xviii, he is the silent listener found in so many of Browning's pieces. His near-immobility and virtual silence are deeply impressive. By paring down the matter provided by the biblical account to the minimum and rejecting all that is unnecessary to his purpose Browning gives the poem its unity.

canvassed by H. W. Yocom, 'Some Additional Sources of Browning's "Saul" ': NQ, 26 July, 1941.

Several critics have remarked that 'Saul' is not a 'dramatic monologue', sometimes in a tone of complaint.[1] But Browning seems never to have used that term, and his poems defy any such over-simplifying formula. As mentioned above, he insisted that his poems were 'dramatic', and 'Saul' is dramatic. That it contains a marked element of narrative does not cut it off from many other of his dramatic poems, any more than does its element of discourse. David is characterized sufficiently in the opening and closing sections. In Saul he has a virtually silent listener and beyond Saul (we may guess) a body of listeners to whom he knows his story will be of momentous religious importance. Browning did not classify the piece as one of his 'Men and Women' poems, in *1863*: it does not belong in the same category as 'Fra Lippo Lippi' or 'Andrea del Sarto'. In his letter he had called it a 'Dramatic Romance', but in the end he classified it as a 'Dramatic Lyric'.

It is a spiritual lyric, an ode, with the marked element of narrative which is often found in this high kind. Light is thrown on its style by Robert Lowth's *De sacri poesi Hebraeorum praelectiones*, first published in 1753 and more than once reprinted in Latin before the English translation by G. Gregory in 1787, a famous book which a man with Browning's deep interest in Hebraic matters is almost certain to have known. Lectures V–XI are particularly relevant. In the summary of VI, for example, we read that

The frequent use of the Metaphor renders a style magnificent, but often obscure: the Hebrew poets have accomplished the sublime without losing perspicuity . . . the imagery which they introduce is in general derived from familiar objects: again, in the use and accomodation of it they pursue a certain custom and analogy: lastly, they make the most free use of that which is most familiar[2]

—a comment which may be considered in relation (for example) to sections v–ix of Browning's poem. Lowth includes in his survey 'Poetic Imagery from Sacred Topics' and 'from Sacred History', as well as considering 'Mystical Allegory' in a chapter which may serve as a comment on 'Saul' as a whole:

The third species of Allegory, which also prevails much in the prophetic poetry, [occurs] when a double meaning is couched under the same words; or when the same production, according as it is differently interpreted, relates to different events, distant in time, and distinct in their nature . . . In the sacred rites of the Hebrews, things, places, times, offices, and such like, sustain as it were a double

---

[1] e.g. Roma A. King, *The Bow and the Lyre: The Art of Robert Browning* (Ann Arbor, Mich., 1957), 103. For the first use of 'monologue dramatique', see p. xxvin above.

[2] *Lectures on the Sacred Poetry of the Hebrews* (1787), 120.

character, the one proper or literal, the other allegorical; and in their writings these
subjects are sometimes treated of in such a manner, as to relate either to the one
sense or the other singly, or to both united. For instance, a composition may treat
of David, of Solomon, of Jerusalem, so as to be understood to relate simply either
to the city itself and its monarchs, or else to those objects, which, in the sacred
allegory of the Jewish religion, are denoted by that city and by those monarchs: or
the mind of the author may embrace both objects at once, so that the very words
which express the one in the plain, proper, historical, and commonly- received
sense, may typify the other in the sacred, interior, and prophetic sense.[1]

Typology, the study of symbolic representation in Scripture, in this case as
forming a link between Jews and Christians, is essential to the under-
standing of 'Saul'. Browning knew that David was taken as a type of
Christ. In Ward Hellstrom's words, 'The climax . . . David's vision of
Christ', is 'the logical and necessary climax toward which the whole poem
moves'.[2]

Although Part the First was printed in short verse in *Dramatic Romances
and Lyrics* in 1845, and is reprinted in that form in our Vol. IV, it is
conceivable that it had originally been written in long verse and was
revised because the format of the *Bells and Pomegranates* pamphlets, with
their double columns, could not accomodate the longer lines.[3] From *1855*
the poem consists of pentameters rhyming in pairs which are longer than
most iambic pentameters because the predominant foot is the anapaest.
The first foot of a line is sometimes disyllabic. A recent critic has pointed
out the metrical similarity of 'Saul' in short verse and 'The Englishman in
Italy', which appeared in the same collection.[4]

In an unusually hostile critique, Roma King complained that the metre
leads to 'a plethora of words beyond those necessary to convey the
argument directly and convincingly',[5] but such an objection questions
the very nature of the poem. In this high ode Browning is remembering
the chorus of Greek tragedy and the style of the Psalms of David. The use
of repetition, as in l. 2, is biblical, as is the very frequent use of 'And',
which opens a line on thirty-six occasions. The transition from one

[1] Ibid. 236.
[2] 'Time and Type in Browning's *Saul*': ELH 33 (1966), 375.
[3] This hypothesis may be weakened, however, by the fact that the long lines are too
long for the typesetting of the poem in *Men and Women*, too. Lines 291 and 292 are the
exceptions.
[4] Daniel Karlin, 'The Sources of "The Englishman in Italy" ': BSN, Winter 1984/5,
29–30.
[5] *The Bow and the Lyre*, 113. An occasional stylistic lapse is undoubted, however, e.g.
in ll. 257–60.

section to another is sometimes effected by splitting a line. There is usually a caesura after the third foot, or in the course of the fourth.

Sharp places the poem among those written in Rome, between late November 1853 and late May 1854.[1]

Date: 1854 (incorporating material from 1845)
1863: Dramatic Lyrics

SAUL.

I.

SAID Abner, "At last thou art come! Ere I tell, ere thou speak,
"Kiss my cheek, wish me well!" Then I wished it, and did
    kiss his cheek.
And he, "Since the King, O my friend, for thy countenance
    sent,
"Neither drunken nor eaten have we; nor until from his tent
"Thou return with the joyful assurance the King liveth yet,   5
"Shall our lip with the honey be bright, with the water be
    wet.
"For out of the black mid-tent's silence, a space of three days,

---

{In *1845* ll. 1–96 appear as *'Part the First'* (see note to l. 96 below), in alternating lines of three and two stresses, 192 in all; the individual sections are not numbered. This arrangement is retained in *1849*, but in *1855P* and subsequent texts the completed poem appears in lines of five stresses, with individual sections numbered.}   2 *1845, 1849* cheek: 4 *1845, 1849* Nor drunken   6 *1845, 1849* be brightened, |—The 7 {new section in *1845, 1849*}

---

1 *Abner*: the captain of Saul's host: 1 Sam. 14: 50. Here he is addressing David.

3 *countenance*: cf. Acts 2: 28: 'thou shalt make me full of joy with thy countenance'. David was 'of a beautiful countenance, and goodly to look to': 1 Sam. 16: 12.

7 *three days*: 'Saul here suggests Christ in the tomb, in the same way, for example, that Jonah was thought to prefigure Christ: "For as Jonas was three days and three nights in the whale's belly; so shall the Son of man be three days and three nights in the heart of the earth" (Mat. 12: 40). Such a suggestion is reinforced when we learn that during Saul's absence the faithful have fasted . . . as the Christian does during the Lenten season. Also, while in the tent Saul has wrestled with the evil spirit as Christ during his entombment descended to Hell and defeated the devil. Saul remains Saul, but he typifies Christ': Hellstrom, 376.

---

[1] *Life*, pp. 166–7.

"Not a sound hath escaped to thy servants, of prayer nor of
  praise,
"To betoken that Saul and the Spirit have ended their strife,
"And that, faint in his triumph, the monarch sinks back
  upon life.   10

II.

"Yet now my heart leaps, O beloved! God's child with his
  dew
"On thy gracious gold hair, and those lilies still living and
  blue
"Just broken to twine round thy harp-strings, as if no wild
  heat
"Were now raging to torture the desert!"

III.

                              Then I, as was meet,
Knelt down to the God of my fathers, and rose on my feet,   15
And ran o'er the sand burnt to powder. The tent was
  unlooped;
I pulled up the spear that obstructed, and under I stooped;
Hands and knees on the slippery grass-patch, all withered
  and gone,

---

8 *1845, 1849* No sound *1855P–63* prayer or of   9 *1845* Have gone their dread
ways.   10 {does not appear in *1845*}   13 *1845, 1849* As thou brak'st them to
14   *1845, 1849* Were raging {no new section in *1845, 1849*}   18 *1845, 1849*
knees o'er the

11 *God's child*: in the Bible good men are sometimes called the children of God. In
1 Sam. 16: 13 we hear how Samuel anointed David, 'and the Spirit of the Lord came
upon [him] from that day forward'.
    his dew: cf. Ps. 110: 3: 'thou hast the dew of thy youth'.
12 *blue*: Mrs Sara Coleridge wrote to John Kenyon 'to enquire whether [Browning]
had authority for the "blue lilies" . . rather than white': Kintner, i. 508. When EBB
asked Browning, he replied: 'lilies are of all colours in Palestine—one sort is particu-
larized as *white* with a dark blue spot and streak—the water lily, lotos, which I think I
meant, is *blue* altogether' 539. EBB reassured Kenyon. Cf. Thomas Moore's note to a
line in *Lalla Rookh*, where he glosses 'Blue water-lilies' as 'The blue lotos, which grows
in Cashmere and in Persia': *Poetical Works* 10 vols. (1840–1), vi. 81 n.
13 *as if no wild heat*: cf. 35.
15 *God of my fathers*: Deut. 1: 21 etc.

That extends to the second enclosure, I groped my way on
Till I felt where the foldskirts fly open. Then once more I
　　prayed,　　　　　　　　　　　　　　　　　　　　　　20
And opened the foldskirts and entered, and was not afraid
But spoke, "Here is David, thy servant!" And no voice
　　replied.
At the first I saw nought but the blackness; but soon I
　　descried
A something more black than the blackness—the vast, the
　　upright
Main prop which sustains the pavilion: and slow into sight　　25
Grew a figure against it, gigantic and blackest of all.
Then a sunbeam, that burst thro' the tent-roof, showed Saul.

IV.

He stood as erect as that tent-prop, both arms stretched out
　　wide
On the great cross-support in the centre, that goes to each
　　side;
He relaxed not a muscle, but hung there as, caught in his
　　pangs　　　　　　　　　　　　　　　　　　　　　　30
And waiting his change, the king-serpent all heavily hangs,

19 *1845, 1849* That leads to　　20 *1845, 1849* open;　　21 *1845, 1849* afraid;
22 *1845, 1849* And spoke, ... replied.　　23 *1845, 1849* And first　　25 *1845,
1849* pavilion,—　　26 *1845, 1849* figure, gigantic, against it, | And　　*1845–56*
all;— *1863S, 1863* all:　　28 *1845–65* tent-prop;　　30 *1845, 1849* So he bent not

19 *the second enclosure*: Hellstrom points out that before the building of the temple by
David's son Solomon, the tabernacle of the Israelites was a tent (Exod. 40: 2) tripartite
in structure.

20 *foldskirts*: OED² has no other example. Ruskin objected to 'skirts'—'as tremen-
dous a long monosyllable as any in the language,'—at the end of a dactyl. '*Fold-skirts*
not a trochee?', Browning replied. 'A spondee possible in English? Two of the "longest
monosyllables" continuing to be each of the old length when in junction?' See
DeLaura, 'Ruskin and the Brownings', 326, and Collingwood, i. 201.

26 *gigantic*: see 1 Sam. 9: 2.

28 *both arms*: a type of the Crucifixion. Hellstrom, 378, remarks that it is significant
that the cruciform figure 'should be in the Holy of Holies, . . . for the Ark of the
Covenant, which was a type of the cross, was kept in the Holy of Holies'.

31 *the king-serpent*: a serpent may be an emblem of good (as in *Queen Mab*), or of
Christ crucified. Cf. John, 3: 14: 'And as Moses lifted up the serpent in the wilderness,

Far away from his kind, in the pine, till deliverance come
With the spring-time,—so agonized Saul, drear and stark,
  blind and dumb.

V.

Then I tuned my harp,—took off the lilies we twine round
  its chords
Lest they snap 'neath the stress of the noontide—those
  sunbeams like swords!   35
And I first played the tune all our sheep know, as, one after
  one,
So docile they come to the pen-door till folding be done.
They are white and untorn by the bushes, for lo, they have fed
Where the long grasses stifle the water within the stream's bed;
And now one after one seeks its lodging, as star follows star   40
Into eve and the blue far above us,—so blue and so far!

VI.

—Then the tune, for which quails on the cornland will
  each leave his mate
To fly after the player; then, what makes the crickets elate
Till for boldness they fight one another: and then, what has
  weight
To set the quick jerboa a-musing outside his sand house—   45

---

33 *1845* and black, blind   37 *1855P* Very docile   *1845* done   *1849* done;
40 *1845, 1849* How one   42 *1845, 1849* Will leave each his   43 *1845, 1849*
To follow the

---

even so must the Son of man be lifted up'. There was a widespread belief that a serpent
could renew itself, as it renews its skin.

33 *stark*: incapable of movement.
34 *chords*: 'The string[s] of a musical instrument': Johnson.
36 *our sheep*: cf. 1 Sam. 16: 11.
37 *folding*: as in 'Love among the Ruins', 51.
37 *So docile*: cf. textual notes. Browning revised 'So docile' (*1845*) to 'Very docile' in proof,
to have an anapaest, but reverted to *1845*, on Kenyon's suggestion: see Peterson, 28–9.
42 *the tune*: Browning was interested in the methods by which quails were captured;
cf. 'The Englishman in Italy', 35.
45 *jerboa*: a small rodent found in the deserts of Africa, which is a great jumper.

There are none such as he for a wonder, half bird and half
    mouse!
God made all the creatures and gave them our love and our
    fear,
To give sign, we and they are his children, one family here.

VII.

Then I played the help-tune of our reapers, their wine-
    song, when hand
Grasps at hand, eye lights eye in good friendship, and great
    hearts expand   50
And grow one in the sense of this world's life.—And then,
    the last song
When the dead man is praised on his journey—"Bear, bear
    him along
"With his few faults shut up like dead flowerets! Are balm-
    seeds not here
"To console us? The land has none left such as he on the
    bier.
"Oh, would we might keep thee, my brother!"—And then,
    the glad chaunt   55
Of the marriage,—first go the young maidens, next, she
    whom we vaunt
As the beauty, the pride of our dwelling.—And then, the
    great march
Wherein man runs to man to assist him and buttress an
    arch
Nought can break; who shall harm them, our friends?—
    Then, the chorus intoned

48 *1845, 1849* To show, we   50 *1845, 1849* Grasps hand,   51 *1845, 1849* life;
.... the low song   53 *1845, 1849* flowrets;   *1855P–65* are   54 *1845* has
got none such   1849 land is left none such   *1845, 1849* bier—   57 *1845, 1849*
dwelling: 58 *1845, 1849* When man   59 *1845* our brothers?

49 *help-tune*: no other example in OED².
    51 *the last song*: cf. the funeral procession of Eglamor in *Sordello*, ii. 169 ff., and 'A
Grammarian's Funeral'.
    53 *balm-seeds*: seeds of comfort.

As the Levites go up to the altar in glory enthroned.   60
But I stopped here: for here in the darkness Saul groaned.

VIII.

And I paused, held my breath in such silence, and listened
    apart;
And the tent shook, for mighty Saul shuddered: and
    sparkles 'gan dart
From the jewels that woke in his turban, at once with a
    start,
All its lordly male-sapphires, and rubies courageous at heart.   65
So the head: but the body still moved not, still hung there
    erect.
And I bent once again to my playing, pursued it unchecked,
As I sang,—

IX.

    "Oh, our manhood's prime vigour! No spirit
    feels waste,
"Not a muscle is stopped in its playing nor sinew unbraced.
"Oh, the wild joys of living! the leaping from rock up to
    rock,   70
"The strong rending of boughs from the fir-tree, the cool
    silver shock
"Of the plunge in a pool's living water, the hunt of the bear,

---

60 *1845, 1849* enthroned—   *1855P–56* enthroned . . .   61 *1845* groaned:
62 *1845, 1849* silence!   *1855P* apart,   63 *1845–63S* shuddered,—   65 *1845*
All the lordly   *1845, 1849* heart;   66 *1845* head,   68 {no new section in
1845, 1849}   *1855P–65* no   69 *1845* No muscle . . . . playing | No sinew
unbraced,—   *1849* No muscle . . . . playing, | No sinew unbraced;—   70 *1845,*
1849 And the . . . . The   71 *1845, 1849* The rending their boughs . . . . the palm-
trees,—| The   72 *1845, 1849* Of a plunge in the pool's   *1849* The haunt of

    60 *Levites*: priests' assistants.

    64 *woke*: cf. Shelley, *Adonais*, 256.

    65 *male-sapphires*: 'male' is applied to precious stones 'on account of depth, brilliance
or other accident of colour': OED².

        courageous: i.e. dark red.

    72 *living water*: as in John 4: 10 (where it is metaphorical, however); cf. Song of
Solomon, 4: 15.

"And the sultriness showing the lion is couched in his lair.
"And the meal, the rich dates yellowed over with gold dust
    divine,
"And the locust-flesh steeped in the pitcher, the full
    draught of wine,   75
"And the sleep in the dried river-channel where bulrushes tell
"That the water was wont to go warbling so softly and well.
"How good is man's life, the mere living! how fit to employ
"All the heart and the soul and the senses for ever in joy!
"Hast thou loved the white locks of thy father, whose
    sword thou didst guard   80
"When he trusted thee forth with the armies, for glorious
    reward?
"Didst thou see the thin hands of thy mother, held up as
    men sung
"The low song of the nearly-departed, and hear her faint
    tongue
"Joining in while it could to the witness, 'Let one more
    attest,
" 'I have lived, seen God's hand thro' a lifetime, and all was
    for best'?   85
"Then they sung thro' their tears in strong triumph, not
    much, but the rest.
"And thy brothers, the help and the contest, the working
    whence grew
"Such result as, from seething grape-bundles, the spirit
    strained true:

73 *1845, 1849* lair: 75 *1845–65* the locust's-flesh steeped   *1855P–56* pitcher;
1863S, 1863 pitcher!   76 *1845, 1849* Where tall rushes tell   77 *1845, 1849*
The water . . . . well,—   78 *1845, 1849* life here, mere   79 *1845, 1849* The
heart   81 *1845, 1849* forth to the wolf hunt | For   82 *1884S* thou kiss the
83 *1845, 1849* The song . . . . And heard her   *1855P–63* and heard her   85 *1845,
1849* thro' that life-time,   *1845–55P, 1856* best . . ."   *1855* best . . .'   *1863S–84S*
best!'   86 *1845, 1849* rest!   88 *1845* spirit so true—   *1849* spirit so true:
1855P–65 true!

75 *locust-flesh*: perhaps the fruit of the carob-tree, *Ceratonia siliqua*. Some suppose this
to have been the 'locusts' eaten by John the Baptist: Matt. 3: 4.
85 *God's hand*: Ps. 104: 28. 'His providential bounty and goodness': Cruden.
87 *working*: ferment.

"And the friends of thy boyhood—that boyhood of wonder
    and hope,
"Present promise and wealth of the future beyond the eye's
    scope,—   90
"Till lo, thou art grown to a monarch; a people is thine;
"And all gifts, which the world offers singly, on one head
    combine!
"On one head, all the beauty and strength, love and rage
    (like the throe
"That, a-work in the rock, helps its labour and lets the gold
    go)
"High ambition and deeds·which surpass it, fame crowning
    them,—all   95
"Brought to blaze on the head of one creature—King Saul!"

X.

And lo, with that leap of my spirit,—heart, hand, harp and
    voice,
Each lifting Saul's name out of sorrow, each bidding rejoice
Saul's fame in the light it was made for—as when, dare I say,
The Lord's army, in rapture of service, strains through its array,   100
And upsoareth the cherubim-chariot—"Saul!" cried I, and
    stopped,

89 *1845, 1849* boyhood | With wonder   90 *1845* And the promise   *1845, 1849*
wealth in the future,— | The eye's eagle scope,—   91 *1845, 1849* monarch,
*{reading of *1855P–72S*, *1889*} *1845, 1849* thine!   *1884S* thine: *1888* hine;
92 *1845* Oh all, all the   *1849* Oh all gifts the   *1845, 1849* combine,   93 *1845,
1849* head the joy and the pride, | Even rage like   *1855P–56* rage, like   *1863S* rage
like   94 *1845, 1849* That opes the .... its glad labour, ... go—   *1855P–63* go:
95 *1845* And ambition that sees a sun lead it | Oh, all of these—all   *1849* And
ambition that sees a sun lead it— | Oh, all of these—all   *1855P–56, 1863* crowning
it,—all   *1863S* crowning it—all   96 *1845, 1849* Combine to unite in one
creature |—Saul! {in *1845* and *1849* the following appears after l. 96:} *1845* (*End of Part
the First.*) *1849* END OF PART THE FIRST.

93 *throe*: cf. *Colombe's Birthday*, v. 111: 'an earthquake's throe'.

99 *the light*: as distinct from the darkness, literal and figurative, in which David had
found him.

100 *The Lord's army*: cf. 1 Sam. 17: 45.
    strains: with effort.

101 *the cherubim-chariot*: cf. Ezek. 10: 3 ff.

And waited the thing that should follow. Then Saul, who
    hung propped
By the tent's cross-support in the centre, was struck by his
    name.
Have ye seen when Spring's arrowy summons goes right to
    the aim,
And some mountain, the last to withstand her, that held (he
    alone,   105
While the vale laughed in freedom and flowers) on a broad
    bust of stone
A year's snow bound about for a breastplate,—leaves grasp
    of the sheet?
Fold on fold all at once it crowds thunderously down to his
    feet,
And there fronts you, stark, black, but alive yet, your
    mountain of old,
With his rents, the successive bequeathings of ages untold—   110
Yea, each harm got in fighting your battles, each furrow
    and scar
Of his head thrust 'twixt you and the tempest—all hail,
    there they are!
—Now again to be softened with verdure, again hold the
    nest
Of the dove, tempt the goat and its young to the green on
    his crest
For their food in the ardours of summer. One long shudder
    thrilled   115
All the tent till the very air tingled, then sank and was stilled
At the King's self left standing before me, released and
    aware.

114 *1855P–63* on its crest   115 *1855P–65* summer!   116 *1863S* then sunk and

    106 *the vale laughed*: cf. Wordsworth, *The Prelude*, iv. 326: 'The sea lay laughing at a distance'.
    107 *leaves grasp*: lets go.
    108 *crowds thunderously*: cf. Keats, *Hyperion*, ii. 8: 'thunderous waterfalls and torrents hoarse'.
    109 *stark*: immobile.

What was gone, what remained? All to traverse, 'twixt hope
    and despair;
Death was past, life not come: so he waited. Awhile his
    right hand
Held the brow, helped the eyes left too vacant forthwith to
    remand   120
To their place what new objects should enter: 't was Saul as
    before.
I looked up and dared gaze at those eyes, nor was hurt any
    more
Than by slow pallid sunsets in autumn, ye watch from the
    shore,
At their sad level gaze o'er the ocean—a sun's slow decline
Over hills which, resolved in stern silence, o'erlap and
    entwine   125
Base with base to knit strength more intensely: so, arm
    folded arm
O'er the chest whose slow heavings subsided.

XI.

                          What spell or what charm,
(For, awhile there was trouble within me) what next should
    I urge
To sustain him where song had restored him?—Song filled
    to the verge
His cup with the wine of this life, pressing all that it yields   130
Of mere fruitage, the strength and the beauty: beyond, on
    what fields,
Glean a vintage more potent and perfect to brighten the eye

118 *1855P–65* all   *1868, 1872S, 1884S* despair.   *1870, 1875* despair,   122 *1884S*
up, dared   126 *1855P–56, 1863, 1865* more intense: so,   *1863S* more intense: so
1855P–65 folded in arm   129 *1863S* Song fills to   131 *1855P–65* beauty!
Beyond,

118 *All to traverse*: i.e. a long journey.
120 *remand*: call back.
130 *the wine of this life*: cf. *Macbeth*, II. iii. 93: 'the wine of life'.

And bring blood to the lip, and commend them the cup
    they put by?
He saith, "It is good;" still he drinks not: he lets me praise
    life,
Gives assent, yet would die for his own part.

XII.

Then fancies grew rife   135
Which had come long ago on the pasture, when round me
    the sheep
Fed in silence—above, the one eagle wheeled slow as in
    sleep;
And I lay in my hollow and mused on the world that might
    lie
'Neath his ken, though I saw but the strip 'twixt the hill
    and the sky:
And I laughed—"Since my days are ordained to be passed
    with my flocks,   140
"Let me people at least, with my fancies, the plains and the
    rocks,
"Dream the life I am never to mix with, and image the show
"Of mankind as they live in those fashions I hardly shall
    know!
"Schemes of life, its best rules and right uses, the courage
    that gains,
"And the prudence that keeps what men strive for."
And now these old trains   145

---

133 *1884S* Bring blood   136 *1855P* I had sought long   *1855P–63* the pastures,
when   137 *1855P–63S* sleep,   139 *1872S, 1884S* sky.   143 *1884S*
know—   145 *1884S* for!"

---

133 *the cup they put by*: cf. ll. 159, 175; and Ps. 116: 13: 'I will take the cup of
salvation'. There is a reference to the wine of the Eucharist.

137 *the . . . eagle wheeled*: cf. Wordsworth, *Descriptive Sketches* (1843), 276.

139 *his ken*: the eagle's field of sight.

141 *Let me people*: cf. Wordsworth, *The Prelude*, i. 546: 'Peopled the mind with forms
sublime or fair'.

142 *image*: imagine.

Of vague thought came again; I grew surer; so, once more
    the string
Of my harp made response to my spirit, as thus—

XIII.

                                    "Yea, my King,"
I began—"thou dost well in rejecting mere comforts that
    spring
"From the mere mortal life held in common by man and by
    brute:
"In our flesh grows the branch of this life, in our soul it
    bears fruit.   150
"Thou hast marked the slow rise of the tree,—how its stem
    trembled first
"Till it passed the kid's lip, the stag's antler; then safely
    outburst
"The fan-branches all round; and thou mindest when these
    too, in turn
"Broke a-bloom and the palm-tree seemed perfect: yet
    more was to learn,
"E'en the good that comes in with the palm-fruit. Our
    dates shall we slight,   155
"When their juice brings a cure for all sorrow? or care for
    the plight

---

153 *1855P–56, 1863–68* thou mindedst when   154 *1855P* palm-tree stood perfect;
155 *1855P* Even the   *1855–65* Ev'n the

146 *vague thought*: a Wordsworthian phrase: see, e.g., 'The White Doe of Rylstone',
325; *The Excursion*, ii. 174 and vii. 941.

150 *the branch of this life*: 'As David moves forward in his narrative, his vision expands
and the imagery more and more suggests . . . the vision of St. John, particularly that of
Revelation . . . The image of the tree to suggest the development through the imper-
fect towards the perfect . . . is a commonplace in Christian writing': Hellstrom, 383.

152 *outburst*: 'rare', OED², but not so in Browning.

153 *fan-branches*: branches spread out like a fan. Cf. 'fan-like' shoots in 'A Forest
Thought', 22: see Vol. I, p. 542.

154 *a-bloom*: no earlier example in OED².

156 *a cure for all sorrow*: an intoxicating liquor is made from the fermented sap of the
date-tree.

"Of the palm's self whose slow growth produced them?
  Not so! stem and branch
"Shall decay, nor be known in their place, while the palm-
  wine shall staunch
"Every wound of man's spirit in winter. I pour thee such
  wine.
"Leave the flesh to the fate it was fit for! the spirit be thine!   160
"By the spirit, when age shall o'ercome thee, thou still shalt
  enjoy
"More indeed, than at first when inconscious, the life of a
  boy.
"Crush that life, and behold its wine running! Each deed
  thou hast done
"Dies, revives, goes to work in the world; until e'en as the
  sun
"Looking down on the earth, though clouds spoil him,
  though tempests efface,   165
"Can find nothing his own deed produced not, must
  everywhere trace
"The results of his past summer-prime,—so, each ray of thy
  will,
"Every flash of thy passion and prowess, long over, shall
  thrill
"Thy whole people, the countless, with ardour, till they too
  give forth
"A like cheer to their sons, who in turn, fill the South and
  the North   170
"With the radiance thy deed was the germ of. Carouse in
  the past!
"But the license of age has its limit; thou diest at last:
"As the lion when age dims his eyeball, the rose at her height,

159 *1855P* wine!   163 *1855P–65* each   167 *1855P* summer-prime:
170 *1872S, 1884S* sons: 171 *1855P–56* past.   172 *1855P–63S, 1872S, 1884S*
last.   *173 {reading of *1855P–84S*, DC, BrU} *1888* heigh   *1889* height

162 *inconscious*: Browning sometimes used this older form: see EBB's comment on
Luria, i. 358.

"So with man—so his power and his beauty for ever take
    flight.
"No! Again a long draught of my soul-wine! Look forth
    o'er the years!   175
"Thou hast done now with eyes for the actual; begin with
    the seer's!
"Is Saul dead? In the depth of the vale make his tomb—bid
    arise
"A grey mountain of marble heaped four-square, till, built
    to the skies,
"Let it mark where the great First King slumbers: whose
    fame would ye know?
"Up above see the rock's naked face, where the record shall
    go   180
"In great characters cut by the scribe,—Such was Saul, so
    he did;
"With the sages directing the work, by the populace chid,—
"For not half, they'll affirm, is comprised there! Which fault
    to amend,
"In the grove with his kind grows the cedar, whereon they
    shall spend
"(See, in tablets 't is level before them) their praise, and
    record   185
"With the gold of the graver, Saul's story,—the statesman's
    great word
"Side by side with the poet's sweet comment. The river's
    a-wave
"With smooth paper-reeds grazing each other when
    prophet-winds rave:

175 _1855P–65_ again   _1855P_ of the spirit! look   _1855–65_ look   _1855P–65_ years—
177 _1855P–65_ in   178 _1855P–63S_ skies.

  175 _soul-wine_: spiritual wine.
  177 _Is Saul dead?_: i.e. when you die.
  179 _the great First King_: of Israel.
  187 _a-wave_: the only other example in OED² is from EBB, 'An Island', st. vi (_Poems_,
  2 vols., 1850, ii. 183).
  188 _paper-reeds_: papyri, the source of the writing material of the ancients.
      prophet-winds: not in OED². Prophetic winds.

"So the pen gives unborn generations their due and their
    part
"In thy being! Then, first of the mighty, thank God that
    thou art!"   190

XIV.

And behold while I sang . . . but O Thou who didst grant
    me that day,
And before it not seldom hast granted thy help to essay,
Carry on and complete an adventure,—my shield and my
    sword
In that act where my soul was thy servant, thy word was
    my word,—
Still be with me, who then at the summit of human
    endeavour   195
And scaling the highest, man's thought could, gazed
    hopeless as ever
On the new stretch of heaven above me—till, mighty to
    save,
Just one lift of thy hand cleared that distance—God's throne
    from man's grave!
Let me tell out my tale to its ending—my voice to my heart
Which can scarce dare believe in what marvels last night I
    took part,   200
As this morning I gather the fragments, alone with my
    sheep,
And still fear lest the terrible glory evanish like sleep!

190 *1863S* being.   *1855P–56* art."   191 *1855P–65* But   192 *1884S*
seldom has granted   195 *1884S* Still help me,   *1855P* who reaching the
196 *1855P* thought can, gazed   200 *1884S* Which scarce dares believe   *1855P–*
56 marvels that night   201 *1872S, 1884S* sheep!   202 *1884S* And fear
1872S, 1884S sleep,

    191 *Thou*: God.
    193 *my shield and my sword*: cf. Deut. 33: 29: 'Happy art thou, O Israel: who is like
unto thee, O people saved by the Lord, the shield of thy help, and who is the sword of
thy excellency!'
    202 *evanish*: the verb occurs in Burns ('Tam o'Shanter', 66), in Tennyson ('Song',
'The lintwhite . . .', 15, in *Poems Chiefly Lyrical*, 1830) and elsewhere in Browning, e.g.
in the Epilogue to *Dramatis Personæ*, 53.

For I wake in the grey dewy covert, while Hebron upheaves
The dawn struggling with night on his shoulder, and
   Kidron retrieves
Slow the damage of yesterday's sunshine.

XV.

I say then,—my song   205
While I sang thus, assuring the monarch, and ever more
   strong
Made a proffer of good to console him—he slowly resumed
His old motions and habitudes kingly. The right-hand
   replumed
His black locks to their wonted composure, adjusted the
   swathes
Of his turban, and see—the huge sweat that his
   countenance bathes,   210
He wipes off with the robe; and he girds now his loins as of
   yore,
And feels slow for the armlets of price, with the clasp set
   before.
He is Saul, ye remember in glory,—ere error had bent
The broad brow from the daily communion; and still,
   though much spent

---

204 *1884S* Dawn

203 *Hebron*: a place SW of Jerusalem, on a mountain. It was the headquarters of David's early rule.

204 *Kidron*: 'the brook Cedron' (John 18: 1), which is dry 'not only in summer, but often in winter, though a storm speedily turns it into a torrent' (Hadow).

204–5 *retrieves / Slow the damage*: cf. Horace, *Odes*, IV. vii. 13: 'Damna tamen celeres reparant caelestia lunæ': 'Yet the swiftly-changing moons repair their losses in the sky'.

206 *assuring*: reassuring.

208 *replumed*: rearranged.

211 *girds . . . his loins*: a common biblical phrase: e.g. 1 Kgs. 18: 46.

212 *of price*: very valuable, as in *2 Henry IV*, V. iii. 95.

213 *error*: Saul had been rebuked by Samuel for disobeying God's law (1 Sam. 15; 16 ff).

214 *the daily communion*: with God.
    spent: worn, diminished.

Be the life and the bearing that front you, the same, God
    did choose,   215
To receive what a man may waste, desecrate, never quite
    lose.
So sank he along by the tent-prop till, stayed by the pile
Of his armour and war-cloak and garments, he leaned there
    awhile,
And sat out my singing,—one arm round the tent-prop, to
    raise
His bent head, and the other hung slack—till I touched on
    the praise   220
I foresaw from all men in all time, to the man patient there;
And thus ended, the harp falling forward. Then first I was
    'ware
That he sat, as I say, with my head just above his vast knees
Which were thrust out on each side around me, like oak-
    roots which please
To encircle a lamb when it slumbers. I looked up to know   225
If the best I could do had brought solace: he spoke not, but
    slow
Lifted up the hand slack at his side, till he laid it with care
Soft and grave, but in mild settled will, on my brow: thro'
    my hair
The large fingers were pushed, and he bent back my head,
    with kind power—
All my face back, intent to peruse it, as men do a flower.   230
Thus held he me there with his great eyes that scrutinized
    mine—
And oh, all my heart how it loved him! but where was the
    sign?

217 *1872S, 1884S* tent-prop, still, stayed   219 *1855P–63* And so sat
221 *1855P–63* all times, to   *1855P–63S* there,   226 *1863S* solace. He
230 *1856* flower,

   215 *that front you*: which are before you.
   217 *stayed*: supported.
   223 *his vast knees*: in 1 Sam. 9: 2 we read that 'from his shoulders and upward' Saul
'was higher than any of the people'.

I yearned—"Could I help thee, my father, inventing a bliss,
"I would add, to that life of the past, both the future and this;
"I would give thee new life altogether, as good, ages hence,   235
"As this moment,—had love but the warrant, love's heart to
        dispense!"

XVI.

Then the truth came upon me. No harp more—no song
        more! outbroke—

XVII.

"I have gone the whole round of creation: I saw and I
        spoke:
"I, a work of God's hand for that purpose, received in my
        brain
"And pronounced on the rest of his handwork—returned
        him again   240
"His creation's approval or censure: I spoke as I saw:
"I report, as a man may of God's work—all's love, yet all's
        law.
"Now I lay down the judgeship he lent me. Each faculty
        tasked
"To perceive him, has gained an abyss, where a dew-drop
        was asked.

234 *1855P–56* this.   *1863S* this!   238 *1855P–65* spoke!   241 *1855P–75*
saw. *1884S* saw,   242 *1884S* "Reported, as man   *1855P–65* law!

237 *No harp more—no song more!*: Elizabeth Bieman comments that some critics have
complained about the unexplained disappearance of Saul from the poem at this point,
and accounts for it thus: 'The Old-Testament power-figure cannot inherit the New-
Testament world explicitly, for the narratives in *Samuel* leave it very clear that David's
ministrations do not save his king in the long run — and that figure of kingship . . .
passes from the Biblical scene long before the King of kings is crowned with thorns':
'The ongoing Testament in Browning's *Saul*', UTQ 43 (1973–4), 164.
        No harp more: from now on David speaks, prophetically.
238 *the whole round of creation*: cf. Carlyle, *Sartor Resartus*, I. iv: para. vii: 'this great
terrestrial and celestial Round'.
239 *work*: creation.
243 *the judgeship*: the right of judging.
244 *an abyss*: an emptiness.

"Have I knowledge? confounded it shrivels at Wisdom laid
    bare. 245
"Have I forethought? how purblind, how blank, to the
    Infinite Care!
"Do I task any faculty highest, to image success?
"I but open my eyes,—and perfection, no more and no less,
"In the kind I imagined, full-fronts me, and God is seen
    God
"In the star, in the stone, in the flesh, in the soul and the
    clod. 250
"And thus looking within and around me, I ever renew
"(With that stoop of the soul which in bending upraises it
    too)
"The submission of man's nothing-perfect to God's
    all-complete,
"As by each new obeisance in spirit, I climb to his feet.
"Yet with all this abounding experience, this deity known, 255
"I shall dare to discover some province, some gift of my
    own.
"There's a faculty pleasant to exercise, hard to hood-wink,
"I am fain to keep still in abeyance, (I laugh as I think)
"Lest, insisting to claim and parade in it, wot ye, I worst
"E'en the Giver in one gift.—Behold, I could love if I durst! 260
"But I sink the pretension as fearing a man may o'ertake
"God's own speed in the one way of love: I abstain for
    love's sake.
"—What, my soul? see thus far and no farther? when doors
    great and small,

254 *1855P–65* feet!   257 *1855P–63S* There's one faculty   260 *1855P–65*
Behold!   262 *1855P–63S* sake!

       a dew-drop: cf. *The Ring and the Book*, viii. 695: 'One dew-drop comfort to
humanity'.

246 *to*: compared with.
249 *full-fronts me*: cf. 215 n.
254 *obeisance*: cf. Fr. obéir. Action or sign of obedience. Cf. 'stoop of the soul'.
259 *wot ye*: you know (arch. and Biblical).
261 *sink*: repress, set aside.

"Nine-and-ninety flew ope at our touch, should the
    hundredth appal?
"In the least things have faith, yet distrust in the greatest of
    all?   265
"Do I find love so full in my nature, God's ultimate gift,
"That I doubt his own love can compete with it? Here, the
    parts shift?
"Here, the creature surpass the Creator,—the end, what
    Began?
"Would I fain in my impotent yearning do all for this man,
"And dare doubt he alone shall not help him, who yet
    alone can?   270
"Would it ever have entered my mind, the bare will, much
    less power,
"To bestow on this Saul what I sang of, the marvellous
    dower
"Of the life he was gifted and filled with? to make such a
    soul,
"Such a body, and then such an earth for insphering the
    whole?
"And doth it not enter my mind (as my warm tears attest)   275
"These good things being given, to go on, and give one
    more, the best?
"Ay, to save and redeem and restore him, maintain at the
    height
"This perfection,—succeed with life's dayspring, death's
    minute of night?
"Interpose at the difficult minute, snatch Saul the mistake,
"Saul the failure, the ruin he seems now,—and bid him
    awake   280

---

267 *1855P–65* here,   269 *1863S* all this for man,   278 *1884S* night:

267 *parts*: roles.
274 *such an earth for insphering the whole*: cf. EBB, 'Adequacy' (in *Poems*, 1850, i. 6–8):
'the clear / Strong stars . . . insphere / Our habitation'.
276 *one more, the best*: immortality ('one' is stressed).
278 *succeed with life's dayspring*: follow the brief night of death with renewed life.
280 *Saul the failure*: cf. 213 n.

"From the dream, the probation, the prelude, to find
   himself set
"Clear and safe in new light and new life,—a new harmony
   yet
"To be run, and continued, and ended—who knows?—or
   endure!
"The man taught enough, by life's dream, of the rest to
   make sure;
"By the pain-throb, triumphantly winning intensified bliss,   285
"And the next world's reward and repose, by the struggles
   in this.

XVIII.

"I believe it! 'T is thou, God, that givest, 't is I who receive:
"In the first is the last, in thy will is my power to believe.
"All's one gift: thou canst grant it moreover, as prompt to
   my prayer
"As I breathe out this breath, as I open these arms to the air.   290
"From thy will, stream the worlds, life and nature, thy
   dread Sabaoth:
"*I* will?—the mere atoms despise me! Why am I not loth
"To look that, even that in the face too? Why is it I dare
"Think but lightly of such impuissance? What stops my
   despair?

---

*284 {reading of DC, BrU, *1889*} *1855P–88* enough by *1855P–56* sure.
286 *1855P–56* the struggle in   287 *1855P–63* 'tis Thou,   *1865* 't is Thou,
292 *1855P* I will,—   *1855P–63S* me! and why . . . . I loth   *1863, 1865* why
293 *1855P–65* why   294 *1855P–65* what

281 *the probation*: 'human life . . . is a state of probation': Paley, Sermon xxxiii.
282 *a new harmony*: cf. 'Abt Vogler', 84.
291 *Sabaoth*: 'an *Hebrew* word that signifies *Hosts* or *Armies. Jehova Sabaoth, The Lord of hosts*, Rom. 9: 29. Whose host all creatures are, whether the host of heaven, or the angels and ministers of the Lord; or the stars and planets, which are as an army ranged in battle-array, and performing the will of God; or the people of the Lord, both of the Old and New Testament, which is truly the army of the Lord, of which God is the General and Commander': Cruden. The word occurs at Rom. 9: 29 and Jas. 5: 4, and is not to be confused with 'Sabbath'. Cruden's *Concordance* is the only book, apart from two Bibles, that Browning's mother is known to have given him. See Kelley and Coley, A 736.
294 *impuissance*: four syllables, with stresses on the first and third, as in 'Cherries', 55, and 'A Pillar at Sebzevar', 140, and EBB, *Aurora Leigh*, ix. 469.

"This;—'t is not what man Does which exalts him, but
   what man Would do!   295

"See the King—I would help him but cannot, the wishes
   fall through.

"Could I wrestle to raise him from sorrow, grow poor to
   enrich,

"To fill up his life, starve my own out, I would—knowing
   which,

"I know that my service is perfect. Oh, speak through me
   now!

"Would I suffer for him that I love? So wouldst thou—so
   wilt thou!   300

"So shall crown thee the topmost, ineffablest, uttermost
   crown—

"And thy love fill infinitude wholly, nor leave up nor down

"One spot for the creature to stand in! It is by no breath,

"Turn of eye, wave of hand, that salvation joins issue with
   death!

"As thy Love is discovered almighty, almighty be proved   305

"Thy power, that exists with and for it, of being Beloved!

"He who did most, shall bear most; the strongest shall stand
   the most weak.

" 'T is the weakness in strength, that I cry for! my flesh, that
   I seek

"In the Godhead! I seek and I find it. O Saul, it shall be

"A Face like my face that receives thee; a Man like to me,   310

---

295 *1855P* does . . . . would   300 *1855P–63S* So wilt Thou—

    295 *what man Would do*: aspiration is one of the main themes of Browning's poetry,
from *Pauline* and *Paracelsus* onwards.

    296 *the wishes fall through*: come to nothing.

    301 *ineffablest*: cf. 'Abt Vogler', ll. 7 and 65: 'the ineffable Name'.

    303 *the creature*: cf. 2 Cor. 5: 17: 'Therefore if any man be in Christ, he is a new
creature: old things are passed away; behold, all things are become new.'

    307 *He who did most, shall bear most*: cf. *King Lear*, v. iii. 325.

    308 *the weakness in strength*: cf. 2 Cor. 12: 9: 'my strength is made perfect in weakness'.

    310 *A Face like my face*: cf. the end of the Epilogue to *Dramatis Personæ*, 'That one
Face, far from vanish, rather grows, / Or decomposes but to recompose, / Become my
universe that feels and knows'.

"Thou shalt love and be loved by, for ever: a Hand like this
　　hand
"Shall throw open the gates of new life to thee! See the
　　Christ stand!"

XIX.

I know not too well how I found my way home in the
　　night.
There were witnesses, cohorts about me, to left and to right,
Angels, powers, the unuttered, unseen, the alive, the aware:　　315
I repressed, I got through them as hardly, as strugglingly
　　there,
As a runner beset by the populace famished for news—
Life or death. The whole earth was awakened, hell loosed
　　with her crews;
And the stars of night beat with emotion, and tingled and
　　shot
Out in fire the strong pain of pent knowledge: but I fainted
　　not,　　320
For the Hand still impelled me at once and supported,
　　suppressed
All the tumult, and quenched it with quiet, and holy behest,
Till the rapture was shut in itself, and the earth sank to rest.

---

311 *1856* forever!　　*1855P, 1855, 1863S* ever!　　312 *1863S* the new gates of life
320 *1855P–56* not.

312 *the Christ*: 'The Messiah or "Lord's Anointed" whose advent was the subject of
Jewish prophecy and expectation': OED², which points out that in the Geneva and
1611 versions of the NT 'the Christ' is often the form.
314 *There were witnesses*: cf. Hebr. 12: 1: 'we also are compassed about with so great
a cloud of witnesses'.
315 *Angels, powers*: cf. Rom. 8: 37–9. See too *Paradise Lost*, x. 34–5.
316 *repressed*: held back.
　　as hardly: with as much difficulty.
　　strugglingly: the only occurrence of the word in OED², after the sixteenth
century, is in Poe, *The Narrative of Arthur Gordon Pym*, ch. xxii, para. 8. In 1845 Poe had
dedicated *The Raven and Other Poems* to EBB, so Browning may well have read the tale.
See Kelley and Coley, A 1876–7.
318 *her crews*: Milton habitually uses 'crew' for Satan's followers.
319 *the stars . . . tingled*: cf. Shelley, *Prometheus Unbound*, i. 134.
323 *the earth sank to rest*: Bieman, 164, cites Heb. 12: 1–2, and Rom. 8: 37–9.

Anon at the dawn, all that trouble had withered from
     earth—
Not so much, but I saw it die out in the day's tender birth;   325
In the gathered intensity brought to the grey of the hills;
In the shuddering forests' held breath; in the sudden wind-
     thrills;
In the startled wild beasts that bore off, each with eye
     sidling still
Though averted with wonder and dread; in the birds stiff
     and chill
That rose heavily, as I approached them, made stupid with
     awe: 330
E'en the serpent that slid away silent,—he felt the new law.
The same stared in the white humid faces upturned by the
     flowers;
The same worked in the heart of the cedar and moved the
     vine-bowers:
And the little brooks witnessing murmured, persistent and
     low,
With their obstinate, all but hushed voices—"E'en so, it is   335
     so!"

---

327 *1855P–56, 1863, 1865* forests' new awe; in   *1863S* forests' new dusk; in
*328 {reading of *1855P–65, 1889*} *1868–88* both oft, each   329 *1855P–56* averted,
in wonder . . . . dread; and the   330 *1855P, 1855, 1863, 1865* awe!   *1856* awe.
331 *1855P* Even the   333 *1855P–63S* vine-bowers.   335 *1855P–56*—E'en
so! . . . . so.

---

327 *wind-thrills*: gusts of wind. The compound is not in OED².
328 *sidling*: looking sideways.
331 *the new law*: that of Christ.
335 *"E'en so, it is so!"*: cf. 'Amen'. Mrs Bronson described Browning's reading of 'the
grand profession of faith' here, as a friend had described it to her: 'his voice failed him
a very little, and when it was ended he turned his back to us, who were gathered about
him in reverent silence, and laying the book quietly on the table, stood so for a
moment': Meredith, 154.

"DE GUSTIBUS—"

'DE gustibus non (est) disputandum' is a Latin proverb, 'about matters of taste there is no arguing'. The thoughts of England in the first part are attributed to an old friend whom it is tempting to identify with 'my own friend Alfred over the sea', as Browning termed Domett in an early letter to EBB.[1] It is no less tempting to identify the second speaker with Browning himself. We do not know when the poem was written.

When Browning rearranged his poems in *1863* ' "De Gustibus—" ' was placed immediately before 'Home-Thoughts, from abroad'.

In the first part the longer lines have four stresses, and the shorter two, and most lines include at least one trisyllabic foot. Lines 5, 7, and 9 are in falling rhythm, the other lines in rising rhythm. The rhyme-scheme is *abbccaddeeeff*. But for ll. 39 and 41–2, the second part consists of iambic tetrameters, often with an anapaest in one foot.

Date: 1853/5
1863: *Dramatic Lyrics*

"DE GUSTIBUS—"

I.

YOUR ghost will walk, you lover of trees,
    (If our loves remain)
    In an English lane,
By a cornfield-side a-flutter with poppies.
Hark, those two in the hazel coppice—   5
A boy and a girl, if the good fates please,

2 *1855P–63S* If loves   6 *1855P* please!

[1] Kintner, i. 17. See too J. McNally, 'The Lover of Trees in "De Gustibus—" ': SBC 3: 1 (1975), 124–7.

Making love, say,—
The happier they!
Draw yourself up from the light of the moon,
And let them pass, as they will too soon,   10
        With the bean-flowers' boon,
        And the blackbird's tune,
        And May, and June!

II.

What I love best in all the world
Is a castle, precipice-encurled,   15
In a gash of the wind-grieved Apennine.
Or look for me, old fellow of mine,
(If I get my head from out the mouth
O' the grave, and loose my spirit's bands,
And come again to the land of lands)—   20
In a sea-side house to the farther South,
Where the baked cicala dies of drouth,
And one sharp tree—'t is a cypress—stands,
By the many hundred years red-rusted,
Rough iron-spiked, ripe fruit-o'ercrusted,   25
My sentinel to guard the sands

---

11 *1872S, 1884S* the beanflower's boon,   22 *1855P–68* baked cicalas die of
23 *1855P–63S* tree ('tis . . . . cypress)

11 *the bean-flowers' boon*: the cultivated bean-plant 'has fragrant violet-tinted white
flowers, whence the often-mentioned "fragrance of the bean-fields" ': OED². Cf. James
Thomson, *Spring*, 498 ff.

15 *precipice-encurled*: surrounded by precipices. Probably a nonce-formation.

16 *gash*: cleft, gorge.
   Wind-grieved: like many of Browning's compound-epithets this sounds like
Greek: cf. ἀνεμόφθορος 'blasted by the wind', in the Greek version of Hos. 8: 7. See
Kelley and Coley, A 239.

19 *bands*: pieces of cloth wrapped round a corpse, but here with a reference to the
fact that the spirit cannot be confined by bonds. See OED *band* sb.¹ 7.

20 *the land of lands*: Italy. Cf. 'Pietro of Abano', 442.

23 *a cypress*: a tree which can grow for centuries. Napoleon, in making the road over
the Simplon, is said to have deviated to avoid a tree reputed to have been in existence
since the time of Caesar. The cones grow darker with age, and become almost black.
The spikes are sharp, the timber is reddish.

25 *iron-spiked*: like the following epithet, probably a nonce-formation.

To the water's edge. For, what expands
Before the house, but the great opaque
Blue breadth of sea without a break?
While, in the house, for ever crumbles   30
Some fragment of the frescoed walls,
From blisters where a scorpion sprawls.
A girl bare-footed brings, and tumbles
Down on the pavement, green-flesh melons,
And says there's news to-day—the king   35
Was shot at, touched in the liver-wing,
Goes with his Bourbon arm in a sling:
—She hopes they have not caught the felons.
Italy, my Italy!
Queen Mary's saying serves for me—   40
　　(When fortune's malice
　　Lost her—Calais)—
　　Open my heart and you will see
　　Graved inside of it, "Italy."
　　Such lovers old are I and she: 45
　　So it always was, so shall ever be!

---

28 *1855P–56* Without the　　29 *1855P–56* sea, and not a　　37 *1855P–56* sling.
38 *1855P* felons!　　42 *1855P–63S* Calais.)　　44 *1855P* "Italy"—
46 *1855P–56* so it still shall be!　　*1863S, 1884S* be.

---

33 *A girl bare-footed*: cf. the girl in 'An Italian in England', 59 ff.

36 *the liver-wing*: 'the right wing of a fowl etc. which, when dressed for cooking, has the liver tucked under it; hence *jocularly*, the right arm': OED².

37 *Bourbon*: Ferdinand II, King of the Two Sicilies (Naples and Sicily), the King Bomba in 'Bishop Blougram's Apology', 715. He was a Bourbon.

39 *Italy, my Italy!*: cf. *Pippa Passes*, iii. 120.

40 *Queen Mary's saying*: Holinshed's *Chronicles*, 6 vols. (1807–8), iv (1808) 137: 'when I am dead and opened, you shall find Calis lieng in my hart' (*sic*).

WOMEN AND ROSES

IN the Introduction we have quoted Browning's remark that this was the first of two or more poems written because he was worried that he had been 'rather lazy', and that it had been 'suggested by a magnificent basket [of roses] that some one had sent [his] wife'.[1] We have tentatively concluded that this occurred in 1853, not 1852. Both poets had a particular fondness for roses, which are mentioned frequently in their love letters. He had 'a garden-full of rose-trees', though he told EBB that it was she who had 'first taught [him] what a rose really *was*'.[2] He often gave her roses. It is the less surprising that roses are mentioned in fifteen of the poems in *Men and Women*.[3]

Mrs Orr describes 'Women and Roses' as 'the impression of a dream', yet it is likely that the opening line, 'I dream of a red-rose tree', relates it to a literary tradition and does not in fact mean that it 'came upon [him] as a kind of dream', as 'Childe Roland' did. Roses are ubiquitous in European love poetry. Eleanor Cook cites a passage from Lorenzo de' Medici, a poet whose work was known to Browning,[4] to indicate the literary tradition which must have been in his mind, and to suggest the remarkable originality and strangeness of his own poem:

> L'altra mattina in un mio piccolo orto
> andavo, e'l sol surgente co' sua rai
> apparia già, non ch'io 'l vedessi scorto.
>   Sonvi piantati drento alcun rosai,
> a'quai rivolsi le mia vaghe ciglie,
> per quel che visto non avevo mai.
>   Eranvi rose candide e vermiglie:
> alcuna a foglia a foglia al sol si spiega;
> stretta prima, poi par s'apra e scompiglie:
>   altra più giovanetta si dislega
> a pena dalla boccia: eravi ancora
> chi le sue chiuse foglie all'aer niega:
>   altra, cadendo, a piè il terreno infiora.

---

[1] See above, p. xii.
[2] Kintner, i.18, 566.
[3] As pointed out by Cook, p. 187.
[4] For his translation of four lines from one of his poems, done in 1846, see Appendix below.

Cosi le vidi nascere e morire
e passar lor vaghezza in men d'un'ora.
    Quando languenti e pallide vidi ire
le foglie a terra, allor mi venne a mente
che vana cosa è il giovenil fiorire.[1]

In this poem the poet sees rose-bushes with blooms at different stages of
their brief lives, and is reminded by them of the transitoriness of youth.
The speaker in Browning's poem, on the other hand, sees roses from three
periods of the world's history—the past, the present, and the future—and
finds that they are all unattainable.

'Women and Roses' consists of four sections of three lines and of four
of nine. The first of the short sections poses the question which of the
three roses on the poet's rose-tree is dearest to him—a question which is
not to be answered. The first of the longer sections describes the beautiful
women of the past, the present, and the future as, 'all to one cadence', they
circle round his rose-tree. The remaining short sections introduce the
longer sections, each of which is devoted to the beautiful women of one
period. As they circle round their particular rose, each is tantalizingly
beyond his reach. One wonders whether Browning's subconscious mind
recalled memories of children in some party game, or figures on a
roundabout at a fair. There is no doubt that a 'dancing ring' appealed to
his imagination: he was to describe his *Romances and Lyrics* as 'this dancing
ring of men & women hand in hand'.[2]

Each of the shorter sections consists of three rhyming trimeters. Ex-
cept the first, each begins with the words 'Dear rose': the first begins
differently and has one anapaest in each line. The longer sections
consist of four-stress lines which rhyme in couplets, except that the
last line of each is the refrain, 'They circle their rose on my rose-tree', so

---

[1] 'Corinto', ll. 163–80, in *Opere*, ed. Attilio Simioni 2 vols. (Bari, 1913–14), i.
211–12. The poem is the first of his *Egloghe*.
    'The other morning I went into a little garden of mine, and the rays of the rising sun
were already visible, though I could not yet see it clearly. Some rose bushes are planted
there to which I turned my wandering gaze as to something I had never seen before.
There were white roses there, and red: some opened themselves to the sun, petal by
petal, tightly bunched at first, then, unfolding, they seemed to separate. Others, the
youngest, gradually unfurled from their buds. Others again held back their shut petals
from the air. Others, falling, made the ground flowery at my feet. So I saw them coming
to birth and dying, their beauty passing away in less than an hour. When I saw the petals
falling to the ground, languid and pale, then it came into my mind how vain a thing is
the flowering of youth.'
[2] Kintner, i. 26.

repeating the initial rhyme-sound of the poem. The alliteration which is noticeable in the longer sections helps to enhance the incantatory effect created by the intricate repetitions. The lesson enforced is the same as that of the Italian poem, which we cite (as does Cook) because it offers the opportunity of an interesting comparison.

'Women and Roses' is a curious construct, which may have begun as a poetic exercise, but which has a haunting quality which ensures that it remains in the mind of the reader.

Date: 1853
1863: Dramatic Lyrics

WOMEN AND ROSES.

I.

I DREAM of a red-rose tree.
And which of its roses three
Is the dearest rose to me?

II.

Round and round, like a dance of snow
In a dazzling drift, as its guardians, go   5
Floating the women faded for ages,
Sculptured in stone, on the poet's pages.
Then follow women fresh and gay,
Living and loving and loved to-day.
Last, in the rear, flee the multitude of maidens,   10
Beauties yet unborn. And all, to one cadence,
They circle their rose on my rose tree.

8 *1855P–56* follow the women   9 *1863–70, 1875* to-day,   11 *1855P–65* Beauties unborn.

5 *drift*: driven snow.
7 *on*: or on.
12 *They circle their rose*: i.e. each group of women circles its rose.

III.

Dear rose, thy term is reached,
Thy leaf hangs loose and bleached:
Bees pass it unimpeached.   15

IV.

Stay then, stoop, since I cannot climb,
You, great shapes of the antique time!
How shall I fix you, fire you, freeze you,
Break my heart at your feet to please you?
Oh, to possess and be possessed!   20
Hearts that beat 'neath each pallid breast!
Once but of love, the poesy, the passion,
Drink but once and die!—In vain, the same fashion,
They circle their rose on my rose tree.

V.

Dear rose, thy joy's undimmed: 25
Thy cup is ruby-rimmed,
Thy cup's heart nectar-brimmed.

VI.

Deep, as drops from a statue's plinth
The bee sucked in by the hyacinth,
So will I bury me while burning,   30
Quench like him at a plunge my yearning,
Eyes in your eyes, lips on your lips!

---

17 *1872S, 1884S* time,   20 *1855P–56* Oh!   22 *1855P–65* But once of
23 *1855P–65* Drink once   *25 {reading of *1884S*} *1855P–72S* undimmed; *1875*
undimmed   *1888, 1889* undimmed,

---

13 *term*: end.
15 *unimpeached*: unhindered, undelayed.
26 *ruby-rimmed*: not in OED².
27 *Thy cup's heart nectar-brimmed*: cf. *The Golden and Silver Ages: Two Plays by Thomas Heywood*, ed. J. Payne Collier, 1851; p. 15 (of *The Golden Age*): '. . . Fetch me his heart. Brim me a bowl / With his warm blood'.
29 *The bee sucked in*: cf. 'In a Gondola', 56 ff and 'Popularity', 46–50.

Fold me fast where the cincture slips,
Prison all my soul in eternities of pleasure,
Girdle me for once! But no—the old measure,   35
They circle their rose on my rose tree.

VII.

Dear rose without a thorn,
Thy bud's the babe unborn:
First streak of a new morn.

VIII.

Wings, lend wings for the cold, the clear!   40
What is far conquers what is near.
Roses will bloom nor want beholders,
Sprung from the dust where our flesh moulders.
What shall arrive with the cycle's change?
A novel grace and a beauty strange.   45
I will make an Eve, be the artist that began her,
Shaped her to his mind!—Alas! in like manner
They circle their rose on my rose tree.

---

34 *1855P–63* pleasure!   35 *1855P–65* me once!   *1855P–63* no—in their old
38 *1856* unborn,   41 *1855P–63* What's far   43 *1855P–63* our own flesh
1884S moulders,

33 *cincture*: girdle.

34 *eternities of pleasure*: cf. *Antony and Cleopatra*, I. iii. 35, and Donne, 'The Legacy',
4: 'lovers' hours be full eternity'.

35 *Girdle*: embrace.

41 *What is far*: cf. Thomas Campbell, *Pleasures of Hope*, i. 7: ' 'Tis distance lends
enchantment to the view.'

48 *They*: i.e. 'Beauties yet unborn'.

PROTUS

THE speaker is acting as a guide to some of the antiquities of Rome. The greater part of the poem (ll. 8–54) is a quotation from an imaginary chronicle. The idea may well have come to Browning between the end of 1853 and the first five months of 1854, when he and EBB were living in Rome. *Protos* is Greek for first, so the name is ironical: the 'First' is Last. So far as chronology is concerned, Browning has deliberately muddied his tracks. The Huns suggest the fourth or fifth century, 'John the Pannonian' at latest the reign of Justinian (between the reconquest of the West and the Longobardic invasion), while the dispatch of a scholarly ex-emperor to the monastery implies a date much later. The point seems to be to reproduce the ethos of the Byzantine empire: classical beauty and learning mixed with the brutal politics of power.

As for 'Half-emperors and quarter-emperors', there were two emperors between 161 and 169 and again between 177 and 180; and thereafter it was not unusual for emperors to make their sons Augusti. In 293 Diocletian and Maximian each took on a deputy and designated successor, called a Caesar: this tetrarchy may be the point of 'quarter-emperors'. Long after the fall of the Western empire in 476 there were often two or three emperors in Constantinople, the senior emperor and his brother or son, or the power behind the throne.

There is irony in the narrator's undiscriminating praise of the two emperors, so completely different, yet equally unfortunate in the end: the beautiful child, thrust aside by the 'hard hand' of John the Pannonian, and John himself, murdered by his sons after six years' reign.

The couplets are so muted that one may well remember the poem as being in blank verse.

Date: 1854
1863: Dramatic Romances

PROTUS.

AMONG these latter busts we count by scores,
Half-emperors and quarter-emperors,
Each with his bay-leaf fillet, loose-thonged vest,
Loric and low-browed Gorgon on the breast,—
One loves a baby face, with violets there,   5
Violets instead of laurel in the hair,
As those were all the little locks could bear.

Now read here. "Protus ends a period
"Of empery beginning with a god;
"Born in the porphyry chamber at Byzant,   10
"Queens by his cradle, proud and ministrant:
"And if he quickened breath there, 't would like fire
"Pantingly through the dim vast realm transpire.
"A fame that he was missing spread afar:
"The world from its four corners, rose in war,   15
"Till he was borne out on a balcony
"To pacify the world when it should see.
"The captains ranged before him, one, his hand
"Made baby points at, gained the chief command.
"And day by day more beautiful he grew   20

---

4 *1855P* low-browed Fury on   9 *1863S* god,   10 *1855P–63S* Byzant;
11 *1855P–56* ministrant.

---

3 *bay-leaf fillet*: laurel band round the head.

4 *Loric*: L. *lorica*, breastplate.

low-browed Gorgon: representations of Medusa (the principal Gorgon) portray her
with her head entwined with snakes, which make her look low-browed. Such an image
was worn as a protection, since it was believed that anyone who encountered a
Gorgon's eyes was turned to stone.

10 *Born in the porphyry chamber*. Cf. Vol. IV, p. 70 n. This indicates that he was the
son of a reigning emperor. Cf. Constantine VII (nominally emperor 908–59). Like
Protus, Constantine was of a scholarly disposition.

12 *quickened breath*: began to breathe.

14 *fame*: rumour.

15 *its four corners*: cf. *The Merchant of Venice*, II. vii. 39: 'From the four corners of the
earth they come', and Donne, Sonnet 7: 'At the round earth's imagined corners'.

"In shape, all said, in feature and in hue,
"While young Greek sculptors, gazing on the child,
"Became with old Greek sculpture reconciled.
"Already sages laboured to condense
"In easy tomes a life's experience: 25
"And artists took grave counsel to impart
"In one breath and one hand-sweep, all their art—
"To make his graces prompt as blossoming
"Of plentifully-watered palms in spring:
"Since well beseems it, whoso mounts the throne,   30
"For beauty, knowledge, strength, should stand alone,
"And mortals love the letters of his name."

—Stop! Have you turned two pages? Still the same.
New reign, same date. The scribe goes on to say
How that same year, on such a month and day,   35
"John the Pannonian, groundedly believed
"A blacksmith's bastard, whose hard hand reprieved
"The Empire from its fate the year before,—
"Came, had a mind to take the crown, and wore
"The same for six years (during which the Huns   40
"Kept off their fingers from us), till his sons
"Put something in his liquor"—and so forth.
Then a new reign. Stay—"Take at its just worth"
(Subjoins an annotator) "what I give
"As hearsay. Some think, John let Protus live   45

---

23 *1855P–63S* Were, so, with

27 *hand-sweep*: not in OED².
28 *prompt*: swift in appearing.
36 *John the Pannonian*: an imaginary soldier from Pannonia, a large country invaded by Caesar and conquered in the reign of Tiberius. It corresponds to western Hungary. Pannonia became a Roman province. It lay to the S and W of the Danube, north of Dalmatia.
  groundedly: on good authority.
40 *the Huns*: a fierce nomadic Asian tribe which invaded Europe *c.* 375. Under Attila, 'The Scourge of God', they overran and ravaged a large part of Europe in the fifteenth century. They played their part in bringing about the fall of the Western Roman Empire.

"And slip away. 'T is said, he reached man's age
"At some blind northern court; made, first a page,
"Then tutor to the children; last, of use
"About the hunting-stables. I deduce
"He wrote the little tract 'On worming dogs,'   50
"Whereof the name in sundry catalogues
"Is extant yet. A Protus of the race
"Is rumoured to have died a monk in Thrace,—
"And if the same, he reached senility."

Here's John the Smith's rough-hammered head. Great eye,   55
Gross jaw and griped lips do what granite can
To give you the crown-grasper. What a man!

47 *blind*: obscure.

50 *worming*: to worm a dog is 'To extract the "worm" or lytta from the tongue', to obviate the risk of its going mad.

54 *senility*: old age.

55 *John the Smith's rough-hammered head*: cf. the description of Hildebrand (Pope Gregory VII) in *Sordello*, v. 161 ff.

56 *griped lips*: cf. 'teeth clenched' in the above passage.

57 *the crown-grasper*: not in OED².

HOLY-CROSS DAY

HOLY CROSS DAY, a feast in honour of the Cross of Christ, is 14 September.[1] We know from John Evelyn, and from Browning's friend G. S. Hillard, that in fact sermons to the Jews occurred on other days too. On 7 January 1645 the former noted:

A sermon was preached to the Jews, at Ponte Sisto, who are constrained to sit till the hour is done; but it is with so much malice in their countenances, spitting, humming, coughing, and motion, that it is almost impossible they should hear a word from the preacher. A conversion is very rare.[2]

Hillard wrote:

By a bull of Gregory XIII. in the year 1584, all Jews above the age of twelve years were compelled to listen every week to a sermon from a Christian priest; usually an exposition of some passages of the Old Testament, and especially those relating to the Messiah, from the Christian point of view. This burden is not yet wholly removed from them, and to this day, several times in the course of a year, a Jewish congregation is gathered together in the Church of St. Angelo in Pescheria, and constrained to listen to a homily from a Dominican friar, to whom, unless his zeal have eaten up his good feeling and his good taste, the ceremony must be as painful as to his hearers.[3]

Since the sermons stopped in 1847, as de Beer informs us, there can be no question of Browning's having witnessed such an occasion. His source will therefore have been hearsay, a guide-book, or (perhaps most probably) Hillard's *Six Months in Italy*. Sharp tells us that the poem was written in the spring of 1854.[4]

---

[1] The day is also known as 'The Exaltation of the Cross'. According to the *Oxford Dictionary of the Christian Church*, on this day 'the exposition of the supposed true Cross at Jerusalem in 629 . . . is commemorated'. The date, 14 September, 'has become attached to it through confusion with a much earlier commemoration kept in Jerusalem in that day, viz. of the dedication in 335 of the basilica built by the Emp. Constantine on the site of the Holy Sepulchre'.

[2] *Diary of John Evelyn*, ed. W. Bray, new ed., rev., 4 vols. (1850–2), i. 136. See too the note by E. S. de Beer, in his authoritative ed. 6 vols. (1955), ii. 291 n.: 'There was a weekly sermon, which a fixed number of Jews, or proportion of the Jewish population of Rome, was obliged to attend. The sermons were first regularly established by Gregory XIII in 1577; they stopped finally in 1847 . . . Despite attempts to maintain order, the congregations behaved very much as they pleased.'

[3] *Six Months in Italy*, 2 vols. (1853), ii. 40–1. Hillard's six months began on 2 September 1847.

[4] In his *Life of Robert Browning*, 167.

Lines 69–120 are said to be 'Ben Ezra's Song of Death' (l. 66). Abraham ben Meir Ibn Ezra (1092/3–1167), whose name is sometimes written Abenezra, as in Browning's favourite early reference books, the *Biographie universelle* and *The Great Historical Dictionary*,[1] was a scholar who wrote in Hebrew and strove to clarify the meaning of many of the books of the Old Testament. He was born and brought up in Spain, and was one of those who brought to other parts of Europe the treasures of knowledge contained in Arabic works. Prompted by l. 66, but without advancing any evidence, DeVane states that Browning 'probably saw' a Song of Death attributed to Ben Ezra in Rome, apparently in the Vatican Library. No such source has been discovered, and Mrs Orr more wisely writes of Ben Ezra's 'supposed death-bed utterance'. She summarizes it well:

> The prayer is an invocation to the justice, and to the sympathy of Christ. It claims His help against the enemies who are also His own. It concedes, as possible, that He was in truth the Messiah, crucified by the nation of which He claimed a crown. But it points to His Christian followers as inflicting on Him a still deeper outrage: a belief which the lips profess, and which the life derides and discredits. It urges, in the Jew's behalf, the ignorance, the fear, in which the deed was done; the bitter sufferings by which it has been expiated. It pleads his long endurance, as testimony to the fact, that he withstands Barabbas now, as he withstood Christ "then;" that he strives to wrest Christ's name from the "Devil's crew," though the shadow of His face be upon him. The invocation concludes with an expression of joyful confidence in God and the future.[2]

This poem demonstrates so clearly Browning's sympathy with the Jews, and his interest in their history and religion, that we can understand the belief which Mrs Orr mentions in the opening sentence of her *Life*, 'that he had Jewish blood in his veins'.[3] The same feeling is evident in 'Saul', 'Ben Karshook's Wisdom', and elsewhere, as in such later poems as 'Rabbi Ben Ezra', the Epilogue to *Dramatis Personæ*, and 'Jochanan Hakkadosh'.

There is an illuminating discussion of the epigraph to the present poem by Barbara Melchiori, who points out that the Biblical references (in what is really a cento of such) 'are taken from passages . . . which teach the supremacy of the Jewish race, and its final triumph'.[4] Thus the quotation

---

[1] 2nd ed., 'Revis'd, Corrected and Enlarg'd' by Jeremy Collier (1701). Cf. our Vol. III, p. 261.

[2] Cf. Browning to Furnivall, 17 February 1888: 'Ben Ezra is not supposed to acknowledge Christ as the Messiah because he resorts to the obvious argument "even on your own showing, and accepting for the moment the authority of your accepted Lawgiver, you are condemned by His precepts—let alone ours" ': *Trumpeter*, 151.

[3] She immediately states that the belief is unfounded.

[4] Melchiori, 92.

or allusion in the second and third lines is 'the prophecy of Zacharias
concerning . . . John the Baptist'. However there is irony in the context,
'which is the Lord's promise to Abraham to free the Jews from their
enemies', a promise mentioned openly in 'Ben Ezra's Song'. While the
dogs referred to in the epigraph are the Jews, 'once again the context
illuminates Browning's irony, for in the Bible it is the Gentile woman who
is the dog'. 'By a masterpiece of irony', in Melchiori's words, 'the Gentiles
here are the Roman Catholics rather than the Protestants.'

Each stanza consists of six tetrameters, rhyming in couplets. Since some
stanzas, notably at the beginning, are in falling metre (consisting of dactyls
and trochees), while later iambs and anapaests predominate, it is best
simply to characterize the piece as written in four-stress lines. Alliteration
is prominent, with phrases which remind us of popular poetry and of
nursery rhymes: *Fee, faw, fum!*, *Rumble and tumble*, *swine in a stye*, *hip to
haunch*, *cog nor cozen*, for example. The caesuras are very marked in most
of the lines, as in st. iii:

> Higgledy piggledy, packed we lie,
> Rats in a hamper, swine in a stye,
> Wasps in a bottle, frogs in a sieve,
> Worms in a carcase, flees in a sleeve.
> Hist! square shoulders, settle your thumbs
> And buzz for the bishop,—here he comes.

It is no surprise that this poem was a favourite of Browning's father, who
'would turn from the Sistine altar-piece' to admire Hogarth's prints and
the work of the Dutch artists 'Brouwer, Ostade, Teniers', as his son
reported.[1] It may be compared with 'The Pied Piper', section ii of
Christmas-Eve (the description of the poor people in the little chapel), and
in the present collection with 'The Heretic's Tragedy'.

Date: 1854
1863: Dramatic Romances

---

[1] Griffin and Minchin, 12.

HOLY-CROSS DAY.

ON WHICH THE JEWS WERE FORCED TO ATTEND AN ANNUAL
CHRISTIAN SERMON IN ROME.

["Now was come about Holy-Cross Day, and now must my lord
preach his first sermon to the Jews: as it was of old cared for in the
merciful bowels of the Church, that, so to speak, a crumb at least
from her conspicuous table here in Rome should be, though but
once yearly, cast to the famishing dogs, under-trampled and   v
bespitten-upon beneath the feet of the guests. And a moving sight in
truth, this, of so many of the besotted blind restif and ready-to-perish
Hebrews! now maternally brought—nay (for He saith, 'Compel
them to côme in') haled, as it were, by the head and hair, and against
their obstinate hearts, to partake of the heavenly grace. What   x
awakening, what striving with tears, what working of a yeasty
conscience! Nor was my lord wanting to himself on so apt an
occasion; witness the abundance of conversions which did
incontinently reward him: though not to my lord be altogether the
glory."—*Diary by the Bishop's Secretary*, 1600.]   xv

What the Jews really said, on thus being driven to church, was
rather to this effect:—

---

sub-title   *1855P*   (ON .... ROME.)   epigraph   ii   *1863S*   for   by   the
viii   *1855P–56* now paternally brought—   xvi   *1855–63* Though what

Title and epigraph: see introduction.
iii   *merciful bowels*: cf. Luke 1: 78 (alternative reading): 'Through the bowels of the
mercy of our God'.
   a crumb: Matt. 15: 27.
   v   *under-trampled*: not in OED². Melchiori points out that trampling is often used in
the OT in connection with the enemies of Israel.
   vi   *bespitten-upon*: not in OED²: cf. Mark 14: 65.
   vii   *besotted*: intellectually or morally blind.
   restif: 'Unwilling to stir; resolute against going forward': Johnson.
   ready-to-perish Hebrews: cf. Deut. 26.5 'A Syrian ready to perish was my father'.
viii   *maternally*: by Mother Church.
   '*Compel them to come in*': Luke 14: 23.
   x   *obstinate hearts*: cf. Deut. 2: 30.
   partake of the heavenly grace: 1 Cor. 10: 27, 30.
   xi   *yeasty*: foamy, 'working'.
   xii   *wanting to himself*: not living up to his own stature.
   xiv   *incontinently*: immediately.
   not to my lord . . . altogether: 1 Cor. 9: 16 ff.

I.

FEE, faw, fum! bubble and squeak!
Blessedest Thursday's the fat of the week.
Rumble and tumble, sleek and rough,
Stinking and savoury, smug and gruff,
Take the church-road, for the bell's due chime   5
Gives us the summons—'t is sermon-time!

II.

Boh, here's Barnabas! Job, that's you?
Up stumps Solomon—bustling too?
Shame, man! greedy beyond your years
To handsel the bishop's shaving-shears?   10
Fair play's a jewel! Leave friends in the lurch?
Stand on a line ere you start for the church!

III.

Higgledy piggledy, packed we lie,
Rats in a hamper, swine in a stye,

6 *1855P–63* sermon-time   11 *1855P–65* leave   12 *1855P–65* church.

1 *Fee, faw, fum!*: cf. *King Lear*, III. iv. 178–80: 'Child Rowland to the dark tower came, / His word was still "Fie, foh, and fum, / I smell the blood of a British man." ' See, as well as the epigraph to 'Childe Roland', 'A Lovers' Quarrel', 131–3. Barbara Melchiori points out (p. 99 and n.) that there is a variant with 'a Christian man!'

bubble and squeak!: a cheap dish of cabbage and potato fried together, sometimes with scraps of meat. Used here to show contempt.

2 *Blessedest Thursday*: this cannot refer to *giovedì grasso*, part of the Carnival season which occurs in late winter. Since 14 September may occur on any day of the week, perhaps we are to imagine that in the year to which the poem refers Holy-Cross Day happens to be a Thursday. The speaker, who knows little of Catholic practices and cares nothing for them, is of course being satirical.

3 *Rumble and tumble*: as in 'The Pied Piper', 109–10.

4 *savoury*: 'Pleasing to the smell': Johnson.
smug: 'Nice; spruce': Johnson.
gruff: 'Sour of aspect; harsh of manners': Johnson.

10 *To handsel*: 'To use or do anything the first time': Johnson. Here, to be the first to be shaved, as a sign of conversion. Cf. the law of the Nazarites, Num. 6: 5, Judg. 13: 5.

11 *Fair play's a jewel*: proverbial: first recorded in Fenimore Cooper, *The Pioneers*, ch. 17 (1823), and Scott, *Redgauntlet* (1824), ch. xxi.

12 *on a line*: as at the beginning of a race.

Wasps in a bottle, frogs in a sieve, 15
Worms in a carcase, fleas in a sleeve.
Hist! square shoulders, settle your thumbs
And buzz for the bishop—here he comes.

IV.

Bow, wow, wow—a bone for the dog!
I liken his Grace to an acorned hog. 20
What, a boy at his side, with the bloom of a lass,
To help and handle my lord's hour-glass!
Didst ever behold so lithe a chine?
His cheek hath laps like a fresh-singed swine.

V.

Aaron's asleep—shove hip to haunch, 25
Or somebody deal him a dig in the paunch!
Look at the purse with the tassel and knob,
And the gown with the angel and thingumbob!
What's he at, quotha? reading his text!
Now you've his curtsey—and what comes next? 30

28 *1855P–65* thingumbob. *30 {reading of *1855P–84S* }*1888, 1889* next DC,
BrU next.

17 *settle your thumbs*: i.e. stop twiddling them in impatience.
18 *buzz*: cf. Evelyn's 'humming' (in introduction above). This may signify contempt,
as in *Hamlet*, II. ii. 389, or a pretence of interest.
19 *Bow, wow, wow*: 'With these words . . . we are back with Old Mother Hubbard in
the realm of nursery rhymes': Melchiori, 100.
20 *an acorned hog*: cf. *Cymbeline*, II. v. 16, 'a full-acorn'd boar'. Orthodox Jews do not
eat the flesh of pigs. Cf. 24.
22 *hour-glass*: to time his sermon with.
23 *chine*: back.
24 *laps*: dewlaps, pendulous folds of flesh about the throat.
28 *thingumbob*: probably a cross, which the speaker does not care to name.
29 *quotha*: forsooth.
30 *curtsey*: by 1755 Johnson already limits the word to the genuflection made by
women.
what comes next: the sermon.

VI.

See to our converts—you doomed black dozen—
No stealing away—nor cog nor cozen!
You five, that were thieves, deserve it fairly;
You seven, that were beggars, will live less sparely;
You took your turn and dipped in the hat,   35
Got fortune—and fortune gets you; mind that!

VII.

Give your first groan—compunction's at work;
And soft! from a Jew you mount to a Turk.
Lo, Micah,—the selfsame beard on chin
He was four times already converted in!   40
Here's a knife, clip quick—it's a sign of grace—
Or he ruins us all with his hanging-face.

VIII.

Whom now is the bishop a-leering at?
I know a point where his text falls pat.
I'll tell him to-morrow, a word just now   45
Went to my heart and made me vow
I meddle no more with the worst of trades—
Let somebody else pay his serenades.

IX.

Groan all together now, whee—hee—hee!
It's a-work, it's a-work, ah, woe is me!   50
It began, when a herd of us, picked and placed,

34 *1855P, 1856* sparely.   47 *1880S* To meddle   48 *1880S–84S* serenades!

32 *nor cog nor cozen!*: the two words, both meaning 'cheat', occur together in Tusser:
see OED², 'Cog', v.³
35 *dipped in the hat*: drew lots.
37 *your first groan*: cf. Rom. 8: 23.
38 *mount*: in the spiritual scale.
42 *his hanging-face*: cf. 'Fra Lippo Lippi', 307.
47 *the worst of trades*: usury.
50 *a-work*: i.e. the religious yeast is 'working' in him. Cf. 'Saul', 94.

Were spurred through the Corso, stripped to the waist;
Jew brutes, with sweat and blood well spent
To usher in worthily Christian Lent.

X.

It grew, when the hangman entered our bounds,   55
Yelled, pricked us out to his church like hounds:
It got to a pitch, when the hand indeed
Which gutted my purse would throttle my creed:
And it overflows when, to even the odd,
Men I helped to their sins help me to their God.   60

XI.

But now, while the scapegoats leave our flock,
And the rest sit silent and count the clock,
Since forced to muse the appointed time
On these precious facts and truths sublime,—
Let us fitly employ it, under our breath,   65
In saying Ben Ezra's Song of Death.

XII.

For Rabbi Ben Ezra, the night he died,
Called sons and sons' sons to his side,
And spoke, "This world has been harsh and strange;

56 *1855P–56* to this church   *1855P– 63* hounds.   58 *1855P–63* creed.
69 *1855P–63S* strange,

---

52 *the Corso*: during the period of Carnival a number of races were run along this street, one of them a race for Jews, who were obliged to run naked. Dr Bonnie J. Blackburn tells us that Pope Paul II moved them to the Via del Corso so that he could watch the finishing-line from his palace in the Piazza di Venezia.

55 *the hangman*: his office included the infliction of other forms of punishment and persecution.

our bounds; those of the ghetto in Rome. In 1814 the Pope allowed a few Jews to live outside it, and in 1847 Pius IX decided to destroy the gates and walls, but he had to bow to public opinion and refrain.

56 *pricked*: drove.

59 *to even the odd*: to complete the reckoning.

61 *scapegoats*: commonly, as here, people who are blamed for the sins (real or imagined) of a whole body. For the original meaning, see Lev. 16.

"Something is wrong: there needeth a change. 70
"But what, or where? at the last or first?
"In one point only we sinned, at worst.

XIII.

"The Lord will have mercy on Jacob yet,
"And again in his border see Israel set.
"When Judah beholds Jerusalem, 75
"The stranger-seed shall be joined to them:
"To Jacob's House shall the Gentiles cleave.
"So the Prophet saith and his sons believe.

XIV.

"Ay, the children of the chosen race
"Shall carry and bring them to their place: 80
"In the land of the Lord shall lead the same,
"Bondsmen and handmaids. Who shall blame,
"When the slaves enslave, the oppressed ones o'er
"The oppressor triumph for evermore?

XV.

"God spoke, and gave us the word to keep, 85
"Bade never fold the hands nor sleep
"'Mid a faithless world,—at watch and ward,

---

70 *1855P–63S* wrong,   77 *1880S* cleave,   84 *1880S–84S* evermore!
*85 {reading of DC, BrU, *1889*}   *1855P–84S* keep: *1888* keep   88 *1855P–63S*
Till the Christ

---

72 *one point*: failing to recognize Christ as the Messiah.

73 *"The Lord will have mercy*: a close following of Isa. 14: 1–2, as Barbara Melchiori points out: 'For the Lord will have mercy on Jacob, and will yet choose Israel, and set them in their own land: and the strangers shall be joined with them, and they shall cleave to the house of Jacob. And the people shall take them, and bring them to their place: and the house of Israel shall possess them in the land of the LORD for servants and handmaids: and they shall take them captives, whose captives they were; and they shall rule over their oppressors'.

76 *stranger-seed*: not in OED[2].

86 *fold the hands*: cf. Prov. 6: 10: 'A little folding of the hands to sleep'.

87 *at watch and ward*: 'Continuous vigilance; guard by night (*watch*) and by day (*ward*)': Brewer, who points out that the phrase originated in feudal times.

"Till Christ at the end relieve our guard.
"By His servant Moses the watch was set:
"Though near upon cock-crow, we keep it yet.   90

XVI.

"Thou! if thou wast He, who at mid-watch came,
"By the starlight, naming a dubious name!
"And if, too heavy with sleep—too rash
"With fear—O Thou, if that martyr-gash
"Fell on Thee coming to take thine own,   95
"And we gave the Cross, when we owed the Throne—

XVII.

"Thou art the Judge. We are bruised thus.
"But, the Judgment over, join sides with us!
"Thine too is the cause! and not more thine
"Than ours, is the work of these dogs and swine,   100
"Whose life laughs through and spits at their creed!
"Who maintain Thee in word, and defy Thee in deed!

XVIII.

"We withstood Christ then? Be mindful how
"At least we withstand Barabbas now!
"Was our outrage sore? But the worst we spared,   105
"To have called these—Christians, had we dared!

---

93 *1855P–63S* if we were too   101 *1855P–84S* creed,   103 *1855P–65* be
105 *1855P–65* but

---

91 *who at mid-watch came*: in Matt. 26: 40 we read how Christ came to his disciples, and found them asleep, and said to Peter, 'What, could ye not watch with me one hour?'

90 *cock-crow*: Matt. 26: 34.

92 *a dubious name*: that of Peter, the doubter.

96 *we gave the Cross*: we Jews, who should have recognized you as the Messiah, crucified you.

97 *bruised*: 'To crush or mangle with [a] heavy blow': Johnson. Cf. Isa. 53: 10.

100 *these dogs and swine*: both considered unclean by the Jews. Cf. ll. 19 and 24.

104 *Barabbas*: at the bidding of the Jews, Pilate released this murderer, rather than Christ: Mark 15: 6ff. Here he represents the Roman Catholic Church.

105 *sore*: extremely serious.

"Let defiance to them pay mistrust of Thee,
"And Rome make amends for Calvary!

XIX.

"By the torture, prolonged from age to age,
"By the infamy, Israel's heritage,   110
"By the Ghetto's plague, by the garb's disgrace,
"By the badge of shame, by the felon's place,
"By the branding-tool, the bloody whip,
"And the summons to Christian fellowship,—

XX.

"We boast our proof that at least the Jew   115
"Would wrest Christ's name from the Devil's crew.
"Thy face took never so deep a shade
"But we fought them in it, God our aid!
"A trophy to bear, as we march, thy band,
"South, East, and on to the Pleasant Land!"   120

[*Pope Gregory XVI. abolished this bad business
of the Sermon.*—R. B.]

107 *1863S* defiance of them   113–14 *1855P* Each heavier to us as these braggarts
waxed,│Each lighter whenever their power relaxed—   115 *1855P–63S* our
proofs, that   116 *1863S* Could wrest   119 *1855P–56* march, a band   final
note *1855P–75* [*The present Pope abolished   1880S–84S* [*The late Pope abolished 1855P
business.*—R.B.]

107 *pay*: repay.
108 *make amends*: because they are equally wicked.
111 *the Ghetto's plague*: the plague constituted by the Ghetto. The ghetto in Rome
was instituted by Paul IV in 1556. The situation of the Jews depended on the character
of the Pope. At certain times the persecution was relaxed. In some periods the men
were supposed to wear yellow hats or vests, yellow being the colour of betrayal.
Cf. Vol. I, p. 453.
114 *the summons to Christian fellowship*: the climax of our indignities.
116 *the Devil's crew*: the Roman Catholic Church.
120 *the Pleasant Land*: 'The passage is taken from Jeremiah in the Old Testament, but
by substituting "Christ's name" for "the name of the Lord" Browning has greatly
altered the meaning. The Lord in Jeremiah was Jehovah, the God of Israel, whereas the
promise to fight in Christ's name can only mean a conversion to Christianity. Rabbi
Ben Ezra's Song of Death therefore concludes in an invitation to the conversion of the
Jews. If this fact had been stressed before, the question of the authenticity of the Song
of Death could hardly have arisen': Melchiori, 110–11.
note: Pope Gregory XVI died on 1 June 1846. The sermons stopped finally in 1847,
which was early in the pontificate of Pius IX, '*The present Pope*', in the words of *1855*.

THE GUARDIAN-ANGEL
A PICTURE AT FANO

THIS poem appears to have been written before any other in *Men and Women*. In the last line there is a reference to Ancona, where we know the Brownings spent a few days in July 1848. Unlike 'Andrea del Sarto' and 'Fra Lippo Lippo' this piece has no literary source.

On 17 July they left Florence for Fano, recommended in Murray's *Handbook for Travellers in Central Italy* as affording 'one of the most agreeable residences in Italy' during the summer months.[1] The *Handbook* states that 'there is scarcely a church which does not present some work by the best, or by less known artists, the study of which would be highly interesting to the traveller who is anxious to trace the history of art in its several schools'.[2] Fano turned out to be far from a delightful place for the Brownings, however, as EBB made clear in a lively letter to her sister in which she refers to 'Murray, the traitor'. It proved 'uninhabitable from the heat', the vegetation 'scorched with paleness, the very air swooning in the sun', with gloomy inhabitants (who included Mrs Wiseman, the Cardinal's mother, 'in a state of permanent moaning' in her 'exile from the common civilities of life'), and a hopeless circulating library. During the three days they remained, however, they found compensation in the beauty of numerous churches, and particularly in 'a divine picture of Guercino's . . . worth going all that way to see'.[3] They visited the painting, in the church of S. Agostino, on three occasions. The poem was written a few days later, in Ancona.

Guercino ('Squinter') lived from 1591 to 1666, his baptismal name being Giovanni Francesco Barbieri. A painter of the High Baroque period, he is too late for Vasari. Browning is likely to have been familiar with one of his paintings from his boyhood, since the Dulwich Gallery has a fine example of his work, *The Woman Taken in Adultery*.[4]

In the Fano painting (reproduced in the first edition of Griffin and Minchin) the central figure is the guardian-angel which gives the poem its title, standing on the ground with wings outstretched. Beside the angel

---

[1] *Handbook* (1843), 111a.   [2] Ibid. 112b.   [3] *Letters of EBB*, i. 380.
[4] See Peter Murray, *Dulwich Picture Gallery: A Catalogue* (Sotheby Parke Bernet, 1980), p. 65.

(which might almost be mistaken for a female figure, because of the delicacy of the features and hair) there kneels a small child, his hands held together, as if in prayer, by the angel. Three cherubim look down on them, from above the clouds. The child's eyes are raised: the angel is looking to the left of the picture: in the right background a turret is visible: the clouds, and the blowing of the angel's drapery, suggest a coming storm. It will be seen that Browning describes the painting fairly accurately. Many years later, when he received a copy of a print made for the Browning Society, he wrote: 'I probably saw the original picture in a favourable *darkness*; it was blackened by taper-smoke, and one fancied the angel all but surrounded with cloud—only a light on the face.'[1]

The poem is highly personal. It is noteworthy that Browning should address Alfred Domett at l. 37, and end with an address to him. Six years earlier Browning had written 'Waring', a fanciful account of Domett's departure from England. Now, in a period of temporary worry and frustration, the sight of a painting by Guercino has greatly moved him, and his mind goes back to his earlier life.

There are eight stanzas of seven lines each. The standard line is an iambic pentameter, and the rhyme-scheme *ababcca*.

Date: 1848
1863: Dramatic Lyrics

¹ Letters, 213.

THE GUARDIAN-ANGEL.
A PICTURE AT FANO.

I.

DEAR and great Angel, wouldst thou only leave
    That child, when thou hast done with him, for me!
Let me sit all the day here, that when eve
    Shall find performed thy special ministry,
And time come for departure, thou, suspending   5
Thy flight, mayst see another child for tending,
    Another still, to quiet and retrieve.

II.

Then I shall feel thee step one step, no more,
    From where thou standest now, to where I gaze,
—And suddenly my head is covered o'er   10
    With those wings, white above the child who prays
Now on that tomb—and I shall feel thee guarding
Me, out of all the world; for me, discarding
    Yon heaven thy home, that waits and opes its door.

III.

I would not look up thither past thy head   15
    Because the door opes, like that child, I know,
For I should have thy gracious face instead,
    Thou bird of God! And wilt thou bend me low
Like him, and lay, like his, my hands together,

title *1855P–56* ANGEL: A   *1863S* *ANGEL*: A   7 *1855P* One more, to stay
with, quiet,   9 *1872S, 1884S* gaze.   10 *1855P–56* head be covered
14 *1855P–63* door!

4 *thy special ministry*: to the child. Cf. Coleridge, 'Frost at Midnight', 1.
16 *like that child*: the child looks past the head of the angel, towards heaven.
18 *Thou bird of God*: in *Purgatorio*, ii. 38 the Angel of God is called 'l'uccel divino'. In
The Ring and the Book, i. 1391, Love is addressed as 'half angel and half bird'.

And lift them up to pray, and gently tether   20
    Me, as thy lamb there, with thy garment's spread?

IV.

If this was ever granted, I would rest
    My head beneath thine, while thy healing hands
Close-covered both my eyes beside thy breast,
    Pressing the brain, which too much thought expands,   25
Back to its proper size again, and smoothing
Distortion down till every nerve had soothing,
    And all lay quiet, happy and suppressed.

V.

How soon all worldly wrong would be repaired!
    I think how I should view the earth and skies   30
And sea, when once again my brow was bared
    After thy healing, with such different eyes.
O world, as God has made it! All is beauty:
And knowing this, is love, and love is duty.
    What further may be sought for or declared?   35

VI.

Guercino drew this angel I saw teach
    (Alfred, dear friend!)—that little child to pray,
Holding the little hands up, each to each
    Pressed gently,—with his own head turned away
Over the earth where so much lay before him   40
Of work to do, though heaven was opening o'er him,
    And he was left at Fano by the beach.

---

33 *1855P–65* all   37 *1855P–63S* friend)—

24 *Close-covered both my eyes*: Browning liked EBB to place her hands over his eyes.
When he first met her he suffered a good deal from headaches. He told Julia Wedgwood
that 'sixteen years ago and more' (i.e. by 1848), once when he could not get to sleep
for the pain, 'my wife took my head in her two little hands, in broad daylight, and I
went to sleep at once': Wedgwood, 102. Cf. 'In a Balcony', 2.

39 *his own head*: the angel's.

42 *by the beach*: Fano is on the Adriatic coast.

VII.

We were at Fano, and three times we went
　　To sit and see him in his chapel there,
And drink his beauty to our soul's content   45
　　—My angel with me too: and since I care
For dear Guercino's fame (to which in power
And glory comes this picture for a dower,
　　Fraught with a pathos so magnificent)—

VIII.

And since he did not work thus earnestly   50
　　At all times, and has else endured some wrong—
I took one thought his picture struck from me,
　　And spread it out, translating it to song.
My love is here. Where are you, dear old friend?
How rolls the Wairoa at your world's far end?   55
　　This is Ancona, yonder is the sea.

50 *1855P–63* work so earnestly

___

48 *dower*: 'Endowment; gift', Johnson's fourth definition.
50 *he did not work thus earnestly*: he painted a great deal, somewhat unevenly.
55 *the Wairoa*: the river Wairoa reaches the sea on the E coast of the North Island of New Zealand, where Domett had gone in 1842.

CLEON

THIS imaginary poet is replying to a letter from Protus,[1] a powerful ruler who has sent him a galley full of gifts, including 'one white she-slave' to serve as his cupbearer. He praises Protus as no ordinary king, and commends the splendid ambition which has led him to undertake the building of a tall tower:

> Whence, all the tumult of the building hushed,
> Thou first of men mightst look out to the East.

In the first forty-two lines the boundless power of the tyrant and the overweening pride of the poet are brilliantly established.

This impression is enhanced in the next long verse-paragraph, in which Cleon acknowledges that he is not only a remarkable poet, but also a sculptor, painter, an innovator in music, and a philosopher who has 'written three books on the soul'. He is, as we would say now, a Renaissance man whose abilities and ranging mind know no bounds, one who has attained 'The very crown and proper end of life'. That is why Protus asks him whether he fears death less than he himself does.

Cleon accepts that Protus is 'worthy of hearing [his] whole mind'. He rejects as a mere play on words the belief that a genius like himself 'lives on' through his works. He confesses that the truth about human life seems to him 'so horrible' that he has sometimes dreamed of personal immortality. If there were such a state, however, Zeus would surely have revealed it; and he has not. The poem ends, with a strong effect of dramatic irony, with Cleon's admission that he cannot forward the letter for the apostle Paul, as Cleon has asked him to do, since he does not know where this 'mere barbarian Jew' is to be found, or indeed whether Paul and Christ are not one and the same. Yet it cannot matter, since 'Their doctrine could be held by no sane man'.

'Karshish' and 'Cleon' have long been regarded as companion poems, a pair of the sort that had appeared as early as January 1836.[2] The contrasting idioms of the garrulous yet highly intelligent Arab physician and the coldly lucid Greek artist point forward to the contrasting styles of the different speakers in *The Ring and the Book*.

---

[1] Cf. the title of the poem 'Protus', in this same volume.

[2] When 'Johannes Agricola' and 'Porphyria's Lover' were published together in the *Monthly Repository*. See our Vol. III, pp. 244 ff.

Since the appearance of an influential article in 1927 it has been customary to associate 'Cleon' with Matthew Arnold's *Empedocles on Etna*, 'A Dramatic Poem' which we know that Browning admired.[1] Having omitted it from his volumes of 1853 and 1855, Arnold reprinted it in his *New Poems* in 1867, with this note:

I cannot deny myself the pleasure of saying that I reprint (I cannot say *republish*, for it was withdrawn from circulation before fifty copies were sold) this poem at the request of a man of genius, whom it had the honour and the good fortune to interest,—Mr. Robert Browning.

Arnold's account of his aim in *Empedocles* is highly relevant here:

I intended to delineate the feelings of one of the last of the Greek religious philosophers, one of the family of Orpheus and Musaeus . . . living on into a time when the habits of Greek thought and feeling had begun fast to change, character to dwindle, the influence of the Sophists to prevail. Into the feelings of a man so situated there entered much that we are accustomed to consider as exclusively modern . . . the dialogue of the mind with itself has commenced; modern problems have presented themselves; we hear already the doubts, we witness the discouragement, of Hamlet and of Faust.[2]

Proof, unavailable to DeVane, that Browning knew Arnold's poem in the year following its publication is to be found in a letter from EBB to her brother George written on 2 May 1853. 'Have you heard a volume of poems by Dr. Arnold's son, ('by A') spoken of in London?', she asked him. 'There is a great deal of thought in them & considerable beauty. Mr. Lytton lent them to us the other day.'[3] The fact that they knew a virtually anonymous little volume of verse, of which fewer than fifty copies had been sold, is further proof of the remarkable way in which the Brownings were able to keep in touch with the English literary scene.

While it is of great interest that Browning's poem was probably prompted by Arnold's, the two could well have been written independently, as similar manifestations of the Victorians' passionate interest in the Greeks and the way in which they contemplated the great problems of life and death. By taking as his speaker an imaginary polymath of the first century A D, rather than an actual philosopher of the fifth century B C,

---

[1] See A. W. Crawford, 'Browning's "Cleon" ': JEGP xxvi (1927), 485–6. There are minor inaccuracies in this article, however. It is not true that Arnold dedicated his *New Poems* (1867) to Browning. The grateful reference to Browning forms the first of the notes at the end of the volume.

[2] Preface to *Poems. A New Edition* (1853), pp. v–vi.

[3] Barrett, 184. Cf. Kelley and Coley, A 101.

as Arnold had done, Browning gave himself greater liberty, and produced
a more successful poem.

Date: 1853/4
1863: Men and Women

CLEON.

"As certain also of your own poets have said".—

CLEON the poet (from the sprinkled isles,
Lily on lily, that o'erlace the sea,
And laugh their pride when the light wave lisps "Greece")—
To Protus in his Tyranny: much health!

    They give thy letter to me, even now: 5
I read and seem as if I heard thee speak.
The master of thy galley still unlades
Gift after gift; they block my court at last
And pile themselves along its portico
Royal with sunset, like a thought of thee: 10
And one white she-slave from the group dispersed
Of black and white slaves (like the chequer-work
Pavement, at once my nation's work and gift,

---

4 *1855P–63* Protos

epigraph: 'For in him [God] we live, and move, and have our being; as certain also of
your own poets have said, For we are also his offspring': Acts 17: 28. The last six words
are from l. 5 of the *Phainomena* of Aratus, a Greek poet of Cilicia born *c.*315BC.
   1 *the sprinkled isles*: cf. l. 63: probably the Sporades, so-called from Gk. σπείρω , *I
scatter*. Cf. *Æneid*, iii. 126–7, 'sparsasque per aequor Cycladas'.
   2 *Lily on lily*: i.e. like so many waterlilies.
     o'erlace: no other example in OED².
   3 *laugh their pride*: cf. *Troilus and Cressida*, I. iii. 163.
   4 *Protus*: an imaginary ruler, from Gk. πρῶτος 'first' or leader. Browning also used
the name in the poem 'Protus', above.
     Tyranny: realm. Gk. τύραννος, absolute power. Here used, without any pejora-
tive sense, of his realm.
   10 *Royal*: golden, crimson.

Now covered with this settle-down of doves),
One lyric woman, in her crocus vest   15
Woven of sea-wools, with her two white hands
Commends to me the strainer and the cup
Thy lip hath bettered ere it blesses mine.

  Well-counselled, king, in thy munificence!
For so shall men remark, in such an act   20
Of love for him whose song gives life its joy,
Thy recognition of the use of life;
Nor call thy spirit barely adequate
To help on life in straight ways, broad enough
For vulgar souls, by ruling and the rest.   25
Thou, in the daily building of thy tower,—
Whether in fierce and sudden spasms of toil,
Or through dim lulls of unapparent growth,
Or when the general work 'mid good acclaim
Climbed with the eye to cheer the architect,—   30
Didst ne'er engage in work for mere work's sake—
Hadst ever in thy heart the luring hope
Of some eventual rest a-top of it,
Whence, all the tumult of the building hushed,
Thou first of men mightst look out to the East: 35
The vulgar saw thy tower, thou sawest the sun.
For this, I promise on thy festival
To pour libation, looking o'er the sea,
Making this slave narrate thy fortunes, speak
Thy great words, and describe thy royal face—   40

---

*19 {reading of *1855P–84S*, DC, BrU, *1889*} *1888* munificence   35 *1855P* East.
1855–63S east.   36 *1855P–63S* tower;

  14 *settle-down*: a 'nonce-word': OED²
  15 *lyric woman*: Gk. λυρικός, a lyrist. Cf. *Balaustion*, 186: 'Balaustion! Strangers, greet
the lyric girl!'
      crocus: saffron-coloured.
  16 *Woven of sea-wools*: 'sea-wools' no doubt means 'wools dyed by some sea-
product'.
  18 *bettered*: rendered more valuable.
  37 *festival*: birthday, as in Fr. *fête*.

Wishing thee wholly where Zeus lives the most,
Within the eventual element of calm.

    Thy letter's first requirement meets me here.
It is as thou hast heard: in one short life
I, Cleon, have effected all those things   45
Thou wonderingly dost enumerate.
That epos on thy hundred plates of gold
Is mine,—and also mine the little chant,
So sure to rise from every fishing-bark
When, lights at prow, the seamen haul their net.   50
The image of the sun-god on the phare,
Men turn from the sun's self to see, is mine;
The Pœcile, o'er-storied its whole length,
As thou didst hear, with painting, is mine too.
I know the true proportions of a man   55
And woman also, not observed before;

---

48 *1855P–56* little chaunt,   *1863S* little chaunt   50 *1855P–63* their nets.

  42 *the eventual element*: cf. the abode of the gods in Odyssey vi. 42–6. The ancients
believed that Mt Olympus reached to the heavens. 'On the top . . . according to the
notions of the poets, there was neither wind, nor rain, nor clouds, but an eternal spring':
Lemprière.

  43 *requirement*: enquiry.

  47 *epos*: epic, long narrative poem. Cf. ll. 285–6, below
     plates: tablets.

  51 *phare*: lighthouse.

  53 *Pœcile*: Browning explained to an enquirer that this means 'a variegated place
anywhere—primarily at Athens where a gallery was so called from the paintings it was
adorned with,—and afterwards, any such gallery—applicable therefore to one in
Cleon's island—wherever *that* may have been': MS letter to Amelia Edwards, 14
January 1879 (Somerville College, Oxford): PK 79: 7.1.
    o'erstoried: no other example in OED².

  55 *the true proportions of a man*: at the beginning of book III of his *De Architectura*
Vitruvius states that religious buildings should have the proportions of a man. Man's
body is a model of proportion because with his arms and legs extended 'it fits into those
"perfect" geometrical forms, the square and the circle. It is impossible to exaggerate
what this simple-looking proposition meant to the men of the Renaissance. To them it
was far more than a convenient rule: it was the foundation of a whole philosophy':
Kenneth Clark, *The Nude* (1956), 13. Browning's friend and neighbour in Florence, the
American painter William Page, was deeply interested in the matter, having come on
the theory independently. Browning told Page (the latter wrote) that he had put the
discovery in 'Cleon', as his wife had in *Aurora Leigh*. [i. 864–9]. Browning had also

And I have written three books on the soul,
Proving absurd all written hitherto,
And putting us to ignorance again.
For music,—why, I have combined the moods, 60
Inventing one. In brief, all arts are mine;
Thus much the people know and recognize,
Throughout our seventeen islands. Marvel not.
We of these latter days, with greater mind
Than our forerunners, since more composite, 65
Look not so great, beside their simple way,
To a judge who only sees one way at once,
One mind-point and no other at a time,—
Compares the small part of a man of us
With some whole man of the heroic age, 70
Great in his way—not ours, nor meant for ours.
And ours is greater, had we skill to know:
For, what we call this life of men on earth,
This sequence of the soul's achievements here
Being, as I find much reason to conceive, 75
Intended to be viewed eventually

---

*60 {reading of *1855P–84S*, DC, BrU, *1889*} *1888* moods   63 *1872S, 1884S* not!
66 *1855P–56* (beside . . . . way)   71 *1855P–63S* ours,   *1863–65, 1884S* ours;
72 *1855P–65, 1884S* know.   73 *1855P–56* Yet, what

referred to the matter in 'Andrea del Sarto', 261–4. See Julia Markus, ' "Andrea del Sarto" . . . and William Page': BIS 2 (1974), 1–2. On 16 November 1854 Browning told Harriet Hosmer, herself a sculptor, that he carried in his mind all he could of Page's 'doctrine about the true proportions of the human figure': *Harriet Hosmer*, ed. Cornelia Carr (1913), 45.

60 *the moods*: modes. Ancient music made use of a large number of scales or modes, which differed from each other in the sequence of the intervals composing them and in tonality. It was to these moods that they attributed the varying ethical effects of music. See Dryden, 'Alexander's Feast'.

63 *our seventeen islands*: since Cleon is a fictitious character, these islands are not to be identified.

68 *mind-point*: not in OED[2].

74 *This sequence*: Progress. In 1881 Browning told Furnivall that 'all that seems *proved* in Darwin's scheme was a conception familiar to me from the beginning: see in *Paracelsus* the progressive development from senseless matter to organized, until man's appearance (Part V) [638–711]. Also in *Cleon*, see the order of "life's mechanics,"—and I daresay in many passages of my poetry': *Trumpeter*, 34.

As a great whole, not analyzed to parts,
But each part having reference to all,—
How shall a certain part, pronounced complete,
Endure effacement by another part?   80
Was the thing done?—then, what's to do again?
See, in the chequered pavement opposite,
Suppose the artist made a perfect rhomb,
And next a lozenge, then a trapezoid—
He did not overlay them, superimpose   85
The new upon the old and blot it out,
But laid them on a level in his work,
Making at last a picture; there it lies.
So, first the perfect separate forms were made,
The portions of mankind; and after, so,   90
Occurred the combination of the same.
For where had been a progress, otherwise?
Mankind, made up of all the single men,—
In such a synthesis the labour ends.
Now mark me! those divine men of old time   95
Have reached, thou sayest well, each at one point
The outside verge that rounds our faculty;
And where they reached, who can do more than reach?
It takes but little water just to touch
At some one point the inside of a sphere,   100
And, as we turn the sphere, touch all the rest
In due succession: but the finer air
Which not so palpably nor obviously,
Though no less universally, can touch
The whole circumference of that emptied sphere,   105
Fills it more fully than the water did;

81 *1855P–63S* Then   *1863, 1865* Then,   91 *1865* same: 92 *1855P–65* Or
where   95 *1855P–65* me—

77 *As a great whole*: cf. 'By the Fire-side', 247–50.
83 *rhomb*: a plane figure with four equal sides and the two opposite angles equal (two being acute and two obtuse).
84 *a lozenge . . . a trapezoid*: a diamond-shaped rhomb, and a quadrilateral figure no two of whose sides are parallel.
97 *The outside verge*: the circumference.

Holds thrice the weight of water in itself
Resolved into a subtler element.
And yet the vulgar call the sphere first full
Up to the visible height—and after, void;   110
Not knowing air's more hidden properties.
And thus our soul, misknown, cries out to Zeus
To vindicate his purpose in our life:
Why stay we on the earth unless to grow?
Long since, I imaged, wrote the fiction out,   115
That he or other god descended here
And, once for all, showed simultaneously
What, in its nature, never can be shown,
Piecemeal or in succession;—showed, I say,
The worth both absolute and relative   120
Of all his children from the birth of time,
His instruments for all appointed work.
I now go on to image,—might we hear
The judgment which should give the due to each,
Show where the labour lay and where the ease,   125
And prove Zeus' self, the latent everywhere!
This is a dream:—but no dream, let us hope,
That years and days, the summers and the springs,
Follow each other with unwaning powers.
The grapes which dye thy wine are richer far,   130
Through culture, than the wild wealth of the rock;
The suave plum than the savage-tasted drupe;
The pastured honey-bee drops choicer sweet;

113 *1855P–56* in its life—   127 *1855P–63* dream. But   129 *1855P–63S*
powers—   *1863* powers;   130 *1863S* are nobler far,

112 *misknown*: misunderstood, as in Carlyle, *Sartor Resartus*, I. iii. para. 3.
115 *imaged*: imagined. Cf. 'A Grammarian's Funeral', 69.
126 *Zeus' self*: i.e. God.
132 *suave*: sweet.
      drupe: 'probably a mistake', Browning commented in his letter to Amelia
Edwards (53 n, above): '. . . in accordance with certain paragraphs about horticulture I
have happened to read, —I meant . . . the rude original fruit whence, by cultivation,
the improved and refined fruit is obtained—as the apple from the crab, the plum from
the sloe. But certainly the original word, both in Greek [δρύππα] and Latin [*druppa*],
is only used for a "mouldy olive": its derivation is uncertain, —and I should hardly think
it refers to the olive only: I must see farther—if it be worth while!'. OED² defines a

The flowers turn double, and the leaves turn flowers;
That young and tender crescent-moon, thy slave,   135
Sleeping above her robe as buoyed by clouds,
Refines upon the women of my youth.
What, and the soul alone deteriorates?
I have not chanted verse like Homer, no—
Nor swept string like Terpander, no—nor carved   140
And painted men like Phidias and his friend:
I am not great as they are, point by point.
But I have entered into sympathy
With these four, running these into one soul,
Who, separate, ignored each other's art.   145
Say, is it nothing that I know them all?
The wild flower was the larger; I have dashed
Rose-blood upon its petals, pricked its cup's
Honey with wine, and driven its seed to fruit,
And show a better flower if not so large: 150
I stand myself. Refer this to the gods
Whose gift alone it is! which, shall I dare
(All pride apart) upon the absurd pretext
That such a gift by chance lay in my hand,
Discourse of lightly or depreciate?   155
It might have fallen to another's hand: what then?
I pass too surely: let at least truth stay!

And next, of what thou followest on to ask.
This being with me as I declare, O king,

136–7 {lines reversed in *1855P*}   136 *1855P–84S* Sleeping upon her   *1855P* as
if on clouds.   *1855–84S* as if on clouds,   137 *1855P* youth—   *139 1855P–*
56, 1863, 1865 like Homer's, no—   142 *1855P–65* by point: *145 {editors'
emendation} *1855P–75* each others' arts.   *1884S* each other's arts.   *1888, 1889*
eachother's art.   150 *1855P–63* large.

drupe as 'A stone-fruit; a fleshy or pulpy fruit enclosing a stone or nut having a kernel,
as the olive, plum, and cherry.'

140 *Terpander*: a lyric poet and musician from Lesbos, *c.*675 BC. 'It is said that he
appeased a tumult at Sparta by the melody and sweetness of his notes': Lemprière.
Cf. *Christmas-Eve*, 674.

141 *Phidias*: the most celebrated of Greek sculptors, d. 432 BC. He was accused of
vanity in having carved his own likeness and that of Pericles on the shield of his statue
of Athena in the Parthenon. It was 39 feet high.

My works, in all these varicoloured kinds,   160
So done by me, accepted so by men—
Thou askest, if (my soul thus in men's hearts)
I must not be accounted to attain
The very crown and proper end of life?
Inquiring thence how, now life closeth up,   165
I face death with success in my right hand:
Whether I fear death less than dost thyself
The fortunate of men? "For" (writest thou)
"Thou leavest much behind, while I leave nought.
"Thy life stays in the poems men shall sing,   170
"The pictures men shall study; while my life,
"Complete and whole now in its power and joy,
"Dies altogether with my brain and arm,
"Is lost indeed; since, what survives myself?
"The brazen statue to o'erlook my grave,   175
"Set on the promontory which I named.
"And that—some supple courtier of my heir
"Shall use its robed and sceptred arm, perhaps,
"To fix the rope to, which best drags it down.
"I go then: triumph thou, who dost not go!"   180

     Nay, thou art worthy of hearing my whole mind.
Is this apparent, when thou turn'st to muse
Upon the scheme of earth and man in chief,
That admiration grows as knowledge grows?
That imperfection means perfection hid,   185
Reserved in part, to grace the after-time?
If, in the morning of philosophy,
Ere aught had been recorded, nay perceived,
Thou, with the light now in thee, couldst have looked

164 *1855P–63* life.   167 *1855P* less even than thyself   168 *1855P–63* men.
169 *1855P–63* nought: 175 *1855P–63* statue that o'erlooks my   176 *1855P*
named,   188 *1855P–63* recorded, aught perceived,
_____

   168 *fortunate*: i.e. most fortunate.
   185 *Imperfection*: cf. Pope, *An Essay on Man*, i. 281: 'Cease then, nor Order Imperfection name'.

On all earth's tenantry, from worm to bird,   190
Ere man, her last, appeared upon the stage—
Thou wouldst have seen them perfect, and deduced
The perfectness of others yet unseen.
Conceding which,—had Zeus then questioned thee
"Shall I go on a step, improve on this,   195
"Do more for visible creatures than is done?"
Thou wouldst have answered, "Ay, by making each
"Grow conscious in himself—by that alone.
"All's perfect else: the shell sucks fast the rock,
"The fish strikes through the sea, the snake both swims   200
"And slides, forth range the beasts, the birds take flight,
"Till life's mechanics can no further go—
"And all this joy in natural life is put
"Like fire from off thy finger into each,
"So exquisitely perfect is the same.   205
"But 't is pure fire, and they mere matter are;
"It has them, not they it: and so I choose
"For man, thy last premeditated work
"(If I might add a glory to the scheme)
"That a third thing should stand apart from both,   210
"A quality arise within his soul,
"Which, intro-active, made to supervise
"And feel the force it has, may view itself,
"And so be happy." Man might live at first
The animal life: but is there nothing more?   215
In due time, let him critically learn
How he lives; and, the more he gets to know
Of his own life's adaptabilities,
The more joy-giving will his life become.
Thus man, who hath this quality, is best.   220

191 *1855P–63* man had yet appeared   195 *1855P–56* "Wilt thou go
201 *1855P–56* slides; the birds . . . . flight, forth . . . . beasts,   *1863S–68* slides, the
birds . . . . flight,   forth . . . . beasts,   209 *1855P–63S* to   this   scheme)
211 *1855P–63* within the soul,   220 *1855P–63* The man

212 *intro-active*: working within, and producing self-awareness.
218 *adaptabilities*: capacity to adapt.

But thou, king, hadst more reasonably said:
"Let progress end at once,—man make no step
"Beyond the natural man, the better beast,
"Using his senses, not the sense of sense."
In man there's failure, only since he left   225
The lower and inconscious forms of life.
We called it an advance, the rendering plain
Man's spirit might grow conscious of man's life,
And, by new lore so added to the old,
Take each step higher over the brute's head.   230
This grew the only life, the pleasure-house,
Watch-tower and treasure-fortress of the soul,
Which whole surrounding flats of natural life
Seemed only fit to yield subsistence to;
A tower that crowns a country. But alas,   235
The soul now climbs it just to perish there!
For thence we have discovered ('t is no dream—
We know this, which we had not else perceived)
That there's a world of capability
For joy, spread round about us, meant for us,   240
Inviting us; and still the soul craves all,
And still the flesh replies, "Take no jot more
"Than ere thou clombst the tower to look abroad!
"Nay, so much less as that fatigue has brought
"Deduction to it." We struggle, fain to enlarge   245
Our bounded physical recipiency,
Increase our power, supply fresh oil to life,
Repair the waste of age and sickness: no,

---

224 *1872S*, *1884S* sense!"   225 *1855P* There's failure in man, only
226 *1863S* and unconscious forms   228 *1855P–63* A spirit . . . . of that life,
235 *1855P–63* alas!   236 *1855P–63* there,   243 *1855P–56* ere you climbed
the *1863S–68* thou climbedst the   248 *1855P–65* sickness. No,

---

224 *the sense of sense*: the meaning of our sensations.
226 *inconscious*: Browning uses both forms of this word. In *Sordello* vi. 148 he revised
'inconsciously' to 'unconsciously', from *1868*. Cf. 'Saul', 162.
236 *The soul now climbs it*: cf. *Paracelsus*, v. 651–2.
243 *thou clombst*: you climbed (arch.)
246 *recipiency*: receptivity.
248 *Repair*: make good.

It skills not! life's inadequate to joy,
As the soul sees joy, tempting life to take.   250
They praise a fountain in my garden here
Wherein a Naiad sends the water-bow
Thin from her tube; she smiles to see it rise.
What if I told her, it is just a thread
From that great river which the hills shut up,   255
And mock her with my leave to take the same?
The artificer has given her one small tube
Past power to widen or exchange—what boots
To know she might spout oceans if she could?
She cannot lift beyond her first thin thread: 260
And so a man can use but a man's joy
While he sees God's. Is it for Zeus to boast,
"See, man, how happy I live, and despair—
"That I may be still happier—for thy use!"
If this were so, we could not thank our lord,   265
As hearts beat on to doing; 't is not so—
Malice it is not. Is it carelessness?
Still, no. If care—where is the sign? I ask,
And get no answer, and agree in sum,
O king, with thy profound discouragement,   270
Who seest the wider but to sigh the more.
Most progress is most failure: thou sayest well.

The last point now:—thou dost except a case—
Holding joy not impossible to one

249 *1855P–65* not: 252 *1855P–56* the water-spurt   260 *1855P–56* first
straight thread.   *1863S* thread.   *1863* thread,   268 *1855P–63* sign
269 *1855P–63* answer: 272 *1855P–63* failure!   *{reading of *1855P–84S*, DC,
BrU, *1889}* *1888* savest   273 *1872S, 1884S* now. Thou

249 *skills*: matters. Arch., as in Shakespeare.
250 *to take*: to reach for it.
252 *a Naiad*: a river nymph (here a statue of one). Cf. 'Up at a Villa', 29–30.
      water-bow: no other example in OED².
258 *boots*: does it help.
266 *beat on to*: throb to.
273 *except a case*: make one exception.

With artist-gifts—to such a man as I   275
Who leave behind me living works indeed;
For, such a poem, such a painting lives.
What? dost thou verily trip upon a word,
Confound the accurate view of what joy is
(Caught somewhat clearer by my eyes than thine)   280
With feeling joy? confound the knowing how
And showing how to live (my faculty)
With actually living?—Otherwise
Where is the artist's vantage o'er the king?
Because in my great epos I display   285
How divers men young, strong, fair, wise, can act—
Is this as though I acted? if I paint,
Carve the young Phœbus, am I therefore young?
Methinks I'm older that I bowed myself
The many years of pain that taught me art!   290
Indeed, to know is something, and to prove
How all this beauty might be enjoyed, is more:
But, knowing nought, to enjoy is something too.
Yon rower, with the moulded muscles there,
Lowering the sail, is nearer it than I.   295
I can write love-odes: thy fair slave's an ode.
I get to sing of love, when grown too grey
For being beloved: she turns to that young man,
The muscles all a-ripple on his back.
I know the joy of kingship: well, thou art king!   300

    "But," sayest thou—(and I marvel, I repeat,
To find thee trip on such a mere word) "what
"Thou writest, paintest, stays; that does not die:
"Sappho survives, because we sing her songs,

280 *1855P* clearer with my   301 {in *1884S* the line does not open a new
paragraph}   *{reading of *1855P–84S*} 1888, 1889 repeat   302 *1855P–84S* thee
tripping on a

288 *Phoebus*: Phoebus Apollo, the god of the Sun, and the type of male beauty, as
Venus is of female.

304 *Sappho*: the most famous female poet of antiquity, was born in Lesbos *c.*612 BC.

"And Æschylus, because we read his plays!"   305
Why, if they live still, let them come and take
Thy slave in my despite, drink from thy cup,
Speak in my place. Thou diest while I survive?
Say rather that my fate is deadlier still,
In this, that every day my sense of joy   310
Grows more acute, my soul (intensified
By power and insight) more enlarged, more keen;
While every day my hairs fall more and more,
My hand shakes, and the heavy years increase—
The horror quickening still from year to year,   315
The consummation coming past escape
When I shall know most, and yet least enjoy—
When all my works wherein I prove my worth,
Being present still to mock me in men's mouths,
Alive still, in the praise of such as thou,   320
I, I the feeling, thinking, acting man,
The man who loved his life so over-much,
Sleep in my urn. It is so horrible,
I dare at times imagine to my need
Some future state revealed to us by Zeus,   325
Unlimited in capability
For joy, as this is in desire for joy,
—To seek which, the joy-hunger forces us:
That, stung by straitness of our life, made strait
On purpose to make prized the life at large—   330
Freed by the throbbing impulse we call death,
We burst there as the worm into the fly,

309 *1855P* Say wiselier that   312 *1855P–56* In power   313 *1872S, 1884S*
my hair falls more   320 *1855P–84S* the phrase of   323 *1855–84S* Shall sleep
328 *1855P–56* us.   330 *1855P–63* make sweet the

305 *Æschylus*: the earliest of the three great tragic dramatists of Athens (525/4–
456 BC). Browning published a near-literal translation of his *Agamemnon* in 1877.

325 *Some future state*: cf. 1 Cor. 15:15ff. Browning often touches on St Paul's
argument for immortality—the apparent futility of human life if there is nothing after
death—the argument here rejected by Cleon.

329 *straitness*: narrowness, limitations.

332 *as the worm into the fly*: the caterpillar, which becomes a butterfly. The Gk. word
ψυχή (*psyche*) means both 'soul' and 'butterfly'. cf. *Pippa Passes*, i. 373–4 and ii. 289 ff.

Who, while a worm still, wants his wings. But no!
Zeus has not yet revealed it; and alas,
He must have done so, were it possible!   335

    Live long and happy, and in that thought die:
Glad for what was! Farewell. And for the rest,
I cannot tell thy messenger aright
Where to deliver what he bears of thine
To one called Paulus; we have heard his fame   340
Indeed, if Christus be not one with him—
I know not, nor am troubled much to know.
Thou canst not think a mere barbarian Jew,
As Paulus proves to be, one circumcised,
Hath access to a secret shut from us?   345
Thou wrongest our philosophy, O king,
In stooping to inquire of such an one,
As if his answer could impose at all!
He writeth, doth he? well, and he may write.
Oh, the Jew findeth scholars! certain slaves   350
Who touched on this same isle, preached him and Christ;
And (as I gathered from a bystander)
Their doctrine could be held by no sane man.

334 *1855P–56* alas!   336 *1855P–84S* die,   337 *1855P–65*   was.
340 *1855P/MS, Fields, Rossetti* To him called   343 *1855P* think that a barbarian
1889 Jew   344 *1855P/MS* be, and circumcised—*Fields, Rossetti* be, and circum-
cised,   *{reading of 1855–84S}* *1855P* circumcised— *1888, 1889* circumcized,
347 *1855P* such a one,   348 *1855P–63* all.   353 *1855P–63* Their doctrines
could
────────
333 *wants*: lacks.
340 *one called Paulus*: in Acts 13–21 we have an account of St Paul's journeyings to
spread the gospel of Christ. 'Christus' is the L. form of Gk. 'Christos', the Anointed
One.
   Browning told Rossetti that 'one called' should be revised to 'him called', and 'one
circumcised' [344] to 'and circumcised' (*Letters*, 42). The revision was never made.
348 *impose*: supply 'on us'.

THE TWINS

WE know a good deal about the occasion of this little poem. On 4 March 1854 EBB wrote to her sister Henrietta: 'Robert and I are going to send Arabel some verses for her bazaar-stall and the Ragged schools'.[1] The bazaar, to provide support for the education of the children of the very poor, was to be held in Baker Street on 19 April. While Arabel was deeply interested in this charity, she felt that she had been 'dragged into' an 'unpleasant position', and it was a case where her sister and brother-in-law felt obliged to help her with verses 'which are to be printed'. On 30 March Browning wrote to Chapman, of Chapman and Hall:

we should like to give her the paper and the printing into the bargain. Here are the poems. Will you kindly get two or three hundred copies struck off, in the simplest fashion, with as much taste as is consistent with cheapness—so that they may be sold, say, at sixpence a copy? No covers, you know, or anything but the plain sheetful, simply doubled into shape—making the best show you can for [the] little we want to spend. Will you have the goodness to get this done *at once* (otherwise all our labor will be thrown away) and charge the same . . . *to our account*—not on any consideration allowing Miss Barrett to interfere—except to correct the proof which you can send her with the copy. Please also to keep the said copy clean—as she will sell the M.S. as an autograph, with other ware of a like character. You must consider, at once, us and the charity and the benevolent public who want as much for their pence as possible.[2]

In a P.S. EBB told Chapman that she considered that 'two or three hundred copies would be inadequate', and that 'the expense attending double the number would be very slight', but left him to decide.

On 3 April EBB wrote to Arabella asking her to correct the proof as carefully as she could, 'as these little things should be particularly accurate'. She continued:

What Robert sends you is not worth much he says . . . being a simple versification of a fable of Martin Luther's—but, in my mind, it is characteristic both of Robert & Luther, & very appropriate to the occasion.[3]

---

[1] Huxley, 203; PK 54: 37. The Ragged School Union had been established in 1844. Browning's lifelong interest in Luther is evident in *Paracelsus* and 'Bishop Blougram's Apology'.

[2] *New Letters*, 71–2.

[3] PK 54: 55. 'The Ragged School cause is one of those unquestionable causes', EBB continues, 'which every man with a sense of justice in him & every woman with a throb of pity in her . . . must give their sympathy.' For the *Keepsake*, see p. 493 below.

She mentioned that Procter ('Barry Cornwall') had promised to give an autograph poem to the bazaar if they both agreed to contribute to the *Keepsake*, in which he was interested—which prompted the suggestion that the sale of a few autographs might be a profitable sideline on the present occasion. On 1 July Browning thanked Chapman for his 'prompt and kind attention to our wishes about those versicles for the charity', adding: 'The plan was none of ours, nor at all to our mind (between ourselves) but since it seemed auspicious to others, we did as you helped us to do'.[1] On 21 October EBB told Arabel that one friend had given her 'five scudi (about a guinea) for the charity', in gratitude for the gift of a copy. Unfortunately 'Our other readers have not shown the same degree of sensibility . . . dropping tears of silver . . in penny pieces'.[2] On 13 February 1855 EBB sent Mrs Martin a copy of the little pamphlet, 'sixpence worth of rhymes', mentioning that they were not now 'purchase-able anywhere', but that they had now been sent a few copies. These were no doubt remainders, since the pamphlet did not sell well. It has a paper cover with the title *Two Poems by Elizabeth Barrett and Robert Browning*, the imprint of Chapman and Hall, and '*Price Sixpence.*' at the foot. Of the sixteen pages, 3–11 have EBB's poem, 'A Plea for the Ragged Schools of London. Written in Rome', with the date '*March 20th* 1854.' at the end, while pp. 13–15 have Browning's poem, dated '*Rome, March 30th, 1854.*'

The source of the poem, as Mrs Orr pointed out, is a passage in the Table Talk of Luther, probably taken from the English translation of Hazlitt's nephew:

Give and it shall be given unto you: this is a fine maxim, and makes people poor and rich . . . There is in Austria a monastery, which, in former times, was very rich, and remained rich so long as it was charitable to the poor; but when it ceased to give, then it became indigent, and is so to this day. Not long since, a poor man went there and solicited alms, which was denied him; he demanded the cause why they refused to give for God's sake? The porter of the monastery answered: We are become poor; whereupon the mendicant said: The cause of your poverty is this: ye had formerly in this monastery two brethren, the one named *Date* (give), and the other *Dabitur* (it shall be given you). The former ye thrust out; the other went away of himself. . . . Beloved, he that desires to have anything, must also give: a liberal hand was never in want, or empty.[3]

[1] *New Letters*, 78.
[2] PK 54: 115; *Letters of EBB*, ii. 185.
[3] *The Table Talk or Familiar Discourse of Martin Luther*, trans. William Hazlitt the younger (1848) 151–2. Cf. Luke 6: 38.

The autograph manuscript of this poem, as of EBB's 'A Plea', is in the Pierpont Morgan Library in New York.

As in the other poem written in response to a request, 'Ben Karshook's Wisdom', Browning uses one of the simplest of English verse-forms, stanzas of four lines each consisting of iambic trimeters (mixed with anapaests) and rhyming *abab*. In other pieces, as in 'Youth and Art', he uses the form more subtly.

Date: 1854
1863: *Dramatic Romances*

THE TWINS.

"Give" and "It-shall-be-given-unto-you."

I.

GRAND rough old Martin Luther
  Bloomed fables—flowers on furze,
The better the uncouther:
  Do roses stick like burrs?

II.

A beggar asked an alms   5
  One day at an abbey-door,
Said Luther; but, seized with qualms,
  The abbot replied, "We're poor!

III.

"Poor, who had plenty once,
  "When gifts fell thick as rain: 10

---

1 *rough*: much about Luther was 'rough'. Browning may be remembering his poems. See *Paracelsus*, iv. 213: 'Halts like the best of Luther's psalms'. Cf. Carlyle's essay on 'Luther's Psalm': *Works*, xxvii. 160 ff.

2 *bloomed fables*: for the transitive use, cf. Num. 17: 8: 'the rod of Aaron . . . brought forth buds, and bloomed blossoms . . .'

furze: gorse, whin, with sticky leaves or needles.

5 *an alms*: as singular, as in Acts 3: 3: 'Who . . . asked an alms'.

"But they give us nought, for the nonce,
    "And how should we give again?"

IV.

Then the beggar, "See your sins!
    "Of old, unless I err,
"Ye had brothers for inmates, twins,   15
    "Date and Dabitur.

V.

"While Date was in good case
    "Dabitur flourished too:
"For Dabitur's lenten face
    "No wonder if Date rue.   20

VI.

"Would ye retrieve the one?
    "Try and make plump the other!
"When Date's penance is done,
    "Dabitur helps his brother.

VII.

"Only, beware relapse!"   25
    The Abbot hung his head.
This beggar might be perhaps
    An angel, Luther said.

---

24 *MS, 1854* "DABITUR joins his   *1855P* "Dabitur help his

16 *Date and Dabitur.* 'Give, and it shall be given unto you', in the Vulgate version:
'Date, et dabitur vobis'.
19 *lenten*: meagre, dismal.
21 *retrieve*: restore, revive.
28 *An angel*: i.e. a messenger from God.

POPULARITY

As we have seen, Browning feared by now that popularity was hardly likely to come his way.[1] In this poem he considers the value of a 'true poet', one whose importance is realized only after death. It may have been inspired, at least in part, by a sonnet sent Keats by an anonymous admirer and recently published by Monckton Milnes in the *Life, Letters and Literary Remains*. It begins

> Star of high promise! Not to this dark age
> Do thy mild light and loveliness belong.[2]

Ironically enough, this poem itself exemplifies in an extreme form certain of the characteristics which were to deny Browning's work any degree of popularity for a further decade. It is not surprising that Ruskin took it as an example of his obscurity in the letter in which he acknowledged *Men and Women*.[3] He wondered, almost desperately, 'how far the purple of [his work] *must* be within this terrible shell; and only to be fished for among threshing of foam & slippery rocks'. In our notes we quote his perplexed comments and Browning's few replies.

The speaker sets out to describe a true poet. God must have a purpose for him. The full beauty of his work will be released in the future, not now. The speaker uses the image of Tyrian purple, so highly prized in antiquity, and its manufacture from molluscs. The poem ends with a reference to poetasters who enliven their verse with hints of the new richness introduced by the new poet—and do very well out of this, enjoying rich food and fine wine. But Keats, who 'fished the murex up', had to be content with very little.

'Popularity' is general in its bearing. Other poets than Keats were also in Browning's mind, notably Shelley—*Adonais* is alluded to at the beginning—and himself.

The metrical form is similar to that of 'Two in the Campagna'. Each stanza consists of four iambic tetrameters followed by a trimeter.

---

[1] See Introduction. For his friends urging him to aim at some measure of popularity, see pp. xi ff.

[2] 2 vols. (1848), i. 254. Altick made this suggestion, VP 1 (1963), 65–6. The writer may well have been Woodhouse.

[3] Above, pp. xxxiv ff.

In our notes to the poem we quote Ruskin's baffled comments from DeLaura, 'Ruskin and the Brownings', 324–7, and Browning's few replies from Dr Philip Kelley's transcription (PK 55:169). The remaining elucidations are our own.

Date: 1853/5
1863: *Dramatic Lyrics*

POPULARITY.

I.

STAND still, true poet that you are!
   I know you; let me try and draw you.
Some night you'll fail us: when afar
   You rise, remember one man saw you,
   Knew you, and named a star!   5

II.

My star, God's glow-worm! Why extend
   That loving hand of his which leads you,

---

1 *1855P–56* are,   3 *1855P–56* us. When   5 *1855P–56* star.

1 *Stand still*: 'Does this mean: literally—stand still? or where was the poet figuratively going—and why couldn't he be drawn as he went?' Ruskin. Browning replied: 'For the reason indicated in the verse, to be sure,—*to let me draw him*—& because he is at present going his way & fancying nobody notices him,—& moreover, "going on" (as we say) against the injustice of that,—& lastly, in as much as one night he'll fail us, as a star is apt to drop out of heaven, in authentic astronomic records, & I want to make the most of my time. So much may be in "stand still" and how much more was (for instance) in that "stay!" of Samuel's (1. xv. 16)'. The Samuel passage begins: 'Stay, and I will tell thee'.
3 *Some night you'll fail us*: 'Why some *night*?—rather than some day?—"Fail us." Now? Die?': Ruskin.
3–4 *when afar / You Rise*: 'Where?—Now?': Ruskin. Cf. 'Waring', 259–60: 'Oh, never star / Was lost here but it rose afar!'
4 *remember*: 'very good—I understand.': Ruskin.
5 *named a star!*: acclaimed him as a great poet. Cf. *Adonais*, 494–5: 'The soul of Adonais, like a star, / Beacons from the abode where the Eternal are'.
6 *My star, God's glow-worm!*: so much more important to me than to God. 'Very fine. I understand and like that': Ruskin, who continues: 'Why ∧ "extend that loving hand." Grammatically, this applies to the Poet. the ellipsis of "Should He" at ∧ throws one quite out—like a step in a floor which one doesn't expect.'

Yet locks you safe from end to end
    Of this dark world, unless he needs you,
Just saves your light to spend?   10

III.

His clenched hand shall unclose at last,
    I know, and let out all the beauty:
My poet holds the future fast,
    Accepts the coming ages' duty,
Their present for this past.   15

IV.

That day, the earth's feast-master's brow
    Shall clear, to God the chalice raising;
"Others give best at first, but thou
    "Forever set'st our table praising,
"Keep'st the good wine till now!"   20

---

11 *1855P* That clenched   12 *1855P–56* beauty.   15 *1855P* That present
20 *1855P–56* now."

8 *Yet locks you safe*: 'How does God's hand lock him; do you mean—keeps him from
being seen?—and how does it make him safe [?]Why is a poet safer or more locked up
than anybody else? I go on—in hope': Ruskin. Line 10 explains.

11 *His clenched hand . . . and let out all the beauty*: 'very good—but I don't understand
why the hand should have held close so long—which is just the point I wanted to be
explained. Why the poet *had to be* locked up': Ruskin. God will need the poet in the
future, unappreciated as he is in the present.

13 *My poet holds the future fast*: 'How? Do you mean he anticipates it in his
mind—trusts in it—I *don't* know if you mean that, because I don't know if poets *do* that.
If you mean that—I wish you had said so plainly': Ruskin. The meaning is that when
God opens his hand the poet's light will shine forth, and accept the praises of future
men.

16 *the earth's feast-master's brow*: 'Who is the earths F.? An Angel? a [*sic*] Everybody?':
Ruskin. The word 'feast-maisters' occurs in J[ohn] H[ealey]'s translation of St Augus-
tine's *De Civitate Dei* (1610), 521. The Gk. original,' ἀρχιτρίκλινος, occurs in John 2: 9.

17 *the chalice raising*: 'This, grammatically, agrees with "*brow*", and makes me uncom-
fortable': Ruskin.

18 *Others give best at first*: a reference to Christ's turning the water into wine: John 2,
particularly 9–10. Ruskin comments: 'very pretty I like that'.

V.

Meantime, I'll draw you as you stand,
  With few or none to watch and wonder:
I'll say—a fisher, on the sand
  By Tyre the old, with ocean-plunder,
A netful, brought to land.   25

VI.

Who has not heard how Tyrian shells
  Enclosed the blue, that dye of dyes
Whereof one drop worked miracles,
  And coloured like Astarte's eyes
Raw silk the merchant sells?   30

---

22 *1855P–56* wonder.   23 *1855P–56* (on   24 *1855P–56* Old) his ocean-
plunder,

---

21 *Meantime, I'll draw you*: 'Do you mean—his Cork?—we have not had anything about painting for ever so long—very well. *Do* draw him then: I should like to have him drawn very much': Ruskin.

22 *With few or none*: cf. Wordsworth, 'Song' ('She dwelt among th'untrodden ways'), 3–4: 'A Maid whom there were none to praise / And very few to love'.

23 *I'll say*: 'Now, where *are* you going to—this is, I believe pure malice against *me*, for having said that painters should always grind their own colours': Ruskin. 'I'll say' means 'I'll put it like this'.

24 *Tyre*: in ancient times, the most famous city of Phoenicia, celebrated for its production of purple from certain shellfish.

25 *netful*: the first occurrence of the word in OED[2].

26 *Who has not heard*: on this stanza Ruskin asks, 'Do you mean—the silk that the merchant sells Raw—or what do you want with the merchant at all[?]'

Tyrian shells: certain gastropod molluscs secrete a liquid from which costly purple or crimson dyes were made, above all at Tyre. In *Æneid*, iv. 262–3 we hear how a cloak hung from the shoulders of Æneas 'ablaze with Tyrian purple—a gift which wealthy Dido had wrought, interweaving the web with thread of gold'. Turner suggests that Browning has 'blue' instead of 'purple' for reasons of rhythm, or 'because of Keats's sonnet to blue eyes, beginning 'Blue! 'Tis the life of heaven': neither hypothesis seems convincing.

29 *Astarte's eyes*: Astarte was 'a powerful divinity of Syria, the same as the Venus of the Greeks': Lemprière.

VII.

And each bystander of them all
  Could criticize, and quote tradition
How depths of blue sublimed some pall
  —To get which, pricked a king's ambition;
Worth sceptre, crown and ball.   35

VIII.

Yet there's the dye, in that rough mesh,
  The sea has only just o'erwhispered!
Live whelks, each lip's beard dripping fresh,
  As if they still the water's lisp heard
Through foam the rock-weeds thresh.   40

IX.

Enough to furnish Solomon
  Such hangings for his cedar-house,
That, when gold-robed he took the throne

---

32 *1856* tradition;   38 *1855P–56* whelks, the lip's-beard

31 *And each bystander*: 'Who are these bystanders—I didn't hear of any before—Are they people who have gone to see the fishing?': Ruskin.

32 *Could criticize, and quote tradition*: 'Criticise what? the fishing?—and why should they—what was wrong in it?—Quote tradition. Do you mean about purple? But if they made purple at the time, it wasn't tradition merely—but experience.—You might as well tell me you heard the colourmen in Long-Acre, quote tradition touching their next cargo of Indigo, or cochineal': Ruskin.

33 *sublimed*: 'I don't know what you mean by "sublimed". Made sublime?—if so—it is not English. To sublime means to evaporate dryly, I believe and has participle "Sublimated"': Ruskin. Johnson gives 'To exalt; to heighten; to improve' as one meaning of the verb.

35 *Worth sceptre, crown and ball*: 'Indeed. Was there ever such a fool of a King?—You ought to have put a note saying who': Ruskin.

36 *Yet there's*: 'Well. I understand that, & it's very pretty': Ruskin.

37 *only just*: only now.
    o'erwhisper'd: no doubt Browning's coinage, for the rhyme.

41 *Enough to furnish Solomon*: 'I don't think Solomons spouse swore.—at least not about blue-bells. I understand this bit, but fear most people won't. How many have noticed a blue-bells stamen?': Ruskin.

42 *his cedar-house*: 1 Kgs. 5: 5–6; 7: 2–3.

In that abyss of blue, the Spouse
Might swear his presence shone   45

X.

Most like the centre-spike of gold
   Which burns deep in the blue-bell's womb,
What time, with ardours manifold,
   The bee goes singing to her groom,
Drunken and overbold.   50

XI.

Mere conchs! not fit for warp or woof!
   Till cunning come to pound and squeeze
And clarify,—refine to proof
   The liquor filtered by degrees,
While the world stands aloof.   55

XII.

And there's the extract, flasked and fine,
   And priced and saleable at last!
And Hobbs, Nobbs, Stokes and Nokes combine
   To paint the future from the past,
Put blue into their line.   60

52 *1855P–56* Till art comes,—comes to   *1863* cunning comes to

44 *abyss of blue*: cf. 33.

   the Spouse: 1 Kgs. 7: 7–8; Song of Solomon 4: 8, etc.

48 *What time*: while.

50 *The bee*: 'I don't understand. I thought there was only one Queen-bee and *she* never was out o'nights—nor came home drunk or disorderly. Besides if she does, unless you had told me what o'clock in the morning she comes home at, the simile is of no use to me': Ruskin.

51 *Mere conchs*: 'Well,' Ruskin asks, 'but what has this to do with the Poet. Who "Pounds" *him*?—I don't understand. World stand[s] aloof—yes—from the purple manufactory, but from Pounding of Poets?—does it?—and if so—who distils—or fines, & bottles them.' The mere shells have to be pounded and treated further before the valuable purple extract is produced.

56 *flasked and fine*: 'Now *is* that what you call painting a poet. Under the whole & sole image of a bottle of Blue, with a bladder over the cork? The Arabian fisherman with his genie was nothing to this': Ruskin.

59 *To paint the future*: 'Why the future. Do you mean *in* the future': Ruskin.

60 *Put blue into their line*: 'I don't understand;—do you mean Quote the Poet, or write articles upon him—or in his style? And if so—was this what God kept him *safe*

XIII.

Hobbs hints blue,—straight he turtle eats:
  Nobbs prints blue,—claret crowns his cup:
Nokes outdares Stokes in azure feats,—
  Both gorge. Who fished the murex up?
What porridge had John Keats? 65

for? to feed Nobbs with Turtle. Is this what you call Accepting the future ages duty.—I don't understand'. The meaning is that these poetasters enrich their verse with valuable new colours or qualities discovered by the 'true poet'. Hobbs and Nobbs are fictitious names, like Stokes and Nokes, which occur in models of legal documents. The latter pair occur in Browning's letter to Domett denying that he is 'difficult on System': *Correspondence*, iv. 261.

61 *he turtle eats*: i.e. he is successful, in the worldly sense.

64 *Who fished the murex up?*: i.e. none of these poetasters.

murex: cf. 26 n., above.

65 *What porridge*: 'Porridge is a Scotch dish, I believe; typical of bad fare. Do you mean that Keats had bad fare? But if he had—how was he kept safe to the worlds end? I don't understand at all!!!!!!!': Ruskin. The meaning is that whereas the derivative poetasters lived well, the genius had poor fare.

THE HERETIC'S TRAGEDY

LIKE 'Johannes Agricola', 'Holy-Cross Day' and 'The Confessional', this is
one of Browning's studies in the perversions of religion. It might have been
inspired by the engravings in Foxe's *Book of Martyrs*. Browning's interest in
the Templars will have been nourished by his early reading of Scott (e.g. *The
Talisman*), while the *Biographie universelle*, which he referred to so often,
provided him (under 'Molai') with a clear account of the life and death of the
last of the Grand Masters of the Templars.[1] There he will have read of the
great importance and wealth of the Order, of its decline, and of the simulta-
neous arrest of all the Templars in France on 13 October 1307. Many and
serious charges were brought against the Order, and those who proved
recalcitrant were delivered to the Inquisition. Jacques du Bourg-Molay and
one other knight were condemned to be burnt in Paris on 18 March 1314:

The stake was erected at the end of the little island on the Seine, at the same place
as the statue of Henri IV. The two knights ascended the stake, which was gradually
lit, and they were burnt over a slow fire . . . To their last gasp, they protested their
innocence and that of their Order . . . It has also been said that the Grand Master,
before dying, had cited the Pope and the King before the tribunal of God.[2]

Two of Chatterton's poems, 'The Tournament' and 'Ælla, a Tragycal
Enterlude, or Discoorseynge Tragedie', may have helped to give Brown-
ing the idea of casting his satire on religious fanaticism in the form of an
Interlude, a genre described by E. K. Chambers as 'a play "between"
speakers, a play in dialogue'.[3] Living at a time when the history of our
earlier drama was being explored with fresh enthusiasm, Browning may
have read some available interlude; but there is no sign of his attempting
to follow any particular model, and the spirit of Chatterton's Thomas
Rowley seems dominant. As Worsfold pointed out, this interlude is
musical, and takes the form of 'an office of the Church',[4] in terrifying
contrast to the horror of what is being done. It is sung, if possible to the

---

[1] The Knights Templar were members of a military and religious Order founded in
the early twelfth century for the protection of the Holy Sepulchre and of Christian
pilgrims visiting the Holy Land. Their name derives from their occupation of a building
on or close to the site of the Temple of Solomon in Jerusalem.
[2] xxix (1821), 278b.
[3] *English Literature at the Close of the Middle Ages* (1945), 15. Chambers adds that 'The
rubrics which introduce their dramatic passages follow no uniform practice'.
[4] Worsfold, ii. 315.

accompaniment of 'lute or clavicithern', the soloist being supported by a chorus. It is introduced by the Abbot, who concludes it with a particularly sinister line.

While this piece and 'Holy-Cross Day' do not appear together in *Men and Women* (any more than 'Fra Lippo Lippi' and 'Andrea del Sarto' appear together), in *1863* and later they do, this poem being preceded by 'Johannes Agricola in Meditation' and followed by 'Holy-Cross Day'.

The lines are iambic tetrameters, with one or two anapaests here and there. The eight-line stanzas rhyme *ababcdcd*. Each stanza except the fifth has a refrain which repeats, wholly or in part, the preceding line.

Date: 1853/5
1863. Dramatic Romances

THE HERETIC'S TRAGEDY.

A MIDDLE-AGE INTERLUDE.

ROSA MUNDI; SEU, FULCITE ME FLORIBUS. A CONCEIT OF MASTER GYSBRECHT, CANON-REGULAR OF SAINT JODOCUS-BY-THE-BAR, YPRES CITY. CANTUQUE, *Virgilius.* AND HATH OFTEN BEEN SUNG AT HOCK-TIDE AND FESTIVALS. GAVISUS ERAM, *Jessides.* v

epigraph   i *1855P–56 (In the original)* ROSA

epigraph (i): the removal of '(*In the original*)' withdrew assistance offered in *1855*.
  ROSA MUNDI: Rose of the World. Cf. Song of Solomon, 2.1.
  SEU, FULCITE ME FLORIBUS: or, support me with flowers. The last three words are the Vulgate text of Song of Solomon, 2.5. Cf. ll. 60 ff. of this poem. In a letter to EBB Browning had quoted the AV, 'Comfort me with apples, for I am sick of love', which forms the epigraph to Quarles, *Emblems*, v. ii.
  (i) CONCEIT: invention.
  (ii) MASTER GYSBRECHT: an imaginary cleric. An Austin canon, or canon regular, as distinct from a secular canon, renounced private property as well as living within the precincts.
  (iii) CANTUQUE: cf. *Æneid*, vii. 754: 'by a charm'. with reference to a priest with magical powers.
  (iv) AND HATH OFTEN: as if on a title-page.
    HOCK-TIDE: the second Monday and Tuesday after Easter Day, a time of festival.

(It would seem to be a glimpse from the burning of Jacques du Bourg-Molay, at Paris, A.D. 1314; as distorted by the refraction from Flemish brain to brain, during the course of a couple of centuries.)

I.

PREADMONISHETH THE ABBOT DEODAET.

THE Lord, we look to once for all,
  Is the Lord we should look at, all at once:
He knows not to vary, saith Saint Paul,
  Nor the shadow of turning, for the nonce.
See him no other than as he is!   5
  Give both the infinitudes their due—
Infinite mercy, but, I wis,
  As infinite a justice too.

[*Organ: plagal-cadence.*

As infinite a justice too.

II.

ONE SINGETH.

John, Master of the Temple of God,   10
Falling to sin the Unknown Sin,

---

viii *1855P–56* centuries.—R.B.)   6 *1855P–56* the Infinites their

(v) GAVISUS ERAM: I had rejoiced. *Jessides*: son of Jesse, David (the psalmist).
(viii) *Flemish*: cf. *Merry Wives*, II. i. 18, the meaning being derogatory, 'boorish'.
DEODAET: St Augustine had a son whom he named Adeodatus, 'given by God'. For the name Deodate see Coleridge, *The Piccolomini or, the First Part of Wallenstein*, I. xi. 8, and *The Death of Wallenstein*, I. v. 10.
3 *He knows not to vary*: Paul does not seem to have said this. Turner suggests Jas. 1: 17: 'the Father . . ., with whom is no variableness, neither shadow of turning'. Cf. Job 23: 13, Ps. 132: 11.
4 *for the nonce*: this has the air of being a tag, put in for the rhyme's sake, so satirizing the speaker. Cf. Chaucer's 'for the nones', General Prologue, 523.
s.d. *plagal cadence*: 'that form of perfect cadence in which the chord major or minor of the subdominant immediately precedes that of the tonic' (OED²), as after 'Amen'.
11 *the Unknown Sin*: the Templars were accused, among other things, of denying God and Christ, spitting on the Cross, idolatry and sacrilege. Cf. ll. 81–4. That which constitutes blasphemy against the Holy Ghost (Luke 12: 10) has never been defined.

What he bought of Emperor Aldabrod,
  He sold it to Sultan Saladin:
Till, caught by Pope Clement, a-buzzing there,
  Hornet-prince of the mad wasps' hive,   15
And clipt of his wings in Paris square,
  They bring him now to be burned alive.
                    [*And wanteth there grace of lute or clavicithern,*
                        ye shall say to confirm him who singeth—
We bring John now to be burned alive.

                              III.

In the midst is a goodly gallows built;
  'Twixt fork and fork, a stake is stuck;   20
But first they set divers tumbrils a-tilt,
  Make a trench all round with the city muck;
Inside they pile log upon log, good store;
  Faggots no few, blocks great and small,
Reach a man's mid-thigh, no less, no more,—   25
  For they mean he should roast in the sight of all.

                          CHORUS.

We mean he should roast in the sight of all.

17 *1855P* They   have   brought   him   18 *1855P* We   have   brought   John
22 *1855* muck,   24 *1855P, 1855, 1863–84S* Faggots not few,   *1856* Fagots not few,

12 *Aldabrod*: no such Emperor is known; Saladin, Sultan of Egypt, lived from 1138
to 1193.

14 *Pope Clement*: Clement V became Pope in 1305. A Gascon, he never went to
Rome, making his residence in Avignon from 1309. He was subservient to the French
King, Philip the Fair, particularly in the proceedings he brought against the Templars.

15 *Hornet-prince*: the most dangerous of heretics, being the Grand Master of the
Templars. Browning may be remembering *The Fable of the Bees*, by Bernard Mandeville,
a satire on the vileness of human nature. Mandeville is addressed in the first of
Browning's *Parleyings* (1887).

17 s.d. *clavicithern*: no other example in OED²: 'clavicytherium', 'An early musical
instrument of the harpsichord type, being really an upright spinet': OED².

21 *tumbrils*: dung-carts, which tilt backwards.

23 *good store*: in abundance.

IV.

Good sappy bavins that kindle forthwith;
   Billets that blaze substantial and slow;
Pine-stump split deftly, dry as pith;   30
   Larch-heart that chars to a chalk-white glow:
Then up they hoist me John in a chafe,
   Sling him fast like a hog to scorch,
Spit in his face, then leap back safe,
   Sing "Laudes" and bid clap-to the torch.   35

CHORUS.

Laus Deo—who bids clap-to the torch.

V.

John of the Temple, whose fame so bragged,
   Is burning alive in Paris square!
How can he curse, if his mouth is gagged?
   Or wriggle his neck, with a collar there?   40
Or heave his chest, which a band goes round?
   Or threat with his fist, since his arms are spliced?
Or kick with his feet, now his legs are bound?
   —Thinks John, I will call upon Jesus Christ.
                       [*Here one crosseth himself.*

---

32 *1855P* they all hoist   41 *1855P–84S* chest, while a

28 *bavins*: sticks 'like those bound up in faggots': Johnson. Cf. *I Henry IV*, III. ii. 61–2.
29 *Billets*: small logs.
32 *they hoist me*: 'me' represents the old ethic dative here, as often in Shakespeare.
   in a chafe: in a fume (here literally).
33 *fast*: tight.
35 *Laudes*: Pss. 148–50, sung as one psalm: part of the Roman Catholic service, a sustained praise sung to God.
   clap-to the torch: put the torch smartly to the wood.
36 *Laus Deo*: praise be to God.
37 *bragged*: made such a noise in the world.
42 *spliced*: bound tightly.

VI.

Jesus Christ—John had bought and sold,   45
    Jesus Christ—John had eaten and drunk;
To him, the Flesh meant silver and gold.
    (*Salvâ reverentiâ.*)
Now it was, "Saviour, bountiful lamb,
    "I have roasted thee Turks, though men roast me!   50
"See thy servant, the plight wherein I am!
    "Art thou a saviour? Save thou me!"

CHORUS.

'T is John the mocker cries, "Save thou me!"

VII.

Who maketh God's menace an idle word?
    —Saith, it no more means what it proclaims,   55
Than a damsel's threat to her wanton bird?—
    For she too prattles of ugly names.
    —Saith, he knoweth but one thing,—what he knows?
    That God is good and the rest is breath;
Why else is the same styled Sharon's rose?   60
    Once a rose, ever a rose, he saith.

---

50 *1855P–63* me.   53 *1855P* It is John   *1855P–63* Save . . . . me!
56 *1855P* bird,—

45 *John had bought and sold*: as Melchiori, 76 ff., points out in a good discussion of this poem, the alleged crime of Jacques 'is twice equated with the crime of Judas'.

46 *had eaten and drunk*: in the Eucharist.

47 *The Flesh meant silver and gold*: 'One of the charges against the Templars was that of omitting the "hoc est corpus" (this is my body) clause in the service of the Eucharist': Worsfold.

(*Salvâ reverentiâ*): if this may be said without irreverence.

50 *Turks*: Infidels, i.e. Muslims; for whom 'Turk' became the general word in English, because by this time it was largely Turks who were expanding the frontiers of Islam: cf. 'Holy-Cross Day', 38.

58 —*Saith, he knoweth but one thing*: John says this.

60 *Sharon's rose*: 'I am the rose of Sharon, and the lily of the vallies': Song of Solomon (Canticles), 2: 1. In the Song of Solomon the Church is the bride of Christ. See Melchiori, 78–9 on this complex passage.

CHORUS.

O, John shall yet find a rose, he saith!

VIII.

Alack, there be roses and roses, John!
    Some, honied of taste like your leman's tongue:
Some, bitter; for why? (roast gaily on!)   65
    Their tree struck root in devil's-dung.
When Paul once reasoned of righteousness
    And of temperance and of judgment to come,
Good Felix trembled, he could no less:
    John, snickering, crook'd his wicked thumb.   70

CHORUS.

What cometh to John of the wicked thumb?

IX.

Ha ha, John pluckerh now at his rose
    To rid himself of a sorrow at heart!
Lo,—petal on petal, fierce rays unclose;
    Anther on anther, sharp spikes outstart;   75
And with blood for dew, the bosom boils;
    And a gust of sulphur is all its smell;
And lo, he is horribly in the toils
    Of a coal-black giant flower of hell!

CHORUS.

What maketh heaven, That maketh hell.   80

---

62 *1865* saith.   64 *1855P–56* tongue.   66 *1855P–63* devil's dung!
72 *1855P–56* John plucks now

64 *leman's*: lover's.
67 *When Paul once reasoned*: 'And as [Paul] reasoned of righteousness, temperance,
and judgment to come, Felix trembled': Acts 24: 25.
70 *crook'd his wicked thumb*: as a sign of contempt.
75 *Anther*: the part of the stamen of a flower containing the pollen.
80 *What maketh heaven*: cf. Inferno, iii. 4–6.

X

So, as John called now, through the fire amain,
 On the Name, he had cursed with, all his life—
To the Person, he bought and sold again—
 For the Face, with his daily buffets rife—
Feature by feature It took its place: 85
 And his voice, like a mad dog's choking bark,
At the steady whole of the Judge's face—
 Died. Forth John's soul flared into the dark.

SUBJOINETH THE ABBOT DEODAET.

God help all poor souls lost in the dark!

85 *1855P–63* place!

 81 *amain*: with all his strength.

TWO IN THE CAMPAGNA

THE 'Campagna di Roma' is a rich and level stretch of territory outside Rome, south-west of the Tiber. With its ruined edifices and its crumbling tombs, set in 'a rich unbroken pasturage' at this time, it was (as it remains) a favourite place for excursions. The Brownings lived in Rome from mid-November 1853 to 28 May 1854. The poem may well have been written during this period, or shortly afterwards.

On 10 May EBB told Miss Mitford that she did not 'pretend to have a rag of sentiment about Rome', adding: 'It's a palimpsest Rome—a watering-place written over the antique—and I haven't taken to it as a poet should, I suppose—only let us speak the truth, above all things'. Yet there was a happy qualification of this view, her delight in the Campagna. She went on to tell her, in the same letter, that 'The pleasantest days . . . we have spent with the Kembles—the two sisters . . who are charming & excellent, both of them & certainly they have given us some exquisite hours on the campagna, upon pic nic excursions . . they, & certain of their friends . . . The talk was almost too brilliant for the sentiment of the scenery.'[1]

'I have been told', William Sharp wrote, 'that [this] poem was as actually personal as . . . the . . . "Guardian Angel". But I do not think stress should be laid on this and kindred localisations. Exact or not, they have no literary value. To the poet, the dramatic poet above all, locality and actuality of experience are, so to say, merely fortunate coigns of outlook'.[2] In any event it is one of the expressions of the mood of a lover which make up a large part of the collection, *Men and Women*. In the words of Mrs Orr, its 'true keynote . . . is the pain of perpetual change, and of the conscious, though unexplained, predestination to it'.[3] It is the work of a man whose youth had been profoundly influenced by Shelley, the poet who had written:

> All things revive in field or grove,
> And sky and sea, but two, which move
> And form all others, life and love.[4]

---

[1] Raymond and Sullivan, iii. 408, 409.
[2] Sharp 159.
[3] *Life* 199.
[4] 'When passion's trance is overpast', 13–15.

It has been rightly described as Browning's most famous expression of his sense of 'the impossibility of real communion between people, even lovers'.[1]

The intricate thought is expressed in a simple metrical form, twelve five-line stanzas each consisting of four iambic tetrameters followed by a single trimeter. The rhyme-scheme is *ababa*.

Date: 1854
1863: Dramatic Lyrics

TWO IN THE CAMPAGNA.

I.

I WONDER do you feel to-day
  As I have felt since, hand in hand,
We sat down on the grass, to stray
  In spirit better through the land,
This morn of Rome and May?   5

II.

For me, I touched a thought, I know,
  Has tantalized me many times,
(Like turns of thread the spiders throw
  Mocking across our path) for rhymes
To catch at and let go.   10

---

*10 {reading of *1855P–84S*, DC, BrU, *1889*} *1888* go

6 *a thought*: cf. *Sordello*, iii. 182 ff.
8 *turns*: twists.
  thread: 'One of the features of the Campagna is the gossamer carpet spun every morning by millions of tiny spiders, which is unnoticed until caught by the sun': Meredith, 172. Cf. *Sordello*, i. 663 ff., and *A Blot in the 'Scutcheon*, II. ii. 195 ff.
9–10 *for rhymes / To catch at*: i.e. to express it.
  and let go: although he had wished and tried to hold it.

---

[1] Daniel Karlin, 'The Sources of "The Englishman in Italy" ': BSN, Winter 1984/5, 36.

III.

Help me to hold it! First it left
  The yellowing fennel, run to seed
There, branching from the brickwork's cleft,
  Some old tomb's ruin: yonder weed
Took up the floating weft,   15

IV.

Where one small orange cup amassed
  Five beetles,—blind and green they grope
Among the honey-meal: and last,
  Everywhere on the grassy slope
I traced it. Hold it fast!   20

V.

The champaign with its endless fleece
  Of feathery grasses everywhere!
Silence and passion, joy and peace,
  An everlasting wash of air—
Rome's ghost since her decease.   25

---

11 *1855P–56* it: first   *1863S* first   18 *1855P–63S* honey-meal,—

11 *Help me to hold it!*: cf. *Sordello*, i. 663 ff. Turner comments that 'Each point on the thread's route (tomb, weed, grassy slope) represents an element in the thought'.

15 *weft*: 'The threads that cross from side to side of a web': OED[2].

17 *five beetles*: 'I suspect', Browning wrote to EBB, '. . . you have found out by this time my odd liking for "vermin" . . . I always loved all those wild creatures God "sets up for themselves" so independently of us': Kintner, i. 356. Beetles are mentioned in *Pippa Passes*, iii. 278, *Paracelsus* v. 673–4, and elsewhere.

18 *honey-meal*: sweet nectar.

21 *The champaign*: the level, open country. The word, stressed on the first syllable, is here used particularly of the 'Campagna di Roma'.

24 *wash of air*: cf. 'the wash of the sea'.

25 *Rome's ghost*: Henry James wrote that the Campagna 'was so bright and yet so sad, so still and yet so charged, to the supersensuous ear, with the murmur of an extinguished life, that you could only say it was intensely and adorably strange, could only impute to the whole overarched scene an unsurpassed secret for bringing tears of appreciation to no matter how ignorant—archaeologically ignorant—eyes': *Italian Hours* (1909), 155–6. (The chapter is dated 1873.)

VI.

Such life here, through such lengths of hours,
　　Such miracles performed in play,
Such primal naked forms of flowers,
　　Such letting nature have her way
While heaven looks from its towers!　　　　　　　　30

VII.

How say you? Let us, O my dove,
　　Let us be unashamed of soul,
As earth lies bare to heaven above!
　　How is it under our control
To love or not to love?　　　　　　　　　　　　35

VIII.

I would that you were all to me,
　　You that are just so much, no more.
Nor yours nor mine, nor slave nor free!
　　Where does the fault lie? What the core
O' the wound, since wound must be?　　　　　　　40

IX.

I would I could adopt your will,
　　See with your eyes, and set my heart
Beating by yours, and drink my fill
　　At your soul's springs,—your part my part
In life, for good and ill.　　　　　　　　　　　45

26 *1855P–65* life there, through   *1863S* such length of   30 *1855P–56* towers. 33
1855P–56   above.   37 *1855P–56*   more—   39 *1855P–65*   what
40 *1855P–68* Of the

26 *here*: note revision: the speaker is supposed to be in the Campagna.
30 *towers*: OED² notes that in early religious use the word 'tower' is 'often applied
to heaven'.
33 *As earth lies bare*: cf. Tennyson, *The Princess*, vii. 167. 'Now lies the Earth all Danaë
to the stars'.

X.

No. I yearn upward, touch you close,
  Then stand away. I kiss your cheek,
Catch your soul's warmth,—I pluck the rose
  And love it more than tongue can speak—
Then the good minute goes.   50

XI.

Already how am I so far
  Out of that minute? Must I go
Still like the thistle-ball, no bar,
  Onward, whenever light winds blow,
Fixed by no friendly star?   55

XII.

Just when I seemed about to learn!
  Where is the thread now? Off again!
The old trick! Only I discern—
  Infinite passion, and the pain
Of finite hearts that yearn.   60

---

54 *1863S* Onward, wherever light   *{reading of *1855P–84S*, DC, BrU, *1889*} *1888*
blow   57 *1884S* again.

48 *I pluck the rose*: cf. *Othello*, v. ii. 13–15: 'When I have pluck'd thy rose, / I cannot give it vital growth again; / It needs must wither' (Pettigrew and Collins).

50 *the good minute*: that in which he feels identified with his lady. Cf. one of EBB's last letters: 'Nobody understands exactly why [Browning gets out of spirits]—except me who am in the inside of him and hear him breathe': *Letters of EBB*, ii. 435.

53 *thistle-ball*: the head of the thistle, consisting of its feathery seeds.

55 *Fixed by no friendly star*: like a ship that has lost its bearings. Pettigrew cites Shakespeare, *Sonnets*, cxvi. 5 ff.

59 *Infinite passion*: cf. Wordsworth, 'Ode [on the day of] A General Thanksgiving', 102: 'And with an infinite pain the spirit aches'; and the last lines of Arnold, 'Philomela', in his *Poems. A New Edition* (1853): 'Eternal Passion! / Eternal Pain!'

A GRAMMARIAN'S FUNERAL

IN this poem one of Browning's central themes, the true nature of success, is illustrated with reference to his passionate love of Greek. Its structure was clearly influenced by lines in *An Essay on Criticism* which Johnson memorably praised in his Life of Pope: 'I cannot forbear to observe that the comparison of a student's progress in the sciences with the journey of a traveller in the Alps is perhaps the best that English poetry can shew.'[1]

> Fir'd at first sight with what the Muse imparts,
> In fearless youth we tempt the heights of Arts,
> While from the bounded level of our mind,
> Short views we take, nor see the lengths behind;
> But, more advanc'd, behold with strange surprize
> New distant scenes of endless science rise!
> So pleas'd at first the tow'ring Alps we try,
> Mount o'er the vales, and seem to tread the sky,
> Th'eternal snows appear already past,
> And the first clouds and mountains seem the last:
> But, those attain'd, we tremble to survey
> The growing labours of the lengthen'd way,
> Th' increasing prospect tires our wand'ring eyes,
> Hills peep o'er hills, and Alps on Alps arise!

The interpretation of the poem was enlivened by R. D. Altick in his article, ' "A Grammarian's Funeral": Browning's Praise of Folly?',[2] in

---

[1] *Lives of the English Poets*, ed. G. Birkbeck Hill 3 vols. (1905), iii. 229, referring to ll. 219–32. Cf. Jack, 170. Imagery of ascent is ubiquitous in Browning, appearing early in the French note to *Pauline*, 811, which states that the poet is concerned with 'the sequence of objectives which it would be possible for him to attain, and of which each one (once attained) should form a sort of plateau from which one could discern other aims'. See too *Sordello*, vi. 276–83:

> They climb; life's view is not at once disclosed
> To creatures caught up, on the summit left,
> Heaven plain above them, yet of wings bereft:
> But lower laid, as at the mountain's foot.
> So, range on range, the girdling forests shoot
> 'Twixt your plain prospect and the throngs who scale
> Height after height, and pierce mists, veil by veil,
> Heartened with each discovery.

[2] SEL 3 (1963), 449–60. The other two articles both appeared in VP 5 (1967): 'Browning's Grammarian: Apparent Failure or Real?', by Martin J. Svaglic (93 ff.), and

which he argued that we should distinguish between the admiration felt by the Grammarian's disciples and the attitude of the poet himself. In a subsequent exchange one scholar maintained the traditional view that 'Browning did mean the grammarian to be viewed with respect', while another went so far as to describe his character as 'unpleasant', and that of his followers as more so. All that we know of Browning makes the latter interpretation hard to accept. The man who habitually travelled with copies of the plays of the three great Greek tragedians in his luggage, and collated four editions of the *Hercules Furens* of Euripides before he wrote *Aristophanes' Apology*, assuming that his readers would be acquainted with the Scholia and other relevant Greek literature,[1] was a better classical scholar than most of his modern critics or editors are likely to be. 'Purely disinterested scholarship [has] always seemed to me to have far more important bearings, moral and intellectual, than are commonly recognized', he wrote in a letter of which only a fragment has been printed.[2] The comments of Browning's contemporaries leave no doubt that they understood that the Grammarian, living in a great age, had in his own way something heroic in his single-mindedness. Like Paracelsus he was one of those who 'aspire to KNOW',[3] although 'know' in lower case may be judged more suitable for his ambition than the grandiose upper case appropriate to the man who aspired to be the Luther of Medicine. 'It always strengthens my backbone to read it', William James wrote to a friend in 1868, 'and I think the feeling it expresses of throwing upon eternity the responsibility of making good your one-sidedness somehow or other . . . is a gallant one, and fit to be trusted if one-sided activity is in itself at all respectable.'[4] It is surely an error to mistake this poem for a 'burial of the pedant', though it remains possible that EBB's description of 'Sibrandus Schafnaburgensis' in these words[5] may have remained in Browning's mind and so helped to prompt its title, and perhaps even the idea of the piece. It is easy to overlook the lines in which we are told that, before he 'Left play for work', the Grammarian had been a man with the 'face and throat' of Apollo himself. It was after a happy youth in which (however) he 'lived nameless' that he had turned to learning, as a fit occupation for an adult man.

'Dactyls and Curlews: Satire In "A Grammarian's Funeral" ', by Robert L. Kelly (105–12).

[1] Domett, 99, cf. DeVane, 377, and l. 60, below.
[2] *Checklist*, 67:33.
[3] *Paracelsus*, i. 282. See too our Vol. I. p. 113.
[4] *The Letters of William James*, ed. Henry James (1926), 129–30.
[5] Kintner, i. 131.

Such scholars as Thomas Linacre and Isaac Casaubon have been suggested as originals for the Grammarian, but he is clearly a generic figure. Browning once wrote out the concluding lines of the poem 'In Memoriam Johannis Conington', a noted Oxford classical scholar who 'had always a special fondness for the Greek tragedians, and especially for Æschylus, whose plays he knew by heart'.[1]

The most striking feature of the verse is the alternation of long and short lines (which rhyme *abab* etc.) The long lines are iambic pentameters, with the first foot usually inverted. The short lines scan / × × / ×, like the conclusion of Greek and Latin hexameters. Alliteration is prominent, particularly in the short lines of the first section and in the last three lines of the poem.

Date: 1853/5
1863: *Dramatic Romances*

A GRAMMARIAN'S FUNERAL,

SHORTLY AFTER THE REVIVAL OF LEARNING IN EUROPE.

LET us begin and carry up this corpse,
　　Singing together.
Leave we the common crofts, the vulgar thorpes,
　　Each in its tether
Sleeping safe on the bosom of the plain,　　　　　　5
　　Cared-for till cock-crow:
Look out if yonder be not day again

---

title *1855P–63, 1872S, 1884S* FUNERAL.　　　*1855P–63* [*Time*—Shortly . . . . Europe.]
*3 {reading of *1855P–84S*} *1888, 1889* thorpes　　　5 *1872S, 1884S* safe in the
6 *1855P–56* cock-crow.

Title: *the revival of learning*: the revival of the study of classical culture (particularly Greek) in the fourteenth and fifteenth centuries. It spread from Italy throughout the rest of Europe, and was the central feature of the Renaissance.
3 *the vulgar thorpes*: the villages where the peasants live.
4 *tether*: limit(s).

---

[1] DNB. For the MS (now in the Berg Collection) see Kelley and Coley, E 153.—A good account of the historical background to this poem is N. G. Wilson, *From Byzantium to Italy: Greek Studies in the Italian Renaissance* (1992).

Rimming the rock-row!
That's the appropriate country; there, man's thought,
    Rarer, intenser,   10
Self-gathered for an outbreak, as it ought,
    Chafes in the censer.
Leave we the unlettered plain its herd and crop;
    Seek we sepulture
On a tall mountain, citied to the top,   15
    Crowded with culture!
All the peaks soar, but one the rest excels;
    Clouds overcome it;
No! yonder sparkle is the citadel's
    Circling its summit.   20
Thither our path lies; wind we up the heights:
    Wait ye the warning?
Our low life was the level's and the night's;
    He's for the morning.
Step to a tune, square chests, erect each head,   25
    'Ware the beholders!
This is our master, famous, calm and dead,
    Borne on our shoulders.

---

7 *1855P–56* if yonder's not the day   12 *1855P–63* censer!   19 *1872S, 1884S*
No,   20 *1855P–63* summit!   21 *1872S* heights!   24 *1855P–63* morning!
25 *1855P–63* erect the head,   *27 {reading of *1855P–1865S, 1872S, 1884S*} *1868,*
1870, 1875, 1888, 1889 famous calm   *28 {reading of *1855P–84S,* DC, BrU, *1889*}
1888 shoulders

  8 *Rimming*: Browning will have found the word in this sense in 'The Gardener's Daughter', 177: 'A length of bright horizon rimm'd the dark'. The piece first appeared in Tennyson's *Poems in Two Volumes* (1842), a collection which Browning studied. Cf. our Vol. III, p. 185.
    rock-row: not in OED².
  11 *Self-gathered*: the only example in OED² is in Tennyson, 'Of old sat Freedom on the heights', also first published in *Poems in Two Volumes*.
  12 *Chafes in the censer*: i.e. grows fragrant, like incense.
  14 *sepulture*: stressed on the second syllable, for the sake of the rhythm. Normally on the first, as in Johnson.
  15 *citied*: cf. Thomson, *Liberty*, i. 305; Keats, *Lamia*, 487.
  17 *excels*: cf. L. *excellere*, to rise above others.
  18 *overcome*: cover.
  22 *warning*: signal (obs.)
  26 *'Ware*: i.e. let them beware!

Sleep, crop and herd! sleep, darkling thorpe and croft,
    Safe from the weather!   30
He, whom we convoy to his grave aloft,
    Singing together,
He was a man born with thy face and throat,
    Lyric Apollo!
Long he lived nameless: how should spring take note   35
    Winter would follow?
Till lo, the little touch, and youth was gone!
    Cramped and diminished,
Moaned he, "New measures, other feet anon!
    "My dance is finished?"   40
No, that's the world's way: (keep the mountain-side,
    Make for the city!)
He knew the signal, and stepped on with pride
    Over men's pity;
Left play for work, and grappled with the world   45
    Bent on escaping:
"What's in the scroll," quoth he, "thou keepest furled?
    "Show me their shaping,
"Theirs who most studied man, the bard and sage,—
    "Give!"—So, he gowned him,   50
Straight got by heart that book to its last page:
    Learned, we found him.
Yea, but we found him bald too, eyes like lead,
    Accents uncertain:
"Time to taste life," another would have said,   55
    "Up with the curtain!"
This man said rather, "Actual life comes next?
    "Patience a moment!
"Grant I have mastered learning's crabbed text,

---

29 *1856* herd! Sleep   41 *1855P–63* way!   42 *1855P–56* city.)   *1863* city,)
52 *1855P–63* him!

34 *Lyric Apollo*: Apollo was the god of poetry and of all the arts, and was celebrated
for his beauty. See Ian Jack, *Keats and the Mirror of Art* (1967), 176 ff.

35 *nameless*: without fame.

48 *their shaping*: what they imagined, wrote, created.

    "Still there's the comment.   60
"Let me know all! Prate not of most or least,
    "Painful or easy!
"Even to the crumbs I'd fain eat up the feast,
    "Ay, nor feel queasy."
Oh, such a life as he resolved to live,   65
    When he had learned it,
When he had gathered all books had to give!
    Sooner, he spurned it.
Image the whole, then execute the parts—
    Fancy the fabric   70
Quite, ere you build, ere steel strike fire from quartz,
    Ere mortar dab brick!

(Here's the town-gate reached: there's the market-place
    Gaping before us.)
Yea, this in him was the peculiar grace   75
    (Hearten our chorus!)
That before living he'd learn how to live—
    No end to learning:
Earn the means first—God surely will contrive
    Use for our earning.   80
Others mistrust and say, "But time escapes:
    "Live now or never!"
He said, "What's time? Leave Now for dogs and apes!
    "Man has Forever."

---

60 *1855P* comment!   61 *1855P–56* all.   62 *1855P–63* easy:
64 *1855P–63* queasy!"   67 *1855P* give—   *1855, 1856* give;   68 *1855P–56*
it!   76 *1855P–63* chorus)   77 *1855P–56* Still before   78 *1855P–56*
learning.   81 *1855P–56* escapes,—   *1863–65S, 1872S, 1884S* escapes!
83 *1855P–65S* leave   *1855P* apes,   84 *1855P* For ever!"

---

68 *Sooner:* until that time.
70 *Fancy:* form a mental picture.
71 *Quite:* completely.
    quartz: building-stone, e.g. sandstone.
75 *peculiar:* a biblical word; cf. Exod. 19: 5: 'then ye shall be a peculiar treasure unto me'.
76 *Hearten:* put your hearts into.

Back to his book then: deeper drooped his head: 85
    Calculus racked him:
Leaden before, his eyes grew dross of lead:
    Tussis attacked him.
"Now, master, take a little rest!"—not he!
    (Caution redoubled,   90
Step two abreast, the way winds narrowly!)
    Not a whit troubled,
Back to his studies, fresher than at first,
    Fierce as a dragon
He (soul-hydroptic with a sacred thirst)   95
    Sucked at the flagon.
Oh, if we draw a circle premature,
    Heedless of far gain,
Greedy for quick returns of profit, sure
    Bad is our bargain!   100
Was it not great? did not he throw on God,
    (He loves the burthen)—
God's task to make the heavenly period
    Perfect the earthen?
Did not he magnify the mind, show clear   105
    Just what it all meant?
He would not discount life, as fools do here,
    Paid by instalment.

---

90 *1855P–63, 1872S, 1884S* redoubled!   91 *1855P–56* narrowly.)   *1863*
narrowly)   *92 {reading of *1855–84S*} *1855P, 1888, 1889* troubled   101 *1856*
did he not throw   104 *1855P* Complete the   105 *1855P* he make the most
of mind,   107 *1855P* He did not   108 *1855P–63* instalment!

---

86 *Calculus*: 'The stone in the bladder' (Johnson), an agonizing complaint.

88 *Tussis*: cough.

95 *soul-hydroptic*: 'hydroptic' (having an insatiable thirst) is a favourite word of
Donne, who is the first writer to use it. He described himself as having 'An hydroptique
immoderate desire of humane learning and languages': *Letters to Several Persons of Honour*
(1651), 51. The compound is no doubt Browning's invention.

97 *draw a circle premature*: draw up the balance-sheet too soon.

103 *the heavenly period*: the original meaning of 'period' is 'circuit'. This is a variant
on the image, common in seventeenth-century elegy, of the imperfect circle of one
who dies too young. Cf. 'Abt Vogler', 72: 'On the earth the broken arcs; in the heaven,
a perfect round'.

105 *magnify the mind*: show forth its greatness. Cf. Luke 1: 46.

He ventured neck or nothing—heaven's success
    Found, or earth's failure: 110
"Wilt thou trust death or not?" He answered "Yes:
    "Hence with life's pale lure!"
That low man seeks a little thing to do,
    Sees it and does it:
This high man, with a great thing to pursue, 115
    Dies ere he knows it.
That low man goes on adding one to one,
    His hundred's soon hit:
This high man, aiming at a million,
    Misses an unit. 120
That, has the world here—should he need the next,
    Let the world mind him!
This, throws himself on God, and unperplexed
    Seeking shall find him.
So, with the throttling hands of death at strife, 125
    Ground he at grammar;
Still, thro' the rattle, parts of speech were rife:
    While he could stammer
He settled *Hoti's* business—let it be!—
    Properly based *Oun*— 130
Gave us the doctrine of the enclitic *De*,

---

111 *1855P* "Will you trust   *1855P–56* he   *{reading of DC, BrU, *1889*} *1855P–56*
"Yes. *1863–84S* "Yes! *1888* "Yes   127 *1855P–56* rife.   129 *1855P* settled
Oti's business—

---

109 *neck or nothing*: proverbial.

116 *ere he knows it*: i.e. before he reaches it.

122 *Let the world mind him!*: i.e. he must be content with *this* world.

124 *Seeking shall find him*: 'Seek, and ye shall find': Matt. 7: 7; Luke 11: 9.

129 *Hoti's business*: grammarians distinguish two kinds of ὅτι, one meaning either 'that' (e.g. introducing indirect speech) or 'because', while the other is the neuter of ὅστις ('whoever'), is sometimes written ὅ, τι, and means (roughly) 'whatever' or 'what' in indirect questions.

130 *Properly based Oun*: οὖν commonly means 'therefore', but can on occasion mean 'certainly, then'.

131 *the enclitic De*: on 2 July 1863 Browning wrote to Tennyson, in explanation: 'There are tritons among minnows, even—so I wanted the grammarian ... to spend his last breath on the biggest of the littlenesses: such an one is the "*enclitic* δε", the "inseparable" [i.e. a suffix], just because it may be confounded with δὲ, *but*, which keeps

Dead from the waist down.
Well, here's the platform, here's the proper place:
    Hail to your purlieus,
All ye highfliers of the feathered race,   135
    Swallows and curlews!
Here's the top-peak; the multitude below
    Live, for they can, there:
This man decided not to Live but Know—
    Bury this man there?   140
Here—here's his place, where meteors shoot, clouds form,
    Lightnings are loosened,
Stars come and go! Let joy break with the storm,
    Peace let the dew send!
Lofty designs must close in like effects: 145
    Loftily lying,
Leave him—still loftier than the world suspects,
    Living and dying.

---

133 *1855P–65S* place.   137 *1855P–63* top-peak!   138 *1855P–63* there.
143 *1855P–63* let

its accent'. He goes on to give examples of the former, for example ὅδε [this here] and ἔρεβόσδε [to Erebos], and continues: 'See Buttmann on these points. It was just this pin-point of a of a puzzle that gave "δέ" its worth rather than the heaps of obvious rhymes to "be" '. This is interesting evidence than Browning knew more Greek than Tennyson (both loved it). He is referring to one of the editions of *A Greek Grammar* by Philip Buttmann, trans. from the German, with additions, by Edward Robinson (Andover, NY, 1833), 313. Buttmann mentions ὅτι = 'because' on p. 317, and οὖν = 'therefore', 'consequently', on p. 428. See Christopher Ricks, 'Two Letters by Browning', TLS 3 June 1965, 464. Browning explained the matter again, more briefly, in a letter to the editor of the *Daily News* on 21 November, 1874: *Letters*, 164.

135 *highfliers*: in the literal sense, suggesting that the Grammarian is a highflier in another sense. Turner records a suggestion that since the swallows and curlews are migrating 'they hint that the Grammarian, too, is taking off for a better place'.

139 *not to Live but Know*: see *Paracelsus* (ii. 624–6), where the protagonist addresses Aprile: 'I too have sought to KNOW as thou to LOVE—/ Excluding love as thou refusedst knowledge. / Still thou hast beauty and I, power'.

ONE WAY OF LOVE

WE have no means of dating this piece, or its companion. They are five-finger exercises which even the most biographical of critics is unlikely to try to associate with the poet's life. Pauline here is yet more evidently 'a mere phantom', in Mill's phrase, than the eponymous heroine of Browning's first published poem.[1]

The poem consists of iambic tetrameters, rhyming in pairs. Lines 5, 11 and 17 lack an initial stressed syllable. Each of them contains an internal rhyme.

Date: 1853/5
1863: *Dramatic Lyrics*

ONE WAY OF LOVE.

I.

ALL June I bound the rose in sheaves.
Now, rose by rose, I strip the leaves
And strew them where Pauline may pass.
She will not turn aside? Alas!
Let them lie. Suppose they die?   5
The chance was they might take her eye.

II.

How many a month I strove to suit
These stubborn fingers to the lute!
To-day I venture all I know.
She will not hear my music? So!   10

title *1865S* SONG.   1 *1865S* sheaves:

1 *I bound the rose in sheaves*: i.e. I made great bunches of roses.
2 *leaves*: petals.

[1] See Vol. I, p. 12.

Break the string; fold music's wing:
Suppose Pauline had bade me sing!

III.

My whole life long I learned to love.
This hour my utmost art I prove
And speak my passion—heaven or hell?   15
She will not give me heaven? 'T is well!
Lose who may—I still can say,
Those who win heaven, blest are they!

11 *1855P–56* wing.   12 *1855P* sing?   15 *1855P–65S* passion.—Heaven
18 *1855, 1856* they.

11 *music's wing*: a traditional image. Cf. Heine's song, 'Auf Flügeln des Gesanges'
(1823).

ANOTHER WAY OF LOVE

WHEREAS the speaker in the previous piece is a man who accepts defeat in love without complaint, in this a woman reacts with spirit to her lover's growing indifference. In the first stanza she describes his manner, in the second she sends him packing, while in the third she asserts her right to choose between taking another lover and using her 'June-lightning' to keep herself free from mankind. Throughout there is a play on the word 'June'. In the first line it is the month, as at the beginning of the previous poem: elsewhere it is also an image for the woman herself.

Each of the three stanzas consists of eight short lines and three long, and rhymes *abcddabceee* (*fghii* etc.) The short lines have two stresses each, the long have four. Stanzas i and iii are in rising rhythm, (consisting of iambs and anapaests), lines 1 and 9 being exceptions: Stanza ii is in falling rhythm (dactyls and trochees), except for ll. 16, 21 and 22. The first stanza, in particular, may remind us that opera was one of the Browning's 'childish' ambitions.[1]

Date: 1853/5
1863: Dramatic Lyrics

ANOTHER WAY OF LOVE.

I.

JUNE was not over
Though past the full,
And the best of her roses
Had yet to blow,
When a man I know   5
(But shall not discover,
Since ears are dull,
And time discloses)

2 *the full*: its mid-point.
4 *blow*: be past their best.
6 *discover*: reveal, name.

[1] See Vol. I, p. 4, and p. 113 above.

Turned him and said with a man's true air,
Half sighing a smile in a yawn, as 't were,—   10
"If I tire of your June, will she greatly care?"

II.

Well, dear, in-doors with you!
    True! serene deadness
Tries a man's temper.
    What's in the blossom   15
    June wears on her bosom?
Can it clear scores with you?
    Sweetness and redness,
    Eadem semper!
Go, let me care for it greatly or slightly!   20
If June mend her bower now, your hand left unsightly
By plucking the roses,—my June will do rightly.

III.

And after, for pastime,
    If June be refulgent
With flowers in completeness,   25
    All petals, no prickles,
    Delicious as trickles
Of wine poured at mass-time,—
    And choose One indulgent
    To redness and sweetness: 30
Or if, with experience of man and of spider,
June use my June-lightning, the strong insect-ridder,
And stop the fresh film-work,—why, June will consider.

---

13 *1855P–63* True,   *18 {reading of *1855P–75*} *1888, 1889* redness.
21 *1855P–65* June mends her bowers now,   22 *1855P–65* plucking their roses,—
32 *1855P–56* She use   33 *1855P–56* To stop   *1855P–63* fresh spinning,—why,

17 *clear scores*: settle the account.

19 *eadem semper*: an ironical echo of Good Queen Bess's motto, 'Semper eadem'. The
girl in the poem is found boring, however, because she is always the same. Cf. Lucretius
iii. 945.

21 *your hand*: which your hand.

29 *One*: another lover.

32 *insect-ridder*: no doubt Browning's coinage.

"TRANSCENDENTALISM: A POEM IN TWELVE BOOKS"

SINCE Mrs Orr tells us that she is indebted to Browning for her note on this poem,[1] we may safely assume that he did not object to her account of it, which may prove helpful:

"Transcendentalism" is addressed to a young poet who is accused of presenting his ideas "naked", instead of draping them, in poetic fashion, in sights and sounds: in other words, of talking across his harp instead of singing to it. He acts on the supposition that, if the young want imagery, older men want rational thoughts. And his critic is declaring this is a mistake. 'Youth, indeed, would be wasted in studying the transcendental Jacob Boehme for the deeper meaning of things which life gives it to see and feel; but when youth is past, we need all the more to be made to see and feel. It is not a thinker like Boehme who will compensate us for the lost summer of our life; but a magician like John of Halberstadt, who can, at any moment, conjure roses up'.

There is a strong vein of humour in the argument, which gives the impression of being consciously overstated. It is nevertheless a genuine piece of criticism.

This last affirmation points us in a more likely direction than that of trying to identify the critic who speaks or the poet whom he is addressing. On these points one can only say that the poet is too earnest and didactic and lacking in imaginative power. The writer of *Sordello* and *Easter-Day* is an obvious candidate, though Altick's statement that 'Browning is addressing himself, or, more specifically, the poet that he had been down to the age of forty',[2] is perhaps too specific. The critic too has a good deal of Browning about him, and we notice that he is providing a Defence of Poetry against such people as Jeremy Bentham, and even against the initial advice given both EBB and himself by 'the great teacher of the age . . . who is also yours and mine'.[3] In 1841, thanking Browning for *Sordello* and *Pippa Passes*, Carlyle had praised both works but added that he seemed not yet 'on the best way for unfolding' his powers, and continued: 'If your own choice happened to point that way, I for one should hail it as a good omen that your next work were written in prose!' In 1845 EBB, who had herself received similar advice, wrote to Browning: 'And does Mr. Carlyle

---

[1] *Handbook*, vii.
[2] R. D. Altick, 'Browning's "Transcendentalism"': JEGP 58 (1959), 24.
[3] Kintner, i. 29; Carlyle, *New Letters*, i. 233–4; Kintner, i. 24; *Letters*, 368 n.

tell you that he has forbidden all "singing" to this perverse and froward
generation, which should work & not sing?' She asked him whether he had
not told the sage 'that song is work', adding that 'to think of putting away,
even for a season, the poetry of the world, was wonderful, and has left me
ruffled in my thoughts ever since'. By 1853, when he thanked Browning
for his Essay on Shelley, Carlyle wrote to him in very different terms: 'Give
us some more of your *writing*, my friend; we decidedly need a man or two
like you . . . Nor do I restrict you to Prose, in spite of all that I have said
and still say: Prose or Poetry, either of them you can master.'

'Transcendentalism' was a word often used in criticism at this time, not
least in reviews of Browning's own work. A writer in the *Athenæum*
complained that *Sordello* 'carries us too far into the regions of *transcendent-
alism*'.[1] Five years later the *Examiner* rejoiced that Browning had 'found
the path again', having earlier lost his way 'in transcendental or other fogs'.
When the *Athenæum* critic of *Christmas-Eve and Easter-Day* censured the
double-poem as 'highly transcendental', ruling that 'transcendentalism
delivered in doggrel verse has . . . the effect of a discord', we note that he
not only made a legitimate critical point but brought the term closer to its
original meaning as a near-synonym for metaphysics. In any case the
general charge that his poetry was obscure and difficult was often ex-
pressed by the use of the word. It is perhaps appropriate that 'Transcend-
entalism' is itself an obscure and confusing poem, perhaps in part because
of a domestic mishap. When Dowden pointed out that Boehme had been
German, not 'Swedish', Browning replied that this 'enormous' blunder
was

only explicable to myself—and hardly that—from the circumstances under which
I well remember having written the poem . . . I was three parts thro' it, when
called to assist a servant to whom a strange accident, partly serious, partly ludicrous,
had suddenly happened; and after a quarter of an hour's agitation, of a varied kind,
I went back to my room and finished what I had begun. I have never touched the
piece since, and really suppose that the putting "Swedish" for "German", or
"Goerlitzist", is attributable just to that—for I knew something of Boehme, and
his autobiography, and how he lived mainly, and died in the Goerlitz where he
was born. But the thought in my head was of that revelation he describes, not of
his nationality; hence, I hope, my blunder—and such excuse as it may admit of.
Depend on it, I will alter the word in the next edition, ay, and look more warily
after what may be other slips of the kind.[2]

---

[1] *Athenæum*, 30 May 1840, 431; *Examiner*, 5 November 1845, 723; *Athenæum*, 6 April
1850, 371.

[2] *Letters*, 103–4. We note that there is no suggestion that the error is deliberate on
Browning's part, to help characterize the speaker. Jakob Boehme (1575–1624) was a

The note which Browning wrote for Mrs Orr, as background to ll. 37–45, suggests that he was now a little vague about his early reading of books relating to magic:

The "magic" symbolized is that of genuine poetry; but the magician, or "mage," is an historical person; and the special feat imputed to him was recorded of other magicians in the Middle Ages, if not of himself.

"Johannes Teutonicus, a canon of Halberstadt in Germany, after he had performed a number of prestigious feats almost incredible, was transported by the Devil in the likeness of a black horse, and was both seen and heard upon one and the same Christmas day to say Mass in Halberstadt, in Mayntz, and in Cologne" ("Heywood's Hierarchy," bk. iv., p. 253).

The "prestigious feat" of causing flowers to appear in winter was a common one. "In the year 876, the Emperor Lewis then reigning, there was one Zedechias, by religion a Jew, by profession a physician, but indeed a magician. In the midst of winter, in the Emperor's palace, he suddenly caused a most pleasant and delightful garden to appear, with all sorts of trees, plants, herbs, and flowers, together with the singing of all sorts of birds, to be seen and heard." (Delrio, "Disquisitio Magicæ," bk. i., chap. iv., and elsewhere; and many other authorities.)[1]

The idiom of the piece, and the handling of the blank verse, are somewhat reminiscent of *Sordello*.

Date: 1853/5
1863: Men and Women

mystical writer, influenced by Paracelsus. What Browning knew was not an autobiography, but *The Life of Jacob Behmen* (1654), reprinted in William Law's edition of his *Works*, 3 vols. (1764), i, pp. xi–xxii. Cf. below, l. 24 n. Browning made the correction in *1868*.

[1] The first quotation is from *The Hierarchie of the Blessed Angells*, by Thomas Heywood (1635). The text of the second, on p. 78 of the 3rd ed. of *Disquisitionum Magicarum Libri Sex*, by M. A. del Rio (1606), is from the chapter headed 'De Magia artificiali': 'Ioannes ex antiquioribus refert, anno 876. tempore Ludouici Imp. Sedechiam quendam religione Iudaeum, professione medicum, stupenda quaedam coram Principibus viris fecisse . . . mediâ brumâ hortum amoenissimum, in Caesaris palatio, arboribus, herbis, floribus, cantillatione auicularum, subitò natis & auditis, producebat.'

"TRANSCENDENTALISM: A POEM IN TWELVE BOOKS."

S T O P playing, poet! May a brother speak?
'T is you speak, that's your error. Song's our art:
Whereas you please to speak these naked thoughts
Instead of draping them in sights and sounds.
—True thoughts, good thoughts, thoughts fit to treasure up!　　5
But why such long prolusion and display,
Such turning and adjustment of the harp,
And taking it upon your breast, at length,
Only to speak dry words across its strings?
Stark-naked thought is in request enough:　　　　　　　　　10
Speak prose and hollo it till Europe hears!
The six-foot Swiss tube, braced about with bark,
Which helps the hunter's voice from Alp to Alp—
Exchange our harp for that,—who hinders you?

　　But here's your fault; grown men want thought, you think;　　15
Thought's what they mean by verse, and seek in verse.
Boys seek for images and melody,
Men must have reason—so, you aim at men.

---

title　*1855P–56*　"TRANSCENDENTALISM:" . . . . BOOKS.　*1863,　1865*
'TRANSCENDENTALISM:' . . . . BOOKS.　1　*1855P–65SP* may　　*16
{reading of DC, BrU, *1889*} *1855P–75* verse: *1888* verse

　　3　*these naked thoughts*: cf. Milton, 'At a Vacation Exercise', 23–4: 'I have some naked thoughts that rove about / And loudly knock to have their passage out'.
　　4　*draping them*: a cliché of classical critical theory. Cf. Pope, *An Essay on Criticism*, 318. In *Sordello*, iii. 248–51 the carping critic Naddo offers to 'school' the troubadour how to 'clothe in a poetic vest / These doings, at Verona'.
　　sights and sounds: this phrase, like 'sounds and sights', occurs a number of times in Browning: e.g. *Sordello*, iii. 29; 'May and Death', 12; *La Saisiaz*, 133.
　　11　*Speak prose*: see introduction.
　　12　*Swiss tube*: the alpenhorn, an instrument of wood and bark used by mountaineers in Switzerland.

Quite otherwise! Objects throng our youth, 't is true;
We see and hear and do not wonder much: 20
If you could tell us what they mean, indeed!
As German Boehme never cared for plants
Until it happed, a-walking in the fields,
He noticed all at once that plants could speak,
Nay, turned with loosened tongue to talk with him.   25
That day the daisy had an eye indeed—
Colloquized with the cowslip on such themes!
We find them extant yet in Jacob's prose.
But by the time youth slips a stage or two
While reading prose in that tough book he wrote   30
(Collating and emendating the same
And settling on the sense most to our mind),
We shut the clasps and find life's summer past.
Then, who helps more, pray, to repair our loss—
Another Boehme with a tougher book   35
And subtler meanings of what roses say,—
Or some stout Mage like him of Halberstadt,
John, who made things Boehme wrote thoughts about?
He with a "look you!" vents a brace of rhymes,

---

19 *1855P* true—*1855, 1856* true,   20 *1855, 1856* much.   22 *1855P–65SP* As
Swedish Bœhme   23 *1865SP* it happened, a-walking   25 *1855P* him:
28–9 {*1863–65SP* have a space between these lines}

19 *Objects throng our youth*: cf. 'May and Death', 9–12: 'Let their new time, as mine
of old, / Do all it did for me: I bid / Sweet sights and sounds throng manifold'. See too
Sordello, i. 648 ff., 'Fra Lippo Lippi', 283 ff.

24 *He noticed*: 'After this . . . he was . . . surrounded by the divine Light, and replen-
ished with heavenly Knowledge; insomuch, as going abroad into the Fields, . . . and
viewing the Herbs and Grass . . . in his inward Light he saw into their Essences, Use and
Properties, which were discovered to him by their Lineaments, Figures, and Signatures.
In like Manner he beheld the whole Creation, and from that Fountain of Revelation
he afterwards wrote his Book, *De Signatura Rerum*': 'The Life', in *The Works of Jacob
Behmen*, ed. William Law (3 vols., 1764), i, p. xiii.

26 *the daisy has an eye*: alluding to the etymology of the word, from the OE form of
'day's eye'. Cf. 'In a Balcony', 837.

27 *cowslip*: Browning may be remembering Johnson's erroneous etymology, 'perhaps
from growing much in pasture grounds, and often meeting the *cow's lip*'.

30 Altick points out that these lines may owe something to Carlyle's 'State of
German Literature', published in 1827: a mystic, he wrote, 'cannot speak to us; he

And in there breaks the sudden rose herself,   40
Over us, under, round us every side,
Nay, in and out the tables and the chairs
And musty volumes, Boehme's book and all,—
Buries us with a glory, young once more,
Pouring heaven into this shut house of life.   45

So come, the harp back to your heart again!
You are a poem, though your poem's naught.
The best of all you showed before, believe,
Was your own boy-face o'er the finer chords
Bent, following the cherub at the top   50
That points to God with his paired half-moon wings.

---

48 *1855P–65SP* you did before,   49 *1855P–65SP* own boy's-face o'er

knows not *our* state, and cannot make known to us his own. His words are an inexplicable rhapsody, a speech in an unknown tongue': *Works*, xxvi. 73.

31 *emendating*: earlier than the first and only example of this clumsy synonym of 'emending' in OED[2].

40 *the sudden rose*: cf. *Sordello*, v. 129.

47 *You are a poem*: the speaker, an older poet, admires the poetic intensity of the younger. As Altick remarks (p. 27), the notion of the poet as poem occurs frequently in Carlyle, who on one occasion paraphrases Milton's ruling that 'he who would not be frustrate of his hope to write well . . . ought himself to be a true poem' (*An Apology for Smectymnuus*, in *Milton on Himself*, ed. J. S. Diekhoff, ed. of 1965, p. 79). In 1845 Browning had told EBB that so far he had never 'begun, even, what I hope I was born to begin and end,—"R.B. a poem" ': Kintner, i. 17.

49 *your own boy-face*: cf. 'Saul', and 'The Boy and the Angel'.

the finer chords: as Turner points out, 'the strings for the highest notes . . . which come nearest the player's head, are thinner than the others'.

50 *following*: looking up at.

51 *his paired half-moon wings*: cf. 'In A Gondola', 95–6; *Sordello* vi. 568 ff.; 'The Guardian-Angel', 10–12.

MISCONCEPTIONS

IN this slight piece the first stanza presents an image of the literal meaning expressed in the second. The speaker is an aspirant lover rejected by the lady in favour of another.

The verse form is unusual, each stanza consisting of five trimeters followed by two tetrameters: the feet are dactyls, but for the last in each line, which is a trochee. The rhyme-scheme of each stanza is *ababbaa*. All rhymes are feminine. The opening of ll. 8, 10, 12, and 13 echo those of ll. 1, 3, 5, and 6.

Date: 1853/5
1863: Dramatic Lyrics

MISCONCEPTIONS.

I.

THIS is a spray the Bird clung to,
   Making it blossom with pleasure,
Ere the high tree-top she sprung to,
   Fit for her nest and her treasure.
   Oh, what a hope beyond measure   5
Was the poor spray's, which the flying feet hung to,—
So to be singled out, built in, and sung to!

II.

This is a heart the Queen leant on,
   Thrilled in a minute erratic,
Ere the true bosom she bent on,   10
   Meet for love's regal dalmatic.
   Oh, what a fancy ecstatic

---

*8 {reading of *1855P–65S, 1872S, 1884S*, DC, BrU, *1889*} *1868, 1870, 1875, 1888* on.

11 *dalmatic*: a robe, similar to an ecclesiastical vestment, worn by kings and emperors at coronations and on other solemn occasions.

Was the poor heart's, ere the wanderer went on—
Love to be saved for it, proffered to, spent on!

14 *1855P* it, matched with, and spent

ONE WORD MORE

'One Word More', which survives in an autograph manuscript dated London, September 22, 1855, was the last-written of these poems.[1] On 3 October EBB told a friend that the collection was 'dedicated to *me* in a poem at the close'.[2] The original title, 'A Last Word', may have been changed, as Pettigrew and Collins suggest, because of 'the unfortunate echo of "A Woman's Last Word" '. The title as we have it may be a reminiscence of EBB's stern injunction, on his premature declaration of love ten years before, that he should leave the subject 'without one word more'.[3] The error of 'Karshook' for 'Karshish' in l. 136 is one of several slips which suggest that the piece was written hurriedly.

In this envoy Browning 'stoop[s] of a sudden under and out of this dancing ring of men & women'[4] to speak 'this once in [his] own person'. EBB was delighted: 'After "one word more" . . Vixi', she wrote in the PS of a letter to Isa Blagden, '—I needn't live one day more, need I? far less write?'[5]

The metre, unrhymed trochaic pentameters, is unique in Browning's work, and can hardly be found elsewhere.[6] The fact that each line ends with an unstressed syllable makes the rhythm reminiscent of Italian verse. Most lines have a slight pause at the end, usually with a mark of punctuation. Alliteration is plentiful, occurring in about half of the lines. Section iii exemplifies this, and includes a telling instance of anaphora. Section viii is also rich in figures of repetition.

Date: 1855
1863: *Men and Women*

---

[1] The MS is in the Pierpont Morgan Library.

[2] PK 55: 160. On the same day she told her sister Henrietta: Huxley, 230.

[3] Kintner, i. 179. Browning used the same words in his last letter to EBB, before their marriage: Kintner, ii 1086.

[4] Ibid., i. 26.

[5] PK 55: 160. 'Vixi', I have lived.

[6] Ruskin forgot this poem when he wrote: 'We may write a pentametre [*sic*] verse in iambs only . . . the historical fact being quite indubitable and unalterable, that no poet has ever attempted to write pentametre in any foot but the iamb, and that the addition of another [trochee] to a . . . tetrametre . . . will instantly make [it] helplessly prosaic and unreadable'. *Elements of English Prosody for use in St. George's Schools* (Orpington 1880), 55–6.

ONE WORD MORE*

TO E. B. B.

1855.

I.

THERE they are, my fifty men and women
Naming me the fifty poems finished!
Take them, Love, the book and me together:
Where the heart lies, let the brain lie also.

II.

Rafael made a century of sonnets,   5
Made and wrote them in a certain volume
Dinted with the silver-pointed pencil
Else he only used to draw Madonnas:

---

* Originally appended to the collection of Poems called "Men and Women," the
greater portion of which has now been, more correctly, distributed under the other
titles of this edition.

---

title *MS* A Last Word. | To E. B. B.   *1855P–65* MORE.   {no date appears in the
title in *MS*, *1855P–56*; in subsequent editions the following date appears:} *1863*, *1865*,
1868–75 London, September, 1855.   *1865SPC/MS* Adapted from "ONE . . . . MORE.
. . . . 1855."   *1865SP, 1865S* ADAPTED FROM "*ONE WORD MORE.* | TO E.B.B. |
London, September, 1855."   note to title {first appears in *1863*, in the present
form except for 'this volume.' instead of 'this edition.' (and certain differences in
accidentals); similarly in *1865*} *1865SPC/MS* {note deleted}   *1865SP, 1865S*
{note omitted}   section numbers {appear in arabic numerals in *MS*, *1855P–56*;
the numbers are cancelled in *1865SPC*, and omitted from *1865SP, 1865S*}
1–2 *1865SPC/MS* {lines deleted}   *1865SP, 1865S* {lines omitted}   2 *MS*,
1855P finished: 3 *1855P–56* together.   4 *MS*, *1855P* heart is, let

1 *women*: women are the speakers in 'A Woman's Last Word', 'Any Wife to any
Husband', 'In A Year' and 'Another Way of Love', while two of the three characters of 'In
A Balcony' are women. In most of the other poems, too, women play a prominent part.

4 *Where the heart lies*: cf. Matt. 6: 21, and l. 142 below.

5 *sonnets*: as F. Page pointed out (TLS, 25 May 1940), the source here is Filippo
Baldinucci's *Notizie dei professori del disegno*, edited by F. Ranalli, 5 vols. (Florence,
1845–7), iv. 26. In the article on Guido Reni we read how, after his death, 'il famoso
libro de' cento sonetti di mano di Raffaello', which Reni had bought in Rome, went
missing, perhaps stolen by a member of his household. For Browning's knowledge of
Baldinucci see p. 47n above. In *Cymbeline*, IV. ii. 394 we have 'century' for a hundred.

7 *silver-pointed pencil*: OED^2 defines 'silver-point' as 'the process of making a drawing
with a silver pencil on specially prepared paper, a drawing made in this way'.

These, the world might view—but one, the volume.
Who that one, you ask? Your heart instructs you.   10
Did she live and love it all her life-time?
Did she drop, his lady of the sonnets,
Die, and let it drop beside her pillow
Where it lay in place of Rafael's glory,
Rafael's cheek so duteous and so loving—   15
Cheek, the world was wont to hail a painter's,
Rafael's cheek, her love had turned a poet's?

III.

You and I would rather read that volume,
(Taken to his beating bosom by it)
Lean and list the bosom-beats of Rafael,   20
Would we not? than wonder at Madonnas—
Her, San Sisto names, and Her, Foligno,
Her, that visits Florence in a vision,
Her, that's left with lilies in the Louvre—
Seen by us and all the world in circle.   25

---

9 *MS* view—[but] one ⟨eye⟩, the volume: 10 *MS* Who⟨se⟩ that ⟨eye⟩ [one], you
11 *MS* life-time—   16 *MS* Cheek, a world . . . . hail, the painter's,   18 {in *MS*
this line is written as continuous with the preceding paragraph; RB has subsequently
indicated that it should open a new paragraph ('3.'); the numbering of the following
paragraph is altered accordingly}   *MS* read th⟨e⟩[at] volume,   25 *MS* and the
whole world

8 *Madonnas*: a series of Madonna and Child pictures painted by Raphael in 1505–6
have led several writers to use the phrase 'the year of the Madonnas'.

12 *his lady of the sonnets*: probably the supposed model for 'La Fornarina' and other
of his paintings. The phrase is often used in connection with Shakespeare's Sonnets.

14 *glory*: halo.

15 *so duteous*: an unhistorical interpretation of Raphael's attitude to women, no
doubt. He never married, but left a generous provision to his favourite mistress: see
'Andrea del Sarto', 136 n.

20 *bosom-beats*: not in OED².

22 *Her, San Sisto names*: the Sistine Madonna (now in Dresden), and the Foligno
Madonna (Vatican Pinacoteca).

23 *Her, that visits Florence*: Browning told W. J. Rolfe that 'The Madonna at Florence is
that called *del Granduca*, which represents her as "appearing to a votary in a vision"—so say
the describers; it is in the earlier manner, and very beautiful'. Of the last here, he wrote: 'I
think I meant *La Belle Jardinière*—but am not sure'. PK 87: 81 (quoted in Cooke, 298).

IV.

You and I will never read that volume.
Guido Reni, like his own eye's apple
Guarded long the treasure-book and loved it.
Guido Reni dying, all Bologna
Cried, and the world cried too, "Ours, the treasure!"   30
Suddenly, as rare things will, it vanished.

V.

Dante once prepared to paint an angel:
Whom to please? You whisper "Beatrice."
While he mused and traced it and retraced it,
(Peradventure with a pen corroded   35
Still by drops of that hot ink he dipped for,
When, his left-hand i' the hair o' the wicked,
Back he held the brow and pricked its stigma,
Bit into the live man's flesh for parchment,
Loosed him, laughed to see the writing rankle,   40
Let the wretch go festering through Florence)—
Dante, who loved well because he hated,
Hated wickedness that hinders loving,
Dante standing, studying his angel,—

26 *MS* read th⟨e⟩[at] volume.   27 *MS* his ⟨eyesight's⟩[own eye's] apple
28 *MS* Laid away the . . . . it;   30 *MS* world with it, Ours—   *1855P–56* world
with it, "Ours—{revised in *1855P/MS, Fields, Rossetti*}   *MS* treasure!   33 *MS*
please? You⟨r own heart⟩ whisper⟨s⟩ "⟨Bice.⟩" [Beatrice.]   35 *MS, 1855P*
Peradventure   41 *MS* Florence. *1855P* Florence,—   42 *MS, 1855P* Dante
then, who loved because   44 *MS* Dante ⟨stood and studied thus⟩ [standing,
studying] his angel,

27 *Guido Reni*: 1575–1642. See 5 n.

33 *'Beatrice'*: Beatrice Portinari, the central figure of the *Vita Nuova* and the *Divina
Commedia*. In ch. xxxv of the former Dante tells us that, a year after her death, he was
drawing an angel as he remembered her. W. M. Rossetti was stupidly literal in objecting
to l. 33: see Cooke, 442. Dante was an excellent draughtsman, and a friend of several artists.

35–6 *corroded / Still*: Browning is not following the true chronology here, since
Dante did not begin the *Divine Commedia* until later in his life.

36 *hot ink*: 'Browning's own figure of speech, not got out of Dante': ibid. Rossetti's
two further comments are of no relevance.

37 *i' the hair o' the wicked*: *Inferno* xxxii. 103 ff., elaborated by Browning.

42 *who loved well*: possibly influenced by a proverb recorded by Thomas Fuller,
'greatest hatred springs from greatest love': *Gnomologia* (1732).

In there broke the folk of his Inferno.   45
Says he—"Certain people of importance"
(Such he gave his daily dreadful line to)
"Entered and would seize, forsooth, the poet."
Says the poet—"Then I stopped my painting."

VI.

You and I would rather see that angel,   50
Painted by the tenderness of Dante,
Would we not?—than read a fresh Inferno.

VII.

You and I will never see that picture.
While he mused on love and Beatrice,
While he softened o'er his outlined angel,   55
In they broke, those "people of importance:"
We and Bice bear the loss for ever.

VIII.

What of Rafael's sonnets, Dante's picture?
This: no artist lives and loves, that longs not
Once, and only once, and for one only,   60
(Ah, the prize!) to find his love a language
Fit and fair and simple and sufficient—
Using nature that's an art to others,

48 MS Entered . . . . would ⟨see,⟩ [sieze,] forsooth, ... poet: 1855P–56 Entered . . . .
poet.   49 MS poet—Then . . . . painting.   50 {in MS this line is written as
continuous with the preceding paragraph; RB has subsequently indicated that it should
open a new paragraph ('6.'); the numbering of the following paragraph ('7.') has not
been altered}   53 MS see th⟨e⟩[at] picture.   54 MS on ⟨heaven⟩ [love] and
⟨on Bice⟩, [Beatrice]   58 {in MS, 1855P–56 this line forms a separate paragraph,
numbered '8.': as a result the numbering of later paragraphs differs from that in 1865–89}
60 MS and but once only,

48 *and would seize*: MS 'see' follows *Vita Nuova*, xxxv. Browning adds the notion that
they wished to 'seize' Dante.

56 *"people of importance"*: 'uomini a' quali si convenia di fare onore'.

57 *Bice*: a familiar form for 'Beatrice'. It also occurs in the MS at ll. 33 and 54, and
in 'Beatrice Signorini' (in *Asolando*).

58 *What of Rafael's sonnets*: in MS and 1855 this line stood alone, as section VIII.

Not, this one time, art that's turned his nature.
Ay, of all the artists living, loving,   65
None but would forego his proper dowry,—
Does he paint? he fain would write a poem,—
Does he write? he fain would paint a picture,
Put to proof art alien to the artist's,
Once, and only once, and for one only,   70
So to be the man and leave the artist,
Gain the man's joy, miss the artist's sorrow.

IX.

Wherefore? Heaven's gift takes earth's abatement!
He who smites the rock and spreads the water,
Bidding drink and live a crowd beneath him,   75
Even he, the minute makes immortal,
Proves, perchance, but mortal in the minute,
Desecrates, belike, the deed in doing.
While he smites, how can he but remember,
So he smote before, in such a peril,   80
When they stood and mocked—"Shall smiting help us?"
When they drank and sneered—"A stroke is easy!"
When they wiped their mouths and went their journey,
Throwing him for thanks—"But drought was pleasant."

---

64 *MS* this time, an art   65 *MS* Out of all   69 *1855P* the artists',
72 *MS, 1855P–56* Save the   73–108 *1865SPC/MS* {lines deleted}   *1865SP,*
1865S   {lines   omitted}   73 *MS* Ah,—for   heaven's . . . . abatement.
77 *MS* Brings, perchance, his mortal   *1855P–63* perchance, his mortal   82 *MS*
⟨T⟩[W]hen they . . . . and smiled—'A   *1855P* and smiled—"A   83 *MS* ⟨Last⟩
[When] they   84 *MS* Throwing ⟨me⟩ [him] for

---

64 *art that's turned his nature*: his own art.
72 *the artist's sorrow*: that of failing to be appreciated.
73 *Heaven's gift takes earth's abatement*: the heavenly gift of poetry is diminished by its reception on earth. As Cook points out, Wordsworth uses 'Heaven's gift' for inspiration in *The Prelude*, xiii. 304. Cf. *Twelfth Night*, I.i. 13 for 'abatement and low price'.
74 *He who smites the rock*: Moses, taken as the type of the poet. Cf. Exod. 17: 1–6 and Numb. 20: 1 ff. See too *Sordello*, iii. 826 ff.: 'While awkwardly enough your Moses smites / The rock, though he forego his Promised Land / Thereby . . .'
78 *Desecrates*: Johnson gives as the meaning of the verb 'To divert from the purpose to which any thing is consecrated'.

Thus old memories mar the actual triumph;   85
Thus the doing savours of disrelish;
Thus achievement lacks a gracious somewhat;
O'er-importuned brows becloud the mandate,
Carelessness or consciousness—the gesture.
For he bears an ancient wrong about him,   90
Sees and knows again those phalanxed faces,
Hears, yet one time more, the 'customed prelude—
"How shouldst thou, of all men, smite, and save us?"
Guesses what is like to prove the sequel—
"Egypt's flesh-pots—nay, the drought was better."   95

x.

Oh, the crowd must have emphatic warrant!
Theirs, the Sinai-forehead's cloven brilliance,
Right-arm's rod-sweep, tongue's imperial fiat.
Never dares the man put off the prophet.

85 *MS* ⟨So past⟩ [Thus old] memories   86 *MS* ⟨So⟩ [Thus] the . . . . disrelish,
87 *MS* ⟨So⟩ [Thus] achievement   89 *MS* gesture—   {in *MS* the following
deleted line appears after l. 89:} ⟨Make precipitate or mar retarding,⟩   90 *MS*
ancient grudge about   91 *MS* {initial reading, subsequently altered} those faces,
phalanxed,   96 {in *MS* this line is written as continuous with the preceding
paragraph; RB has subsequently indicated that it should open a new paragraph ('11.');
the numbering of the following paragraph ('12.') has not been altered}   97 *MS* the
⟨prophet⟩ [Sinai]-forehead's   98 *MS* rod-sweep and tongue's regal fiat—

85 *actual*: present (Fr.)
88 *O'er-importuned brows*: importuned too much, the poet finds that he is less pleased
to fulfil the request.
90 *an ancient wrong*: that of having been under-rated in the past.
91 *phalanxed*: as in Byron, *Childe Harold's Pilgrimage*, i. 797.
95 *Egypt's flesh-pots*: cf. Exod. 16: 2–3.
   the drought was better: so they will say, in their ingratitude.
97 *Theirs*: as if by right.
   The Sinai-forehead's cloven brilliance: to convince the people of his divine authority,
Moses asked to see the 'glory' of God. The reply was that no man would see God's face
and live, but that he might see the 'back parts' of God from a 'clift of the rock' on the
brow of Mount Sinai. When Moses descended with 'the two tables of testimony' his
face was shining, so that the people 'were afraid to come nigh him': Exod. 34: 30. See
too Numb. 20: 7–11. A colleague comments: ' "cloven" because, the Hebrew word for
"shone", *qāran*, being related to that for "horn", *qeren*, Exod. 34: 29, was rendered in
the Vulgate "ignorabat quod cornuta esset facies sua" '.
98 *rod-sweep*: cf. Exod. 17: 9.

XI.

Did he love one face from out the thousands,   100
(Were she Jethro's daughter, white and wifely,
Were she but the Æthiopian bondslave,)
He would envy yon dumb patient camel,
Keeping a reserve of scanty water
Meant to save his own life in the desert;   105
Ready in the desert to deliver
(Kneeling down to let his breast be opened)
Hoard and life together for his mistress.

XII.

I shall never, in the years remaining,
Paint you pictures, no, nor carve you statues,   110
Make you music that should all-express me;
So it seems: I stand on my attainment.
This of verse alone, one life allows me;
Verse and nothing else have I to give you.
Other heights in other lives, God willing: 115
All the gifts from all the heights, your own, Love!

XIII.

Yet a semblance of resource avails us—
Shade so finely touched, love's sense must seize it.

---

101 *MS* Were   102 *MS* bondslave,   103 *MS* Why—he'd envy
104 *MS* ⟨Dowered with his⟩ ⟨Gifted⟩ ⟨a⟩ [Keeping a] reserve . . . . scanty ⟨drinking⟩,
[water]   105 *MS* desert,   106 *MS* desert ⟨might he yield it⟩ [to] ⟨be
yielded⟩ [deliver]   108 *MS* together ⟨to⟩ [for] his   111 *MS* me.
112 *MS* attainment: 113 *MS, 1855P* me,   114 *MS* you,   *1855P* you;

---

101 *Jethro's daughter*: Zipporah: Exod. 2: 21.
102 *the Æthiopian bondslave*: see Num. 12. 1.
110 *carve you statues*: in Florence Browning frequented the studio of his friend Story,
and loved to model in clay. See Henry James, *William Wetmore Story and his Friends*,
2 vols. (1903), ii. 53 and 68.
111 *all-express*: the only other instance of the compound in OED² is from *Festus*, by
P. J. Bailey: see Kelley and Coley, A 146–7.
115 *other lives*: cf. 'Evelyn Hope', 29–30.
118 *Shade*: shade of difference.
    finely touched: cf. *Measure for Measure*, I. i. 36.

Take these lines, look lovingly and nearly,
Lines I write the first time and the last time. 120
He who works in fresco, steals a hair-brush,
Curbs the liberal hand, subservient proudly,
Cramps his spirit, crowds its all in little,
Makes a strange art of an art familiar,
Fills his lady's missal-marge with flowerets. 125
He who blows thro' bronze, may breathe thro' silver,
Fitly serenade a slumbrous princess.
He who writes, may write for once as I do.

XIV.

Love, you saw me gather men and women,
Live or dead or fashioned by my fancy, 130
Enter each and all, and use their service,
Speak from every mouth,—the speech, a poem.
Hardly shall I tell my joys and sorrows,
Hopes and fears, belief and disbelieving:
I am mine and yours—the rest be all men's, 135
Karshish, Cleon, Norbert and the fifty.
Let me speak this once in my true person,

---

119 *MS* Take this verse, look   120 *MS* Verse I   121 *MS* steals a ⟨paint-⟩
[an oil-] brush,   122 *MS* the ⟨callous⟩ [liberal] hand,   131 *MS* and ⟨claim⟩
[use] their   135 *1865SPC/MS*, *1865S* men's.   136 *1865SPC/MS* {line
deleted}   *1865SP*, *1865S* {line omitted}   *MS*, *1855P–63*, *1865*, *1868* Karshook, Cleon,

120 *the first time*: Browning had never written trochaic pentameters before.
Cf. introduction.

121 *in fresco*: fresco-painting is large-scale water-colour painting on walls etc.
hair-brush: a brush of fine hairs.

125 *missal-marge*: no other example in OED².

130 *Live or dead*: the most obvious of the living was Cardinal Wiseman, the main
model for Bishop Blougram.

133 *Hardly*: scarcely at all.

136 *Karshish*: 'Karshish is the proper word, referring as it does to him of the
"Epistle"—*Karshook* (Heb. a Thistle) just belongs to the snarling verses I remember to
have written but forget for whom': *Letters* 196 (Browning to Furnivall, 15 September
1881). For 'Ben Karshook's Wisdom', see below, Appendix. Although there had been
a character called Karshook in *The Return of the Druses*, this error is surprising, and bears
out the impression that 'One Word More' may have been written hurriedly. It was not
put right until *1872*.
     Norbert: in 'In a Balcony'.

Not as Lippo, Roland or Andrea,
Though the fruit of speech be just this sentence:
Pray you, look on these my men and women,   140
Take and keep my fifty poems finished;
Where my heart lies, let my brain lie also!
Poor the speech; be how I speak, for all things.

XV.

Not but that you know me! Lo, the moon's self!
Here in London, yonder late in Florence,   145
Still we find her face, the thrice-transfigured.
Curving on a sky imbrued with colour,
Drifted over Fiesole by twilight,
Came she, our new crescent of a hair's-breadth.
Full she flared it, lamping Samminiato,   150
Rounder 'twixt the cypresses and rounder,
Perfect till the nightingales applauded.
Now, a piece of her old self, impoverished,
Hard to greet, she traverses the houseroofs,
Hurries with unhandsome thrift of silver,   155
Goes dispiritedly, glad to finish.

138 *1865SPC/MS* {line   deleted}   *1865SP*,   *1865S* {line   omitted}
*139 {reading of DC, BrU, *1889*} *MS*, *1888* sentence   *1855P–63*, *1865–75* sentence—
140 *1865SPC/MS*, *1865SP*, *1865S* you, take and keep my   141 *1865SPC/MS*
{line deleted}   *1865SP*, *1865S* {line omitted}   *MS* finished,   142 *MS*, *1855P*
heart is, let   147 *MS*, *1855P* with colours,   148 *MS* Drifted ⟨us o'er⟩ [over]
Fiesole   151 *MS* Rounded ⟨a-top⟩ ['twixt] the cypress⟨-walk⟩[es] and
156 *MS* ⟨All⟩ [Goes] dispiritedly[,] ⟨and⟩ glad

142 *Where my heart lies*: see l. 4.
143 *be how I speak, for all things*: poor as my expression is, let it serve to express my
thanks for everything.
145 *Here in London*: they left Florence on 20 June 1855, and reached London on 12
July.
146 *thrice-transfigured*: the MS is dated 22 September, so that the moon had waxed
and waned three times.
150 *lamping*: OED has two earlier examples of the transitive use, one from Bailey's
Festus (1852). Cf. l. 111 n, above, and *The Ring and the Book*, vi. 1173.
    Samminiato: the church of San Miniato al Monte, SE of Florence.
154 *houseroofs*: see Ruskin's objection to 'foldskirts' as a trochee, in 'Saul', 20 (p. 364,
above), and Browning's reply. Here too what might well be a spondee becomes a
trochee because of the natural pronunciation of the compound.

XVI.

What, there's nothing in the moon noteworthy?
Nay: for if that moon could love a mortal,
Use, to charm him (so to fit a fancy)
All her magic ('t is the old sweet mythos)   160
She would turn a new side to her mortal,
Side unseen of herdsman, huntsman, steersman—
Blank to Zoroaster on his terrace,
Blind to Galileo on his turret,
Dumb to Homer, dumb to Keats—him, even!   165
Think, the wonder of the moonstruck mortal—
When she turns round, comes again in heaven,
Opens out anew for worse or better!
Proves she like some portent of an iceberg
Swimming full upon the ship it founders,   170
Hungry with huge teeth of splintered crystals?
Proves she as the paved work of a sapphire
Seen by Moses when he climbed the mountain?
Moses, Aaron, Nadab and Abihu
Climbed and saw the very God, the Highest,   175

157 {in MS this line is written as continuous with the preceding paragraph; RB has subsequently indicated that it should open a new paragraph ('17.')}   *158 {reading of MS, 1855P–75, DC, BrU, 1889} 1888 mortal   159 MS ⟨Have⟩ [Use] to ⟨grace⟩ [charm] him   *{reading of MS, 1855P–75} 1888 fancy BrU, 1889 fancy, 160 MS her ⟨pleasure⟩ [magic] ('tis   162 MS of shepherd, huntsman, 167 MS Wh⟨at⟩[en she] turns round, ⟨and⟩ comes   168 MS, 1855P–63 better? 169 MS Proves ⟨it⟩ [she like] some ⟨white⟩ portent   171 Fields splintered chrystal?   172–3 MS Proves ⟨it⟩ [she] as when Moses climbed the mountain, | Saw the paved-work of a stone, a sapphire,   173 1855P mountain—

158 *love a mortal*: as in Keats's *Endymion*, based on an ancient myth.

163 *Zoroaster*: one of the great teachers of the East, of uncertain date. His teaching contrasts the powers of light with those of darkness. In *Paracelsus*, v. 187 he is 'Persic Zoroaster, lord of stars!'

164 *Galileo*: Galileo Galilei (1564–1642), the great astronomer, who discovered that the earth goes round the sun, a discovery which he was obliged to renounce ('e pur si muove', he is supposed to have said to himself). Born in Pisa, he is thought to have used the Leaning Tower for experiments.

165 *Homer*: no doubt mentioned because of the Homeric 'Hymn to the Moon', translated by Shelley.

Stand upon the paved work of a sapphire.
Like the bodied heaven in his clearness
Shone the stone, the sapphire of that paved work,
When they ate and drank and saw God also!

XVII.

What were seen? None knows, none ever shall know.   180
Only this is sure—the sight were other,
Not the moon's same side, born late in Florence,
Dying now impoverished here in London.
God be thanked, the meanest of his creatures
Boasts two soul-sides, one to face the world with,   185
One to show a woman when he loves her!

XVIII.

This I say of me, but think of you, Love!
This to you—yourself my moon of poets!
Ah, but that's the world's side, there's the wonder,
Thus they see you, praise you, think they know you!   190
There, in turn I stand with them and praise you—
Out of my own self, I dare to phrase it.
But the best is when I glide from out them,
Cross a step or two of dubious twilight,
Come out on the other side, the novel   195
Silent silver lights and darks undreamed of,
Where I hush and bless myself with silence.

---

176 *MS* sapphire: *178 {reading of *MS, 1868–75*, DC, BrU, *1889*} *1855P–65S*
paved-work, *1888* work   179 *MS* Whe⟨re⟩[n] they   180 *MS* Wh⟨ich⟩[at]
were   186 *MS* woman if he   *MS, 1855P–63* her.   190 *MS, 1855P–63*
you.   191 *1865, 1868, 1870* you.   192 *MS, 1855P* self—(I   *MS* it)
1855P it:)   {in *MS* the following line appears after l. 192:} Seeing—mine with all
the eyes—our wonder.   197 *MS* with beauty.

---

176 *a sapphire*: 'Then went up Moses, and Aaron, Nadab, and Abihu, and seventy of
the elders of Israel: And they saw the God of Israel: and there was under his feet as it
were a paved work of a sapphire stone, and as it were the body of heaven in his
clearness. And upon the nobles of the children of Israel he laid not his hand: also they
saw God, and did eat and drink': Exod. 24: 9–11.

185 *soul-sides*: apparently Browning's coinage: not in OED².

XIX.

Oh, their Rafael of the dear Madonnas,
Oh, their Dante of the dread Inferno,
Wrote one song—and in my brain I sing it,   200
Drew one angel—borne, see, on my bosom!

R. B.

198 {in *MS* this line is written as continuous with preceding paragraph}
201 *MS* ⟨   ⟩ {illegible deleted word} [Drew] one   {in *MS* the following date
and initials appear at the end of the poem:} <u>London, Sept 22. 1855.</u>   <u>R.B.</u> {the initials
'R.B.' also appear in *1863–75*}

198 *XIX*: not a separate section in MS.

APPENDIX

FUGITIVES

Quatrain on Correggio

> Could I, heart-broken, reach his Place of birth
> And stand before his Pictures—could I chuse
> But own at once "the sovereign'st thing on earth
> "Is Parma-city for an inward bruise?"

These lines were printed in part of an undated letter from Browning to Mrs Jameson in Sotheby's catalogue for a sale on 10 December 1913, and collected by W. Whitla in his privately-printed *Six Stray Verses by Robert Browning* (Oxford, 1966). They now appear in *Correspondence*, v. 258, in a letter dated '?mid-March 1842'. Immediately before the verses Browning wrote: 'At which of the Colnaghis can one see the Correggio you spoke of one evening at Carlyle's? I am just now hungry for his pictures, and mean whenever I am sore at heart to go and get well before the great cupola at—but why not versify, since that, or something like it, is my trade?' Correggio (named after his birthplace, a town near Parma), was born Antonio Allegri *c.*1490 and lived until 1534. There were two Colnaghi shops at this time, one at 14 Pall Mall East, the other at 23 Cockspur Street.

Correggio's work in Parma includes the remarkable adornment of the cupola of the church of San Giovanni. In another church there, San Antonio, there is a painting of the Virgin with Mary Magdalena, which includes 'a boy, representing a little angel, . . . who is smiling so naturally that all who look on him are moved to smile also; nor is there any one, however melancholy his temperament, who can behold him without feeling a sensation of pleasure'. This observation in Vasari's *Lives* (ii. 406) may have been in Browning's mind as he wrote these lines. Whitla reprinted them, with comments, in 'Four More Fugitives by Robert Browning'; NQ, December 1974, 449–50, mentioning that the quotation is from *1 Henry IV*, 1. iii. 57–8 (with 'Is' for 'Was'). He reminds us that there is a pun here based 'on the supposed etymology of "spermaceti" which the commentators on Shakespeare's text note was fancifully connected with Parma, and which was believed to have the power of dissolving coagulated blood beneath the skin or in the organs'.

Translation from Lorenzo de' Medici

'SEE those lines in the Athenæum on Pulci with Hunt's translation', Browning wrote to EBB on 8 February 1846, in a postscript to his letter: '—all wrong—"*che non si sente*," being—"that one does not *hear* him" i.e. the ordinarily noisy fellow—and the rest, male, pessime! Sic verte, meo periculo, mî ocelle!'

> Where's Luigi Pulci, that one don't the man see?
> He just now yonder in the copse has '*gone it*' (*n*'andò)
> Because across his mind there came a fancy;
> He'll wish to fancify, perhaps, a sonnet![1]

The *Athenæum* for the previous day carried a 'Second Notice' of Leigh Hunt's *Stories from the Italian Poets*, 2 vols. (1846) which mentions Pulci's familiar friendship with Lorenzo de' Medici and quotes lines 81–4 from the latter's poem about hawking, 'La Caccia col Falcone':

> —Luigi Pulci ov'è, che non si sente?—
> —Egli se n'andò dianzi in quel boschetto,
> ché qualche fantasia ha per la mente:
> vorrá fantasticar forse un sonetto.

Hunt's translation follows:

> "And where's Luigi Pulci? I saw *him*".[3]
> "Oh, in the wood there. Gone, depend upon it,
> To vent some fancy in his brain—some whim,
> That will not let him rest till it's a sonnet."[4]

Translation of lines attributed to Pietro d'Abano

'Now Ba thinks nothing can be worse than that?', Browning wrote in the same letter. 'Then read *this* which I really told Hunt and got his praise for. Poor dear wonderful persecuted Pietro d'Abano wrote this quatrain on the people's plaguing him about his mathematical studies and wanting to burn him—he helped to build Padua Cathedral, wrote a Treatise on Magic still extant, and passes for a conjuror in his country to this day . . . Well, this quatrain is said, I believe truly, to have been discovered in a well near Padua some fifty years ago.

---

[1] Kintner, i. 443–4. The Latin translates 'badly done, very badly done!' (like a schoolmaster's grade) and 'Render it this way, at my risk (on my authority), my darling!'

[2] *Opere*, ed. Attilio Simioni, 2 vols., Bari, 1913–14, ii. 23.

[3] Italicized because the narrator has just been mentioning other friends.

[4] Vol. i, p. 286.

> Studiando le mie cifre, col compasso
> Rilevo, che presto sarò sottera—
> Perchè del mio saper si fa gran chiasso,
> E gl'ignoranti m'hanno mosso guerra'.

'Affecting, is it not, in its simple, child like plaining?', he asks. 'Now so, if I remember, I turned it—word for word—

> Studying my ciphers, with the compass
> I reckon—who soon shall be below ground,
> Because of my lore they make great "rumpus,"
> And against me war makes each dull rogue round.

Say that you forgive me tomorrow!' No doubt she did, but she added her own translation.[1]

In the preface to a revised edition of *The Reliques of Father Prout* (i.e. F. S. Mahony, cf. p. 210–11, above), we read: 'From Florence the poet Browning has sent for this edition some lines lately found in the Euganeian hills, traced on a marble slab that covered the bones of Pietro di Abano, held in his old age to be an astrologer.'[2] Writing to Furnivall in 1881 (*Trumpeter*, 36–7), Browning slightly corrected Mahony's Italian text. According to Prout 'the poet has supplied this vernacular, rendering *verbatim*': "Studying my cyphers with the compass, / I find I shall soon be under the daisy; / Because of my lore folks make such a rumpus, / That every dull dog is thereat *unaisy*." This had been tampered with by Prout in fun. 'I told him of the thing at Florence', Browning commented, 'and did it *impromptu* into this doggerel: "Studying my cyphers with the compass, / I gather I soon shall be below ground, / Because of my lore men make great rumpus, / And war on myself makes each dull rogue round" '. In 1880 he published a poem entitled 'Pietro of Abano' in *Dramatic Idyls. Second Series*. As a note to l. 40 he gave the Italian text, adding 'They were extemporaneously Englished thus: not as Father Prout chose to prefer them.' In this version he has 'I soon shall be' in l. 2, 'folks' for 'they' in l. 3, and 'And war on myself' at the beginning of l. 4.

Impromptu verses on E.B.B.

'Robert tells me two or three times a day that I dont love him, & once with ever so many impromptu verses he said & sung it . . (did I tell you what an improvisatore he was?) said & sung that I did'nt love him . .

[1] Kintner, i. 443–4.
[2] 'New Edition, Revised and largely Augmented' (1860), p. iv.

> "That I only deceive
> Beguile him and leave
> At the treason to grieve.
> While like fair mother Eve
> I laugh in my sleeve!"

& all because I object to turning him out of his chair, when my sofa is as near the fire . . or because I dont sit with a shawl over my head, or some such fantastical reason': EBB to Arabella Moulton-Barrett, 22–3 December 1847: PK 47: 69. Probably improvised not long before.

To Miss Unger

> Dear Miss Unger,
> You're young: but though younger
> You ought to have known that one's ardour it damps,
> To have to transmit you these valueless stamps.
> The Postman will say—all you've done, Miss, is undone:
> What goes in St. Frisco don't go here in London.

These lines were first published on pp. 48–9 of the 1900 *Appendix* to *The Rowfant Library: A Catalogue of Printed Books* [etc.] *Collected by Frederick Locker-Lampson* (1886). It is stated that they are in Browning's autograph in a copy of *Christmas-Eve and Easter-Day*, and were 'written at Florence the year of publication' of that poem, i.e. 1850. Miss Unger of San Francisco had obviously sent Browning American stamps for his reply to her request for an autograph. W. Whitla reprinted the lines in his *Six Stray Verses by Robert Browning* (Oxford, 1966), with the comment that an agreement was reached between the United States and Great Britain for the exchange of mail in 1848.

Epigram on Justina Deffell

On 30 April 1853 EBB wrote to Arabel: 'I had a visit the other day from Justina Deffel. She is not charming, you know, . . she abused Italy, depreciated art, climate, scenery, in the most trenchant way—swore that all the trees were pollarded—!!!!!—Do you understand that Robert was all but uncivil to her after *that*? It was the way, the manner, the tone of voice. Oh, he took such a hatred to her—he never "saw such a hateful woman in his life." ' EBB added: 'it isn't her fault that she cant see beauty,—with a blind soul.' The Deffells lived in Harley Street, near the Barretts. At the end of the letter EBB transcribed 'Robert's last word of crossness against her', adding: 'he wrote it in pencil & threw it to me, promising that he wdṇt. be cross anymore.—

> How much upon a level
> Lie these expressions two—
> We see just-in-a Devil
> What we see just in *you*'.

PK 53: 38.

Epigram on the Grand Duke of Tuscany

> The Grand Duke wash'd and kiss'd the poor men's feet,
> You'll say His Grace is gracious to inferiors:
> But even Tuscan toes must now taste sweet
> To one who kisses Austria's posteriors.

These lines by Browning occur in a letter from Robert Lytton to John Forster written in 1853. They were first printed by Michael Meredith in 'News and Comment' in BSN 1990/1. The Brownings had been deeply disillusioned by Leopold II. On 12 September 1847, their first wedding anniversary, they had watched a splendid procession filing past, as 'the Duke & his family stood in tears . . . to receive the thanks of his people'. They were delighted by the prospect of liberty for Italy. It was very different when the Duke returned to Florence, to rule with Austrian troops, after the battle of Novara in 1849: it was no longer possible to regard him as an enlightened ruler. In Part II of *Casa Guidi Windows*, written at this time, EBB addressed him as 'thou false Duke Leopold' (l. 40). Cf. 'Old Pictures in Florence', 261.

BEN KARSHOOK'S WISDOM

On 13 March 1854 Bryan Waller Procter ('Barry Cornwall') asked a favour of Browning: 'I want you to send me a scrap of verse—& to prevail on your wife to send me another—for the Keepsake. The year before last I got something from Carlyle—& something from Tennyson. Now I come to the Brownings'.[1]

He explained that the Annual was 'edited by Miss Power (Lady Blessington's niece)—a young woman who is very respectable—& very

---

[1] PK 54: 38.

hard-working—& wretchedly poor', having 'been neglected by some that ought not to have forgotten her'. She had suffered from 'the small pox in its worst form' and was now 'working for bread'. On 13 April Procter wrote again, urging haste. It seems that EBB sent her poem, 'My Kate', right away. Browning's is dated 27 April. Whereas EBB's contribution appeared in *The Keepsake* for 1855 (late in 1854), Browning's was not published until the following year. He did not include it in *Men and Women*, or in any of his collected editions. Furnivall reprinted it, however, in the Chronological List of Browning's works in the *Proceedings of the Browning Society*, 56. In a letter to him Browning referred to it as 'snarling verses I remember to have written but forget for whom': *Trumpeter*, 24. It should be added that there is a character called Karshook in *The Return of the Druses*.

The origin of this little poem, as Judith Berlin-Lieberman[1] has pointed out, is an anecdote about Rabbi Eliezer ben Hyrkanos, a celebrated Jewish teacher. She refers to an anecdote about him in the Talmud:

R. Eliezer said: Repent one day before your death. His disciples asked him, Does then one know on what day he will die? Then all the more reason that he repent to-day, he replied, lest he die to-morrow, and thus his whole life is spent in repentance.[2]

In the first and second centuries AD the Sadducees, who were conservative Jews, did not accept the developed oral tradition of the Law promoted by the Pharisees, and did not believe in life after death.

BEN KARSHOOK'S WISDOM

I

'Would a man 'scape the rod?'
  Rabbi Ben Karshook saith,
'See that he turn to God
  'The day before his death.'

'Ay, could a man inquire   5
  'When it shall come!' I say.

---

[1] *Robert Browning and Hebraism* (Azriel Press, Jerusalem, 1934), 30 ff.
[2] Trans. H. Freedman, ed. I. Epstein, ii (1972), 153a (*Hebrew–English Edition of the Babylonian Talmud*, Soncino Press, London, Jerusalem, New York).

The Rabbi's eye shoots fire—
   'Then let him turn to-day!'

II

Quoth a young Sadducee:
   'Reader of many rolls,   10
'Is it so certain we
   'Have, as they tell us, souls?'

'Son, there is no reply!'
   The Rabbi bit his beard:
'Certain, a soul have *I*—   15
   '*We* may have none,' he sneer'd.

Thus Karshook, the Hiram's-Hammer,
   The Right-hand Temple-column,
Taught babes in grace their grammar,
   And struck the simple, solemn.   20
Rome, *April* 27, 1854.

---

10 *rolls*: books.

17–18 *Hiram's-Hammer*: this is a reference to Hiram of Tyre, a worker in brass who was Solomon's master craftsman: 1 Kgs 7.13 ff. As Berlin-Lieberman points out, Browning is remembering a passage in the Talmud. In the Hebrew–English edn. of the Babylonian Talmud cited above we read that when Rabbi Johanan fell ill, his disciples addressed him as 'Lamp of Israel, pillar of the right hand, mighty hammer!': Berakoth 28b.

INDEX OF TITLES

INDEX OF FIRST LINES